OT 40
Operator Theory: Advances and Applications
Vol. 40

Birkhäuser Verlag
Basel · Boston · Berlin

The Gohberg Anniversary Collection

Volume I: The Calgary Conference and Matrix Theory Papers

Edited by

H. Dym
S. Goldberg
M. A. Kaashoek
P. Lancaster

1989

Birkhäuser Verlag
Basel · Boston · Berlin

Volume Editorial Office:

Department of Mathematics
and Computer Science
Vrije Universiteit
Amsterdam, The Netherlands

CIP-Titelaufnahme der Deutschen Bibliothek

The **Gohberg anniversary collection** / [vol. ed. office: Dep. of Mathematics and Computer Science, Vrije Univ., Amsterdam, The Netherlands]. Ed. by H. Dym ... – Basel ; Boston ; Berlin : Birkhäuser
(Operator theory ; ...)
ISBN 3-7643-2283-7 (Basel ...)
ISBN 0-8176-2283-7 (Boston)
NE: Dym, Harry [Hrsg.]; Vrije Universiteit <Amsterdam> / Faculteit der Wiskunde en Informatica; Gochberg, Izrail': Festschrift
Vol. 1. The Calgary conference and matrix theory papers. – 1989

The **Calgary conference and matrix theory papers** / [vol. ed. office: Dep. of Mathematics and Computer Science, Vrije Univ., Amsterdam, The Netherlands]. Ed. by H. Dym ... – Basel ; Boston ; Berlin : Birkhäuser, 1989
(The Gohberg anniversary collection ; Vol. 1)
(Operator theory ; Vol. 40)
ISBN 3-7643-2307-8 (Basel ...) Pb.
ISBN 0-8176-2307-8 (Boston)
NE: Dym, Harry [Hrsg.]; 2. GT

Printed in Germany on acid-free paper
ISBN 3-7643-2283-7 (complete set)
ISBN 3-7643-2307-8 (vol. 1)
ISBN 3-7643-2308-6 (vol. 2)
ISBN 0-8176-2283-7 (complete set)
ISBN 0-8176-2307-8 (vol. 1)
ISBN 0-8176-2308-6 (vol. 2)

Table of contents of Volume I

Part B: Papers on Matrix Theory and its Applications

Editorial Preface

The Gohberg Anniversary Collection is dedicated to Israel Gohberg. It contains the proceedings of the international conference on "Operator Theory: Advances and Applications", which was held in Calgary, August 22 - 26, 1988, on the occasion of his 60th birthday. The two volumes present an up to date and attractive account of recent advances in operator theory, matrix theory and their applications. They include contributions by a number of the world's leading specialists in these areas and cover a broad spectrum of topics, many of which are on the frontiers of reseach. The two volumes are a tribute to Israel Gohberg; they reflect the wide range of his mathematical initiatives and personal interests.

This first volume is split into two parts. The first part consists of "Mathematical Tales" by I. Gohberg and a biographical text composed by the Editors from letters written by Gohberg's former colleagues and co-workers in Kishinev, from speeches delivered at the conference and from various personal notes, including "Reminiscences" by M.G. Krein. This part also contains Gohberg's curriculum vitae, his list of publications and the Calgary Conference program.

The second part of this volume consists of papers on matrix theory and its applications. It includes original research papers on Toeplitz matrices and other specific classes of structured matrices, on efficient inversion of matrices and problems in numerical linear algebra, on completion problems for partially defined matrices, on stability and classification of invariant subspaces, and the study of invariant factors.

The Editors are grateful to the Department of Mathematics and Computer Science of the Vrije Unversiteit for providing secretarial assistance. In particular, they thank Marijke Titawano for her work.

The Editors

Part A

The Calgary Conference, honoring Israel Gohberg

on the occasion of his 60th birthday

Israel Gohberg

Acknowledgements

These anniversary volumes owe their existence to the conference on "Operator Theory: Advances and Applications", held in honour of Israel Gohberg's 60th birthday at the University of Calgary, Canada, from August 22nd to 26th, 1988. This conference was made possible by the financial support of:

The National Sciences and Engineering Research Council, Canada,

The National Science Foundation, U.S.A.,

The Office of Naval Research, U.S.A.,

The United States Army,

The University of Calgary,

Control Data, Canada,

Nathan and Lily Silver, Israel,

as well as by the willingness of many invited participants to seek other sources of funding. The help of all these agencies and individuals is gratefully acknowledged by the organizers.

The organizers would also like to record their thanks to several individuals at the University of Calgary for their support of the conference in various forms. To P.J. Krueger, Vice-President Academic for his opening address. To Dean D.A. Armstrong of the Faculty of Science for financial support of the social program. To P.J. Browne, Head of the Department of Mathematics and Statistics for support and assistance in meeting substantial over-head costs. To Jim Peacock of the Department of Communications Media for excellent group phothographs, some of which appear in this volume. To Madeleine Aldridge of the Conference Office and her staff for their cheerful assistance through many months of preparations, and to Lorne Williams of "Summer Conference Housing" for his friendly and accomodating approach to a difficult task.

International Organizing Committee:

P. Lancaster, Chairman, The University of Calgary,

H. Dym, Weizmann Institute,

S. Goldberg, University of Maryland,

M.A. Kaashoek, Vrije Universiteit, Amsterdam.

With the assitstance of:

H. Bart (Rotterdam), J.A.Ball (Blacksburg), C. Foias (Bloomington),

J.W. Helton (San Diego), L. Lerer (Haifa), L. Rodman (Williamsburg).

Local Organizing Committee:

P. Lancaster (Chairman), P.J. Browne, P.A. Binding,

Madeleine Aldridge (for the Conference Office).

International Conference on
OPERATOR THEORY: ADVANCES & APPLICATIONS
A Conference to mark the 60th birthday of I. Gohberg

PROGRAM

Time	Event	Place
SUNDAY, AUGUST 21		
8:30 a.m.-6:00 p.m.	Hiking excursions.	
7:00 p.m.-10:00 p.m.	Registration and Reception	Faculty Club
MONDAY, AUGUST 22		
SESSION 1 - Chair:	P. Lancaster, University of Calgary	E 243
8:30 a.m.-8:45 a.m.	Welcome and Opening Remarks P.J. Krueger, Vice-President (Academic) University of Calgary	
8:45 a.m.-9:35 a.m.	Plenary lecture: Harry Dym, The Weizmann Institute of Science, Israel - "*Reproducing Kernel Spaces and Interpolation*"	
	REFRESHMENTS AND GREETINGS	
SESSION 2 - Chair:	S. Goldberg, University of Maryland	E 243
10:10 a.m.-11:00 a.m.	Plenary lecture: M.M. Djrbashian, Armenian Academy of Sciences, U.S.S.R. - "*Differential operators of fractional order and boundary value problems in the complex domain*"	
11:00 a.m.-11:30 a.m.	Invited paper: Joseph A. Ball, Virginia Tech - "*A Beurling-Lax invariant subspace representation theorem for rational matrix functions*"	
11:30 a.m.-12:00 p.m.	Invited paper: T. Ando, Hakkaido University, Japan - "*Operator means and operator inequalities*"	
	LUNCH	

SESSION 3 - Chair: C. Davis, University of Toronto E 243

1:10 p.m.-2:05 p.m. Plenary lecture:
Donald Sarason, University of California at Berkeley - "*Some function-theoretic questions connected with the AAK parameterization*"

2:05 p.m.-3:00 p.m. Plenary lecture:
Alexander Dynin, Ohio State University - "*Multivariable Gohberg-Krupnik Operator Algebras*"

COFFEE/TEA

SESSION 4a - Chair: P.A. Binding, University of Calgary E 243

3:30 p.m.-4:00 p.m. Invited paper:
B. Textorius, University of Linköping, Sweden - "*Directing mappings and spectral functions*"

4:00 p.m.-4:30 p.m. Invited paper:
H. De Snoo, University of Groningen, Netherlands - "*Spectral theory for equations with λ-depending boundary conditions*"

4:30 p.m.-5:00 p.m. Invited paper:
A. Dijksma, University of Groningen, Netherlands - "*Unitary colligations and characteristic functions in Krein spaces*"

5:00 p.m.-5:30 p.m. Contributed paper:
W. Allegretto, University of Alberta - "*Second Order Elliptic Equations with Degenerate Weight*"

SESSION 4b - Chair: I. Koltracht, University of Connecticut E 241

3:30 p.m.-4:00 p.m. Invited paper:
M. Tismenetsky, IBM Scientific Center, Haifa - "*Inversion of Block Toeplitz and Related Matrices*"

4:00 p.m.-4:30 p.m. Invited paper:
R. Ellis, University of Maryland - "*Orthogonal Systems Related to Infinite Hankel Matrices*"

4:30 p.m.-5:00 p.m. Invited paper:
T. Shalom, Tel Aviv University, Israel - "*On Bezoutian of Non-square Matrix Polynomials and Inversion of Matrices with Non-square Blocks*"

5:00 p.m.-5:30 p.m. Invited paper:
A. Ben-Artzi, Tel Aviv University, Israel - "*Nonstationary Inertia Theorems, Dichotomy and Applications*"

TUESDAY, AUGUST 23:

SESSION 5 - Chair: B.A. Francis, University of Toronto — E 243

8:30 a.m.-9:20 a.m. — Plenary lecture:
P. Dewilde, Technical University of Delft, Netherlands - "*Approximate Matrix Extensions and Applications in Modelling Theory*"

9:20 a.m.-9:50 a.m. — Invited lecture:
H. Baumgärtel, Academy of Science, D.R. Germany - "*On Causal Nets of Operator Algebras*"

REFRESHMENTS

SESSION 6 - Chair: H. Dym, Weizmann Institute — E 243

10:10 a.m.-11:00 a.m. — Plenary lecture:
T. Kailath, Stanford University, California - "*Generalized Gohberg-Semencul formulas*"

11:00 a.m.-11:30 a.m. — Invited paper:
B. Korenblum, SUNY, New York - "*Unimodular Mobius-Invariant Contracting Divisors for the Bergman Space*"

11:30 a.m.-12:00 p.m. — Invited paper:
S. Prössdorf, Academy of Sciences of the GDR, Berlin - "*Numerical Analysis for Singular Integral Equations*"

LUNCH

SESSION 7 - Chair: P. Lancaster, University of Calgary — E 243

1:10 p.m.-2:00 p.m. — Plenary lecture:
K.R. Davidson, University of Waterloo - "*Finite Dimensional Problems in Operator Theory*"

2:00 p.m.-2:30 p.m. — Invited paper:
C. Davis, University of Toronto - "*The norm of a dispersion mapping*"

2:30 p.m.-3:00 p.m. — Invited paper:
E.M. Semenov, University of Voronezh, U.S.S.R. - "*The Geometrical Properties of Operators Acting on* L_p"

COFEE/TEA

SESSION 8a - Chair: D.C. Lay, University of Maryland E 243

3:30 p.m.-4:00 p.m. Contributed paper:
K.F. Taylor, University of Saskatchewan - "*Projections in group* C^**-algebras*"

4:00 p.m.-4:30 p.m. Contributed paper:
J.H. Fourie, Potchefstroom University, South Africa - "*On Ultra Weak Type Topologies on* L(E,F)"

SESSION 8b - Chair: L. Rodman, College of William & Mary, VA E 241

3:30 p.m.-4:00 p.m. Contributed paper:
A.F. Dos Santos, Instituto Superior Técnico, Portugal - "*General Wiener-Hopf Operators and convolution equations on a finite interval*"

4:00 p.m.-4:30 p.m. Contributed paper:
A.B. Kon, Technion, Haifa, Israel - "*Inverse of Wiener-Hopf Type Operators*"

SESSION 9 - Chair: R.S. Phillips, Stanford University Village Park Inn

5:15 p.m.-6:15 p.m. Plenary session:
I. Gohberg, Tel Aviv University, Israel - "*Mathematical Tales and Gossips*"

6:15 p.m.-7:00 p.m. Cocktails -- Cash Bar

7:00 p.m.-10:00 p.m. Banquet
After-dinner speaker: S. Goldberg, University of Maryland

WEDNESDAY, AUGUST 24:

SESSION 10a - Chair: P. DeWilde, Technical University of Delft E 243

8:30 a.m.-9:00 a.m. Invited paper:
I. Koltracht, University of Connecticut - "*Efficient Algorithms for Structured matrices and kernels*"

9:00 a.m.-9:30 a.m. Contributed paper:
P.G. Spain, University of Glasgow, Scotland - "*Numerical Approximation of Hankel Operators*"

9:30 a.m.-10:00 a.m. Contributed paper:
V. Pan, SUNYA, Albany, New York - "*Fast and efficient parallel inversion of (block) Toeplitz matrices*"

10:00 a.m.-10:30 a.m. Contributed paper:
Q. Ye, University of Calgary - "*Variational Properties and Rayleigh Quotient Algorithms for Hermitian Matrix Pencils*"

SESSION 10b - Chair: H. Bart, Erasmus University, Rotterdam E 241

8:30 a.m.-9:00 a.m. Contributed paper:
B. Mityagin, Ohio State University, Columbus - *"Logarithm of Products of Operator Exponentials"*

9:00 a.m.-9:30 a.m. Contributed paper:
J. Janas, Institute of Mathematics PAN, Poland - *"Operators of ω type and their properties"*

9:30 a.m.-10:00 a.m. Contributed paper:
K. Stroethoff, University of Montana - *"Compact Hankel operators on the Bergman space"*

10:00 a.m.-10:30 a.m. Contributed paper:
T.H. Kuo, National Chiao Tung University, Taiwan - *"Operator Versions of the Convergence of Regular Measures on F-Spaces"*

REFRESHMENTS

11:00 a.m.-9:30 p.m. Excursion to the Mountains.

THURSDAY, AUGUST 25:

SESSION 11 - Chair: J.W. Helton, University of California at San Diego E 243

8:30 a.m.-9:20 a.m. Plenary lecture:
H. Widom, University of California, Santa Cruz - *"Generalized Wiener-Hopf Determinants"*

9:20 a.m.-9:50 a.m. Invited lecture:
E.V. Meister, Technische Hochschule Darmstadt, F.R.G. - *"Wiener-Hopf factorization of certain non-rational matrix functions in mathematical physics"*

REFRESHMENTS

SESSION 12 - Chair: M. Tismenetsky, IBM, Haifa, Israel E 243

10:10 a.m.-11:00 a.m. Plenary lecture:
M.A. Kaashoek, Vrije Universiteit, Amsterdam - *"Regular matrix polynomials"*

11:00 a.m.-11:30 a.m. Invited paper:
R.C. Thompson, University of California at Santa Barbara - *"Divisibility relations Satisfied by the Invariant Factors of a Matrix Product"*

11:30 a.m.-12:00 a.m. Invited paper:
H. Schneider, University of Wisconsin - *"Max Balancing of a weighted directed graph"*

LUNCH

SESSION 13a - Chair: R. Arocena, Universidad del Uruguay E 243

1:10 p.m.-2:00 p.m. Plenary lecture:
B. Gramsch, University of Mainz, West Germany - "*Frechet fibre bundles in the operator theory with applications to algebras of pseudodifferential operators*"

2:00 p.m.-2:30 p.m. Invited lecture:
M. Cotlar, Universidad Central de Venezuela - "*Lifting theorems in scattering systems with two evolution groups*"

2:30 p.m.-3:00 p.m. Invited lecture:
R. Mennicken, Universität Regensburg, West Germany - "*Equivalence of Boundary Value Operators and their characteristic matrices*"

SESSION 13b - Chair: K. Glover, Cambridge University E 241

2:00 p.m.-2:30 p.m. Invited lecture:
H. Bart, Erasmus University, The Netherlands - "*Complementary Triangular Forms of Upper Triangular Toeplitz Matrices*"

2:30 p.m.-3:00 p.m. Invited lecture:
L. Lerer, Israel Institute of Technology, Haifa - "*Inverse problems for block Toeplitz matrices, orthogonal matrix polynomials and coprime symmetric factorizations*"

COFFEE/TEA

SESSION 14a - Chair: H. Schneider, University of Wisconsin E 243

3:30 p.m.-4:00 p.m. Invited paper:
C.R. Johnson, College of William & Mary, Virginia - "*Matrix Completion Problems: Explicit Formulae and Solutions*"

4:00 p.m.-4:30 p.m. Invited paper:
F. Van Schagen, Vrije Universiteit, Amsterdam - *Eigenvalues of Completions of Submatrices*"

4:30 p.m.-5:00 p.m. Contributed paper:
L. Elsner, Universität Bielefeld, F.R.G. - "*On the spectral radius of entrywise functions of matrices*"

5:00 p.m.-5:30 p.m. Invited paper:
H. Woerdeman, Vrije Universiteit, Amsterdam - *Strictly Contractive and Positive Completions for Block Matrices*"

SESSION 14b - Chair: C. Sadosky, Howard University, Washington E 241

3:30 p.m.-4:00 p.m. Invited paper:
Y. Rodin, Illinois - "*The Riemann boundary problem on Riemann surfaces, integrable systems and soliton theory*"

4:00 p.m.-4:30 p.m. Contributed paper:
P.J. Browne, University of Calgary - "*Two Parameter Eigencurve Theory*"

4:30 p.m.-5:00 p.m. Contributed paper:
F. Farid, University of Calgary - "*Spectral Properties of Diagonally Dominant Infinite Matrices*"

5:00 p.m.-5:30 p.m. Invited paper:
L.S. Frank, Catholic University of Nijmegen - "*Coercive Singular Perturbations: Reduction to Regular Perturbations and Applications*"

6:00 p.m.-8:00 p.m. Wine and Cheese Party Faculty Club

FRIDAY, AUGUST 26:

SESSION 15 - Chair: K. Clancey, University of Georgia E 243

8:30 a.m.-9:20 a.m. Plenary lecture:
R.S. Phillips, Stanford University, California - "*Moduli Space, Heights and Isospectral Sets of Planar Domains*"

9:20 a.m.-9:50 a.m. Invited paper:
H. Isaev, Azerbaijan Academy of Sciences, Baku - "*Multi-parameter spectrums*"

REFRESHMENTS

SESSION 16 - Chair: J.A. Ball, Virginia Polytech Institute E 243

10:10 a.m.-11:00 a.m. Plenary lecture:
J.W. Helton, University of California at San Diego - (TITLE TO BE ANNOUNCED)

11:00 a.m.-11:30 a.m. Invited paper:
K. Glover, Cambridge University, England - "*Maximum Entropy and Risk Aversion*"

11:30 a.m.-12:00 a.m. Invited paper:
R. Duducava, Georgian Academy of Science, Tbilisi - "*Regularization of the Singular Integral Operators*"

LUNCH

SESSION 17a - Chair: C.R. Johnson, College of William & Mary, Virginia — E 243

1:15 p.m.-1:45 p.m. — Invited paper:
D.C. Lay, University of Maryland -
"Negative Eigenvalues of Selfadjoint Extensions of Band Matrices"

1:45 p.m.-2:15 p.m. — Invited paper:
A.C.M. Ran, Vrije Universiteit, Amsterdam -
"On strong α-stability of invariant subspaces of matrices"

2:15 p.m.-2:45 p.m. — Invited paper:
L. Rodman, College of Mary & William, Virginia -
"Stability of invariant lagrangian subspaces and Riccati equations"

SESSION 17b - Chair: L.S. Frank, Catholic University of Nijmegen — E 241

1:15 p.m.-1:45 p.m. — Invited paper:
K. Clancey, University of Georgia -
"Theta Functions and Representing Measures on Multiply Connected Domains"

1:45 p.m.-2:15 p.m. — Contributed paper:
R. Arocena, Universidad del Uruguay -
"A class of translation invariant forms, dilations of commutants and maximum entropy"

2:15 p.m.-2:45 p.m. — Contributed paper:
D. Shemesh, Rafael, Haifa - *"Subspaces Which are Left Invariant Under Certain Families of Operators"*

COFFEE/TEA

SESSION 18 - Chair: M.A. Kaashoek, Free University, Amsterdam — E 243

3:10 p.m.-3:45 p.m. — Invited paper:
I.M. Spitkovski, Academy of Sciences, Odessa -
"Almost periodic factorization"

3:45 p.m.-4:00 p.m. — Concluding Remarks

Israel Gohberg with the members of the organizing committee

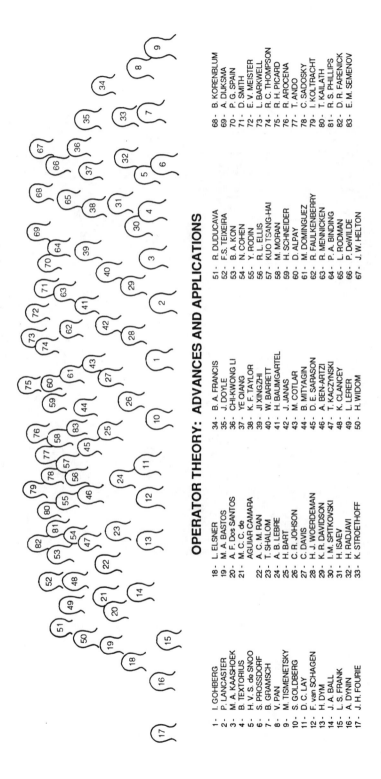

OPERATOR THEORY: ADVANCES AND APPLICATIONS

1 - I. GOHBERG
2 - P. LANCASTER
3 - M. A. KAASHOEK
4 - B. TEXTORIUS
5 - H. V. S. de SNOO
6 - S. PROSSDORF
7 - B. GRAMSCH
8 - V. PAN
9 - M. TISMENETSKY
10 - S. GOLDBERG
11 - D. C. LAY
12 - F. van SCHAGEN
13 - H. DYM
14 - J. A. BALL
15 - L. S. FRANK
16 - A. DYNIN
17 - J. H. FOURIE
18 - L. ELSNER
19 - M. A. BASTOS
20 - A. F. Dos SANTOS
21 - M. C. C. de AGUIAR CAMARA
22 - A. C. M. RAN
23 - T. SHALOM
24 - A. B. LEBRE
25 - H. BART
26 - C. R. JOHSON
27 - C. DAVIS
28 - H. J. WOERDEMAN
29 - K. R. DAVIDSON
30 - I. M. SPITKOVSKI
31 - H. ISAEV
32 - H. RADJAVI
33 - K. STROETHOFF
34 - B. A. FRANCIS
35 - J. DOYLE
36 - CHI-KWONG LI
37 - YE QIANG
38 - K. F. TAYLOR
39 - JI XINGZHI
40 - W. BARRETT
41 - H. BAUMGARTEL
42 - J. JANAS
43 - M. COTLAR
44 - B. MITYAGIN
45 - D. E. SARASON
46 - A. BEN-ARTZI
47 - T. KACZYNSKI
48 - K. CLANCEY
49 - L. LERER
50 - H. WIDOM
51 - R. DUDUCAVA
52 - F.S. TEIXEIRA
53 - B. A. KON
54 - N. COHEN
55 - Y. RODIN
56 - R. L. ELLIS
57 - KUO TSANG-HAI
58 - M. MORAN
59 - H. SCHNEIDER
60 - D. ALPAY
61 - M. DOMINGUEZ
62 - R. FAULKENBERRY
63 - R. MENNICKEN
64 - P. A. BINDING
65 - L. RODMAN
66 - P. DeWILDE
67 - J. W. HELTON
68 - B. KORENBLUM
69 - A. DIJKSMA
70 - P. G. SPAIN
71 - D. SMITH
72 - E. V. MEISTER
73 - L. BARKWELL
74 - R. C. THOMPSON
75 - R. H. PICARD
76 - R. AROCENA
77 - T. ANDO
78 - C. SADOSKY
79 - I. KOLTRACHT
80 - T. KAILATH
81 - R. S. PHILLIPS
82 - D. R. FARENICK
83 - E. M. SEMENOV

INTRODUCTION

R. S. PHILLIPS

I am very gratified to have been asked to give this introductory talk for our honoured guest, Israel Gohberg. I should like to begin by spending a few minutes talking shop.

One of the great tragedies of being a mathematician is that your papers are read so seldom. On the average ten people will read the introduction to a paper and perhaps two of these will actually study the paper. It's difficult to know how to deal with this problem. One strategy which will at least get you one more reader, is to collaborate with someone. I think Israel early on caught on to this, and I imagine that by this time most of the analysts in the world have collaborated with him. He continues relentlessly in this pursuit; he visits his neighbour Harry Dym at the Weizmann Institute regularly, he spends several months a year in Amsterdam working with Rien Kaashoek, several weeks in Maryland with Seymour Goldberg, a couple of weeks here in Calgary with Peter Lancaster, and on the rare occasions when he is in Tel Aviv, he takes care of his many students.

I should remark that all this activity has not gone unnoticed: At the University of Tel Aviv he occupies the Silver Chair of mathematics (one must distinguish between *the* Silver Chair and *a* silver chair), he is a member of the Royal Dutch Academy and he has received the Israel Rothschild Prize in Mathematics, and, as I understand it, he is favoured to win the most travelled mathematician award.

This all began about 40 years ago, at which time he was a protégé of Mark Krein. The two of them formed one of the most successful collaborations in mathematics, and the resulting books and papers are outstanding. One of the consequences of this collaboration was that he became a member of the Moldavian Academy. However, I really believe that Israel blossomed after he left the Soviet Union in 1974. Since then his output and influence has been truly prodigious.

The feeling of good-will which pervades this conference is in good part due to the fact that we are celebrating Israel's sixtieth birthday. I suppose I should say his approximate birthday since Don Sarason has cast some doubt as to the exact date of his birth. In any case, it is a great pleasure to present Israel on this occasion.

MATHEMATICAL TALES

I. GOHBERG

I want to thank Ralph very much for his kind introduction. Now I am going to relate some stories from my career in mathematics, mostly from the times when I lived in the Soviet Union, before immigrating to Israel.

1. UNIVERSITY STUDIES AND MY FIRST PAPERS

The high school I graduated from in 1946 was in a village called Vasilevsky Sovhoz, not far from Frunze the capital of the Kirgizian Soviet Socialist Republic, where my mother, sister and myself lived during the time of World War Two. This republic borders on continental China. During my final three years I had a wonderful mathematics teacher, whom I will never forget. He was M.S. Shumbarsky, a young man recently graduated from the Warsaw University under the instructorship of Professor K. Borsuk.

During my first two years after high school I studied in Frunze, at the Pedagogical Institute. Apart from a small stipend given to all students by the authorities, I was supported by my mother. She worked very hard in a small country hospital where she was the only midwife, and consequently always on call. My mother had to be very inventive to be able to keep my sister and herself on her small salary, as well as to help me. This postwar period was a very difficult time. Food and clothing were rationed. I could not afford to eat at the student menza, so every week I brought food from home. I lived in a student residence together with seven other students in one room. My high school teacher, M.S. Shumbarsky, often visited me when I came home for weekends, and during long hours we would discuss the new material which I had studied and read during the past week. He always brought food with him, hidden under his coat (I think he did not want his wife to know.) They had no children. I had very good teachers (unusually so for such a remote place). I remember with gratitude G. Ja. Sukhomlinov (his name appears at the beginning of functional analysis) and G. Ja. Bykov (an expert in differential equations). My favourite professor of this period was D.L. Picus, who obtained his Ph.D. from V.F. Kagan in Moscow University. I will always remember his very interesting lectures and conversations. From him I learned about the most popular unsolved problems in mathematics.

In 1947 I won a Stalin stipend. It was a high award and nearly every academic institution of higher education awarded a small number of them. Financially my new stipend was three to four times larger than the old one, and I could now support myself, and even offer some help to my mother and sister. During the following academic year (1947/1948) I had my first small mathematical success. I invented my first theorem and found an interesting proof of a well known one. During this year I realized that I did not want to continue my studies at a Pedagogical Institute, where a lot of time was spent on training to be a high school teacher. I was more interested in a university education and in research. My professors also advised me to move to a university. There was no university in Frunze at that time, so I discussed the matter with my mother and she offered me the necessary moral and financial support. We also decided to take advantage of this situation to return to the area from which we originally came. In the summer of 1948 I left Frunze and the Stalin stipend, and moved back to the West. By coincidence, D.L. Picus was moving to Kishinev, and he helped me to transfer to Kishinev to continue my studies there. The following academic year I was busy adjusting to the university curriculum, and I also started to support myself partially by tutoring.

I was lucky; when I was in my fourth year at this university a young doctor from Leningrad came to work there. As he himself said, he taught us everything he knew. He was very knowledgeable as well as a good lecturer, and I listened to everything he had to say. This was I.A. Itscovitch, a former Ph.D. student of S.G. Mikhlin, and I am grateful to him for introducing me to singular integral equations, to Fredholm operators, to index, and to all those topics in which later on I started to work actively. In 1949 I already had my first results which were published a little later, in 1951.

D.L. Pikus introduced me to S.M. Nikolsky, and advised me to send him my first results for evaluation. S.M. Nikolsky was interested in these topics and had made nice contributions to this area. He recommended my manuscript to A.N. Kolmogorov, who presented my first two papers to "Doklady." In 1951, they were published in this journal whilst I was still in my fifth year. At the same time, in another part of the world, in Ibadan (Nigeria), F.V. Atkinson obtained similar results. He published them in 1951 in Russian in "Mathematichesky Sbornik." Also in 1951, in the United States, a paper of B. Yood with similar results appeared. As B. Yood discovered, this story started with an earlier paper of J.A. Dieudonne, published in France in 1943, during the war, (see the paper: J.A. Dieudonne, Integral Equations and Operator Theory, 580-589, 1985). I am happy to share these results with good friends.

In the autumn of 1950, I decided to visit M.G. Krein. Somehow I had heard that Krein was a nice man and would talk to me if I came. So I decided to go to Odessa to visit him. I could travel by train, but there was the question of an hotel. Hotels in Odessa were always full, so how could I find a place? One had to pay under the table and I didn't know how to do that. I had once heard from my uncle that his wife had family living in Odessa, so I wrote to my uncle. He wrote to the relatives in Odessa and they agreed to accept me for a couple of days. So I came to Odessa to these relatives.

I didn't even know the telephone number of Krein, but I knew where he was working; I already knew some of his work. He was at the Marine Engineering Institute in Odessa. This was a semi-military academic institution, so the professors wore uniforms and held ranks, which were denoted by the braid on their uniforms. An ordinary person could not enter; one needed to have some special identity card, which I for sure did not have, but I saw some students running in waving something in their hands. I also ran in waving something, and so I came to Krein's office. At that time he held the chair in theoretical mechanics. Some time earlier he had been dismissed from the Odessa University. I came up to the secretary sitting at a desk and said that I would like to meet Professor Krein. She

A cartoon from my student years done by a friend and fellow student, Zobov. It is entitled "Twenty Years Hence"
The two men at the right and left are the colonels who taught us military subjects once a week at the university
I am in the centre

said, "He will be here in an hour. There will be a seminar." I waited. After an hour I saw two men with all this braid and insignia on their uniforms - colonels, captains, whatever - two men, one looked very ordinary and the second fat and distinguished, who I was sure must be Krein. I went up to him and asked, "Are you Mark Grigorievich Krein?" "No, " he said, "This one is." Krein invited me to his seminar and I listened to his talk. It was a very interesting talk on the behaviour of a stretched string, on extreme mass distributions. After his talk, he spoke to me. I showed him my first results; they were about Fredholm operators and index. He invited me to his home in the evening, and there we had our first long conversation. He drew my attention to two topics. The first was commutative normed rings, today we would say commutative Banach algebras. I did not know anything about it. "You don't know about this?" he said. This was in 1950. He said this was essential for a mathematical education. I felt terrible, non-educated. Then he showed me a couple of papers which had just appeared on infinite Toeplitz matrices. He said that they looked interesting to him. I am not sure if these two papers are known in the West, they are by Rappaport, who was the first to see the connection between Toeplitz matrices and singular integral equations. These topics became very important in my career.

At the end of our meeting I told M.G. Krein that I would be happy to listen to his lectures and to be under his direction. He answered that, unfortunately, he could not take me as a graduate student. Later I learned that his institution would not accept Jewish Ph.D. students. After World War Two M.G. had only two or three Jewish Ph.D. students, all war veterans. One of them was I.S. Iokhvidov who returned from the war with the rank of major, and the second M.A. Krasnoselsky, who, if I am not mistaken, returned with the rank of captain.

When I returned to my hosts I related to them what a great impression M.G. Krein had made on me. While I was leaving Odessa and thanking them for their hospitality, they asked me how much the professor had charged me. I told them, nothing. They could not believe this because they were used to dealing with professors of medicine. This meeting with M.G. Krein was a very important beginning.

In 1951 I graduated from Kishinev University with a degree equivalent to a masters degree in the West. This was just before the tragedy of the Jewish doctors in the

Soviet Union. During the last years of Stalin antisemitism grew rapidly and the situation for the Jews was fast worsening. I could not find a university which would accept me as a Ph.D. student. I tried hard. I asked in my own university, but the Dean did not even want to discuss it with me. I asked S.M. Nikolsky about possibilities in Moscow (he was then Vice Director of the Steklov Institute). He answered that for reasons which I would probably understand, it would be impossible. In some places they would get away with it by saying that strong students do not need to be accepted for the Ph.D. programme because they can write their thesis without any help; only the weak ones, who need help, have to be accepted to the Ph.D. programme. This policy enabled the universities to accept communist party activists who were weak students. I got a compulsory assignment to a high school in a small town on the border with Rumania (Ungeny). In Moldavia there is a lot of wine, and the previous teacher in mathematics drank too much and could no longer teach, so they sent me in his place. M.G. Krein wrote a highly complimentary review on my Diploma (master) thesis. This, together with a recommendation of my former professors, V.A. Andrunakievich and I.F. Volkov, made an impression on the Minister of Education of the Moldavian Soviet Republic, A.N. Krachun, who took the responsibility of changing my assignment. Finally I was sent to work at a two-year teachers' college in Soroki, a more interesting place. I never was a Ph.D. student; I wrote my Ph.D. thesis externally in my spare time and defended it in Leningrad. This became possible in 1954 after Stalin's death, when the situation improved.

The advice Krein gave me was very useful. In my diploma thesis, there was already a chapter on normed rings in which I found maximal ideals. I generated an algebra with all linear singular integral operators with continuous coefficients on a closed contour, and factored it by the compact operators (it was known that this is a commutative ring) and found the maximal ideals. This result enabled something new to be found, namely the conditions necessary for a singular integral operator to satisfy the F. Noether theorems. The proof was based on the fact that for a linear singular integral operator the F. Noether theorems hold if and only if they have a bounded regularizer, or what is the same, that the singular integral operator has a bounded inverse, modulo the ideal of compact operators. This was in 1950. Later, I showed these results to M.G. Krein, who liked them. I showed these results also to I.M. Gelfand, and they both advised me to publish them in Uspekhi, where they appeared later as a short paper. There was a problem with this paper which I am going to relate.

I was very proud of this paper. As I remember, it appeared in the second issue of 1952. I was so happy that I even subscribed to Uspekhi! I didn't have enough money, but I did it anyway, and so each number of the journal was delivered to my home. When I received number six I could hardly believe my eyes. The title of a two page paper included in this issue of the journal was "On a note of I.C. Gohberg," the author was F.D. Gakhov. Later I was told by some former students of Gakhov that my paper had discouraged some of his graduate students from working with nonbounded regularizers. To raise the morale of his students Gakhov had presented the matter in his paper in the following way: he wrote that in my paper I had introduced the artificial condition of boundedness of the regularizer just to be able to use theorems from abstract functional analysis. He had left out the crucial fact that this is the condition which is equivalent to the F. Noether theorems. The end of F.D. Gakhov's paper is ridiculous. It contains the conclusion that "the theorem proved by I.C. Gohberg has a conditional character and holds only under restrictions on the choice of the regularizer which the author made." This remark of his applies to any correct theorem in the world and thus all of them are conditional. Later I was told by M.G. Krein that he thought this little paper of Gakhov was directed somehow against abstract mathematics in general. I heard that A.N. Kolmogorov also got this impression, but it is obvious that they were all afraid to do or say anything officially; 1952 was a bad time. Till now the paper of Gakhov remains unchallenged. In general, I do not understand how a respected journal like Uspekhi could publish such a paper.

Some of F.D.Gakhov's students were very good mathematicians. I have a high regard for I.B. Simonenko from Rostov, who made very important contributions to the theory of singular integral operators. I met him for the first time in the late fifties and many times thereafter. It was always a pleasure to discuss mathematics with him.

2. MY FIRST YEARS OF WORK

I was assigned to work at a teachers institute in Soroki, a small town in the north of Moldavia. This was a two year college type institute which trained teachers for the 5-7 grades of elementary school. A large number of the students were quite weak. The administration judged a teacher by the marks he gave his students. My work was even more complicated because a large part of my lectures had to be in Moldavian (a Rumanian dialect), and I had to start lecturing with an extremely limited knowledge of this language. I did not imagine then that some twenty-four years hence I would have the same problems with English in the United States and with Hebrew in Israel.

I worked for two years in Soroki, from 1951 to 1953. These were the most difficult years of Stalin's rule, and years of the severest antisemitism. A Jewish teacher could be dismissed, or worse, sent to jail, as a result of an accusation by a student who failed to pass an examination. Later I learned that I was about to be dismissed on just such grounds, but I was saved by Stalin's death.

The director in Soroki was a mathematician by the name of V.G. Cheban, a very pleasant man. Before World War Two he was a graduate student of A.N. Kolmogorov. He got his Ph.D. degree much later in mechanics at Moscow University. He supported my work with M.G. Krein and allowed me to travel to Odessa whenever possible.

In 1953 my director was promoted to director of the Pedagogical Institute at Beltsy (the third largest town in Moldavia). He had me transferred also to Beltsy where my job was much more interesting. This was a four year university type institution. Whilst working there I wrote my Ph.D. thesis externally. During the autumn semester of 1953 I taught a 40-46 hours a week (which was my yearly work load). This enabled me to spend the spring semester of 1954 in Leningrad, where I completed my thesis and defended it at the Leningrad Pedagogical Institute. The opponents (readers of the thesis) were G.P. Akilov and S.G. Mikhlin.

In Leningrad I met S.G. Mikhlin for the second time. I visited him for the first time in 1951 and it was a great pleasure to meet him again. He showed interest in my work and was always very kind to me and supportive. I remember with gratitude our interesting mathematical conversations and discussions. He and his papers had an important influence on me, and I consider him as one of my teachers. I was very glad to meet V.I. Smirnov, a famous mathematician and a very interesting man of high personal integrity. For a long time we corresponded and he discussed with me various problems which appeared whilst he was writing a new edition of his volume containing the theory of integral equations. I attended on a regular basis the seminar of V.I. Smirnov and the seminar of L.V. Kantorovich. The latter was studying the book of L. Schwartz on distributions. We were using a pirate edition of this book printed in the USSR. I recall with pleasure my meetings with M.S. Birman, V.A. Jakubovich, L.D. Faddeev (who was then a student), A.I. Koshelev, and O.A. Ladyzhenskaja. A few years later I also met M.Z. Solomjak and N.K. Nikolsky.

After the defence my salary doubled and I was able to bring my mother from Kirgizia to Beltsy and to arrange for my sister to transfer from Frunze to Kishinev. She was a student of medicine and such a move was no trivial matter. Mrs. A.N. Krachun, who was now in an even higher position (vice premier) in the government of Moldavia, helped me for the second time, and I remember her help with gratitude. We were always a close family and after the death of my father we felt even closer, and it was very important for us to be together. (My sister and her family are now living in Israel. She is a pediatric surgeon and has a Ph.D. In 1985 she was awarded the title "Woman of the Year.")

The nearest USSR university town to Beltsy from the north was Chernovitsy, which had a well established university. I often visited this town because my sister lived there with her family. On each occasion that I visited I also met with my colleagues and good friends K.M. Fischman and S.D. Eidelman. We had many interesting mathematical discussions since our interests were quite close and we understood each other well. We also studied interesting papers together. This very pleasant and useful connection continued for many years with visits and lectures, however we never produced anything jointly.

At the beginning of 1956 I.M. Gelfand and S.V. Fomin organized a conference in Functional Analysis in Moscow University. This conference was the first conference in which I participated and lectured. It was the time when I.M. Gelfand and his colleagues were writing the now famous volumes on generalized functions and their manifold applications. It was expected that the new theory would have a very strong influence and would introduce order into many fields.

The conference opened with an introduction by M.V. Keldysh and a talk by the famous physicist L.D. Landau. According to the programme he was to present the lecture "Functional analysis methods and theoretical physics." I think it was expected that he would explain how distributions solve difficult problems in physics. I remember how L.D. Landau started by remarking that he did not know what functional analysis was doing in the title of his talk and he would speak about the state of affairs in theoretical physics. I understood that the influence of distributions was already behind him.

I found the conference very interesting and I very much enjoyed many of the talks and the very pleasant meetings. There for the first time I met B.Sz.-Nagy. I knew about his important contributions from M.G. Krein, and I was very happy to be introduced to him. We also had common interests, and I tried to have a talk with him. Unfortunately I did not speak English and my German was not very good, but we soon discovered that we could talk in Rumanian, and this is how we communicated until I learned English. I very much liked B.Sz.-Nagy's papers, and on a few occasions I found in his work answers to questions which were bothering me. Later I followed with great interest his joint papers with C. Foias. Their important series of papers were often discussed at M.G. Krein's seminars. I met C. Foias for the first time ten years later at the congress in Moscow. I feel that my interests in mathematics are very close to those of C. Foias and B.Sz.-Nagy, and it is a pleasure to have such good mathematical neighbours and friends.

At this conference I met a number of very active young mathematicians. Ju.M. Berezansky, S.V. Fomin, M.A. Krasnoselsky, A.G. Kostjuchenko, S.G. Krein (M.G.'s younger brother), G.E. Shilov and M.I. Vishik. I was very impressed by their talks and research plans. On the last day of the conference, following a talk on J. von Neumann algebras, Gelfand pondered in his remarks on how it could be that such a beautiful theory had no applications (which was the situation at that time). At the end of the conference in his concluding remarks, the famous topologist, P.S. Alexandrov, said that I.M. Gelfand had stated the law of the conservation of beauty. If a theory is beautiful then it must have applications.

After this conference I went to Leningrad where Bella and I got married. This was the best thing that ever happened to me, and I now understand fully just how lucky I was. My wife was a medical student in her final year. We had met a few years earlier in Frunze when my sister introduced me to her friend and classmate in the Institute. After the wedding Bella and I spent a few days together; this was the beginning of our honeymoon, which I think continues even today. My wife works as a medical doctor. We have two lovely daughters, Zvia and Yanina, married respectively to Nissim and Arie. They also have children - Tali, Jonathan and Keren (who was born soon after the Calgary conference). From Leningrad I went to Beltsy and Odessa, where I worked together with M.G. Krein on writing the first draft of the expository paper on Fredholm operators and index.

Later in Beltsy I got the chair in mathematics, and so to my regular duties of lecturing (18 to 24 hours a week) and research, was added also the responsibilities entailed in training teachers of mathematics.

In 1959 I was invited to join the Moldavian branch of the main academy in Kishinev. I applied and was accepted. I left the chair and a better salary and moved to Kishinev. This institution was trying to organize a strong mathematical group because it was preparing to be transformed into the Moldavian Academy of Science. Almost every republic already had its own academy. At the beginning we were attached to the Department of Physics, headed by T.I. Malinovsky, a well known crystallographer. Very soon this academy was inaugurated and an institute of mathematics was established. My colleagues and myself (as chairman) formed the department of functional analysis of the new institute. In the institute there were also two other departments of theoretical mathematics. One of these was the department of algebra, with the group of V.A. Andrunakievich, which was interested in the theory of rings and modules, and the group of the late V.D. Belousov which specialized in quasigroup theory. V.D. Belousov was a pleasant man and a very good mathematician. We worked together in Beltsy (he was born there) and we became friends. By the way, Belousov was the only one of my colleagues who had spent an academic year in the United States (Madison, University of Wisconsin). From him I got my first picture of academic life in a university in the United States. He was very excited about this period, but he had to be very careful when speaking about it at home. His stories had to be balanced, and he had to describe not only the positive, but also an exaggerated negative side of American life, otherwise he would be in trouble, especially since he was a communist party member. The other department was the department of differential equations and dynamical systems, with I.U. Bronshtein, K.S. Sibirsky and B.A. Stcherbakov as its senior people. Their interests were mostly in the theory of invariants of ordinary differential equations and topological theory of dynamical systems. V.A. Andrunakievich was appointed director of this institute. We were happy with this choice since he was a very good mathematician and a very intelligent person. During my student years V.A. Andrunakievich was a professor at Kishinev University where I took his courses in linear algebra and number theory and wrote a joint paper with him. In the early fifties he left Kishinev for Moscow, fearing that his mathematical career, and maybe much more, was in danger. The person he feared was the Dean of the Faculty of Physics and Mathematics at Kishinev University, an extremely weak mathematician, as well as a man of low morals, and an active party member. When the academy was inaugurated V.A. Andrunakievich (a full professor of the Mendeleev Institute in Moscow, and an ethnic Moldavian) was the only mathematician to be appointed a full member. The initial members of the academy were appointed by the government of the republic. V.A. Andrunakievich soon returned to Kishinev and this time the Dean was unable to harm him. Shortly after the Dean disappeared from Kishinev.

3. WORKING WITH M.G. KREIN

The work I did together with M.G. Krein was an important part of my life, especially the two books we wrote together. At this point we already had the experience of writing together two large expository papers (the paper about Fredholm operators and the paper about Wiener-Hopf operators). In 1958 we started to write these two books as one book on perturbation theory. At the beginning I found it very difficult. I was not familiar enough with the background, and I had a great deal to learn. The discussions I had with M.G. Krein whilst we were working together were very important for me. In a very simple and elegant way he soon introduced me to new areas. Whatever he told me was nicely connected and motivated, and had an interesting historical perspective. Heuristic remarks always shed light on difficult formal considerations. In this way I was able to learn the background very quickly and to grasp the global picture.

In writing Mark Grigorievich is extremely demanding of himself and of everyone working with him. If, by a complete change in the writing of a paper or a chapter, he could improve it by even a small fraction, he would not think twice. It was never a question of whether it was worthwhile or not. If you can improve it you have to do so. Papers that were almost ready would lie for years until they attained perfection. He maintained that the writing of a paper is no less scientifically important than proving the result, because whilst polishing up a paper one can find new proofs, new presentations, new connections and new mathematics.

Probably some readers noticed that the paper on systems of Wiener-Hopf integral equations of I. Gohberg and M.G. Krein appeared before Krein's paper on a single Wiener-Hopf equation. At the same time the first published paper was a continuation of the second. The explanation of this is as follows. The 200 page typescript of Krein's paper was actually ready much before the paper of Gohberg and Krein was written. But M.G. decided that his paper needed a few small additions and some polishing. This work was not attractive, especially taking into consideration the fact that in such a huge paper every small change easily turns into a snowball of changes throughout the entire manuscript, so M.G. kept on postponing it. Work on systems was fresh and much more interesting, so he was more interested in working with me on systems. I remember this paper on systems was written in a very short time. In three or four months we produced a major part of the results and wrote the paper. We sent the manuscript to "Uspekhi" and it was accepted. M.G.'s paper was still waiting, and I proposed to M.G. that I help him to finish his paper. Some time later I came to Odessa for a month for this purpose, and at the end of this period the fat manuscript was sent to "Uspekhi." The work we had to do was mostly technical. The whole family was worried about this manuscript because the situation had a bad effect on M.G. and I remember how happy Raisa Lvovna (M.G.'s wife) was when we showed her the receipt from the Post Office. I also remember a celebration. After M.G.'s paper on Wiener-Hopf equations was published he presented me with a reprint with the inscription "To the midwife of this paper..." Some of M.G.'s manuscripts were never published. I would especially like to mention his large manuscript on the theory and applications of cones in Banach space written before World War Two. This manuscript was very popular in Voronezh and was used by M.A. Krasnoselsky and his students when they developed the theory of positive solutions of operator equations. Shortly after World War Two M.G. Krein wrote a large manuscript together with M.S. Brodsky on representation of topological groups. This manuscript was never submitted for publication because M.G. thought it needed some additions and some polishing.

Even today in the Soviet Union the formulae in typescripts are written in by hand. At the beginning of our collaboration M.G. wrote the formulae in the first copy of the paper; he did not trust me enough to do this. When I said "But I think I can do it," he answered, "Yes, but I like to write them in myself because while doing so I again think over the proofs and the whole material."

The plans of the books changed many times; the whole concept was changed, we made unexpected additions and extensions, including results which were still fresh. At a later stage we developed the theory of singular values, the very same singular values which are now so popular even for matrices. Very few people knew of them at that time and only a few papers had appeared in the literature. It was very time consuming, but later it was extremely enjoyable and satisfying.

We decided to include in the book a number of very interesting recent results of M.V. Keldysh on completeness and distribution of eigenvalues for certain classes of nonselfadjoint operators. These results were published without proofs in a four page short note in Doklady. We tried to get the proofs from the author, but were informed that they do not exist. The detailed manuscript with the complete proofs disappeared. At that time M.V. Keldysh was President of the Academy of Sciences of USSR. This post can be compared with the post of a member of the government responsible for science. He was also responsible for the theoretical part of the USSR cosmos project. In official reports and the reminiscences of the first cosmonauts (as the USSR astronauts are called), there were two persons who were not called by their real names. These were the "chief designer" and the "chief theoretician." We all knew that M.V. Keldysh was the chief theoretician, and S.P. Koroleov the chief designer, but it was forbidden to publish their names in the press. This information was disclosed officially much later. During these years M.V. Keldysh was very busy and there was no chance that he would have time to recover the proofs

This photograph was taken around 1958 when work was begun on the book with M.G. Krein. On the right G.N. Chebotarev, Professor of Mathematics at Kazan University son of N.G. Chebotarev, who was M.G. Krein's teacher. M.G. Krein is in the centre, I am on the left.

of his results. With the help of some colleagues we recovered the proofs of an important part of these results. So the first time these results of M.V. Keldysh with complete proofs appeared was in our first book. I met M.V. Keldysh personally in 1966 at the Congress in Moscow. He told me that he liked the exposition of his results in our book and that it differs from his original presentation. The original manuscript of M.V. Keldysh was found much later (I do not know the circumstances) and was published in Uspekhi in 1971.

In 1961 I took part in the Fourth Soviet Mathematical Congress in Leningrad. V.B. Lidsky, who is well known for his excellent contributions in operator theory, was scheduled to present a joint talk with M.V. Keldysh about the theory of nonselfadjoint operators. A day before he had to give this important invited talk he felt that he was loosing his voice. He feared that he would loose it completely during his talk, so he asked me to prepare myself to take over should he not be able to continue. The talk was not written down, so V.B. spent a couple of hours instructing me. The following day, after a long evening of work, I was really ready to take over at any point. Fortunately it was not necessary for me to do so, and V.B. Lidsky gave a very nice talk. But the incident was very useful and gave me an opportunity to go over the theory and to discuss the details with V.B. Lidsky under the pressure which usually precedes lecturing. He was a very good friend and I enjoyed discussing mathematics with him. Unfortunately our interests later went different ways.

There were areas which did not exist before we started to write the book, for instance the theory of factorization of operators (this theory generalizes the multiplicative lower upper triangular decomposition of matrices to the infinite dimensional case). The same is true for the theory of transformation of triangular truncation with applications to differential operators. All of these results were obtained during the writing of the book. It was very satisfactory for us to see later in papers of T. Kailath and his colleagues how these theories work beautifully in applications. In general our research paths and those of T. Kailath and his colleagues often cross, and it is always a pleasure when this happens.

When selecting material or discussing expositions or proofs, we sometimes had differing opinions, and this usually led to an argument. In general M.G. is a fighter and he can make himself very convincing. But he would also listen attentively to my arguments.

During such discussions we sometimes exchanged positions - I would adopt his position and he mine. But we always ended up on a cheerful note with a common point, jokes often being used to illustrate important arguments.

I think it took us around five to six years to write the books, initially as one volume. I spent two or three months a year in Odessa for joint work, part of this time during my vacation, on M.G. Krein's dacha on the shores of the Black Sea. On occasion we would even allow ourselves an hour off for a swim. Sometimes my family would join me in Odessa and I had some difficulty in dividing my time betweeen them and M.G., but most of the time we were working in Krein's apartment. A small room there got the official title of Izia's office. Whilst I was in Odessa M.G. spent most of his time writing the book and discussing it with me. He would never allow me to eat out, this wonderful family always insisted that I eat with them. Members of the family would answer the telephone, and the caller would be told that he could speak with M.G. only if it were urgent since M.G. is busy, Izia is here. Some of my Odessa friends threatened to beat me up since I took up too much of Mark Grigorievich's attention.

When I started to work together with M.G. Krein and our first joint papers appeared I received congratulations and a warning; a friend warned me that readers would only remember that M.G. Krein had written the paper, and the name of the coauthor would not be remembered, not even its existence. He also thought that in reviews and references I would get little credit for joint work with M.G. Krein. Now I see he was wrong (maybe with very rare exceptions). From the very outset I understood that working together with M.G. was the best thing that could have happened to me. I had heard many tales about what a difficult person M.G. Krein was, but during the twenty four years during which we worked together I found him to be otherwise. True he was demanding, and it may be for this reason that he got the name of being difficult. He set very high standards for himself, and I found his demands of others to be fare and reasonable.

After we wrote our first paper on Fredholm operators and index I suggested that his name appear before mine on the manuscript. I explained to M.G. that this would be to the benefit of the paper, which would be more appreciated and attract more attention. He refused, maintaining that he would not write a joint work with a person who could not be an equal partner, and that he always used the alphabetical order of names in joint papers and any change will cause speculation in the mind of the readers. After a while I drew his attention to a paper by "M.G. Krein and M.A. Krasnoselsky." He laughed and remarked that the difference is only of the third degree. In our joint work we never gave specific indications of who did what. M.G. considered joint work as the work of a team, and after deciding that we would work together on certain topics, we then would not disinguish who did what in these topics. In research it is not always obvious what is the more important. Sometimes it is an idea or the choice of topics or the timing, sometimes the conjecture, or the proof, sometimes the concept, sometimes a definition, a remark or finding an error, and a counterexample. M.G. would compare joint research with a team of sportsmen, especially in a long term collaboration. Each player passes the ball on to another player, and it is impossible to delineate which pass was the most important.

These principles worked very well and during the twenty four years of our collaboration we never had any misunderstanding.

While writing the books we always worked with other people, and there were some topics where we acted as contractors. For instance, if we needed something in an area where our colleagues were better than us, then we would ask them to prove a certain theorem for us. They also kept us informed about new results and new improvements, so the material just grew before us. Among those colleagues who helped us were the following: M.S Birman, M.S. Brodsky, Ju.P. Ginzburg, G.E. Kisilevsky, S.G. Krein, B. Ja. Levin, V.B. Lidsky, Ju. I. Lyubich, V.I. Macaev, A.S. Markus, L.A. Sakhnovich, E.M. Semenov, Ju. L. Shmuljan, and M.Z. Solomyak.

The writing of the book took up more and more time. I would return home to Kishinev and my wife would ask if the book was finished yet. "There is still a little more work to be done," I would tell her. Each time, "Did you finish?" and each time I would reply that a little more remains to be done. As I remember, my wife finally stopped asking. She probably gave up all hope. It is still told in Odessa, now as a joke, though at the time it was true, how Sahnovich met me and asked, "How is the book going?" "Well, it's eighty five per cent ready," I replied. "Then why do you look so sad? That's wonderful." "Yes," I answered, "but if you had asked me yesterday I would have said it was ninety five per cent ready." Our students and friends made fun of us; I.S. Iokhvidov even wrote a little poem on the eve of the new year in 1963. I am grateful to Chandler Davis for translating this poem into English:

Around the festive table, all our friends
Have come to mark our new book's publication.
The fresh and shiny volume in their hands,
They offer Izia and me congratulations.
The long awaited hour is here at last.
The sourest sceptic sees he was mistaken,
And, smiling, comes to cheer us like the rest,
And I'm so delighted, ... I awaken.

From M.G. Krein's dream, New Year's Eve, 1963.

In the spring of 1963 Krein agreed to allow me to fill in the formulae in the first copy. I filled in almost 1500 pages of formulae; more than 1000 pages of manuscript for the book, then came 250 pages which were my second thesis which I was preparing at the same time. There were also a few papers which we were submitting. All in all I filled in 1500 pages. At that time my family lived in two small rooms. Our daughters were small then, and at ten o'clock everyone went to sleep. From ten in the evening till two in the morning was my time for filling in formulae. My friends helped me to fill in the second and third copies. Soon I went to Moscow to submit the book. The publisher said it was too long, so we had another problem. We divided it into two and made two volumes, the first on non-selfadjoint operators, and the second on Volterra operators.

On the same trip to Moscow I submitted my second thesis to Moscow University. The Dean was N.V. Efimov, a famous geometer and a very nice man, but he was not interested in having me or coping with my defence. One extra Jew to defend in Moscow University brings only difficulties. He tried to convince me that I really did not want to defend my thesis in Moscow University. By chance Professor A.G. Kurosch, the famous algebraist, a very straight forward man, dropped into Efimov's office. Whenever Efimov came up with yet another argument to convince me, he would intervene. "You don't sound convincing," he would tell Efimov, "Why should you not take this thesis?" Finally Efimov took the thesis, but said that I would have to wait my turn as there was a long line of candidates. In February of 1964, I defended my thesis in Moscow University. This was no formality but a real defence, with presentations and questions put and a secret ballot held at the end at a meeting of a highly qualified scientific council. Four abstained, still more than two thirds voted for me, and so I passed approval. In my case the opponents (the official readers of my thesis) were S.G. Mikhlin, M.A. Naimark, and G.E. Shilov. A special review came from the Institute of Applied Mathematics and was signed by M.V. Keldysh and V.B. Lidsky.

I continued working on the book together with M.G.Krein. After dividing it into two, it went to the copy editor. With the copy editor we were both lucky and unlucky. He was F.V. Shirokov, a university professor in mathematics, with the Russian language as well as mathematics at his finger tips. Shirokov was, I think, the best copy editor I have ever seen. He was extremely demanding. First of all he insisted that I sit with him while he read the manuscript. I had no alternative. Secondly he would try to understand all the proofs in detail. He would suddenly burst out, "I don't like this proof." "So give another one!" "No, no, I don't like this proof." Sometimes he forced us to work very hard. It would take us weeks to change a proof till it met with his satisfaction. Sometimes his demands lead us to a better understanding of the material or new results. He had good taste and the exposition was thereby improved essentially. In general he acted as an attorney for the reader. "The reader will not like that. The reader will not understand." We did not understand where this power of attorney came from, but we took his remarks very seriously. Eventually the books appeared, the first in 1965 and the second in 1967.

A. Feinstein translated the books into English for the AMS Tranlations programme. He did an excellent job. Professor Ando, who made a second English translation, sent us a list of misprints. Feinstein also had a list of misprints, and we ourselves also found some. Each of the three parties found around 80 misprints, and surprisingly enough there was almost no intersection between these lists. I was told that the first book in English is an AMS bestseller, and a third printing came out this year.

At the Mathematical Congress held in Moscow in 1966 a mathematician by the name of Gokr appeared there for the first time. M.G. Krein gave a plenary talk, and he had to refer frequently to our joint papers, and somehow it was awkward for him to have to repeat our two names each time, so he introduced Gokr as a short form of Gohberg-Krein. "This is done by Gokr, this is a paper of Gokr," he would say. I remember M.V. Keldysh, turning to ask M.I. Vishik, who was sitting near him in the audience, "Who is this Gokr?" I had helped M.G. Krein to prepare this talk, and it took some weeks of hard but interesting work. Part of the talk was based on our books, but it contained many other things as well.

At this congress I met C. Foias for the first time, during the preparation of M.G. Krein's talk (he helped in its translation into French). At this congress I also met R.G. Douglas, P.D. Lax, N. Levinson, R.S. Phillips and I.J. Schoenberg. All of these meetings were very pleasant and very useful.

For many years M.G. Krein ran a mathematical seminar at the Scientists House in Odessa. I lectured there and listened to many excellent talks. It was always interesting with a very pleasant atmosphere. During my visits to Odessa I also attended other seminars of M.G. Krein at the various institutions where he worked. At these seminars I met very nice people and excellent mathematicians, among them the famous old generation of Krein students: M.S. Livsic, author of the theory of characteristic operator functions; D.P.Milman who coauthored the extremal points theorems; V.P. Potapov, known for his contributions to the theory of matrix functions and their multiplicative decompositions, and M.A. Rutman, the coauthor of the theory of cones in Banach spaces. I would like to include M.S. Brodsky also in this group. In the late fifties he started to work on the theory of nonselfadjoint operators and made very important contributions. Among the younger generation I met V.M. Adamjan, D.Z. Arov, M.L. Brodsky, Ju. P. Ginzburg, I.S. Iokhvidov, I.S. Kac, K.R. Kovalenko, B.R. Mukminov, A.A. and L.A. Nudelman, G.Ja. Popov, L.A. Sakhnovich, Ju. L. Schmuljan, and V.G. Sizov. All were formal or informal Ph.D. students of M.G. Krein, except Mukminov and Sakhovich who were students of Livsic, and Ginzburg of Potapov; Sizov I do not remember. H. Langer from Dresden and V.I. Macaev from Kharkov were often guests of M.G. and lectured at his seminars. Langer once spent a full academic year in Odessa and was already considered a native "Odesid;" we called him Heinz Kurtovich.

I also met M.G.'s Armenian students, V.A.Javrjan, F.E.Melik-Adamjan and Sh. N. Saakjan. They were sent for extended periods of time from Erevan to Odessa to write their Ph.D. thesis with M.G.

So I was introduced to an interesting group whose achievements I was able to follow. The interests of this group were wide and extended my horizon. In this way I learned about operator theory in spaces with indefinite scalar products, interpolation theory, theory of cones in Banach space, theory of operator functions, theory of characteristic functions, scattering theory and other areas of analysis. Later this knowledge proved to be very important for me. As a matter of fact, no one from Odessa University attended M.G. Krein's seminars. They probably did not even realize what they were missing. I think it was one of the best seminars in analysis and its applications in which I have participated. As I already mentioned, M.G. Krein was dismissed from Odessa University earlier on, and all of those mathematicians mentioned above worked in other academic institutions.

For more than twelve years I worked intensively with M.G. Krein. The remaining years he was mostly busy with other projects and we worked less intensively, but we always met and thought about joint plans and joint projects. We also planned a third book. Working with M.G. was a joy and an important school for me. I never was a formal student of his, but he was more than an ordinary instructor for me. He was a great teacher and is a very good friend.

4. GELFAND'S SEMINAR

I used to like to visit Moscow University and to stay as a guest at the student residence which occupies the wings of the skyscraper. The middle part is used for academic purposes and consists mostly of halls, classrooms, libraries and offices. (Professors do not have their own offices in the universities of the USSR.) Concentrated on four or five floors of this building are to be found one of the best mathematics libraries in the world, very good book stores, and halls in which many important seminars and meetings take place. There are also caffeterias, menzas, restaurants, a concert hall and cinemas. The library was especially good; almost every mathematical journal and book from all over the world was to be found there. Newly published books in mathematics made their first appearance in the book stores in this building. One could meet Soviet and foreign mathematics stars, and attend many important seminars, lectures and conferences. The Moscow Mathematical Society made this their meeting place. Even the bureaucratic procedure to register as a guest at the student residence was pleasant. First one had to get the recommendation of the head of the Chair of Functional Analysis, which for a long time was held by D.E. Menshov. One then needed the recommendation of the Chairman of the Department of Mathematics, P.S. Alexandrov. After that permission of the Dean (for a long time A.N. Kolmogorov), was needed. Finally one had to get the approval of the Rector, I.G. Petrovsky. For a young mathematician, as I was then, all of this was like touching the history of mathematics. In the libraries, halls and caffeterias, etc., one could meet friends and colleagues from the whole of the Soviet Union, hear the latest mathematical news, rumours and gossip, and one could also work quietly. And all of this within one building. Unfortunately it was not always possible to obtain a place in this residence. The entrance to the building was strictly guarded and a special identity card was needed to enter, but without giving away any secrets, I can say that it was possible to stay at the residence without having an officially approved place.

In 1962 I visited Moscow University and I was fortunate to be able to stay at the student residence. At the invitation of G.E. Shilov I gave a course in the theory of nonselfadjoint operators. This course was based on the rough version of the manuscript of the Gohberg and Krein book. I had a good audience; I remember B.C.Mitjagin (at that time a Ph.D. student of G.E. Shilov), and D.A. Raikov sitting in at this course. I enjoyed this work very much, and this course also served as a useful experiement for us in process of writing the book.

Gelfand's seminar is a seminar which is held at Moscow University already more than 45 years, and I am certain there has never been another seminar quite like it. First of all at least 50 people holding a second doctors' degree attended, and many others, including very strong high school students. Gelfand's behaviour was very unusual. Sometimes he would say who should sit in the first row and who in the second, and he would move people around. He would criticize freely, but not only criticize. Here is an example. The Moscow University professor, G.E. Shilov, one of his former students as well as a close friend and collaborator, is lecturing and writing on the blackboard a linear differential equation with coefficient depending on t. "Yura," Gelfand exclaims, "cross out the t." "But Israel Moiseevich," Shilov explains, "It's more general this way, the proofs are much more complicated. I went through them and I want to keep it." "Yura, cross out the t!" "Israel Moiseevich, it's more difficult, and very non trivial. I don't want to do it." "Yura, don't do cheap generalizations, cross out the t." I also recall other examples of this type. In some cases Gelfand gave the lecturer three minutes in which to state some result. He calculated thus: "Look, there are 50 professors here. You get three minutes. That's 3 x 50, or 150 minutes of highly qualified professors' time. That's a lot of time!" The meetings of the seminar were very interesting - many different modern topics were discussed, sharp questions asked, with illuminating discussions and comments. I often had the feeling that I was being enriched. On the other hand the seminar somehow had the flavour of a circus; it was a show and somewhat intimidating because someone could be hurt. There were those who could not take it. Not everyone was criticized by Gelfand. When a foreign speaker was talking, the seminar would take on the form of a regular seminar. He would not criticize foreigners, and he refrained from criticizing S.V. Fomin, as well as some others.

Whilst visiting Moscow University I attended Gelfand's seminar regularly, and he invited me to speak there. In general the seminar met formally on Mondays at 6.30. Everyone would turn up at 6.30, but Gelfand would come a little later. People would stand around, Gelfand speaking to one, to another, to a third, and so on. Meantime everyone is standing around and waiting. Around eight o'clock the seminar would start, and talks would continue up to ten. The same thing was repeated each time. On the day he invited me to give a talk, there were many other talks, and ten minutes before ten he said, "All right, who else? Ah, yes, Gohberg." I opened my talk with two general sentences: "There are different classes of linear non-selfadjoint operators, some of them, by their properties, close to selfadjoint, and some of them very different. For instance the Volterra operators which have only one point of spectrum." I don't think I had said anything else before Gelfand got up and started to develop his philosophy. In his opinion there has to be a better definition of a linear operator and a better definition of a space, and I thought he expected the whole picture would change and be nicer. I had heard such remarks from him on previous occasions, but I never heard constructive suggestions. I had spoken for two minutes, he the remaining eight, and this was the end of my talk. I was shattered. Somehow I felt I was presenting not only my results, but also the results of others, and I had done such a terrible job of it. These others were not there, and could do nothing to defend themselves. I thought about this a lot and decided that whether he allowed me to speak or not, I would get up at the next meeting and say that what he had said was wrong, that there are a lot of deep results of many people, and so on. During the following week, while planning my revolt, I met Shilov and told him of my intention. He started to laugh, "Don't do it. You'll be the laughing stock! Nobody pays any attention, that's his style. Don't do it, it's wrong," and so on. Finally he convinced me and so I kept quiet.

I did lecture in Gelfand's seminar two or three times. He even invited me once to lecture for a full session. In general Gelfand would ask you to lecture, and after ten minutes he would take over. That was usual practice. But when I lectured - I gave a talk on factorization - I spoke for almost the whole two hours. He put questions, wrote things down in a notebook, and discussed with other people. I thought that I had made a very good impression, but later I found out that I was wrong.

Much later, closer to 1970, I had a very interesting experience. I was visiting Moscow and Gelfand, seeing me in the audience, promptly invited me to lecture. "I'm not ready," I remonstrated. "I don't want to lecture." I did not want to experience those pains again. He insisted. "But I'm not ready." And still he insisted. He then put forward a theory that you should lecture when you are not ready, because then you will say only what you remember and will not give all the details and nonsense which no one wants to hear. So finally I lectured. I decided that this time I would say what I was not given a chance to say on the first occasion. But without philosophizing. I started by simply stating theorems, and it came much better. He put questions, showed interest and discussed results, and I enjoyed it very much.

I had some interesting conversations with I.M. Gelfand during a conference on Operator Theory held in Tihany (Hungary) in the summer of 1970, and on the way from Budapest to Moscow. We even discussed working together, but unfortunately it never worked out.

In general the conference in Tihany (which was held directly after the congress in Nice) was very important for me. There I met for the first time a large number of Western colleagues; L. Coburn, Ch. Davis, P. Halmos, H. Helson, J.W. Helton, M.A. Kaashoek, P. Massani, J.D. Pincus. Many of these acquaintances helped me very much later on.

It was a pleasure to meet Gelfand recently when he visited Tel Aviv to receive his Wolf Prize. At the same time he received the Wolf Prize on behalf of both Kolmogorov and Krein.

5. DEPARTMENT OF FUNCTIONAL ANALYSIS IN KISHINEV

During my last ten years in Kishinev (1964-1974) I headed the Department of Functional Analysis of the Institute of Mathematics at the Moldavian Academy. Around 100 to 200 researchers worked in this institute, as well as some Ph.D. students, whilst in the department there were no more than ten persons. The senior researchers in this department, apart from myself, were I.A. Feldman and A.S. Markus, both of whom were more or less former students of mine. The remaining colleagues held positions of junior researchers, post doctoral fellows, or Ph.D. students. A seminar, also attended by mathematicians from other institutions, was held regularly. N. Ja. Krupnik, from Kishinev University, at one time an informal student of mine, was another senior participant in this seminar. A pleasant, friendly and enthusiastic atmosphere pervaded the department and the seminar.

We worked mainly on problems of nonselfadjoint operators and operator functions, Wiener-Hopf operators, Toeplitz operators, singular integral operators, and equations of transport. One of our specialities was factorization of operator functions and operators. It was during these years that the books of I.A. Feldman with I.Gohberg, and I. Gohberg with N.Ja. Krupnik were written. We had a large number of graduate students of Moldavian origin (this was required), as well as graduate students from other republics and countries. I am proud of R.V. Duduchava from Tbilisi, now one of the leading young professors there, and of G. Heinig and J. Leiterer from GDR, both of them outstanding experts in their areas. All three were my Ph.D. students. I am happy that students of mine now play an important role in Kishinev in higher education, in research and in other areas.

The research group was very critical, though with good will and good taste. All results obtained were thoroughly discussed and criticized with good humour. All members of the group worked hard and results were appreciated. I think that in certain areas of operator theory we had a very good reputation, both inside and outside the Soviet Union. I am happy that our results of these years are often used and quoted, and that some of them have interesting applications to different areas, including electrical engineering. In obtaining these results important contributions were made also by our younger colleagues. I would like to mention M.A. Barkar, V.M. Brodsky, M.S. Budjanu, I.S. Chebotaru, R.V. Duduchava, V.M. Eni, V.D. Frolov, L.S. Goldenstein, G. Heinig, J. Leiterer, L.E. Lerer, V.I. Levchenko, I.V. Mereutsa, V.I. Paraska, B.A. Prigorsky, G.I. Russu, A.A. Semencul (Sementsul), E.M. Shpigel, E.I. Sigal, O.I. Soibelman, V.P. Soltan, N. Vizitei, M.K. Zambitsky, and V.A. Zolotarevsky.

The institute published a journal "Matematicheskie Issledovanija." Formally I was an associate editor of this journal, but in practice I organized the journal and edited the analysis section. On looking back I see that we published many important papers in operator theory. The journal was exchanged with many Western universities, and it is a pity it no longer exists.

Members of the department were also interested in matrix theory and numerical methods, and we obtained good results in these areas. For a while we worked actively in combinatorial geometry, and our results attracted the interest of other mathematicians. Based on this research, jointly with V.G. Boltjansky, I wrote two small books on combinatorial geometry, now translated into many languages. I enjoyed this work very much. Boltjansky is a very strong mathematician with a very broad knowledge, as well as an excellent lecturer and a very pleasant person with whom to work. Along with all of this, he has a special talent for writing mathematics, and his first draft is, as a rule, the final work. (By the way, I worked together with Boltjansky on the index problem. We stopped when the first paper of M. Atiyah and I. Singer appeared.) V.G. often visited us and we also met many times in Moscow.

Colleagues from various cities throughout the USSR, as well as a number of foreign mathematicians, visited us. We interacted with many of them, and here are some examples. We had good connections with groups of mathematicians from Chernovitsy, Kharkov, Leningrad, Moscow, Odessa, Rostov, Tbilisi, and Voronezh. V.I. Macaev (Matsaev) was very often our guest. Our paths first crossed in Odessa when he was a Ph.D. student (Kharkov) and lectured in M.G.'s seminar. His contributions to operator theory were very impressive, some of which are included in the first book of Gohberg and Krein. For a long time V.I. worked together with A.S. Markus, and they produced very interesting results in the theory of operator polynomials and operator functions. Macaev and Markus were customers of J. Leiterer and myself. We proved for them theorems of factorization of operator functions, and they used these theorems. E.M. Semenov (Voronezh) visited us a number of times. He was a former student of S.G. Krein, and we had common interests. It was while he was helping us with the book that we first met. In Voronezh there was a strong school of functional analysis and we felt close to this group. Members of the department and our students often participated in the famous mathematical winter schools in the neighbourhood of Voronezh. I remember the visit to us of M.A. Shubin (Moscow) whom I met for the first time in Moscow University when he was a Ph.D. student of M.I. Vishik and many times later. A very useful visit was the visit of M.V. Maslennikov (Moscow), a well known expert in transport equations. Some of these equations can be transformed into Wiener-Hopf equations. We were very interested in these connections, I.A. Feldman especially so. He had very nice results in this area and it was planned that he would use them for his second doctoral thesis. B.S. Mitjagin (Moscow) and N.K. Nikolsky (Leningrad) were also among our important visitors. Our first visitors from the West were Chandler Davis, Seymour Goldberg and Israel Halperin. Our first visitors from Eastern European countries were H. Baumgaertel, S. Proessdorf, H. Langer and J. Bognar.

During the last ten years I also lectured at the Kishinev University, in a part time position. Each year I gave a year long course on special topics for senior undergraduate and Ph.D. students. It contained chapters on operator theory with different applications to differential and integral equations and numerical methods. I was a member of the chair of cybernetics and computer science headed by P.S. Soltan. He is a very enthusiastic and inventive mathematician, and an interesting person. He was a Ph.D. student of P.S. Alexandrov and V.G. Boltjansky and studied in Moscow University. Our common interests were in combinatorial geometry.

As a result of these activities, within a short period of time and with very modest means available, a centre of analysis was created in Kishinev. Our connections with the university made it easier for us to prepare and to choose our future students. The speciality of this centre was operator theory, integral equations and their applications. M.G.'s help and influence was of great importance.

We experienced difficulties in having Jews accepted to this department; the usual semi-official response was that the percentage of Jews in our department was already too high. There was also a problem when it came to accepting a Jewish Ph.D. student. The usual procedure was that a Jew applying for the Ph.D. programme would be rejected automatically at the entrance examination on Marxism, unless the ground was well prepared. This preparation took the form of under the table bargaining with the administration, and there were instances where it was successful. There was also a serious problem when it came to finding an appropriate job for a Jew after he received his degree. The scenario was usually as follows: I would call people whom I knew and suggest that they hire a Ph.D. student of mine who was graduating. Having described the student, the first reaction would usually be: "Sure, we'll take him, we have had good experience with your students, let him come tomorrow." Usually they would take him, if the student was not Jewish. In the case of a Jewish student I would get a call: "Sorry, the administration will not give permission, I already took a Jewish student two years ago." In one year four students of mine of various ethnic origins graduated, all of them very good. In one day I found jobs for the three non Jews, but for the Jew it took more than a year.

In 1968 things worsened. In the Soviet Union the defence of the first or second doctoral degree has to obtain additional approval by a special committee sitting in Moscow (Higher Certification Commission). This was usually only a formality especially for a good Ph.D. thesis, but from 1968 it was almost impossible for Jews to pass; the second doctoral degree was no longer available at all to Jews, except in some very special cases. When the policy of this committee changed, A.G. Kurosh and G.E. Shilov resigned from it.

During these bad years this committee was chaired first by V.A. Ilyin (professor at Moscow University), and then later by V.S. Vladimirov (now director of the Steklov Institute, academician, and hero of socialist labour). Accounts I have heard about discussions which took place in this committee are unbelievable. As an example see the book of G. Freiman, "It Seems I am a Jew," Fefer and Simons Inc., London, Amsterdam, 1980.

A.S. Markus defended an excellent second doctorate in Voronezh University, and it was highly acclaimed by main experts in the area. It was passed by a unanimous secret vote of a very qualified scientific council. However this special certification committee in Moscow did not approve Markus' thesis, rejection based on one negative review, instigated by the committee itself. It took the committee a very long time to find a person willing to write such a review, but finally they found one. A very good thesis of Ju. L. Shmuljan from Odessa was also rejected, and there were many similar cases. I was very disappointed. I considered this a personal injury and I did my utmost to fight it. It was a drawback for all the department, generally affecting the whole atmosphere within the department and the Institute. A.S. Markus never made another attempt, I.A. Feldman, who had excellent results on Wiener-Hopf and transport equations with which to form the second thesis never completed it, and only recently was N.Ja. Krupnik able to defend his second thesis in Tbilisi.

In the late sixties and early seventies it became much more difficult to publish the work of Jewish mathematicians, and sometimes even of Ph.D. students of Jewish instructors. An editorial board, headed by L.S. Pontrjagin, was set up to control the editorial policy in mathematics throughout the entire Soviet Union. I am sure that many excellent books did not appear because of the discriminatory policy of this board. These changes were very painful for us.

In 1968 to 1970 I was allowed to visit some Eastern European countries. Later I was not so lucky; in the early seventies I was not allowed to go to Poland or to Bulgaria, and my Jewish frields are not allowed to travel abroad even today. By the way, in each of the lucky cases I had to set out from Moscow, because there I had to pick up my passport and to receive instructions. I also had to return home via Moscow in order to return the passport and to hand in a report, entailing a lot extra travelling. For instance to spend four or five days in Rumania, which was only a short distance from my home, I had to travel thousands of kilometres.

6. ELECTIONS TO THE ACADEMY

The Academy of Science of the USSR is the main academy in the Soviet Union. However each republic has its own Academy of Science. Election to an academy is very prestigious, bringing with it many benefits, among them essential financial benefits. From 1968, the year of the death of S.N. Bernstein, until 1984 no Jews were full members in the Department of Mathematics of the main academy. I.M. Gelfand was a corresponding member. Only in 1984 was he elected to full membership; this was possible only after the death of I.M. Vinogradov. M.G. Krein is a corresponding member of the Ukrainian Academy (since 1939). There is a joke in this connection: "The Ukrainian Academy must be the strongest in the world because M.G. Krein is only a corresponding member there." The Academy of the Moldavian Republic is one of the youngest and smallest among the academies. I was elected to it as a corresponding member at the beginning of 1970.

Full and corresponding members are elected to the academies by a secret vote held at a meeting of all members. Prior to the elections there is a very complicated preparatory procedure. The first part of the procedure is carried out in secret, the second part is more open. The most important part is probably the first: one has to be proposed and then the candidate has to obtain the approval of a number of institutions, including party offices, KGB, academy offices on the republic level and on the Moscow level. A list of those candidates who passed the first part successfully is published in the press. The second part of the procedure for the republic academies consists of two secret votes, the first in Moscow in the Department of Mathematics of the main academy. These results are supposed to play an advisory role only, but in reality they have much more weight. The last vote is held at meetings of the academy.

The first time I was proposed in 1965 my name was dropped at the end of the first part of the procedure. A friend who knew the details told me later that it was not for reasons of myself personally, but was connected with my father who was arrested by the Soviets on 23rd August, 1940, my birthday, two months after they took over Bessarabia.

He was sentenced by a troika to eight years imprisonment, and I never saw him again. My father died in the Gulag a couple of years later, exactly where or when we do not know. We had to keep the story of my father a secret otherwise I would not have been accepted to the university or be able to work at the academy, and my sister would have had the same sort of difficulties. This information was passed on to the academy by the KGB when my candidacy was discussed, and as a result I was rejected. In 1966 a court which reexamined my father's case found that he had not committed any crime. His case was closed and, as with many others, he was posthumously rehabilitated. In 1969 I was proposed to the academy for the second time. I had very good recommendations and my candidacy somehow passed the initial procedures successfully. I have no details on this. I had thought that the rest would go through smoothly, but I was wrong. It soon became apparent that there was a problem; that someone was making trouble. I do not know precisely how things developed, but I was told that M.V. Keldysh became involved. He knew some of my work and supported me. M.V. Keldysh was informed about my case by P.S. Alexandrov. I was also strongly supported by the following members of the main academy: I.M. Gelfand, L.V. Kantorovich, N.I. Muskhelishvili, V.I. Smirnov, S.L. Sobolev, and I.N. Vekua. They were all familiar with at least some of my work. Later a vote took place at a meeting of the Department of Mathematics in the main academy in Moscow, and I passed with a two third majority. At this point it seemed as if a happy end was in sight. The final elections in Kishinev were scheduled for the 2nd January 1970, and I was the only candidate. I learned later that three or four days prior to the elections a letter reached the Moldavian Academy (the same letter was also sent to the Department of Science of the Central Committee of the Communist Party of the USSR). This letter was signed by the Director of the Steklov Institute, academician I.M. Vinogradov, hero of socialist labour. He wrote that in his opinion I am not suited to the position of a corresponding member of the Moldavian Academy because there is some doubt as to whether my papers with M.G. Krein are correct (he referred to a letter of G.E. Shilov in "Uspekhi" 1966, which has nothing to do with our work), and also that I do not have any outstanding results of my own. It appears to me that Vinogradov did not expect such a development and his letter was a last minute blow below the belt. I am sure he did not have any idea about my work or joint work with M.G. Krein. Probably this letter was based on a report. By the way, I was told recently that, after his death, a suitcase full of reports was found in a safe place in his home. Fortunately for me the letter of Vinogradov arrived too late. Everything was already officially approved, and it was much easier for the bureaucrats to go ahead. The elections went through and I was elected unanimously.

It is well known that antisemitism was an important issue in the activities of Director Vinogradov. He was very successful and under his directorship, the Steklov Institute in Moscow - the central institute of mathematics of the USSR - became Judenfrei. B.N. Delone told me during a visit to Kishinev, that any topic discussed with I.M. Vinogradov always comes down to antisemitism. I know that Vinogradov did not forget me, and in 1976 (two years after my emigration) he continued to make unpleasant remarks about me.

I did not know I.M. Vinogradov personally. I had met him face to face only once briefly at the Steklov Institute in Moscow at the beginning of 1960, when I was approved for the degree of senior researcher. I knew he was famous for his outstanding contributions to number theory, and at the university I studied his text book on this subject. I was surprised later when to learn that he had practically no Ph.D. students, and is a poor lecturer. I had attended a rather strange lecture which he had given to the USSR Mathematical Congress in 1956. This was a unique plenary lecture delivered in the largest hall of the Moscow University, before an audience of around 1500 to 2000. I think it was intended to be the lecture of the world's greatest mathematician, but it turned out differently. Whenever he used the blackboard he would forget about the microphone, so it was rather like watching a silent movie. Then he suddenly took the microphone and spoke into it very loudly, reading out formulae from a manuscript. He was confused and it was impossible to follow him so people started to fidget and get up and leave. He also overstepped the allotted time. Later I heard that he blamed P.S. Alexandrov, who chaired that particular session, for the fiasco. During the final part of the lecture P.S. Alexandrov signalled to him; he interpreted these signs to mean "Beautiful, go on," but they were in fact meant to convey to him, "Finish, your time is over."

In 1971 I visited Tbilisi and participated in the Ph.D. defence of my student R.V. Duduchava. There I met for the first time N.I. Muskhelishvili, a famous mathematician.

I have a high regard for him and his school, and for their contributions to the theory of integral equations with singular kernels. N.I. Muskhelishvili was a very interesting man, one of the very few who was a member of the Supreme Soviet (the parliament of the USSR) from the beginning (1936) till his death. He was very influencial and held many important posts in the main and Georgian academies. I visited him and thanked him for his support in my election to the Moldavian Academy. He answered modestly that he had done nothing exceptional, only fulfilled his duty. I told him that I had heard that his support was important, to which he replied that it may be so because some "bad characters had to be balanced." He presented me with a copy of the latest edition of his book "Singular Integral Equations," which I like very much. During this visit I also met other well known Georgian mathematicians: G.S. Chogoshvili, B.V. Khvedelidze and G.F. Mandzhavidze. Khvedilidze and I had mutual interests and we were friends for a long time.

In 1972 I was nominated as a candidate for full membership of the academy. This time Vinogradov and his friends were more careful. At a very early stage a special committee which was sent to Kishinev was also instructed to oversee my candidacy. This committee came to the conclusion that the Moldavian Academy did not need a full member, and that they would be better off with two corresponding members instead (my name was not mentioned at all). I followed developments regarding my nomination, and friends told me that progress went well before this special committee arrived. It was made up of N.N. Bogolubov, Chairman, A.N. Tichonov, A.A. Dorodonitsyn, A.N. Shirshov, and S.M. Nikolsky - a very powerful committee. They came to their decision and I was disappointed. But one can never know what is for the best. Had I been elected, who knows how many years I would have had to wait for permission to emigrate.

I would like to relate how my career as a member of the Moldavian Academy ended. When I left for Israel I could not take with me any documents showing that I was a corresponding member of the academy. I had a special identification card (which helped me in hotels, or to go to a movie without standing in line, or to a restaurant). I wanted to keep this identification, but I was not allowed to do so. When I arrived in Israel I asked the Ministry of Foreign affairs to get some document for me showing that I was indeed a corresponding member of the Moldavian Academy. At that time I thought it important for me to have such a document. By the way, during the almost 15 years since then I have never been asked for this identification. The Ministry sent a letter to the Dutch embassy in Moscow, which represents Israel in USSR, and the Dutch embassy asked for this document. After six months I received a reply from the Minister of Foreign Affairs saying that they had received a letter from the Soviet Union in which they state that they are unable to give me a document showing that I was indeed a member of the Academy of Science in Moldavia since I no longer appear on the list of members of this academy.

7. TOWARDS EMIGRATION

For a long time I had thought of emigrating to Israel, but the idea was more a dream than a real possibility. In 1969 things started to change, and more and more people were able to emigrate for reasons given as reunification of families. We had many relatives in Israel, uncles, aunts, and entire families. With the agreement of all my family I started to plan our emigration. At the same time I also took the necessary steps at my place of work. I refrained from taking on any new students, and I saw to it that almost all of my students would finish their theses before I applied for emigration. By the way, two of my Ph.D. students from Kishinev University defended their theses after I applied for an exit visa, my name as instructor was replaced by another, and the students were not allowed to mention me at all. I stopped working (part time) at Kishinev University. I tried to complete joint work which was in process, and many other things had to be taken care of. I followed closely the progress of the emigration process of people in a position similar to mine, and I remember what an impression the case of Boris Korenblum (Professor of Kiev Polytechnic Institute) made on me. The following is his story.

In order to apply for a visa at that time one had to prepare various papers, one of them a reference from one's employer. An initial meeting of one's colleagues would be arranged where some of those present (often communist party members) would discuss the applicant's behaviour and as a rule come to the conclusion that since he is a person who intends to leave the Socialistic Homeland for a capitalistic country, then he is a traitor. After this meeting the administration would give a letter of reference based on what had been said at this meeting. Where Boris Korenblum was concerned the authorities decided to make a show case. The meeting was planned as if a session of the Scientific Council (Senate). The Rector was the first to speak. He said that Professor Korenblum had received a free education in the Soviet Union, and just when he could be useful and serve his country, he wishes to leave it and to emigrate to another country, and not even a friendly one. The Rector closed by asking "Is this fair?" B. Korenblum was allowed to answer the Rector. He said that he wanted to begin by stating some facts from his biography. He graduated from high school before the Second World War and was accepted to the university. When war broke out he volunteered and joined the Red Army, and spent the whole of the war fighting at the front. After he was demobilized at the end of the war he was allowed, as a veteran, to graduate from the university externally (by sitting examinations without actually attending classes). He never was a graduate student. He wrote his Ph.D. thesis in his spare time and defended it externally. In the same way he obtained also his second doctoral degree. B. Korenblum closed by asking if the Rector could perhaps explain how it is that he, Korenblum, who had volunteered in the World War Two to fight and to endanger his life for the Soviet Union, no longer accepted this country as his own and planned to emigrate to another. I do not remember any more details of this meeting which was a complete fiasco for the Rector. The result was that B. Korenblum applied for a visa and was given an extremely short time (much less than others) in which to leave the USSR. By the way my family and myself, apart from my mother, had to go through such meetings. Even my twelve year old daughter. Worst of all was the meeting at the university to discuss my elder daughter. She was given an extra haranguing on my behalf also since I had already stopped working there and no longer in their hands.

During these years various stories were circulated. Once a university colleague asked me if the following rumours which were being spread were true. According to these rumours the Rector of Kishinev University had suggested to me that I change my patronymic names, Israel Tsudikovich. He maintained that students had complained that my name was too Zionistic and they felt uncomfortable pronouncing it. My reputed answer to the rector was that I refused to make any changes, explaining that the first name was given me by my parents, and the second is the name of my father, who is no longer alive. I also said that it was not the business of my students what my name is. Such an answer was considered extremely bold for that time, and my colleague told me that it gave him great satisfaction to hear of it. I had to disappoint him - this story was all fiction. Others also asked me similar questions about my name. I can only guess that my name was the subject of discussion at a certain administrative level, but probably no decision was taken as to any action.

Soon after I applied for a visa to Israel my sister was told by someone who neither knew that she was my sister, nor was close to academic circles, that the following was reputed to have happened in my case: I applied for a visa to a conference. When it was refused I threw the paper with the refusal into the face of the authorities, threatening that I would not let it go at that. I decided to leave the Soviet Union, and when I applied for an emigration visa, people standing in a long line waiting for visas allowed me and my family to make the application without standing in line, and I am probably already in Israel.

In reality the process of obtaining a visa for emigration was much more difficult and painful for my family and myself, with many refusals and a long waiting time. I was demoted and subjected to all kinds of discriminations, and as a result I resigned from my job.

On another occasion my wife was told that she should look out for my safety. Someone had overheard in a conversation at the academy that a group of people was planning to prevent my emigration by the use of brute force. There were many cases where people who had applied for an exit visa were brutally attacked, and after hearing this my family never let me out of the house without someone accompanying me. At the time I wondered about this, but it was only when we reached Israel that my wife told me the whole story.

During this difficult period of being a refusenik my family and I received a lot of support from the West. A businessman from England, Gerald Wise, often called us on the telephone. This gave us great moral support. We felt as if the entire Jewish people, the entire free world, was behind him. Gerald informed my colleagues in the West of my difficulties, and shortly after I received an important call from Chandler Davis, who became very active in my case. We received letters and telephone calls from other colleagues and friends in the United States and Israel. I was told that I was also supported at a meeting of the Bourbaki seminar.

During the darkest period, when the future of my family and myself was in real danger, two couples from the United States visited Kishinev for a few days in order to help us and other refuseniks. One couple was the New York lawyer, Alvin Hellerstein and his wife, and a special prosecutor of the State of New York, Maurice Nadjari and his wife. It is impossible to describe how much this visit meant to us. My family and myself will always remember with gratitude all those who helped us in our struggle to emigrate from the Soviet Union to Israel.

I had thought that my emigration would not greatly harm the Department of Functional Analysis in Kishinev or my friends, and I was sure that my friends would be able to replace me. Unfortunately they were not allowed to do so, and within a short time the Department of Functional Analysis was closed and its members dispersed among other departments. This does not mean that my colleagues stopped working. Recently I was very happy to see two excellent new books, one by N. Ja. Krupnik, "Banach Algebras with Symbol and Singular Integral Operators," Kishinev, Stiintsa, 1984; the English translation appeared in the OT series of Birkhaeuser Verlag, 1987 (OT 26). The other book is by A.S. Markus, "Introduction to the Spectral Theory of Polynomial Operator Bundles," Kishinev, Stiintsa, 1986, English translation appeared in the AMS translation series in 1988. The journal was closed down and a series of brochures, virtually unavailable in the West, is being published in its place. In publications of the Moldavian Academy (as well as of the Ukrainian Academy) it is forbidden to quote my papers or even to mention my name, so my colleagues cannot quote their own joint papers with me. This applies also to some publications of the main academy, even when the editor is G.I. Marchuk, President of the Academy of Science of the USSR. Soon after I emigrated, V.M. Bychkov and K.S. Sibirsky wrote a brochure "Development of Mathematics in Moldavian SSR." A complete section is devoted to functional analysis and integral equations, and my name does not appear there at all (see review by Ch.Davis in Historia Mathematica, 1976, pages 235-236). More than that, rumours are occasionally spread in Kishinev that I had died. My relatives discovered that the source of these rumours was the Institute of Mathematics, where I had been working. At the end of one of their weekly meetings, it was announced that they had been informed that I could not find a job in Israel and that I had died. It was suggested they stand in silence in my memory. Why these rumours were spread I do not know, but obviously they were exaggerated.

8. EPILOGUE

I arrived in Israel with my family at the end of July 1974, and it was not at all clear to me how my career would progress. I had left behind 26 Ph.D.s (candidates) whom I had educated, my friends, and my teacher, Mark Gregorievich Krein. I knew I would miss all of them and I realized that it would probably take a very long time before I would have a group to work together with. In the West things developed much better than I had expected, and as a result I have a home country. This is Israel, and Tel Aviv University is my home university. I hold the Silver Chair donated by those wonderful people, Nathan and Lily Silver. And I have even more; I have second homes and wonderful friends, groups of colleagues and students with whom I work. My friends and colleagues now include not only mathematicians, but also engineers. I feel at home in the Netherlands at the Free University of Amsterdam, in the United States at the University of Maryland in College Park. I regularly visit the Weizmann Institute in Israel, and the University of Calgary in Canada, as well as many other places. Last but not least I would like to mention my visits to Basel, Switzerland, to my publisher, Birkhaeuser Verlag.

9. ACKNOWLEDGEMENTS

The material presented above is based on a talk given at the Conference on Operator Theory held in Calgary, August 22 to August 28, 1988, to mark my 60th birthday. This talk preceded the birthday banquet. The other talks given at this conference were of a much more serious nature.

I would like to thank my colleagues and friends, former and present students, and all participants from many countries for attending this conference and making it such a success. I would like to thank the organizing committees and my very good friends H. Dym, S. Goldberg, M.A. Kaashoek and especially P. Lancaster, for their efforts and friendship. Thanks to all those who conveyed to me their congratulations.

My sincere gratitude is addressed to the University of Calgary, the Department of Mathematics and the Conference Department, for the excellent organization of this conference. Support of the conference by United States organizations, institutions of Canada, and Nathan and Lily Silver from Israel, is highly appreciated. My thanks to the Lancaster family for their kindness, friendship and outstanding hospitality.

I am happy that my family was present at this conference, sharing with me the warmth and wonderful atmosphere. I am grateful to them for their patience, and for sharing with me my problems and difficulties, and for bearing with my frequent travels. I am only very sorry that my mother could not be with us. She died in Israel five years ago. She brought my sister and myself up on her own, under extremely difficult conditions. She was my first and most important teacher.

Tel Aviv
December 1988

Four generations:
Clara (Israel's mother) with son, granddaughter and great-grandson.
The picture was taken on Clara's 80th birthday, January 1983.

GOHBERG MISCELLANEA

This biographical text is composed by the Editors from reminiscences, notes, letters and speeches prepared by Gohberg's former students, colleagues and friends on the occasion of his sixtieth birthday.

Israel Gohberg was born on August 23, 1928 in the town of Tarutino, in the southern part of Bessarabia, then part of Rumania. His father, Cudic (Tsudic), was a printer and his mother, Clara, was a midwife.

Cudic Gohberg was arrested in the Summer of 1940, for reasons which were never made clear, and sent to a labor camp. He was never heard from again. In June 1941, when the Germans moved deep into the Soviet Union, Clara Gohberg fled to Frunze, the capital of Kirgizia in Central Asia, with Israel and his younger sister Fanny. In Frunze, Israel completed his elementary and high school education and then, in 1946, he entered the Pedagogical Institute with plans to switch to engineering as that was the only vocation that he was aware of which would use his already evident mathematical talents. This was a great disappointment to his mother who wanted him to study medicine. His mother's wish to have a doctor in the family was fulfilled by his sister who became a surgeon and, as an added bonus, introduced Israel to his future wife, Bella, who was one of her classmates in medical school.

THE EARLY YEARS

S. Goldberg (College Park, Maryland, U.S.A.)

Israel Gohberg's life can best be summarized as one filled with outstanding accomplishments, despite the trials and tribulations which he and his family endured. We have seen in his "Mathematical Tales" the obstacles he had to overcome throughout his professional career. I shall now touch upon some of his experiences in his early youth; a detailed account would constitute a very interesting book.

Israel was born in Tarutino, Bessarabia, on August 23, 1928. His was a closely knit, devoted and loving family consisting of his parents and paternal grandparents. His sister Feia was born 5 years later. Israel's mother Clara worked as a nurse-midwife and his father owned a one-man print shop dealing with announcements and invitations. The Gohbergs were a typical Jewish family in Tarutino.

On Israel's twelfth birthday the Soviet secret police arrested his father without any formal charges. He was dragged away and tried by three officials (Troika) and sentenced to eight years at hard labor in a Gulag in Siberia. The so called trial took place without the presence of a defense witness or a defense lawyer. He was never seen by the family again. Clara was now the sole support of her two children. After pleading with various authorities and writing many letters, she learned years later that her husband perished in the labor camp.

In June 1941, the German army invaded the Soviet Union forcing the Gohbergs to flee for their lives. This was the start of the family's trek East from village to village seeking food and shelter which was to last throughout the war. The journey often took place in carts and open trains in bitter cold, accompanied by snow and rain. In order to survive, the Gohbergs worked as farm hands, with Israel also mending shoes to obtain additional food. During this time, Clara made sure that her children attended school and kept up with their home work.

Some of the schools which Israel attended did not offer an environment conducive to studies. Many of the students were much older than Israel and were waiting to be drafted into the Army. Nevertheless, Israel worked hard and did exceedingly well in his classes. In fact, he was later awarded scholarships. In applying for these grants, he was always concerned that the authorities would learn of his father's demise in a Gulag and would deny Israel any support.

After more than twenty years, Clara received a terse note that her husband was posthumously declared "free of guilt". No apology or compensation was offered to the family.

The experiences of the Gohberg's which, in small part, I've described above, were told to me by Clara. She was an exceptional person whose courage, devotion and judgment enabled the children to survive some terrible times. Her endeavors motivated her two children to excel in their professions - Feia became a prominent pediatric surgeon who received a "woman of the year" award from a major Israeli magazine.

Israel was awarded a Stalin Fellowship after his first year of study at the Frunze Pedagogical Institute. Two years later, in 1948, he was encouraged by one of his professors to transfer to Kishinev University. Israel's mother and sister joined him in Kishinev in 1954. By this time Israel was already working with M.G.Krein.

REMINISCENCES

M.G. Krein (Odessa, U.S.S.R.)

I have had a number of students I feel proud of. The list includes M.A. Krasnoselski, H.K. Langer, M.S. Livsic, M.A. Naimark and V.P. Potapov. In this brilliant company a conspicuous place is occupied by Israel Gohberg.

I first met Israel Gohberg in 1950. I was then on the faculty of the Odessa Marine Engineering Institute. I gave a seminar talk on (as far as I can remember) the inverse problem for the oscillating string with "beads" and noticed the face of an unfamiliar young man in the audience. After the talk he came up and asked me whether I could spare some time for him. This young man was Israel Gohberg. I invited him to come to my house the same evening. He came and showed me some unpublished manuscripts and asked me to suggest possible continuations. This work was done under the supervision of Docent Itskovich of Kishinev University. After perusing the manuscripts I concluded that they ought to be published. (It turned out that one had already been presented to "Doklady of the USSR Academy of Sciences" with the help of S.M. Nikolskii, who at that time was not yet an academician.) I suggested to Israel Gohberg that he study the paper of I.M. Gelfand, D.A. Raikov and G.E. Silov on normed rings which had appeared just before the war in "Uspehi". I had a reprint of that paper and asked I. Gohberg to look for it in one of my bookcases. I remember well that at this very moment, with his face turned to the bookcase and his back to me, he said that he would be happy to work under my supervision.

I cannot now remember exactly whether he was a graduate student or an undergraduate student at that time (however, it seems possible that he was never in "aspiranture", the regular graduate program). I do remember having sent a personal letter to the Education Minister of Moldavia about a work assignment for I. G. after his graduation. In particular, I wrote that his diploma work could serve as a base for a Ph.D. dissertation and requested that he be placed in an environment favorable for research. As a result of this letter, he was assigned to the Beltsy Pedagogical Institute, and later he moved to Kishinev, the capital of Moldavia.

Despite a huge teaching load, he managed to find opportunities (and in this, I must mention that he was helped by the administration) to travel to Odessa to see me. His research advanced successfully and fruitfully.

At one of our metings (in 1955) I suggested that we write a joint paper for "Uspehi". This marked the beginning of a long and fruitful collaboration in a broad field of problems which I look back on with a sense of joy and satisfaction. Israel Gohberg's energy, his easy accessibility and cheerfulness, quickly made him a favorite of both the Odessa circle of mathematicians and of my whole family. His visits invariably brought joy and excitement.

In these days of I.G's birthday celebration I transmit to him my affection and respect and extend to him my best wishes for many years of vitality, health and creativity.

For want of a better place, Israel used to work on the dining room table in his home, filling reams of paper with calculations and mathematical symbols. His sister recalls how at the end of one particularly long day he picked up the accumulated stack of papers, handed them to his mother and said "you see all this, you can put it in the garbage". This caused his family concern. It was especially worrisome because it was difficult for them to understand what he and Krein were doing. "We ask ourselves questions and then try to answer them", was the best explanation that Israel could manage. "Then why don't you ask yourselves easier questions?". was his mother's immediate commonsense reply.

Enough hard questions were answered to insure Israel's rapid advancement on the Russian academic ladder. In relatively short order he was appointed Head of the Department of Functional Analysis in the Institute of Mathematics at the Moldavian Academy of Science. In addition to this full-time position, he also held a half-time teaching position at Kishinev University. Advanced students at the University often participated in seminars at the Academy. Leonid Lerer, then a third-year student at the University, attended a seminar on s-numbers which was given by Israel Gohberg at the Moldavian Academy in 1962-63. Leonid recalls that he and the other students were completely magnetized by these lectures. They left feeling that they had been exposed to one of the most exciting chapters of modern mathematics; many of them later became his students.

Letter of A. Markus, N. Krupnik and I. Feldman (Kishinev, U.S.S.R.)

Dear Israel Cudicovich,

We have it from an absolutely reliable source that on the 23rd of August 1988 you will be 60 years old. You were nearly half as young when in Kishinev a small group of mathematicians started to work under your leadership. The fifteen years during which we worked together in Kishinev were very fruitful years, and it is with mixed feelings of joy and sadness that we, your first students, recall those years. Your boundless energy, your cheerfulness and your limitless interest in mathematics, were to some extent passed on to us. During the following fourteen years you were far from us, but this did not prevent you from obtaining an entire series of first class results, to publish a number of papers and monographs, become the laureate of the Rothschild

Prize, and to travel extensively all over the world (unfortunately we cannot say the same for ourselves).

Continuing in the arithmetic line of this letter, and basing ourselves on Jewish tradition, we wish you a healthy, happy, creative, active life till 120. Hearty greetings to Bella Jakovlevna, your children and grandchildren. Please convey our wishes for much success to the participants of the conference, which by good luck coincided with your anniversary.

Affectionately,

Kishinev, 25 July, 1988 — A. Markus, N. Krupnik and I. Feldman

Speech of R. Duduchava (Tbilisi, U.S.S.R.), delivered at the banquet

I am authorized to transfer to you greetings from Professor I. Simonenko from Rostov. He wrote me that all the mathematicians in Rostov like you as much as before and they think that you are just on a long business trip abroad.

Ten days ago I was in Kishinev and met there your former collaborators, Naum Krupnik, Israel Feldman and Alexander Markus. This meeting was not occasional of course. I must underline that the friendly atmosphere, which you leave among your pupils and collaborators in the Sovjet Union, is preserved and we have very tight and friendly relations. They (Krupnik, Feldman and Markus) also asked me to transfer to you their best wishes on the occasion of your 60th birthday. They regret very much that they cannot express their feelings personally.

In conclusion I would like to say several words in my own name as well.

I am very grateful to you as a person and as a mathematician. When I came to Kishinev 20 years ago I was an inexperienced young man. What I know now and what I am now, is mostly due to you. I will never forget those two and a half years in Kishinev, which were among the best in my life. You and your nice family supported me, even when I had difficulties in my private life.

I wish you a long and happy life so that you can still do a lot of kind and necessary work in this world.

MY YEARS IN KISHINEV

G. Heinig (Karl-Marx-Stadt, G.D.R.)

The years from 1971 to 1974 I spent at Kishinev State University for Ph. D. studies. These years were very important for me, from the view-point of my scientific career they were surely the most important in my life. In Kishinev I found a fertile mathematical climate, excellent teachers and good friends. Most of what I know how to do in mathematics I learned there.

The man who taught me this subject was Professor Gohberg. He embodied for me and the other students all the qualities that a mathematician should possess. We appreciated him for his superlative mathematical research activity and for his outstanding results but also for his abilities as an expositor and teacher of modern mathematics. Still more striking was his permanent care for the personal matters of his students. On holidays he used to invite his students to his house. There they got an unforgettable impression of the excellent cuisine of the Gohberg women. As I got to know, Professor Gohberg is not only an outstanding adviser but also an ideal co-worker. "Mathematics should be done like football" - these are his words. The enormous number of co-authors of his papers shows that he is an excellent player and game organizer.

There is no doubt that at the time I stayed in Kishinev the Gohberg team was one of the most active research groups in the world in the fields of operator theory and integral equations. Many issues of the Kishinev journal "Mathematicheskie Issledovanija" of that time are still important now. Active members of the group were A. Markus, N. Krupnik, I. Feldman, A. Semencul and others. The seminar of the group became a model for me how to run a real research seminar. Many outstanding mathematicians such as V. Macaev, B. Mityagin, H. Langer, S. Prössdorf, R. Duduchava gave talks in the seminar regularly. Especially I remember with pleasure the sometimes controversial but always productive discussions between Professor Gohberg and A. Markus.

What I also learned in Kishinev is that serious mathematics does not exclude humor. Professor Gohberg was a master in joke telling. I wish that he will retain this humor for many years. I wish him further successful research, many good students and, last but not least, good health.

In 1964 Seymour Goldberg visited Kishinev. He came to discuss the book that he was writing on unbounded operators. He spent a few days discussing mathematics with Israel with the aid of an interpreter and a little Yiddish. This was Israel's first meeting with an American mathematician. Other contacts with Western mathematicians were made in 1970 when Israel was permitted to participate in the Tihany Conference in Hungary which was organized by B. Sz.-Nagy. There he met L.A. Coburn, J.D. Pincus, M.A. Kaashoek, J.W. Helton, P.R. Halmos, F.F. Bonsall, Chandler Davis and P. Masani for the first time, and renewed his acquaintanceship with Ciprian Foias and Heinz Langer.

FIRST MEETING

S. Goldberg (College Park, Maryland, U.S.A.)

I first met the Gohbergs in Kishinev in April, 1964. The family then consisted of Clara, Israel, his wife Bella, and their daughters Zvia and Yanina. The purpose of my visit was to discuss with Israel the manuscript of my book "Unbounded Linear Operators". I knew of Israel's seminal work in operator theory and was sure he would offer valuable suggestions.

Israel greeted me with a "bear hug" and invited me to have dinner with his family at their apartment. I was accompanied by Israel's colleagues - I.A. Feldman, A.S. Markus, - and an interpreter who was also an mathematician. We had a wonderful dinner which was prepared by Bella and Clara. When introduced to Clara, I had the impression that she was a very frightened woman. I tried to converse with her in Yiddish, which she pretended not to understand. It was obvious to me that she knew the language since Israel spoke it fluently. Years later, Clara told me (in Yiddish) that she was very worried that, by entertaining an American, the family would suffer dire consequences. This is certainly understandable in view of the tragic loss of her husband during the Stalin reign of terror.

The next day, a reception was held in my honor at Kishinev University to enable me to meet administrators and various faculty members. I was informed that I was the first mathematician from the West to visit Kishinev on an official basis. They all were very friendly and wanted to know about life in America; in particular, how university faculty fared. When I informed them that my teaching load was six hours, they were surprised that I meant six hours per week, not per day. This was substantially less than their teaching loads. Many eyebrows were raised when I announced that my trip to various cities in the Soviet Union was sponsored by the U.S. Air Force. Later I learned that the authorities wanted to know whether I was really a mathematician visiting for professional reasons or an agent on some secret mission. Recall that this was about the time that a Yale professor, visiting the U.S.S.R, was accused of being a spy.

After several more days in Kishinev, I bid a sad farewell to my new friends. We did not believe that we would ever meet again. Who would have thought that ten years later the Gohbergs would join us for dinner in our home in Maryland. To this day, Israel shakes his head in disbelief.

What amazes me is that in spite of the hardships encountered by Israel, he remains a warm, kind and gregarious human being. He is an inspiration and a delight to all those who know him.

The Moldavian Academy was a forty-minute walk from Kishinev University. Leonid Lerer recalls that he often walked with Israel from the University to the Academy and that during these walks many problems, mathematical and other, were thrashed out. On one of these walks Leonid revealed that he was thinking of applying for permission to immigrate to Israel. Gohberg encouraged him in this even though it could well have been a cause of future embarrassment for him. Leonid applied and received permission some four months later. Israel followed suit in November 1973. However, his application was rejected and the Gohbergs went through a very difficult period. The combined pressure applied by many foreign friends and colleagues, who were familiar with and sympathetic to the case, finally led to reversal. In June 1974 Israel received permission to leave. Late in July the Gohbergs left Kishinev by train for Vienna enroute to Israel. Household furnishings and "approved books" were sent ahead. Unfortunately many reprints and unpublished manuscripts had to be left behind; only a small portion of this material arrived later in Israel with the help of the Dutch embassy, which was and still is representing Israel in the U.S.S.R..

FROM TWO SIDES

L. Lerer (Haifa, Israel)

My initial acquaintance with Israel Gohberg came during my student years at Kishinev. Thanks to his lucid and captivating lectures, seminars and informal discussions, I was introduced to a wide range of exciting mathematical theories and problems. Since then Gohberg has been my "guiding star", and his judgement and support have played a very important role for me.

Gohberg arrived in Israel full of ideas for far-reaching projects. Despite a long exhausting journey of several days, while still on the way from Ben-Gurion Airport to an absorption center in Tel-Aviv, he told me about some of his plans. Very soon we started to work together.

Our first joint works gave me a unique opportunity to learn at close range from a great mathematician. One cannot help being impressed by Gohberg's unerring instinct for what is important and potentially fruitful, and by his striking talent for analyzing a complicated problem via a transparent and motivating special case. The high standards he applies to himself and to his co-workers, and his diciplined work habits taken together with his unimpeachable honesty, kindness and a very special sense of humor, create a wonderful school for every young mathematician working with Gohberg.

I had the privilege of going through this school at a very important stage of my development. At that time we often worked at Gohberg's appartment , where a warm friendly atmosphere reigned thanks to his wife Bella Jakovlevna, his late mother "babushka" Clara, and his lovely daughters Zvia and Janina.

The above remarks, as incomplete as they are, indicate that working with Gohberg is an enjoyable and exciting experience. Fortunately, our collaboration continues and many projects are in progress. From the bottom of my heart I wish Israel Gohberg many healthy years of enjoying his great love - Mathematics.

Israel the mathematician received offers from most of the universities in Israel the state. He chose Tel-Aviv University because he felt that he could play a useful role in shaping the growth of its Mathematics Department, which was then still young and unformed.

Israel Gohberg at Tel-Aviv University

D. Amir (Tel-Aviv, Israel)

Those who know Izia Gohberg and are familiar with his wonderful sense of humor will certainly understand why it seems natural to me to begin my Gohberg recollections with a Jewish joke.

A young man, not very rich and not too clever, comes to a matchmaker to ask for a bride. The matchmaker says: "I have got something very special for you: She is from a very good family, rich, young and beautiful too". The man says: "This seems perfect to me; but, how come such a wonderful girl is still unmarried - doesn't she have any faults?" The matchmaker answers: "To tell you the truth - she has one small problem: Once a year she becomes insane for one day". The young man reflects for a while and says: "One day a year is not that bad. I am willing to marry her. In fact, I would like to marry her as soon as possible. Why don't we go there at once?". The matchmaker calms him down: "You can't do it now ; we have to wait till the day she becomes insane and then she may consent to marry you... .".

When we received Gohberg's C.V. in 1974, just after he applied to emigrate from the USSR, naturally we became very enthusiastic. It was obvious that here was a distinguished mathematician, highly esteemed and holding a high position in the USSR in spite of his Jewishness. He was very rich, in publications of course. I believe his publication list contained 137 works at that time, including several books. He was known to be an outstanding teacher, with 25 Ph.D. students to his credit. Moreover, he was even willing to marry us, i.e., to join Tel-Aviv

University. But there was still some tiny problem. Mother Russia did not approve of the marriage. His application was refused with the excuse that, if allowed to emigrate, "he would take out with him the ideas of his colleagues...".

Nevertheless, in June 1974, The Mother's consent finally being acquired, we received a telegram from Kishinev telling us the good news. On July 28th he arrived in Vienna and on the next day - he was finally in Israel. Two days later he was already studying in an Ulpan (an intensive Hebrew course for newcomers) and shortly thereafter he accepted a position as a Professor of Mathematics at Tel-Aviv.University. This, besides showing how eager we were to absorb him, shows also how fast Izia adapts to new conditions, like a cat always manages to fall on its feet... . In fact, he adapted so fast that in the same fall he already went, for the first time in his life, to visit the real West, i.e., the U.S.

I was serving then as the Chairman of the Department of Pure Mathematics. I still remember how he came to my room and handed me an invitation which he had received from Stony Brook and an application to go there for a short visit. I looked at the papers and said: "That's O.K. You may go". He remained seated, waiting for something else to be said by me - some "only" or "but...". He just could not believe that this was all the procedure needed when you want to go abroad... . Anyhow, as you all know very well, he learnt this, too, quite fast.

There's this joke about the guy who, when told that his wife is being unfaithful to him, and that with more than one man, answers as follows: "My late father, may he rest in peace, was a successful merchant. Before he died he said to me: My son, this is the advice I can give you: It is much better to share a good business with several people, then to be the single owner of a bad one..". Thus, we had to share Izia with the Weizmann Institute, Stony Brook, College Park, Calgary, and Amsterdam... . Still Gohberg is a wonderful business investment, bearing Tel-Aviv University's name, and making his home here in Israel .

And what a home! Most of us have experienced, more than once, the proverbial "Russian hospitality" in that warm home. His charming wife, Bella, the Doctor, helped by their daughters, and sometimes even by his sister, made evenings at the Gohberg's unforgettable experiences. In the first years there was "Babushka" too, Izia's wonderful mother, who kept an eye on each of us to make sure that we are all well fed.

Gohberg turned out, of course, to be as popular in Tel-Aviv, as he had been in Kishinev, and as he is everywhere. As a teacher he is strongly beseiged by the students. When I taught the introductory course in Hilbert Spaces in the second semester, while he gave the same course in the first semester, the distribution of students was about 5:1 in his favour, and others didn't score better... . He holds a local record in the number of graduate students, and many of them can be seen queuing in the corridor to his office. As everybody knows, he is very diligent, and is an ideal partner for research and publication. His current list of publications holds about 300 papers, among them a dozen or more books, and he is still only 60 years young! On top of that, one has to add his other activities: Founding and editing the journal "Integral Equations and Operator Theory" and the book series "Operator Theory: Advances and Applications", running the Israel seminar on Operator Theory, and initiating and organizing the biannual Otto Toeplitz Memorial Lectures etc..

Some of this unbelievably intensive activity should probably be attributed to the very special Gohberg personality, some of the ingredients of which are a basic optimism and a rare sense of humor, which did not let him down during the worst political or physical crises and enabled him to recover and bloom again each time. Thus it seems appropriate to conclude with a classical traditional Jewish story.

A traveller walked in the desert. After ten days in which he met no city, no inn, no tree, no water and no living soul, he found a tree standing on a sweet water spring. He sat down, cooled himself under the thick shadow of the beautiful tree, ate from the tree's tasty fruit, drank the water and rested. When he had to leave he said: "Oh tree, what blessing can I wish you? You are sitting on water, you are beautiful, your shadow is thick and your fruit is plentiful and delicious! The only blessing I can add to all that is : - LET THERE BE MANY MORE LIKE YOU WITH US!

Letter of B. Trachtenbrot (Tel-Aviv, Israel)

Dear Israel,

I hereby join your many friends, colleagues and students in greeting you on the occasion of your anniversary.

As early as the fifties you had made a name for yourself as one of the most brilliant mathematicians of your generation. Even though my area of expertise is far from your field of research, I always followed with great interest the development of your scientific career. There were personal reasons also for my interest and admiration. After all, we are what in Russian is called "Zemliaki" (fellow countrymen), and I was very impressed and moved by your contribution towards scientific development in the Bessarabia region, in which we were both of us born, and from which I departed many years ago.

You were the first of the senior academy members who reached and realized the difficult and courageous decision to make aliya to Israel. In this way you encouraged me as well as others to work towards aliya.

You succeeded in raising in the old-new homeland a young generation of students as well as continuing in your excellent research. You achieved this thanks to your superlative talents and to your never-ending conscientious work.

Best wishes to you, your family, your students and your admirers.

Much success in your life's endeavor.

Sincerely,
Boris Trachtenbrot and wife Bertha.

Shortly after his arrival in Israel, Ronald Douglas and Joel Pincus invited him to visit Stony Brook for the Fall semester. Israel requested permission from his Department Chairman to accept the invitation. Permission was promptly granted. Israel, unaccustomed as he was to the freedom of the West, was sure that the Department Chairman had not understood the question properly. He therefore repeated it twice more, each time receiving assurances that it was okay to go, before he was ready to believe that he could really go. In mid October 1974 Israel made his first trip to the United States.

At Stony Brook arrangements had been made for room and board with David and Barbara Ebin, an orthodox Jewish family, because it was believed that M.G. Krein was orthodox, and therefore that Israel must be so too. This was based on the observation that Krein kept his head covered and was very careful about what he ate. These conditions, although necessary, where not sufficient. Nevertheless the boarding arrangements were very satisfactory to all parties concerned, and exposed Israel to customs which he had been isolated from in the Soviet Union and brought him new friends. Stony Brook offered him a full time position , but Israel decided to stay permanently in Tel-Aviv.

In January and February of 1975, Israel was invited to the University of Maryland at College Park, by Seymour Goldberg. At Maryland he met Rien Kaashoek, who was visiting David Lay. They showed him their work. There were some strong differences of opinion. Prompted by Rien, Israel presented a couple of informal lectures on promising directions for future research and on open problems. One of these, the problem of linearizing analytic operator functions, caught Rien and David's fancy and led to a program for joint research. A paper of Gohberg, Kaashoek and Lay was completed in the Spring of 1976. More importantly, however, this chance meeting marked the beginning of the Dutch connection which was to blossom and expand in subsequent years.

THE DUTCH CONNECTION

M.A. Kaashoek (Amsterdam, The Netherlands)

Israel Gohberg's first visit to Amsterdam took place in December 1975. We had met before in 1970 at the Hilbert Space Operators and Operator Algebras conference in Tihany and, much more intensively, at College Park, Maryland in the beginning of 1975. The latter meeting, although unplanned, turned out to be most important. At that time Israel was in College Park for two months, as a guest of Seymour Goldberg, and lectured on various topics from his work with M.G. Krein, N. Krupnik, and J. Leiterer. I was in College Park for the Spring semester and planned to work with David Lay on problems related to papers of Gohberg-Sigal, not knowing that Israel would be in town. Israel was quite critical about a paper Harm Bart, David Lay and I had written, and for me our first meetings in College Park can be best described in terms which are sometimes used in the Dutch weather forecast: heavy storms and critical conditions at the dikes. But the winds were warm and the atmosphere was friendly. Before Israel left College Park at the end of February 1975 the first main results for a Gohberg-Kaashoek-Lay paper on linearization and factorization existed, there was a set of notes (never published, but still worth doing so) of two stimulating lectures of Israel about open problems on operators and operator-valued functions, there were plans for further collaboration, and I had the permission of my chairman to invite Israel to Amsterdam for the Autumn semester of 1976. Israel's visit to Amsterdam in December 1975 was just the first in a long chain.

In the Autumn semester of 1976 Israel developed a great deal of activities in Amsterdam. He gave an advanced course on singular integral equations and Toeplitz operators and ran a wonderful seminar on matrix polynomials, including the fresh and new Gohberg-Lancaster-Rodman results. Israel, Harm Bart and I were planning to work on related problems for rational matrix functions using the approach of the theory of characteristic operator functions. Harm and I were introduced to the latter subject in one long afternoon session, where Israel explained to us the main ideas of the theory by browsing through the Brodskii book. After the session both of us felt that we had known the subject all our lives. Such experiences we had many times. That semester, in lectures, seminars and informal discussions, Israel introduced the operator theory group in Amsterdam to the beautiful way of mathematical thinking in (what I shall call for simplicity) the Gohberg-Krein school, and we learned much about the great mathematical achievements in Odessa and Kishinev. We also experienced the stimulating and joyful working atmosphere that Israel knows how to create, which involves many hours of intensive mathematical discussions (larded with relaxing stories and jokes) and also non-mathematical affairs as mushroom dinners, bicycle rides and family visits. In short it was a great period.

At the end of the 1976 Autumn semester it was decided that each year Israel would come to Amsterdam for two or three short periods, each of a couple of weeks. The contract would be for three years, but for each short period a formal appointment was needed and each time all forms would have to be filled in. In the Dutch context, with its well-developed tax and social security system, the number of forms is not negligible. Hence each period started with a couple of hours of filling in forms and answering questions which are not meant for persons who were born in Rumania, emigrated from the U.S.S.R to Israel and came to Amsterdam to do mathematics. Soon Israel's file at the personnel department of the Vrije Universiteit exceeded the place reserved for it and he knew more about the Dutch working conditions than most of us. In 1983 the three year contract was replaced by an appointment as an extra-ordinary professor. We appreciate the appointment and miss the forms.

By now Israel is well established in Amsterdam, and the results of his visits are clearly visible. During the past years many new ideas emerged, new students were attracted and joined the group, new connections were made, with the mathematical system theory people and the electrical engineers, new books appeared, dissertations were written and many papers published.

Israel's activities in Amsterdam are not restricted to the Vrije Universiteit. He has developed contacts all over the country. Also he has brought many mathematicians to Amsterdam. Several have become good friends and co-workers. His many mathematical achievements are well recognized and highly appreciated in the Netherlands. In 1985 her majesty the Queen appointed him a foreign member of the Royal Dutch Academy, and, as one may guess from the size of the country, it is more difficult to become a foreign member than an ordinary one. I wish that in Amsterdam we may enjoy his visits for many years to come.

Speech of L. Frank (Nijmegen, The Netherlands), delivered during the conference

The Gohberg-Krein theory of convolution operators on the half-line is one of those fundamental contributions to Operator Theory which is extensively used in many different fields of Pure and Applied Mathematics.

Coercive Singular Perturbations is one illustration of the important role that this class of operators plays in Singular Perturbation Theory. Therein, in order to reduce a coercive singular perturbation to a regular one in a constructive way, one needs the symbolic calculus with a small parameter (modulo operators with small norms), whose version without parameter (modulo smoothing operators) was developed earlier by Boutet de Monvel. The core of Boutet de Monvel's calculus and its version with a small parameter is the Gohberg-Krein theory mentioned above.

Thus, not only as an admirer, but also as a user of the fundamental results by I. Gohberg and M.G. Krein, I consider it a special privilege to have been invited to give a talk at the conference honoring the 60th birthday of Israel Gohberg.

I first saw Professor Gohberg at the Moscow State University at one of the sessions of Gelfand's much celebrated Monday seminar. At that time, Israel Gohberg was not yet a corresponding member of the Moldavian Academy of Sciences. I met Israel Gohberg for the second time in 1974 at the Hebrew University of Jerusalem after his alya (immigration) to Israel. At that time he was no longer on the list of the members of the Moldavian Academy of Sciences. The last time I saw Israel Gohberg (before coming to the Conference honoring his 60th birthday) was in Nijmegen, at my home University, where he gave a talk on determinants and traces for some classes of linear operators. At this time he was already a foreign member of the Dutch Royal Academy of Sciences. Quite a way to go along and further up to the International Conference honoring the 60th birthday of Israel Gohberg.

Albert Einstein said once: "If my Relativity Theory is true, Germany will claim that I am German and France will say that I am a Citizen of the World. However, if my Relativity Theory turns out to be wrong, then France will claim that I am German and Germany will say that I am Jewish".

It is my belief that in the case of Israel Gohberg each country where he feels at home, is happy to claim Israel Gohberg's belonging to its scientific elite, even if he happens to be only a part-time Dutchman, Canadian and American, being a full-time Israeli.

From Maryland, Israel also made short excursions to Toronto and Calgary at the invitation of Chandler Davis and Peter Lancaster, respectively. The visit to Calgary was to prove particularly fruitful.

GOHBERG IN CANADA

P.Lancaster (Calgary, Alberta, Canada)

I was surprised and pleased to receive a letter from M.G.Krein in 1968 requesting a copy of the monograph on "Lambda-Matrices and Vibrating Systems" that grew out of my doctoral thesis. It showed that my work had attracted some attention in the U.S.S.R.. Subsequently, I got to know the Gohberg-Krein book on non-selfadjoint operators, as well as several important papers that had appeared in translation by Gohberg and Krein, Gohberg and Markus, and Gohberg and

Sigal. So I was very glad to hear from Chandler Davis in 1974 that Israel Gohberg had emigrated, and would be able to visit North America in early 1975.

As a result, he first came to Calgary in February of 1975. This was not a long visit, but enough to begin to identify problem areas where we might work together. But that was not our only common ground. It was a cold month with plenty of snow, and we still remember his delight in our cottage in the mountains and in the clear winter weather. Since then he has enjoyed our wilderness in most seasons of the year and, along the way, we have joined in some most enjoyable mathematics.

We met again in the following year while I was on sabbatical leave in Scotland. After this visit and my later visit to Tel Aviv, the shape of our first researches on matrix polynomials began to emerge. I probably met Israel's Ph.D. student, Leiba Rodman, at about that time who, under Israel's guidance, was already producing very interesting results on analytic matrix functions. So began a very productive and enjoyable three-way collaboration. Since those early years we have been able to meet, for shorter or longer periods, in Tel-Aviv, or Calgary, or elsewhere, on an annual basis.

Since we first met I have been fascinated by Israel's powers of gentle persuasion. His extraordinary talent in stimulating mathematical investigations is very much in evidence in these volumes. But he never needs to explicitly persuade anyone to join with him on a mathematical adventure. One needs only to show enthusiasm for a problem that he considers interesting and worth-while, and there is a good chance that something interesting and worth-while will actually be produced; after some intense effort and several revisions, to be sure. He seems always to be able to bring out the best mathematical talents in those around him, whether they are beginners, engineers, pure or applied mathematicians.

During these years of joint activity warm, and very rewarding relationships have evolved between our three families. It is a privilege, not only to have worked with a genius of our time, and with Leiba Rodman, but also to have shared many happy times, and a few sad times, with their families.

I am very glad to have had the opportunity to help in providing a sixtieth birthday present in the form of the Calgary conference and these volumes. In these pages, and at Calgary in August of 1988, we have been fortunate to bring together Israel's immediate family, and many members of his extended family of collaborators and admirers representing his career both in the U.S.S.R. and in the West.

At the end of February 1975, upon returning to Tel-Aviv, Israel found Leiba Rodman on his doorstep. Leiba wanted Israel to be his Ph.D. advisor. Israel agreed and suggested Matrix Polynomials as a research topic. By the Spring of 1976 they had their first results. This, as Leiba writes, was the easy part. Writing it in acceptable form took longer--"he would make me rewrite drafts many times. Although it was a privilege to work with a great master in creating mathematics, it was often frustrating due to his high demands and expectations. There was a point in my Ph.D. work (after being told to rewrite a draft for the eighth time) when I seriously contemplated quitting. Why I did not quit, I do not know... I do know that doing a Ph.D. with Gohberg means going through an outstanding school of mathematics".

A paper of Peter Lancaster was found to be relevant to Leiba's and Israel's work on matrix polynomials. Peter who was then on sabbatical in Scotland, came to visit Tel-Aviv in the Spring of 1976. This led to the first Gohberg-Lancaster-Rodman publication and marked the beginning of another successful partnership.

In the Spring of 1975 Israel also started to lecture in Tel-Aviv University using the English language which he had picked up during his visits to the United States and Canada, lecturing in Hebrew later. The same semester he also accepted a half-time position at the Weizmann Institute of Science. This led in due course to a long and fruitful collaboration with Harry Dym.

ISRAEL AT THE WEIZMANN INSTITUTE

H.Dym (Rehovot, Israel)

I first met Israel Gohberg in the Spring of 1975 when he joined the Weizmann Institute as a half-time faculty member. That Spring he delivered a series of lectures on Topics in Operator Theory. They were outstanding. He had a gift for focusing on the essence, of presenting just enough to give the flavor and the main results without overwhelming the listener with technical details. It all seemed so clear, so natural and so elegant. It was only later, upon reviewing the lecture that one realized how deep many of the results were.

These virtuoso performances were to be repeated many times in the years to come on a number of different topics ranging from highlights of his books with Krein and with Feldman to the newly developing theory of matrix polynomials.

In the early days at Weizmann our contacts were limited. I listened to his lectures, and asked him an occasional question connected with some problems I was working on at the time, which, as it happened, were based on an operator theoretic interpretation of Szegö's formula. Israel used to come to the Institute twice a week. On one of these days he would lecture. He spent most of the rest of the time talking with his newly acquired student, Sonia Levin (daughter of the well-known refusenik Alexander Lerner). Still this was not enough to keep a man of his vitality fully occupied. He used to sit in an office two doors down the hall from mine. His door was always open and as I passed by from time to time, I could not help feeling that it was a tremendous waste just to leave him to his own devices and, more than that, I sensed that he too would welcome some active intervention with the "natives".

In the Spring of 1976 I approached him and expressed an interest in working with him. He was receptive. We didn't get much done in the remaining few weeks of that semester, but contact had been initiated.

In the Fall semester, Israel returned from Amsterdam with a question on extensions which was to mark the real beginning of our collaboration. Our meetings were somewhat sporadic in the beginning. Israel had many invitations and I had a less exotic invitation to do a couple of months of military service. Nevertheless we had amassed some results before I left for a partial sabbatical in May of 1978. That Summer, while visiting Tom Kailath, I stumbled across Burg's Ph.D. thesis. If memory serves me correctly, I just happened upon it in the xerox room. This was to prove to be a wonderful find. The search for analogues of Burg's maximum entropy principle in the context of a variety of different extension problems was to turn out to be a major influence on much of our subsequent work. We continued to collect results throughout the coming academic year.

Some weeks later, in the Summer of 1979, we met again in the Van Gogh museum in Amsterdam on a Sunday afternoon. It was one of those grey days which the Dutch excel in; rain just around the corner and never quite making it beyond a sprinkle here and there--perfect museum weather. I came in from Delft with the family and met Israel at the museum. Irene and the boys went to look at the paintings and Israel and I seated ourselves on a couple of comfortable armchairs to formulate strategy. A fat loose-leaf of notes was placed on a nearby table amidst a stack of art magazines and catalogues. They were picked up from time to time by passing browsers, but they were always replaced very quickly. It was a fruitful meeting which led to some nice refinements of our accumulated results and agreement on the general lines of three separate papers, all of which appeared not so long thereafter. Curiously enough, the one which we thought to be just a side issue in the general context of our developing machinery, seems to have attracted the most interest.

I learned a great deal working with Israel. It was equivalent to serving an apprenticeship with a master craftsman. Even more than that, it was a living connection with the great Russian school of Functional Analysis of Achiezer and Krein. Israel was an ideal teacher and colleague. He seemed to remember everything that he had ever worked on, where to find it, and how to explain it. Moreover, he was always patient, always cheerful, and always, always optimistic. When Israel first met my youngest son Michael, he asked him "How many children are there in your class?". "Forty-one" was the reply. "Wonderful" said Israel, "so many friends".

For many years it was Israel's habit to come to the Weizmann Institute early on Sunday mornings. One morning he came very late. It turned out that he had had a traffic accident enroute. Another car had hit his car in the rear. As accidents go, it was relatively minor, but still the expense and inconvenience was far from negligible. After settling in, he called his wife to tell her what happened."But why did he do that to you" was her immediate wifely response. "Bellachka", said Israel, ever so gently, "this question you have to put to him, not to me".

Israel spent the Fall semester of 1975 at Stony Brook, where he gave a graduate course on Fredholm operators and an undergraduate course on linear algebra. That semester he met Kelvin Clancey who was also visiting Stony Brook while on sabbatical leave from Athens, Georgia. This was the beginning of their joint work, which continued later with visits of Israel to Athens and produced a number of nice papers and a book on factorization of matrix functions and singular integral operators.

By the Fall of 1976 a number of collaborations were in operation. Permutations of these, supplemented by students and colleagues of the original partners, generated many new collaborations. Moreover, the roster of partners kept growing as Gohberg shuttled between Israel, Amsterdam, the United States and Canada.

In 1978 the first issue of Integral Equations and Operator Theory, a new journal under his editorship, appeared. In 1979 it was followed by the first volume in the accompanying series of books: Operator Theory: Advances and Applications (also under his editorship). Both of these ventures succeeded because of his optimism, enthusiasm and hard work. With characteristic forethought, Israel had enough collaborations running by this time to sustain the Journal over its initial critical period. In 1979 the first Toeplitz Lectures Series were set up. Peter Lax and Ciprian Foias, the latter then a recent refugee from Rumania, were the first guest lecturers. One of the other highlights of that event was a party in Israel's house catered by the Gohberg women: Mother,wife, sister and two daughters, whose combined energies and talents were truly awesome. His wife and sister took a few days off from their medical careers to cook and bake. It was a spectacular party that was surpassed only by the Toeplitz Memorial Conference Party which was held at his home two years later.

This Calgary conference is testimony to the success of all these activities. Hugo Woerdeman, perhaps the youngest participant, spoke for us all when he observed:"Professor Gohberg is still so young too! He could sit back and relax and look back on a wonderful career as a mathematician. But he still does all this travelling and is still so active. I am glad he is doing all this and I hope that he continues because I learned a great deal from him and hope to learn a lot more".

Letter of B. Khvedelidze (Tbilisi, U.S.S.R.), read at the banquet

Dear Israel !

With my whole heart I would like to congratulate you on the occasion of your sixtieth birthday.

Thanks to the organizers for inviting me to the conference, dedicated to this event. I regret very much that the doctors at the last moment advised me to cancel this trip which I was so much looking forward to make.

Since I lost the opportunity to join your pupils, collaborators and colleagues during the celebration in Calgary, I decided to express in writing my admiration of you as a person and as a mathematician.

Your fundamental investigations in many topics of functional analysis certainly influenced their development and determined their current substance. These investigations brought you worldwide fame. I appreciate especially your result on integral equations with singular kernels, which completed the investigations in this field.

I must also express my gratitude for educating my student R. Duduchava, who became an experienced expert in integral equations under your guidance.

My colleagues and I remember well the nice meetings with you here in Tbilisi and in Kishinev. During these meetings you impressed me as an honest, kind and sensitive person. I pray to God that we may have more scientists like you.

Unfortunately we haven't seen each other for a long time and it's a pity for me to miss the opportunity to correct this situation.

Due to the last positive changes in our lives I hope I will be able to invite you very soon as a cherished guest of honor.

Sincerely yours,

Tbilisi, 15 August, 1988 — Professor Boris Khvedlidze

Speech of M.M. Drzjabashian (Yerevan, U.S.S.R.), delivered at the banquet

Dear colleagues and friends,

We are gathered together here today to mark with honor the 60th birthday of one of the outstanding mathematicians of our time, Professor Israel Cudikovich Gohberg.

All of us heartily greet and congratulate you, dear celebrant, your wonderful family, your daughters and wife, on this festive day. Wherever you may be, and wherever your creative activity and your organizational ability develops, you serve the gratifying and noble task of the development of the science which all of us here love - mathematics - the science to which you devoted all your energy and talent.

I think it would not be out of place here to recall what is perhaps known to only a few of you, that from ancient times the people of Armenia had an interest in the science of mathematics. Even in the 11th century a then famous scholar and political figure in Armenia, Gregory Magister, occupied himself with mathematics. A visit to the Matenadaran, in Yerevan, will serve to convince oneself of this fact. This is where the ancient manuscripts of the Armenian people are kept, and where eleven pages of an old translation of the "Elements" of Euclid in the Armenian language was miraculously kept safe from the Mongol-Seljuq barbarians. Because of these barbarians, it was only after a very long period of time that Armenian mathematics started to develop once more, in fact only recently, during the last four or five decades.

The people of Armenia worked the land, and they were particularly successful at tending vineyards and producing wine. Exactly 60 years ago, in this sunny land, there was an exceptionally good grape harvest, and from this harvest of Armenian grapes it was decided to produce a very good cognac, which is now exactly 60 years old. Allow me on this day to present to you as a souvenir, a bottle of this Armenian cognac which is precisely 60 years old. Allow me also to convey my heartfelt wish to you and your family that you should open this 60 year old bottle of cognac in good health on the day of your one hundredth birthday, with your grandchildren and your greatgrandchildren, gathered around you.

The present notes form only a partial biography. Mathematics is hardly discussed, and many important events and meetings are not touched upon. These topics remain for a next version. Moreover, it is our hope that many new developments will take place and that new sections will have to be added later.

The Editors

I. Gohberg with (some of) his co-authors

Front row (from left to right): K. Clancey, D. Alpay, R.L. Ellis, I. Gohberg, L. Rodman, H. Dym, M.A. Kaashoek; second row: J.A. Ball, D.C. Lay, T. Kailath, H.J. Woerdeman, S. Goldberg, L. Lerer; last row: A.C.M. Ran, I. Koltracht, P. Lancaster, F. van Schagen, H. Bart, A. Ben-Artzi, T. Shalom.

I. Gohberg and (former) students

First diagonal (from top to bottom): I. Koltracht, L. Lerer, I. Gohberg, L. Rodman; second diagonal: M. Tismenetsky, B.A. Kon, A. Ben-Artzi, T. Shalom; third diagonal: H.J. Woerdeman, N. Cohen, R. Duduchava.

ISRAEL GOHBERG

TEL-AVIV UNIVERSITY
Raymond and Beverly Sackler
Faculty of Exact Sciences
School of Mathematical Sciences
Department of Pure Mathematics

CURRICULUM VITAE

DATE AND PLACE OF BIRTH:	August 23, 1928, Tarutino, USSR
MARITAL STATUS:	Married, two children

EDUCATION:

M.Sc. Mathematics
Kishinev University, Kishinev,
Moldavian Soviet Republic, USSR
Date of award: July 1951

Kandidat of Sciences, Ph.D. Mathematics
Leningrad Pedagogical Institute, USSR
Date of award: April 1954

Doctor of Sciences, Mathematics
Moscow State University, USSR
Date of award: February 1964

ACADEMIC AND PROFESSIONAL EXPERIENCE:

1951-1953	Assistant Professor, Soroki Teacher's Institute, Moldavian Soviet Republic, USSR
1953-1959	Assistant Professor, Associate Professor, Chairman of the Department of Mathematics, Beltsky Pedagogical Institute, Moldavian Soviet Republic, USSR
1959-1974	Senior Researcher and Head of the Department of Functional Analysis, Institute of Mathematics of the Academy of Science, Moldavian Soviet Republic, USSR
1966-1973	Professor at Kishinev University, USSR (part-time)
1974-	Professor, Tel Aviv University, Israel

1975-1983	Professor, Weizmann Institute of Science, Rehovot, Israel (part-time)
1981-	Incumbent of the Nathan and Lily Silver Chair in Mathematical Analysis and Operator Theory, Tel Aviv University
1983-	Professor, Vrije Universiteit, Amsterdam, The Netherlands (part-time)
	Visiting and adjunct professor for various extended periods at State University of New York at Stony Brook, New York, U.S.A. University of Calgary, Alberta, Canada University of Georgia, Athens, GA, U.S.A. University of Maryland, College Park, MD. U.S.A. Vrije Universiteit, Amsterdam, The Netherlands.
ACADEMIC AWARDS:	
1970	Elected corresponding member of the Academy of Sciences of MSSR, USSR (In 1974 removed from the list of members of this Academy)
1985	Elected Foreign Member of the Royal Netherlands Academy of Arts and Sciences
1986	Awarded Rothschild Prize in Mathematics
EDITORIAL WORK:	
1978-	Editor of the international journal "Integral Equations and Operator Theory" published by Birkhauser Verlag, Basel
	Editor of the book series "Operator Theory: Advances and Applications" published by Birkhauser Verlag, Basel
	Member of editorial board of the journals: "Applicable Analysis" (Gordon and Breach Science Publishers); "Asymptotic Analysis" (North-Holland); "Applied Mathematics Letters" (Pergamon Press).

Supervised thirty-seven doctoral students

December 1988

December 1988

Professor Israel GOHBERG.

LIST OF PUBLICATIONS

Books.

1. I. Gohberg, M. Krein.
Vvedenie v Teoriju Linejnyh Nesamosopriazennyh Operatorov v Gilbertovom Prostranstve. Nauka, Moscow, 448 pages (Russian) 1965.

1a. I. Gohberg, M. Krein.
Introduction to the theory of linear nonselfadjoint operators. American Mathematical Society, Providence, 378 pages (translated from Russian) 1969; second printing 1978, third printing 1983, fourth printing 1988.

1b. I. Gohberg, M. Krein.
Introduction a la Theorie des Operateurs Lineaires Non Autoadjoints dans un Espace Hilbertien. Dunod, Paris, 372 pages (French, translated from Russian) 1971.

2. I. Gohberg, M. Krein.
Teorija Volterovhy Operatorov v Gilbertovom Prostranstve i Ejo Prilozenia. Nauka, Moscow, 508 pages (Russian) 1967.

2a. I. Gohberg, M. Krein.
Theory and Applications of Volterra Operators in Hilbert Space. American Mathematical Society, Providence, (Translated from Russian) 430 pages, 1970.

3. I. Feldman, I. Gohberg.
Proektionnyc Metody Reshenia Uravnenij Wiener-Hopfa. Akademija Nauk MSSR, Kishinev, 164 pages (Russian) 1967.

4. I. Feldman, I. Gohberg.
Uravnenija v Sveortkah i Proektionnye Metody ih Reshenia. Nauka, Moscow, 352 pages (Russian) 1971.

4a. I. Feldman, I. Gohberg.
Faltungsgleichungen und Projektionsverfahren zu Ihrer Losung.
Akademie-Verlag, Berlin, 276 pages (German, translated from Russian) 1974.

4b. I. Feldman, I. Gohberg.
Faltungsgleichungen und Projektionsvesfahren zu ihrer Losung. Mathematische Reihe 49. Birkhaeuser Verlag, 275 pages (Translated from Russian) 1974.

4c. I. Feldman, I. Gohberg.
Convolution Equations and Projection Methods for their Solution. American Mathematical Society, Providence, 262 pages (Translated from Russian) 1974.

5. I. Gohberg, N. Krupnik.
Vvedenije v Teoriju Odnomernyh Singuliarnyh Integralnyh Operatorov. Shtiinta, Kishinev, 428 pages (Russian) 1973.

5a. I. Gohberg, N. Krupnik.
Einfuhrung in die Theorie der Eindimensionalen Singularen Integraloperatoren. Birkhauser Verlag, Basel, 379 pages (German, translated from Russian) 1979.

6. V.G. Boltyanskii, I. Gohberg.
Teoremy i Zadachi Kombinatornoj Geometrii. Nauka, Moscow, 108 pages (Russian), 1965.

6a. V.G. Boltyanskii, I. Gohberg.
Satze und Probleme der Kombinatorishcen Geometrie. Deutsche Verlag der Wissenschaftern, Berlin, 128 pages (German, translated from Russian) 1972.

6b. V.G. Boltyanskii, I. Gohberg.
Tetelek es Faladtok A Kombinatorikus Geome.riabol. Tankoyvkiado, Budapest, 112 pages (Hungarian, translated from Russian) 1970.

6c. V.G. Boltyanskii, I. Gohberg.
Results and Problems in Combinatorial Geometry. Cambridge University Press, 108 pages (Translated from Russian) 1985.

7. V.G. Boltyanskii, I. Gohberg.
Razbienie Figur na Menshie Chasti. Nauka, Moscow, 88 pages (Russian), 1971.

7a. V.G. Boltyanskii, I. Gohberg.
Division de Figuras en Partes Menores. Mir, Moscow, 106 pages, (Spanish, translated from Russian) 1973.

7b. V.G. Boltyanskii, I. Gohberg.
The Decomposition of Figures into Smaller Parts, 75 pages, University of Chicago Press, 75 pages (Translated from Russian), 1980.

7c. V.G. Boltyanskii, I. Gohberg.
Alakzatok Felbontasa Kisebb Reszekre. Tankonyvkiad, Budapest, 93 pages, (Hungarian, translated from Russian) 1976.

8. H. Bart, I. Gohberg, M.A. Kaashoek.
Minimal Factorization of Matrix and Operator Functions. Operator Theory: Advances and Applications, Vol. 1. Birkhauser Verlag, 236 pages 1979.

9. I. Gohberg, S. Goldberg.
Basic Operator Theory Birkhauser Verlag, 285 pages, 1981.

10. K. Clancey, I. Gohberg.
Factorization of Matrix Functions and Singular Integral Operators. Operator Theory: Advances and Applications, Vol. 3. Birkhauser Verlag, 234 pages, 1981.

11. I. Gohberg, P. Lancaster, L. Rodman.
Matrix Polynomials. Academic Press, 409 pages, 1982.

12. I. Gohberg, P. Lancaster, L. Rodman.
Matrices and Indefinite Scalar Products. Operator Theory: Advances and Applications, Vol. 8. Birkhauser Verlag, 374 pages, 1983.

13. I. Gohberg, P. Lancaster, L. Rodman.
Invariant Subspaces of Matrices with Applications. Canadian Math. Soc. Series of Monographs and Advanced Texts, John Wiley & Sons, 629 pages, 1986.

Articles.

1. I. Gohberg.
On linear equations in Hilbert space. Dokl. Acad. Nauk SSSR, 76, no. 4, 9-12 (Russian) (1951), MR 13, 46 (1952).

2. I. Gohberg.
On linear equations in normed spaces. Dokl. Akad. Nauk SSSR, 76, no. 4, 447-480 (Russian) (1951). MR 13, 46 (1952).

3. I. Gohberg.
On Linear operators depending analytically upon a parameter. Dokl. Akad. Nauk SSSR, 78, no. 4, 629-632 (Russian) (1951); MR 13, 46 (1952).

4. V.A. Andrunakievich, I. Gohberg.
On linear equations in infinite-dimensional spaces. Uch. zap. Kishinev. Univ., Vol. V, 63-67 (Russian), (1952).

5. I. Gohberg.
On an application of the theory of normed rings to singular integral equations. Uspehi Mat. Nauk 7, 149-156 (Russian) (1952); MR 14, 54 (1953).

6. I. Gohberg.
On the index of an unbounded operator. Mat. Sb 33(75), I, 193-198 (Russian) (1953). MR 15, 233 (1954).

7. I. Gohberg.
On systems of singular integral equations. Uc. Zap Kisinevsk. Univ. 11, 55-60 (Russian) (1954); MR 17, 163 (1956); MR 17, 75 (1950).

8. I. Gohberg.
On zeros and zero elements of unbounded operators. Dokl. Akad. Nauk SSSR 101, 9-12 (Russian) (1955); MR 17, 284 (1956).

9. I. Gohberg.
Some properties of normally solvable operators. Dokl. Akad. Nauk SSSR 104, 9-11 (Russian) (1955); MR 17, 647 (1956)

10. I. Gohberg, A.S. Markus.
On a characteristic property of the kernel of a linear operator. Dokl. Akad. Nauk. SSSR 101, 893-896 (Russian) (1955); MR 17, 769 (1956).

11. I. Gohberg.
The boundaries of applications of the theorems of F. Noether. Uch. zap Kishinev Univ, Vol. 17, 35-43 (Russian) (1955).

12. I. Gohberg, A.S. Marcus.
On stability of certain properties of normally solvable operators. Mat. Sb. 40 (82), 453-466 (Russian) (1956); MR 19, 45 (1958).

13. I. Gohberg, M.G. Krein.
On the basic propositions of the theory of systems of integral equations on a half-line with kernels depending on the difference of arguments. Proc. III Math. Congr. SSSR, Vol. 2, (Russian) 1956.

14. I. Gohberg, M.G. Krein.
The application of the normed rings theory to the proof of the theorems of solvability of systems of integral equations. Proc. III Math. Cong. SSSR, Vol. 2, 1956.

15. I. Gohberg.
On the index, null elements and elements of the kernel of an unbounded operator. Uspehi Mat. Nauk (N.S) 12, No.1 (73), 177-179 (Russian) (1957); MR 19, 45 (1958); English Transl. Amer. Math. Soc. Transl. 2(16) 391-392, 1960; MR 22 #8374.

16. I. Gohberg, L.S. Goldenstein, A.S. Markus.
Investigations of some properties of linear bounded operators with connection to their q-norm. Uch. zap. Kishinev Univ. Vol. 29, (Russian) 1957.

17. I. Gohberg, M.G. Krein.
The basic propositions on defect numbers root numbers and indices of linear operators. Uspehi Mat. Nauk 12, No. 2 (74), 43-118 (1957); English transl. Amer. Math. Soc. Transl. (2) 13, 185-264 (1960); MR 20 #3459; MR 22 # 3984.

18. I. Gohberg, M.G. Krein.
Systems of integral equations on a half-line with kernels depending on the difference of arguments. Uspehi Mat. Nauk 13, No.2 (80), 3-72 (1958); English transl. Amer. Math. Soc. Transl. 2 (14), 217-287 (1960);MR 21 #1506; MR 22 #3954.

19. I. Gohberg, M.G. Krein.
On the stability of a system of partial indices of the Hilbert problem for several unknown functions. Dokl. Akad. Nauk SSSR 119, 854-857 (1958); MR 21 #3547.

20. I. Gohberg.
On the number of solutions of a homogeneous singular integral equation with continuous coefficients. Dokl. Akad. Nauk SSSR 122, 327-330 (Russian) (1958); MR 20 #4748 (1959).

21. I. Gohberg.
Two remarks on index of a linear bounded operator. Uch. zap. Belz Pedagog. Inst. No. 1, 13-18 (Russian) (1959).

22. I. Gohberg, M.G. Krein.
On a dual integral equation and its transpose I. Teoret. Prikl. Mat. No. 1, 58-81, Lvov (Russian) (1958); MR 35 #5877.

23. I. Gohberg.
On bounds of indexes of matrix-functions. Uspehi Nat. Nauk 14, No. 4 (88), 159-163 (Russian) (1959); MR 22 #3993.

24. I. Gohberg, A.S. Markus.
Two theorems on the gap between subspaces of a Banach space. Uspehi Mat. Nauk 14, No. 5 (89) 135-140 (Russian) (1959); MR 22 #5880.

25. I. Gohberg, M.G. Krein.
On completely continuous operators with spectrum concentrated at zero. Dokl. Acad. Nauk SSSR, 128, No. 2, 227-230 (Russian) (1959); MR 24 #A1022.

26. I. Gohberg, A.S. Markus.
Characteristic properties of the pole of a linear closed operator. Uch. zap Belz. Pedagog. Inst. No. 5, 71-75 (Russian) (1960).

27. I. Gohberg.
A remark of standard factorization of matrix-functions. Uch. zap. Belz. Pedegog Inst. No. 5, 65-69 (Russian) (1960).

28. I. Gohberg, A.S. Markus.
Characteristic properties of certain points of spectrum of bounded linear operators. Izv. Vyso. Ucel Zaved. Matematik No. 2 (15) 74-87 (Russian) (1960); MR 24 #A1626.

29. I. Gohberg, L.S. Goldenstein.
On a multidimensional integral equation on a half-space whose kernel is a function of the difference of the arguments, and on a discrete analogue of this equation. Dokl. Acad. Nauk SSSR 131, No. 1, 9-12 (Russian) (1960); Soviet Math. Dokl. 1, 173-176 (1960); MR 22 #8298.

30. I. Gohberg.
On the theory of multidimensional singular integral equations. Dokl. Acad Nauk SSSR 133, No. 6, 1279-1282 (Russian) (1960); Soviet Math. Dokl. 1, 960-963 (1961); MR 23 #A2015.

31. I. Gohberg.
Some topics of the theory of multidimensional singular integral equations. Izv. Mold. Akad. Nauk No. 10 (76), 39-50 (Russian) (1960).

32. I.A. Feldman, I. Gohberg, A.S. Markus.
On normally solvable operators and ideals associated with them. Bul. Akad. Stiince RSS Moldoven. No. 10 (76), 51-70 (1960); English transl., Amer. Math. Soc. Transl. (2) 61, 63-84 (1967); MR 36 #2004.

33. I. Gohberg, A.S. Markus.
One problem on covering of convex figures by similar figures. Izv. Mold. Acad. Nauk 10 (76), 87-90 (Russian) (1960).

34. I. Gohberg, A.S. Markus.
Some remarks about topologically equivalent norms. Izv. Mold. fil. Acad. Nauk SSSR 10 (76), 91-95 (Russian) (1960).

35. I. Gohberg, M.G. Krein.
On the theory of triangular representations of non-selfadjoint operators. Dokl. Acad Nauk SSSR 137, No. 5, 1034-1037 (1961); Soviet Math. Dokl. 2, 392-395 (1961);MR 25 #3370.

36. I. Gohberg, M.G. Krein.
On Volterra operators with imaginary component in one class or another. Dokl. Acad. Nauk SSSR 139, No. 4, 779-782 (1961); Soviet Math. Dokl. 2, 983-986 (1961); MR 25 #3372.

37. I. Gohberg, M.G. Krein.
The effect of some transformations of kernels of integral equations upon the equations' spectra. Ukrain. Mat. Z 13, No. 3, 12-28 (1961); English transl., Amer. Math. Soc. Transl. 2(35) 263-295 (1964); MR 27 #1788.

38. I. Gohberg, A.S. Markus.
On the stability of bases in Banach and Hilbert spaces. Izv. Moldavsk. Fil. Akad. Nauk SSSR, No. 5, 17-35 (Russian) (1962); MR 37 # 1955.

39. I. Gohberg, A.S. Markus.
On some inequalities between eigenvalues and matrix elements of linear operators. Izv. Moldavsk. Fil. Akad. Nauk SSSR, No. 5, 103-108 (Russian) (1962).

40. I. Gohberg.
Tests for one-sided invertibility of elements in normed rings and their applications. Dokl. Akad. Nauk SSSR 145, No. 5, 971-974 (1962); Soviet Math. Dokl.3, 1119-1123 (1962); MR 25 #6147.

41. I. Gohberg.
A general theorem concerning the factorization of matrices-functions in normed rings, and its applications. Dokl. Akad. Nauk SSSR 146, No. 2, 284-287 (1962); Soviet Math. Dokl. 3, 1281-1284 (1962); MR 25 #4376.

42. I. Gohberg, M.G. Krein.
On the problem of factorization of operators in Hilbert space. Dokl. Akad. Nauk SSSR 147, No. 2, 279-282 (1962); Soviet Math. Dokl. 3, 1578-1582 (1962); MR 26 #6777.

43. I. Gohberg.
On factorization of operator-functions Uspehi Mat. Nauk 18, No. 2, 180-182 (Russian) (1963).

44. I. Gohberg.
On relations between the spectra of the Hermitian components of nilpotent matrices and on the integral of triangular truncation. Bul. Akad. Stiiuce RSS Moldoven, No. 1, 27-37 (Russian) (1963); MR 35 #2168.

45. I. Gohberg.
On normal resolvability and the index of functions of an operator. Izv. Acad Nauk Mold. SSR, No. 11, 11-24 (Russian) (1963); MR 36 #6965.

46. M.S. Brodskii, I. Gohberg, M.G. Krein, V. Matsaev.
On some new investigations on the theory of non-self-adjoint operators Proc. IV All-union Math. Congress, Vol. 2, 261-271 (Russian) (1964); MR 36 #3153.

47. I. Gohberg, A.S. Markus.
Some relations between eigenvalues and matrix elements of linear operators. Mat. Sb. 64 (106), No. 4, 481-496 (1964); English transl., Amer. Math. Soc. transl. (2), 52, 201-216 (1966); MR 30 #457,

48. I. Gohberg, M.G. Krein.
Criteria for completeness of the system of root vectors of a contraction. Ukrain. Mat. Z. 16, No. 1, 78-82 (1964); English transl., Amer. Math Soc. Transl., (2) 54, 119-124 (1966); MR 29 #2651.

49. I. Gohberg, M.G. Krein.
On factorization of operators in Hilbert space. Acta Sci. Math., Szeged, 25, No. 1-2, 90-123 (1964); English transl., Amer. Math. Soc. Transl. (2) 51, 155-188 (1966); MR 29 #6313.

50. I. Gohberg.
A factorization problem in normed rings, functions of isometric and symmetric operators and singular integral equations. Uspehi Mat. Nauk 19, No. 1 (115), 71-124; Russian Math. Survey 19, No. 1, 63-144 (1964);MR 29 #487.

51. I. Gohberg.
The factorization problem for operator functions. Izv. Akad. Nauk SSSR, Ser. Mat. 28, No. 5, 1055-1082 (Russian) (1964) MR 30 #5182.

52. V.G. Ceban, I. Gohberg.
On a reduction method for discrete analogues of equations of Wiener-Hopf type. Ukrain Mat. Z 26, No. 6, 822-829 (1964); English transl., Amer. Math. Soc. transl. (2) 65, 41-49 (1967). MR 30 #2244.

53. M.S. Budjanu, I. Gohberg.
A general theorem about factorization of matrix-functions. Studies in Algebra and Math. Anal Izd. "Kartja Mold".Kishinev, 116-121, 1965. MR 36 #726.

54. I. Gohberg, M.K. Zambickii.
On normally solvable operators in spaces with two norms. Bull. Akad. Nauk Mold. SSR, No. 6, 80-84 (Russian) (1964). MR 36 #3143.

55. I.A. Feldman, I. Gohberg.
On approximative solutions of some classes of linear equations. Dokl. Akad. Nauk SSSR 160, No. 4, 750-753 (1965); Soviet Math. Dokl. 6, 174-177 (1965). MR 34 #6572.

56. I. Gohberg, M.G. Krein.
On the multiplicative representation of the characteristic functions of operators closed to unitary ones. Dokl. Acad. Nauk SSSR 164, No. 4, 732-735, (1965); Soviet Math. Dokl. 6, 1279-1283, (1965); MR 33 #571.

57. I.A. Feldman, I. Gohberg.
On reduction method for systems of Wiener-Hopf type. Dokl. Akad. Nauk SSSR 165, No. 2, 268-271, (1965); Soviet Math. Dokl. 6, 1433-1436, (1965); MR 32 #8085.

58. I. Gohberg, M.K. Zambickii.
On the theory of linear operators in spaces with two norms. Ukrain. Mat. Z. 18, No. 1, 11-23, (1966); MR 33 #4676.

59. I. Gohberg.
A generalization of theorems of M.G. Krein of the type of the Wiener-Levi theorems. Mat. Issled. 1, No. 1, 110-130, (Russian) (1966); MR 34 #3366.

60. M.A. Barkar, I. Gohberg.
On factorization of operators relative to a discrete chain of projections in Banach space. Mat. Issled. I, No. 1, 32-54, (1966); English transl., Amer. Math. Soc. Transl. 2 (90), 81-103, (1970); MR 34 #6539.

61. M.A. Barkar, I. Gohberg.
On factorization of operators in a Banach space. Mat. Issl. 1, No. 2, 98-129, (Russian) (1966); MR 35 #780.

62. I.A. Feldman, I. Gohberg.
On truncated Wiener-Hopf equations. Abstracts of Short Scientific Reports, Intern. Congress of Math. (Moscow), Section 5, 44-45, (Russian) (1966).

63. I. Gohberg, M.G. Krein.
On triangular representations of linear operators and on multiplicative representations of their characteristic functions. Dokl. Acad. Nauk SSSR, 175, NO.2, 272-275, (1967); MR 35 #7157.

64. I.A. Feldman, I. Gohberg.
On indices of multiple extensions of matrix functions. Bull. Akad. Nauk Mold. SSR, No.6, 76-80, (Russian) (1967); MR 37 #4658

65. I. Gohberg, M.G. Krein.
On a description of contraction operators similar to unitary ones. Funkcional Anal. i Priloz, 1, No. 1, 38-68, (1967); Functional Anal. and Appl. Vol. 1, 1, 38-60 (1967); MR 35 #4763

66. I. Gohberg.
On Toeplitz matrices composed of the Fourier coefficients of piece-wise continuous functions. Funkcional Anal. i Priloz., 1, No. 2, 91-92, (1967); Function Anal. Appl. 1, 166-167, (1967); MR 35 #4763.

67. M.S. Budjanu, I. Gohberg.
On factorization problem in abstract Banach algebras I. Splitting algebras. Mat. Issled 2, No. 2, 25-61, (1967); English transl., Amer. Math Soc. Transl. (2); MR #5697.

68. M.S. Budjanu, I. Gohberg.
On factorization problem in abstract Banach algebras II. Irreducible algebras. Mat. Issled 2, No. 3, 3-19, (1967); English transl., Amer. Math. Soc. Transl. (2); MR 37 #5698.

69. I. Gohberg, O.I. Soibelman.
Some remarks on similarity of operators. Mat. Issled. 2, No. 3, 166-170, (Russian) (1967); MR 37 #3387.

70. M.S. Budjanu, I. Gohberg.
On multiplicative operators in Banach algebras. I. General propositions. Mat. Issled 2, No. 4, 14-30, (Russian) (1967); MR 379 #1972. (English transl. Amer. Mat. Soc. Trans. (2), vol. 90, 211-223, 1970.

71. I. Gohberg, N. Ia. Krupnik.
On the norm of the Hilbert transfrom in Lp spaces. Funkcional Anal. i Priloz, 2, No. 2, 91-92, (1968); Functional Anal. Appl. 2, 180-181, (1968).

72. I. Gohberg, N.Ia. Krupnik.
On the spectrum of one-dimensional singular integral operators with piece-wise continuous coefficients. Mat. Issled. 3, No. 1 (7), 18-30, (1968); English transl., Amer. Math. Soc. Transl. (2) 103, 181-193, (1973); MR 41 #2469.

73. M.S. Budjanu, I. Gohberg.
General theorems on the factorization of matrices-functions I. The fundamental theorem. Mat. Issled 3, No. 2 (8), 87-103 (1968); English transl., Amer. Math. Soc. Transl. (2) 102, 1-14 (1973); MR 41 #4246a.

74. M.S. Budjanu, I. Gohberg.
General theorems on the factorization of matrices-functions II. Some tests and their consequences. Mat. Issled 3, No. 3 (9), 3-18 (1968); English transl., Amer. Math. Soc. Transl. (2) 102, 15-26 (1973); MR 41 #4246b.

75. I.A. Feldman, I. Gohberg.
On Wiener-Hopf integral difference equations. Dokl. Akad, Nauk SSSR 183, No. 1, 25-28 (1968); Soviet Math. Dokl. 9, 1312-1316 (1968); MR 44 #3096.

76. I. Gohberg, N. Ia. Krupnik.
On the spectrum of singular integral operators in Lp spaces. Studia Math. 31, 347-362 (Russian) (1968); MR 38 #5068.

77. N.N. Bogolyubov, I. Gohberg, G.E. Shilov.
Mark Grigorevich Krein (on his sixtieth birthday). Uspehi Mat. Nauk, 23, No.3, 197-214 (1968); Russian Math. Surveys, 23, No. 3, 177-192, (May-June 1968); MR 37 #5077

78. I. Gohberg, N. Ia. Krupnik.
On the spectrum of singular integral operators in Lp spaces with weight. Dokl. Acad. Nauk. SSSR 185, No.4 745-748 (1969); Soviet Math. Dokl. 10, 406-410 (1969); MR 40 #1817.

79. I. Gohberg, N.Ia. Krupnik.
On an algebra generated by Toeplitz matrices. Funkcional Anal. i Priloz, 3, No. 2, 46-59 (1969); Functional Anal. Appl. 3, 119-127 (1969); MR 40 #3323.

80. I.A. Feldman, I. Gohberg.
Integro-difference Wiener-Hopf equations. Acta Sci. Math., Szeged, 30, No. 3-4, 199-224 (Russian) (1969); MR 40 #7880.

81. I. Gohberg, N.Ia. Krupnik.
Systems of singular integral equations in Lp spaces with a weight. Dokl. Akad. Nauk SSSR 186, No. 5, 998-1001 (1969); Soviet Math. Dokl. 10, 688-651 (1969); MR 40 #1818.

82. I. Gohberg, N.Ia. Krupnik.
On quotient norm of singular integral operators. Mat. Issled 4, No. 3, 136-139 (Russian) (1968); MR 41 4306.

83. I. Gohberg, N.Ia. Krupnik.
On the algebra generated by Toeplitz matrices in hp spaces. Mat. Issled 4, No. 3, 54-62 (Russian) (1969).

84. V.M. Brodskii, I. Gohberg, M.G. Krein.
General theorems on trianglular representations of linear operators and multiplicative representations of their characteristic functions. Funk. Anal. i Priloz, 3, No. 4, 1-27 (1969); MR 40 #4794.

85. I. Gohberg, N.Ia. Krupnik.
On composite linear singular integral equations. Mat. Issled. 4, No. 4, 20-32 (1969); English transl., Amer. Math. Soc. Transl. (2) (to appear); MR 43 #996.

86. I. Gohberg, N.Ia. Krupnik.
The symbols of one-dimensional singular integral operators on an open contour. Dokl. Akad Nauk SSSR 191, 12-15 (1970); Soviet Math. Dokl. 11, 299-303 (1970); MR 41 #9060.

87. V.M. Brodskii, I. Gohberg, M.G. Krein.
The definition and basic properties of the characteristic function of a knot. Funkt. Anal. i Proloz, No. 4, 1, 88-90 (1970).

88. I. Gohberg, N.Ia. Krupnik.
On the algebra generated by the one-dimensional singular integral operators with piecewise continuous coefficients. Funkcional Anal. i Priloz 4, No. 3, 26-36 (1970); Functional Anal. App. 4, 193-201 (1970); MR 42 #5057.

89. I. Gohberg, M.G. Krein.
New inequalities for the eigenvalues of integral equations with smooth kernels. Mat. Issled 5, No. 1 (15), 22-39 (Russian) (1970);MR 44 #818.

90. I. Gohberg, N.Ia. Krunnik.
Singular integral equations with continuous coefficients on a composite contour. Mat. Issled No. 5, 1, 22-39 (Russian) (1970)

91. I. Gohberg, N.Ia. Krupnik.
On singular integral equations with unbounded coefficients. Mat. Issled 5, No. 3 (17), 46-57 (Russian) (1970); MR 45 #980.

92. I. Gohberg, A.A. Semencul.
Toeplitz matrices composed of the Fourier coefficients of functions with discontinuities of almost periodic type. Mat. Issled. 5, No. 4, 63-83 (Russian) (1970); MR 44 #7379.

93. I. Gohberg, N.Ia. Krupnik.
Banach algebras generated by singular integral operators. Colloquia Math. Soc. Janos Bolyai 5. Hilbert space operators, Tihany (Hungary), 239-267 (Russian) (1970).

94. I. Gohberg, E.M. Spigel.
A projection method for the solutin of singular integral equations. Dokl. Akad Nauk SSSR 196, No. 5, 1002-1005 (1971); Soviet Math. Dokl. 12, 289-293 (1971); MR 43 # 3755.

95. V.M. Brodskii, I. Gohberg, M.G. Krein.
On characteristic functions of an invertible operator. Acta Sci. Math. Szeged, No. 32, 1-2, 141-164 (Russian) (1971).

96. I. Gohberg, N.Ia. Krupnik.
Singular integral operators on a composite contour. Proc. Georgian Akad Nauk 64, 21-24 (Russian, Georgian and English summaries) (1971); MR 45 #4223.

97. I. Gohberg.
On some questions of spectral theory of finite-meromorphic operator-functions. Izv. Arm. Akad. Nauk, No. 6, 2-3, 160-181 (Russian) (1971).

98. I. Gohberg.
The correction to the paper "On some questions of spectral theory of finite-meromorphic operator-functions". Izv. Arm. Acad. Nauk, No. 7, 2, 152 (Russian)(1972).

99. I. Gohberg, N.Ia. Krupnik.
Singular integral operators with piecewise continuous coefficients and their symbols. Izv. Akad. Nauk SSSR. Ser. Mat. 35, 940-964 (Russian)(1971); MR 45 #581.

100. I. Gohberg, V.I. Levcenko.
Projection method for the solution of degenerate Wiener-hopf equations. Funkcional Anal. in Priloz., 5, No.4, 69-70 (Russian) (1971); MR 44 #7317.

101. I. Gohberg, E.I. Sigal.
An operator generalization of the logarithmic residue theorem and Rouche's theorem. Mat. Sb. (N.S.) 84 (126), 607-629 (1971); English transl. Math. USSR, sb. 13, 603-625 (1971). MR 47 #2409.

102. I. Gohberg, E.I. Sigal.
Global factorization of a meromorphic operator-function and some of its applications. Mat. Issled. 6, No. 1 (19), 63-82 (Russian)(1971); MR 47 #2410

103. I. Gohberg, E.I. Sigal.
The root multiplicity of the product of meromorphic operator functions. Mat. Issled. 6, No. 2 (20), 30-50, 158 (Russian)(1971);MR 46 #2461.

104. I. Gohberg, E.M. Spigel.
On the projection method of solution of singular integral equations with polynomial coefficients. Mat. Issled. 6, No. 3, 45-61 (Russian) (1971); MR 44 #7380.

105. I. Gohberg, V.I. Levcenko.
On the convergence of a projection method of solution of a degenerated Wiener-Hopf equation. Mat. Issled. 6, No. 4, 20-36 (Russian) (1971). MR 45 # 918.

106. I. Gohberg, J. Leiterer.
The canonical factorization of continuous operator functions with respect to the circle. Funk Anal. i Priloz 6, No. 1 73-74 (1972); Functional Anal. Appl. 6, 65-66 (1972); MR 45 #2519.

107. I. Gohberg, J. Leiterer.
On factorization of continuous operator funtions with respect to a contour in Banach algebras. Dokl. Akad. Nauk SSSR, 206, 273-276 (1972); English transl. Soviet Math. Dokl. 13, 1195-1199 (1972).

108. I. Gohberg, J. Leiterer.
Factorization of operator functions with respect to a contour I. Finitley meromorphic operator functions. Math. Nachrichten 52, 228-259 (Russian) (1972).

109. I. Gohberg, N. Ia. Krupnik.
A formula for the inversion of finite Toeplitz matrices. Mat. Issled 7, No. 2, 274-283 (Russian) (1972)

110. I. Gohberg, A.A. Semencul.
On the inversion of finite Toeplitz matrices and their continuous analogues. Mat. Issled 7, No. 2, 201-223, (Russian) (1972).

111. I. Gohberg, V.I. Levcenco.
On a projection method for a degenerate Wiener-Hopf equation. Mat. Issled. 7, No. 3, 238-253 (Russian) (1972).

112. I. Gohberg. J. Leiterer.
General theorems on a canonic factorization of operator-functions with respect to a contour. Mat. Issled. No. 7, 3, 87-134 (Russian) (1972).

113. I. Gohberg, J. Leiterer.
On holomorphic vector-functions of one variable. Mat. Issled. No. 7, 4, 60-84 (Russian) (1972).

114. I. Gohberg, J. Leiterer.
The factorization of operator-functions with respect to a contour II. Canonic factorization of operator-functions closed to unit ones. Math. Nachrichten, No. 54, 1-6, 41-74 (Russian) (1973).

115. I. Gohberg, J. Leiterer.
The factorizaion of operator-functions with respect to a contour III Factorization in algebras. Math. Nachrichten, No. 55, 1-6, 33-61 (Russian) (1973).

116. I. Gohberg, J. Leiterer.
On co-cycles, operator-functions and families of subspaces. Mat. Issled. No. 8, 2, (1973).

117. I. Gohberg, J. Leiterer.
On holomorphic functions of one variable II. Functions in a domain. Mat. Issled. No. 8, 1, 37-58 (Russian) (1973)

118. I. Gohberg, N. Ia. Krupnik.
On algebras of singular integral operators with a shift. Mat. Issled No. 8, 2, (Russian) (1973).

119. I. Gohberg, N. Ia. Krupnik.
On one-dimensional singular integral operators with a shift. Izv. Arm. Acad. Nauk, No. 1, 3-12 (Russian) (1973).

120. I. Gohberg, J. Leiterer.
Criterion of the possibility of the fatorization of operator-function with respect to a contour. Dokl. Acad. Nauk SSSR, 209, 3, 529-532 (Russian) (1973).

121. I. Gohberg, J. Leiterer.
General theorems on the factorization of operator-functions with respect to a closed contour. I. Holomorphic functions. Acta. Sci. Math., Szeged, 30, 103-120 (Russian) (1973).

122. I. Gohberg, J. Leiterer.
General theorems on the factorization of operator-functions II. Generalizations. Acta. Sci. Math. Szeged (Russian) (1973).

123. I. Gohberg, J. Leiterer.
On a local principle in the problem of the factorization of operator-functions. Funk. Anal. i Priloz. No. 7, 3 (Russian) (1973)

124. I. Gohberg, J. Leiterer.
The local principle in the problem of the factorization of continuous operator-functions. Revue Rounainie de Math. Pures et Appl., XIX, 10, (Russian) (1973).

125. I. Gohberg, N. Ia. Krupnik.
On a symbol of singular integral operators on a composite contour. Proc. Tbilisi Simp. Mech. Sploshnich Sred, Tbilisi, (Russian) (1973).

126. I. Gohberg, N. Ia. Krupnik.
On the local principle and on algebras generated by Toeplitz's matrices. Annalele stiintifice ale Univ. "Al. I. Cuza", Iasi, section I a) Matematica, XIX, F. I, 43-72 (Russian) (1973).

127. I. Gohberg, J. Leiterer.
Familes of holomorphic subspaces with removable singularities. Math. Nachrichten 61, 157-173(Russian) (1974).

128. I. Gohberg, G. Heinig.
On the inversion of finite Toeplitz matrices. Math. Issled. No. 8, 3, 151-155 (Russian) (1973).

129. I. Gohberg, G. Heinig.
Inversion of finite Toeplitz matrices composed from elements of a non-commutative algebra. Rev. Roum. Math. Pures et Appl. 20, 5, 55-73 (Russian) (1974)

130. I. Gohberg, G. Heinig.
On matrix-valued integral operators on a finite interval with matrix kernels which depend on the difference of arguments. Re. Roumaine Math. Pures Appl., 20, 1. 55-73 (1975).

131. I. Gohberg, G. Heinig.
Matrix resultant and its generalizations, I. The resultant operator for matrix valued polynomials. Acta Sci. Math. (Szeged), T.37, 1-2, 1975, 41-61.

132. I. Gohberg, S. Prossdorf.
Ein Projektionsverfahren zue Losung entarteter Systeme von diskreten Wiener-Hopf-Gleichungen. Math. Nachr., Band 65, 19-45 (1975).

133. I. Gohberg, G. Heinig.
Matrix resultant and its generalizations, II. Continual analog of the resultant operator. ACta Math. Acad. Sci. Hungar. T.28 (3-4), 189-209 (1976).

134. I. Gohberg, J. Leiterer.
Uber algebren steitiger operator functionen. Studia Math., T. 57, 1-26 (1976).

135. I. Gohberg, M.A. Kaashoek, D.C. Lay.
Spectral classification of operators and operator functions. Bull. Amer. Math. Soc. 82, 587-589 (1976).

136. I. Gohberg, L.E. Lerer.
Resultant of matrix polynomials. Bull. Amer. Math. Soc. 82, 4 (1976).

137. K. Clancey, I. Gohberg.
Local and global factorizations of matrix-valued functions. Trans. Amer. Math. Soc., Vol. 232, 155-167 (1977).

138. I. Gohberg, M.A. Kaashoek, D.C. Lay.
Equivalence, linearization and decomposition of holomorphic operator functions. J. Funct. Anal., Vol. 28, No. 1, 102-144 (1978).

139. I. Gohberg, P. Lancaster, L. Rodman.
Spectral analysis of matrix polynomials, I. Canonical forms and divisors. Linear Algebra and its Appl., 20, 1-44 (1978).

140. I. Gohberg, P. Lancaster , L. Rodman.
Spectral analysis of matrix polynomials, II. The resolvent form and spectral divisors. Linear Algebra and its Appl. 21, 65-88 (1978).

141. I. Gohberg, L.E. Lerer.
Resultant operators of a pair of analytic functions. Proceedings Amer. Math. Soc., Vol. 72, No. 1, 65-73 (1978).

142. I. Gohberg, L.E. Lerer.
Singular integral operators as a generalization of the resultant matrix. Applicable Anal., Vol. 7, 191-205 (1978).

143. I. Gohberg, M.A. Kaashoek, F. van Schagen.
Common multiples of operator polynomials with analytic coefficients. Manuscripta Math., 25, 279-314 (1978).

144. I. Gohberg, M.A. Kaashoek, L. Rodman.
Spectral analysis of families of operator polynomials and a generalized Vandermonde matrix, I. The finite-dimensional case. Topics in Functional Analysis. Adv. in Math., Supplementary Studies, Vol. 3, 91-128 (1978).

145. I. Gohberg, M.A. Kaashoek, L. Rodman.
Spectral analysis of families of operator polynomials and a generalized Vandermonde matrix II. The infinite dimensional case. J. Funct. Anal., Vol. 30, No. 3, 358-389 (1978).

146. I. Gohberg, P. Lancaster , L. Rodman.
Representations and divisibility of operator polynomials. Canad. J. Math., Vol. XXX, No. 5, 1045-1069 (1978).

147. I. Gohberg, L. Rodman.
On spectral analysis of non-monic matrix and operator polynomials, I. Reduction to monic polynomials. Israel J. Math., Vol. 30, Nos. 1-2, 133-151 (1978).

148. I. Gohberg, L. Rodman.
On spectral analysis of non-monic matrix and operator polynomials, II. Dependence on the finite spectral data. Israel J. Math., Vol. 30, No. 4, 321-334 (1978).

149. I. Gohberg, L. Lerer, L. Rodman.
Factorization indices for matrix polynomials. Bull. Amer. Math. Soc., Vol. 84, No. 2, 275-277 (1978).

150. I. Gohberg, L. Lerer, L. Rodman.
On canonical factorization of operator polynomials, spectral divisors and Toeplitz matrices. Integral Equations Operator Theory, Vol. 1, 176-214 (1978).

151. H. Bart, I. Gohberg, M.A. Kaashoek.
Operator polynomials as inverses of characteristic functions. Integral Equations Operator Theory, Vol. 1, 1 18 (1978).

152. H. Bart, I. Gohberg, M.A. Kaashoek.
Stable factorizations on monic matrix polynomials and stable invariant subspaces. Integral Equations Operator Theory, Vol. 1, 496-517 (1978).

153. I. Gohberg, S. Levin.
Asymptotic properties of Toeplitz matrix factorization. Integral Equations Operator Theory, Vol. 1, 518-538 (1978).

154. I. Gohberg, M.A. Kaashoek.
Unsolved problems in matrix and operator theory, I. Partial multiplicities and additive perturbations. Integral Equations Operator Theory, Vol. 1, 278-283 (1978).

155. K. Clancey, I. Gohberg.
Localization of singular integral operators. Math. Z. 169, 105-117 (1979).

156. H. Dym, I. Gohberg.
Extensions of matrix valued functions with rational polynomial inverses. Integral Equations Operator Theory, Vol. 2, 503-528 (1979).

157. I. Gohberg, P. Lancaster, L. Rodman.
Perturbation theory for divisors of operator polynomials. SIAM J. Math. Anal., Vol. 10, No. 6, 1161-1183 (1979).

158. I. Gohberg, L. Rodman.
On the spectral structure of monic matrix polynomials and the extension problem. Linear Algebra Appl., 24, 157-172 (1979).

159. I. Gohberg, P. Lancaster, L. Rodman.
On selfadjoint matrix polynomials. Integral Equations Operator Theory, Vol. 2, 434-439 (1979).

160. I. Gohberg., L. Lerer.
Factorization indices and Kronecker indices of matrix polynomials. Integral Equations Operator Theory, Vol. 2, 199-243 (1979).

161. I. Gohberg, M.A. Kaashoek.
Unsolved problems in matrix and operator theory, II. Partial multiplicities for products. Integral Equations Operator Theory, Vol. 2, 116-120 (1979).

162. I. Gohberg, S. Levin.
On an open problem for block Toeplitz matrices. Integral Equations Operator Theory, Vol. 2, 121-129 (1979).

163. E. Azoff, K. Clancey, I. Gohberg.
On the spectra of finite-dimensional perturbations of matrix multiplication opertors. Manuscripta Math. 30, 351-360 (1980).

164. I. Gohberg, L. Lerer, L. Rodman.
Stable factorizations of operator polynomials. I.Spectral divisors simply behaved at infinity. J. Math. Anal. Appl. 74, 401-431 (1980).

165. I. Gohberg, L. Lerer, L. Rodman.
Stable factorizations of operator polynomials. II. Main results and applications to Toeplitz operators. J. Math. Anal. Appl. 75, 1-40 (1980).

166. I. Gohberg, M.A. Kaashoek, F. van Schagen.
Similarity of operator blocks and canonical forms, I. General results, feedback equivalence and Kronecker indices. Integral Equations Operator Theory, Vol. 3, 350-396 (1980).

167. I. Gohberg, P. Lancaster, L. Rodman.
Spectral analysis of selfadjoint matrix polynomials. Annals of Mathematics, 112, 33-71 (1980).

168. H. Dym, I. Gohberg.
On an extension problem, generalized Fourier analysis, and an entropy formula. Integral Equations Operator Theory, 3, 143-215 (1980).

169. H. Bart, I. Gohberg, M.A. Kaashoek, P. van Dooren.
Factorizations of transfer functions. SIAM J. Control and Optimization, 18, No. 6, 675-696 (1980).

170. I. Gohberg, M.A. Kaashoek, F. van Schagan.
Similarity of operator blocks and canonical forms. II. Infinite dimensional case and Wiener-Hopf factorization. Operator Theory: Advances and Applications, 2, 121-170 (1981).

171. I. Gohberg, M.A. Kaashoek, L. Lerer, L. Rodman.
Common multiples and common divisors of matrix polynomials, I. Spectral method. Indiana University Mathematics Journal, 30 No. 3, 321-356 (1981).

172. H. Dym, I. Gohberg.
Extensions of band matrices with band inverses. Linear Algebra and its Applications, 36, 1-14 (1981).

173. I. Gohberg, L. Rodman.
Analytic matrix functions with prescribed local data. Journal d'Analyse Mathematique, 40, 90-128 (1981).

174. H. Bart, I. Gohberg, M.A. Kaashoek.
Wiener-Hopf integral equations, Toeplitz matrices and linear systems. Toeplitz Centennial, Operator Theory: Advances and Applications, Vol. 4, Birkhauser Verlag, 85-135 (1982).

175. I. Gohberg, P. Lancaster, L. Rodman.
Factorization of selfadjoint matrix polynomials with constant signature. Linear and Multilinear Algebra, 11, 209-224 (1982).

176. E. Azoff, K. Clancey, I. Gohberg.
Singular points of families of Fredholm integral operators. Toeplitz Centennial, Operator Theory: Advances and Applications, Vol. 4, Birkhauser Verlag, 57-65 (1982).

177. E. Azoff, K. Clancey, I. Gohberg.
On line integrals of rational functions of two complex variables. Proceedings American Mathematical Society, 88, 229-235 (1982).

178. I. Gohberg. L. Lerer.
On non-square sections of Wiener-Hopf operators., Integral Equations Operator Theory, Vol. 5, No. 4, 518-532 (1982).

179. H. Bart, I. Gohberg, M.A. Kaashoek.
Convolution equations and linear systems. Integral Equations and Operator Theory, Vol. 5, No. 3, 283-340 (1982).

180. H. Dym, I. Gohberg.
Extensions of triangular operators and matrix functions. Indiana University Mathematics Journal, Vol. 31, No. 4, 579-606 (1982).

181. H. Dym, I. Gohberg.
Extensions of matrix valued fuctions and block matrices. Indiana University Mathematics Journal, Vol. 31, No. 5, 733-765 (1982).

182. I. Gohberg, M.A. Kaashoek, F. van Schagen.
Rational matrix and operator functions with prescribed singularities. Integral Equations Operator Theory, Vol. 5, No. 5, 673-717 (1982).

183. I. Gohberg, P. Lancaster, L. Rodman.
Perturbations of H-selfadjoint matrices, with applications to differential equations. Integral Equations and Operator Theory, Vol. 5, No. 5, 718-757 (1982).

184. I. Gohberg, M.A. Kaashoek, L. Lerer, L. Rodman.
Common multiples and common divisors of matrix polynomials, II. Vandermonde and resultant matrices. Linear and Multilinear Algebra, 159-203 (1982).

185. I. Gohberg, S. Goldberg.
Finite Dimensional Wiener-Hopf equations and factorizations of matrices. Linear Algebra and its Applications, 48, 219-236 (1982).

186. I. Gohberg, L. Rodman.
Analytic operator valued functions with prescribed local data. Acta Sci. Math., Szeged, 45, 189-199 (1983).

187. I. Gohberg, L. Lerer, L. Rodman.
Wiener-Hopf factorization of piecewise matrix polynomials. Linear Algebra and its Applications, Vol. 52,53, 315-350 (1983).

188. H. Dym, I. Gohberg.
On unitary interpolants and Fredholm infinite block Toeplitz matrices. Integral Equations & Operator Theory, 6, 863-878 (1983).

189. H. Dym, I. Gohberg.
Extensions of kernels of Fredholm operators. Journal d'Analyse Mathematique, 42, 51-97 (1982/83).

190. H. Dym, I. Gohberg.
Unitary interpolants, factorization indices and infinite Hankel block matrices. Journal of Functional Analysis, Vol. 54, No. 3, 229-289 (1983).

191. H. Dym, I. Gohberg.
Hankel integral operators and isometric interpolants on the line. Journal of Functional Analysis, Vol. 54, No. 3, 290-307 (1983).

192. I. Gohberg, P. Lancaster, L. Rodman.
A sign characteristic for selfadjoint meromorphic matrix functions. Applicable Analysis, 16, 165-185 (1983).

193. H. Bart, I. Gohberg, M.A. Kaashoek.
The coupling method for solving integral equations. Operator Theory: Advances and Applictions, 12, 39-73 (1984).

194. I. Gohberg, M.A. Kaashoek, L. Lerer, L. Rodman.
Minimal divisors of rational matrix functions with prescribed zero and pole structure. Operator Theory: Advances and Applications, 12, 241-275 (1984).

195. I. Gohberg, M.A. Kaashoek.
Time varying linear systems with boundary conditions and integral operators, I. The transfer operator and its properties. Integral Equations and Operator Theory, 7, 325-391 (1984).

196. I. Gohberg, S. Goldberg.
Extensions of triangular Hilbert-Schmidt operators. Integral Equations and Operator Theory, 7, 743-790 (1984).

197. I. Gohberg, M.A. Kaashoek, F van Schagen.
Non-compact integral operators with semiseparable kernels and their discrete analogues: Inversion and Fredholm properties. Integral Equations and Operator Theory, 7, 642-703 (1984).

198. H. Bart, I. Gohberg, M.A. Kaashoek.
Wiener-Hopf factorization and realization. Lecture Notes in Control and Information Sciences, Mathematical Theory of Networks and Systems, Springer-Verlag, 58, 42-62 (1984).

199. I. Gohberg, P. Lancaster, L. Rodman.
A sign characteristic for selfadjoint rational matrix functions. Lecture Notes in Control and Infromation Sciences, Mathematical Theory of Networks and Systems, Springer-Verlag, 58, 263-269 (1984).

200. J.A. Ball, I. Gohberg.
A commutant lifting theorem for triangular matrices with diverse applications. Integral Equations and Operator Theory, 8, 205-267 (1985).

201. H. Bart, I. Gohberg, M.A. Kaashoek.
Fredholm theory of Wiener-Hopf equations in terms of realization of their symbols. Integral Equations and Operator Theory, 8, 590-613 (1985).

202. I. Gohberg, T. Kailath, I. Koltracht.
Linear complexity algorithms for semiseparable matrices. Integral Equations and Operator Theory, 8, 780-804 (1985).

203. I. Gohberg, P. Lancaster, L. Rodman.
Perturbation of analytic hermitian matrix functions. Applicable Analysis, 20, 23-48 (1985).

204. R.L. Ellis, I. Gohberg, D. Lay.
Factorization of Block Matrices. Linear Algebra and its Applications 69, 71-93 (1985).

205. I. Gohberg, I, Koltracht.
Numerical solution of integral equations, fast algorithms and Krein-Sobolev equation. Numer. Math. 47, 237-288 (1985).

206. J.A. Ball, I. Gohberg.
Shift invariant subspaces, factorization, and interpolation for matrices. I. The canonical case. Linear Algebra and its Applications, 1-64 (1985).

207. H. Dym, I. Gohberg.
A maximum entropy principle for contractive interpolants. Journal of Functional Analysis 65, 83-125 (1986).

208. I. Gohberg, L. Rodman.
Interpolation and local data for meromorphic matrix and operator functions. Integral Equations and Operator Theory 9, 60-94 (1986).

209. I. Gohberg, M.A. Kaashoek.
On minimality and stable minimality of time-varying linear systems with well-posed boundary conditions. Int. J. Control 43, 5, 1401-1411 (1986).

210. I. Gohberg, L. Rodman.
On distance between lattices of invariant subspaces of matrices. Linear Algebra Appl. 76, 85-120 (1986).

211. I. Gohberg, T. Kailath, I. Koltracht.
Efficient solution of linear systems of equations with recursive structure. Linear Algebra and its Applications 80, 81-113 (1986).

212. H. Bart, I. Gohberg, M.A. Kaashoek.
Wiener-Hopf factorization, inverse Fourier transforms and exponentially dichotomous operators. Journal of Functional Analysis 68, No. 1, 1-42 (1986).

213. I. Gohberg, M.A. Kaashoek.
Similarity and reduction of time varying linear systems with well-posed boundary conditions. SIAM J. Control and Optimization 24, No. 5, 961-978 (1986).

214. I. Gohberg, S. Rubinstein.
Stability of minimal fractional decompositions of rational matrix functions. Operator Theory: Advances and Applications 18, Birkhauser, Basel, 249-270 (1986).

215. J.A. Ball, I. Gohberg.
Classification of shift invariant subspaces of matrices with Hermitian form and completion of matrices. Operator Theory: Advances and Applications 19, Birkhauser, Basel, 23-85 (1986).

216. R.L. Ellis, I. Gohberg, D.C. Lay.
The maximum distance problem in Hilbert space. Operator Theory: Advances and Applications 19, Birkhauser, Basel, 195-206 (1986).

217. H. Bart, I. Gohberg, M.A. Kaashoek.
Wiener-Hopf equations with symbols analytic in a strip. Operator Theory: Advances and Applications 21, Birkhauser, Basel, 39-74 (1986).

218. I. Gohberg, M.A. Kaashoek, L. Lerer, L. Rodman.
On Toeplitz and Wiener-Hopf operators with contourwise rational matrix and operator symbols. Operator Theory: Advances and Applications 21, Birkhauser, Basel, 75-127 (1986).

219. I. Gohberg, M.A. Kaashoek.
Minimal factorization of integral operators and cascade decompositions of systems. Operator Theory: Advances and Applications 21, Birkhauser, Basel, 157-230 (1986).

220. H. Bart, I. Gohberg, M.A. Kaashoek.
Explicit Wiener-Hopf factorization and realization. Operator Theory: Advances and Applications 21, Birkhauser, Basel, 235-316 (1986).

221. H. Bart, I. Gohberg, M.A. Kaashoek.
Invariants for Wiener-Hopf equivalence of analytic operator functions. Operator Theory: Advances and Applications 21, Birkhauser, Basel,317-355 (1986).

222. H. Bart, I. Gohberg, M.A. Kaashoek.
Multiplication by diagonals and reduction to canonical factorization. Operator Theory: Advances and Applications 21, Birkhauser, Basel, 357-372 (1986).

223. I. Gohberg, P. Lancaster, L. Rodman.
Quadratic matrix polynomials with a parameter. Advances in Applied Mathematics 7, 3, 253-281 (1986).

224. R.L. Ellis, I. Gohberg, D.C. Lay.
Band extensions, maximum entropy and permanence principle. In Maximum Entropy and Bayesian Methods in Applied Statistics (J. Justice, Ed.), Cambridge University Press (1986).

225. I. Gohberg, P. Lancaster, L. Rodman.
On Hermitian solutions of the symmetric algebraic Riccati equation. SIAM Journal of Control and Optimization 24, 6, 1323-1334 (1986).

226. I. Gohberg, M.A. Kaashoek, L. Lerer.
Minimality and irreducibility of time-invariant boundary-value systems. nt. J. Control 44, 2, 363-379 (1986).

227. J.A. Ball, I. Gohberg.
Pairs of shift invariant subspaces of matrices and nonconical factorization. Linear and Multilinear Algebra 20, 27-61 (1986).

228. A. Ben-Artzi, R.L. Ellis, I. Gohberg, D.C. Lay.
The maximum distance problem and band sequences. Linear Algebra and its Applications 87, 93-112 (1987).

229. J.A. Ball, I. Gohberg, L. Rodman.
Minimal factorization of meromorphic matrix functions in terms of local data. Integral Equations and Operator Theory 10, 3, 309-348 (1987).

230. I. Gohberg, M.A. Kaashoek.
An inverse spectral problem for rational matrix functions and minimal divisibility. Integral Equations and Operator Theory 10, 437-465 (1987).

231. H. Bart, I. Gohberg, M.A. Kaashoek.
The state space method in problems of analysis. Proceedings of the First International Conference on Industrial and Applied Mathematics (ICIAM 87), 1-16, (1987).

232. I. Gohberg, S. Rubinstein.
Cascade decompositions of rational matrix functions and their stability. Int. J. Control 46 2, 603-629 (1987).

233. I. Gohberg, M.A. Kaashoek, L. Lerer.
On minimality in the partial realization problem. System & Control Letters 9, 97-104 (1987).

234. I. Gohberg, I. Koltracht, P. Lancaster.
Second order parallel algorithms for Fredholm integral equations with continuous displacement kernels. Integral Equations and Operator Theory 10, 577-594 (1987).

235. I. Gohberg, T. Kailath, I. Koltracht, P. Lancaster.
Linear complexity parallel algorithms for linear systems of equations with recursive structure. Linear Algebra and its Applications 88/89, 271-315 (1987).

236. R.L. Ellis, I. Gohberg, D.C. Lay.
Invertible selfadjoint extensions of band matrices and their entropy. SIAM J. Alg. Disc. Meth. 8, 3, 483-500 (1987).

237. I. Gohberg, S. Goldberg.
Semi-separable operators along chains of projections and systems. Journal of Mathematical Analysis and Applications 125, 1, 124-140 (1987).

238. I. Gohberg, M.A. Kaashoek.
Minimal representations of semiseparable kernels and systems with separable boundary conditions. J. Math. Anal. Appl. 124, 2, 436-458 (1987).

239. I. Gohberg, M.A. Kaashoek, F. van Schagen.
Szego-Kac-Achiezer formulas in terms of realizations of the symbol. J. Functional Analysis 74, 1, 24-51 (1987).

240. I. Gohberg, T. Kailath, I. Koltracht.
A note on diagonal innovation matrices. IEEE Transactions on Acoustics, Speech, and Signal Processing, Vol. ASSP-35, No. 7, 1068-1069, (1987)

241. A. Ben-Artzi, I. Gohberg.
Nonstationary Szego theorem, band sequences and maximum entropy. Integral Equations and Operator Theory 11, 10-27 (1988).

242. R.L. Ellis, I. Gohberg, D.C. Lay.
On two theorems of M.G. Krein concerning polynomials orthogonal on the unit circle. Integral Equations and Operator Theory 11, 87-104 (1988).

243. I. Gohberg, M.A. Kaashoek, F. van Schagen.
Rational contractive and unitary interpolants in realized form. Integral Equations and Operator Theory 11, 105-127 (1988).

244. H. Dym, I. Gohberg.
A new class of contractive interpolants and maximum entropy principles. Operator Theory: Advances and Applications 29, 117-150, Birkhauser, Basel (1988).

245. I. Gohberg, M.A. Kaashoek, L. Lerer.
Nodes and realization of rational matrix functions: Minimality theory and applications. Operator Theory: Advances and Applications 29, 181-232, Birkhauser, Basel (1988).

246. A. Ben-Artzi, I. Gohberg.
Fredholm properties of band matrices and dichotomy. Operatory Theory: Advances and Applications 32, 37-52, Birkhauser, Basel (1988).

247. J.A. Ball, I. Gohberg, L. Rodman.
Realization and interpolation of rational matrix functions. Operator Theory: Advances and Applications 33, 1-72, Birkhauser, Basel (1988).

248. I. Gohberg, M.A. Kaashoek, A.C.M. Ran.
Interpolation problems for rational matrix functions with incomplete data and Wiener-Hopf factorization. Operator Theory: Advances and Applications 33, 73-108, Birkhauser, Basel (1988).

249. I. Gohberg, M.A. Kaashoek.
Regular rational matrix functions with prescribed pole and zero structure. Operator Theory: Advances and Applications 33, 109-122, Birkhauser, Basel (1988).

250. D. Alpay, I. Gohberg.
Unitary rational matrix functions. Operator Theory: Advances and Applications 33, 175-222, Birkhauser, Basel (1988).

251. I. Gohberg, S. Rubinstein.
Proper contractions and their unitary minimal completions. Operator Theory: Advances and Applications 33, 223-247, Birkhauser, Basel (1988).

252. A. Ben-Artzi, I. Gohberg.
Lower upper factorizations of operators with middle terms. J. Functional Analysis 77, 2, 309-325 (1988).

253. I. Gohberg, S. Goldberg.
Factorizations of semi-separable operators along continuous chains of projections. Journal of Mathematical Analysis and Applications, 133, 1, 27-43(1988)

254. D. Alpay, I. Gohberg.
On orthogonal matrix polynomials. Operator Theory: Advances and Applications, 34, 25-46, Birkhauser, Basel (1988)

255. A. Ben-Artzi, I. Gohberg.
Extension of a theorem of M.G. Krein on orthogonal polynomials for the nonstationary case. Operator Theory: Advances and Applications, 34, 65-78, Birkhauser, Basel (1988)

256. I. Gohberg, L. Lerer.
Matrix generalizations of M.G. Krein theorems on orthogonal polynomials. Operator Theory: Advances and Applications, 34, 137-202 Birkhauser, Basel (1988)

257. I. Gohberg, M.A. Kaashoek.
Block Toeplitz operators with rational symbols. Operator Theory: Advances and Applications, 35, 385-440, Birkhauser, Basel (1988)

258. I. Gohberg, M.A. Kaashoek, P. Lancaster.
General theory of regular matrix polynomials and band Toeplitz operators. Integral Equations and Operator Theory 11, 776-882 (1988)

Part B

Papers on Matrix Theory and its Applications

The second part of this volume consists of papers on matrix theory and its applications. It includes original research papers on Toeplitz matrices and other specific classes of structured matrices, on efficient inversion of matrices and problems in numerical linear algebra, on completion problems for partially defined matrices, on stability and classification of invariant subspaces, and the study of invariant factors.

Operator Theory:
Advances and Applications, Vol. 40

SOME MATRIX INEQUALITIES IN MULTIPORT NETWORK CONNECTIONS

Tsuyoshi Ando and Fumio Kubo

Dedicated to Professor I. Gohberg on the occasion of his 60th birthday.

Connections of resistive multiport electrical networks give rise to several questions concerning comparisons among certain functions of impedance matrices of branch networks. In the present paper, some matrix inequalities, related to symmetric function means of an n-tuple of positive definite matrices, are proved to answer a part of the conjectures of Anderson, Morley and Trapp.

1. INTRODUCTION AND RESULTS

An N-port electrical network is a black box with 2N external terminals divided into pairs, each called a *port*. It is assumed that only resistors are hidden inside the box and that electrical current flows into the box from one terminal of each port and out of the box from the other terminal of the same port. Then current is represented by a vector $x \in \mathbb{C}^N$ and the aggregate of resistors by an N×N positive semi-definite matrix A, called the *impedance matrix* of the network. The vector Ax then represents the voltage drop across ports, and $\langle x|Ax\rangle$ does the energy of the network when current x flows into it, where $\langle\cdot|\cdot\rangle$ denotes inner product.

Throughout the paper the word *vector* means an element of $\mathbb{C}^N$. For positive integer M, an M-column $\begin{bmatrix} x_1 \\ \vdots \\ x_M \end{bmatrix}$ with components in $\mathbb{C}^N$ will be called an M-*block vector* while an element of $\mathbb{C}^M$ will be called an M-*numerical vector*.

Given two positive semi-definite matrices A, B, Anderson and Duffin [1] introduced the notion of *parallel sum* A:B as what corresponds to the impedance matrix of the network obtained by connecting in parallel one network with impedance A and another with B (see Figure (I)). When both A, B are invertible, A:B is nothing but $(A^{-1}+B^{-1})^{-1}$. Remark that the ordinary sum A+B represents the impedance matrix of the network obtained by series connection (see Figure (II)).

Anderson and Trapp [3] gave a variational description for parallel sum:

(1) $$\langle x|(A:B)x\rangle = \inf\{\langle u|Au\rangle + \langle v|Bv\rangle : x = u + v\}$$

or equivalently

(2) $$\langle x|(A:B)x\rangle = \inf_y\{\langle x-y|A(x-y)\rangle + \langle y|By\rangle\}.$$

Formula (1) is used to define parallel sum for non-invertible A, B. According to the Kirchhoff law, in parallel connection, current x flowing into the network is divided as x = u + v with u into one branch network and v into another. Formula (1) gives a mathematical interpretation to the Maxwell law that branch currents are so determined as to make minimum the energy of the total network.

Since the operation of parallel addition is seen associative, we can consider $A_1:\cdots:A_n$ for an n-tuple of positive semi-definite matrices, $\prod_{j=1}^{n}:A_j$ in short. Incidentally notice the obvious relations:

(3) $$A/k = \overbrace{A:\cdots:A}^{k} \quad \text{and} \quad kA = \overbrace{A+\cdots+A}^{k} \quad \text{for } k = 1,2,\cdots.$$

For an n-tuple of positive numbers $\alpha = (\alpha_1,\cdots,\alpha_n)$, Marcus and Lopes [6] defined *symmetric function means* (or Marcus-Lopes means) $E_{k,n}(\alpha)$ by

(4) $$E_{k,n}(\alpha) := e_{k,n}(\alpha)/e_{k-1,n}(\alpha) \qquad \text{for } 1 \le k \le n,$$

where $e_{k,n}(\alpha)$ is the normalized k-th elementary symmetric function of $\alpha = (\alpha_1,\cdots,\alpha_n)$, that is, $e_{o,n}(\alpha) \equiv 1$ and

$$e_{k,n}(\alpha) := \{\sum_{1\le i_1<\cdots<i_k\le n} \prod_{j=1}^{k} \alpha_{i_j}\}/\binom{n}{k} \quad \text{for} \quad 1 \le k \le n.$$

Using an equivalent version of definition (4), Anderson, Morely and and Trapp [2] introduced two kinds of *symmetric function means for an n-tuple* $A = (A_1,\cdots,A_n)$ of positive semi-definite matrices:

$$\mathfrak{S}_{1,n}(A) := \{\sum_{j=1}^{n} A_j\}/n \qquad \text{(arithmetic mean)}$$

$$s_{n,n}(A) := n\{\prod_{j=1}^{n}:A_j\} \qquad \text{(harmonic mean)}$$

and recurrently

(5) $\mathfrak{S}_{k,n}(A) :=$

$$:= \sum_{j=1}^{n} \{(A_j/n-k+1):(\mathfrak{S}_{k-1,n-1}(A_{(j)})/k-1)\} \quad \text{for } 2 \le k \le n$$

and

(6) $$s_{k,n}(A) := \prod_{j=1}^{n}:\{kA_j + (n-k)s_{k,n-1}(A_{(j)})\} \quad \text{for } 1 \le k \le n-1,$$

where $A_{(j)}$ denotes the $(n-1)$-tuple $(A_1,\cdot\cdot,A_{j-1},A_{j+1},\cdot\cdot,A_n)$.

Starting with series connection for $n\mathfrak{S}_{1,n}(A)$ and parallel connection for $s_{n,n}(A)/n$, in view of (3), the recurrent definitions make it possible to give network interpretations to $\mathfrak{S}_{k,n}(A)$ and $s_{k,n}(A)$. Thus the networks with impedance matrix $\mathfrak{S}_{k,n}(A)$ or $s_{k,n}(A)$ can be constructed from those with $A_1,\cdots,A_n$ by using series and parallel connections only.

By definition both $\mathfrak{S}_{k,n}(A)$ and $s_{k,n}(A)$ are invariant under permutations of indices. The following relations hold for an n-tuple $A = (A_1,\cdots,A_n)$ of invertible matrices

(7) $$\mathfrak{S}_{k,n}(A^{-1})^{-1} = s_{n-k+1,n}(A) \quad \text{for} \quad 1 \le k \le n,$$

where $A^{-1} = (A_1^{-1},\cdots,A_n^{-1})$, and

(8) $$s_{1,n}(A) = \mathfrak{S}_{1,n}(A) \quad \text{and} \quad \mathfrak{S}_{n,n}(A) = s_{n,n}(A).$$

In the present paper we are concerned with order relations among those two kinds of means. Here for two positive semi-definite matrices A, B order relation $A \geq B$ means that $A-B$ is positive semi-definite, or equivalently

(9) $$\langle x|Ax\rangle \geq \langle x|Bx\rangle \quad \text{for all } x.$$

Besides the easily proved inequalities

$$\mathfrak{S}_{1,n}(A) \geq \mathfrak{S}_{k,n}(A) \geq \mathfrak{S}_{n,n}(A),$$

$$s_{1,n}(A) \geq s_{k,n}(A) \geq s_{n,n}(A) \quad \text{for } 2 \leq k \leq n-1,$$

not much is known about order relations among $\mathfrak{S}_{j,n}(A)$ and $s_{k,n}(A)$ $(j,k = 2,\cdots,n-1)$. If all A_j are scalars, that is, $A = \alpha$, then both $\mathfrak{S}_{k,n}(\alpha)$ and $s_{k,n}(\alpha)$ coincide with the Marcus-Lopes mean $E_{k,n}(\alpha)$ (see [2]). Therefore it follows via spectral theory that if A is a commuting n-tuple then

$$\mathfrak{S}_{k,n}(A) = s_{k,n}(A)$$

$$\geq s_{k+1,n}(A) = \mathfrak{S}_{k+1,n}(A) \quad \text{for } 2 \leq k \leq n-2.$$

The equality $\mathfrak{S}_{k,n}(A) = s_{k,n}(A)$ is not valid in general for $2 \leq k \leq n-1$ (see [2]).

Anderson, Morley and Trapp [2] raised the following two challenging conjectures:

$(*)_{k,n}$ $$\mathfrak{S}_{k,n}(A) \geq s_{k,n}(A) \quad \text{for } 2 \leq k \leq n-1,$$

and

$(\#)_{k,n}$ $$\mathfrak{S}_{k,n}(A) \geq \mathfrak{S}_{k+1,n}(A) \quad \text{for } 2 \leq k \leq n-2,$$

(or by (7) equivalently

$$s_{k,n}(A) \geq s_{k+1,n}(A) \quad \text{for } 2 \leq k \leq n-2).$$

Remark that since in view of formula (1) the map $(A,B) \mapsto A:B$ is jointly continuous from above, that is, $A_1 \geq A_2 \geq \cdots \to A$ and $B_1 \geq B_2 \geq \cdots \to B$ implies $A_1:B_1 \geq A_2:B_2 \geq \cdots \to A:B$, we may confine our attention only to the case of an n-tuple of invertible matrices.

Mathematically, inequality $(*)_{k,n}$ is rather mysterious, because for any commuting n-tuple the inequality must reduce to equality. Among others, Anderson, Morley and Trapp [2] settled $(*)_{2,3}$ positively. Independently Ando [4] proved it by a completely different method.

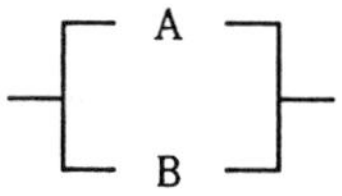

Fig. (I)

Fig. (II)

Fig. (III)

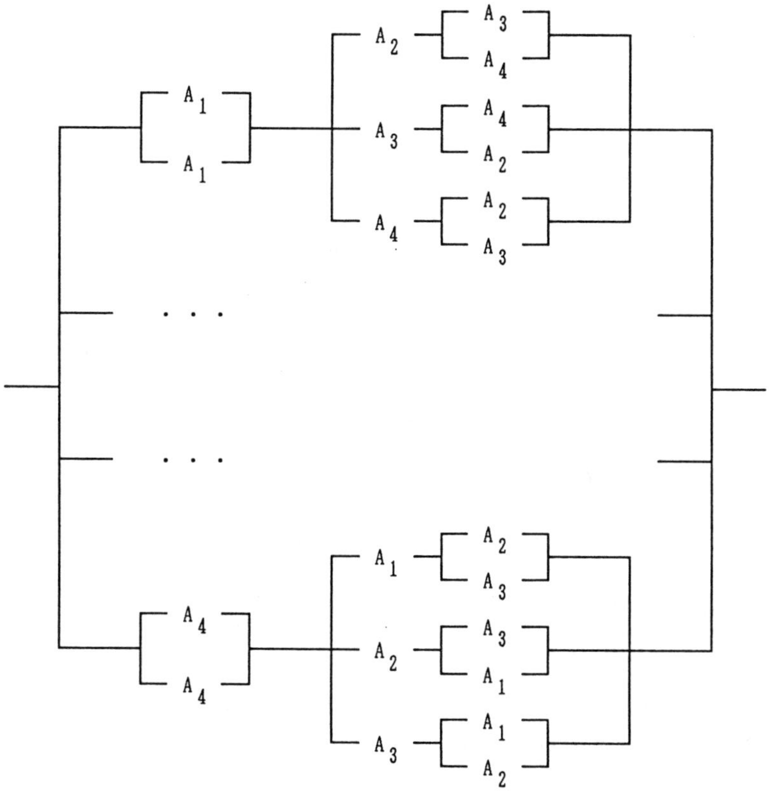

Fig. (IV)

In the present paper, developing the method used in [4] we shall settle conjecture $(*)_{2,n}$ affirmatively for all $n \geq 3$. However this, at the same time, settles $(*)_{n-1,n}$ for all $n \geq 3$ In fact, applying $(*)_{2,n}$ to A^{-1} we obtain

$$\mathfrak{S}_{2,n}(A^{-1}) \geq s_{2,n}(A^{-1}),$$

and hence

$$\mathfrak{S}_{2,n}(A^{-1})^{-1} \leq s_{2,n}(A^{-1})^{-1}$$

by the order inverting property of the map $X \longmapsto X^{-1}$ on the set of positive definite matrices. Now $(*)_{n-1,n}$ follows by (7).

To help visual understanding, let us mention that $\mathfrak{S}_{2,4}(A)$ represents the impedance matrix of 3 parallel copies of the network in Figure (III) while $s_{2,4}(A)$ does that of 4 series copies of the network in Figure (IV).

2. REDUCTION

Let us state the result once again.

Theorem. *For any n-tuple* $A = (A_1, \cdots, A_n)$ *of positive definite matrices*

$(*)_{2,n}$ $$\mathfrak{S}_{2,n}(A) \geq s_{2,n}(A).$$

Proof. By definition of order (9) we have to show that

(10) $$\langle y|\mathfrak{S}_{2,n}(A)y\rangle \geq \langle y|s_{2,n}(A)y\rangle \quad \text{for all } y.$$

Since by (7) $s_{2,n}(A) = \mathfrak{S}_{n-1,n}(A^{-1})^{-1}$ and

$$\langle y|\mathfrak{S}_{n-1,n}(A^{-1})^{-1}y\rangle = \sup_x \{|\langle x|y\rangle|^2/\langle x|\mathfrak{S}_{n-1,n}(A^{-1})x\rangle\},$$

matrix inequality $(*)_{2,n}$ is equivalent to the following:

$$\langle x|\mathfrak{S}_{n-1,n}(A^{-1})x\rangle^{1/2} \cdot \langle y|\mathfrak{S}_{2,n}(A)y\rangle^{1/2} \geq |\langle x|y\rangle| \quad \text{for all } x,y.$$

Further in view of the arithemtic-geometric means inequality this is reduced to the following:

(11) $$\langle x|\mathfrak{S}_{n-1,n}(A^{-1})x\rangle + \langle y|\mathfrak{S}_{2,n}(A)y\rangle \geq 2|\langle x|y\rangle| \quad \text{for all } x,y.$$

For computational convenience, replace x and y in (11) by $\sqrt{2\cdot(n-2)!}\,x$ and $\sqrt{n-1}\,y$, respectively. Then it is to prove the inequality

$$(12)\qquad 2\cdot(n-2)!\langle x|\mathfrak{S}_{n-1,n}(A^{-1})x\rangle + (n-1)\langle y|\mathfrak{S}_{2,n}(A)y\rangle \geq 2\sqrt{2(n-1)!}\,|\langle x|y\rangle|.$$

Our first task is to find variational expressions for $\langle x|\mathfrak{S}_{n-1,n}(A^{-1})x\rangle$ and $\langle y|\mathfrak{S}_{2,n}(A)y\rangle$. Let us begin with easier one $\langle y|\mathfrak{S}_{2,n}(A)y\rangle$. Since by (5)

$$(n-1)\mathfrak{S}_{2,n}(A) = \sum_{j=1}^{n}\{A_j:(\sum_{k=1}^{n-1}A_{j+k})\},$$

where indices are understood mod n, it follows from the variational formula (2) that

$$(n-1)\langle y|\mathfrak{S}_{2,n}(A)y\rangle = \inf_{y_1,\cdots,y_n}\sum_{j=1}^{n}\Big\{A_j[y-y_j] + \sum_{k=1}^{n-1}A_{j+k}[y_j]\Big\}.$$

Here we use, for notational simplicity, $A[z]$ instead of $\langle z|Az\rangle$. Grouping together the terms $A_j[\cdot]$ for each j we obtain

$$(13)\qquad (n-1)\langle y|\mathfrak{S}_{2,n}(A)y\rangle = \inf_{y_1,\cdots,y_n}\sum_{j=1}^{n}\Big\{A_j[y-y_j] + \sum_{k=1}^{n-1}A_j[y_{j+k}]\Big\}.$$

For later use, let us introduce some notations. Given a vector y and n vectors $y_1,\cdots,y_n$, define an n-block vector by

$$\overleftarrow{y}(n;j) := \begin{bmatrix} y-y_j \\ y_{j+1} \\ \vdots \\ y_{j+n-1}\end{bmatrix} \qquad \text{for } 1 \leq j \leq n,$$

where indices are understood mod n. For $\ell \neq j$, let us use also the notation

$$\underleftarrow{y}(n-1;j|\ell) := \begin{bmatrix} y-y_j \\ y_{j+1} \\ \vdots \\ y_{j+k-1} \\ y_{j+k+1} \\ \vdots \\ y_{j+n-1}\end{bmatrix} \qquad \text{with } k = \ell-j \mod n.$$

Now let us turn to a variational expression for

$$2(n-2)!\mathfrak{S}_{n-1,n}(A^{-1})$$
$$= \sum_{j=1}^{n} \{(n-2)!A_j^{-1}\}:\{2(n-3)!\mathfrak{S}_{n-2,n-1}(A_{(j)}^{-1})\},$$

it follows from (2) by induction on n that

(14) $$2(n-2)!\langle x|\mathfrak{S}_{n-1,n}(A^{-1})x\rangle$$
$$= \inf\Big\{ \sum_{j_1=1}^{n} (n-2)!A_{j_1}^{-1}[x-x_{j_1}]$$
$$+ \sum_{k=2}^{n-2} \sum_{\substack{j_k=1 \\ j_k\notin\{j_1,\cdots,j_{k-1}\}}}^{n} (n-k-1)!A_{j_k}^{-1}[x_{j_1,\cdots,j_{k-1}} - x_{j_1,\cdots,j_k}]$$
$$+ \sum_{\substack{j_{n-1}=1 \\ j_{n-1}\notin\{j_1,\cdots,j_{n-2}\}}}^{n} A_{j_{n-1}}^{-1}[x_{j_1,\cdots,j_{n-1}}]\Big\},$$

where $A^{-1}[z]$ stands for $\langle z|A^{-1}z\rangle$ as before. Here infimum is taken over all possible $x_{j_1,\cdots,j_k}$ where $1 \le k \le n-1$, $1 \le j_k \le n$ and $j_p \ne j_q$ for $p \ne q$.

To rewrite the expression in $\{\cdots\}$ on the right hand side of (14), starting with $N_3 = 3$ and $\vec{\delta}^{(3)} = \begin{bmatrix} 1 \\ 1 \\ 1 \end{bmatrix}$, define N_n and $\vec{\delta}^{(n)}$ inductively by

$$N_n = 1+(n-1)N_{n-1} \quad \text{and} \quad \vec{\delta}^{(n)} = \begin{bmatrix} \sqrt{(n-2)!} \\ \vec{\delta}^{(n-1)} \\ \vdots \\ \vec{\delta}^{(n-1)} \end{bmatrix} \Big\} n-1.$$

Then $\vec{\delta}^{(n)}$ is an N_n-numerical vector, and

$$N_n = (n-1)!\sum_{k=1}^{n-1}\frac{1}{(n-k)!} .$$

Given a vector x and $N_{n+1}-1$ number of vectors $x_{j_1,\cdots,j_k}$ where $1 \le k \le n-1$, $1 \le j_p \le n$ and $j_p \ne j_q$ for $p \ne q$, we are going to define N_n-block vectors $\vec{x}(n;j)$ for

$1 \leq j \leq n$. For $n = 3$, let

$$\vec{x}(3;j) = \begin{bmatrix} x-x_j \\ x_{j+1} \\ x_{j+2} \end{bmatrix} \quad \text{for} \quad 1 \leq j \leq 3,$$

where indices are understood mod 3. Assuming that the definition for the case $n-1$ has been settled, let

$$\vec{x}(n;j) = \begin{bmatrix} x-x_j \\ \underset{\to}{x}(n-1;j|j+1) \\ \underset{\to}{x}(n-1;j|j+2) \\ \vdots \\ \underset{\to}{x}(n-1;j|j+n-1) \end{bmatrix} \quad \text{for} \quad 1 \leq j \leq n,$$

where for $1 \leq \ell \leq n$ with $\ell \neq j$ $\underset{\to}{x}(n-1;j|\ell)$ is defined as $\vec{x}(n-1;1)$ with $x = x_\ell$ and $x_{i_1,\cdots,i_p} = x_{\ell,i'_1,\cdots,i'_p}$ and

$$i' = \begin{cases} j+i-1 & \text{for} \quad 1 \leq i \leq \ell-j, \\ j+i & \text{for} \quad \ell-j+1 \leq i \leq n-1 \end{cases} \qquad \text{mod } n.$$

Starting with the entrywise product $\vec{\delta}^{(3)} \circ \vec{x}(3;j)$, define $\vec{\delta}^{(n)} \circ \vec{x}(n;j)$ as the entrywise product of the N_n-numerical vector $\vec{\delta}^{(n)}$ and the N_n-block vector $\vec{x}(n;j)$; more precisely $\vec{\delta}^{(n)} \circ \vec{x}(n;j)$ is defined inductively by

$$\vec{\delta}^{(n)} \circ \vec{x}(n;j) = \begin{bmatrix} \sqrt{(n-2)!}(x-x_j) \\ \vec{\delta}^{(n-1)} \circ \underset{\to}{x}(n-1;j|j+1) \\ \vdots \\ \vec{\delta}^{(n-1)} \circ \underset{\to}{x}(n-1;j|j+n-1) \end{bmatrix}.$$

Represent $\vec{\delta}^{(n)} \circ \vec{x}(n;j)$'s as N_n-block vectors;

$$\vec{\delta}^{(n)} \circ \vec{x}(n;j) = \begin{bmatrix} z_{1j} \\ z_{2j} \\ \vdots \\ z_{N_n,j} \end{bmatrix} \quad \text{for} \quad 1 \leq j \leq n. \tag{15}$$

Then it is seen via inductive consideration that $\{\cdots\}$ on the right hand side of (14) is equal to $\sum_{j=1}^{n} \sum_{i=1}^{N_n} A_j^{-1}[z_{ij}]$. Therefore we have shown

$$(16) \qquad 2(n-2)!\langle x|\mathfrak{G}_{n-1,n}(A^{-1})x\rangle = \inf\{\sum_{j=1}^{n} \sum_{i=1}^{N_n} A_j^{-1}[z_{ij}]\}.$$

Here infimum is taken over all $\{z_{ij}\}$, obtained from all possible $x_{j_1,\cdot\cdot,j_k}$, where $1 \le k \le n-1$, $1 \le j_k \le n$ and $j_p \ne j_q$ for $p \ne q$.

From (13) and (16) we can see that inequality (12) with x,y is reduced to the following; for any choice of $x_{j_1,\cdots,j_k}$, where $1 \le k \le n-1$, $1 \le j_k \le n$ and $j_p \ne j_q$ for $p \ne q$, and any choice of $y_1,\cdot\cdot,y_n$

$$(17) \qquad \sum_{j=1}^{n} \{ \sum_{i=1}^{N_n} A_j^{-1}[z_{ij}] + A_j[y-y_j] + \sum_{k=1}^{n-1} A_j[y_{j+k}]\} \ge 2\sqrt{2(n-1)!}\,|\langle x|y\rangle|,$$

where z_{ij} are determined by (15).

A key tool for the proof of (17) is provided with the following formula due to Flanders [5].

Lemma. *For any pair of block vectors (of possibly different length),* $\vec{x} = \begin{bmatrix} x_1 \\ \vdots \\ x_\ell \end{bmatrix}$ *and* $\overleftarrow{y} = \begin{bmatrix} y_1 \\ \vdots \\ y_m \end{bmatrix}$ *the following identity holds:*

$$\inf\{ \sum_{i=1}^{\ell} \langle x_i|A^{-1}x_i\rangle + \sum_{j=1}^{m} \langle y_j|Ay_j\rangle \ : \ A \textit{ is positive definite}\} = 2\|G[\vec{x}|\overleftarrow{y}]\|_1,$$

where $G[\vec{x}|\overleftarrow{y}]$ *is the correlation matrix of* $\vec{x}$ *and* $\overleftarrow{y}$, i.e.

$$G[x|y] = [\langle x_i|y_j\rangle]_{\substack{i=1,\cdots,\ell \\ j=1,\cdots,m}}$$

and $\|G\|_1$ *denotes the trace norm,* i.e. $\|G\|_1 = \mathrm{tr}((G^*\cdot G)^{1/2})$.

According to this lemma, (13) and (15), inequality (17) will follow if the following is proved:

$$(18)\qquad \sum_{j=1}^{n} \| G[\vec{\delta}^{(n)} \circ \vec{x}(n;j) | \overleftarrow{y}(n;j)] \|_1 \geq \sqrt{2(n-1)!}\, |\langle x|y\rangle|.$$

Let us reduce (18) further to a more manageable form, by using a duality between trace norm $\|\cdot\|_1$ and *spectral norm* $\|\cdot\|_\infty$; for any pair of rectangular matrices $T = [t_{ij}]$, $V = [v_{ij}]$ of same size

$$\|T\|_1 \geq |tr(T\cdot V^*)|/\|V\|_\infty.$$

Incidentally remark that

$$(19)\qquad tr(T\cdot V^*) = \sum_{i,j} t_{ij}\overline{v}_{ij}.$$

Now inequality (18) will follow if there exists a non-zero $N_n \times n$ matrix V_n such that

$$(20)\qquad \sum_{j=1}^{n} tr(G[\vec{\delta}^{(n)} \circ \vec{x}(n;j) | \overleftarrow{y}(n;j)] \cdot V_n^*)$$
$$= \sqrt{2(n-1)!}\, \|V_n\|_\infty \langle x|y\rangle.$$

3. CONSTRUCTION OF V_n

We are going to construct by induction an $N_n \times n$ matrix V_n with the help of an auxiliary matrix U_n. For $n = 3$ let

$$U_3 = \begin{bmatrix} 0 & 1 & 1 \\ 0 & 0 & 1 \\ 0 & 1 & 0 \end{bmatrix} \quad \text{and} \quad V_3 = \begin{bmatrix} 2 & 1 & 1 \\ 1 & -1 & 2 \\ 1 & 2 & -1 \end{bmatrix}.$$

Assuming that

$$U_{n-1} = [\, \vec{u}_1^{(n-1)}, \ldots, \vec{u}_{n-1}^{(n-1)} \,] \qquad \text{and}$$
$$V_{n-1} = [\, \vec{v}_1^{(n-1)}, \ldots, \vec{v}_{n-1}^{(n-1)} \,]$$

have been defined, where $\vec{u}_j^{(n-1)}$ and $\vec{v}_j^{(n-1)}$ are N_{n-1}-numerical vectors for $1 \leq j \leq n-1$, define

$$U_n = [\, \vec{u}_1^{(n)}, \ldots, \vec{u}_n^{(n)} \,] \qquad \text{and}$$
$$V_n = [\, \vec{v}_1^{(n)}, \ldots, \vec{v}_n^{(n)} \,]$$

by

$$\vec{u}_1^{(n)} = 0, \quad \vec{u}_k^{(n)} = \begin{bmatrix} \sqrt{(n-2)!} \\ \left.\begin{matrix} \vec{u}_{k-1}^{(n-1)} \\ \vdots \\ \vec{u}_{k-1}^{(n-1)} \end{matrix}\right\} k-2 \\ \vec{0}^{(n-1)} \\ \left.\begin{matrix} \vec{u}_{k}^{(n-1)} \\ \vdots \\ \vec{u}_{k}^{(n-1)} \end{matrix}\right\} n-k \end{bmatrix} \quad \text{for} \quad 2 \leq k \leq n,$$

where $\vec{0}^{(n-1)}$ is the N_{n-1}-numerical zero vector, and

$$\vec{v}_1^{(n)} = \begin{bmatrix} (n-1)\sqrt{(n-2)!} \\ \left.\begin{matrix} \vec{v}_{1}^{(n-1)} \\ \vdots \\ \vec{v}_{1}^{(n-1)} \end{matrix}\right\} n-1 \end{bmatrix}$$

$$\vec{v}_k^{(n)} = \vec{u}_k^{(n)} + \begin{bmatrix} 0 \\ \left.\begin{matrix} \vec{v}_{k-1}^{(n-1)} \\ \vdots \\ \vec{v}_{k-1}^{(n-1)} \end{matrix}\right\} k-2 \\ -\vec{v}_1^{(n-1)} \\ \left.\begin{matrix} \vec{v}_{k}^{(n-1)} \\ \vdots \\ \vec{v}_{k}^{(n-1)} \end{matrix}\right\} n-k \end{bmatrix} \quad \text{for} \quad 2 \leq k \leq n.$$

We have already used the notation $\vec{\delta}^{(n)} \circ \vec{x}(n;j)$. Starting with the entrywise product $\vec{u}_k^{(3)} \circ \vec{\delta}^{(3)} \circ \vec{x}(3;j)$, define $\vec{u}_k^{(n)} \circ \vec{\delta}^{(n)} \circ \vec{x}(n;j)$ inductively by

$\vec{u}_1^{(n)} \circ \vec{\delta}^{(n)} \circ \vec{x}(n;j) = 0$ and for $2 \leq k \leq n$

$$\vec{u}_k^{(n)} \circ \vec{\delta}^{(n)} \circ \vec{x}(n;j) = \begin{bmatrix} \sqrt{(n-2)!}\sqrt{(n-2)!}(x-x_j) \\ \vec{u}_{k-1}^{(n-1)} \circ \vec{\delta}^{(n-1)} \circ \underset{\rightarrow}{x}(n-1;j|j+1) \\ \vdots \\ \vec{u}_{k-1}^{(n-1)} \circ \vec{\delta}^{(n-1)} \circ \underset{\rightarrow}{x}(n-1;j|j+k-2) \\ \vec{0}^{(n-1)} \\ \vec{u}_{k}^{(n-1)} \circ \vec{\delta}^{(n-1)} \circ \underset{\rightarrow}{x}(n-1;j|j+k) \\ \vdots \\ \vec{u}_{k}^{(n-1)} \circ \vec{\delta}^{(n-1)} \circ \underset{\rightarrow}{x}(n-1;j|j+n-1) \end{bmatrix}.$$

And $\vec{v}_k^{(n)} \circ \vec{\delta}^{(n)} \circ \vec{x}(n;j)$ $(k = 1,\cdot\cdot,n)$ are defined correspondingly.

In the sequel, for an M-block vector $\vec{w} = \begin{bmatrix} w_1 \\ \vdots \\ w_M \end{bmatrix}$, we shall use $\mathbf{Tr}_M(\vec{w})$ to denote the sum of all component vectors of $\vec{w}$, that is,

$$\mathbf{Tr}_M(\vec{w}) = \sum_{i=1}^{M} w_i .$$

Proposition 1. *Fix* x *and* y. *Then for any choice of* $x_{j_1},\dots,j_k$ $(1 \le k \le n-1,\ 1 \le j_p \le n,$ *and* $j_p \ne j_q$ *for* $p \ne q)$ *and* y_j $(1 \le j \le n)$ *the following identity holds for the traces of correlation matrices:*

$$(21)_n \qquad \sum_{j=1}^{n} \mathrm{tr}\left(\mathbf{G}\left[\vec{\delta}^{(n)} \circ \vec{x}(n;j) | \overleftarrow{y}(n;j)\right] \cdot \mathbf{V}_n^*\right) = n!\langle x|y\rangle .$$

Proof. In place of $(21)_n$ we shall prove, by induction, the following two relations:

$$(22)_n \qquad \sum_{j=1}^{n} \mathrm{tr}\left(\mathbf{G}\left[\vec{\delta}^{(n)} \circ \vec{x}(n;j) | \overleftarrow{y}(n;j)\right] \cdot \mathbf{U}_n^*\right) = (n-1)! \sum_{j=1}^{n} \langle x|y_j\rangle$$

and

$$(23)_n \qquad \sum_{j=1}^{n} \mathrm{tr}\left(\mathbf{G}\left[\vec{\delta}^{(n)} \circ \vec{x}(n;j) | \overleftarrow{y}(n;j)\right] \cdot (\mathbf{V}_n^* - \mathbf{U}_n^*)\right)$$
$$= n!\langle x|y\rangle - (n-1)! \sum_{j=1}^{n} \langle x|y_j\rangle .$$

Since by the definitions of $\vec{x}(3;j)$ and $\overleftarrow{y}(3;j)$

$$\sum_{j=1}^{3} \mathbf{G}\left[\vec{\delta}^{(3)} \circ \vec{x}(3;j) | \overleftarrow{y}(3;j)\right]$$

$$= \begin{bmatrix} \sum_{j=1}^{3} \langle x-x_j | y-y_j \rangle & \sum_{j=1}^{3} \langle x-x_j | y_{j+1} \rangle & \sum_{j=1}^{3} \langle x-x_j | y_{j+2} \rangle \\ \sum_{j=1}^{3} \langle x_{j+1} | y-y_j \rangle & \sum_{j=1}^{3} \langle x_{j+1} | y_{j+1} \rangle & \sum_{j=1}^{3} \langle x_{j+1} | y_{j+2} \rangle \\ \sum_{j=1}^{3} \langle x_{j+2} | y-y_j \rangle & \sum_{j=1}^{3} \langle x_{j+2} | y_{j+1} \rangle & \sum_{j=1}^{3} \langle x_{j+2} | y_{j+2} \rangle \end{bmatrix}$$

and since

$$U_3 = \begin{bmatrix} 0 & 1 & 1 \\ 0 & 0 & 1 \\ 0 & 1 & 0 \end{bmatrix} \quad \text{and} \quad V_3 - U_3 = \begin{bmatrix} 2 & 0 & 0 \\ 1 & -1 & 1 \\ 1 & 1 & -1 \end{bmatrix},$$

we can easily check the validity of $(22)_3$ and $(23)_3$, and hence of $(21)_3$. Assume that $(22)_{n-1}$ and $(23)_{n-1}$, and hence $(21)_{n-1}$, are true. By (19) it follows from the definitions of $\vec{\delta}^{(n)}$, $\vec{x}(n;j)$, $\overleftarrow{y}(n;j)$, U_n and V_n that

$$\sum_{j=1}^{n} \mathrm{tr}\left(G\left[\vec{\delta}^{(n)} \circ \vec{x}(n;j) | \overleftarrow{y}(n;j)\right] \cdot U_n^*\right)$$

$$= \sum_{j=1}^{n} \sum_{k=1}^{n-1} \Big\{ (n-2)! \langle x-x_j | y_{j+k} \rangle$$

$$+ \sum_{p=1}^{k-1} \langle \mathrm{Tr}_{N_{n-1}} (\vec{u}_k^{(n-1)} \circ \vec{\delta}^{(n-1)} \circ \underset{\rightarrow}{x}(n-1; j | j+p)) | y_{j+k} \rangle$$

$$+ \sum_{p=k+1}^{n-1} \langle \mathrm{Tr}_{N_{n-1}} (\vec{u}_{k+1}^{(n-1)} \circ \underset{\rightarrow}{x}(n-1; j | j+p)) | y_{j+k} \rangle \Big\}$$

$$= (n-1)! \sum_{j=1}^{n} \langle x | y_j \rangle - (n-2)! \sum_{j=1}^{n} \sum_{\substack{\ell=1 \\ \ell \neq j}}^{n} \langle x_j | y_\ell \rangle$$

$$+ \sum_{j=1}^{n} \sum_{\substack{\ell=1 \\ \ell \neq j}}^{n} \Big\{ \sum_{k=\tilde{\ell}_j - j+1}^{n-1} \langle \mathrm{Tr}_{N_{n-1}} (\vec{u}_k^{(n-1)} \circ \vec{\delta}^{(n-1)} \circ \underset{\rightarrow}{x}(n-1; j | \ell)) | y_{j+k} \rangle$$

$$+ \sum_{k=1}^{\tilde{\ell}_j - j-1} \langle \mathrm{Tr}_{N_{n-1}} (\vec{u}_{k+1}^{(n-1)} \circ \vec{\delta}^{(n-1)} \circ \underset{\rightarrow}{x}(n-1; j | \ell)) | y_{j+k} \rangle \Big\}$$

$$= (n-1)! \sum_{j=1}^{n} \langle x | y_j \rangle - (n-2)! \sum_{\ell=1}^{n} \sum_{\substack{j=1 \\ j \neq \ell}}^{n} \langle x_\ell | y_j \rangle$$

$$+ \sum_{\ell=1}^{n} \sum_{\substack{j=1 \\ j\neq\ell}}^{n} \{ \sum_{k=2}^{\tilde{\ell}_j - j} \langle \mathrm{Tr}_{N_{n-1}} (\vec{u}_k^{(n-1)} \circ \vec{\delta}^{(n-1)} \circ \underset{\rightarrow}{x}(n-1;j|\ell)) | y_{j+k-1} \rangle$$

$$+ \sum_{k=\tilde{\ell}-j+1}^{n-1} \langle \mathrm{Tr}_{N_{n-1}} (\vec{u}^{(n-1)} \circ \vec{\delta}^{(n-1)} \circ \underset{\rightarrow}{x}(n-1;j|\ell)) | y_{j+k-1} \rangle \},$$

where $\tilde{\ell}_j = \ell$ or $\ell+n$ according as $\ell > j$ or $\leq j$. Here we see from the definition of $\underset{\rightarrow}{x}(n-1;j|\ell)$ and $\underset{\leftarrow}{y}(n-1;j|\ell)$ that the expression $\sum_{\substack{j=1 \\ j\neq\ell}}^{n} \{\cdots\}$ in the last summand coincides with

$$\sum_{\substack{j=1 \\ j\neq\ell}}^{n} \mathrm{tr} \left(G\left[\vec{\delta}^{(n-1)} \circ \underset{\rightarrow}{x}(n-1;j|\ell) | \underset{\leftarrow}{y}(n-1;j|\ell) \right] \cdot U_{n-1}^{*} \right),$$

which is equal to $(n-2)! \sum_{\substack{j=1 \\ j\neq\ell}}^{n} \langle x_\ell | y_j \rangle$ by assumption $(22)_{n-1}$. This proves $(22)_n$.

Before entering the proof of $(23)_n$, let us prove the following identity:

$$(24)_n \qquad \sum_{j=1}^{n} \mathrm{Tr}_{N_n} (\vec{v}_1^{(n)} \circ \vec{\delta}^{(n)} \circ \vec{x}(n;j)) = n!x.$$

Since $\vec{v}_1^{(3)} = [2,1,1]^t$, $\vec{\delta}^{(3)} = [1,1,1]^t$ and

$$\sum_{j=1}^{3} \vec{x}(3;j) = \begin{bmatrix} 3x - \sum_{j=1}^{3} x_j \\ \sum_{j=1}^{3} x_{j+1} \\ \sum_{j=1}^{3} x_{j+2} \end{bmatrix}$$

we can easily check the validity of $(24)_3$. Assume that $(24)_{n-1}$ is true. Then by the definitions of $\vec{\delta}^{(n)}$, $\vec{x}(n;j)$ and V_n

$$\sum_{j=1}^{n} \mathrm{Tr}_{N_n} (\vec{v}_1^{(n)} \circ \vec{\delta}^{(n)} \circ \vec{x}(n;j))$$

$$= (n-1)! \sum_{j=1}^{n} (x - x_j)$$

$$+ \sum_{j=1}^{n} \sum_{\substack{\ell=1 \\ \ell\neq j}}^{n} \mathrm{Tr}_{N_{n-1}} (\vec{v}_1^{(n-1)} \circ \vec{\delta}^{(n-1)} \circ \underset{\rightarrow}{x}(n-1;j|\ell))$$

$$= n!x - (n-1)! \sum_{j=1}^{n} x_j$$

$$+ \sum_{\ell=1}^{n} \sum_{\substack{j=1 \\ j\neq \ell}}^{n} \mathrm{Tr}_{N_{n-1}} (\vec{v}_1^{(n-1)} \circ \vec{\delta}^{(n-1)} \circ \underset{\rightarrow}{x}(n-1;j|\ell))$$

$$= n!x - (n-1)! \sum_{j=1}^{n} x_j + \sum_{\ell=1}^{n} (n-1)!x_\ell \qquad \text{by } (24)_{n-1}$$

$$= n!x.$$

This proves $(24)_n$.

Now returning to the proof of $(23)_n$, we see from the definitions of U_n and V_n that on the left hand side of $(23)_n$ the contribution from diagonal entries of

$$\sum_{j=1}^{n} G\left[\vec{\delta}^{(n)} \circ \vec{x}\ (n;j) | \overleftarrow{y}(n;j)\right] \cdot (V_n^* - U_n^*)$$

is

$$(n-1)! \sum_{j=1}^{n} \langle x-x_j | y-y_j \rangle$$

$$- \sum_{j=1}^{n} \sum_{\substack{\ell=1 \\ \ell\neq j}}^{n} \langle \mathrm{Tr}_{N_{n-1}} (\vec{v}_1^{(n-1)} \circ \vec{\delta}^{(n-1)} \circ \underset{\rightarrow}{x}(n-1;j|\ell) | y_\ell \rangle$$

$$= (n-1)! \sum_{j=1}^{n} \langle x-x_j | y-y_j \rangle - \sum_{\ell=1}^{n} (n-1)! \langle x_\ell | y_\ell \rangle \qquad \text{by } (24)_{n-1}$$

$$= n!\langle x|y\rangle - (n-1)! \sum_{j=1}^{n} \langle x|y_j\rangle - (n-1)! \sum_{j=1}^{n} \langle x_j|y\rangle.$$

Therefore for the proof of $(23)_n$ we have to show that the contribution from off-diagonal entries is equal to $(n-1)! \sum_{j=1}^{n} \langle x_j|y\rangle$. It follows from the definitions of $\vec{x}(n;j)$, $\overleftarrow{y}(n;j)$, U_n and V_n that the contribution from off-diagonal entries is

$$\sum_{j=1}^{n} \{ \sum_{p=1}^{n-1} \langle \mathrm{Tr}_{N_{n-1}} (\vec{v}_1^{(n-1)} \circ \vec{\delta}^{(n-1)} \circ \underset{\rightarrow}{x}(n-1;j|j+p)) | y-y_j \rangle$$

$$+ \sum_{k=1}^{n-1} \Big\{ \sum_{p=1}^{k=1} \langle \mathbf{Tr}_{N_{n-1}} (\vec{v}_k^{(n-1)} \circ \underset{\rightarrow}{x}(n-1;j|j+p)) | y_{j+k} \rangle$$

$$+ \sum_{p=k+1}^{n-1} \langle \mathbf{Tr}_{N_{n-1}} (\vec{u}_{k+1}^{(n-1)} \circ \vec{\delta}^{(n-1)} \circ \underset{\rightarrow}{x}(n-1;j|j+p)) | y_{j+k} \rangle \Big\}\Big\}$$

$$= \sum_{\ell=1}^{\infty} \sum_{\substack{j=1 \\ j\neq\ell}}^{n} \Big\{ \langle \mathbf{Tr}_{N_{n-1}} (\vec{v}_1^{(n-1)} \circ \underset{\rightarrow}{x}(n-1;j|\ell)) | y-y_j \rangle$$

$$+ \sum_{k=2}^{\tilde{\ell}_j - j} \langle \mathbf{Tr}_{N_{n-1}} (\vec{v}_k^{(n-1)} \circ \vec{\delta}^{(n-1)} \circ \underset{\rightarrow}{x}(n-1;j|\ell)) | y_{j+k-1} \rangle$$

$$+ \sum_{k=\tilde{\ell}_j - j+1}^{n-1} \langle \mathbf{Tr}_{N_{n-1}} (\vec{v}_k^{(n-1)} \circ \vec{\delta}^{(n-1)} \circ \underset{\rightarrow}{x}(n-1;j|\ell)) | y_{j+k} \rangle \Big\}$$

where $\tilde{\ell}_j = \ell$ or $\ell + n$ according as $\ell > j$ or $\leq \ell$. Since the expression $\sum_{\substack{j=1 \\ j\neq\ell}}^{n} \{\cdots\}$ is nothing but

$$\sum_{\substack{j=1 \\ j\neq\ell}}^{n} \mathbf{Tr}_{N_{n-1}} \Big(G\Big[\vec{\delta}^{(n-1)} \circ \underset{\rightarrow}{x}(n-1;j|\ell) \,|\, \underset{\leftarrow}{y}(n-1;j|\ell)\Big] \cdot V_{n-1}^{*} \Big),$$

which is equal to $(n-1)!\langle x_\ell | y \rangle$ by $(21)_{n-1}$, we arrive at $(23)_n$. This completes the proof. □

Proposition 2. $\|V_n\|_\infty = n\sqrt{(n-1)!/2}$.

Proof. First remark that $\|V_n\|_\infty^2$ coincides with the maximum eigenvalue of $V_n^* V_n$. Since the (ℓ,k)-entry of $V_n^* V_n$ is $\langle \vec{v}_k^{(n)} | \vec{v}_\ell^{(n)} \rangle$ for $k,\ell = 1,\cdots,n$, the assertion will follow if the following two relations are proved:

$$(25)_n \qquad \langle \vec{v}_1^{(n)} | \vec{v}_\ell^{(n)} \rangle = \begin{cases} n!(n-1)/2 & \text{for } \ell = 1 \\ n!/2 & \text{for } \ell \neq 1, \end{cases}$$

$$(26)_n \qquad \langle \vec{v}_k^{(n)} | \vec{v}_\ell^{(n)} \rangle = \begin{cases} n!(n-1)/2 & \text{for } \ell = k \geq 2 \\ -n!/2 & \text{for } \ell \neq k \text{ and } \ell,k \geq 2. \end{cases}$$

In fact, $(25)_n$ and $(26)_n$ imply that

$$V_n^* V_n = \{\frac{n!(n-1)}{2} + \frac{n!}{2}\}I - \frac{n!}{2}[-1,1,\cdots,1]^t\cdot[-1,1,\cdots,1]$$

$$= \frac{n^2(n-1)!}{2}\{I - \frac{1}{n}[-1,1,\cdots,1]^t\cdot[-1,1,\cdots,1]\},$$

and $\|V_n\|_\infty = n\sqrt{(n-1)!/2}$ follows from the fact that $\frac{1}{n}[-1,1,\cdots,1]^t\cdot[-1,1,\cdots,1]$ is a rank-one Hermitian projection.

For the proof of $(25)_n$ we need the following relation:

$(27)_n$ $$\sum_{k=2}^{n} \vec{v}_k^{(n)} = \sum_{k=2}^{n} \vec{u}_k^{(n)} = \vec{v}_1^{(n)}.$$

Since $(27)_3$ is obvious, assume that $(27)_{n-1}$ is true. Now it follows from the definitions of U_n and V_n that

$$\sum_{k=2}^{n} \vec{v}_k^{(n)} = \begin{bmatrix} 0 \\ -\vec{v}_1^{(n-1)} + \sum_{k=2}^{n-1} \vec{v}_k^{(n-1)} \\ \vdots \\ -\vec{v}_1^{(n-1)} + \sum_{k=2}^{n-1} \vec{v}_k^{(n-1)} \end{bmatrix} + \sum_{k=2}^{n} \vec{u}_k^{(n)} = \sum_{k=2}^{n} \vec{u}_k^{(n)}$$

$$= \begin{bmatrix} (n-1)\sqrt{(n-2)!} \\ \sum_{k=2}^{n-1} \vec{u}_k^{(n-1)} \\ \vdots \\ \sum_{k=2}^{n-1} \vec{u}_k^{(n-1)} \end{bmatrix} = \begin{bmatrix} (n-1)\sqrt{(n-2)!} \\ \vec{v}_1^{(n-1)} \\ \vdots \\ \vec{v}_1^{(n-1)} \end{bmatrix} = \vec{v}_1^{(n-1)} \quad \text{by } (27)_{n-1}$$

which proves $(27)_n$.

Now let us turn to the proof of $(25)_n$. Since $(25)_3$ is obvious, assume that $(25)_{n-1}$ is true. Then we have by the definition of V_n

$$\langle\vec{v}_1^{(n)}|\vec{v}_1^{(n)}\rangle = (n-1)^2(n-2)! + (n-1)\langle\vec{v}_1^{(n-1)}|\vec{v}_1^{(n-1)}\rangle$$

$$= (n-1)(n-1)! + (n-1)(n-1)!(n-2)/2 \quad \text{by } (25)_{n-1}$$

$$= n!(n-1)/2.$$

On the other hand, since it is readily seen by induction on n that $\langle\vec{v}_1^{(n)}|\vec{v}_k^{(n)}\rangle$ is constant for $2 \le k \le n$, we have by $(27)_n$

and the already proved part of $(25)_n$

$$\langle \vec{v}_1^{(n)} | \vec{v}_\ell^{(n)} \rangle = \frac{1}{n-1} \langle \vec{v}_1^{(n)} | \sum_{k=2}^{n} \vec{v}_k^{(n)} \rangle$$

$$= \frac{1}{n-1} \langle \vec{v}_1^{(n)} | \vec{v}_1^{(n)} \rangle = n!/2.$$

this proves $(25)_n$.

For the proof of $(26)_n$ we need the following relation:

$$(28)_n \qquad \langle \vec{v}_k^{(n)} | \vec{u}_k^{(n)} \rangle = n!/2 \quad \text{and}$$

$$\langle \vec{u}_k^{(n)} | \vec{u}_k^{(n)} \rangle = (n-1)! \qquad \text{for} \quad 2 \le k \le n.$$

Since $(28)_3$ is obvious, assume that $(28)_{n-1}$ is true. Then for $2 \le k \le n$, we have by the definitions of U_n and V_n

$$\langle \vec{v}_k^{(n)} | \vec{u}_k^{(n)} \rangle = (n-2)!$$

$$+ (k-2) \langle \vec{v}_{k-1}^{(n-1)} + \vec{u}_{k-1}^{(n)} | \vec{u}_{k-1}^{(n-1)} \rangle$$

$$+ (n-k) \langle \vec{v}_k^{(n-1)} + \vec{u}_k^{(n-1)} | \vec{u}_k^{(n-1)} \rangle$$

$$= (n-2)! + (n-2)\{(n-1)!/2 + (n-2)!\} \qquad \text{by } (28)_{n-1}$$

$$= n!/2.$$

In a similar way, for $2 \le k \le n$, we have

$$\langle \vec{u}_k^{(n)} | \vec{u}_k^{(n)} \rangle = (n-2)! + (n-2)(n-2)! = (n-1)!.$$

This proves $(28)_n$.

Now let us turn to the proof of $(26)_n$. Since $(26)_3$ is obvious, assume that $(26)_{n-1}$ is true. Then by $(28)_{n-1}$, $(26)_{n-1}$ and $(25)_{n-1}$ it follows from the definitions of U_n, V_n that

$$\langle \vec{v}_k^{(n)} | \vec{v}_k^{(n)} \rangle = (n-2)!$$

$$+ (k-2) \langle \vec{v}_{k-1}^{(n-1)} + \vec{u}_{k-1}^{(n-1)} | \vec{v}_{k-1}^{(n-1)} + \vec{u}_{k-1}^{(n-1)} \rangle$$

$$+ \langle \vec{v}_1^{(n-1)} | \vec{v}_1^{(n-1)} \rangle$$

$$+ (n-k) \langle \vec{v}_k^{(n-1)} + \vec{u}_k^{(n-1)} | \vec{v}_k^{(n-1)} + \vec{u}_k^{(n-1)} \rangle$$

$$= (n-2)! + (n-1)!(n-2)/2$$
$$+ (n-2)\{(n-1)!(n-2)/2 + 2\cdot(n-1)!/2 + (n-2)!\}$$
$$= n!(n-1)/2.$$

Finally since it is readily seen by induction that $\langle \vec{v}_k^{(n)} | \vec{v}_\ell^{(n)} \rangle$ is constant for $k \neq \ell$, $(k,\ell = 2,\cdots,n)$, we have for $k \neq \ell$

$$\langle \vec{v}_k^{(n)} | \vec{v}_\ell^{(n)} \rangle = \frac{1}{n-2} \langle \vec{v}_k^{(n)} | \sum_{\substack{p=2 \\ p\neq k}}^{n} \vec{v}_p^{(n)} \rangle$$

$$= \frac{1}{n-2} \langle \vec{v}_k^{(n)} | \vec{v}_1^{(n)} - \vec{v}_k^{(n)} \rangle \qquad \text{by } (27)_n$$

$$= \frac{1}{n-2} \{n!/2 - n!(n-1)/2\} \qquad \text{by } (25)_n$$

$$= - n!/2.$$

This proves $(26)_n$ and completes the proof of Proposition 2. □

Now the desired inequality (20) follows immediately from Propositions 1 and 2. This completes the proof of Theorem.

4. CONCLUDING REMARKS

It seems that our method could yield $(*)_{k,n}$ for all $k = 2,\cdots,n-1$. In fact, we have already checked that for $n = 5$ this is really true. For larger n, however, the construction of a matrix, corresponding to $\mathbf{V}_n$, seems quite complicated and requires much deeper combinatorial consideration. We shall report further progress in a subsequent paper.

REFERENCES

1. W. N. ANDERSON, Jr. and R. J. DUFFIN, *Series and parallel addition of matrices,* J. Math. Anal. Appl., 26 (1969), 576-594.
2. W. N. ANDERSON, Jr., T. D. MORLEY and G. E. TRAPP *Symmetric function means of positive operators*, Linear Alg. Appl., 60 (1984), 129-143.
3. W. N. ANDERSON, Jr. and G. E. TRAPP, *Shorted operators* II, SIAM J. Appl. Math., 28 (1975), 61-71.
4. T. ANDO, *An inequality between symmetric function means of positive operators*, Acta Sci. Math., 45 (1983) 19-22.

5. H. FLANDERS, *An extremal problem in the space of positive definite matrices*, Linear Multilinear Alg., 3 (1975), 33-39.

6. M. MARCUS and L. LOPES, *Inequalities for symmetric functions and Hermitian matrices*, Canad. J. Math., 9 (1957), 305-312.

Tsuyoshi Ando
Division of Applied Mathematics
Research Institute of
Applied Electricity
Hokkaido University
Sapporo 060, Japan

Fumio Kubo
Department of Mathematics
Faculty of Science
Toyama University
Toyama 930, Japan

Operator Theory:
Advances and Applications, Vol. 40

COMPLEMENTARY TRIANGULAR FORMS OF UPPER TRIANGULAR TOEPLITZ MATRICES

H. Bart and G.Ph.A. Thijsse

Dedicated to Israel Gohberg on the occasion of his sixtieth birthday, with admiration

The problem considered is the following. Given two upper triangular Toeplitz matrices A and Z, when does there exist an invertible matrix S such that $S^{-1}AS$ is upper triangular and $S^{-1}ZS$ is lower triangular ? The motivation for considering simultaneous reduction to complementary triangular forms of pairs of matrices comes from systems theory. For upper triangular Toeplitz matrices, a complete answer is given. The argument involves a detailed analysis of a certain directed graph associated with A and Z. Along the way information is obtained about the structure of the similarity S. The results actually hold for a class of matrices strictly larger than that consisting of the upper triangular Toeplitz matrices.

0. INTRODUCTION AND MAIN RESULTS

This paper deals with a particular case of the following general problem (cf. [4]): *Given two square matrices A and Z, when does there exist an invertible matrix S such that $S^{-1}AS$ is upper triangular and $S^{-1}ZS$ is lower triangular* ? In other words, when do A and Z admit *simultaneous reduction to complementary triangular forms* ?

The initial motivation for considering this problem comes from systems theory. Indeed, there is a close connection with the problem of complete factorization of a transfer function.

It is illuminating to give some details. A *complete factorization* of a rational $n \times n$ matrix function $W(\lambda)$ is a factorization of the form

$$W(\lambda) = \left(I_n + \frac{1}{\lambda - \alpha_1} R_1\right) \quad . \quad . \quad . \quad \left(I_n + \frac{1}{\lambda - \alpha_m} R_m\right),$$

where $R_1,\ldots,R_m$ are $n \times n$ matrices of rank 1 and a certain minimality condition is satisfied (no "pole-zero cancellations"). Not every rational $n \times n$ matrix function admits a complete factorization, and it is here that the connection with complementary triangularization comes in: Write $W(\lambda)$ in the form

$$(0.1) \qquad W(\lambda) = I_n + C(\lambda I_m - A)^{-1}B,$$

where A is an $m \times m$ matrix, B is an $m \times n$ matrix and C is an $n \times m$ matrix. Systems theory tells us that such a *realization* of $W(\lambda)$ exists whenever $W(\lambda)$ is analytic at ∞ and $W(\infty) = I_n$. Suppose the realization (0.1) is *minimal* (i.e., m has the smallest possible value). Then $W(\lambda)$ admits complete factorization if and only if A and $A-BC$ admit simultaneous reduction to complementary triangular forms. For details (including a brief review of the relevant background material from systems theory), see [4] and [5]; cf. also [1], [2], [3], [10], [11] and [12].

Now let us return to the problem of complementary triangularization of pairs of matrices A, Z. As far as the authors are aware, the first result concerning this issue is that A and Z do admit simultaneous reduction to complementary triangular forms whenever A or Z is diagonable. This result is implicitly contained in the proof of [3], Theorem 1.6, a fact which was noted (around 1981) by I. Gohberg. Other results on complementary triangularization may be found in [1], [4] and [5]. As a rule, these results are concerned with special classes of matrices.

Here we restrict ourselves to the case when A and Z are upper triangular Toeplitz matrices. To avoid trivialities, we assume that neither A nor Z is the zero matrix. We also assume that A and Z are both strictly upper triangular (otherwise subtract the diagonal). Thus A and Z are of the form

$$A = a_\alpha J^\alpha + \ldots + a_{m-1}J^{m-1}, \qquad Z = z_\omega J^\omega + \ldots + z_{m-1}J^{m-1},$$

where J is the upper triangular nilpotent $m \times m$ Jordan block, $1 \leq \alpha,\omega \leq m-1$ and $a_\alpha, z_\omega \neq 0$. The numbers α and ω are unique, and we shall call them the *type* of A and Z, respectively. It turns out that these types alone determine whether or not A and Z can be brought simultaneously into complementary triangular forms.

THEOREM 0.1. *Let A and Z be strictly upper triangular $m \times m$ Toeplitz matrices of type α and ω, respectively, $1 \leq \alpha,\omega \leq m-1$. Then A and Z admit simultaneous reduction to complementary triangular forms if and only if*

$\alpha + \omega > m$, *α does not divide ω and ω does not divide α.*

Presently we shall comment on the proof of Theorem 0.1, but first we want to discuss one of its consequences. The point is that (the if part of) Theorem 0.1 enables us to obtain a sufficient condition for two polynomials in a given matrix to admit simultaneous reduction to complementary triangular forms. Of course we consider nonvanishing polynomials only. It is convenient to introduce some notation.

Let μ be a complex number, and let $p(\lambda)$ be a (scalar) polynomial. The order of μ as a zero of the polynomial $p(\lambda)-p(\mu)$ will be denoted by $m_p(\mu)$. If μ is an eigenvalue of a (square) matrix H, then $m_H(\mu)$ stands for the largest partial multiplicity of μ as an eigenvalue of H. In other words, $m_H(\mu)$ is the size of the largest Jordan block corresponding to μ in the Jordan form of H.

COROLLARY 0.2. *Let H be an $m \times m$ matrix, and let $p(\lambda)$ and $q(\lambda)$ be (nonvanishing scalar) polynomials. Suppose that for each eigenvalue μ of H either the conditions*

$$(i) \quad \begin{cases} m_p(\mu) + m_q(\mu) > m_H(\mu), \\ m_p(\mu) \textit{ does not divide } m_q(\mu), \\ m_q(\mu) \textit{ does not divide } m_p(\mu), \end{cases}$$

or the condition

$$(ii) \qquad \max\{m_p(\mu),\ m_q(\mu)\} \geqq m_H(\mu)$$

is satisfied. Then $p(H)$ and $q(H)$ admit simultaneous reduction to complementary triangular forms.

This result is obtained by bringing H into (upper triangular) Jordan form and applying Theorem 0.1 to the appropiate polynomials in the Jordan blocks. Examples can be given to show that the converse of Corollary 0.2 does not hold.

Now, let us comment on the proof of Theorem 0.1. The proof of the only if part is easy. It is given in Section 1. The proof of the if part is considerably more involved and presented in Sections 2-4.

One of the main points is the detailed analysis of a certain directed graph associated with the given matrices A and Z. This analysis is carried out in Sections 2 and 3. Section 3 deals with a specialization of the problem at hand: *Let J be the upper triangular nilpotent $m \times m$ Jordan block, and let α and ω be integers, $1 \leqq a, \omega \leqq m-1$. When does there exist an $m \times m$ permutation matrix Π such that $\Pi^{-1}J^{\alpha}\Pi$ is upper triangular and $\Pi^{-1}J^{\omega}\Pi$ is lower* *triangular*? Answer: if and only if the graph associated with the matrices J^{α} and J^{ω} contains no cycles. An equivalent requirement is that

$$\alpha + \omega \geqq m + \gcd(\alpha,\omega), \tag{0.2}$$

where $\gcd(\alpha,\omega)$ is the greatest common divisor of α and ω.

Another ingredient in the proof of Theorem 0.1 is the simultaneous reduction of A and Z to "simple" forms. The class of simple matrices that we have in mind here contains the powers of the upper triangular nilpotent $m \times m$ Jordan block. For certain combinations of m, α and ω (in fact when (0.2) is satisfied), this subclass is even sufficiently large. In general, however, one has to allow for appropriate perturbations. For details, see Theorem 4.4. The proof of Theorem 4.4 is given in [7]; cf. also [6].

Theorem 0.1 is concerned with strictly upper triangular Toeplitz matrices. As a matter of fact we shall establish a slightly stronger result which applies to sharply upper triangular matrices. The concept of a sharply upper triangular matrix is introduced in Section 1. It is a straightforward generalization of the notion of an upper triangular Toeplitz matrix.

The if part of Theorem 0.1 (and of its generalization Theorem 4.1) guarantees the existence of an invertible matrix S such that $S^{-1}AS$ is upper triangular and $S^{-1}ZS$ is lower triangular. It is possible to improve the result by supplying information about additional properties of S. In Section 4 it is proved that when (0.2) is satisfied, i.e., $\alpha+\omega \geqq m+\gcd(\alpha,\omega)$, then S can be chosen in the form $S = U\Pi$, where U is an invertible upper triangular matrix and Π is a permutation matrix. In case $m < \alpha+\omega < m+\gcd(\alpha,\omega)$, the situation is more complicated. One is then forced to perturb the matrix Π (additively) by a matrix R of rank $1+\gamma$, where $\gamma = m+\gcd(\alpha,\omega)-\alpha-\omega$ is the number of cycles in the graph associated with A and Z. Note that γ, and hence rank R, is small compared to m, α and ω.

A few remarks about notation and terminology: All matrices to be considered have complex entries. The $n \times n$ identity matrix is denoted by I_n or simply I. The superscript T signals the operation of taking the transpose. Whenever this is convenient matrices are identified with (linear) operators. The image of a matrix (operator) M is denoted by Im M, its null space by Ker M. The symbol ■ stands for "end of proof", "end of remark" or "end of example".

1. PRELIMINARIES AND FIRST RESULTS

Let $A = (a_{ij})_{i,j=1}^{m}$ be an $m \times m$ matrix. We call A *sharply upper triangular* if there exists a nonnegative integer α such that

(1.1) $a_{ij} = 0, \qquad j < i+\alpha;\ i,j = 1,\ldots,m,$

(1.2) $a_{i,i+\alpha} \neq 0, \qquad i = 1,\ldots,m-\alpha.$

A few remarks are in order. Sharply upper triangular matrices are upper triangular indeed (for α is non-negative). Upper triangular Toeplitz matrices are sharply upper triangular. If A is sharply upper triangular and $A \neq 0$, then there is precisely one integer α among $0,\ldots,m-1$ such that (1.1) and (1.2) are satisfied. This integer is called the *type* of A. The $m \times m$ zero matrix is sharply upper triangular, and any of the integers m, $m+1,\ldots$ may serve as its type. Finally, the matrix A is sharply upper triangular of type 0 if and only if A is upper triangular and invertible.

Let A and Z be $m \times m$ matrices. Recall that A and Z are said to *admit simultaneous reduction to complementary triangular forms* if there exists an invertible $m \times m$ matrix S such that $S^{-1}AS$ is upper triangular and $S^{-1}ZS$ is lower triangular. In this paper we are interested in the case when A and Z are both sharply upper triangular of *positive* type. This covers the situation where A and Z are both strictly upper triangular Toeplitz matrices.

We begin with two lemmas on nilpotent matrices. Note that sharply upper triangular matrices of positive type are nilpotent.

LEMMA 1.1. *Let A and Z be nilpotent $m \times m$ matrices. Suppose Ker $Z \subset$ Im A or Ker $A \subset$ Im Z. Then A and Z do not admit simultaneous reduction to complementary triangular forms.*

PROOF. Suppose there exists an invertible $m \times m$ matrix S such that $U = S^{-1}AS$ is upper triangular and $L = S^{-1}ZS$ is lower triangular. Since A and Z are nilpotent, the diagonals of U and L consist of zero entries only. Let $e = (0\ldots0\ 1)^T$ be the m-th unit vector in $\mathbb{C}^m$. Then $ZSe = SLe = S0 = 0$, so $Se \in \mathrm{Ker}\ Z$. If Ker $Z \subset$ Im A, it follows that $e \in S^{-1}[\mathrm{Im}\ A] = \mathrm{Im}\ U$. But this is impossible, for U is strictly upper triangular. The argument for the case when Ker $A \subset$ Im Z is analogous.■

LEMMA 1.2. *Let A and Z be nilpotent $m \times m$ matrices. Suppose Im A = Im Z and Ker A = Ker Z. Then either $A = Z = 0$ or A and Z do not admit simultaneous reduction to complementary triangular forms.*

PROOF. Suppose there exists an invertible $m \times m$ matrix S such that $U = S^{-1}AS$ is upper triangular and $L = S^{-1}ZS$ is lower triangular. Since A and Z

are nilpotent, the diagonals of U and L consist of zero entries only. Clearly Im U = Im L and Ker U = Ker L. It follows that the first column, the last column, the first row and the last row of U consist of zero entries only. The same is true with U replaced by L. Now let U_1 and L_1 be the matrices that are obtained by crossing out the first and last row and the first and last column of U and L, respectively. Then Im U_1 = Im L_1 and Ker U_1 = Ker L_1, and the argument can be repeated. In a finite number of steps we get $U = L = 0$, which amounts to the same as $A = Z = 0$. ■

The next result is a modest generalization of the only if part of Theorem 0.1.

PROPOSITION 1.3. *Let A and Z be sharply upper triangular $m \times m$ matrices of type α and ω, respectively, $1 \leqq \alpha,\omega \leqq m-1$. If A and Z admit simultaneous reduction to complementary triangular forms, then $\alpha + \omega > m$, α does not divide ω and ω does not divide α.*

PROOF. First assume that $\alpha+\omega \leqq m$. It is easy to see that Ker Z is spanned by the first ω unit vectors in $\mathbb{C}^m$ and that Im A is spanned by the first $m-\alpha$ unit vectors in $\mathbb{C}^m$. Hence $\alpha+\omega \leqq m$ implies Ker $Z \subset$ Im A. Now apply Lemma 1.1.

Next, assume that $\alpha = \omega$. Then Ker A = Ker Z and Im A = Im Z. Since $\alpha = \omega \leqq m-1$, we have $A,Z \neq 0$. Now apply Lemma 1.2. Finally, observe that the case when α divides ω or ω divides α can be reduced to the situation $\alpha = \omega$ by taking an appropriate power of A or Z. ■

2. THE GRAPH ASSOCIATED WITH THE PROBLEM

Throughout this section m, α and ω will be positive integers satisfying

(2.1) $\alpha + \omega \geqq m.$

With these integers we associate a directed graph $\mathcal{D}(m;\alpha,\omega)$ as follows. The vertices of $\mathcal{D}(m;\alpha,\omega)$ are the numbers $1,\ldots,m$, and for p and q in the vertex set $\mathbb{N}_m = \{1,\ldots,m\}$ there is a (directed) arc connecting p and q if $q = p+\alpha$ or $q = p-\omega$. Thus the arcs in $\mathcal{D}(m;\alpha,\omega)$ may be identified with the ordered pairs $(1,\alpha+1)$, $(2,\alpha+2),\ldots,(m-\alpha,\alpha)$, $(\omega+1,1)$, $(\omega+2,2),\ldots,$ $(m,m-\omega)$ as far as they belong to $\mathbb{N}_m \times \mathbb{N}_m$. In other words, the adjacency matrix of $\mathcal{D}(m;\alpha,\omega)$ is $J^\alpha+(J^T)^\omega$, where J is the nilpotent upper triangular $m \times m$ Jordan block.

Let $p \in \mathbb{N}_m$. By (2.1) there is at most one $q \in \mathbb{N}_m$ such that (q,p) is an arc. Analogously, there is at most one $q \in \mathbb{N}_m$ such that (p,q) is an arc. In other words, the indegree and outdegree of p are at most one. Since α and ω are both positive, there is no arc connecting p with itself. Thus $\mathcal{D}(m;\alpha,\omega)$ contains no loops. The terminology used here is taken from [8].

Again let $p \in \mathbb{N}_m$. We call p an *initial vertex* of $\mathcal{D}(m;\alpha,\omega)$ if the indegree of p is zero. Analogously p is said to be a *terminal vertex* of $\mathcal{D}(m;\alpha,\omega)$ if the outdegree of p is zero. Put $\alpha_0 = \min\{\alpha,m\}$ and $\omega_0 = \min\{\omega,m\}$. Then p is an initial vertex if and only if $m-\omega_0+1 \leqq p \leqq \alpha_0$ and p is a terminal vertex if and only if $m-\alpha_0+1 \leqq p \leqq \omega_0$. There do exist initial (terminal) vertices if and only if $\alpha+\omega > m$, and in that case the number of initial vertices is the same as that of the terminal vertices, namely $\alpha_0+\omega_0-m$.

Let $p_1,\dots,p_k$ be vertices of $\mathcal{D}(m;\alpha,\omega)$. We write

$$p_1 \rightarrow p_2 \rightarrow \ . \ . \ . \rightarrow p_k \tag{2.2}$$

if for each $j = 1,\dots,k-1$ there is an arc connecting p_j and p_{j+1}. In that case (2.2) or, more precisely, the ordered sequence $p_1,\dots,p_k$, is called a *walk*.

A walk (2.2) is said to be a *chain* if p_1 is an initial vertex and p_k is a terminal vertex. This implies that $p_1,\dots,p_k$ are distinct. The number k is called the *length* of the chain. A chain of length 1 consists of one single element which is an initial vertex and a terminal vertex at the same time. Two chains in $\mathcal{D}(m;\alpha,\omega)$ coincide if and only if they have a common vertex.

A walk (2.2) is said to be a *cycle* if $p_1,\dots,p_k$ are distinct and $p_k \rightarrow p_1$. The number k is then called the *length* of the cycle. If (2.2) is a cycle, then so is

$$p_t \rightarrow \ . \ . \ . \rightarrow p_k \rightarrow p_1 \rightarrow \ . \ . \ . \rightarrow p_{t-1}. \tag{2.3}$$

Here $t=1,\dots,k$. It is convenient to make no distinction between the cycles appearing in (2.3). With this convention, two cycles in $\mathcal{D}(m;\alpha,\omega)$ coincide if and only if they have a common vertex. Since $\mathcal{D}(m;\alpha,\omega)$ has no loops, each cycle in $\mathcal{D}(m;\alpha,\omega)$ has length at least 2. If $\alpha \neq \omega$, then each cycle in $\mathcal{D}(m;\alpha,\omega)$ has length at least 3.

Each vertex of $\mathcal{D}(m;\alpha,\omega)$ belongs to precisely one chain or precisely one cycle. Chains and cycles are mutually disjoint. So the vertex set $\mathbb{N}_m$ is the disjoint union of the chains and cycles in $\mathcal{D}(m;\alpha,\omega)$.

We shall now enter into a more detailed analysis of $\mathcal{D}(m;\alpha,\omega)$. It is convenient to start with a lemma concerning the case $m = \alpha+\omega$. Clearly the graph $\mathcal{D}(\alpha+\omega;\alpha,\omega)$ has neither initial nor terminal vertices, and so it has only cycles and no chains.

LEMMA 2.1. *Let p and q be vertices of* $\mathcal{D}(\alpha+\omega;\alpha,\omega)$. *Then p and q belong to the same cycle in* $\mathcal{D}(\alpha+\omega;\alpha,\omega)$ *if and only if* $p - q$ *is divisible by* δ, *where* δ *is the greatest common divisor of* α *and* ω.

PROOF. Assume p and q belong to the same cycle in $\mathcal{D}(\alpha+\omega;\alpha,\omega)$. Then there exist integers h and k such that

$$p = q + h\alpha - k\omega, \tag{2.4}$$

and hence $p-q$ is divisible by δ. This proves the only if part of the lemma.

Next suppose that δ divides $p-q$. Then p can be written in the form (2.4) with h and k integers, $kh \geqq 0$. We may assume that $h,k \geqq 0$ (otherwise interchange the roles of p and q). Define

$$q_0 = q, \qquad q_{j+1} = \begin{cases} q_j+\alpha & \text{if} \quad q_j \leqq \omega, \\ q_j-\omega & \text{if} \quad q_j > \omega. \end{cases}$$

Then $q_0, q_1, \ldots$ are vertices of $\mathcal{D}(\alpha+\omega;\alpha,\omega)$. Since $q_j \to q_{j+1}$, $j=0,1,\ldots$, all vertices $q_0, q_1, \ldots$ belong to the same cycle in $\mathcal{D}(\alpha+\omega,\alpha,\omega)$. Put

$$t_0 = 0, \qquad t_{j+1} = \begin{cases} t_j + 1 & \text{if} \quad q_j \leqq \omega, \\ t_j & \text{if} \quad q_j > \omega. \end{cases}$$

Then, for $j = 0,1,\ldots$,

$$q_j = q + t_j\alpha - (j-t_j)\omega. \tag{2.5}$$

Observe that $t_j \leqq h$ and $j-t_j \leqq k$ for $j=0,\ldots,h+k$. In particular $t_{h+k} = h$. Combining this with (2.4) and (2.5), one gets $q_{h+k} = p$. But then $q = q_0$ and $p = q_{h+k}$ belong to the same cycle. ■

Next, let us return to the general case $\alpha+\omega \geqq m$.

THEOREM 2.2. *Suppose* $\alpha + \omega \geqq m$, *and put*

$$\nu = \alpha_0 + \omega_0 - m, \qquad \gamma = \max\{0, m + \delta - \alpha - \omega\}, \tag{2.6}$$

where $\alpha_0 = \min\{\alpha,m\}$, $\omega_0 = \min\{\omega,m\}$, *and* δ *is the greatest common divisor of* α *and* ω. *Then the vertex set of the graph* $\mathcal{D}(m;\alpha,\omega)$ *is the disjoint union of* ν *chains and* γ *cycles. If* $m \leqq \alpha + \omega \leqq m + \delta$, *then all chains have length* $(\alpha + \omega - \delta)\delta^{-1}$ *and all cycles have length* $(\alpha + \omega)\delta^{-1}$.

If $m = \alpha+\omega$, then, as we already observed earlier, there are only cycles; if $\alpha+\omega \geqq m+\delta$ there are only chains. In case $m < \alpha+\omega < m+\delta$, there exist both cycles and chains, and the number of cycles does not exceed δ-1.

PROOF. First, assume that $m = \alpha+\omega$. For $j = 1,\ldots,\delta$, let C_j be the cycle in $\mathcal{D}(\alpha+\omega;\alpha,\omega)$ containing the vertex j.

Let $1 \leqq p,q \leqq \delta$, and suppose $C_p \cap C_q \neq \emptyset$. Then $C_p = C_q$, and p and q belong to the same cycle in $\mathcal{D}(\alpha+\omega;\alpha,\omega)$. Hence δ divides $p-q$ by Lemma 2.1. Since $0 \leqq p-q < \delta$, it follows that $p = q$. We conclude that $C_1,\ldots,C_\delta$ are mutually disjoint.

Next, let s be any vertex in $\mathcal{D}(\alpha+\omega;\alpha,\omega)$, and let r be the remainder of $s-1$ upon division by δ. Then $1 \leqq r+1 \leqq \delta$, and $p-(r+1)$ is divisible by δ. It follows that $p \in C_{r+1}$.

We have now proved that the vertex set of $\mathcal{D}(\alpha+\omega;\alpha,\omega)$ is the disjoint union of the cycles $C_1,\ldots,C_\delta$. To see that each of these cycles has length $(\alpha+\omega)\delta^{-1}$, we show that, for $j = 1,\ldots,\delta$, the cycle C_j can be obtained from C_1 by adding j-1 to each vertex in C_1.

Let j be one of the integers $1,\ldots,\delta$. It is clear from Lemma 2.1 that $\alpha+\omega-\delta+j$ belongs to C_j. In fact $\alpha+\omega-\delta+j$ is the largest integer in C_j. Specializing to $j=1$, we see that $\alpha+\omega-\delta+1$ is the largest integer in C_1. Adding j-1 to each vertex in C_1, we obtain a cycle containing j. The desired result now follows from the fact that C_j is the unique cycle in $\mathcal{D}(\alpha+\omega;\alpha,\omega)$ containing j.

Next we study the case $m < \alpha+\omega$. In this situation the graph $\mathcal{D}(m;\alpha,\omega)$ is an induced subgraph of $\mathcal{D}(\alpha+\omega;\alpha,\omega)$. Indeed, $\mathcal{D}(m;\alpha,\omega)$ can be obtained from $\mathcal{D}(\alpha+\omega;\alpha,\omega)$ by omitting the v vertices $m+1,\ldots,\alpha+\omega$ together with the incident arcs. The effect of this is that some (or all) cycles in $\mathcal{D}(\alpha+\omega;\alpha,\omega)$ break up into chains. The details are as follows.

As above, let $C_1,\ldots,C_\delta$ be the different cycles constituting $\mathcal{D}(\alpha+\omega;\alpha,\omega)$. We know that the maximal integer in C_j is $\alpha+\omega-\delta+j$. Now if $\alpha+\omega \geqq m+\delta$, then in the process of obtaining $\mathcal{D}(m;\alpha,\omega)$ from $\mathcal{D}(\alpha+\omega;\alpha,\omega)$ all these maximal elements are omitted. Hence all cycles in $\mathcal{D}(\alpha+\omega;\alpha,\omega)$ break up into chains in $\mathcal{D}(m;\alpha,\omega)$. The number of chains is equal to the number of initial (terminal) vertices, that is $\alpha_0+\omega_0-m = \nu$.

Finally, assume $m < \alpha+\omega \leqq m+\delta$. Then $\alpha+\omega-\delta+j$ does not exceed m when $j = 1,\ldots,\gamma$, where γ is as in (2.6). So $C_1,\ldots,C_\gamma$ are not only cycles in $\mathcal{D}(\alpha+\omega;\alpha,\omega)$ but also in $\mathcal{D}(m;\alpha,\omega)$. All these cycles have length $(\alpha+\omega)\delta^{-1}$. For $j = \gamma+1,\ldots,\delta$, the maximal element $\alpha+\omega-\delta+j$ in C_j does exceed m and is therefore omitted in the process of obtaining $\mathcal{D}(m;\alpha,\omega)$ from $\mathcal{D}(\alpha+\omega;\alpha,\omega)$. In fact $m+1,\ldots,\alpha+\omega$ disappear from $C_{\gamma+1},\ldots,C_\gamma$, respectively. But $m+1,\ldots,\alpha+\omega$ are precisely the vertices that are removed from $\mathcal{D}(\alpha+\omega;\alpha,\omega)$ in order to get $\mathcal{D}(m;\alpha,\omega)$. Thus the v cycles $\mathcal{C}_{\gamma+1},\ldots,\mathcal{C}_\delta$ in $\mathcal{D}(\alpha+\omega;\alpha,\omega)$ break up into chains in $\mathcal{D}(m;\alpha,\omega)$, each cycle turning into exactly one chain of length $(\alpha+\omega)\delta^{-1}-1$. ∎

Implicitly the proof of Theorem 2.2 contains a detailed description of the cycles and chains in $\mathcal{D}(m;\alpha,\omega)$, at least for the case $m \leqq \alpha+\omega \leqq m+\delta$. We shall use this information in Section 4 below.

3. PERMUTATIONS AND POWERS OF THE JORDAN BLOCK

The main problem discussed in this paper reads as follows: Given two sharply upper triangular $m \times m$ matrices A and Z, when does there exist an invertible $m \times m$ matrix S such that $S^{-1}AS$ is upper triangular and $S^{-1}ZS$ is lower triangular ? In this section we specialize in two ways. First of all, it is assumed that A and Z are powers of the upper triangular nilpotent $m \times m$ Jordan block. Secondly it is required that S belongs to the class of permutation matrices. In Section 4 below we shall see that the results have significance for the general problem too.

We begin with some definitions. Let m be a positive integer, and let $\sigma : \mathbb{N}_m \to \mathbb{N}_m$ be a permutation of the numbers $1,\ldots,m$. With σ we associate the $m \times m$ matrix Π_σ by stipulating that the j-th column of Π_σ is $e_{\sigma(j)}$. Here $e_1,\ldots,e_m$ is the standard basis in $\mathbb{C}^m$. The inverse of σ will be denoted by σ^{-1}. Note that $\Pi_{\sigma^{-1}} = \Pi_\sigma^{-1} = \Pi^T$.

Let κ be an integer, $1 \leqq \kappa \leqq m-1$. The permutation σ is called *κ-increasing* if $\sigma(j+\kappa) > \sigma(j)$, $1 \leqq j,j+\kappa \leqq m$. Analogously, σ is said to be *κ-decreasing* if $\sigma(j+\kappa) < \sigma(j)$, $1 \leqq j,j+\kappa \leqq m$.

THEOREM 3.1. *Let m, α and ω be integers, $1 \leqq \alpha,\omega \leqq m-1$, and let J be the upper triangular nilpotent $m \times m$ Jordan block. The following statements are equivalent:*

(*i*) *there exists an $m \times m$ permutation matrix Π such that $\Pi^{-1}J^\alpha\Pi$ is upper triangular and $\Pi^{-1}J^\omega\Pi$ is lower triangular;*

(*ii*) *there exists a permutation σ of the numbers $1,\ldots,m$ which is α-increasing and ω-decreasing;*

(*iii*) *$\alpha + \omega > m$ and the graph $\mathcal{D}(m;\alpha,\omega)$ contains no cycles;*

(*iv*) *$\alpha + \omega \geqq m + \delta$.*

Here δ is the greatest common divisor of α and ω.

Recall that $\mathcal{D}(m;\alpha,\omega)$ is the directed graph with adjacency matrix $J^\alpha+(J^T)^\omega$. For details, see Section 2.

PROOF. The equivalence of (iii) and (iv) is clear from the results of Section 2.

Let τ be a permutation of the numbers $1,\ldots,m$, and consider $\Pi_\tau^{-1}J^\alpha\Pi_\tau$. It is easy to see that this matrix is upper triangular if and only if the inverse τ^{-1} of τ is α-increasing (cf. Remark 3.2 below). This proves the equivalence of (i) and (ii).

Let σ be as in (ii), and put $\tau = \sigma^{-1}$. Then $\tau(1) \leqq \alpha$ and $\tau(1)+\omega > m$. So $m < \alpha+\omega$, and the directed graph $\mathcal{D}(m;\alpha,\omega)$ is well-defined (see Section 2). Clearly, along a walk in $\mathcal{D}(m;\alpha,\omega)$ the permutation σ is increasing. But then $\mathcal{D}(m;\alpha,\omega)$ cannot contain a cycle. This settles that (ii) implies (iii).

The reverse implication follows from a standard characterization of cyclic graphs (see e.g. [9], Section 2.5). For the rather simple graph $\mathcal{D}(m;\alpha,\omega)$ considered here, the situation is as follows. Assume (iii) is satisfied. Then the vertex set $\mathbb{N}_m$ of the graph $\mathcal{D}(m;\alpha,\omega)$ is the disjoint union of chains. Suppose there are ν chains $\mathcal{G}_1,\ldots,\mathcal{G}_\nu$, the n-th chain $\mathcal{G}_n$ being given by

$$(3.1) \qquad g_{n1} \to g_{n2} \to \cdots \to g_{nk_n}.$$

Here $n = 1,\ldots,\nu$, $1 \leqq k_n \leqq m$ and $k_1+\ldots+k_\nu = m$. Let τ be the permutation of the numbers $1,\ldots,m$ obtained by taking the ordered union of $\mathcal{G}_1,\ldots,\mathcal{G}_\nu$, where the n-th chain $\mathcal{G}_n$ has the order suggested by (3.1). So

$$\tau\left(t + \sum_{s=1}^{n-1} k_s\right) = g_{nt}, \qquad t = 1,\ldots,k_n;\ n = 1,\ldots,\nu.$$

Then $\sigma=\tau^{-1}$ is α-increasing and ω-decreasing. ■

REMARK 3.2. Let $X = (x_{ij})_{i,j=1}^m$ and $Y = (y_{ij})_{i,j=1}^m$ be $m \times m$ matrices, and let τ be a permutation of the numbers $1,\ldots,m$. Then $\Pi_\tau^{-1}X\Pi_\tau$ *and* $\Pi_\tau^{-1}Y\Pi_\tau$ are upper triangular and lower triangular, respectively, if and only if $\tau^{-1}(p) \leqq \tau^{-1}(q)$ whenever $x_{pq} \neq 0$ or $y_{qp} \neq 0$. Define the directed graph $\mathcal{D}(X,Y)$ as follows. The vertices of $\mathcal{D}(X,Y)$ are the numbers $1,\ldots,m$, and for p and q in the vertex set $\mathbb{N}_m=\{1,\ldots,m\}$ there is a (directed) arc connecting p and q if $x_{pq} \neq 0$ or $y_{qp} \neq 0$. There exists a permutation matrix Π such that $\Pi^{-1}X\Pi$ is upper triangular and $\Pi^{-1}Y\Pi$ is lower triangular if and only if $\mathcal{D}(X,Y)$ has no cycles (different from loops). ■

The property of complementary triangularization of a pair of matrices can be expressed (in a coordinate free manner) in terms of matching chains of invariant subspaces (cf. [4], Section 1). In the situation considered here, things can be translated into another combinatorial condition on m, α and ω ("shift invariance property") which is equivalent to (i)-(iv) appearing in Theorem 3.1. For details, see [6], Section 3.

4. COMPLEMENTARY TRIANGULAR FORMS

The following result contains Theorem 0.1 from the Introduction as a special case.

THEOREM 4.1. *Let A and Z be sharply upper triangular $m \times m$ matrices of type α and ω, respectively, $1 \leqq \alpha,\omega \leqq m-1$. Then A and Z admit simultaneous reduction to complementary triangular forms if and only if $\alpha + \omega > m$, α does not divide ω and ω does not divide α.*

The only if part of the theorem is already covered by Proposition 1.3. In this section we shall deal with the if part. Thus, assuming that $\alpha+\omega > m$, α does not divide ω and ω does not divide α, we shall construct an invertible matrix S such that $S^{-1}AS$ is upper triangular and $S^{-1}ZS$ is lower triangular. It turns out that S can be chosen in a special form. The details are given in the next two theorems.

THEOREM 4.2. *Let A and Z be sharply upper triangular $m \times m$ matrices of type α and ω, respectively, $1 \leqq \alpha,\omega \leqq m-1$. The following two statements are equivalent:*

(*i*) *There exist an invertible upper triangular $m \times m$ matrix U and an $m \times m$ permutation matrix Π such that $\Pi^{-1}U^{-1}AU\Pi$ is upper triangular and $\Pi^{-1}U^{-1}ZU\Pi$ is lower triangular;*

(*ii*) $\alpha + \omega \geqq m + \delta$.

Here δ is the greatest common divisor of α and ω.

Condition (ii), together with the assumption $\alpha,\omega < m$, implies that α does not divide ω and ω does not divide α.

THEOREM 4.3. *Let A and Z be sharply upper triangular $m \times m$ matrices of type α and ω, respectively, $1 \leqq \alpha,\omega \leqq m-1$. Suppose α does not divide ω, ω does not divide α and $m < \alpha + \omega < m + \delta$, where δ is the greatest common divisor of α and ω. Then there exists an invertible $m \times m$ matrix S such that $S^{-1}AS$ is upper triangular and $S^{-1}ZS$ is lower triangular. The matrix S can be chosen in the form $S = U(\Pi+R)$, where U is an invertible upper triangular $m \times m$ matrix, Π is an $m \times m$ permutation matrix and R is an $m \times m$ matrix of rank $1+m+\delta-\alpha-\omega$.*

In the situation of Theorem 4.3, the rank of R is at most δ. So the rank of R is small compared to α and ω.

In the proof of Theorems 4.2 and 4.3, we shall use the following result, taken from [7]; cf. also [6].

THEOREM 4.4. *Let A and Z be sharply upper triangular $m \times m$ matrices of positive type α and ω, respectively. Put*

$$\gamma = \max\{0,\ m + \delta - \alpha - \omega\},$$

where δ is the greatest common divisor of α and ω, and let J be the upper triangular nilpotent $m \times m$ Jordan block. Then there exist an invertible upper triangular $m \times m$ matrix U and an invertible upper triangular $\gamma \times \gamma$ matrix A_0 such that

$$(4.1) \qquad U^{-1}AU = \begin{bmatrix} A_0 & 0 \\ 0 & I_{m-\gamma} \end{bmatrix} J^{\alpha} = \begin{bmatrix} 0 & A_0 & 0 \\ 0 & 0 & I_{m-\alpha-\gamma} \\ 0 & 0 & 0 \end{bmatrix}, \qquad U^{-1}ZU = J^{\omega}.$$

In particular, if $\alpha+\omega \geqq m+\delta$, there exists an invertible upper triangular $m \times m$ matrix U such that $U^{-1}AU = J^{\alpha}$ and $U^{-1}ZU = J^{\omega}$.

The first part of (4.1) means that $U^{-1}AU$ is sharply upper triangular of type (α,γ) in the sense of [6] and [7]. In view of the results of Section 1, we are mainly interested in the situation where $1 \leqq \alpha,\omega \leqq m-1$, $\alpha+\omega > m$, α does not divide ω and ω does not divide α. In that case γ is the number of different cycles in the graph $\mathcal{D}(m;\alpha,\omega)$ introduced in Section 2. Also $\gamma < \delta$. Since α does not divide ω and ω does not divide α, this means that γ is small compared to α, ω and m. So $U^{-1}AU$ may be viewed as a small perturbation of J^{α}. Theorem 4.4 can be extended to a result on polynomials in a given matrix H. The argument is along the same lines as that concerning Corollary 0.2. We leave the details to the reader.

PROOF OF THEOREM 4.2. Suppose (i) is satisfied. Put $A_1 = U^{-1}AU$, $Z_1 = U^{-1}ZU$, and let τ be the permutation of the numbers $1,\ldots,m$ such that $\Pi = \Pi_{\tau}$. Then A_1 and Z_1 are sharply upper triangular of type α and ω, respectively. Further $\Pi_{\tau}^{-1}A_1\Pi_{\tau}$ is upper triangular and $\Pi_{\tau}^{-1}Z_1\Pi_{\tau}$ is lower triangular. This implies that the inverse τ^{-1} of τ is α-increasing and ω-decreasing (cf. Remark 3.2). Hence $\alpha+\omega \geqq m+\delta$ by Theorem 3.1.

Next, assume $\alpha+\omega \geqq m+\delta$. By Theorem 4.3 there exists an invertible upper triangular $m \times m$ matrix U such that $U^{-1}AU = J^{\alpha}$ *and* $U^{-1}ZU = J^{\omega}$. Here J is the upper triangular nilpotent $m \times m$ Jordan block. Now apply Theorem 3.1 to get a permutation matrix Π such that $\Pi^{-1}J^{\alpha}\Pi$ is upper triangular and $\Pi^{-1}J^{\omega}\Pi$ is lower triangular. ■

It is possible to prove to Theorem 4.2 without using Theorem 4.4. An outline of the argument can be found in [6], Section 3.

PROOF OF THEOREM 4.3. Without loss of generality we may assume that $\alpha < \omega$. For if not, then $\omega < \alpha$ and we interchange the roles of A and Z.

Put $\gamma = m+\delta-\alpha-\omega$, and let J be the upper triangular nilpotent $m \times m$ Jordan block. By Theorem 4.4, there exists an invertible upper triangular $m \times m$ matrix U such that $U^{-1}AU$ and $U^{-1}ZU$ are as in (4.1). For convenience, we write A_1 instead of $U^{-1}AU$. We shall prove that there exists an $m \times m$ permutation matrix Π and an $m \times m$ matrix R of rank $1+\gamma$ such that $(\Pi+R)^{-1}A_1(\Pi+R)$ is upper triangular and $(\Pi+R)^{-1}J^{\omega}(\Pi+R)$ is lower triangular. For this we return to the analysis of the graph $\mathcal{D}(m;\alpha,\omega)$ given in the proof of Theorem 2.2.

First, consider $\mathcal{D}(\alpha+\omega;\alpha,\omega)$. The vertex set $\mathbb{N}_m = \{1,\ldots,m\}$ of $\mathcal{D}(\alpha+\omega;\alpha,\omega)$ is the disjoint union of δ cycles $C_1,\ldots,C_\delta$. Here C_j is the cycle that contains the vertex j. All these cycles have length $s = (\alpha+\omega)\delta^{-1}$.

Recall that $\mathcal{D}(m;\alpha,\omega)$ is obtained from $\mathcal{D}(\alpha+\omega;\alpha,\omega)$ by omitting the vertices $m+1,\ldots,\alpha+\omega$ together with the incident arcs. As we have seen, the effect of this is that $C_1,\ldots,C_\gamma$ remain cycles (of length s) in $\mathcal{D}(m;\alpha,\omega)$ and that $C_{\gamma+1},\ldots,C_\delta$ turn into chains $C'_{\gamma+1},\ldots,C'_\delta$ of length $s-1$ in $\mathcal{D}(m;\alpha,\omega)$. For $j = 1,\ldots,\gamma$, write the cycle C_j in $\mathcal{D}(m;\alpha,\omega)$ as

$$c_{j1} \to c_{j2} \to \cdots \to c_{js}$$

with $c_{j1} = j$ and (hence $c_{js} = \omega+j$). Also, for $j = \gamma+1,\ldots,\delta$, write the chain C'_j in $\mathcal{D}(m;\alpha,\omega)$ as

$$c'_{j1} \to c'_{j2} \to \cdots \to c'_{j,s-1}$$

with initial vertex $c'_{j1} = m-\omega+j-\gamma = j+\alpha-\delta$ and terminal vertex $c'_{j,s-1} = m-\alpha+j-\gamma = j+\omega-\delta$.

Let us have a closer look at the chain C'_δ. This chain starts with α, ends with ω and contains the vertex δ (cf. Lemma 2.1) Since $\alpha < \omega$ (by assumption) and α does not divide ω, the numbers α, ω and δ are distinct. So C'_α can be written as

$$\alpha \to \ldots \to \omega-\alpha+\delta \to \omega+\delta \to \delta \to \alpha+\delta \to \ldots \to \omega$$

and C'_δ contains at least four different vertices (hence $s \geqq 5$). Write $\omega+\delta = c'_{\delta t}$. Then $2 \leqq t \leqq s-3$ and $c'_{\delta,t+1} = \delta$.

We introduce a permutation τ (or, equivalently, an ordering) of the numbers $1,\ldots,m$ as follows. First, we take the first part $\alpha \to \ldots \to \omega+\delta$ of the chain C'_δ. Then we take the ordered union of the cycles $C_1,\ldots,C_\gamma$. We proceed by taking the remaining part $\delta \to \alpha+\delta \to \ldots \to \omega$ of the chain C'_δ, and we finish by taking the ordered union of the chains $C'_{\gamma+1},\ldots,C'_{\delta-1}$. Thus

$$\begin{array}{ll} \tau(k) = c'_{\delta k}, & k = 1,\ldots,t; \\ \tau(t + (j-1)s + k) = c_{jk}, & j = 1,\ldots,\gamma;\ k = 1,\ldots,s; \\ \tau(t + \gamma s + k) = c'_{\delta,t+k}, & k = 1,\ldots,s-1-t; \\ \tau(\gamma + j(s-1) + k) = c'_{jk} & j = 1,\ldots,s-1;\ k = \gamma+1,\ldots,\delta-1. \end{array}$$

Note that the inverse τ^{-1} of τ is α-increasing but that it fails to be ω-decreasing. Roughly speaking, the latter property is violated at the beginning and the end of the cycles. This is why we are forced to perturb the simple permutation similarity $\Pi = \Pi_\tau$ by an appropriate matrix R.

Let $e_1,\ldots,e_m$ be the standard basis in $\mathbb{C}^m$. Define the $m \times m$ matrix R by

$$Re_k = \begin{cases} (-1)^{\gamma-j}\, e_{\omega+\delta} & k = t+js; \quad j = 1,\ldots,\gamma; \\ e_j, & k = t+1+js;\ j = 1,\ldots,\gamma; \\ 0, & k = 1,\ldots,m, \text{ otherwise.} \end{cases}$$

Clearly R has rank $1+\gamma$. Put $S = \Pi_\tau+R$, so

$$Se_k = \begin{cases} e_{\omega+j} + (-1)^{\gamma-j}e_{\omega+\delta}, & k = t+js; \quad j = 1,\ldots,\gamma; \\ e_{j+1} + e_j, & k = t+1+js;\ j = 1,\ldots,\gamma-1; \\ e_\delta + e_\gamma, & k = t+1+\gamma s; \\ e_{\tau(k)}, & k = 1,\ldots,m, \text{ otherwise.} \end{cases}$$

Then S is invertible. It remains to prove that $S^{-1}A_1S$ is upper triangular and $S^{-1}J^\omega S$ is lower triangular. In other words, for $k = 1,\ldots,m$ we need to show that $S^{-1}A_1Se_k$ is a linear combination of $e_1,\ldots,e_k$ and that $S^{-1}J^\omega Se_k$ is a linear combination of $e_k,\ldots,e_m$. Along the lines suggested by the definition of Se_k given above, we distinguish several possibilities for k.

1. Suppose k is of the form $k = t+js$ with $1 \leqq j \leqq \gamma$. Then $Se_k = e_{\omega+j} + (-1)^{\gamma-j}e_{\omega+\delta}$. Recall that A_1 is sharply upper triangular of type (α,γ). Since $\alpha \leqq \omega-\delta$ and $\alpha+\omega > m$, we have $\alpha+\gamma < \omega$. Hence $A_1Se_k = e_{\omega-\alpha+j} + (-1)^{\gamma-j}e_{\omega-\alpha+\delta} = Se_{k-1} + (-1)^{\gamma-j}Se_{t-1}$. So

$$S^{-1}A_1Se_k = e_{k-1} + (-1)^{\gamma-j}e_{t-1}.$$

Further $J^\omega Se_k = e_j + (-1)^{\gamma-j}e_\delta = \sum_{\nu=j}^{\gamma} (-1)^{\nu-j}Se_{t+\nu s+1}$. Hence $S^{-1}J^\omega Se_k$ is a linear combination of $e_{k+1},\ldots,e_m$.

2. Suppose k is of the form $k = t+1+js$ with $1 \leqq j \leqq \gamma-1$. Then $Se_k = e_{j+1} + e_j$. Since $\gamma < \delta$, it follows that $A_1Se_k = J^{\omega}Se_k = 0$. A similar argument works when $k = t+1+\gamma s$ (hence $Se_k = e_\delta + e_\gamma$) or $k = t+1$ (hence $Se_k = e_1$).

3. Suppose k is of the form $k = t+(j-1)s+2$ with $1 \leqq j \leqq \gamma$. Then $Se_k = e_{\alpha+j}$ for $\tau(k) = c_{j2} = \alpha+j$. Since A_1 is as in the first part of (4.1), the vector $A_1Se_k = A_1e_{\alpha+j}$ can be written as a linear combination of $e_1,\dots,e_j$. Now $Se_{t+1} = e_1$, $Se_{t+s+1} = e_2 + e_1,\dots,Se_{t+(j-1)s+1} = e_j + e_{j-1}$. So A_1Se_k is a linear combination of $Se_{t+1}, Se_{t+s+1},\dots,Se_{t+(j-1)s+1}$. Hence $S^{-1}A_1Se_k$ is in the linear hull of $e_1,\dots,e_{k-1}$. Further $J^{\omega}Se_k = J^{\omega}e_{\alpha+j} = 0$, for $\alpha+j \leqq \alpha+\gamma < \omega$.

4. For the remaining values of k, we have $Se_k = e_{\tau(k)}$ with (among other things) $\tau(k) \neq \alpha+1,\dots,\alpha+\gamma$. So either $A_1Se_k = 0$ (when $\tau(k) \leqq \alpha$) or $A_1Se_k = e_{\tau(k)-\alpha}$ (when $\tau(k) > \alpha$), and in the latter case $S^{-1}A_1Se_k = e_{k-1}$. Finally $J^{\omega}Se_k = 0$ (when $\tau(k) \leqq \omega$) or $J^{\omega}Se_k = e_{\tau(k)-\omega}$ (when $\tau(k) > \omega$), and in the latter case $S^{-1}J^{\omega}Se_k = e_{k+1}$. ■

We illustrate the proof of Theorem 4.3 with an example.

EXAMPLE 4.5. Take $m = 14$, $\alpha = 6$ and $\omega = 9$. Then $\delta = 3$ and $\gamma = 2$. Let J be the upper triangular nilpotent 14×14 Jordan block, and let $Z = J^9$. Also, let A be the 14×14 matrix given by

$$Ae_k = \begin{cases} 0, & k = 1,\dots,6, \\ ae_1, & k = 7, \\ be_1 + ce_2, & k = 8, \\ e_{k-6}, & k = 9,\dots,14. \end{cases}$$

Here $e_1,\dots,e_{14}$ is the standard basis in $\mathbb{C}^{14}$. The graph $\mathcal{D}(14;6,9)$ has two cycles, namely

$$1 \to 7 \to 13 \to 4 \to 10, \qquad 2 \to 8 \to 14 \to 5 \to 11,$$

and one chain, namely

$$6 \to 12 \to 3 \to 9.$$

So in this case the values $\tau(1),\dots,\tau(14)$ of the permutation τ introduced in the proof of Theorem 5.3 are

$$6,\ 12,\ 1,\ 7,\ 13,\ 4,\ 10,\ 2,\ 8,\ 14,\ 5,\ 11,\ 3,\ 9,$$

respectively. The nonzero columns of R are $Re_7 = -e_{12}$, $Re_8 = e_1$, $Re_{12} = e_{12}$ and $Re_{13} = e_2$. Clearly the rank of R is 3 ($= 1+\gamma$). Putting $S = \Pi_\tau+R$, one has that $S^{-1}AS$ is upper triangular and $S^{-1}ZS$ is lower triangular. Indeed, the nonzero columns of $S^{-1}AS$ are $S^{-1}ASe_2 = e_1$, $S^{-1}ASe_4 = ae_3$, $S^{-1}ASe_5 = e_4$, $S^{-1}ASe_7 = e_6 - e_1$, $S^{-1}ASe_9 = ce_8 + (b-c)e_3$, $S^{-1}ASe_{10} = e_9$, $S^{-1}ASe_{12} = e_{11} + e_1$, $S^{-1}ASe_{14} = e_{13} - e_8 + e_1$, and the nonzero columns of $S^{-1}ZS$ are $S^{-1}ZSe_2 = e_{13} - e_8 + e_3$, $S^{-1}ZSe_5 = e_6$, $S^{-1}ZSe_7 = e_8 - e_{13}$, $S^{-1}ZAe_{10} = e_{11}$ and $S^{-1}ZSe_{12} = e_{13}$. ■

REFERENCES

1. Alpay, D. and I. Gohberg: Unitary rational matrix functions and orthogonal matrix polynomials, to appear.
2. Bart, H.: Transfer functions and operator theory, *Linear Algebra Appl.* 84 (1986), 33-61.
3. Bart, H., I. Gohberg and M.A. Kaashoek: *Minimal Factorization of Matrix and Operator Functions*, Operator Theory: Advances and Applications, Vol. 1, Birkhäuser, Basel, 1979.
4. Bart, H. and H. Hoogland: Complementary triangular forms of pairs of matrices, realizations with prescribed main matrices, and complete factorization of rational matrix functions, *Linear Algebra Appl.* 103: 193-228 (1988).
5. Bart, H. and P.S.M. Kop Jansen: Upper triangularization by lower triangular similarities, *Linear Algebra Appl.* 103: 229-248 (1988).
6. Bart, H. and G.Ph.A. Thijsse: Complementary triangular forms and simultaneous reduction to simple forms of upper triangular Toeplitz matrices, Report 8804/B, Econometric Institute, Erasmus University, Rotterdam, 1988.
7. Bart, H. and G.Ph.A. Thijsse: Similarity invariants for pairs of upper triangular Toeplitz matrices, to appear.
8. Bondy, J.A. and U.S.R. Murty: *Graph Theory with Applications*, McMillan, London, 1976.
9. Carré, B.: *Graphs and Networks*, Clarendon Press, Oxford, 1979.
10. DeWilde, P. and J. Vandewalle: On the factorization of a nonsingular rational matrix, *IEEE Trans. Circuits and Systems*, *Vol. CAS*-22(8) (1975), 387-401.
11. Gohberg, I., P. Lancaster and L. Rodman: *Invariant Subspaces of Matrices with Applications*, Canadian Math. Soc. Series of Monographs and Advanced Texts, John Wiley & Sons, New York, 1986.
12. Sahnovic, L.A.: On the factorization of an operator-valued transfer function, *Soviet Math. Dokl.* 17 (1976), 203-207.

H. Bart
G.Ph.A. Thijsse
Econometric Institute
Erasmus University Rotterdam
Postbus 1738
3000 DR Rotterdam

Operator Theory:
Advances and Applications, Vol. 40

COMPARING A MATRIX TO ITS OFF-DIAGONAL PART

Rajendra Bhatia, * Man-Duen Choi and Chandler Davis †

Let $\mathcal{O}$ be the operation which for any $n \times n$ complex matrix replaces all its diagonal entries by zeroes. For various matrix norms, we study $\max_A |||\mathcal{O}A|||/|||A|||$. Upper and lower bounds are obtained, but they agree only for the c_p norms with $p = 1, 2, \infty$. For these latter norms, the value of the maximum is also obtained with A restricted to the subset $A \geq 0$.

Dedicated to Israel Gohberg on the occasion of his sixtieth birthday

1. INTRODUCTION

The operation on $\mathcal{M}_n$, the space of $n \times n$ complex matrices, which replaces each matrix by its diagonal,

$$\mathcal{D} : \mathcal{M}_n \to \mathcal{M}_n \tag{1.1}$$

$$(\mathcal{D}A)_{ij} = \begin{cases} A_{ij} & (i = j) \\ 0 & (i \neq j), \end{cases}$$

has been important in matrix studies for many decades. This is sometimes because $\mathcal{D}A$ is used as an approximant to A, and sometimes because the operation $\mathcal{D}$ has an averaging role resembling the conditional expectation in probability [3, Section 3]. Because $\mathcal{D}A$ is literally an average – a convex combination – of N unitary transforms of A,

$$\mathcal{D}A = \sum_{k=0}^{N-1} \lambda_k U_k^* A U_k \qquad (U_k^* U_k = 1,\ \lambda_k > 0,\quad \Sigma\lambda_k = 1) \tag{1.2}$$

* This author thanks the University of Toronto and NSERC (Canada) for a visit during which some of this work was done.

† This author thanks the Indian Statistical Institute and NSERC (Canada) for a visit during which some of this work was done.

(as we will discuss below), it is norm-reducing: $|||\mathcal{D}A||| \le |||A|||$, if $|||\cdot|||$ denotes any weakly unitarily invariant [2] norm on $\mathcal{M}_n$.

Consideration of $\mathcal{D}$ often entails consideration of the corresponding "residual"

$$\mathcal{O} = \mathcal{I} - \mathcal{D} : \mathcal{M}_n \to \mathcal{M}_n \tag{1.3}$$

($\mathcal{I}$ denotes the identity operation on $\mathcal{M}_n$), which replaces each matrix by its off-diagonal part. Here it is not so clear what the norm of the operation is. In this paper we will give some results on this subject.

The norms we study will be the c_p norms [5], [6], $1 \le p \le \infty$. Recall that if the singular values of A are $\sigma_1(A) \ge \sigma_2(A) \ge \ldots \ge \sigma_n(A) \ge 0$, then the c_p norms for finite p are defined by

$$\|A\|_p = \left(\sum_{i=1}^{n} \sigma_i(A)^p \right)^{1/p},$$

while $\|A\|_\infty$ is just the bound norm: $\|A\|_\infty = \sigma_1(A)$. By $c_p(n)$ we mean $\mathcal{M}_n$ with the c_p norm. Recall also that the definition $\langle A, B\rangle = \operatorname{tr}(A^*B)$ identifies $c_p(n)$ with the dual space to $c_{p'}(n)$, where p' as usual denotes the conjugate exponent to $p : \frac{1}{p} + \frac{1}{p'} = 1$. But the adjoints of $\mathcal{I}, \mathcal{D}, \mathcal{O}$ on $c_p(n)$ are easily computed to be respectively $\mathcal{I}, \mathcal{D}, \mathcal{O}$ on $c_{p'}(n)$. This means that the quantity we are trying to find,

$$\|\mathcal{O}\|_p = \max\{\|\mathcal{O}A\|_p : \|A\|_p = 1\},$$

satisfies $\|\mathcal{O}\|_{p'} = \|\mathcal{O}\|_p$, cutting our work in half.

A few facts are clear even for the more general quantity

$$|||\mathcal{O}||| = \max\{|||\mathcal{O}A||| : |||A||| = 1\}$$

coming from any weakly unitarily invariant norm. It is obvious that $|||\mathcal{O}||| \ge 1$, since $\mathcal{O}A = A$ if A is already off-diagonal. It is obvious that $|||\mathcal{O}||| \le 2$, since $\mathcal{O}A = A - \mathcal{D}A$ and each term on the right has norm at most $|||A|||$.

We proceed in Section 2 to give results on $|||\mathcal{O}|||$ and $\|\mathcal{O}\|_p$. In Section 3 we extend the results to other, related mappings.

The facts are distinctly simpler when $\mathcal{O}$ is considered only on the subset of positive semidefinite matrices. This is the subject of Section 4. Section 5 mentions some open questions.

2. THE NORM OF THE OFF-DIAGONAL MAP

The first positive result uses only weak unitary invariance of the norm, which by definition is the identity

$$|||A||| = |||U^*AU||| \tag{2.1}$$

for all A and all unitary U. For the c_p norms we find more detailed information.

THEOREM 2.1. *For every weakly unitarily invariant norm,*

$$|||\mathcal{O}A||| \le \left(2 - \frac{2}{n}\right) |||A||| \,. \tag{2.2}$$

In particular for c_p we have

$$\begin{aligned} \|\mathcal{O}\|_p &\le \left(2 - \frac{2}{n}\right)^{2/p-1} \qquad (1 \le p \le 2) \\ \|\mathcal{O}\|_p &\le \left(2 - \frac{2}{n}\right)^{1-2/p} \qquad (2 \le p \le \infty)\,. \end{aligned} \tag{2.3}$$

These inequalities are sharp for $p = 1, 2, \infty$. For $n = 2$ they are sharp for all norms.

REMARK. Conclusion (2.3) could be written as the single inequality $\|\mathcal{O}\|_p \le (2 - \frac{2}{n})^{|1/p-1/p'|}$, making visible the symmetry between conjugate exponents which we pointed out above.

PROOF. Let us give an explicit form to the expression (1.2) of $\mathcal{D}A$ as an average of unitary transforms of A. Let U denote the diagonal unitary $U = \operatorname{diag}(1, \omega, \omega^2, \dots, \omega^{n-1})$, where ω is a primitive n-th root of unity. Then it is easy to see that

$$\mathcal{D}A = \frac{1}{n} \sum_0^{n-1} U^{*k} A U^k \,.$$

Indeed, the right-hand sum is $1/n$ times the Schur product of A by the matrix whose (i,j)-entry is $\sum_{k=0}^{n-1} \omega^{k(i-j)} = n\delta_{ij}$. (The notation has been chosen so that the sum begins with $U^{*0}AU^0 = A$.)

This allows us to write

$$\mathcal{O}A = A - \mathcal{D}A = \frac{n-1}{n}A - \frac{1}{n}\sum_1^{n-1} U^{*k}AU^k .$$

By the triangle inequality and weak unitary invariance,

$$|||\mathcal{O}A||| \le \frac{n-1}{n}|||A||| + \frac{1}{n}\sum_1^{n-1} |||U^{*k}AU^k||| = 2\frac{n-1}{n}|||A||| .$$

This is the desired conclusion.

For $n = 2$ it simply says that $\mathcal{O}$ is a contraction. But it has already been pointed out that $\mathcal{O}A$ can be equal to A, so this bound 1 must be sharp.

For $p = 2$, $\|A\|_2^2 = \langle A, A\rangle = \sum_{i,j} |A_{ij}|^2$, and this can not be increased by replacing some of the elements A_{ij} by zeroes. This gives the bound $\|\mathcal{O}\|_2 \le 1$, in agreement with (2.3), which again is obviously sharp.

Now we must treat either $p = 1$ or $p = \infty$: as already remarked, they must give the same value by duality. For $p = 1$ the example is a little easier. Take E to be the matrix whose entries are all ones. Its singular values are $n, 0, \ldots, 0$, so $\|E\|_1 = n$. Since $\mathcal{O}E$ is obtained from E by subtracting a multiple of the identity, its singular values are easy to compute: $\mathcal{O}E = E - I$ has eigenvalues $n-1, -1, \ldots, -1$, so $\|\mathcal{O}E\|_1 = 2(n-1)$. For this example, then, $\|\mathcal{O}E\|_1/\|E\|_1 = 2(n-1)/n$ in agreement with the bound in (2.3), so that bound is sharp.

It may be illuminating to show where the norm is attained for $p = \infty$ as well, though the proof does not require it. Instead of E, consider $F = E - \frac{n}{2}I$, with eigenvalues $\frac{n}{2}, -\frac{n}{2}, \ldots, -\frac{n}{2}$ and so with $\|F\|_\infty = \frac{n}{2}$. Again $\mathcal{O}F = \mathcal{O}E$ with singular values $n-1, 1, \ldots, 1$: $\|\mathcal{O}F\|_\infty = n - 1 = 2\frac{n-1}{n}\|F\|_\infty$.

It remains to derive the bounds for intermediate values of p. But these follow from those we have already found above by the Calderón-Lions interpolation theorem [5, Chapter IX]. The proof is complete.

This has given, however, no reason for confidence that the values given for cases other than $p = 1, 2$, and ∞ are good ones. We rather think they are not.

The simplification in the computation of singular values which made the discussion of E above so easy will occur whenever $\mathcal{O}$ is applied to a normal matrix all of whose diagonal entries are the same. In particular, we could use any circulant matrix, that is, any $A = (A_{ij})_{i,j}$ such that the value of A_{ij} depends only on the value of $i - j \mod n$. This enables us to give a lower bound to $\|\mathcal{O}\|_p$.

PROPOSITION 2.1. *$\|\mathcal{O}\|_p$ is bounded below by*

$$\left[t^{p-1} + (1-t)^{p-1}\right]^{1/p} \left[t^{p'-1} + (1-t)^{p'-1}\right]^{1/p'} . \tag{2.3}$$

Here t can assume any value k/n', for integers k, n' with $1 \le k < n' \le n$.

Notice that the result (2.3) exhibits the expected symmetries: it is unchanged if p is replaced by its conjugate exponent, or if t is exchanged with $1 - t$.

PROOF. Apply $\mathcal{O}$ in particular to a circulant matrix A with eigenvalues $\lambda_1, \ldots, \lambda_n$. The eigenvalues of $\mathcal{O}A$ are then $\lambda_1 - \bar{\lambda}, \ldots, \lambda_n - \bar{\lambda}$, where $\bar{\lambda}$ denotes $\frac{1}{n}\sum_1^n \lambda_j$. Specialize A still further by setting $\lambda_j = s$ for $1 \le j \le k$ and $\lambda_j = -1$ for $k+1 \le j \le n$; then the eigenvalues of $\mathcal{O}A$ are $(s+1)(1-\frac{k}{n})$ for $1 \le j \le k$ and $-(s+1)\frac{k}{n}$ for $k+1 \le j \le n$. Therefore $\|\mathcal{O}\|_p^p$ is greater than or equal to

$$\frac{\|\mathcal{O}A\|_p^p}{\|A\|_p^p} = \frac{(s+1)^p\left[t(1-t)^p + (1-t)t^p\right]}{ts^p + 1 - t} .$$

Here we have made the assumption $s \ge 0$, which loses nothing. We have also set $k = tn$, that is, we have assumed that $n' = n$ in the statement of the Proposition; it is clear how to extend to the slight generalization there given.

For each admissible t we have a lower bound depending upon a positive parameter s. We find by an elementary computation that the expression is maximized by choosing $s = \left(\frac{1-t}{t}\right)^{p'-1}$. This is substituted in the above lower bound, and the result after taking the pth root and simplifying is (2.3), q.e.d.

To illustrate, consider the case $p = 9$. Using values of t around .05 we infer from the Proposition that $\|\mathcal{O}\|_9 > 1.51$. For $n = 20$ (only for n that big do such values of t

become available), Theorem 2.1 tells us that $\|\mathcal{O}\|_9 \leq 1.9^{7/9} < 1.65$. Tighter bounds might be wished for.

REMARK. The proof of Proposition 2.1 consists essentially of bounding below the norm, as an operator on $\ell_p(n)$, of the matrix whose i,j-entry is $\delta_{ij} - \frac{1}{n}$.

3. SOME EXTENSIONS

In this section we consider the applicability of the ideas which have been introduced to a wider class of mappings of $\mathcal{M}_n$ to itself.

Typical, and next simplest after $\mathcal{D}$, is the mapping $\mathcal{X}$ given by

$$(\mathcal{X}A)_{ij} = \begin{cases} A_{ij} & (i=j \quad \text{or} \quad i+j=n+1) \\ 0 & (\text{otherwise}) \end{cases}$$

(the reader is invited to see on a picture why $\mathcal{X}$ is the best name for this transformation).

Let us display $\mathcal{X}$ as an average of unitary similarities, as we did $\mathcal{D}$. Then it will follow that $\mathcal{X}$ is norm-reducing for any weakly unitarily invariant norm on $\mathcal{M}_n$, and we will be able to follow the pattern of analysis of the residual $\mathcal{Y} = \mathcal{I} - \mathcal{X}$. The formula is

$$\mathcal{X}A = \frac{1}{N}\sum_{k=0}^{N-1} V^{*k}AV^k ,$$

with the following definitions. The dimensionality n of the space is now either $2N-1$ or $2N$; and $V = \operatorname{diag}(1, \omega, \omega^2, \ldots, \omega^{N-1}, \ldots, \omega, 1)$ (with either one or two occurrences of ω^{N-1} according as n is odd or even). It is easy to verify the correctness of the formula.

THEOREM 3.1. *For $\mathcal{Y}$ acting on space of $2N-1$ or $2N$ dimensions,*

$$|||\mathcal{Y}A||| \leq \left(2 - \frac{2}{N}\right) \|A\|$$

for every weakly unitarily invariant norm. In particular, for c_p,

$$\|\mathcal{Y}\|_p \leq \left(2 - \frac{2}{N}\right)^{\frac{2}{p}-1} \quad (1 \leq p \leq 2)$$

$$\|\mathcal{Y}\|_p \leq \left(2 - \frac{2}{N}\right)^{1-\frac{2}{p}} \quad (2 \leq p \leq \infty) .$$

For every norm, $|||\mathcal{Y}|||$ is at least as large as $|||\mathcal{O}|||$ for the corresponding norm on N-space (when both are defined); consequently the inequalities found are sharp for $p = 1, 2, \infty$.

PROOF. The last sentence is clear, for among the matrices to which $\mathcal{Y}$ may be applied are those of the form $\begin{pmatrix} A & 0 \\ 0 & 0 \end{pmatrix}$ for $n \times n$ matrices A, and $\mathcal{Y}\begin{pmatrix} A & 0 \\ 0 & 0 \end{pmatrix} = \begin{pmatrix} \mathcal{D}A & 0 \\ 0 & 0 \end{pmatrix}$ in this case. The first sentence is also clear, for the proof of (2.2) used only the form of the expression of $\mathcal{D}$ in terms of unitary transforms, and that remains the same for $\mathcal{X}$. Finally, the added ingredients for proving the assertions of (2.3) were the special nature of the c_2 norm, and interpolation in p; those apply equally well in the present case. This completes the proof.

Despite the possible aesthetic appeal of the mapping $\mathcal{X}$, it does not stand out in any intrinsic way from the larger class of mappings on $\mathcal{M}_n$ which we now specify.

DEFINITION. By a stencil, we will mean a subset of $\{1, \ldots, n\} \times \{1, \ldots, n\}$. Given a stencil $\mathcal{S}$, a linear mapping $\mathcal{F} : \mathcal{M}_n \to \mathcal{M}_n$ will be called the $\mathcal{S}$-map in case, for every $(i,j) \in \mathcal{S}$ and every A, $(\mathcal{F}A)_{ij} = A_{ij}$, while for every $(i,j) \notin \mathcal{S}$ and every A, $(\mathcal{F}A)_{ij} = 0$.

THEOREM 3.2. *Assume $\mathcal{F}$ is the $\mathcal{S}$-map for some stencil $\mathcal{S}$, and assume that $\mathcal{F}$ is given by a convex combination of unitary transforms as in (1.2). Then $\mathcal{S}$ is an equivalence relation.*

Conversely, given any equivalence relation $\mathcal{S}$ on $\{1, \ldots, n\}$, with equivalence classes $\mathcal{I}_1, \ldots, \mathcal{I}_N$, the corresponding stencil-map $\mathcal{F}$ may be represented as an arithmetic mean of unitary transforms as follows. Let V be the diagonal unitary whose (i,i)-entry is ω^{K-1} if $i \in \mathcal{I}_K$, where ω is a primitive N-th root of unity. Then

$$\mathcal{F}A = \frac{1}{N} \sum_{k=0}^{N-1} V^{*k} A V^k .$$

No representation of this $\mathcal{F}$ as a convex combination of unitary transforms uses fewer than N terms.

For the mapping $\mathcal{I} - \mathcal{F}$ (which replaces by zero just those entries of a matrix whose indices are in $\mathcal{S}$), the conclusions of Theorem 3.1 hold.

PROOF. Assume $\mathcal{F}$, an $\mathcal{S}$-map, is given by

$$\mathcal{F}A = \sum_{k=0}^{N-1} \lambda_k U_k^* A U_k .$$

Then $\mathcal{F}I = I$, so $\{(i,i) : i \in \{1, \ldots, n\}\} \subseteq \mathcal{S}$, that is, $\mathcal{S}$ is reflexive.

For any $(i,j) \in \mathcal{S}$ consider $E_{ij} \in \mathcal{M}_n$, the matrix with 1 in the (i,j)-entry and zeroes elsewhere. In the representation assumed for $\mathcal{F}E_{ij}$, the 1 in the (i,j)-entry is obtained as a convex combination of terms each of which has modulus at most 1, therefore each of them is 1. This requires that each U_k commute with E_{ij}. To clear clashes of notation, let U denote any one of the U_k. Directly from definitions we compute that $U_{ii} = U_{jj}$ and that all other entries of U in the i-th and j-th row and column are zero.

What do these conclusions yield as we let i,j vary? Each U is diagonal. If $(i,j) \in \mathcal{S}$ and $(j,k) \in \mathcal{S}$ then for each U, $U_{ii} = U_{jj} = U_{kk}$. Then the formula shows that E_{ji} and E_{ik} are invariant under $\mathcal{F}$. It has been proved that $\mathcal{S}$ is an equivalence relation.

Next let us prove that the number of terms N in *any* expression (1.2) of $\mathcal{F}$ as a convex combination is larger than or equal to the number of equivalence classes. For any pair of distinct equivalence classes, choose members i,j. Remember that the i-th diagonal entry of U_k is a complex number depending only on the equivalence class of i, call it α_k; define β_k similarly starting from j. Now $\mathcal{F}E_{ij} = 0$, that is, $\sum_k \lambda_k \bar{\alpha}_k \beta_k = 0$. Consider the column vectors

$$\begin{bmatrix} \alpha_1 \\ \vdots \\ \alpha_N \end{bmatrix}, \quad \begin{bmatrix} \beta_1 \\ \vdots \\ \beta_N \end{bmatrix};$$

we have just proved they are orthogonal with respect to the inner product got from the coefficients λ_k, and they are surely not zero. But there are as many of them as there are equivalence classes. Therefore there is room for no more than N equivalence classes, as alleged.

For the converse, given $\mathcal{S}$ an equivalence relation with N classes, the formula shown for the $\mathcal{S}$-map works, by what has already been said. The proof of the conclusions of Theorem 3.1 remains the same. Theorem 3.2 is proved.

Thus the stencil-maps considered are all pinchings, which makes them trace-preserving averagings onto subalgebras, but even a little more special than that [3]. Similar questions could be raised for $\mathcal{I} - \mathcal{F}$ with somewhat more general norm-reducing $\mathcal{F}$; for example, for $\mathcal{F}$ given by any expression like (1.2). When will one be able to bound $|||\mathcal{I} - \mathcal{F}|||$ strictly below 2? In this connection the following result seems worth noting.

(Here the invariance we refer to is the property $|||UAV||| = |||A|||$ for all unitary U and V. This property, usually called unitary invariance [6], we here call strong unitary invariance to distinguish it from weak unitary invariance.)

THEOREM 3.3. *Assume the linear mapping $\mathcal{F} : \mathcal{M}_n \to \mathcal{M}_n$ satisfies $\mathcal{F}I = I$. The following are equivalent:*

(i) $\mathcal{F}$ is norm-reducing on c_1;

(ii) $\mathcal{F}$ is norm-reducing with respect to all strongly unitarily invariant norms:

(iii) for every hermitian A there exist unitaries U_k and convex coefficients λ_k such that $\mathcal{F}A = \sum_k \lambda_k U_k^* A U_k$.

PROOF. This is essentially a concatenation of known results.

Assume (i), and take any A with $0 \le A \le I$. In the coordinate system whose basis vectors are the right singular vectors of $\mathcal{F}A$, the diagonal entries of $\mathcal{F}A$ are the singular values times the inner products of right with left singular vectors. Let $\mathcal{D}$ denote the diagonal operator in this system. We know that

$$\text{Re tr } \mathcal{F}A \; = \; \text{Re tr } \mathcal{D}(\mathcal{F}A) \; \le \|\mathcal{D}(\mathcal{F}A)\|_1 \; \le \; \|\mathcal{F}A\|_1 \; \le \; \|A\|_1 \; = \; \text{tr } A,$$

and the same for $I - A$. Adding, $\text{Re tr } \mathcal{F}A + \text{Re tr } \mathcal{F}(I - A) = \text{Re tr } \mathcal{F}I = \text{tr } I = \text{tr } A + \text{tr } (I - A)$. Therefore all the above inequalities are equalities. This is only possible if all the inner products of respective singular vectors are 1, so that $\mathcal{F}A \ge 0$. We have proved that $\mathcal{F}$ is positivity-preserving; also that it preserves traces of positive matrices, which by linearity implies that it preserves traces of all matrices.

It is known that a linear map which preserves the identity, traces, and positivity (a 'doubly stochastic' map) has properties (ii) and (iii) [1, Theorem 7.1]. Note that it is not true that such a map must allow a representation as in (iii) with coefficients and unitaries independent of the choice of A; see [1, Appendix B].

The converses (ii) $\Rightarrow$ (i) and (iii) $\Rightarrow$ doubly stochastic are immediate, completing the proof.

The most important averaging map of $\mathcal{M}_n$ to itself, perhaps, is the normalized trace, $\tau(A) = \frac{1}{n}(\text{tr}\, A)I$. It behooves us to make explicit how it fits into the scheme of this paper.

It is plain that τ satisfies the equivalent conditions of Theorem 3.3: (i) is immediate, and there is a familiar choice of representation (iii); namely, assuming without loss of generality that A is diagonal, we let U_k in (iii) be the kth power of

$$V = \begin{bmatrix} 0 & 0 & 0 & \dots & 1 \\ 1 & 0 & 0 & \dots & 0 \\ 0 & 1 & 0 & \dots & 0 \\ & & \dots & & \\ 0 & 0 & \dots & 1 & 0 \end{bmatrix}$$

($k = 0, \dots, n-1$) and we set $\lambda_k = \frac{1}{n}$ for all k. This illustrates the observation made at the end of the proof above that the representations mentioned in (iii) may depend upon the choice of A.

It is nonetheless easy to get away from this dependence. In an arbitrary coordinate system, not tied to any fixed A, we let U be the diagonal matrix used in the proof of Theorem 2.1, and we let V be the permutation matrix just defined. Then the representation (iii) holds for τ if k is a multi-index $k = (k_1, k_2)$ with each k_s running from 0 to $n-1$, and if $\lambda_k = \frac{1}{n^2}$ for all k and $U_k = U^{k_1} V^{k_2}$. The argument of Theorem 2.1 adapted to this expression gives $|||\mathcal{I} - \tau||| \leq 2 - \frac{2}{n^2}$; but a better bound is available.

THEOREM 3.4. *For every weakly unitarily invariant norm* $|||\ \ |||$ *we have* $|||\mathcal{I} - \tau||| \leq |||\mathcal{O}|||$. *Therefore the bounds (2.2) and (2.3) found for* $|||\mathcal{O}|||$ *are valid for* $|||\mathcal{I} - \tau|||$. *In* c_1, c_2, *and* c_∞ *the bounds are sharp.*

PROOF. Here we do use a coordinate system depending on the given A. Indeed, $A - \tau A$ has zero trace, so by a known theorem [4] coordinates can be chosen so that all its diagonal entries are zero. But in that situation $\tau A = \mathcal{D} A$. It follows that all the bounds on norms of $\mathcal{I} - \mathcal{D}$ apply to $\mathcal{I} - \tau$. To show the bounds in c_1, c_2, and c_∞ are sharp, the same examples work. This completes the proof.

One might try generalizing the stencil-maps, considering linear maps which rather than replacing certain entries by zeroes just diminished them. We have no positive results to offer in this connection. However, we note that it is harder than might be supposed for such a mapping to be norm-reducing.

PROPOSITION 3.1. *If $|||\ \ |||$ is a strongly unitarily invariant norm on $\mathcal{M}_n$ with the property that whenever A and B satisfy*

$$|A_{ij}| \le |B_{ij}| \qquad \text{for all} \quad i, j$$

they satisfy $|||A||| \le |||B|||$, then $|||\ \ |||$ must be a positive multiple of the c_2 norm.

PROOF. Making the assumption that $|||E_{11}||| = 1$ – the conventional normalization – we will prove that $|||\ \ |||$ is the c_2 norm. It is familiar [6] that $|||A|||$ is given by $\Phi(s_1, \ldots, s_n)$ for some symmetric gauge function Φ; here $s_1 \ge \ldots \ge s_n$ again denote the singular values of A. Zero singular values are without effect. We can prove Proposition 3.1 by induction on n. It is true for $n = 1$ where all symmetric gauge functions coincide by the convention.

LEMMA. *For any two positive real numbers α and β, there exist positive real a, b, c such that the singular values of $\begin{bmatrix} a & b \\ b & c \end{bmatrix}$ are $(\alpha^2 + \beta^2)^{1/2}$ and 0 while the singular values of $\begin{bmatrix} a & b \\ b & -c \end{bmatrix}$ are α and β.*

This is an easy computation if we set

$$b = \left(\frac{\alpha\beta}{2}\right)^{1/2}, \qquad a + c = \left(\alpha^2 + \beta^2\right)^{1/2}, \qquad a - c = \alpha - \beta\,.$$

Returning to the proof of the Proposition, we consider any set of singular values $s_1 \ge \ldots \ge s_n > 0$; assuming the inductive hypothesis, we are to prove that $\Phi(s_1, \ldots, s_n)^2 = s_1^2 + \cdots + s_n^2$. Consider the matrices $A_\pm$ defined by

$$A_\pm = \begin{bmatrix} s_2 & & & & \\ & \ddots & & & \\ & & s_{n-1} & & \\ & & & a & b \\ & & & b & \pm c \end{bmatrix}.$$

We choose a, b, c using the Lemma so that A_- has singular values $s_1, \ldots, s_n$ and A_+ has singular values $s_0, s_2, \ldots, s_{n-1}, 0$, where s_0 denotes $\left(s_1^2 + s_n^2\right)^{1/2}$. Now $|||A_+||| = |||A_-|||$ by our hypothesis, because the two matrices have moduli of all elements equal. The inductive hypothesis can be applied to A_+. We conclude

$$\begin{aligned} |||A_-|||^2 &= |||A_+|||^2 = s_0^2 + s_2^2 + \cdots + s_{n-1}^2 \\ &= s_1^2 + s_2^2 + \cdots + s_n^2, \qquad \text{q.e.d.} \end{aligned}$$

The proof has established a somewhat stronger statement than given above, namely,

PROPOSITION 3.1′. *If $|||\ \ |||$ is a strongly unitarily invariant norm on $\mathcal{M}_n$ with the property that whenever A and B are real symmetric matrices with*

$$|A_{ij}| = |B_{ij}| \qquad \text{for all} \qquad i,j$$

they satisfy $|||A||| = |||B|||$, then $|||\ \ |||$ must be a positive multiple of the c_2 norm.

4. RESTRICTION TO POSITIVE MATRICES

THEOREM 4.1. *Assume $A \geq 0$. Then*

$$\|\mathcal{O}A\|_\infty \leq (1 - \frac{1}{n})\|A\|_\infty$$

$$\|\mathcal{O}A\|_2 \leq (1 - \frac{1}{n})^{1/2}\|A\|_2$$

$$\|\mathcal{O}A\|_1 \leq (2 - \frac{2}{n})\|A\|_1 .$$

All three constants are sharp.

PROOF. The bound for the c_1 norm is the one already proved. The other two inequalities have constants less than 1, but that is not shocking because $\mathcal{O}A$ is no longer allowed to be the same as A.

Let us prove the inequality for c_∞. Return to the expression

$$\mathcal{O}A = \frac{n-1}{n}A - \frac{1}{n}\sum_{j=1}^{n-1} U^{*k}AU^k .$$

If $A \geq 0$, this expresses $\mathcal{O}A$ in the form $P_1 - P_2$, where $P_1 = \frac{n-1}{n}A \geq 0$ and $P_2 \geq 0$. But for any decomposition of a hermitian as a difference of two $P_i \geq 0$, its norm is bounded by $\max \|P_i\|$. Therefore $\|\mathcal{O}A\| \leq \frac{n-1}{n}\|A\|$.

To prove the result for the c_2 norm, note that if $A \geq 0$ then for all i,j

$$|A_{ij}|^2 \leq A_{ii}A_{jj} \leq \frac{1}{2}\{A_{ii}^2 + A_{jj}^2\} ,$$

so that

$$\|\mathcal{O}A\|_2^2 = \sum_{i \neq j} |A_{ij}|^2 \leq (n-1) \sum |A_{ii}|^2 = (n-1)\|\mathcal{D}A\|_2^2 .$$

But also $\mathcal{O}A \perp \mathcal{D}A$, hence

$$\begin{aligned} \|A\|_2^2 &= \|\mathcal{O}A\|_2^2 + \|\mathcal{D}A\|_2^2 \\ &\geq (1 + \frac{1}{n-1})\|\mathcal{O}A\|_2^2 = \frac{n}{n-1}\|\mathcal{O}A\|_2^2 , \end{aligned}$$

the inequality asserted.

We already saw above that the above inequality for c_1 reduces to equality when for A we choose E, the (positive) matrix of ones. The same is true, for the same matrix, of the inequalities for c_2 and c_∞.

The proof is complete.

5. CONCLUDING REMARKS

Beside the gap between upper and lower bounds in Section 2, there are some other questions to which we hope to return on another occasion.

QUESTION 1. What are the constants in Theorem 4.1 for other values of p? For all we know, the matrix E may be extremal in that problem for all p, as it is for $p = 1, 2, \infty$.

QUESTION 2. For D a diagonal matrix and B an off-diagonal matrix, we have considered $\min \frac{\|B+D\|}{\|B\|}$ in Section 2, while in Section 4 we considered the same minimum with the side condition that $B + D \geq 0$. Now under that side condition, it also makes sense to inquire about $\min \|D\|$ instead of $\min \|B + D\|$ (for fixed hermitian B).

REFERENCES

1. T. Ando: Majorization, doubly stochastic matrices and comparison of eigenvalues, Lecture Notes, Sapporo, 1982; to appear in *Linear Algebra and its Applications.*

2. R. Bhatia and J.A.R. Holbrook: Unitary invariance and spectral variation, *Linear Algebra and Appl.* **95** (1987), 43-68.

3. Ch. Davis: Various averaging operations onto subalgebras, *Illinois J. Math.* **3** (1959), 538-553.

4. W.V. Parker: Sets of complex numbers associated with a matrix, *Duke Math. J.* **15** (1948), 711-715.

5. M. Reed and B. Simon: Methods of Modern Mathematical Physics, II: Fourier Analysis, Self-adjointness, Academic Press, 1975.

6. R. Schatten: Norm Ideals of Completely Continuous Operators, Springer, Berlin, 1960.

Indian Statistical Institute
Delhi Centre
7 SJS Sansanwal Marg
New Delhi 110016, INDIA

Department of Mathematics
University of Toronto
Toronto, CANADA M5S 1A1

Department of Mathematics
University of Toronto
Toronto, CANADA M5S 1A1

Operator Theory:
Advances and Applications, Vol. 40

RANKS OF COMPLETIONS OF PARTIAL MATRICES

Nir Cohen, Charles R. Johnson* , Leiba Rodman*, and Hugo J. Woerdeman

Dedicated to Israel Gohberg on the occasion of his sixtieth birthday

For an n-by-m array with some entries specified and the remainder free to be chosen from a given field, we study the possible ranks occurring among all completions. For any such partial matrix the maximum rank may be nicely characterized and all possible ranks between the minimum and maximum are attained. The minimum is more delicate and is not in general determined just by the ranks of fully specified submatrices. This focusses attention upon the patterns of specified entries for which the minimum is so determined. It is shown that it is necessary that the graph of the pattern be (bipartite) chordal, and some evidence is given for the conjecture that this is also sufficient.

1. INTRODUCTION

A *partial matrix* is an n-by-m array A certain of whose entries are specified elements of a given underlying field $\mathbb{F}$ and whose remaining entries are free to be chosen from $\mathbb{F}$. We denote the unspecified entries by ?'s , so that a simple example of a partial matrix over the field of rational numbers would be

$$\begin{bmatrix} -1 & ? & 0 \\ ? & 1/2 & ? \end{bmatrix} .$$

By a *completion* $B = (b_{ij})$ of a partial matrix $A = (a_{ij})$ we simply mean an ordinary n-by-m matrix over $\mathbb{F}$ whose entries coincide with those of A in all the positions in which A has specified entries. For example,

$$\begin{bmatrix} -1 & 3 & 0 \\ -1/6 & 1/2 & 0 \end{bmatrix}$$

is a completion of the preceding example of a partial matrix. Thus a completion of a partial matrix A may be thought of as a particular specification of the unspecified entries of A.

Problems concerning ranks of completions of partial matrices have been studied in the literature in various contexts. We mention briefly some of the previous works. Completions of matrices with unspecified diagonals have been studied in [FS] (in connection with certain

* The works of these authors was supported in part by National Science Foundation grant DMS 8802836.

econometric models) and in [F,FM2]. Related problems were studied in [FM1]. Ranks of completions of Hermitian matrices appeared in [Dn, FK]. In [KW, W1] key results in the minimal rank completion problem are obtained in a finite dimensional as well as in an infinite dimensional setting. The importance of these results to systems theory is explained in these two papers. We mention also the connection with the partial realization problem in the linear systems theory [K, W2] , and with Schur complements and related ideas [C]. The reference [MS] serves as a general introduction to the various connections between the rank of a matrix and the ranks of its submatrices.

We shall generally be interested in the following problem. Given a partial matrix A, what are the possible ranks occurring among all completions of A. We denote throughout the minimal rank over all completions of A by mr (A) and the maximal rank over all completions by MR(A). It is not difficult to see that all integer values between mr (A) and MR(A) are attained as ranks of completions of A. Indeed, if B is a minimal rank completion of A and C a maximal rank completion of A, then changing B into C by changing one entry of B into the corresponding one of C at a time changes the rank by at most one at each step, so that all intermediate ranks are also attained. Thus, it suffices to know mr(A) and MR(A).

Of the two, MR(A) is more easily analyzed and may be simply described, for an arbitrary partial matrix, in terms of the ordinary ranks of rectangular submatrices (maximal ones suffice) consisting entirely of specified entries. This is discussed in section 2 and may be viewed as a generalization of the classical Frobenius-König result, (see [S] and its references), which is the special case in which all the specified entries are equal to 0.

The case of minimal rank is more difficult and, in general, mr(A) cannot be described solely in terms of the ranks of fully specified submatrices (except in case $\mathbb{F}$ is the field of two elements). For this reason we concentrate attention upon the *pattern* $J \subseteq \mathbb{Z} \times \mathbb{Z}$ consisting of the ordered pairs of indices associated with the specified entries of a partial matrix A. To focus upon the pattern, any partial matrix whose pattern is J will said to be *subordinate* to J. When we wish to emphasize the pattern J of a partial matrix A, we write mr(A, J) in place of mr(A) (and MR(A,J) in place of MR(A)). Our particular interest is in determining those patterns J for which mr (A, J) may be described entirely in terms of the ranks of specified submatrices of the partial matrix A for all partial matrices subordinate to J. (This is the case for many patterns, in particular the block triangular patterns analyzed in [W1, W2, KW, Dv]). This particular question is reminiscent of one studied for positive definite completions of partial Hermitian matrices [GJSW, JR], and, indeed, the full solution we suspect is importantly similar to that one, though there are notable technical differences.

Since our problem is permutation equivalence invariant, it is natural to describe the pattern J for the specified entries of an n-by-m partial matrix in terms of a (bipartite) graph on n+m vertices $u_1, ..., u_m, v_1, ..., v_n$. The (bipartite) graph of a partial matrix subordinate to J then has an undirected edge connecting u_i and v_j if and only if the i , j entry is specified.

We say that a pattern J is *scalar rank determined* if mr (A_1, J) = mr (A_2, J) whenever A_1 and A_2 are partial matrices subordinate to J such that the ranks of corresponding fully specified submatrices of A_1 and A_2 coincide. (Thus, mr (A, J) is entirely determined by the ranks of fully specified submatrices of A for all partial matrices subordinate to J.) An analogous and formally stronger condition on a pattern J is that of *block rank determined* in which specified positions of J may be replaced by (specified) matrices and unspecified entries by blocks of unspecified entries in a consistent way to produce a "block" partial matrix. Such a resulting block partial matrix will still be referred to as subordinate to J.

We conjecture that the scalar rank determined patterns are exactly those whose graphs are *bipartite chordal* (no minimal simple circuit of length 6 or more, [G]). If so, the notions of scalar rank determined and block rank determined (a technical notion that arises in our partial analysis) would coincide, as they do in the case of the previously analysed triangular patterns [KW, W1, W2] . We prove the necessity of this conjecture in section 3 and note several special cases of sufficiency in sections 4-6.

The present work has come about through an effort to generalize the nice results of [W1] about "triangular" patterns by characterizing all (scalar or block) rank determined patterns. In fact, the formula we conjecture to hold for determining mr (.) in the case of bipartite chordal patterns is based upon the minimum rank of certain triangular subpatterns of the given pattern, and thus ultimately uses expressions from this paper. A pattern for which this formula in terms of triangular subpatterns is valid for all subordinate block (respectively scalar) matrices is called *block triangular rank determined* (respectively, *scalar triangular rank determined*). We conjecture that both properties are also equivalent to bipartite chordality. In section 3 we compare the several concepts mentioned in this introduction. In particular, if this central conjecture is correct, not only would all bipartite chordal patterns be rank determined, but we would have a formula for the minimum rank.

Section 4-6 mention some additional triangular rank determined patterns consistent with our conjecture.

2. MAXIMAL RANKS

We start with the description of the maximal rank of completions. A *pattern* J is just a subset of $\underline{n} \times \underline{m} = \{1, ..., n\} \times \{1, ..., m\}$; an $n \times m$ partially defined matrix $A = \left[A_{ij}\right]_{i=1}^{n}\ {}_{j=1}^{m}$ with blocks A_{ij} of size $p_i \times q_j$ is called *subordinate* to J if

(i) A_{ij} are $p_i \times q_j$ matrices over $\mathbb{F}$ for $(i,j) \in J$;

(ii) A_{ij} are unspecified blocks of size $p_i \times q_j$ for $(i,j) \notin J$.

The unspecified blocks of A will be denoted by "?". The maximal completion rank of a matrix A subordinate to a pattern J is defined as

$$MR(A;J) = \max\{\operatorname{rank} B : B \text{ is a completion of } A\}.$$

We assume that each block A_{ij} of A, whether specified or not, is of the given size $p_i \times q_j$. In order to obtain a nice formula for MR, we relate it to

$$mr(A;J) = \min(\operatorname{rank} B : B \text{ is a completion of } A\}$$

through the following observation:

LEMMA 2.1. *Let* A *be subordinate to* $J \subseteq \underline{n} \times \underline{m}$. *Set* $p = n + m$, $K = \{\underline{n} \times (\underline{p} \setminus \underline{m})\} \cup \{(\underline{p} \setminus \underline{n}) \times \underline{m}\} \cup J$. *Then* B *is a maximal rank completion of* A *in J if and only if, for some matrix* C, $\begin{bmatrix} B & I \\ I & C \end{bmatrix}$ *is a minimal rank completion of* $D := \begin{bmatrix} A & I \\ I & ? \end{bmatrix}$ *in* K. *Moreover*,

$$MR(A,J) + mr(D,K) = p.$$

<u>Proof</u>. We need the following formula ([W1], see also [Dv])

$$\text{(2.1)} \qquad mr \begin{bmatrix} X & Y \\ Z & ? \end{bmatrix} = \operatorname{rank} \begin{bmatrix} X \\ Z \end{bmatrix} + \operatorname{rank} [X \quad Y] - \operatorname{rank} X.$$

Here X, Y, Z are fully specified matrices of suitable sizes and ? is an unspecified rectangular block. (Actually, (2.1) is a particular case of (3.2) in the next section). Using (2.1) we have

$$mr\left(\begin{bmatrix} B & I \\ I & ? \end{bmatrix}, K \cup \underline{n} \times \underline{m}\right) = p - \operatorname{rank} B.$$

Choosing B of maximal rank minimizes the left hand side, and we get as desired $mr(D,K) = p - MR(A,J)$. □

Apply this observation to a matrix A subordinate to a *rectangular* pattern J : $A = \begin{bmatrix} E & ? \\ ? & ? \end{bmatrix}$ of size $n \times m$. Here E is a fully specified p x q block. Let K be the pattern described in Lemma 2.1, and let $D = \begin{bmatrix} A & I \\ I & ? \end{bmatrix}$ be subordinate to K. Using the formula for the minimal rank given at the end of Section 5 (pattern (6) with F, G, H empty), we compute

$$mr(D;K) = \max(n, m, p + q - \operatorname{rank} E).$$

By Lemma 2.1

$$MR(A;J) = \min(m, n, (n-p) + (m-q) + \operatorname{rank} E).$$

By the way, one can prove this directly also or deduce it from the interlacing formulas appearing in Theorem 3.1 in [dS] (see also [T]). We are thus led to associate with every rectangular pattern J and subordinate matrix A as above the number

$$\rho(A,J) = (n - p) + (m - q) + \operatorname{rank} E.$$

This definition extends to trivial rectangular patterns (p=0 or q=0) by simply setting rankE=0. We have just proven the following result for the special case in which J is rectangular (we denote by A_K the partial block matrix subordinate to the subpattern K, obtained by replacing A_{ij} with "?" for all $(i,j) \in J \setminus K$).

THEOREM 2.2. *Let* A *be a* p×q *matrix, subordinate to some pattern* J ⊂ n̲×m̲.
Then MR (A,J) = min ρ(A$_K$, K), *where* K *runs over all the maximal rectangular subpatterns of*
J, *including the trivial ones of size* 0-by-m *and* n-by-0.

Note that this result holds for arbitrary patterns, whether bipartite chordal or not.

P̲r̲o̲o̲f̲. Because of basic known inequalities for the rank of a conventional matrix
MR (A,J) ≤ minρ(A$_K$, K) ; thus, we have to show that MR (A,J) ≥minρ(A$_K$,K) . Let K be a
maximal rectangular subpattern of J on which the above minimum is obtained. Up to row and
column permutations we have

$$A = \begin{bmatrix} U & V & * \\ W & ? & * \\ * & * & * \end{bmatrix}, \qquad A_K = \begin{bmatrix} U & V & ? \\ ? & ? & ? \\ ? & ? & ? \end{bmatrix}$$

of size (α+1+β)× (γ+δ+ε) . Here * represents irrelevant partially defined blocks. The basic
recurring step is to show that one can always find X such that

(2.2) $\text{rank} \begin{bmatrix} U & V \\ W & X \end{bmatrix} = \text{rank} [U,V] + 1$.

For if (2.2) is true we can continue by induction on the number of rows and columns in A.

To prove (2.2) we examine three possible cases :

C̲a̲s̲e̲ 1̲. rank $\begin{bmatrix} U \\ W \end{bmatrix}$ >rankU. Here (2.2) holds for all X, due to (2.1).

C̲a̲s̲e̲ 2̲ .rank $\begin{bmatrix} U \\ W \end{bmatrix}$ =rankU>rank[U,V]-δ. This means that up to column permutation
V=[V' , V"], where rank [U,V'] = rank [U V] and V' is of size α×η , with η=rank[U,V]-rankU.
Under the same partition, X=[X' , X"], where we choose X' arbitrary. We have

$$\text{rank} \begin{bmatrix} U & V' \\ W & X' \end{bmatrix} = \text{rank}[U,V'] = \text{rank}[U,V] .$$

But then, Theorem 5.1 in [KW] yields that $\begin{bmatrix} U & V' & V" \\ W & X' & ? \end{bmatrix}$ has a u̲n̲i̲q̲u̲e̲ minimal rank completion (also
compare with (2.1) for that pattern). Choose any X" different than the minimal rank one, and
(2.2) is obtained.

C̲a̲s̲e̲ 3̲. rank $\begin{bmatrix} U \\ W \end{bmatrix}$ =rankU=rank[U,V]-δ. This case can never occur, as it leads to the following
contradiction: let L be the rectangular subpattern of J with subordinate matrix $A_L = \begin{bmatrix} U & ? & ? \\ W & ? & ? \\ ? & ? & ? \end{bmatrix}$. Then

ρ(A$_L$, L) = rankU + β + δ + ε = ρ(A$_K$, K) − 1
contradicting the choice of K. ▯

Theorem 2.2 provides a nice generalization of the classical result of Frobenius/König.
(The determinantal version of this result may be found in [HL]). The latter result, though
originally stated not in terms of rank, but in terms of singularity vs nonsingularity of a square

matrix, is (essentially) the special case of the former in which all specified entries are 0; thus the ranks of all specified blocks are 0 and do not appear. Of course, the classical result also was not stated in terms of ranks of completions of partial matrices. See [S], and its classical references, for a fuller view of the development of the classical result.

To conclude this section, we re-examine its starting point, i.e. Lemma 2.1. using the result of Theorem 2.2:

LEMMA 2.3. *In the notation of Lemma* 2.1 *we have*

$$\text{mr}\,(D,K) = \max(p_L + q_L - \text{rank}A_L),,$$

where L *runs over all the maximal rectangular subpatterns of* J, *including the two trivial ones*; *and for each* L *the matrix* A_L *is of size* $p_L \times q_L$.

3. MINIMAL RANK COMPLETIONS

We now state precisely the minimal rank completion problem for a given (commutative) field $\mathbb{F}$. We assume throughout the rest of the paper that $\mathbb{F}$ is not the field consisting of two elements 0 and 1. Our objects are partially defined n×m block-matrices and their patterns. As in the previous section, consider a pattern $J \subseteq \underline{n} \times \underline{m}$ and an n×m partial matrix $A = \left[A_{ij}\right]_{i=1}^{n}\,{}_{j=1}^{m}$ subordinate to J. We assume that the blocks (specified or not) A_{ij} are of size $\upsilon_i \times \mu_j$. If all the blocks are 1×1, we shall refer to A as a *scalar (partially defined) matrix*, risking slight abuse of notation.

An n×m block matrix $\left[B_{ij}\right]_{i=1}^{n}\,{}_{j=1}^{m}$ with block entries B_{ij} of size $\upsilon_i \times \mu_j$ (all matrices over $\mathbb{F}$) is called a *completion* of the n×m matrix $A = \left[A_{ij}\right]_{i=1}^{n}\,{}_{j=1}^{m}$ subordinate to J if $B_{ij} = A_{ij}$ for all $(i,j) \in J$.

Given a matrix A subordinate to J, denote by mr (A;J) the minimal possible rank of all the completions of A. A completion B which attains this minimum is called a *minimal rank completion.*

In this and the next sections we study the minimal ranks of completions of a given block matrix A, and compute it in many cases in terms of the ranks of fully specified submatrices of A.

A subset K of a pattern J is called a *subpattern* of J. Given a partial block matrix A subordinate to J, its *restriction* to K is the partial block matrix A_K, obtained by replacing A_{ij} by "?" for all $(i,j) \in J\backslash K$. Obviously, A_K is subordinate to K and

$$\text{mr}\,(A;J) \geq \text{mr}\,(A_K; K).$$

We call K *rectangular* if K is of the form I×J for some sets $I \subseteq \underline{n}$ and $J \subseteq \underline{m}$. For rectangular patterns mr $(A_K;K)$ is simply the rank of A_K.

A pattern J is called *scalar rank determined* if, for every partial scalar matrix A subordinate to J, mr (A, J) depends only on the ranks of the various rectangular restrictions of A. If in this definition also block partial matrices A with any sizes of blocks $\upsilon_1, ..., \upsilon_n$ and $\mu_1, ..., \mu_m$ are allowed, we call J *block rank determined.* The latter property is in principle stronger than the former, but see Conjecture 3.3 below. The example of

(3.1) $J = \underline{3}\times\underline{3} \setminus \{ (1,1) , (2,2) , (3,3) \}$

will show that in general rectangular restriction ranks are insufficient to determine mr. Indeed, if A is a 3×3 matrix with non zero entries off the main diagonal and unspecified diagonal entries then mr (A,J) is either one or two, depending on the specific entry values. An easy analysis shows that for

$$A = \begin{bmatrix} ? & a & b \\ d & ? & c \\ e & f & ? \end{bmatrix} \qquad (a , b , c , d , e , f \neq 0)$$

the minimal rank of A is 1 if ace = bdf, and 2 otherwise. However , all the rectangular restrictions of A are invariably of rank 1.

An important class of rank determined patterns is the class of *triangular patterns*. A pattern J is called *left upper triangular* if it has the property that (k,l) $\in$ J and r≤k and s≤l implies (r,s) $\in$ J. More generally, J is called *triangular* if there exist permutations σ on $\underline{n}$ and τ on $\underline{m}$ such that

$$J_{\sigma\tau} \ := \{ (\sigma(i) , \tau (j)) : (i , j) \in J \}$$

is left upper triangular . It is easy to see that J is triangular if and only if (i, j) $\in$ J and (k,r) $\in$ J implies that at least one of (i, r) and (k , j) is in J.

The following formula holds for a left upper triangular pattern J (proved in [W1]), extending by permutation to all triangular patterns. Let J be left upper triangular, and set

$$q = \max \{k : (k , 1) \in J \}$$

$$p_j = \max \{k: (j,k) \in J \} \qquad (j = 1 , ..., q).$$

Then for any partial block matrix $A = [A_{ij}]$ subordinate to J we have

$$\text{(3.2)}\ \operatorname{mr} (A;J) = \sum_{j=1}^{q} \operatorname{rank} \begin{bmatrix} A_{11} & \cdots & A_{1,p(j)} \\ \vdots & & \vdots \\ A_{j1} & \cdots & A_{j,p(j)} \end{bmatrix} - \sum_{j=1}^{q-1} \operatorname{rank} \begin{bmatrix} A_{11} & \cdots & A_{1,p(j)-1} \\ \vdots & & \vdots \\ A_{j1} & \cdots & A_{j,p(j)-1} \end{bmatrix} .$$

Formula (3.2) shows that triangular patterns are indeed rank determined.

Define the *triangular minimal rank* of A with respect to J by

$$\operatorname{tmr} (A;J) = \max \{\operatorname{mr} (A_K : K) : K \subseteq J \text{ and K is triangular } \} .$$

Note that by inclusion the inequality tmr (A, J) ≤ mr (A , J) holds in general. Every pattern J for which mr (A,J) = tmr (A , J) holds for all A subordinate to J, will also be rank determined, since computation of mr(A , J) reduces to the triangular case. Such a pattern J will be called *block triangular rank determined.*

If mr (A , J) = tmr (A , J) is true only for scalar (but not necessarily for block) matrices A subordinate to J, we call J *scalar triangular rank determined.* At first sight this is a weaker property, but see Conjecture 3.3.

The 3×3 matrices missing their diagonal (mentioned in (3.1.)) provide an example of patterns which are not scalar triangular rank determined. By the way, all partial matrices checked so far satisfy mr ≤ 2tmr . It is an open question whether this equalities holds in general.

Matrix patterns may be conveniently described by *bipartite graphs*. Given a pattern J, the corresponding (undirected) bipartite graph G (J) has vertices $\{v_1, ..., v_n, u_1, ..., u_m\}$; and (v_i, u_j) is an edge in G (J) if and only if (i, j) ∈ J . A bipartite graph G is called *chordal* if there are no minimal cycles of length ≥ 6 in G. Note that all the cycles are of even length ≥ 4 . See, e.g., [G] for further properties of bipartite chordal graphs.

So far we have defined five crucial properties of patterns J :

I. block rank determined;

II. scalar rank determined;

III. block triangular rank determined;

IV. scalar triangular rank determined;

V. the corresponding graph G (J) is bipartite chordal.

We mention the obvious implications among these properties; obviously I implies II and III implies IV. Also III implies I and IV implies II. We next prove that II implies V.

THEOREM 3.1. *If the pattern* J *is scalar rank determined, then the corresponding graph* G(J) *is bipartite chordal.*

To make the proof of Theorem 3.1 more transparent, it is convenient to introduce a useful notion of reduction. A pattern $K \subseteq \underline{p} \times \underline{q}$ will be called a *reduction* of the pattern $J \subseteq \underline{n} \times \underline{m}$ if the graph G(K) is a subgraph of G(J) (i.e., G(K) is obtained from G (J) by deleting some vertices together with all incident edges).

LEMMA 3.2. *Properties* I *through* V *are preserved under reduction.*

Proof. Let K be a reduction of J. We can complete any (block or scalar) matrix A subordinate to K to a matrix B subordinate to J by filling in B_{ij} with (block or scalar) zeros whenever (i,j) ∈ J\K. If J is (scalar) rank determined then for all such A mr (A,K) = mr (B,J) is determined by the ranks of rectangular restrictions of B, which are zero completions of rectangular restrictions of A. So K must be (block or scalar) rank determined. Similarly, if J is (block or scalar) triangular rank determined then for all A as above

$$mr (A,K) = mr (B,J) = tmr (B,J) = tmr (A,K)$$

so that K is (block or scalar) triangular rank determined. Finally, if G(J) is bipartite chordal then so is G(K), since minimal cycles in G (K) are minimal in G(J). □

Proof of Theorem 3.1. Let J be scalar rank determined but not bipartite chordal, so there is a minimal cycle of length ≥ 6 in G(J). Assume by induction that the theorem is valid for all patterns with smaller number of rows and columns. If this minimal cycle does not include all vertices in G(J) then by removing the vertices not in this cycle (together with all adjacent edges) we obtain a pattern $\hat{J}$ which is rank determined by Lemma 3.1 but G $(\hat{J})$ is not bipartite chordal. This is a contradiction in view of the induction hypothesis.

To finish the proof it remains to show that a pattern J whose graph G(J) consists of the minimal cycle of length ≥ 6 including all the vertices is not rank determined. Applying a permutation, if necessary, we can assume that a matrix A subordinate to J is in form

$$\begin{bmatrix} a_1 & b_1 & ? & ? & \dots & ? & ? \\ ? & a_2 & b_2 & ? & \dots & ? & ? \\ \cdot & \cdot & \cdot & \cdot & \cdot & \cdot & \cdot \\ ? & ? & ? & ? & \dots & a_{n-1} & b_{n-1} \\ b_n & ? & ? & ? & \dots & ? & a_n \end{bmatrix}$$

Let a_i , b_j be all non-zero; then the ranks of all rectangular restriction of A are equal to 1. On the other hand, it is not difficult to see that

$$\mathrm{mr}\,(A\,;J) = \begin{cases} 1 & \text{if} \quad a_1 a_2 \dots a_n = b_1 b_2 \dots b_n, \\ 2 & \quad \text{otherwise}. \end{cases}$$

Thus, J is not rank determined.□

Theorem 3.1 leads naturally to the following open problem. Let J be a pattern. For any partial scalar matrix A subordinate to J let S_A be the collection of all ranks of fully specified submatrices of A. If A and B are subordinate to J and $S_A = S_B$, what can we say about the size of $|\,\mathrm{mr}\,(A) - \mathrm{mr}\,(B)\,|$? An analogous problem can be formulated for partial block matrices as well. According to the definition, in case J is scalar rank determined, we have that $S_A = S_B$ implies $\mathrm{mr}(A) = \mathrm{mr}(B)$, and the proof of Theorem 3.1 shows that for patterns J with G(J) not bipartite chordal there exist partial scalar matrices A and B subordinate to J such that $S_A = S_B$ but $\mathrm{mr}\,(A) - \mathrm{mr}\,(B) = 1$.

We believe that a statement stronger than Theorem 3.1 is true.

CONJECTURE 3.3. *All five properties defined above are equivalent for any pattern* J.

Due to the trivial implications and Theorem 3.1, we see that conjecture 3.3 would be true if only V implied III. Actually, it will be shown below that the weaker implication, from V to IV, would also suffice. For this we need the following definition.

A pattern K is called an *amplification* of a pattern J if G (K) is obtained from G(J) by replacing each vertex v in G(J) by a finite number of vertices $w_1(v)$, ..., $w_{p(v)}(v)$ $(p(v)\geq 1)$ such that $(w_i(v)\,,\, w_j\,(u))$ is an edge in G(K) if and only if (v,u) is an edge in G(J) . It is easy to check that an amplification of a chordal bipartite graph is again chordal bipartite.

LEMMA 3.4. *If any amplification of* J *is scalar triangular rank determined then* J *is block triangular rank determined.*

Proof. Let the block matrix A be subordinate to J. There exists a unique amplification K of J to which A is subordinate as a scalar matrix. Now the maximal triangular subpatterns of K and those of J correspond to precisely the same submatrices in A. Therefore if K is scalar triangular rank determined we get

$$\text{tmr}(A;J) = \text{tmr}(A;K) = \text{mr}(A;K) = \text{mr}(A;J).$$

Since A was arbitrary, we conclude that J is block triangular rank determined.□

COROLLARY 3.5. *If* V *implies* IV *then* V *implies* III.

Proof. Let G(J) be bipartite chordal. Then, as is easy to see, so are all its amplifications. If V implies III we conclude that all the amplifications are scalar triangular rank determined. But then by Lemma 3.4 J itself is block triangular rank determined.□

Finally, we remark that a study of patterns can be reduced to the patterns J for which G(J) is connected.

PROPOSITION 3.6. *Assume that* G(J) *has* k *connected components* $G(J_1), \ldots, G(J_p)$. *Then for every block matrix* A *subordinate to* J *we have*

$$\text{mr}(A;J) = \max\{\text{mr}\, A_{J_1};J_1),\ldots,\text{mr}(A_{J_p};J_p)\}.$$

Proof. Letting $A_i = A_{J_i}$, set

$m = \max \text{mr}(A_i;J_i)$. If B_i is a minimal completion of A_i, B_i factors as C_iD_i where C_i has m columns and D_i has m rows. Now it turns out that

$$B = \begin{bmatrix} C_1 \\ C_2 \\ \cdot \\ \cdot \\ C_k \end{bmatrix} [D_1\ D_2 \ldots D_k]$$

is a completion of A and rank B = m . □

It follows from Proposition 3.6 that each of the properties I - V holds for J if and only if it holds for every subpattern $J_1, \ldots, J_p$, where $G(J_i)$ $(i = 1, \ldots, p)$ are the connected components of G(J).

In analogy with the minimal rank situation, we can also define the triangular maximal rank of A as

$$\text{TMR}(A;J) = \min\{\text{MR}(A_K;J) : K \subseteq J \text{ is maximal triangular}\}.$$

It turns out, however, that MR = TMR holds universally. Indeed, due to inclusion the inequalities

$$\text{MR}(A,J) \le \text{TMR}(A,J) \le \min \rho(A_K, K)$$

hold for the matrix A subordinate to J (here K runs over all the maximal rectangular subpatterns of A). In Theorem 2.2, however, a K has been found for which MR (A, J) = $\rho(A_K, K)$. Therefore the above three values must be equal.

4. A SEQUENTIAL SIMPLIFICATION

The following procedure can be applied in finding mr for certain classes of partial matrices. It evolved from an attempt to prove Conjecture 3.3.

THEOREM 4.1. *Let* J *be some pattern. Suppose that we can find a sequence of distinct points* α_1 *through* α_p *not in* J *such that each pattern* $J_j = J\cup\{\alpha_1, ..., \alpha_j\}$ *has a unique maximal triangular subpattern containing* α_j . *Then if* J_p *is scalar triangular rank determined, so is* J.

We first prove this result for the special case when p=1 and J_1 is triangular:

LEMMA 4.2. *Let* $J\subseteq \underline{n}\times\underline{m}$ *be a triangular pattern missing one element (i.e., there exists* $\alpha\in\underline{n}\times\underline{m}$ *such that* $J\cup\{\alpha\}$ *is triangular). Then* J *is scalar triangular rank determined.*

Proof. We shall use induction on the depth N=min{n,m} of J. For N≤2 J is triangular and the assertion is trivial. So fix a pattern J with depth N, say left upper triangular with a missing entry α, and assume the Lemma is true for all triangular patterns missing one element of smaller depth.

We choose a scalar matrix A subordinate to J such that

(4.1) $\qquad N \geq mr(A;J) > tmr(A;J)$.

Using allowable (i.e., such that they do not introduce unspecified entries into the specified spots in A) elementary row operations, we can successfully remove n–mr (A;J) rows from A which depend linearly (as partially defined vectors) or higher rows, without affecting the minimal rank, hence without violating (4.1). We can similarly eliminate m-mr (A;J) columns using allowable elementary column operations. Therefore we may as well assume that

(4.2) $\qquad N = n = m = mr(A;J) > tmr(A;J)$.

Obviously α cannot lie in the rows and columns omitted, otherwise we get a triangular pattern and (4.2) is violated. Therefore we still have a triangular pattern omitting a single entry.

Note that by (4.2) any completion of A has rank N.

Assume that α=(k,r). Denote by K the pattern J minus row k, and by L the pattern J minus column r. Since both K and L are triangular subpatterns of A, by (4.2) obviously

(4.3) $\qquad mr(A_K;K) = mr(A_L;L) = N-1$.

In fact, due to their size, any completion of A_K in K or of A_L in L will have rank N–1. Note that mr $(A_{K\cap L}, K\cap L)$ can be either N–1 or N–2. In fact, we claim that

(4.4) $\qquad mr(A_{K\cap L}; K\cap L) = N-2$.

For suppose all the completions of $A_{K\cap L}$ have rank N–1. Let B be such a completion let C and D be arbitrary minimal completions (of rank N–1) of A_K and A_L that agree with B; and let E be a minimal completion of A that agrees with C and D. Then by (3.2) and the above

$$\text{rank}E = \text{rank}C + \text{rank}D - \text{rank}B = N-1$$

contradicting (4.2).

So $A_{K\cap L}$ is an $(N-1) \times (N-1)$ partial matrix of minimal rank N–2, subordinate to a left upper triangular pattern. Therefore we can annihilate the specified entries of a certain row in $A_{K\cap L}$, say row p, by elementary row operations using the previous rows. Such operations are allowable since they never add a multiple of an unspecified entry to a specified one, and since they do not change the overall rank. Similarly we can annihilate the specified entries of a certain column, say column q, by allowable elementary column operations using the previous columns.

The analysis in [W2, §1] shows that if $(p,q) \notin J$ then all the minimal completions of A will have the same entry value at (p,q). This stands in contradiction with the fact that <u>any</u> completion of A has rank N. So we must have $(p,q) \in J$.

Having annihilated row p and column q in $A_{K\cap L}$, we observe that entries (p,r) and (k,q) in A are non zero since mr (A;J)=N.

Let M be the pattern obtained from J by unspecifying entries (k,j) for $j < q$, as well as (i,r) for i>p. Since $(p,q) \in J$, the subpattern M of J is triangular. From (3.2) it is easy to get

$$\text{tmr}(A;J) \geq \text{mr}(A_M;M) = (A_{K\cap L}; K\cap L) + 2 = N.$$

This contradicts (4.2), and the proof is complete. □

A propos, if J is a triangular pattern missing one entry α, it is not hard to describe all the maximal triangular subpatterns of J. If R_j, j=1, ..., p, are all the maximal rectangular subpatterns of $J \cup \{\alpha\}$ which contain α, then T_j, j=1, ..., p, are all the maximal triangular subpatterns of J, where T_j is obtained from J by removing the entries in the row and column of α which lie outside of R_j.

<u>Proof of Theorem 4.1</u>. By induction it suffices to check the theorem for p=1. We assume that α is not in J, and that $J_1 = J \cup \{\alpha\}$ contains a unique maximal triangular subpattern L containing α. We also assume that J_1 is scalar triangular rank determined.

Let A be scalar matrix subordinate to J. We want to establish that tmr (A,J). Pick $x \in \mathbb{F}$; denote by A_x the completion of A to J_1 with value x at α, and $t_x = \text{mr}(A_x, J_1)$. If $\text{mr}((A_x)_K, K) = t_x$ for some maximal triangular subpattern $K \neq L$ of J_1, then $K \subseteq J$ implies the equality $\text{mr}(A,J) = \text{tmr}(A,J) = t_x$.

If, on the other hand, L is the only maximal triangular subpattern of J_1 such that $\text{mr}((A_x)_L, L) = t_x$, it may happen that for some y the value of $\text{mr}((A_y)_L, L)$ drops to $\text{mr}((A_x)_L, L) - 1$, in which case we easily conclude that $\text{mr}(A, J) = \text{tmr}(A,J) = t_x - 1$.

Otherwise, $\text{mr}((A_y)_L, L) = t_x$ independently of y , so by definition $\text{mr}(A_M, M) = t_x$, where $M = L \setminus \{\alpha\}$. M is a triangular array missing an entry, so by Lemma 4.2 $\text{tmr}(A_M, M) = t_x$. Since $M \subseteq J$ we have

$$\text{tmr}(A_J, J) \geq t_x = \text{mr}(A_x, J_1) \geq \text{mr}(A_J, J) \geq \text{tmr}(A_J, J)$$

so equality again prevails. □

Suppose that for a pattern J a sequence of points α_1 , ..., α_p has been found according to Theorem 4.1 and such that J_p is scalar triangular rank determined. Then J is scalar triangular rank determined by Theorem 4.1, but one can also show independently that J has a bipartite chordal graph. In this sense Theorem 4.1 proves a particular case of Conjecture 3.3. The converse is not true: the pattern $J=\underline{3}\times\underline{3} \setminus \{ (1,1), (3,3) \}$ has both these properties, but no appropriate sequence α, ..., α_p exists.

Finally, we remark that an analogue of Lemma 4.2 concerning triangular patterns plus one entry is valid as well : Namely, let J be a triangular pattern, and let $\alpha \notin J$; then $J\cup\{\alpha\}$ is scalar triangular rank determined. We omit the proof of this statement, because it is not clear to us how to utilize this result in a proof of a theorem similar to Theorem 4.1.

5. MISCELLANEOUS RESULTS ON THE MINIMAL RANK

In this section we collect various results and special cases on minimal rank and triangular rank determined patterns, as well as prove Conjecture 3.3 in special cases.

THEOREM 5.1. *Assume that* $p>n$ *and* $q>m$. *Let* $J\subseteq \underline{n}\times\underline{m}$ *be any pattern* . Let $J'\subseteq (\underline{p}\setminus\underline{n}) \times (\underline{q}\setminus\underline{m})$ *be a triangular pattern and let* $J'' = \underline{n}\times (\underline{q}\setminus\underline{m})$. *Then the pattern* $K = J\cup J''$ $\subset \underline{n}\times\underline{q}$ *is block triangular rank determined if and only if the pattern* $K = J\cup J''\cup J' \subset \underline{p}\times\underline{q}$ *is block triangular rank determined.*

Proof. We shall actually prove more: if A is subordinate to L then

(5.1) $\quad \mathrm{mr}(A;L) - \mathrm{tmr}(A;L) = \mathrm{mr}(A_K;K) - \mathrm{tmr}(A_K;K)$.

By simple iteration on the lower block rows of A it suffices to consider the case where p=n+1, q=m+1, $J' = \{n+1\}\times\{m+1\}$ and $A_{J'}$ is $1 \times \mu_{m+1}$. The following statements are then obviously equivalent for a subpattern M of J.

(i) M is maximal triangular in J;

(ii) $M'' := [M,J'']$ is maximal triangular in K;

(iii) $M' := \begin{bmatrix} M & J'' \\ ? & J' \end{bmatrix}$ is maximal triangular in L.

Choose M as in (i) such that $\mathrm{mr}(A_{M''}; M'')$ is maximized. Then

(5.2) $\quad \mathrm{mr}(A_{M''} : M'') = \mathrm{tmr}(A_K;K)$,

$\quad \mathrm{mr}(A_{M'}; M') = \mathrm{tmr}(A)$.

If $A_{J''}$ is linearly dependent on $A_{J'}$, then the two left hand sides in (5.2) are equal, and moreover

(5.3) $\quad \mathrm{mr}(A_{M'}; M') = \mathrm{mr}(A)$,

proving (5.1).

If on the other hand $A_{J''}$ is linearly dependent on $A_{J'}$, then the two left hand sides in (5.2) differ by 1, as well as the two quantities in (5.3), so that (5.1) still holds. □

It would be interesting to check whether the following particular case of Conjecture 3.3 is true.

CONJECTURE 5.2. *Let* $J \subseteq \underline{n} \times \underline{m}$ *be any pattern, and for some* $q > m$ *let* K *be* $J \cup (\underline{n} \times (\underline{q} \setminus \underline{m}))$. *Then* J *is block triangular rank determined if and only if* K *is block triangular rank determined.*

It is again expected that we should have

$$\mathrm{mr}\,(A_J\,;J) - \mathrm{tmr}\,(A_J\,;J) = \mathrm{mr}\,(A;K) - \mathrm{tmr}\,(A;K)$$

for all A subordinate to K.

For various pattern classes one can calculate mr by inductive arguments, such as in the following two examples.

LEMMA 5.3. *The pattern* $J_n = \{ (i,1), (1,i), (i,i) : i=1, \ldots, n\}$ *consisting of a row, a column and a diagonal is block triangular rank determined.*

Proof. The cases n=1,2 are trivial. To check for n=3, let A be subordinate to J_3. Using allowable elementary (i.e., such that do not introduce unspecified entries into the specified spots of A) row and column operations we can bring A to the form

$$\left[\begin{array}{cccc|cc|cc}
I & 0 & 0 & 0 & 0 & 0 & 0 & 0 \\
0 & 0 & 0 & 0 & I & 0 & 0 & 0 \\
0 & 0 & 0 & 0 & 0 & 0 & I & 0 \\
0 & 0 & 0 & 0 & 0 & 0 & 0 & 0 \\
\hline
0 & I & 0 & 0 & 0 & 0 & ? & ? \\
0 & 0 & 0 & 0 & 0 & X & ? & ? \\
\hline
0 & 0 & I & 0 & ? & ? & 0 & 0 \\
0 & 0 & 0 & 0 & ? & ? & 0 & Y
\end{array}\right]$$

of, say, size $(\alpha+\beta+\gamma+\delta+\varepsilon+\zeta+\eta+\vartheta) \times (\alpha+\varepsilon+\eta+\iota+\beta+\kappa+\gamma+\lambda)$. Now J_3 has two maximal triangles $K=J_3 \setminus \{ (3,3) \}$ and $L = J_3 \setminus \{ (2,2) \}$. It is easy to compute (where $a \vee b$ denotes max (a,b))

$$\mathrm{mr}\,(A,J) = \alpha+\beta+\gamma+\varepsilon+\eta+\mathrm{rank}\,X \vee \mathrm{rank}\,Y =$$

$$= (\alpha+\beta+\gamma+\varepsilon+\eta+\mathrm{rank}X) \vee (\alpha+\beta+\gamma+\varepsilon+\eta+\mathrm{rank}Y) = \mathrm{mr}\,(A_K, K) \vee \mathrm{mr}\,(A_L, L)$$

and hence J_3 must be block triangular rank determined.

We now proceed by induction on $n \geq 4$. Write

$$J_n = J_{n-1} \cup \{ (n,1), (1,n), (n,n) \}.$$

By the induction hypothesis J_{n-1} is triangular rank determined, and by two applications of Theorem 5.1 so is $J_n \setminus \{ (n, n) \}$. The maximal triangular subpatterns of J_n are M_i (i=2, ...,n):

$$M_i = \{(1,j), (j,1) : = j=1, \ldots, n\} \cup \{(i,i)\}.$$

The maximal triangular subpatterns of $J \setminus \{(n,n)\}$ are M_i (i=2, ..., n–1).

Now consider a block matrix A subordinate to J_n. Let B be a restriction of a rank minimal completion of A to $J \cup (\underline{(n-1)} \times \underline{(n-1)})$. The matrix B is subordinate to J_3, hence is triangular rank determined:

$$\mathrm{mr}\,(B,J_3) = \mathrm{mr}\,(B_K, K) \vee \mathrm{mr}\,(B_l, L).$$

But B_K is subordinate to $J \setminus \{(n,n)\}$, which has been shown to be triangular rank determined, hence

$$\mathrm{mr}\,(B_K\,, K) \;=\; \max_{i=2}^{n-1} \mathrm{mr} \quad (A_{M_i}\;,\; M_i\,)\;;$$

while $L \subseteq J_3$ has been identified here with $M_n \subseteq J_n$, hence

$$\mathrm{mr}\,(B_L\,, L) \;=\; \mathrm{mr}\,(A_M\,, M_n\,)\,.$$

Putting all these equalities together we find

$$\mathrm{mr}\,(A;J_n\,) \le \;\mathrm{mr}\,(B;J_3\,) \;=\; \max_{i=2}^{n} \;\mathrm{mr}\,(A_{M_i}\;,\; M_i\,) \;=\; \mathrm{tmr}\,(A,J_n\,)$$

as claimed □

LEMMA 5.4. *A pattern of the form*

(5.3) $E = \{\; 1,1)\;,\,(1,2)\;,\,(2,2)\;,\,(2,3)\;,\,...\}$

is block triangular rank determined.

Proof. Denote by E_n the pattern of this type which has n elements in the right handside of (5.3).

First we show that if $\begin{bmatrix} A & B & ? \\ ? & C & D \end{bmatrix}$ is subordinate to E_4 then one can find a matrix X such that

(i) $\mathrm{mr}\,(\begin{bmatrix} A & B & ? \\ X & C & D \end{bmatrix}, E_4 \cup \{\;(2,1)\;\}\;) = \mathrm{mr}\,(\begin{bmatrix} A & B \\ ? & C \end{bmatrix}, E_3\,) \vee \mathrm{mr}\left(\begin{bmatrix} B & ? \\ C & D \end{bmatrix}, E_3\right),$

(ii) $\mathrm{rank}\,[X,C,D] = \mathrm{rank}\,[C,D]$.

Indeed, using allowable elementary row and column operations we may bring $\begin{bmatrix} A & B & ? \\ ? & C & D \end{bmatrix}$ to the form

$$\begin{bmatrix} 0 & I & 0 & 0 & ? \\ U & 0 & 0 & 0 & ? \\ \hline ? & P & 0 & 0 & 0 \\ ? & 0 & I & 0 & 0 \\ ? & 0 & 0 & 0 & V \end{bmatrix},$$

where the partition is of size, say, $(\alpha+\beta+\gamma+\delta+\varepsilon)\times(\eta+\alpha+\delta+\zeta+\theta)$, and the rows of P are linearly independent. Using (3.2) one verifies that

$$\mathrm{mr}\left(\begin{bmatrix} A & B \\ ? & C \end{bmatrix}, E_3\right) = \alpha+\delta+\mathrm{rank}\,U\,;$$

$$\mathrm{mr}\left(\begin{bmatrix} B & ? \\ C & D \end{bmatrix}, E_3\right) = \alpha+\delta+\mathrm{rank}\,V\,.$$

The same equality (3.2) shows that (i) and (ii) are satisfied for

$$X = \begin{bmatrix} O \\ O \\ VZU \end{bmatrix},$$

where the $\theta \times \beta$ matrix Z is chosen so that

(5.4) $\mathrm{rank}\,V + \mathrm{rank}\,U - \mathrm{rank}\,(VZU) = \max\,(\mathrm{rank}\,V, \mathrm{rank}\,U).$

The existence of Z satisfying (5.4) is not difficult to verify : assume, for instance, that rank U $\le$ rank V. Then choose Z so that Z (Range U) $\cap$ Ker V = {0} .

Now we are in a position to use induction on n to show that E_n is scalar triangular rank determined. The case n=3 is trivial, and n=4 follows from (i) above. For notational simplicity we shall only illustrate the case n=5. Let

$$A = \begin{bmatrix} A & B & ? \\ ? & C & D \\ ? & ? & E \end{bmatrix}$$

be the partial block matrix in question. Find X such that (i) , (ii) above is satisfied. We obtain the partial matrix

$$B = \begin{bmatrix} A & B & ? \\ X & C & D \\ ? & ? & E \end{bmatrix}$$

which is subordinate to E_4 , hence is triangular rank determined:

$$\mathrm{mr}\ (B,E_4) = \mathrm{mr} \begin{bmatrix} A & B & ? \\ X & C & D \end{bmatrix} \vee \mathrm{mr} \begin{bmatrix} X & C & D \\ ? & ? & E \end{bmatrix}.$$

Combined with (i) , (ii) above this gives

$$\mathrm{mr}\ (B,E_4) = \mathrm{mr} \begin{bmatrix} A & B \\ ? & C \end{bmatrix} \vee \mathrm{mr} \begin{bmatrix} B & ? \\ C & D \end{bmatrix} \vee \mathrm{mr} \begin{bmatrix} C & D \\ ? & E \end{bmatrix}$$

hence mr (A,E_5) = tmr (A,E_5).

Generalizing this process to the case n>5 is left as an exercise for the interested reader. □

We conclude this section with a table of mr values for some partial block matrices of simple pattern. The formulas are based on the identity mr = tmr and (3.2). We denote matrix blocks by A,B, ... and fully unspecified blocks by "?".

(1) mr [A,?] = rankA.

(2) $\mathrm{mr} \begin{bmatrix} A & ? \\ ? & B \end{bmatrix} = \max\ \{\mathrm{rank}A, \mathrm{rank}B\}$.

(3) $\mathrm{mr} \begin{bmatrix} A & ? \\ B & C \end{bmatrix} = \mathrm{rank} \begin{bmatrix} A \\ B \end{bmatrix} + \mathrm{rank}[B,C] - \mathrm{rank}C$.

(4) $\mathrm{mr} \begin{bmatrix} A & B & ? \\ ? & C & D \end{bmatrix} = \mathrm{rank} \begin{bmatrix} B \\ C \end{bmatrix} + \max\ \{\mathrm{rank}[A,B]-\mathrm{rank}B,\ \mathrm{rank}[C,D]-\mathrm{rank}C\}$.

(5) $\mathrm{mr} \begin{bmatrix} A & C & E \\ B & ? & F \\ ? & D & G \end{bmatrix} = \mathrm{rank}\ [A,C,E] + \mathrm{rank} \begin{bmatrix} E \\ F \\ G \end{bmatrix} +$

$$+\max\left\{\operatorname{rank}\begin{bmatrix}A & E\\ B & F\end{bmatrix}-\operatorname{rank}[A,E]-\operatorname{rank}\begin{bmatrix}E\\ F\end{bmatrix},\ \operatorname{rank}\begin{bmatrix}C & E\\ D & G\end{bmatrix}-\operatorname{rank}[C,E]-\operatorname{rank}\begin{bmatrix}E\\ G\end{bmatrix}\right\}.$$

(6) $$\operatorname{mr}\begin{bmatrix}A & C & ? & F\\ B & ? & ? & G\\ ? & D & E & H\end{bmatrix} = \max\ \{\alpha,\beta,\gamma\}\ ,\ \text{where}$$

$$\alpha = \operatorname{rank}\ [A,C,F] + \operatorname{rank}\begin{bmatrix}F\\ G\\ H\end{bmatrix} + \operatorname{rank}\begin{bmatrix}A & F\\ B & G\end{bmatrix} - \operatorname{rank}[A,F] - \operatorname{rank}\begin{bmatrix}F\\ G\end{bmatrix},$$

$$\beta = \operatorname{rank}\ [D,E,H] + \operatorname{rank}\begin{bmatrix}F\\ G\\ H\end{bmatrix} + \operatorname{rank}\begin{bmatrix}C & F\\ D & H\end{bmatrix} - \operatorname{rank}[D,H] - \operatorname{rank}\begin{bmatrix}F\\ H\end{bmatrix},$$

$$\gamma = \operatorname{rank}\ [A,C,F] + \operatorname{rank}\begin{bmatrix}F\\ G\\ H\end{bmatrix} + \operatorname{rank}\begin{bmatrix}C & F\\ D & H\end{bmatrix} - \operatorname{rank}\ [C,F] - \operatorname{rank}\begin{bmatrix}F\\ H\end{bmatrix}.$$

6. COMPLETION WITH MINIMAL RANK 1.

In this section we consider the partial matrices with minimal completion rank 1.

We prove the following particular case of Conjecture 3.3.

THEOREM 6.1. *Let* A *be subordinate to* J. If G (J) *is bipartite chordal and* tmr (A;J)=1 *then* mr(A;J) = 1.

The proof of this theorem is based on complete characterization of partial matrices whose minimal rank is 1 or triangular minimal rank is 1.

Given a pattern J with the corresponding bipartite graph G(J). A subset $K \subseteq J$ is called a *cycle* in G(J) if K is of the form

(6.1) $\{(v_1, u_1), (v_1, u_2), (v_2, u_2), ..., (v_k, u_k), (v_k, u_1)\}$

for distinct $v_1, v_2, ..., v_k$ and distinct $u_1, ..., u_k$. In other words, G(K) is a cycle in G (J). We say that $K \subseteq J$ is a *3-line* in G(J) if K is of the form

(6.2) $\{(v_1, u_1), (v_1, u_2), (v_2, u_1)\}$

where $v_1 \neq v_2$, $u_1 \neq u_2$ and $(v_2, u_2) \notin J$. In other words, the subgraph of G(J) corresponding to the four vertices v_1, v_2, u_1, u_2 is a line consisting of 3 edges.

Let now A be a partial scalar matrix subordinate to J, and let a_{vu} be the entry in A corresponding to the edge (v,u) in G(J). The matrix A = $[a_{ij}]$ will be called *singular* with respect to a cycle K in G(J) (given by (6.1)) if

$$a_{v_1u_1}\ a_{v_2u_2} \cdots a_{v_ku_k} = a_{v_1u_2}\ a_{v_2u_3} \cdots a_{v_{k-1}u_k}\ a_{v_ku_1}\ .$$

The matrix A will be called *singular* with respect to a 3-line K in G(J) (given by (6.2)) if either $a_{v_1u_1} \neq 0$ or $a_{v_1u_2}\ a_{v_2u_1} = 0$ (or both).

LEMMA 6.2 *Let* A *be a non-zero scalar matrix subordinate to a pattern* J *(not necessarily chordal). Then*
(i) tmr (A;J) = 1 *if and only if* A *is singular with respect to all 4-cycles (i.e., cycles with 4 edges) and all 3-lines in* G (J);
(ii) mr (A;J) = 1 *if and only if* A *is singular with respect to all cycles and all* 3-*lines in* G(J).

Proof . The definition of singularity of A with respect to 4-cycles and 3-lines easily implies the "only if" part in (i). Assume that A is singular with respect to all 4-cycles and all 3-lines. We have to prove that for any triangular subpattern K of J there exists a rank 1 completion B of A_K . The matrix B will be built from A_K by specifying one previously unspecified entry at a time.

Using the hypothesis that K is triangular, without loss of generality (performing, if necessary, permutations of rows and columns of A_K), we can assume that the entry to be specified is in the (i_o, j_o) position, all the entries (i,j) with $i=i_o$ and $j > j_o$, or with j=jo and $i < i_o$ are specified in A_K, and if the entry (i,j) is specified in A_K, then so are all entries (i ',j ') with $i' \leq i$ and $j' \geq j$. Denote by a_{ij} the specified entry in the (i,j) position in A_K . Denote by A_K (x) the partial matrix obtained from A_K by replacing ? in the (i_o, j_o) position with $x \in \mathbb{F}$
Assume first that $a_{i_0j} = 0$ and $a_{ij} \neq 0$ for some $j > j_o$ and $i > i_o$. As A_K is singular with respect to all 4-cycles and 3-lines, it follows that $a_{i_0j'} = 0$ for all indices $j' > j_o$. In this case A_K (0) is singular with respect to all its 4-cycles and 3-lines. Analogously the case when $a_{ij'} \neq 0$, $a_{ij_0} = 0$ for some $i < i_o$ is taken care of.

Next, assume that the cases treated in the previous paragraph do not appear. Then for any value of x $A_K(x)$ is singular with respect to all its 3-lines. To make sure that $A_K(x)$ is also singular with respect to all its 4-cycles, choose x as follows: if $a_{ij} \neq 0$ for some $i < i_o$, $j > j_o$ put x $= a_{ij_0} \, a_{i_0j} \, / \, a_{ij}$. As A_K is singular with respect to all 4-cycles, this definition of x is independent of the choice of indices (i,j) such that $i < i_o$, $j > j_o$ and $a_{ij} \neq 0$. (If $a_{ij} = 0$ for all $i < i_o$, $j < j_o$ choose x arbitrarily).

Let B be the completion of A_K constructed by specifying one previously unspecified entry at a time as prescribed above. Then all 2×2 submatrices of B are singular by induction. So rank B = 1 , and we have proved (i).

We pass now to the proof of (ii). The "only if" part is easy (cf. the proof of Theorem 3.1) Now assume that A is singular with respect to all cycles and 3-lines in G(J). Again we will specify one unspecified entry at a time. Let (i_o, j_o) be an unspecified entry of A, and let A(x) be the partial matrix obtained from A by replacing ? in the (i_o, j_o) position with $x \in \mathbb{F}$. If for some i and j both entries a_{i_0j} and a_{ij} are specified in A and $a_{i_0j} = 0$, $a_{ij} \neq 0$, then (as in the proof of the part (i)) we verify that A(0) is singular with respect to all its 3-lines and cycles. Analogously, A(0) is singular with respect to all its 3-lines and cycles in case $a_{ij_0} = 0$, $a_{ij} \neq 0$ for some i,j . Excluding these cases it follows that A(x) is singular with respect to all its 3-lines. To ensure that A(x) is also singular with respect to all its cycles, choose x as follows. Let

(6.3) $\{(v_1, u_1), (v_1, u_2), \ldots, (v_k, u_k), (v_k, u_1)\}$

be a cycle in $G(J \cup (i_0, j_0))$ which was not a cycle in $G(J)$, so one of the edges in this cycle is (i_0, j_0), say $(v_1, u_1) = (i_0, j_0)$, and assume that $p := a_{v_2u_2} a_{v_3u_3} \ldots a_{v_ku_k} \neq 0$, $q := a_{v_1u_2} a_{v_2u_3} \ldots a_{v_ku_1} \neq 0$. Then put $x = q(p)$. Again, the property that A is singular with respect to all its cycles ensures that the value of x is independent of the choice of cycle (6.3) (subject to the above conditions).

Applying this procedure to fill in all unspecified entries of A one by one, we obtain a completion B of A with rank B=1, and the part (ii) is proved. □

Proof of Theorem 6.1. Assume mr $(A;J) \geq 2$. Then by Lemma 6.2 A contains a regular cycle A_K. If K is a 4-cycle we are done, again by Lemma 6.2. Otherwise, since J is chordal, K has a chord dividing K into two cycles, strictly shorter than K. One of them is again regular, etc. By descending induction on the lengths of these cycles, we must finally get a 2×2 regular cycle, hence tmr $(A;J) \geq 2$. □

An interesting corollary of Lemma 6.2 is obtained concerning partial matrices with missing diagonal:

COROLLARY 6.3. *Let be given a partial matrix*

$$A = \begin{bmatrix} ? & q_{12} & q_{13} & \cdots & q_{1n} \\ q_{21} & ? & q_{23} & \cdots & q_{2n} \\ q_{31} & q_{32} & ? & \cdots & . \\ . & . & . & ? & q_{n-1\,n} \\ q_{n1} & q_{n2} & q_{n3} & \cdots & ? \end{bmatrix}, \quad q_{ij} \in \mathbb{F} \ (i \neq j)$$

with missing diagonal, and assume $n \geq 3$. *Then there exist* $x_1, \ldots, x_n \in \mathbb{F}$ *such that*

$$\text{rank} \begin{bmatrix} x_1 & q_{12} & \cdots & q_{1n} \\ q_{21} & x_2 & \cdots & q_{2n} \\ q_{31} & q_{32} & \cdots & q_{3n} \\ . & . & . & . \\ q_{n-1\,1} & q_{n-1\,2} & \cdots & q_{n-1\,n} \\ q_{n1} & q_{n2} & \cdots & x_n \end{bmatrix} = 1$$

if and only if the following conditions are satisfied:

(i) *every fully specified* 2×2 *submatrix of* A *has rank* 1;

(ii) *every* 2×2 *submatrix* of A *with precisely one* ? *admits a rank* 1 *completion. In other words, if* $q_{ij} = 0$ *for some* $i \neq j$ *then for every* $k \neq i, j$ *the equality* $q_{ik} q_{kj} = 0$ *holds*;

(iii) *for every triple of distinct indices* i, j, k *the equality* $q_{ij} q_{jk} q_{ki} = q_{ik} q_{kj} q_{ji}$ *holds*.

The proof follows immediately from Lemma 6.2 upon the observation that the graph G(J) for the pattern J of A contains only 4-cycles and 6-cycles.

A result close to Corollary 6.3 was proved in [FS] by different methods. A special case of Corollary 6.3 was proved in [J] in connection with a problem in probability theory.

REFERENCES

[C] Carlson, D.: Generalized inverse invariance, partial orders and rank minimization problems for matrices, Current Trends in Matrix Theory (eds. F. Uhlig, R. Grone), N. Holland, (1987), 81-88.

[D,n] Dancis, J.: The possible inertias for a Hermitian matrix and its principal submatrices, Lin Alg. Appl. 85 (1987), 121-151.

[Dv] Davis, C.: Completing a matrix so as to minimize its rank, Operator Theory: Advances and Applications, 29, (1988), 87-95.

[F] Fiedler, M.: A characterization of tridiagonal matrices, Linear Algebra and Appl. 2 (1969), 191-197.

[FK] Fritzsche, B.; Kirstein, B.: An extension problem for non-negative Hermitian block Toeplitz matrices, Math. Nachr. 130 (1987), 121-135.

[FM1] Fiedler, M.; Markham, T.L.: Completing a matrix when certain entries of its inverse are specified, Lin. Alg. Appl. 74, (1986), 225-237.

[FM2] Fiedler, M.; Markham, T.L.: Rank preserving diagonal completions of a matrix, Lin. Alg. Appl., 85, (1987), 49-56.

[FS] Furth, D.; Sierksma, G.: The rank and eigenvalues of main diagonal perturbed matrices, Report 87-07-OR, Econometrisch Instituut, R.U.Groningen, The Netherlands.

[G] Golumbic, M.C.: Algorithmic graph theory and perfect graphs, Academic Press, New York, (1980).

[GJSW] Grone, R.; Johnson, C.R.; Marques de Sá, E.; Wolkowitz, H.: Positive definite completions of partial Hermitian matrices, Linear Algebra and Appl. 58, (1984), 109-124.

[HL] Hartfiel, D.J.; Loewy, R.: A determinant version of the Frobenius-König theorem, Linear and Multilinear Algebra 16, (1984), 155-165.

[J] Johnson, C.R.: Bayesian deduction of marginal from conditional probabilities, Linear and Multilinear Algebra 11, (1982), 333-350.

[JR] Johnson, C.R.; Rodman, L.: Inertia possibilities of completions of partial Hermitian matrices, Linear and Multilinear Algebra 16, (1984), 179-195.

[K] Kalman, R.E.: On partial realizations, transfer functions and canonical forms, Acta Polyt. Scand. Math., Comp. Sci. Series, MA 31, (1979), 9-31.

[KW] Kaashoek, M.A.; Woerdeman, H.J.: Unique minimal rank extensions of triangular operators, J. Math. Anal. Appl. 131, (1988), 501-516.

[MS] Marsaglia, G.; Styan, G.P.: Equalities and inequalities for ranks of matrices, Linear and Multilinear Algebra 2, (1974), 269-292.

[dS] de Sá, E.M.: Imbedding conditions for λ-matrices, Lin. Alg. Appl. 24 (1979), 33-50.

[S] Schneider, H.: The concepts of irreducibility and full indecomposability of a matrix in the works of Frobenius, König and Markov, Linear Algebra and its Applications 18, (1977), 139-162.

[T] Thompson, R.C.: Interlacing inequalities for invariant factors, Lin. Alg. Appl. 24 (1979), 1-32.

[W1] Woerdeman, H.J.: The lower order of lower triangular operators and minimal rank extensions, Integral Equations and Operator Theory 10 (1987), 859-879.

[W2] Woerdeman, H.J.: Minimal rank completions for block matrices, to appear in Linear Algebra and Appl.

Nir Cohen
Department of Theoretical Mathematics
Weizmann Institute of Science
Rehovot, 76100 ISRAEL

Hugo J. Woerdeman
Department of Mathematics
Vrije Universiteit
De Boelelaan 1081
1081 HV Amsterdam
The NETHERLANDS

Charles R. Johnson and Leiba Rodman
Department of Mathematics
College of William and Mary
Williamsburg, Va 23185
U.S.A.

Operator Theory:
Advances and Applications, Vol. 40

FINITE DIMENSION PROBLEMS IN OPERATOR THEORY

Kenneth R. Davidson
University of Waterloo

Dedicated to Israel Gohberg on the occasion of his sixtieth birthday.

We will survey four open problems about matrices which have important implications for infinite dimensional problems. The main theme of these problems is that a solution in M_n with norm estimates which are independent of dimension provides infinite dimensional information as well.

This paper is the text of a survey talk I gave at the University of Calgary in August 1988 at the conference honouring Professor Israel Gohberg. It was my purpose to illustrate how finite dimensional problems arise naturally in infinite dimensional contexts. The main theme is - quantitative norm estimates in the finite dimensional case which do not depend on dimension yield important for operators on Hilbert space as well.

These problems are not original. Indeed, they have all been around for quite a while in some form, although much of the interest in these problems has been quite recent. Many infinite dimensional problems can be cast in a finite dimensional context, and it is often a fruitful approach. In this talk, I have attempted to choose problems which are attractive in finite dimensions and may stand on their own even without the infinite dimensional context. So perhaps this will attract the attention of more mathematicians.

Recall that the operator norm of a matrix T in M_n is given by its action on $\mathbb{C}^n$ with the Euclidean norm:

$$\|T\| = \sup_{x\neq 0} \frac{\|Tx\|}{\|x\|} .$$

This is also computed as the first "singular value", namely the largest eigenvalue of $(T^*T)^{1/2}$.

The first problem is an old favourite of mine.

PROBLEM 1. Let A and B be Hermitian $n\times n$ matrices. If $\|AB-BA\|$ is <u>small</u>, are A and B <u>close</u> to a commuting pair of Hermitian matrices?

To be more precise, we formulate this in a quantitative way. Given $\varepsilon > 0$, is there a $\delta > 0$ so that if $\|A\| \leq 1$, $\|B\| \leq 1$, and $\|AB-BA\| < \delta$, then there are Hermitian matrices A' and B' such that $A'B' = B'A'$ and $\|A-A'\|+\|B-B'\| < \varepsilon$?

Note that for any fixed dimension n, the function $f(A,B) = \|AB-BA\|$ is a continuous function on the compact set of all pairs of $n\times n$ Hermitian matrices in the unit ball. The zero set is precisely the set of commuting pairs. So the uniform continuity of f yields an appropriate $\delta = \delta(\varepsilon,n)$ depending on n. Implicit in this problem is that δ must not depend on n. Equivalently, if $\delta(\varepsilon,n)$ is the best possible value, is $\lim_{n\to\infty} \delta(\varepsilon,n) > 0$?

This problem can be recast in an interesting way. Form the matrix $T = A+iB$. Note that T is normal if and only if A commutes with B. Indeed,

$$T^*T-TT^* = 2i(AB-BA).$$

So $\|T^*T-TT^*\|^{1/2}$ is a homogeneous quantity equivalent to $\|AB-BA\|$; and the distance to a commuting pair $\{A',B'\}$ is equivalent to the distance of T to the normal operators. We recast problem 1 in a stronger form:

PROBLEM 1'. Is there a universal constant C so that for every matrix T of any size,

$$\operatorname{dist}(T,\mathcal{N}ormals) \leq C\|T^*T-TT^*\|^{1/2} ?$$

Problem 1 has a number of variants, such as using unitary matrices, arbitrary matrices, triples of Hermitian matrices, etc. Most of these other versions have negative answers. This might be taken as negative evidence in our case. However, Voiculescu has observed that these other cases seem to exhibit a higher dimensional topological obstruction which cannot occur in the Hermitian case. I will give two examples.

EXAMPLE 1. Consider the $n \times n$ unitary matrices

$$U_n = \begin{bmatrix} 0 & & & & 1 \\ 1 & 0 & & \bigcirc & \\ & 1 & 0 & & \\ \bigcirc & & & 0 & \\ & & & 1 & 0 \end{bmatrix} \quad \text{and} \quad V_n = \begin{bmatrix} \omega & & & \\ & \omega^2 & & \bigcirc \\ & & \omega^3 & \\ \bigcirc & & & \ddots \\ & & & & \omega^n \end{bmatrix}$$

where $\omega = e^{2\pi i/n}$. Notice that $U_n V_n U_n^{-1} V_n^{-1} = \bar{\omega} I$ so that $\|U_n V_n - V_n U_n\| = |1-\bar{\omega}| = 2 \sin \pi/n$ which tends to 0 as n increases.

Nevertheless, Voiculescu [26] was able to show that this pair was bounded away from pairs of commuting unitaries independent of n. Modifying an argument of Choi which we mention in Example 2, Loring was able to show that $\{U_n, V_n\}$ is bounded away from arbitrary commuting pairs independent of n. Finally, Exel and Loring [17] gave a very elementary argument to show that this pair is bounded away from all commuting pairs by at least $1/3$. Here is a brief sketch of their argument.

The multiplicative commutator $UVU^{-1}V^{-1}$ has determinant 1, so the path

$$f(t) = \det((1-t)I + tUVU^{-1}V^{-1}), \qquad 0 \le t \le 1$$

is a loop. Taking the pair U_n, V_n, one obtains a loop in $\mathbb{C}\backslash\{0\}$ with winding number -1 around 0. On the other hand, if $UV = VU$, this is the constant function so it has index 0. Now if U and V are unitaries for which there is a commuting pair A, B satisfying $\|U-A\| \le 1/3$ and $\|V-B\| \le 1/3$, a simple argument shows that the function f is homotopic in $\mathbb{C}\backslash\{0\}$ to a constant; thus it has index 0. Consequently, $\{U_n, V_n\}$ is not close to such a pair.

EXAMPLE 2. Consider the $n+1 \times n+1$ matrices

$$A_n = \begin{bmatrix} 0 & & & & \\ & \frac{1}{n} & & \bigcirc & \\ & & \frac{2}{n} & & \\ & \bigcirc & & \ddots & \\ & & & & 1 \end{bmatrix} \quad \text{and} \quad B_n = \begin{bmatrix} 0 & b_1 & & & \bigcirc \\ & 0 & b_2 & & \\ & & \ddots & \ddots & \\ & \bigcirc & & \ddots & b_n \\ & & & & 0 \end{bmatrix}$$

where $b_j = \frac{2}{n}[j(n+1-j)]^{1/2}$. The point is that A is diagonal with entries slowly increasing from 0 to 1; and B is a weighted shift with weights slowly increasing from 0 to 1 and back down to 0 again. It is easy to verify that $\|A_nB_n-B_nA_n\| < 1/n$ and $\|B_n^*B_n-B_nB_n^*\| \leq 4/n$.

The technique developed by Berg [4] for approximating weighted shifts by normal operators shows that B_n is asymptotically close to some sequence of normal matrices N_n. In [14], I showed that $\{A_n,B_n\}$ is bounded away by at least 1/10 from the commuting pairs $\{A,B\}$ in which $A = A^*$ but B is arbitrary. On the other hand, the pairs $\{A_n,\mathrm{Re}(B_n)\}$ and $\{A_n,\mathrm{Im}(B_n)\}$ $\{\mathrm{Re}(B_n),\mathrm{Im}(B_n)\}$ are each asymptotically close to commuting Hermitian pairs. Finally, Choi [11] gave an algebraic argument to show that the distance from $\{A_n,B_n\}$ to arbitrary commuting pairs tends to 1/2 as n increases.

One can get estimates that depend on n. Pearcy and Shields [22] show that if $A = A^*$ and B is arbitrary, then the distance to a commuting pair $\{A_1 = A_1^*,B_1\}$ is at most $(n-1/2)^{1/2}\|AB-BA\|^{1/2}$. Choi's argument above shows that this is sharp. Szarek [25] has used my methods to show that in the Hermitian case, the dependence on n is no worse than $O(n^{1/4})$.

On the positive side are certain <u>absorption</u> theorems. This means that if the pair $\{A,B\}$ is augmented to a pair $\{A\oplus C,B\oplus D\}$ in which C and D are appropriate commuting Hermitian matrices, then the extra "room" enables one to approximate this new pair by a commuting pair. We will state the results in the context of Problem 1', since it is in this form that they are applied.

In [14], I showed that if T is any matrix in M_n (or in $B(H)$), there is a normal matrix N in M_n with $\|N\| \leq \|T\|$ so that

$$\text{dist}(T \oplus N, \mathcal{N}\text{ormals}) \leq 75\|T^*T-TT^*\|^{1/2}.$$

In the infinite dimensional case, it can occur that $\|T^*T-TT^*\|$ is very small, but T is far from normals because of having non-zero Fredholm index. In this case, the normal operator N can be taken to have spectrum the disk of radius $\|T\|$. This effectively obliterates all index obstructions. It is quite conceivable that the same thing happens in some quantitative way in the finite dimensional case.

It is desirable to control the spectrum of N in terms of quantitative properties of T. The prototypical result of this kind is due to Berg and myself [5]: If T is a matrix in M_n with $\|T\| \leq R$ and $\|T^{-1}\| \leq r^{-1}$, then there is a normal matrix N in M_n with spectrum in the annulus $\{\lambda: r \leq |\lambda| \leq R\}$ such that

$$\text{dist}(T \oplus N, \mathcal{N}\text{ormals}) \leq 100\|T^*T-TT^*\|^{1/2}.$$

This result is the key to our "constructive", operator theoretic proof of the Brown-Douglas-Fillmore Theorem [10]: If T is an operator such that T^*T-TT^* is compact, and if $\text{ind}(T-\lambda I) = 0$ whenever $\lambda \notin \sigma_e(T)$, then there is a compact operator K such that $T-K$ is normal.

When the spectrum is "nice", such as an annulus, we obtain estimates of $\|K\|$ in terms of $\|T^*T-TT^*\|^{1/2}$. In order to deal with more complicated spectra, we use conformal mapping techniques which lose our explicit control on the norm. Nevertheless, we are able to prove the asymptotic result - namely $\|K\|$ tends to 0 as $\|T^*T-TT^*\|$ tends to zero, - subject to certain necessary quantitative conditions that keep $\sigma(T)$ close to the essential spectrum. It is precisely our inability to answer Problem 1 that forces this restriction on us.

The second problem is, ostensibly, the easiest of a whole class of problems about using unitary invariants to provide a lower bound on the distance between two operators.

PROBLEM 2. Compute the distance between the unitary orbits of two normal matrices.

Now a normal matrix M in M_k is determined up to unitary equivalence by its spectrum $\sigma(M) = \{\mu_1,\ldots,\mu_k\}$. More precisely, the unitary orbit $U(M) = \{UMU^*: U \text{ unitary}\}$ consists of all matrices of the diagonal form $\mathrm{diag}\{\mu_1,\ldots,\mu_k\}$ with respect to any orthonormal basis.

Let N be another normal matrix in M_k with spectrum $\sigma(N) = \{\nu_1,\ldots,\nu_k\}$. Recall that if N commutes with M, then they can be simultaneously diagonalized. This amounts to a pairing of the eigenvalues. One such pairing achieves the minimum difference (subject to the commutativity hypothesis)

$$\|M-N\| \geq \mathrm{spd}(N,M) \equiv \min_{\pi \in S_k} \max_{1\leq j\leq k} |\mu_j - \nu_{\pi(j)}| .$$

This minimum is called the spectral distance, which we denote by spd(N,M). This leads to an old conjecture:

PROBLEM 2'. Is $\mathrm{dist}(U(M),U(N)) = \mathrm{spd}(M,N)$?

There are many partial results for special cases. All are based on nice geometry of the spectra of M and N. It is easy to prove the conjecture for $k = 2$, but it remains unknown even for $k = 3$.

The earliest result is due to Weyl [27] in 1912. He verifies the conjecture for N and M Hermitian. Here is the basic idea. First, the optimal pairing is obtained by taking $\mu_1 \leq \mu_2 \leq \ldots \leq \mu_k$ and $\nu_1 \leq \nu_2 \leq \ldots \leq \nu_k$. Suppose $\mathrm{spd}(M,N) = d = \mu_j - \nu_j$. The following sketch illustrates $k = 6$, $j = 3$.

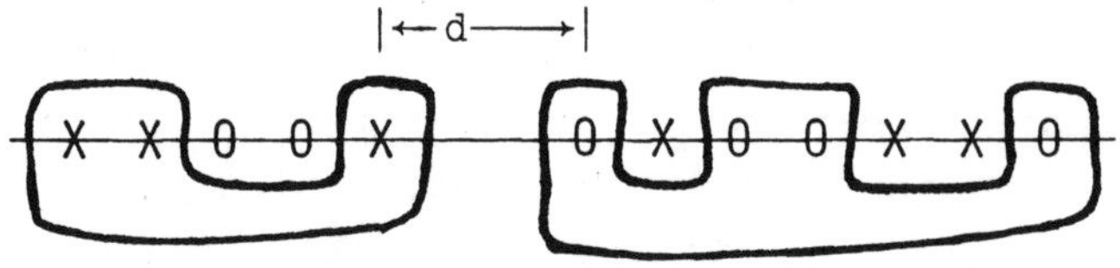

N 3-dim M 4-dim

Form the spectral subspace $\mathcal{N}$ for N corresponding to the eigenvalues $\{\nu_1,\dots,\nu_j\}$, and similarly form the spectral subspace $\mathcal{M}$ for M corresponding to $\{\mu_j,\dots,\mu_k\}$. As $\dim \mathcal{N} + \dim \mathcal{M} > k$, there must be a unit vector u in the intersection $\mathcal{N} \cap \mathcal{M}$. Now (Mu,u) is a convex combination of $\{\mu_j,\dots,\mu_k\}$ and hence exceeds μ_j. Likewise $(Nu,u) \le \nu_j$. Hence

$$\|M-N\| \ge ((M-N)u,u) \ge \mu_j-\nu_j = d.$$

Other results have more recently been obtained. Sunder [24] verified the conjecture for $M = M^*$ and $N = -N^*$. Bhatia and Davis [6] verified it for unitary matrices, and subsequently, Bhatia and Holbrook [7] verified the conjecture for scalar multiples of unitaries.

The deepest result on this problem is due to Bhatia, Davis and McIntosh [8]. They used a Fourier transform technique to establish the existence of a universal constant $C > 1/3$ such that

$$\text{dist}(\mathcal{U}(M),\mathcal{U}(N)) \ge C \text{ spd}(M,N).$$

Their argument is very pretty. Moreover, it does not use any special geometric considerations.

It is interesting to note that the spectral distance can be formulated for operators on Hilbert space. Azoff and Davis [3] extended Weyl's theorem, while I [13] extended the Bhatia, Davis, McIntosh theorem to the infinite dimensional context. Moreover, if $\sigma(N) = \sigma_e(N)$, (that is, N has no isolated eigenvalues of finite multiplicity), then $\text{dist}(\mathcal{U}(M),\mathcal{U}(N)) = \text{spd}(M,N)$. So the only obstruction to the conjecture in the infinite dimensional case is precisely the finite dimensional problem.

Finally, I mention a partial result of unknown significance due independently to Elsner and to Djokovic and myself, both unpublished. Recall that the singular value $s_k(A)$ is the k-th largest eigenvalue of $(A^*A)^{1/2}$. It is clear that the condition $s_2(A) < s_1(A)$ is generic. The conjecture 2' is equivalent to the following condition being generic among all pairs of unitary orbits of normal $k \times k$ matrices: There exist $M_0 \in \mathcal{U}(M)$ and $N_0 \in \mathcal{U}(N)$ such that

1) $\|M_0 - N_0\| = \mathrm{dist}(\mathcal{U}(M), \mathcal{U}(N))$
2) $s_2(M_0 - N_0) < s_1(M_0 - N_0)$.

The third problem deals with so-called "matrix filling" problems, which amount to computing the distance to subspaces of $\mathcal{M}_k$ determined by a set of non-zero matrix entries. I defer the actual problem that I have in mind to the end of the discussion.

The first result of this type is due to Krein [20]. The problem is to minimize the norm of the Hermitian matrix $\left\|\begin{bmatrix} A & B \\ B^* & X \end{bmatrix}\right\|$ by appropriate choice of X. Clearly, $\|[A\ B]\| = \|AA^* + BB^*\|^{1/2}$ is a lower bound. It turns out to be the precise answer. The general, non Hermitian analogue was solved by Parrot [21] and Davis, Kahan, Weinberger [16]. They showed that

$$\inf_X \left\|\begin{bmatrix} A & B \\ C & X \end{bmatrix}\right\| = \max\left\{\|[A\ B]\|,\ \left\|\begin{bmatrix} A \\ C \end{bmatrix}\right\|\right\}.$$

Moreover, the latter paper explicitly exhibits all possible X values achieving the minimum.

EXAMPLE 3. This result is a special case of a distance formula due to Arveson [2] for computing the distance to block upper triangular matrices (and more generally, to a nest subalgebra of $\mathcal{B}(\mathcal{H})$). Let $0 = \mathcal{M}_0 \subset \mathcal{M}_1 \subset \ldots \subset \mathcal{M}_k = \mathcal{H}$ be a finite chain of subspaces of a (finite dimensional) Hilbert space $\mathcal{H}$. Let $\mathcal{T}$ denote the algebra of all matrices which leave each $\mathcal{M}_j$ invariant - namely the block upper triangular matrices with respect to the given decomposition. If P_j is the orthogonal projection onto $\mathcal{M}_j$, then

$$\mathcal{T} = \{T:\ P_j^{\perp} T P_j = 0, \quad 1 \le j < k\} .$$

Arveson's distance formula states that for any matrix A,

$$\mathrm{dist}(A, \mathcal{T}) = \max_{1 \le j \le k} \|P_j^{\perp} A P_j\|.$$

The following proof, due to Power [23], shows the role of the 2×2 case already mentioned. Given A, one can think of $A-T$ for an unknown T in $\mathcal{T}$ as having the strictly lower triangular matrix entries fixed while the upper triangular entries remain to be chosen to our advantage. The quantity $\|P_j^{\perp}AP_j\|$ measures the norm of one of the maximal rectangles in this partially completed matrix. Consider the following diagram:

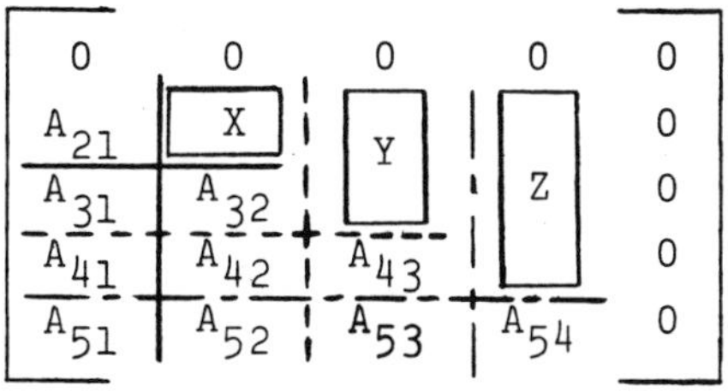

We can, arbitrarily, set the first row and last column to zero. Considering the first two columns as a partially completed 2×2 matrix, we can fill in X without increasing the norm of the maximal rectangles. Then with X fixed, we consider the first three columns as a 2×2 matrix with missing entry Y. Again, this is completed without increasing the norm. After k steps, the matrix is complete with norm $\max_{1\le j\le k} \|P_j^{\perp}AP_j\|$.

How general is this kind of result? For any subalgebra $\mathcal{A}$ of $\mathcal{M}_n$, let $\operatorname{Lat} \mathcal{A}$ denote the collection of invariant subspaces of $\mathcal{A}$. Dually, given a lattice $\mathcal{L}$ of subspaces, let $\operatorname{Alg} \mathcal{L}$ denote the set of matrices which leave each element of $\mathcal{L}$ invariant. An algebra $\mathcal{A}$ is said to be reflexive if $\mathcal{A} = \operatorname{Alg} \operatorname{Lat} \mathcal{A}$.

Fix a reflexive algebra $\mathcal{A}$. Let $T \in \mathcal{M}_n$, $A \in \mathcal{A}$ and $L \in \operatorname{Lat} \mathcal{A}$. Then

$$\|T-A\| \ge \|P_L^{\perp}(T-A)P_L\| = \|P_L^{\perp}TP_L\|.$$

Now take the sup over $\operatorname{Lat} \mathcal{A}$ and the inf over A in $\mathcal{A}$ to obtain

$$\operatorname{dist}(T,\mathcal{A}) \ge \sup_{L \in \operatorname{Lat} \mathcal{A}} \|P_L^{\perp}TP_L\| \equiv \beta_{\mathcal{A}}(T).$$

Since $\mathcal{M}_n$ is finite dimensional, and $\beta_{\mathcal{A}}$ is a seminorm with kernel precisely $\mathcal{A}$, the quantity $\beta_{\mathcal{A}}(T)$ is an equivalent measure of the distance. The <u>distance constant</u> for $\mathcal{A}$ is the smallest $C < \infty$ so that

$$\operatorname{dist}(T,\mathcal{A}) \le C\beta_{\mathcal{A}}(T)$$

for all T in $\mathcal{M}_n$. This constant is important even when it is not 1 as for the triangular algebras.

EXAMPLE 4. Fix an orthonormal basis $\{e_1,\dots,e_n\}$ for $\mathbb{C}^n$, and let $\mathcal{D}_n$ be the corresponding algebra of diagonal matrices. Then Lat $\mathcal{D}_n$ consists of $\{\mathcal{L}_\sigma = \operatorname{span}\{e_k : k \in \sigma\} : \sigma \in 2^n\}$ as σ runs over all subsets of $\{1,\dots,n\}$. Let P_σ be the corresponding orthogonal projection. Then

$$\operatorname{dist}(T,\mathcal{D}_n) \le 2 \sup_{\sigma\in 2^n} \|P_\sigma^\perp T P_\sigma\| .$$

To see this, let $U_\sigma = 2P_\sigma - I$. This is a self adjoint unitary - a symmetry. The set $\{U_\sigma : \sigma \in 2^n\}$ forms the group of diagonal matrices with ± 1 as entries. Compute

$$\begin{aligned} T-U_\sigma T U_\sigma^* &= (TU_\sigma - U_\sigma T)U_\sigma^* = 2(TP_\sigma - P_\sigma T)U_\sigma \\ &= 2(P_\sigma^\perp T P_\sigma - P_\sigma T P_\sigma^\perp)U_\sigma^* \end{aligned} .$$

This is a difference of two terms with orthogonal domains and ranges. Hence

$$\|T-U_\sigma T U_\sigma^*\| = 2 \max\{\|P_\sigma^\perp T P_\sigma\|, \|P_{\sigma^c}^\perp T P_{\sigma^c}\|\} \le 2\beta_{\mathcal{D}_n}(T).$$

Now average over the whole group. Set

$$A = 2^{-n} \sum_\sigma U_\sigma T U_\sigma^* .$$

One computes $AU_\tau = U_\tau A$ for all τ, whence $A \in \mathcal{D}_n$. Moreover, $\|T-A\| \le 2\beta_{\mathcal{D}_n}(T)$ and the proof is complete.

Next, I will show that $C > 1$ even for $n = 3$. Take $T = \begin{bmatrix} 1 & 1 & 1 \\ 1 & 1 & 1 \\ 1 & 1 & 1 \end{bmatrix}$. Then it is easy to see that $\beta_{\mathcal{D}_3}(T) = \sqrt{2}$. Any closest diagonal D can be replaced by any permutation of the basis entries. Averaging yields a scalar matrix λI as the closest diagonal matrix. Since $\sigma(T) = \{0,3\}$, we see that $\mathrm{dist}(T,\mathcal{D}_3) = 3/2$.

Christensen [12] has generalized the result above to all injective von Neumann algebras. It is unknown for more general von Neumann algebras.

Not all nice looking algebras have well behaved distance constants. Let $\mathcal{T}$ be the algebra of 2×2 upper triangular matrices. Set $\mathcal{T}^{(1)} = \mathcal{T}$, and for $n \geq 1$, set $\mathcal{T}^{(n+1)} = \mathcal{T}^{(n)} \otimes \mathcal{T}$ be the algebra of 2×2 upper triangular matrices with entries in $\mathcal{T}^{(n)}$ acting on $\mathbb{C}^{2^{n+1}}$ in the natural way. Power and I [15] showed that the distance constant for $\mathcal{T}^{(n)}$ tends to infinity with n.

The invariant subspace lattice of $\mathcal{T}^{(n)}$ has width n, meaning that it is generated by n commuting chains. So, in the limit, the "infinite tensor product" $\mathcal{T}^{(\infty)}$ has infinite width which may be a significant factor in its failure to have a distance formula. With this in mind, we consider the following test case of width 2 algebras. Let $\mathcal{T}_n$ be the algebra of $n\times n$ upper triangular matrices. Define $\mathcal{T}_n \otimes \mathcal{T}_n$ to be the subalgebra of M_{n^2} of $n\times n$ upper triangular matrices with entries in $\mathcal{T}_n$.

PROBLEM 3. Are the distance constants for $\mathcal{T}_n \otimes \mathcal{T}_n$ uniformly bounded for $n \geq 1$?

A positive solution will have a significant impact on the study of commutative subspace lattice (CSL) algebras, especially regarding similarity invariants, perturbations, etc., which required the distance formula in the analysis of the nest algebra case.

The last problem has become known as the paving problem. Naturally, the constant $1/2$ could be replaced by any ε in $(0,1)$.

PROBLEM 4. Is there an integer N so that:
Given $T = (t_{ij}) \in M_k$, $k \geq 1$ with $t_{ii} = 0$, $1 \leq i \leq k$ and $\|T\| \leq 1$, then there exist N <u>diagonal</u> projections $P_1,\dots,P_N$

with $\sum_{j=1}^{N} P_j = I$ and $\max_{1\le j\le N} \|P_j T P_j\| \le 1/2$.

This problem was introduced by Anderson [1]. It is equivalent to an old problem about C* algebras first studied by Kadison and Singer [19] and attributed by them to Segal and Kaplansky. Fix a diagonal algebra $\mathcal{D}$ with respect to an orthonormal basis $\{e_n, n \ge 1\}$ of a Hilbert space $\mathcal{H}$. Recall that a state is a positive linear functional φ on a C* algebra with $\varphi(1) = 1$. The extreme points of the set of all states are called pure states.

PROBLEM 4'. Does every pure state on $\mathcal{D}$ have a unique extension to $\mathcal{B}(\mathcal{H})$?

The algebra $\mathcal{D}$ is isomorphic to ℓ^∞, which has maximal ideal space equal to the Stone-Cech compactification of the positive integers. The multiplicative linear functionals are precisely the pure states. By the Hahn-Banach theorem (or actually by a theorem of Krein in this context), every state on $\mathcal{D}$ has an extension to a state on $\mathcal{B}(\mathcal{H})$. For a pure state, the extreme points of the set of possible extensions are pure. Let Δ denote the map of $\mathcal{B}(\mathcal{H})$ onto $\mathcal{D}$ which sends an operator T to its diagonal. Since this is a contractive positive map, one extension of a state φ is readily obtained by $\varphi \circ \Delta$.

Halperin, Kaftal and Weiss [18] gave another reformulation of this problem asking if $\mathcal{D}$ has the relative Dixmier property. Let $\mathcal{U}_d$ denote the unitary group of $\mathcal{D}$.

PROBLEM 4". For every T in $\mathcal{B}(\mathcal{H})$, is

$$\operatorname{conv}\{UTU^*: U \in \mathcal{U}_d\}^{-\|\cdot\|} \cap \mathcal{D}$$

nonempty? (where $^{-\|\cdot\|}$ denotes norm closure.)

Although many different attacks have been made on this problem, information is quite scarce. Halpern, Kaftal and Weiss have written several papers with partial results for specific classes of operators. An easy case is for T with $t_{ij} \ge 0$, where N = 4 will suffice.

A deep result was obtained by Bourgain and Tzafiri [9] for quite different reasons. They showed, using probabilistic methods, that there is an integer N so that: Given T in M_k, $k \geq 1$ with zero diagonal and $\|T\| = 1$, then there is one diagonal projection P such that rank $P \geq k/N$ and $\|PTP\| \leq 1/2$.

This implies that any dependence of N on k grows no worse than $O(\log k)$.

Radjavi has informed me that he considered the problem of finding arbitrary projections (not necessarily diagaonal). In this basis free version, one need only assume trace(T) = 0. He showed that there is an integer N so that one can always partition the identity into N orthogonal projections P_j with $\|P_j T P_j\| \leq 1/2$. However, he warns me that he has not written the argument out carefully. Unfortunately, this result is unlikely to have much bearing on the diagonal case.

In conclusion, let me say again that many infinite dimensional problems have important finite dimensional versions. Also, one need not be interested in infinite dimensions to be interested in this kind of dimension free analysis. It is also important in numerical analysis to have estimates of this kind.

REFERENCES

[1] J. Anderson, Extensions, restrictions and representations of states on C*-algebras, Trans. Amer. Math. Soc. 249 (1979), 303-329.

[2] W. Arveson, Interpolation problems in nest algebras, J. Func. Anal. 20 (1975), 208-233.

[3] E. Azoff and C. Davis, On distances between unitary orbits of self adjoint operators, Acta Sci. Math. (Szeged) 47 (1984), 419-439.

[4] I.D. Berg, On approximation of normal operators by weighted shifts, Mich. Math. J. 21 (1974), 377-383.

[5] I.D. Berg and K. Davidson, Almost commuting matrices and a quantitative version of the Brown, Douglas, Fillmore Theorem, preprint 1987.

[6] R. Bhatia and C. Davis, A bound for spectral variation of a unitary operator, Lin. Mult. Alg. 15 (1984), 71-76.

[7] R. Bhatia and J. Holbrook, Short normal paths and spectral variation, Proc. Amer. Math. Soc. 94 (1985), 377-382.

[8] R. Bhatia, C. Davis and A. McIntosh, Perturbations of spectral subspaces and solution of linear operator equations, Lin. Alg. Appl. 52/53 (1983), 45-67.

[9] J. Bourgain and L. Tzafriri, Invertibility of large submatrices with applications to the geometry of Banach spaces and harmonic analysis, Israel J. Math. 57 (1987), 137-224.

[10] L. Brown, R. Douglas and P. Fillmore, Unitary equivalence modulo the compact operators and extensions of C* algebras in "Proc. Conf. on Operator Theory", Lect. Notes Math 345, pp.58-128, Springer-Verlag, Berlin-New York-Heidelberg 1973.

[11] M.D. Choi, Almost commuting matrices need not be nearly commuting, Proc. Amer. Math. Soc. 102 (1988), 529-533.

[12] E. Christensen, Perturbations of operator algebras II, Indiana Univ. Math. J. 26 (1977), 891-904.

[13] K. Davidson, The distance between unitary orbits of normal operators, Acta Sci. Math. (Szeged) 50 (1986), 213-223.

[14] K. Davidson, Almost commuting Hermitian matrices, Math. Scand. 56 (1985), 222-240.

[15] K. Davidson and S. Power, Failure of the distance formula, J. London Math. Soc. (2)32 (1984), 157-165.

[16] C. Davis, W. Kahan and W. Weinberger, Norm preserving dilations and their applications to optimal error bounds, SIAM J. Numer. Anal. 19 (1982), 445-469.

[17] R. Exel and T. Loring, Assymptotically commuting unitary matrices, preprint 1988.

[18] H. Halpern, V. Kaftal and G. Weiss, The relative Dixmier property in discrete crossed products, J. Func. Anal., to appear.

[19] R. Kadison and I. Singer, Extensions of pure states, Amer. J. Math. 81 (1959), 547-564.

[20] M. Krein, The theory of self adjoint extensions of semi bounded Hermitian transformations and its applications, Mat. Sb. 20 (1947), 431-495; 21 (1947), 365-404 (in Russian).

[21] S. Parrott, On a quotient norm and the Sz. Nagy Foias lifting theorem, J. Func. Anal. 30 (1978), 311-328.

[22] C. Pearcy and A. Shields, Almost commuting matrices, J. Func. Anal. 33 (1979), 332-338.

[23] S. Power, The distance to the upper triangular operators, Math. Proc. Camb. Phil. Soc. 88 (1980), 327-329.

[24] V. Sunder, Distance between normal operators, Proc. Amer. Math. Soc. 84 (1982), 483-484.

[25] S. Szarek, On almost commuting Hermitian operators, preprint 1988.

[26] D. Voiculescu, Assymptotically commuting finite rank unitaries without commuting approximants, Acta. Sci. Math. (Szeged) 451 (1983), 429-431.

[27] H. Weyl, Der asymptotische Verteilunggesetz der Eigenwerte linearer partieller Differentialgleichungen, Math. Ann. 71 (1912), 441-479.

Pure Mathematics Department
University of Waterloo
Waterloo, Ontario
Canada N2L 3G1

Operator Theory:
Advances and Applications, Vol. 40

MATRICES WITH DISPLACEMENT STRUCTURE, GENERALIZED BEZOUTIANS, AND MOEBIUS TRANSFORMATIONS

Georg Heinig and Karla Rost

Dedicated to our teacher Professor I.Gohberg on occasion of his 60th birthday with admiration

Matrices are considered the entries of which fulfil a difference equation (called ω-structured matrices) and a class of generalized Bezoutians is introduced. It is shown that A is a generalized Bezoutian iff its inverse is ω-structured. This result generalizes the Gohberg/Semencul theorem and other facts concerning Toeplitz matrices.

1. INTRODUCTION

It is well-known and easily checked that the inverse of a Toeplitz matrix $[a_{i-j}]$ (or a Hankel matrix $[s_{i+j}]$) is not necessarily Toeplitz (Hankel) again. But it turned out that these inverses are Toeplitz-like (Hankel-like): They can be represented as product sum of Toeplitz and Hankel matrices. Such a representation is provided by the celebrated Gohberg/Semencul formula [GS]. It establishes the inverse matrix from its first and last columns. Other inversion formulas and related results were obtained by Gohberg/Krupnik [GK], the authors [HR1] and many others (see for example [BH],[T1],[T2],[BAS1]).

Lander [L] observed that matrices represented by the Gohberg/Semencul formula are just Bezoutian matrices, well-known from root separation problems, and he proved that the inverse of a nonsingular (Toeplitz or Hankel) Bezoutian is Toeplitz or Hankel.

The Gohberg/Semencul formula was generalized to the noncommutative (in particular block) case in [GH] by Gohberg and one of the authors. Inverses of block Hankel matrices turned out to be Bezoutians in the sense of Anderson/Jury [AJ] (see also [LT]). Recently it was shown by Tewodros and one of the authors [HT] that the inverse of an Anderson/Jury Bezoutian is block Hankel. Related results are contained in [BAS2] and [KK].

In the present paper we consider a class of structured matrices that contains the classes of block Hankel and Toeplitz matrices as special cases. On the other hand we introduce a generalized Bezoutian concept. The main aim is to show that the classical connection between structured matrices and Bezoutians remains to be true in the more general situation. The main tool of investigation in this paper will be Moebius transformations . A more direct approach will be offered in [HR3].

To be more precise we give now the definitions of the matrix classes under consideration. Throughout the paper Z will denote the algebra of all dxd matrices with complex entries and Z^{mxn} the space of mxn matrices with entries from Z. I will be the dxd unity matrix. For a given matrix $\omega = [\omega_{kl}] \in \mathbb{C}^{pxq}$ (k=0,...,p-1;l=0,...q-1) we denote by $Str_{mn}(\omega)$ or simply $Str(\omega)$ the class of matrices $A=[a_{ij}] \in Z^{mxn}$ (i=0,...,m-1;j=0,...,n-1) the entries of which fulfil the difference equations

$$\sum_{k=0}^{p-1} \sum_{l=0}^{q-1} a_{i-k,j-l}\,\omega_{kl} = 0 \qquad (1.1)$$

$$(i=p-1,\dots,m-1;\, j=q-1,\dots,n-1).$$

Let us note that $Str(\alpha\omega)=Str(\omega)$ for $\alpha\in\mathbb{C}$, $\alpha\neq 0$.

The matrices from $Str(\omega)$ will be called (block) matrices with an ω- displacement structure or ω-structured matrices. The class $Str(\omega)$ was introduced in [HR2]. Another concept of displacement structure (similar to our Bezoutian concept) was introduced in [LAK]. In the present paper we restrict ourselves to the case p=q=2, since the results we obtained for more general cases are not complete yet. Let us note, however, that some of the results can be generalized to the case rank ω =2.

Obviously for the choice $\omega = \omega_H := \begin{bmatrix} 0 & 1 \\ -1 & 0 \end{bmatrix}$ $Str(\omega)$ will be the class of block Hankel and for the choice $\omega = \omega_T := \begin{bmatrix} 1 & 0 \\ 0 & -1 \end{bmatrix}$ $Str(\omega)$ will be the class of block Toeplitz matrices. To define the class of ω-Bezoutians it is convenient to introduce some notation. For $A = [a_{ij}] \in Z^{mxn}$ we denote by $A(\lambda,\mu)$ the polynomial in two variables

$$A(\lambda,\mu) = \sum_{i=0}^{m-1} \sum_{j=0}^{n-1} a_{ij}\lambda^i \mu^j \qquad (1.2)$$

The variables λ and μ will be considered as complex parameters. Introducing block vectors

$$l(\lambda) = l_n(\lambda) := [\lambda^i I]_0^{n-1}, \qquad l_n(\infty) = [0,\dots,0,I]^T$$

(1.2) can be written in the form

$$A(\lambda,\mu) = l_m(\lambda)^T A l_n(\mu). \qquad (1.3)$$

It is convenient to define $A(\lambda,\mu)$ also for $\lambda=\infty$ or $\mu=\infty$ by (1.3). Identifying vectors from Z^n with column matrices from Z^{nx1} the definition above makes also sense for vectors.

The matrix $B \in Z^{mxn}$ will be called ω-Bezoutian if

$$\omega(\lambda,\mu)B(\lambda,\mu) = \sum_{i=1}^{p+q} g_i(\lambda)f_i(\mu) \qquad (1.4)$$

for some $g_i \in Z^{m+p-1}$, $f_i \in Z^{n+q-1}$. The class of all mxn ω-Bezoutians will be denoted by $Bez(\omega) = Bez_{mn}(\omega)$.

In the case of an Hermitian ω this concept was introduced in [LABK] and was used for solving root localization problems.

For $\omega = \omega_H$ we have $\omega(\lambda,\mu) = \lambda-\mu$, for $\omega = \omega_T$ we have $\omega(\lambda,\mu) = 1-\lambda\mu$. The corresponding Bezoutians will be called Hankel or Toeplitz Bezoutians, respectively. The classical Hankel are those ones with n=m, d=1, $f_1 = g_2$, $f_2 = -g_1$, the classical Toeplitz Bezoutians are those with n=m, d=1,

$$f_1(\lambda) = g_2(\lambda^{-1})\lambda^n, \quad f_2(\lambda) = -g_1(\lambda^{-1})\lambda^n.$$

The main result of our paper is the following one.

THEOREM 1.1. A nonsingular matrix A possesses an ω-displacement structure if and only if A^{-1} is an $\hat{\omega}$-Bezoutian, where

$$\hat{\omega} = \begin{bmatrix} 0 & 1 \\ 1 & 0 \end{bmatrix} \omega^T \begin{bmatrix} 0 & 1 \\ 1 & 0 \end{bmatrix}.$$

For the Toeplitz case the "only if" part follows from [GH] and the "if" part is contained in [HT]. However, we shall present below in Section 4 an alternative proof of the "if" part that is a little bit more instructive. Our approach of proving Theorem 1.1 consists in the reduction of the general case to the Toeplitz or Hankel case. This reduction will be carried out with the help of a class of matrices that is isomorphic to the class of Moebius transforms in the Riemann sphere $\mathbb{C}_\infty$. The corresponding transforms are related to the so-called Frobenius/Fischer transforms linking the algebraic moment problem with the geometric one (see [Ioh],[HR1]).

We conjecture that Theorem 1.1 remains to be true for arbitrary mxn matrices ω with rank$\omega = 2$. However, it is easily seen that the theorem fails for rank$\omega > 3$. For example, if $\omega = \mathrm{diag}(1,-2,1)$, then $A = \mathrm{diag}(1,2,\ldots,n)$ belongs to Str(ω), but A^{-1} is not Bezoutian-like. Let us furthermore remark that in the case of rank$\omega = 1$ the classes Str(ω) and Bez(ω) contain only matrices of low rank.

In the continuation [HR3] of the present paper the problem of inversion of ω-structured matrices will be considered in more detail. In particular, the Gohberg/Semencul, the Gohberg/Krupnik and other inversion formulas from [HR1] will be generalized. Moreover fast inversion algorithms will be presented.

The rest of the paper is built as follows. In Section 2 we introduce the concept of Moebius matrices and study Moebius transforms of ω-structured matrices. In that way a result from [HR1] will be generalized. In Section 3 the same transformations for Bezoutians are considered. The proof of Theorem 1.1 is contained in Section 4. Moreover some refinement of this result is presented.

2. MOEBIUS TRANSFORMS OF STRUCTURED MATRICES

We associate any complex 2x2 regular matrix $\varphi = \begin{bmatrix} a & c \\ b & d \end{bmatrix}$ with the Moebius function $\varphi(\lambda) = \frac{a\lambda + b}{c\lambda + d}$ mapping $\mathbb{C}_\infty := \mathbb{C} \cup \{\infty\}$ onto $\mathbb{C}_\infty$ and with the operator $M_n(\varphi) = M(\varphi)$ acting in Z^n according to the rule

$$(M_n(\varphi)x)(\lambda) := x(\varphi(\lambda))(c\lambda + d)^{n-1} \qquad (2.1)$$

The matrix of the operator $M_n(\varphi)$ with respect to the canonical basis in Z^n will also be denoted by $M_n(\varphi)$. Matrices of this form will be called Moebius matrices. Let us note some elementary facts.

PROPOSITION 2.1.

(1) The mapping $\varphi \longrightarrow M_n(\varphi)$ is a group isomorphism from $GL(\mathbb{C}^2)$ onto the class of Moebius matrices.

(2) The group of Moebius matrices is generated by matrices $M_n(\varphi)$ with φ of the following forms:

$$\text{(a) } \varphi = \begin{bmatrix} 1 & 0 \\ b & 1 \end{bmatrix} \quad \text{(b) } \varphi = \begin{bmatrix} a & 0 \\ 0 & 1 \end{bmatrix} \quad \text{(c) } \varphi = \begin{bmatrix} 0 & 1 \\ 1 & 0 \end{bmatrix}. \qquad (2.2)$$

(3) $M_n(\varphi)^T 1(\lambda) = 1(\varphi(\lambda))(c\lambda + d)^{n-1}$. (2.3)

Proof. (1) is easily verified; (2) follows from (1) and the fact that the φ of the forms (a),(b),(c) generate $GL(\mathbb{C}^2)$. Relation (3) follows from

$$1(\lambda)^T M_n(\varphi)x = x(\varphi(\lambda))(c\lambda + d)^{n-1}$$
$$= 1(\varphi(\lambda))^T x(c\lambda + d) . \quad \square$$

Throughout this paper ω will be the matrix

$$\omega = \begin{bmatrix} \alpha & \gamma \\ \beta & \delta \end{bmatrix} \in GL(\mathbb{C}^2).$$

Moebius matrices can be used to transform matrices with a certain ω-structure into matrices with another structure. This is the main result of this section.

THEOREM 2.1. The transformation

$$A \longrightarrow M_m(\varphi_1)^T A M_n(\varphi_2) \qquad (2.4)$$

in $Z^{m\times n}$ maps $Str(\omega)$ onto $Str(\omega')$ with

$$\omega' = \varphi_1^{-1} \omega \varphi_2^{-T} . \qquad (2.5)$$

We shall prove this theorem for rank one matrices from $Str(\omega)$ and show that these matrices form a complete system. Following this idea we have to describe the class of all rank one matrices in Str(ω).

PROPOSITION 2.2. The general form of a rank one matrix $A \in$ Str(ω) is given by

$$A = l(s)Rl(t)^T \qquad (2.6)$$

with $R \in Z$, rank $R = 1$, $s,t \in \mathbb{C}_\infty$ and $t = \xi(s)$, where

$$\xi(s) := -\frac{\gamma s + \delta}{\alpha s + \beta} \qquad \left(s = -\frac{\beta t + \delta}{\alpha t + \gamma}\right). \qquad (2.7)$$

Proof. We start with the proof for the scalar case $d=1$. Suppose that $A \in \mathbb{C}^{m\times n}$, rank $A = 1$ and $A = [\ b_i c_j\ ]$. Then by definition

$$\alpha b_i c_j + \beta b_{i-1} c_j + \gamma b_i c_{j-1} + \delta b_{i-1} c_{j-1} = 0. \qquad (2.8)$$

Now we have to distinguish different cases.

(1) Case: All b_i, c_i are nonzero. In this case we obtain from (2.8) $c_j/c_{j-1} = \xi(b_i/b_{i-1})$ for all i and j. Hence the ratios c_j/c_{j-1} and b_i/b_{i-1} are constants, say t and s. It follows that A has the form (2.6) with (2.7).

(2) Case: For some $j=k$, $c_k = 0$ and $c_{k-1} \neq 0$. In this case (2.8) implies, putting $j=k$,

$$\gamma b_i + \delta b_{i-1} = 0 \qquad (i=1,\dots,m-1) \qquad (2.9)$$

therefore

$$(\alpha b_i + \beta b_{i-1})c_j = 0 \quad (j=1,\dots,n-1). \qquad (2.10)$$

If $\alpha b_i + \beta b_{i-1} = 0$ for $i=1,\dots,m-1$ then (2.9) implies $b_i = 0$ for $i = 0,\dots,m-1$ and thus $A = 0$. Hence $c_j = 0$ for $j=1,\dots,n-1$. Consequently $c = [c_j]$ is a multiple of the first unit vector $l(0)$. For b_i we obtain from (2.9) that $b_i = (-\delta/\gamma)^i b_0$ if $\gamma \neq 0$ and $b_i = 0$ $(i=0,\dots,m-2)$ if $\gamma = 0$. In the first case $b = [b_i] = b_0 l(-\delta/\gamma)$, in the second one b is a multiple of $l(\infty)$. In both cases b is a multiple of $l(\xi^{-1}(0))$, which proves (2.6),(2.7).

(3) Case: $c_j = 0$ for $j=0,\ldots,k-1$ and $c_j \neq 0$ for $j=k,\ldots,n-1$. If $k<n-1$ then, in view of (2.8), $\alpha b_i + \beta b_{i-1} = 0$ for all i. By (2.9) we conclude $b_i = 0$ for all i. Consequently $k=n-1$. In this case c is a multiple of $l(\infty)$, and $\alpha b_i + \beta b_{i-1} = 0$ yields $b = \text{const}\ l(\xi^{-1}(\infty))$.

Analogously the corresponding cases for b can be considered, which completes the proof for the scalar case.

Let us consider now the general case. Suppose that $A \in \mathrm{Str}(\omega)$, $A = [B_i C_j^T]$, $B_i, C_j \in \mathbb{C}^d$. If b_{pi} denotes the p th component of B_i and c_{qj} the q th component of C_j then $A_{pq} := [b_{pi} c_{qj}]$ is a scalar rank one matrix from $\mathrm{Str}(\omega)$. Repeating the arguments above we conclude $A_{pq} = r_{pq} l(s_{pq}) l(t_{pq})^T$ for some $r_{pq} \in \mathbb{C}$, $s_{pq} \in \mathbb{C}_\infty$ and $t_{pq} = \xi(s_{pq})$. We have to show that the s_{pq} actually do not depend on p,q. In view of the special form of A_{pq} we have

$$r_{pq} = b_{p0} c_{q0} \tag{2.11}$$

Moreover, for $s_{pq}, t_{pq} \neq \infty$ we get, putting $i=1, j=0$ and $i=0, j=1$,

$$b_{p1} c_{q0} = r_{pq}\, s_{pq}\ , \quad b_{p0} c_{q1} = r_{pq}\, t_{pq}\ .$$

Taking (2.11) into account and the fact that $g_p = 0$ or $h_q = 0$ leads to $A_{pq} = 0$ we conclude that s_{pq} depends only on p and t_{pq} depends only on q. Thus $t_{pq} = t$, $s_{pq} = s$ and $A = l(s) R l(t)^T$, where $R = [r_{pq}]$. For $s_{pq} = \infty$ or $t_{pq} = \infty$ this representation is proved in similar way. □

The next proposition is a simple consequence of the relation (2.3).

PROPOSTION 2.3. Suppose that

$$A = l_m(s)Rl_n(t)^T, \quad \varphi_i = \begin{bmatrix} a_i & c_i \\ b_i & d_i \end{bmatrix} \in GL(\mathbb{C}^2) \quad (i=1,2).$$

Then

$$M(\varphi_1)^T A M(\varphi_2) = (c_1 s + d_1)^{m-1}(c_2 t + d_2)^{n-1} l(\varphi_1(s)) R l(\varphi_2(t))^T \tag{2.12}$$

PROOF OF THEOREM 2.1. In view of part (2) of Prop.2.1 it suffices to prove the theorem for φ_i being of one of the forms (2.2). Moreover, we may assume that one of the φ_i, say φ_2, is the identity. We start proving the theorem for rank one matrices $A \in Str(\omega)$ of the form (2.6). We have to show that $A' := M_m(\varphi_1)^T A \in Str(\omega')$ for

$$\omega' = \begin{bmatrix} \alpha' & \gamma' \\ \beta' & \delta' \end{bmatrix} = \varphi_1^{-1}\omega \quad .$$

We consider the 3 cases of (2.2).

(1) Case: φ_1 is given by (2.2),(a). By Prop.2.3 we have

$$A' = l(s')Rl(t)^T, \quad \omega' = \begin{bmatrix} \alpha & \gamma \\ \beta - b\alpha & \delta - b\gamma \end{bmatrix}$$

with $s' = s + b$. Furthermore,

$$t = -\frac{\gamma s + \delta}{\alpha s + \beta} = -\frac{\gamma(s' - b) + \delta}{\alpha(s' - b) + \beta} = -\frac{\gamma' s' + \delta'}{\alpha' s' + \beta'} .$$

Hence $A' \in Str(\omega')$, by Prop.2.2.

(2) Case: φ_1 is of the form (2.2),(b). In this case

$$A' = l(as)Rl(t)^T, \qquad \omega' = \begin{bmatrix} \alpha/a & \gamma/a \\ \beta & \delta \end{bmatrix} .$$

On the other hand $t = -(\gamma' s' + \delta)/(\alpha' s' + \beta)$ with $s' = as$, $\gamma' = \gamma/a$, $\alpha' = \alpha/a$. Thus $A' \in Str(\omega')$.

(3) Case: φ_1 is given by (2.2),(c). Applying again Prop.2.3 we get

$$A' = l(s^{-1})Rl(t)^T s^{m-1} \qquad \omega' = \begin{bmatrix} \beta & \delta \\ \alpha & \gamma \end{bmatrix}.$$

Since $t = -(\gamma/s' + \delta)/(\alpha/s' + \beta)$ with $s' = 1/s$ we conclude $A' \in Str(\omega')$.

Analogously one can show that $AM_n(\varphi_2) \in Str(\omega')$ with $\omega' = \omega\varphi_2^{-1}$ and φ_2 of the form (2.2). In that way we proved that rank one matrices from Str(ω) will be transformed by the transformation (2.4) into matrices from Str(ω'), where ω' is given by (2.5).

It remains to show that the system of rank one matrices is complete in Str(ω). It is well-known and easily checked that rank one block Hankel matrices form a complete system. Now we choose φ_1, φ_2 in such way that

$$\varphi_1 \omega \varphi_2^T = \omega_H \qquad (= [\begin{smallmatrix} 0 & 1 \\ -1 & 0 \end{smallmatrix}]).$$

Then the transformation (2.4) provides a one-to-one map from the class of rank one block Hankel matrices onto the class of rank one matrices in Str(ω). Taking into account that the space Str(ω) has the same dimension as Str(ω_H) we conclude the completeness of the rank one matrix system in Str(ω). □

From Theorem 2.1 it becomes clear that for any pair (ω, ω') and for fixed φ_1 there exists exactly one φ_2, up to a multiplicative constant, such that the transformation (2.4) maps Str(ω) onto Str(ω'). It seems to be of some interest to ask what can be done using only transformations $M(\varphi_i)$ with

$$\varphi_i = [\begin{smallmatrix} a_i & 0 \\ b_i & 1 \end{smallmatrix}] \qquad (\text{ i.e. } \varphi_i(\lambda) = a_i\lambda + b_i) \qquad (2.13)$$
$$(i=1,2)$$

In case that $\alpha \neq 0$ φ_1, φ_2 of the form (2.13) can be found by the LU-factorization of ω such that

$$\varphi_1 [\begin{smallmatrix} 1 & 0 \\ 0 & -1 \end{smallmatrix}] \varphi_2^T = \omega ,$$

in case that $\alpha = 0$ one can find φ_1, φ_2 satisfying

$$\varphi_1 [\begin{smallmatrix} 0 & 1 \\ -1 & 0 \end{smallmatrix}] \varphi_2^T = \omega .$$

Thus we obtain the following

COROLLARY 2.1. The class Str(ω) can be

transformed by means of transformations (2.13) onto the class of block Toeplitz matrices if $\alpha \neq 0$ and onto the class of block Hankel matrices if $\alpha = 0$.

Since Hankel matrices cannot be transformed into Toeplitz matrices in such a way the set of all Str(ω) splits into two subclasses. This fact will also be essential for the construction of inversion algorithms in [HR3].

Since the matrices $M(\varphi)$ with φ of the form (2.13) are upper triangular we conclude from Cor.2.1 that matrices $A \in \mathrm{Str}(\omega)$ are LU-equivalent (in the sense of [HR1],I,3.6) to Toeplitz matrices if $\alpha \neq 0$ and to Hankel matrices if $\alpha = 0$. In that way the results concerning generalized LU-factorization from [HR1] can readily be transmitted to matrices from Str(ω).

Theorem 2.1 enables us to generalize a result from [HR1] (Th.4.1,I). First we generalize this result from the scalar Hankel to the block Hankel case.

LEMMA 2.1. A transformation $A \longrightarrow C_1 A C_2$ ($C_1 \in Z^{mxm}$, $C_2 \in Z^{nxn}$ maps the class of mxn block Hankel matrices into itself if and only if for some $a,b \in Z$, $\varphi \in GL(\mathbb{C}^2)$

$$C_2 = D(a)M_n(\varphi) \quad \text{and} \quad C_1^T = D(b)M_m(\varphi) \qquad (2.14)$$

where $D(c) := \mathrm{diag}(c,\dots,c)$ (c=a or c=b). The map is onto iff a and b are nonsingular.

Proof. Suppose that

$$A = [\ s_{i+j}\ ]\ , \qquad s_i = [\ s_i^{pq}\ ]_1^d\ ,$$
$$C_k = [\ c_{kij}\ ]\ , \qquad c_{kij} = [\ c_{kij}^{pq}\ ]_1^d \qquad (k=1,2)$$

and define

$$A_{pq} := [\ s_{i+j}^{pq}\ ]_{i,j} \quad , C_{kpq} := [\ c_{kij}^{pq}\ ]_{i,j}\ .$$

Fix now p=P and q=Q. We choose matrices A for which $A_{pq} = 0$ for $p \neq P$ and $q \neq Q$ and apply the result for the scalar case ([HR1],Theorem 4.1,I). We conclude that

$$C_{2Qq} = b_{Qq} M(\varphi_q), \quad C_{1pP}^T = a_{pP} M(\varphi'_p)$$

for constants b_{Qq} and a_{Pp} and $\varphi'_p = \varphi_q$. Hence φ_q actually do not depend on p and q. This leads to a representation (2.14). □

THEOREM 2.2. Suppose that $\omega, \omega' \in GL(\mathbb{C}^2)$. A transformation $\Phi : A \longrightarrow C_1 A C_2$ ($C_1 \in Z^{m\times m}$, $C_2 \in Z^{n\times n}$) maps the class Str(ω) onto Str(ω') if and only if

$$C_2 = M_n(\varphi)D(a), \quad C_1^T = M_m(\omega\varphi^{-T}\omega'^{-1})D(b)$$

for some $a,b \in Z$ and $\varphi \in GL(\mathbb{C}^2)$. The map Φ is onto iff a and b are nonsingular.

Proof. The sufficiency part is a consequence of Theorem 2.1. The necessity part will be proved by reducing the general case to the case of Lemma 2.1.

Define $\psi = \omega\omega_H$, $\psi' = \omega'\omega_H$. Then $M(\psi)^T A$, $M(\psi')^T A'$ are Hankel if $A \in$ Str(ω), $A' \in$ Str(ω'). Moreover, $M(\psi^{-1})^T H \in$ Str(ω) if H is Hankel. Hence the transformation

$$H \longrightarrow M(\psi')^T C_1 M(\psi^{-1}) H C_2$$

maps block Hankel matrices into block Hankel matrices. By Lemma 2.1 there exist $\varphi \in GL(\mathbb{C}^2)$, $a,b \in Z$ such that

$$C_2 = M(\varphi)D(a) \text{ and } M(\psi')^T C_1 M(\psi^{-1}) = M(\varphi)^T D(b). \quad \square$$

3. MOEBIUS TRANSFORMATIONS OF BEZOUTIANS

In Subsection 3.1 we consider Moebius transforms of ω-Bezoutians. In 3.2 we generalize the classical Bezoutian concepts for the scalar case, 3.3 is dedicated to the case of Hermitian ω.

3.1. To begin with we give an equivalent definition of an ω-Bezoutian. Each $\omega = \begin{bmatrix} \alpha & \gamma \\ \beta & \delta \end{bmatrix} \in GL(\mathbb{C}^2)$ will be associated with the transformation $\nabla(\omega)$: $Z^{m\times n} \longrightarrow Z^{(m+1)\times(n+1)}$ defined by

$$\nabla(\omega)A := [\alpha a_{ij} + \beta a_{i-1,j} + \gamma a_{i,j-1} + \delta a_{i-1,j-1}]_{0}^{m}{}_{0}^{n} \quad (3.1)$$

where $A = [\, a_{ij}\,]_0^{m-1}{}_0^{n-1}$ and $a_{ij} := 0$ if $i \notin \{0,\dots,m-1\}$ or $j \notin \{0,\dots,n-1\}$.

LEMMA 3.1.

$$(\nabla(\omega)A)(\lambda,\mu) = \omega(\lambda,\mu)A(\lambda,\mu)\,. \quad (3.2)$$

The proof is straightforward. From Lemma 3.1 and the definition of an ω-Bezoutian we conclude

PROPOSITION 3.1. The matrix B is an -Bezoutian iff rank $\nabla(\omega)B \le 2$.

LEMMA 3.2. Suppose that $C \in \mathbb{C}^{m\times n}$, $\varphi_i = \begin{bmatrix} a_i & c_i \\ b_i & d_i \end{bmatrix} \in GL(\mathbb{C}^2)$ $(i=1,2)$ and

$$C' := M_m(\varphi_1)CM_n(\varphi_2)^T.$$

Then

$$C'(\lambda,\mu) = C\,(\varphi_1(\lambda),\varphi_2(\mu))(c_1\lambda+d_1)^{m-1}(c_2\mu+d_2)^{n-1}. \quad (3.3)$$

Proof. By definition and Prop.2.1,(3) we have

$$\begin{aligned} C'(\lambda,\mu) &= 1_m(\lambda)^T M_m(\varphi_1)CM_n(\varphi_2)^T 1_n(\mu) \\ &= 1_m(\varphi_1(\lambda))^T C 1_n(\varphi_2(\mu))(c_1\lambda+d_1)^{m-1}(c_2\mu+d_2)^{n-1} \\ &= C(\varphi_1(\lambda),\varphi_2(\mu))(c_1\lambda+d_1)^{m-1}(c_2\mu+d_2)^{n-1}\,. \;\square \end{aligned}$$

From Lemma 3.2 we get the following assertion.

LEMMA 3.3. Let C and φ_i as in Lemma 3.2 and

$$\hat{\varphi}_i := j\varphi_i^T j\,, \quad \omega' := \hat{\varphi}_1^T \omega \hat{\varphi}_2 \qquad \left(j := \begin{bmatrix} 0 & 1 \\ 1 & 0 \end{bmatrix} \right).$$

Then

$$M_{m+1}(\varphi_1)(\nabla(\omega)C)M_{n+1}(\varphi_2)^T = \nabla(\omega')(M_m(\varphi_1)CM_n(\varphi_2)^T) \quad (3.4)$$

Proof. Denoting $C' := M_{m+1}(\varphi_1)(\nabla(\omega)C)M_{n+1}(\varphi_2)^T)$ we have according to (3.2) and (3.3)

$$C'(\lambda,\mu) = \omega(\varphi_1(\lambda),\varphi_2(\mu))C(\varphi_1(\lambda),\varphi_2(\mu))(c_1\lambda+d_1)^m * \\ *(c_2\mu+d_2)^n.$$

By applying Lemma 3.2 we obtain

$$\begin{aligned} C'(\lambda,\mu) &= \omega(\varphi_1(\lambda),\varphi_2(\mu))(c_1\lambda+d_1)(c_2\mu+d_2)(M(\varphi_1)CM(\varphi_2)^T(\lambda,\mu) \\ &= \omega'(\lambda,\mu)(M(\varphi_1)CM(\varphi_2)^T)(\lambda,\mu) \ , \end{aligned}$$

where

$$\omega' = M_2(\varphi_1)\omega M_2(\varphi_2)^T.$$

It remains to remark that $M_2(\varphi_i) = j\varphi_i j$ (i=1,2), thus $\omega' = j\varphi_1 j\omega j\varphi_2^T j$. □

THEOREM 3.1. The transformation

$$B \longrightarrow M_n(\varphi_1)BM_m(\varphi_2)^T \qquad (3.5)$$

maps the class of mxn ω-Bezoutians onto the class of ω'-Bezoutians, where $\omega' = \hat{\varphi}_1^T \omega \hat{\varphi}_2$. Moreover, if

$$B(\lambda,\mu) = \frac{1}{\omega(\lambda,\mu)} \sum_{i=1}^{2} g_i(\lambda)f_i(\mu)$$

and $B' = M(\varphi_1)BM(\varphi_2)^T$, then

$$B'(\lambda,\mu) = \frac{1}{\omega'(\lambda,\mu)} \sum_{i=1}^{2} (M(\varphi_1)g_i)(\lambda)(M(\varphi_2)f_i)(\mu).$$

The theorem is an immediate consequence of (3.4) and Prop.3.1.

Mappings of the form (3.5) will be called Moebius transformations of Bezoutians. From Theorem 3.1 one may easily deduce the statements from [HR1],I,4.4 concerning Hankel and Toeplitz Bezoutians.

3.2. In this subsection we consider only the scalar case d=1. Our aim is to generalize the classical Hankel and Toeplitz Bezoutian concepts. Recall that a Hankel

Bezoutian B in the classical sense is given by

$$B(\lambda,\mu) = (g(\lambda)f(\mu) - f(\lambda)g(\mu))/(\lambda-\mu).$$

The nxn matrix B is called the Hankel Bezoutian of g and f. For $\omega = \begin{bmatrix} \alpha & \gamma \\ \beta & \delta \end{bmatrix}$, let η denote the matrix $\begin{bmatrix} -\gamma & \delta \\ -\alpha & \beta \end{bmatrix}$. We introduce the notation $g^{\#}(\lambda) := (M_n(\eta)g)(\lambda)$ for vectors $g \in \mathbb{C}^n$. In particular, for $\omega = \omega_H$ we have $g^{\#} = g$. The transformation $g(\lambda) \longrightarrow g^{\#}(\lambda)$ is called polynomial reflection. Let us point out that $g^{\#}(\lambda)$ depends (in general) not only on ω but also on n.

DEFINITION. For $g, f \in \mathbb{C}^{n+1}$ the nxn matrix B with the generating function

$$B(\lambda,\mu) = (g(\lambda)f^{\#}(\mu) - f(\lambda)g^{\#}(\mu))/\omega(\lambda,\mu) \tag{3.6}$$

will be called the (classical) ω-Bezoutian of $g(\lambda)$ and $f(\lambda)$ (or of the vectors g and f) and will be denoted by $\mathrm{Bez}_\omega(g,f)$.

For Hermitian ω this Bezoutian concept was introduced in [LABK]. Let us point out that the definition of $\mathrm{Bez}_\omega(g,f)$ depends on n, in general. For example, in the Toeplitz case $\omega = \begin{bmatrix} 1 & 0 \\ 0 & -1 \end{bmatrix}$ we have $B(\lambda,\mu) = \mu^{n-1}$ for $B = \mathrm{Bez}_\omega(1,\lambda)$.

In order to show that the definition makes sense we have to prove that the right-hand side of (3.6) is in fact a polynomial. For this it suffices to verify that the numerator vanishes for all (λ,μ) for which $\omega(\lambda,\mu) = 0$. The latter condition is equivalent to $\lambda = \eta(\mu)$. After this substitution we get for the numerator

$$g(\eta(\mu))f^{\#}(\mu) - f(\eta(\mu))g^{\#}(\mu) = 0.$$

Thus (3.6) defines in fact a Bezoutian.

Now we study Moebius transforms of classical

Bezoutians.

PROPOSITION 3.2. For $\varphi_1, \varphi_2 \in GL(\mathbb{C}^2)$

$$M_n(\varphi_1)Bez_\omega(g,f)M_n(\varphi_2)^T = Bez_{\omega'}(g',f'),$$

where $\omega' = \varphi_1^T\omega\varphi_2$ and

$$g' = \frac{1}{\det\varphi_1} M_{n+1}(\varphi_1)g , \quad f' = M_{n+1}(\varphi_1)f$$

Proof. We denote

$$B := Bez_\omega(g,f) \quad \text{and} \quad B' := M_n(\varphi_1)BM_n(\varphi_2)^T.$$

By Theorem 3.1 B' is an ω'-Bezoutian and

$$\omega'(\lambda,\mu)B'(\lambda,\mu) = g_1(\lambda)f_1(\mu) - g_2(\lambda) f_2(\mu) ,$$

where

$$g_1 = M(\varphi_1)g, \quad g_2 = M(\varphi_1)f, \quad f_1 = M(\varphi_2)f^{\#}, \quad f_2 = M(\varphi_2)g^{\#}.$$

In order to show that B' is classical we have to clarify what is polynomial reflection with respect to ω', i.e. we have to evaluate the matrix η' corresponding to ω'.

By definition

$$\eta = j\,\omega^T\begin{bmatrix} -1 & 0 \\ 0 & 1 \end{bmatrix} \quad \text{and} \quad \eta' = j\,\omega'^T\begin{bmatrix} -1 & 0 \\ 0 & 1 \end{bmatrix}.$$

Since $\omega' = j\varphi_1 j\omega j\varphi_2^T j$ we conclude

$$\eta' = \varphi_2 j\,\omega^T j\,\varphi_1^T j\begin{bmatrix} -1 & 0 \\ 0 & 1 \end{bmatrix} = \varphi_2\eta\varphi_1^{-1}\det\varphi_1.$$

Hence

$$M(\eta')g_1 = M(\varphi_2\eta)g \det\varphi_1 = \det\varphi_1 f_2, \; M(\eta')g_2 = \det\varphi_1\, f_1.$$

We obtain

$$\omega'(\lambda,\mu)B'(\lambda,\mu) = \frac{1}{\det\varphi_1}(g_1(\lambda)(M(\eta')g_2)(\mu) - g_2(\lambda)(M(\eta')g_1)(\mu)).$$

Thus $B'(\lambda,\mu) = Bez_{\omega'}(g',f')$. □

In all what follows let spec(g) denote the projective spectrum of $g(\lambda)$, $g \in \mathbb{C}^n$, i.e. the set of all complex roots of $g(\lambda)$ inclusively ∞ if the highest order coefficient of $g(\lambda)$ vanishes. From the properties of the

Hankel Bezoutian we can conclude the following fact.

COROLLARY 3.1. The matrix $Bez_\omega(g,f)$ is nonsingular if and only if $spec(g) \cap spec(f)$ is empty.

Next we show that any Bezoutian can be reduced in some sense to a classical one. This reduction is based on the following

LEMMA 3.4. Suppose that B is an ω-Bezoutian,

$$\omega(\lambda,\mu)B(\lambda,\mu) = g_1(\lambda)f_1(\mu) + g_2(\lambda)f_2(\mu), \qquad (3.7)$$

and let one of the following conditions be fulfilled:

(a) B is square and $spec(g_1) \cap spec(g_2) = \emptyset$

(b) $spec(f_1) \cap spec(f_2) = spec(g_1) \cap spec(g_2) = \emptyset$.

Then B is classical, $B = \varepsilon\, Bez_\omega(g_1,g_2)$ for some $\varepsilon \in \mathbb{C}$.

Proof. Since $\omega(\eta(\mu),\mu) = 0$ we have $g_1^\#(\mu)f_1(\mu) - g_2^\#(\mu)f_2(\mu) = 0$. Hence $g_1^\#(\mu)/g_2^\#(\mu) = -f_2(\mu)/f_1(\mu)$. If now (a) or (b) is fulfilled we get $f_2 = -\varepsilon g_1^\#$, $f_1 = \varepsilon g_2^\#$ and $\omega(\lambda,\mu)B(\lambda,\mu) = \varepsilon(g_1(\lambda)g_2^\#(\mu) - g_2(\lambda)g_1^\#(\mu))$.

For the formulation of the next proposition we introduce some notation. For $h = [\, h_i \,]_0^r \in \mathbb{C}^{r+1}$ we denote by $D_p(h)$ the matrix

$$D_p(h) = \left.\begin{bmatrix} h_0 & h_1 & \dots & h_r & & 0 \\ & h_0 & h_1 & \dots & h_r & \\ & & \ddots & \ddots & & \ddots \\ 0 & & & h_0 & h_1 & \dots & h_r \end{bmatrix}\right\} p \; .$$

Then $D_p(h)^T$ is the matrix of the operator of multiplication by $h(\lambda)$. For $g_1, g_2 \in \mathbb{C}^n$ the notation $gcd(g_1,g_2)$ will mean the vector of coefficients of the greatest common divisor of $g_1(\lambda)$ and $g_2(\lambda)$ supplemented with s zeros if s denotes the common multiplicity of ∞ provided that ∞ is a common zero of $g_1(\lambda)$ and $g_2(\lambda)$, i.e. $d = gcd(g_1,g_2)$ means that $d(\lambda)$ is the g.c.d. of $g_1(\lambda)$ and $g_2(\lambda)$ and $d \in \mathbb{C}^k$, $k = \deg d + s$.

PROPOSITION 3.3. Let B be an mxn ω-Bezoutian defined by (3.7) and let

$$h_1 := \gcd(g_1, g_2), \quad h_2 := \gcd(f_1, f_2),$$
$$g(\lambda) := g_1(\lambda)/h_1(\lambda), \quad f(\lambda) := g_2(\lambda)/h_2(\lambda).$$

Then, for some $\varepsilon \in \mathbb{C}$,

$$B = \varepsilon D_p(h_1)^T \mathrm{Bez}_\omega(g,f) D_q(h_2). \tag{3.8}$$

Proof. Suppose $g_i(\lambda) = g_i^o(\lambda)h_1(\lambda)$, $f_i(\lambda) = f_i^o(\lambda)h_2(\lambda)$ then

$$\omega(\lambda,\mu)B(\lambda,\mu) = h_1(\lambda)(g_1^o(\lambda)f_1^o(\mu) + g_2^o(\lambda)f_2^o(\mu))h_2(\mu).$$

It remains to apply Lemma 3.4. □

COROLLARY 3.2. Any nonsingular Bezoutian is classical.

3.3. Let us discuss in more detail the case of Hermitian ω (i.e. $\alpha, \delta \in \mathbb{R}$, $\bar{\beta} = \gamma$) and Hermitian matrices $A \in \mathrm{Str}(\omega)$ (or $B \in \mathrm{Bez}(\omega)$). In the Toeplitz case ω is already Hermitian, for the Hankel case we get an Hermitian ω replacing ω_H by $\begin{bmatrix} 0 & \sqrt{-1} \\ -\sqrt{-1} & 0 \end{bmatrix}$. We denote the class of Hermitian matrices in $\mathrm{Str}(\omega)$, $\mathrm{Bez}(\omega)$ by $\mathrm{Str}^*(\omega)$, $\mathrm{Bez}^*(\omega)$, respectively.

We ask for transformations $A \longrightarrow C^*AC$ mapping $\mathrm{Str}^*(\omega)$ into $\mathrm{Str}^*(\omega')$. This problem can also be formulated in the language of quadratic forms. Let us call forms $A(x,x) = x^*Ax$ for $A \in \mathrm{Str}^*(\omega)$ ω-forms. So we ask for transformations of coordinates for which ω-forms go over into ω'-forms. An immediate consequence of Theorem 2.2 is

PROPOSITION 3.4. The transformation Φ: $A \longrightarrow C^*AC$

($A,C \in \mathbb{C}^{n\times n}$) maps $Str^*(\omega)$ into (onto) $Str^*(\omega')$ iff $C = M(\varphi)$ for some $\varphi \in GL(\mathbb{C}^2)$ and $\omega = \varepsilon\varphi\omega'\varphi^*$, where ε is a nonzero real.

COROLLARY 3.3. Φ maps $Str^*(\omega)$ onto itself iff, for some $\varepsilon \in \mathbb{C}$, $\varepsilon\varphi$ is ω-unitary.

COROLLARY 3.4. For given Hermitian ω and $\omega' \in GL(\mathbb{C}^2)$ there exists a transformation Φ mapping $Str^*(\omega)$ onto $Str^*(\omega')$ iff ω and ω' are both definite or both indefinite.

For Hermitian $\omega \in GL(\mathbb{C}^2)$ we define

$$K_\omega := \{ \lambda \in \mathbb{C} : \omega(\lambda, \bar{\lambda}) = 0 \}.$$

It is easily verified that K_ω is empty if ω is definite. In case that ω is indefinite K_ω represents just a circle with centre $-\bar{\beta}/\delta$ and radius $\sqrt{|\beta|^2 - \alpha\delta}/|\delta|$ if $\delta \neq 0$ or a straight line if $\delta = 0$. In the Toeplitz case K_ω is the unit circle, in the Hankel case K_ω is the real axis. We show now how K_ω changes by transforming ω.

LEMMA 3.5. Let $\omega, \omega' \in GL(\mathbb{C}^2)$ be Hermitian and $\omega = \varphi\,\omega'\varphi^*$. Then $\mu \in K_{\omega'}$ iff $\varphi(\mu^{-1})^{-1} \in K_\omega$.

Proof. We have $\mu \in K_\omega$ iff

$$0 = \omega(\mu, \bar{\mu}) = [\ 1 \ \ \mu\ ]\varphi\omega'\varphi^*[\ \tfrac{1}{\bar{\mu}}\ ]. \tag{3.9}$$

Let $\varphi = [\begin{smallmatrix} a & c \\ b & d \end{smallmatrix}]$, then (3.9) means

$$0 = [\ a + b\mu \quad c + d\mu\ ]\,\omega'[\ \begin{smallmatrix} \bar{a} + \bar{b}\bar{\mu} \\ \bar{c} + \bar{d}\bar{\mu} \end{smallmatrix}\ ]$$

which is equivalent to

$$\omega'(\ \varphi(\mu^{-1})^{-1}\ ,\ \overline{\varphi(\mu^{-1})^{-1}}) = 0,$$

i.e. equivalent to $\varphi(\mu^{-1})^{-1} \in K_{\omega'}$. □

The curve K_ω uniquely determines the class $Bez(\omega)$. Therefore, we could (as Lev-Ari/Bistritz/Kailath [LABK] do) speak of K_ω-Bezoutians instead of ω-Bezoutians.

A consequence of Theorem 2.1 is the following statement.

COROLLARY 3.5. Let $\psi(\lambda) = (a\lambda + b)/(c\lambda + d)$ transform $K_{\omega'}$ onto K_ω and let $\psi = \begin{bmatrix} a & c \\ b & d \end{bmatrix}$. Then the transformation $A \longrightarrow M(\varphi)^* AM(\varphi)$ with $\varphi = j\psi j$ maps $Str^*(\omega)$ onto $Str^*(\omega')$.

By means of Cor.3.5 the root localization theorems for the real line (Hermite theorem) and the unit circle (Schur/Cohn theorem) can be generalized to arbitrary circles and straight lines. This is contained in [LABK]. Furthermore, theorems of Jacobi/Borchardt type could be generalized.

4. INVERSES OF STRUCTURED MATRICES AND BEZOUTIANS

The main aim of this section is the proof of Theorem 1.1. The proof will be carried out in 4.2 according to the "tea pot principle", i.e. the reduction to the Hankel case. For this case the "only if" part is quite well-known from [GH]. A proof of the "if" part is contained, in principle, in [HT], but we present an alternative proof in 4.1. In 4.3 we give a more precise description of the inverses of structured matrices generalizing the corresponding facts for Hankel matrices. For simplicity we restrict ourselves in 4.3 to the scalar case. However, all arguments can readily be generalized to the block case.

4.1. THEOREM 4.1. If B is a nonsingular block Hankel Bezoutian then B^{-1} is block Hankel.

For the proof we need the following

LEMMA 4.1. Let $G_1, G_2, F_1, F_2 \in Z$ be such that

(a) $G_1 F_1 + G_2 F_2 = 0$

(b) $[\ G_1 \quad G_2\ ],\ [\ F_1 \quad F_2\ ]^T$ have full rank.

Then there exists a matrix $C \in Z^{2x2}$ satisfying

$$C = \begin{bmatrix} * & F_1 \\ * & F_2 \end{bmatrix}, \qquad C^{-1} = \begin{bmatrix} G_1 & G_2 \\ * & * \end{bmatrix} \tag{4.1}$$

Proof. Choose $U_1, U_2, V_1, V_2 \in Z$ such that

$$M := \begin{bmatrix} G_1 & G_2 \\ U_1 & U_2 \end{bmatrix}, \quad N := \begin{bmatrix} V_1 & F_1 \\ V_2 & F_2 \end{bmatrix}$$

are nonsingular. Then

$$MN = \begin{bmatrix} R_1 & 0 \\ R_0 & R_2 \end{bmatrix}$$

with nonsingular $R_1, R_2 \in Z$. This implies

$$\begin{bmatrix} I & 0 \\ 0 & R_2^{-1} \end{bmatrix} MN \begin{bmatrix} R_1^{-1} & 0 \\ -R_2^{-1} R_0 R_1^{-1} & I \end{bmatrix} = \begin{bmatrix} I & 0 \\ 0 & I \end{bmatrix}.$$

Introducing $X_i := R_2^{-1} U_i$, $Y_i := V_i R_1^{-1} - F_i R_2^{-1} R_0 R_1^{-1}$ $(i=1,2)$ this can be written in the form

$$\begin{bmatrix} G_1 & G_2 \\ X_1 & X_2 \end{bmatrix} \begin{bmatrix} Y_1 & F_1 \\ Y_2 & F_2 \end{bmatrix} = \begin{bmatrix} I & 0 \\ 0 & I \end{bmatrix}.$$

It remains to put

$$C := \begin{bmatrix} Y_1 & F_1 \\ Y_2 & F_2 \end{bmatrix}. \quad \square$$

Proof of Theorem 4.1. We assume that

$$\nabla(\omega_H) B = g_1 f_1^T + g_2 f_2^T \tag{4.2}$$

with $g_i, f_i \in Z^{n+1}$ $(i=1,2)$. Let $G_i \in Z$ denote the last component of g_i and F_i that one of f_i^T. We intend to show that there is a representation (4.2) with $G_1 = F_2 = I$, $G_2 = F_1 = 0$.

By definition of $\nabla(\omega_H)$,

$$G_1 F_1 + G_2 F_2 = 0 .$$

Furthermore, $L := G_1 f_1^T + G_2 f_2^T$ is the last row of B. Since L has full rank the matrix $[\ G_1 \quad G_2\ ]$ has also full rank.

Analogously $[\ F_1\ \ F_2\ ]^T$ has full rank. By Lemma 4.1 there exists a matrix C satisfying (4.1). We put now

$$[\ \tilde{g}_1\ \ \tilde{g}_2\ ] := [\ g_1\ \ g_2\ ]C\ ,\ [\ \tilde{f}_1\ \ \tilde{f}_2\ ]^T = C^{-1}[\ f_1\ f_2\ ]^T.$$

Then we have

$$\tilde{g}_1\tilde{f}_1^T + \tilde{g}_2\tilde{f}_2^T = g_1 f_1^T + g_2 f_2^T$$

and, for the last components $\tilde{G}_i, \tilde{F}_i$ of g_i, f_i^T,

$$[\ \tilde{G}_1\ \ \tilde{G}_2\ ] = [\ I\ 0\ ]\ ,\ [\ \tilde{F}_1\ \ \tilde{F}_2\ ]^T = [\ 0\ I\ ]^T.$$

In that way we constructed a representation (4.2) with $G_1 = F_2 = I$, $G_2 = F_1 = 0$.

Suppose

$$g_1 = [\ {g_1' \atop I}\ ],\ g_2 = [\ {g_2' \atop 0}\ ],\quad f_1^T = [\ f_1'^T\ 0\ ],\ f_2^T = [\ f_2'^T\ I].$$

Then

$$\nabla(\omega_H)B = \begin{bmatrix} g_1' f_1'^T + g_2' f_2'^T & g_2' \\ f'^T & 0 \end{bmatrix} \tag{4.3}$$

and $f_1'^T = e^T B$, $g_2' = -Be$ with $e := [\ 0\ \dots\ 0\ I\ ]^T$. Cancelling in (4.3) the last row and the last column we obtain

$$BS^T - SB = g_1' f_1'^T + g_2' f_2'^T ,$$

where S denotes the block down shift. Applying B^{-1} from both sides we conclude

$$S^T B^{-1} - B^{-1} S = xe^T + ey^T$$

for some $x, y \in Z^n$. This implies that B^{-1} is block Hankel.

4.2. PROOF OF THEOREM 1.1. Put $\varphi := \omega\omega_H$. Then $H := M(\varphi)^T A$ is block Hankel for all $A \in Str(\omega)$ according to Theorem 2.1. If now A is nonsingular then $H^{-1} = A^{-1}M(\varphi^{-1})^T$ is a (block) Hankel Bezoutian. Applying Theorem 3.1 we conclude that $A^{-1} = H^{-1}M(\varphi)^T$ belongs to $Bez(\omega')$, where

$$\omega' = \omega_H \hat{\varphi} = \omega_H j(\omega\omega_H)^T j = j\,\omega^T j = \hat{\omega}\,.$$

Hence $A^{-1} \in Bez(\hat{\omega})$. Using the same arguments in reverse order and applying Theorem 4.1 we obtain $B^{-1} \in Str(\omega)$ if B Bez($\hat{\omega}$).

4.3. In all what follows we consider the scalar case $Z = \mathbb{C}$.

There are different possiblities for the construction of the inverse of a Toeplitz matrix. The Gohberg/Semencul formula provides a construction of the inverse from its first and last columns, the Gohberg/Krupnik formula from its first two columns. Other approaches use so-called fundamental solutions [HR1]. The most natural approach seems to be, in our opinion, the construction with the help of solutions of a certain associated homogeneous equation. Let us formulate this result for the Hankel case.

PROPOSITION 4.1. Let $H = [\ s_{i+j}\ ]_0^{n-1}$ be non-singular and H' the (n-1)x(n+1) Hankel matrix

$$H' = [\ s_{i+j}\ ]_{0}^{n-2}\ {}_{0}^{n} \qquad (4.4)$$

and let {u,v} be a basis of ker H'. Then

$$H^{-1} = \varepsilon\, Bez(u,v) \quad , \qquad (4.5)$$

where $\varepsilon \in \mathbb{C}$ and "Bez" denotes the Hankel Bezoutian.

This result is in principle contained in [HR1] and explicitly formulated in [Ab]. In [HR1] one can see that formula (4.5) implies all classical inversion formulas.

Now we are going to generalize Prop.4.1 to ω-structured matrices. First of all we generalize the transformation $H \rightarrow H'$. For this we adopt some notational conventions. Suppose $\omega = [\begin{smallmatrix} \alpha & \gamma \\ \beta & \delta \end{smallmatrix}]$. If A is an mxn matrix then A_1, A_2 will denote the (m-1)xn matrices defined by

$$A = [\begin{smallmatrix} A_1 \\ * \end{smallmatrix}] = [\begin{smallmatrix} * \\ A_2 \end{smallmatrix}].$$

Now we introduce a linear transformation $\partial : Str_{mn}(\omega) \longrightarrow Str_{m-1,n+1}(\omega)$ as follows. If $A = [\ a_{ij}\ ]$, $A' = \partial A = [\ a'_{ij}\ ]$ then

$$\begin{aligned} a'_{ij} &:= \beta a_{ij} + \alpha a_{i+1,j} \quad (j=0,\dots,n-1; i=0,\dots,m-2) \\ a'_{in} &:= -\gamma a_{i+1,n-1} - \delta a_{i,n-1} \quad . \end{aligned} \tag{4.6}$$

It is easily checked that in fact $A' \in Str(\omega)$ and

$$a'_{ij} = -\gamma a_{i+1,j-1} - \delta a_{i,j-1} \quad (j=1,\dots,n;\ i=0,\dots,m-2).$$

This can be written in the form

$$A' = [\ \alpha A_2 + \beta A_1 \quad *\ ] = [\ * \quad -\gamma A_2 - \delta A_1\ ].$$

Obviously, for $\omega = \omega_H$ ∂A will be just the matrix defined by (4.4).

THEOREM 4.2. If $A \in Str(\omega)$ is nonsingular then dim ker $\partial A = 2$. Let $\{u,v\}$ be a basis of ker A then

$$A^{-1} = \varepsilon \, Bez_{\hat{\omega}}(u,v)$$

for some $\varepsilon \in \mathbb{C}$, $\varepsilon \neq 0$.

The proof rests on the following two lemmas. The first one is technical, the second one seems to be of independent interest. It shows that Moebius transformations intertwine with the transformation ∂ .

LEMMA 4.2. Let $A \in Str(\omega)$ be of the form $A = 1_m(s)1_n(t)^T$ where $s,t \neq \infty$. Then

$$A' = (\alpha s + \beta) 1_{m-1}(s) 1_{n-1}(t)^T . \tag{4.7}$$

Proof. According to the definition we have for $A' = [\ a'_{ij}\ ]$

$$\begin{aligned} a'_{ij} &= \beta a_{ij} + \alpha a_{i+1,j} = \beta s^{i-1} t^{j-1} + \alpha s^i t^{j-1} \\ &= (\alpha s + \beta) a_{ij} \qquad (i=0,\dots,m-2;\ j=0,\dots,n) \end{aligned}$$

and

$$a'_{in} = -\gamma a_{i+1,n-1} - \delta a_{i,n-1} = -\gamma s^i t^{n-2} - \delta s^{i-1} t^{n-2}$$
$$= -(\gamma s + \delta) t^{-1} a_{in}.$$

Since in view of Prop.2.2 $t = \xi(s) := -(\gamma s + \delta)/(\alpha s + \beta)$ we conclude (4.7). □

LEMMA 4.3. Let A be an mxn ω-structured matrix, $\varphi_1, \varphi_2 \in GL(\mathbb{C}^2)$ and $C := M_m(\varphi_1)^T A M_n(\varphi_2)$. Then

$$C' = M_{m-1}(\varphi_1)^T A' M_{n+1}(\varphi_2). \tag{4.8}$$

Proof. Repeating the arguments of the proof of Theorem 2.1 we restrict ourselves to the case of a rank one matrix A , φ_2 being of the form (2.2) and φ_1 being the identity. We consider the 3 cases of (2.2).

(1) Case: φ_1 is of the form (2.2),(a). According to Prop.2.1 (3)

$$C = M_m(\varphi_1)^T 1_m(s) 1_n(t)^T = 1_m(s+b) 1_n(t)^T \in Str(\tilde{\omega}),$$

where

$$\tilde{\omega} = \begin{bmatrix} \alpha & \gamma \\ \beta - \alpha b & \delta - \gamma b \end{bmatrix}.$$

Hence, in view of (4.7) and (2.3),

$$C' = (\alpha s + \beta) 1_{m-1}(s+b) 1_{n+1}(t)^T.$$

On the other hand, by (4.7),

$$M_{m-1}(\varphi_1)^T A' = (\alpha s + \beta) 1_{m-1}(s+b) 1_{n+1}(t)^T ,$$

which proves (4.8).

(2) Case: φ_1 is of the form (2.2),(b). In this case

$$C = 1_m(as) 1_n(t)^T \in Str(\tilde{\omega}), \quad \tilde{\omega} = \begin{bmatrix} \alpha/a & \gamma/a \\ \beta & \delta \end{bmatrix}$$

and, on the other hand,

$$M_{m-1}(\varphi_1)^T A' = (\alpha s + \beta) 1_{m-1}(as) 1_{n+1}(t)^T$$

which proves (4.8).

(3) Case: φ_1 is of the form (2.2),(c). In this case

$$C = 1_m(s^{-1})1_n(t)^T s^{m-1} \in \mathrm{Str}(\tilde{\omega}), \quad \tilde{\omega} = \begin{bmatrix} \beta & \delta \\ \alpha & \gamma \end{bmatrix}$$

and

$$M_{m-1}(\varphi_1)^T A' = (\alpha s + \beta) 1_{m-1}(s^{-1}) 1_n(t)^T s^{m-1} (\beta s^{-1} + \alpha).$$

Thus (4.8) is proved in all 3 cases. □

Proof of Theorem 4.2. Put $\varphi = -\omega\omega_H$. Then $H = M_n(\varphi)^T A$ is Hankel, by Theorem 2.1, and $\partial H = M_{n-1}(\varphi)^T \partial A$ according to Lemma 4.3. Hence $\ker \partial H = \ker \partial A$, in particular $\dim \ker \partial A = 2$. Let now $\{u,v\}$ be a basis of $\ker \partial A$. Then according to Prop.4.1

$$H^{-1} = \varepsilon \,\mathrm{Bez}(u,v) = A^{-1} M_n(\varphi^{-1})^T.$$

Applying Theorem 3.1 we conclude

$$A^{-1} = \varepsilon \,\mathrm{Bez}(u,v) M_n(\varphi)^T = \varepsilon \,\mathrm{Bez}_{\omega'}(u,v),$$

where

$$\omega' = \omega_H \hat{\varphi} = \omega_H j \,\omega_H \omega^T j = \hat{\omega} \;. \;\square$$

Let us note that there are many possibilities for evaluating the constant ε occuring in Theorem 4.2. Let us describe a general approach. Choose two vectors $p,q \in \mathbb{C}^n$ satisfying $p^T q \neq 0$. Denoting $f := A^T p$, $g := \mathrm{Bez}_{\hat{\omega}}(u,v)q$ we obtain $f^T g \neq 0$ and $\varepsilon = p^T q \,/\, f^T g$. Special convenient choices for p and q are unit vectors. More discussion on inversion formulas can be found in [HR3].

REFERENCES

[Ab] Abukov,V.M., Kernel structure and the inversion of Toeplitz and Hankel matrices. (in Russian) Izvestija vuzov (Mat.) 7 (290),1986, 3-8.

[AJ] Anderson,B. and Jury,E., Generalized Bezoutian and Sylvester matrices in multivariable linear control. IEEE Trans.on a.c., AC-21,4 (1976),551-556.

[BH] Baxter, G. and Hirschman,I.I., An explicit inversion formula for finite-section Wiener-Hopf operators. Bull.AMS 70 (1964), 820-823.

[BAS1] Ben-Artzi,A. and Shalom,T., On inversion of Toeplitz and close to Toeplitz matrices. Linear Algebra and Appl.75 (1986), 173-192.

[BAS2] - " -, On inversion of block Toeplitz matrices. Int. Equ. and Op.Theory 8,6 (1985), 751-779.

[GH] Gohberg,I. and Heinig,G., Inversion of finite Toeplitz matrices composed of elements of a non-commutative algebra. (in Russian) Rev. Roumaine Math. Pures and Appl.19,5 (1974), 623-663.

[GK] Gohberg,I. and Krupnik,N.Ja., A formula for the inversion of finite-section Toeplitz matrices. (in Russian) Mat.Issled. 7,2 (1972), 272-284.

[GS] Gohberg,I. and Semencul,A.A., On inversion of finite-section Toeplitz matrices and their continuous analogues. (in Russian) Mat.Issled. 7,2 (1972), 201-224.

[HR1] Heinig,G. and Rost,K., Algebraic methods for Toeplitz-like matrices and operators. Akademie-Verlag, Berlin 1984 and Operator theory, Vol.13, Birkhäuser Basel 1984.

[HR2] - " - , On the inverses of Toeplitz-plus-Hankel matrices. Lin.Alg.and Appl.(to appear 1988)

[HR3] - " - , Inversion of matrices with displacement structure (to appear)

[HT] Heinig,G. and Tewodros,A., On the inverse of Hankel and Toeplitz mosaic matrices. Seminar Analysis, Teubner-Verlag Leipzig (to appear 1989).

[Ioh] Iohvidov,I.S., Hankel and Toeplitz matrices and

forms. Birkhäuser Basel 1982.

[KK] Kailath,T. and Koltracht,I., Matrices with block Toeplitz inverses. Lin.Alg.and Appl. 75 (1986),145-153.

[L] Lander,F.I., The Bezoutian and the inversion of Hankel and Toeplitz matrices. Mat.Issled. 9,2 (1974), 69-87.

[LT] Lerer,L. and Tismenetsky,M., Generalized Bezoutian and the inversion problem for block Toeplitz matrices. Int.Equ. and Op.Theory 9,6 (1986), 790-819.

[LABK] Lev-Ari,H., Bistritz,Y. and Kailath,T., Generalized Bezoutians and families of efficient root-location procedures. IEEE Trans. on Circ. and Syst.(to appear)

[LAK] Lev-Ari,H. and Kailath T., Triangular factorization of structured Hermitian matrices. Operator Theory, Vol.18, Birkhäuser Basel 1986.

[T1] Trench, W.F., An algorithm for the inversion of finite Toeplitz matrices. SIAM J.Appl.Math. 12 (1964), 515-522.

[T2] - " - , A note on Toeplitz inversion formulas. (to appear)

Technische Universität Karl-Marx-Stadt
Sektion Mathematik
Postfach 964
Karl-Marx-Stadt
DDR-9010
German Democratic Republic

Operator Theory:
Advances and Applications, Vol. 40

GENERALIZED GOHBERG-SEMENCUL FORMULAS FOR MATRIX INVERSION

T. Kailath and J. Chun

Dedicated to Israel Gohberg with admiration and appreciation.

We give a constructive and elementary proof of the Gohberg-Semencul formula for the inverse of a Toeplitz matrix. Our approach suggests a natural generalization of the formula to matrices with displacement structure.

1. INTRODUCTION.

In 1972, Gohberg and Semencul [10] published some striking formulas for the inverse of a Toeplitz matrix, which we shall further elaborate and extend. First we note that the results of [10] became more generally known to English-speaking readers with the publication of the monograph [7, Chap 3, pp. 86-99], which also presents several extensions of the results in [10]. Secondly, on closer examination it became clear that (at least) some of the Gohberg-Semencul formulas were "integrated" or "summed" versions of certain recursions of Trench [19] for the elements of the inverses of (symmetric) Toeplitz matrices; also that the polynomial form of these recursions were essentially the Christoffel-Darboux formulas for the Szego polynomials orthogonal on the unit circle (see [14], where the continuous analog of these formulas was also noted to be what is known as Sobolev's resolvent identity in radiative transfer theory.) Finally, we note that by now the Gohberg-Semencul formulas are widely known and often used and cited; a noteworthy application has been to $O(n \log^2 n)$ algorithms for solving Toeplitz linear equations [2], [3].

Though Gohberg and Semencul considered more general Toeplitz matrices, we shall start with Hermitian positive-definite Toeplitz matrices,

This work was supported in part by the Air Force Office of Scientific Research, Air Force Systems Command under Contract AF83-0228 and the U.S. Army Research Office, under Contract DAAL03-86-K-0045.

$$\mathbf{T} = (\, c_{i-j} \,) \in C^{n \times n}, \qquad c_0 = 1, \qquad c_{-i} = \bar{c}_i, \tag{1}$$

where the bar denotes the complex conjugate. Assume that we have the Cholesky factorization of $\mathbf{T}^{-1}$,

$$\mathbf{T}^{-1} = \mathbf{U}\mathbf{U}^*, \qquad \mathbf{U} \equiv \begin{bmatrix} a_{0,0} & a_{1,1} & \cdot & a_{n-1,n-1} \\ & a_{1,0} & \cdot & a_{n-1,n-2} \\ & & \cdot & \cdot \\ & & & \cdot \\ & & & a_{n-1,0} \end{bmatrix}, \tag{2}$$

where the superscript * denotes conjugate transpose. Then, among other expressions, Gohberg and Semencul showed that $\mathbf{T}^{-1}$ could be written as

$$\mathbf{T}^{-1} = \mathbf{L}(\mathbf{a}^{\#})\mathbf{L}^*(\mathbf{a}^{\#}) - \mathbf{L}(\mathbf{a})\mathbf{L}^*(\mathbf{a}), \tag{3}$$

where $\mathbf{L}(\mathbf{a})$ and $\mathbf{L}(\mathbf{a}^{\#})$ are lower triangular Toeplitz matrices whose first columns are

$$\mathbf{a} \equiv [0, a_{n-1,n-1}, \cdots, a_{n-1,1}]^T \qquad \mathbf{a}^{\#} \equiv [\bar{a}_{n-1,0}, \bar{a}_{n-1,1}, \cdots, \bar{a}_{n-1,n-1}]^T,$$

where the superscript T denotes the transpose. Among other interesting consequences, the expression (3) shows that $\mathbf{T}^{-1}$ is completely determined by the last column of $\mathbf{T}^{-1}$.

Products of the form $\mathbf{LU}$, where $\mathbf{L}$ and $\mathbf{U}$ denote lower and upper-triangular matrices, respectively, have a nice nesting property: the submatrix composed of the first m rows and columns is just (in an obvious notation) $\mathbf{L}_m \mathbf{U}_m$. Using this remark, it is not hard to see that (3) implies the following recursive formula,

$$[\mathbf{T}^{-1}]_{i+1,j+1} = [\mathbf{T}^{-1}]_{i,j} + \bar{a}_{n-1,i}a_{n-1,j} - a_{n-1,n-i}\bar{a}_{n-1,n-j}, \qquad 1 \le i, j \le n-1, \tag{4}$$

which was in fact first derived by Trench [19] in 1964. Moreover, if we associate $\mathbf{T}^{-1}$ with the *generating function*

$$K_{n-1}(z,x) \equiv \sum_{i=0}^{n-1}\sum_{j=0}^{n-1}[\mathbf{T}^{-1}]_{i+1,j+1}z^i\bar{x}^j,$$

then (2) shows that

$$K_{n-1}(z,x) = \sum_{i=0}^{n-1} A_i(z)\bar{A}_i(x),$$

where

$$A_i(z) \equiv a_{i,0}z^i + a_{i,1}z^{i-1} + \cdots + a_{i,i}, \qquad 0 \le i \le n-1.$$

Furthermore, as noted by Kailath, Vieira and Morf [14], (4) yields the Christoffel-Darboux formula [6, p. 3], [11, p. 41],

$$K_{n-1}(z,x)(1-z\bar{x}) = A_{n-1}^{\#}(z)\bar{A}_{n-1}^{\#}(x) - z\bar{x}A_{n-1}(z)\bar{A}_{n-1}(x),$$

where $A_{n-1}^{\#}(z)$ is the *reverse polynomial* $A_{n-1}^{\#}(z) \equiv z^n \bar{A}_{n-1}(z^{-1})$.

Gohberg and Semencul also derived various generalizations of the formula (3), e.g., to non-Hermitian Toeplitz matrices with only $\mathbf{T} \in C^{n \times n}$ and its first leading principal submatrix being nonsingular, alternate forms corresponding to forms of the Christoffel-Darboux formula based on $\mathbf{T} \in C^{(n+1)\times(n+1)}$, and forms corresponding to "backwards" summation of the recursions (4). Their proofs were completely algebraic.

The present contribution grew out of our studies on constructive algorithms [4] for fast triangular and orthogonal factorizations of matrices given in a so-called displacement representation (see [13]). We discovered that one of these constructions not only gave a Gohberg-Semencul formula for the inverse of a Toeplitz matrix, but also indicated a natural method of extending the formulas to general non-Toeplitz matrices.

The *displacement* of a matrix $\mathbf{A} \in C^{n \times n}$ has been defined as [13]

$$\nabla \mathbf{A} \equiv \mathbf{A} - \mathbf{Z}_n \mathbf{A} \mathbf{Z}_n^*,$$

where $\mathbf{Z}_n$ is the $n \times n$ lower shift matrix with ones on the first subdiagonal and zeros everywhere else. Suppose that $\nabla \mathbf{A}$ is expressed as a sum of outer products,

$$\nabla \mathbf{A} = \sum_{i=1}^{\alpha} \mathbf{x}_i \mathbf{y}_i^*.$$

Then it is easy to see, using the nilpotency of $\mathbf{Z}_n$, that $\mathbf{A}$ can be written as a sum of products,

$$\mathbf{A} = \sum_{i=1}^{\alpha} \mathbf{L}(\mathbf{x}_i)\mathbf{L}^*(\mathbf{y}_i), \tag{5}$$

where as before $\mathbf{L}(\mathbf{x})$ denotes a lower triangular Toeplitz matrix with the first column $\mathbf{x}$. The expression in (5) is called the *displacement representation* of $\mathbf{A}$. For Hermitian matrices we can refine this to the form,

$$\mathbf{A} = \sum_{i=1}^{p} \mathbf{L}(\mathbf{x}_i)\mathbf{L}^*(\mathbf{x}_i) - \sum_{i=p+1}^{p+q} \mathbf{L}(\mathbf{x}_i)\mathbf{L}^*(\mathbf{x}_i). \tag{6}$$

For a simple example, consider a Hermitian Toeplitz matrix, $\mathbf{T} = (c_{i-j})$, $c_0 = 1$. Then we can see that

$$\nabla \mathbf{T} = \mathbf{T} - \mathbf{Z}_n \mathbf{T} \mathbf{Z}_n^* = \begin{bmatrix} 1 & \bar{c}_1 & \cdot & \cdot & \bar{c}_n \\ c_1 & & & & \\ \cdot & & & & \\ c_n & & & & \end{bmatrix} = \mathbf{x}_1\mathbf{x}_1^* - \mathbf{x}_2\mathbf{x}_2^*,$$

where

$$\mathbf{x}_1 = [\, 1, c_1, \cdots, c_n \,]^T, \quad \mathbf{x}_2 = [\, 0, c_1, \cdots, c_n \,]^T.$$

It follows, as noted in (6), that

$$\mathbf{T} = \mathbf{L}(\mathbf{x}_1)\mathbf{L}^*(\mathbf{x}_1) - \mathbf{L}(\mathbf{x}_2)\mathbf{L}^*(\mathbf{x}_2). \tag{7}$$

The fact that the Gohberg-Semencul formula (3) for $\mathbf{T}^{-1}$ has a similar form as (7) is not an accident. In fact, it was shown in [13] that if the matrix $\mathbf{A}$ has the form (5), then $\tilde{\mathbf{I}}\mathbf{A}^{-1}\tilde{\mathbf{I}}$ (where $\tilde{\mathbf{I}}$ is the matrix with ones on the reverse-diagonal and zeros elsewhere) has the representation,

$$\tilde{\mathbf{I}}\mathbf{A}^{-1}\tilde{\mathbf{I}} = \sum_{i=1}^{\alpha} \mathbf{L}(\mathbf{x}_i)\mathbf{L}^*(\mathbf{y}_i), \qquad \text{or} \quad \mathbf{A}^{-1} = \sum_{i=1}^{\alpha} \mathbf{L}^*(\mathbf{x}_i)\mathbf{L}(\mathbf{y}_i) \tag{8}$$

with certain vectors $\{\mathbf{x}_i, \mathbf{y}_i\}$. (We may note that if we insist on a lower-upper type representation for $\mathbf{A}^{-1}$, we can always obtain this but with $\alpha + 2$ terms in general). The formula (8) would be a generalization of the Gohberg-Semencul formula to arbitrary matrices, except that the proof in [13] did not show how to actually construct a displacement representation of $\tilde{\mathbf{I}}\mathbf{A}^{-1}\tilde{\mathbf{I}}$ or $\mathbf{A}^{-1}$ from a displacement representation of $\mathbf{A}$.

This construction will be supplied in this paper for a large class of matrices, and in principle for all matrices. To do so, we shall first generalize in Sec 2, the earlier notion of displacement representation. Then we shall show that a certain partial triangularization procedure of the 2×2 block matrix,

$$\mathbf{A} = \begin{bmatrix} \mathbf{A}_{1,1} & \mathbf{A}_{1,2} \\ \mathbf{A}_{2,1} & \mathbf{A}_{2,2} \end{bmatrix}, \quad \mathbf{A}_{1,1} = \text{strongly nonsingular}, \tag{9}$$

easily yields a displacement representation of the so called Schur-complement of $\mathbf{A}_{1,1}$, i.e., a representation

$$\mathbf{A}_{2,2} - \mathbf{A}_{2,1}\mathbf{A}_{1,1}^{-1}\mathbf{A}_{1,2} = \sum_{i=1}^{p} \mathbf{L}(\mathbf{x}_i)\mathbf{L}^*(\mathbf{y}_i) - \sum_{i=p+1}^{p+q} \mathbf{L}(\mathbf{x}_i)\mathbf{L}^*(\mathbf{y}_i).$$

As an example, we shall obtain the Gohberg-Semencul formula for a Toeplitz matrix by applying the procedure to the block matrix

$$\mathbf{A} = \begin{bmatrix} \mathbf{T} & \mathbf{I} \\ \mathbf{I} & \mathbf{O} \end{bmatrix},$$

where the Schur complement of $\mathbf{T}$ is just $-\mathbf{T}^{-1}$. Then in Sec 3, we shall apply the procedure in Sec 2 to various matrices, e.g.,

$$\begin{bmatrix} \mathbf{T}^*\mathbf{T} & \mathbf{I} \\ \mathbf{I} & \mathbf{O} \end{bmatrix}, \quad \begin{bmatrix} \mathbf{T}_1 & \mathbf{T}_2 \\ \mathbf{T}_2^* & \mathbf{O} \end{bmatrix}, \quad \begin{bmatrix} \mathbf{T}^*\mathbf{T} & \mathbf{T}^* \\ \mathbf{T} & \mathbf{I} \end{bmatrix}, \quad \begin{bmatrix} \mathbf{T}^*\mathbf{T} & \mathbf{T}^* \\ \mathbf{I} & \mathbf{O} \end{bmatrix},$$

to obtain *generalized Gohberg-Semencul formulas,* or, equivalently, *displacement representations,* of the matrices,

$$(\mathbf{T}^*\mathbf{T})^{-1}, \quad \mathbf{T}_2^*\mathbf{T}_1^{-1}\mathbf{T}_2, \quad \mathbf{T}(\mathbf{T}^*\mathbf{T})^{-1}\mathbf{T}^*, \quad (\mathbf{T}^*\mathbf{T})^{-1}\mathbf{T}^*.$$

2. GENERALIZED DISPLACEMENT REPRESENTATIONS AND SCHUR COMPLEMENTS.

First, we shall generalize the concept of displacement representation, and then give a fast triangularization algorithm for a certain 2×2 block matrix. During the triangularization procedure, displacement representations for the Schur complement of the (1, 1) block will naturally arise.

The following sum-of-products representation of a matrix $\mathbf{A} \in C^{m \times n}$ is called a (generalized) *displacement representation* of $\mathbf{A}$ with respect to the *displacement operators* $\{\mathbf{F}_1, \mathbf{F}_2\}$:

$$\mathbf{A} = \sum_{i=1}^{\alpha} \mathbf{K}_n(\mathbf{x}_i, \mathbf{F}_1)\mathbf{K}_n^*(\mathbf{y}_i, \mathbf{F}_2),$$

where $\mathbf{F}_1 \in C^{n \times n}$ and $\mathbf{F}_2 \in C^{n \times n}$ are nilpotent matrices of index less than or equal to n, i.e., $\mathbf{F}_1^n = \mathbf{F}_2^n = \mathbf{O}$, and $\mathbf{K}_n(\mathbf{x}_i, \mathbf{F}_1) \in C^{m \times n}$ and $\mathbf{K}_n(\mathbf{y}_i, \mathbf{F}_2) \in C^{n \times n}$ are the so called Krylov matrices,

$$\mathbf{K}_n(\mathbf{x}_i, \mathbf{F}_1) \equiv [\mathbf{x}_i, \mathbf{F}_1\mathbf{x}_i, \ldots, \mathbf{F}_1^{n-1}\mathbf{x}_i], \quad \mathbf{K}_n(\mathbf{y}_i, \mathbf{F}_2) \equiv [\mathbf{y}_i, \mathbf{F}_2\mathbf{y}_i, \ldots, \mathbf{F}_2^{n-1}\mathbf{y}_i].$$

The matrix pair, $\{ \mathbf{X}, \mathbf{Y} \}$, where $\mathbf{X} \equiv [\mathbf{x}_1, \mathbf{x}_2, \ldots, \mathbf{x}_\alpha]$ and $\mathbf{Y} \equiv [\mathbf{y}_1, \mathbf{y}_2, \ldots, \mathbf{y}_\alpha]$ is called a *generator* of $\mathbf{A}$ (with respect to $\{\mathbf{F}_1, \mathbf{F}_2\}$), and is denoted $G_\alpha(\mathbf{A}, \mathbf{F}_1, \mathbf{F}_2)$. The number α is called the *length* of the generator (with respect to $\{\mathbf{F}_1, \mathbf{F}_2\}$). A generator of $\mathbf{A}$ with the minimal possible length is called a *minimal* generator. The length of the minimal generator of $\mathbf{A}$ is called the *displacement rank* of $\mathbf{A}$ (with respect to $\{\mathbf{F}_1, \mathbf{F}_2\}$), and denoted as $\alpha(\mathbf{A}, \mathbf{F}_1, \mathbf{F}_2)$.

If the matrix $\mathbf{A}$ is Hermitian, then $\mathbf{A}$ can be represented as

$$\mathbf{A} = \sum_{i=1}^{p} \mathbf{K}_n(\mathbf{x}_i, \mathbf{F})\mathbf{K}_n^*(\mathbf{x}_i, \mathbf{F}) - \sum_{i=p+1}^{p+q} \mathbf{K}_n(\mathbf{x}_i, \mathbf{F})\mathbf{K}_n^*(\mathbf{x}_i, \mathbf{F}), \tag{10}$$

and the generator $G_{p+q}(\mathbf{A}, \mathbf{F}, \mathbf{F})$ can be written as $\{ \mathbf{X}, \mathbf{X}\Sigma \}$, where $\mathbf{X} = [\mathbf{x}_1, \ldots, \mathbf{x}_{p+q}]$ and $\Sigma \equiv \mathbf{I}_p \oplus -\mathbf{I}_q$.

A displacement representation of a matrix $\mathbf{A}$ can be obtained by using the following lemma, whose simple proof we shall omit.

LEMMA. *For any* $\mathbf{A} \in C^{m\times n}$, *if* $\mathbf{F}_1$ *or* $\mathbf{F}_2$ *is nilpotent, there exists* $\alpha \le min(m, n)$ *such that*

$$\mathbf{A} = \sum_{i=1}^{\alpha} \mathbf{K}_n(\mathbf{x}_i, \mathbf{F}_1)\mathbf{K}_n^*(\mathbf{y}_i, \mathbf{F}_2) \qquad \textit{if and only if} \qquad \mathbf{A} - \mathbf{F}_1\mathbf{A}\mathbf{F}_2^* = \sum_{i=1}^{\alpha} \mathbf{x}_i\mathbf{y}_i^*.$$

In later developments an important role will be played by 2×2 block matrices (9). For simplicity, we shall first consider a Hermitian matrix,

$$\mathbf{A} \equiv \begin{bmatrix} \mathbf{A}_{1,1} & \mathbf{A}_{1,2} \\ \mathbf{A}_{1,2}^* & \mathbf{A}_{2,2} \end{bmatrix} \in C^{(n+m)\times(n+m)}, \quad \mathbf{A}_{1,1} \in C^{n\times n}, \quad \mathbf{A}_{2,2} \in C^{m\times m}, \tag{11}$$

where $\mathbf{A}_{1,1}$ is a Hermitian positive definite matrix, and $\mathbf{A}_{2,2}$ is a Hermitian matrix.

For the matrix $\mathbf{A}$ in (11) we shall choose both displacement operators as

$$\mathbf{F} = \begin{bmatrix} \mathbf{Z}_n & \mathbf{O} \\ \mathbf{O} & \mathbf{Z}_m \end{bmatrix}.$$

With this choice, $\mathbf{K}_{n+m}(\mathbf{x}_i, \mathbf{F})$ in (10) will have the form

$$\mathbf{K}_{n+m}(\mathbf{x}_i, \mathbf{F}) \equiv \begin{bmatrix} \mathbf{L}(\mathbf{x}_{1,i}) & \mathbf{O} \\ \mathbf{L}(\mathbf{x}_{2,i}) & \mathbf{O} \end{bmatrix} \in C^{(n+m)\times(n+m)}, \quad \mathbf{L}(\mathbf{x}_{1,i}) \in C^{n\times n}, \quad \mathbf{L}(\mathbf{x}_{2,i}) \in C^{m\times m},$$

where $[\ \mathbf{x}_{1,i}^T, \mathbf{x}_{2,i}^T\ ] \equiv \mathbf{x}_i^T$, and $\mathbf{L}(\mathbf{x}_{1,i})$ and $\mathbf{L}(\mathbf{x}_{2,i})$ are lower triangular Toeplitz matrices whose first columns are $\mathbf{x}_{1,i}$ and $\mathbf{x}_{2,i}$, respectively. The $\mathbf{O}$'s denote rectangular null matrices of appropriate sizes.

Generators of Schur complements.

We shall now show how to obtain the displacement representation (with respect to $\mathbf{Z}_m$ and $\mathbf{Z}_m$) of the matrix $\mathbf{A}_s$,

$$\mathbf{A}_s \equiv \mathbf{A}_{2,2} - \mathbf{A}_{1,2}^*\mathbf{A}_{1,1}^{-1}\mathbf{A}_{1,2},$$

which is the so-called Schur complement of $\mathbf{A}_{1,1}$.

1. Obtain a generator of $\mathbf{A}$, say $\{\ \mathbf{X}, \mathbf{X}\Sigma\ \}$, $\Sigma = \mathbf{I}_p \oplus -\mathbf{I}_q$.
2. Form the matrix Δ,

$$\Delta \equiv \Big[\ \mathbf{K}(\mathbf{x}_1, \mathbf{F}), \cdots \mathbf{K}(\mathbf{x}_p, \mathbf{F}), \mathbf{K}(\mathbf{x}_{p+1}, \mathbf{F}), \cdots, \mathbf{K}(\mathbf{x}_{p+q}, \mathbf{F})\ \Big] \tag{12a}$$

$$= \left[\begin{bmatrix} \mathbf{L}(\mathbf{x}_{1,1}) & \mathbf{O} \\ \mathbf{L}(\mathbf{x}_{2,1}) & \mathbf{O} \end{bmatrix} \cdots \begin{bmatrix} \mathbf{L}(\mathbf{x}_{1,p}) & \mathbf{O} \\ \mathbf{L}(\mathbf{x}_{2,p}) & \mathbf{O} \end{bmatrix} \begin{bmatrix} \mathbf{L}(\mathbf{x}_{1,p+1}) & \mathbf{O} \\ \mathbf{L}(\mathbf{x}_{2,p+1}) & \mathbf{O} \end{bmatrix} \cdots \begin{bmatrix} \mathbf{L}(\mathbf{x}_{1,p+q}) & \mathbf{O} \\ \mathbf{L}(\mathbf{x}_{2,p+q}) & \mathbf{O} \end{bmatrix} \right]. \tag{12b}$$

3. Post-multiply Δ by a *J-unitary* matrix $\mathbf{\Theta}$, where $\mathbf{J} \equiv \mathbf{I}_{(n+m)p} \oplus -\mathbf{I}_{(n+m)q}$ (i.e., the matrix $\mathbf{\Theta}$ is such that $\mathbf{\Theta J \Theta}^* = \mathbf{J}$), that will transform Δ as follows (We shall show how to do this in the proof):

$$\text{(i) } \mathbf{K}(\mathbf{x}_1, \mathbf{F}) \rightarrow \begin{bmatrix} \mathbf{L} & \mathbf{O} \\ \mathbf{M} & \mathbf{L}_1 \end{bmatrix}, \quad \mathbf{L} \text{ is lower-triangular; } \mathbf{L}_1 \text{ is lower triangular Toeplitz}$$

$$\text{(ii) } \mathbf{K}(\mathbf{x}_i, \mathbf{F}) \rightarrow \begin{bmatrix} \mathbf{O} & \mathbf{O} \\ \mathbf{L}_i & \mathbf{O} \end{bmatrix}, \quad \mathbf{L}_i \text{ is lower triangular Toeplitz,} \quad 2 \le i \le p+q.$$

The result will be

$$\tilde{\Delta} \equiv \Delta\mathbf{\Theta} = \left[\begin{bmatrix} \mathbf{L} & \mathbf{O} \\ \mathbf{M} & \mathbf{L}_1 \end{bmatrix} \begin{bmatrix} \mathbf{O} & \mathbf{O} \\ \mathbf{L}_2 & \mathbf{O} \end{bmatrix} \cdots \begin{bmatrix} \mathbf{O} & \mathbf{O} \\ \mathbf{L}_{p+q} & \mathbf{O} \end{bmatrix} \right]. \tag{13}$$

Then it turns out that

$$\mathbf{A}_{1,1} = \mathbf{L}\mathbf{L}^*, \tag{14a}$$

$$\mathbf{A}_{1,2}^* = \mathbf{M}\mathbf{L}^*, \tag{14b}$$

$$\mathbf{A}_s \equiv \mathbf{A}_{2,2} - \mathbf{A}_{1,2}^*\mathbf{A}_{1,1}^{-1}\mathbf{A}_{1,2} = \sum_{i=1}^{p} \mathbf{L}_i\mathbf{L}_i^* - \sum_{i=p+1}^{p+q} \mathbf{L}_i\mathbf{L}_i^*. \tag{14c}$$

Note that the generator of $\mathbf{A}_s$ has the same p and q as the given generator of A itself, a fact first discovered by Morf [17] and used by him to derive "divide-and-conquer"-type algorithms (see also [3]).

PROOF. The results in (14a, b) follow immediately by equating the (1, 1) and (2, 1) blocks on both sides of the equality,

$$\mathbf{A} = \Delta\mathbf{J}\Delta^* = \Delta\mathbf{\Theta}\mathbf{J}\mathbf{\Theta}^*\Delta^* = \tilde{\Delta}\mathbf{J}\tilde{\Delta}^*. \tag{15}$$

Furthermore, equating the (2, 2) blocks of (15) gives

$$\mathbf{A}_{2,2} = \mathbf{M}\mathbf{M}^* + \sum_{i=1}^{p} \mathbf{L}_i\mathbf{L}_i^* - \sum_{i=p+1}^{p+q} \mathbf{L}_i\mathbf{L}_i^*,$$

from which the equality (14c) follows by noting that

$$\mathbf{M}\mathbf{M}^* = \mathbf{A}_{1,2}^*\mathbf{L}^{-*}\mathbf{L}^{-1}\mathbf{A}_{1,2} = \mathbf{A}_{1,2}^*\mathbf{A}_{1,1}^{-1}\mathbf{A}_{1,2}.$$

The only thing left to do is to show how to construct $\mathbf{\Theta}$ so as to obtain $\tilde{\Delta}$ of the form (13). This can be done in several ways, but perhaps the simplest and the most useful is to construct $\mathbf{\Theta}$ as a product of $(p+q)(n+m) \times (p+q)(n+m)$ circular (or Givens) and hyperbolic rotations. (For some applications, circular and hyperbolic Householder reflections may also be useful). Givens rotations $\mathbf{G}_{i,j}(\kappa)$ and hyperbolic rotations $\mathbf{H}_{i,j}(\kappa)$, with *reflection coefficient* κ, are defined as identity matrices except for the following four entries,

$$[\mathbf{G}_{i,j}(\kappa)]_{i,i}=[\mathbf{G}_{i,j}(\kappa)]_{j,j}=\frac{1}{(1+|\kappa|^2)^{1/2}},\quad [\mathbf{G}_{i,j}(\kappa)]_{i,j}=\frac{-\kappa}{(1+|\kappa|^2)^{1/2}},\quad [\mathbf{G}_{i,j}(\kappa)]_{j,i}=\frac{\bar{\kappa}}{(1+|\kappa|^2)^{1/2}},$$

$$[\mathbf{H}_{i,j}(\kappa)]_{i,i}=[\mathbf{H}_{i,j}(\kappa)]_{j,j}=\frac{1}{(1-|\kappa|^2)^{1/2}},\quad [\mathbf{H}_{i,j}(\kappa)]_{i,j}=\frac{-\kappa}{(1-|\kappa|^2)^{1/2}},\quad [\mathbf{H}_{i,j}(\kappa)]_{j,i}=\frac{-\bar{\kappa}}{(1-|\kappa|^2)^{1/2}}.$$

For a given row vector $\mathbf{x}^T$, we can *annihilate* x_i, *pivoting with* x_j, by post multiplying $\mathbf{x}^T$ with $\mathbf{G}_{i,j}(\kappa)$ or $\mathbf{H}_{i,j}(\kappa)$ with the reflection coefficient, κ chosen as the ratio x_j/x_i. Now we can describe how to convert Δ to $\tilde{\Delta}$. (We encourage readers to jump to the example below, and then return to complete the rest of this proof.)

We annihilate $\{\ \mathbf{L}(\mathbf{x}_{1,2}), \mathbf{L}(\mathbf{x}_{1,3}), \ldots, \mathbf{L}(\mathbf{x}_{1,p+q})\ \}$ in (12b) with n *sweeps* (0th, 1st, $\cdot\cdot$, $(n-1)$st sweeps). The kth sweep annihilates the kth sub-diagonals of the $p-1$ matrices, $\{\ \mathbf{L}(\mathbf{x}_{1,2}), \mathbf{L}(\mathbf{x}_{1,3}). . , \mathbf{L}(\mathbf{x}_{1,p})\ \}$ with Givens rotations, and the kth sub-diagonals of the q matrices, $\{\ \mathbf{L}(\mathbf{x}_{1,p+1}), \mathbf{L}(\mathbf{x}_{1,p+2}). . , \mathbf{L}(\mathbf{x}_{1,p+q})\ \}$ with hyperbolic rotations, pivoting with the diagonal elements in $\mathbf{L}(\mathbf{x}_{1,1})$ in both cases.

In the kth sweep, if $k > n-m$, then we apply 'dummy' rotations to the $(n-k+1)$st to the mth columns of $\mathbf{K}(\mathbf{x}_i, \mathbf{F})$, pivoting with the $(n+1)$st to $(m+k)$th columns of $\mathbf{K}(\mathbf{x}_1, \mathbf{F})$, in order to keep the Toeplitz structure in $\{\ \mathbf{L}(\mathbf{x}_{2,2}), \mathbf{L}(\mathbf{x}_{2,3}). . , \mathbf{L}(\mathbf{x}_{2,p+q})\ \}$. This will introduce a non-zero lower triangular Toeplitz matrix in the (2, 2) block of $\mathbf{K}(\mathbf{x}_1, \mathbf{F})$. After the $(n-1)$st sweep, we shall have $\tilde{\Delta}$ in (13).

□

EXAMPLE (A Gohberg-Semencul formula for Toeplitz matrices).

Let $\mathbf{T} = (c_{i-j})$ be an $n \times n$ Hermitian positive definite Toeplitz matrix. Consider the matrix

$$\mathbf{A} \equiv \begin{bmatrix} \mathbf{T} & \mathbf{I}_n \\ \mathbf{I}_n & \mathbf{O} \end{bmatrix}. \tag{16}$$

For $\mathbf{F} \equiv \mathbf{Z}_n \oplus \mathbf{Z}_n$, it is easy to see that the displacement rank of $\mathbf{A}$ with respect to $\{\mathbf{F}, \mathbf{F}\}$ is two, and that a generator $G_2(\mathbf{A}, \mathbf{F}, \mathbf{F})$ is given by $\{\mathbf{X}, \mathbf{X}\Sigma\}$, where

$$\mathbf{X} \equiv \begin{bmatrix} \mathbf{x}_{1,1} & \mathbf{x}_{1,2} \\ c_0^{-1/2}\mathbf{e}_1 & c_0^{-1/2}\mathbf{e}_1 \end{bmatrix}, \qquad \Sigma \equiv 1 \oplus -1,$$

where

$$\mathbf{x}_{1,1} = c_0^{-1/2}\cdot[c_0, c_1, \cdots, c_{n-1}]^T, \quad \mathbf{x}_{1,2} = c_0^{-1/2}\cdot[0, c_1, \cdots, c_{n-1}]^T, \quad \mathbf{e}_1 = [\ 1, 0, \cdots, 0\ ]^T.$$

With this generator, the matrix Δ in (12) will have the form

$$\Delta = \begin{bmatrix} \mathbf{L}(\mathbf{x}_{1,1}) & \mathbf{O} & \mathbf{L}(\mathbf{x}_{1,2}) & \mathbf{O} \\ c_0^{-1/2}\mathbf{I}_n & \mathbf{O} & c_0^{-1/2}\mathbf{I}_n & \mathbf{O} \end{bmatrix}. \tag{17}$$

We shall show how to transform the matrix Δ into a matrix $\tilde{\Delta}$ of the form (13),

$$\tilde{\Delta} = \begin{bmatrix} \mathbf{L} & \mathbf{O} & \mathbf{O} & \mathbf{O} \\ \mathbf{U} & \mathbf{L}_1 & \mathbf{L}_2 & \mathbf{O} \end{bmatrix}.$$

Since the Schur complement of $\mathbf{T}$ in (16) is $-\mathbf{T}^{-1}$, formula (14c) will yield

$$\mathbf{T}^{-1} = \mathbf{L}_2\mathbf{L}_2^* - \mathbf{L}_1\mathbf{L}_1^*.$$

To reduce the notational burden, we shall illustrate the procedure for going from (12) to (13) for a 3×3 matrix,

$$\mathbf{T} = \begin{bmatrix} 1 & \bar{\alpha}_1 & \bar{\alpha}_2 \\ \alpha_1 & 1 & \bar{\alpha}_1 \\ \alpha_2 & \alpha_1 & 1 \end{bmatrix}, \qquad \mathbf{x}_{1,1} = [1, \alpha_1, \alpha_2]^T, \qquad \mathbf{x}_{1,2} = [0, \alpha_1, \alpha_2]^T.$$

First, we post-multiply the matrix Δ (we shall suppress the last null column of Δ in (17), because these $\mathbf{O}$'s are not altered during the procedure) with hyperbolic rotations $\mathbf{H}_{2,7}(\kappa_1)$ and $\mathbf{H}_{3,8}(\kappa_1)$, where $\kappa_1 \equiv \alpha_1$, to annihilate the 1st sub-diagonal of $\mathbf{L}(\mathbf{x}_{1,2})$ pivoting with the diagonal of $\mathbf{L}(\mathbf{x}_{1,1})$. To preserve the Toeplitz structure at the (2, 3) block of Δ, we also apply a "dummy" hyperbolic rotation $\mathbf{H}_{4,9}(\kappa_1)$ to the 3rd column of the (2, 3) block pivoting with the 1st (null) column of the (2, 2) block. This will introduce a nonzero element β_4 in the lower left corner of the (2, 2) block as shown below.

$$\Delta = \begin{bmatrix} 1 & & & & & & & & \\ \alpha_1 & 1 & & & & & \alpha_1 & & \\ \alpha_2 & \alpha_1 & 1 & & & & \alpha_2 & \alpha_1 & \\ & & & & & & & & \\ 1 & & & & & & 1 & & \\ & 1 & & & & & & 1 & \\ & & 1 & & & & & & 1 \end{bmatrix} \rightarrow \begin{bmatrix} 1 & & & & & & & & \\ \alpha_1 & \beta_1 & & & & & & & \\ \alpha_2 & \beta_2 & \beta_1 & & & & \beta_3 & & \\ & & & & & & & & \\ 1 & \beta_4 & & & & & \beta_5 & & \\ & \beta_5 & \beta_4 & & & & \beta_4 & \beta_5 & \\ & & \beta_5 & \beta_4 & & & & \beta_4 & \beta_5 \end{bmatrix} \equiv \Delta_1$$

Next we apply a hyperbolic rotation $\mathbf{H}_{3,7}(\kappa_2)$, where $\kappa_2 \equiv \beta_3/\beta_1$, to annihilate the remaining element β_3 in the (1, 3) block, and then apply two dummy hyperbolic rotations $\mathbf{H}_{4,8}(\kappa_2)$ and $\mathbf{H}_{5,9}(\kappa_2)$ to preserve the Toeplitz structure in the (2, 3) block, see below.

$$\Delta_1 = \begin{bmatrix} 1 & & & & & & & & \\ \alpha_1 & \beta_1 & & & & & & & \\ \alpha_2 & \beta_2 & \gamma_1 & & & & & & \\ & & & & & & & & \\ 1 & \beta_4 & \gamma_2 & & & & \gamma_4 & & \\ & \beta_5 & \gamma_3 & \gamma_2 & & & \gamma_3 & \gamma_4 & \\ & & \gamma_4 & \gamma_3 & \gamma_2 & & \gamma_2 & \gamma_3 & \gamma_4 \end{bmatrix} = \begin{bmatrix} \mathbf{L} & \mathbf{O} & \mathbf{O} \\ \mathbf{U} & \mathbf{L}_1 & \mathbf{L}_2 \end{bmatrix} = \tilde{\mathbf{\Delta}}. \tag{18}$$

In this particular example, the persymmetricity of $\mathbf{T}$, and hence of $\mathbf{T}^{-1}$, makes the last column of $\mathbf{U}$ equal to the reverse of the first column of $\mathbf{L}_2$. Notice that this expression is not unique because we can apply hyperbolic rotations $\mathbf{H}_{4,7}(\kappa)$, $\mathbf{H}_{5,8}(\kappa)$ and $\mathbf{H}_{6,9}(\kappa)$ with *any* $|\kappa| < 1$ to $\tilde{\mathbf{\Delta}}$ in (18) without destroying the lower triangular Toeplitz structure in $\mathbf{L}_1$ and $\mathbf{L}_2$.

Generalized Schur algorithm.

In the above example, we need two sweeps, and each sweep consists of three hyperbolic rotations, $\{\mathbf{H}_{2,7}(\kappa_1), \mathbf{H}_{3,8}(\kappa_1), \mathbf{H}_{4,9}(\kappa_1)\}$, $\{\mathbf{H}_{3,7}(\kappa_1), \mathbf{H}_{4,8}(\kappa_1), \mathbf{H}_{5,9}(\kappa_1)\}$. The hyperbolic rotations in a given sweep are identical; notice also that they are applied to two successively shifted columns. Therefore, it is enough to keep track only of the two relevant columns. With this consideration, we can re-formulate the previous procedure more compactly as follows, yielding a so-called generalized Schur algorithm:

1. Post-multiply $\mathbf{X}$ by $p+q-1$ hyperbolic rotations that will annihilate the top-most non-zero row of $\mathbf{X}$ except for the element in the first column.
2. Pre-multiply the first column of $\mathbf{X}$ with $\mathbf{F}$ (i.e., shift-down appropriately).
3. Go to 1.

To annihilate n rows out of $n+m$ rows, we shall need approximately $4(p+q-1)\sum_{k=m}^{n+m} k = 2(p+q-1)\times(n^2+2nm+2m+n)$ multiplications. This will be less than the $O(n^3)$ multiplications needed to obtain the factors of a matrix $\mathbf{A}_{1,1}$ and its inverse unless $p+q$ is nearly n. There are many interesting matrices (see Sec 3) for which $p+q \ll n$.

Non Hermitian matrices.

For non-Hermitian rectangular matrices $\mathbf{A}$ in (9), one can formulate a similar procedure. We form the matrices Δ_1 and Δ_2 as

$$\Delta_1 \equiv \left[\mathbf{K}(\mathbf{x}_1, \mathbf{F}_1), \cdots, \mathbf{K}(\mathbf{x}_\alpha, \mathbf{F}_1) \right], \quad \Delta_2 \equiv \left[\mathbf{K}(\mathbf{y}_1, \mathbf{F}_2), \cdots, \mathbf{K}(\mathbf{y}_\alpha, \mathbf{F}_2) \right],$$

and annihilate the elements in Δ_1 and Δ_2 by post-multiplying Δ_1 and Δ_2 with *spinor matrices,* instead of Givens and hyperbolic rotations. A spinor matrix is defined as the identity except for the following four entries,

$$[\mathbf{S}_{i,j}]_{i,i} = [\mathbf{S}_{i,j}]_{j,j} = \frac{1}{(1+\kappa_1\bar{\kappa}_2)^{1/2}}, \quad [\mathbf{S}_{i,j}]_{i,j} = \frac{-\kappa_1}{(1+\kappa_1\bar{\kappa}_2)^{1/2}}, \quad [\mathbf{S}_{i,j}]_{j,i} = \frac{\bar{\kappa}_2}{(1+\kappa_1\bar{\kappa}_2)^{1/2}}.$$

Because of the invariance property that

$$\mathbf{A} = \Delta_1 \cdot \Delta_2^* = \Delta_1 \mathbf{S}_{i,j} \cdot \mathbf{S}_{i,j}^{-1} \Delta_2^*,$$

a similar procedure to that in the Hermitian case will give a displacement representation of $\mathbf{A}_s$,

$$\mathbf{A}_s \equiv \mathbf{A}_{2,2} - \mathbf{A}_{2,1}\mathbf{A}_{1,1}^{-1}\mathbf{A}_{1,2} = \sum_{i=1}^{\alpha} \mathbf{L}_i \mathbf{U}_i, \tag{19}$$

where $\mathbf{L}_i$ and $\mathbf{U}_i^*$ are lower triangular Toeplitz matrices.

3. SOME GENERALIZED GOHBERG-SEMENCUL FORMULAS.

The first step of the procedure to obtain a generator for the matrix $\mathbf{A}_s = \mathbf{A}_{2,2} - \mathbf{A}_{2,1}\mathbf{A}_{1,1}^{-1}\mathbf{A}_{1,2}$ is to find a generator of the matrix

$$\mathbf{A} = \begin{bmatrix} \mathbf{A}_{1,1} & \mathbf{A}_{1,2} \\ \mathbf{A}_{2,1} & \mathbf{A}_{2,2} \end{bmatrix}.$$

This can be done by using the lemma in Sec 2. In this section, we shall give generators of some interesting **A**'s, from which the corresponding Gohberg-Semencul formulas for the matrices of interest will be evident.

EXAMPLE 1 (Generator of inverse).

Let **B** be an $n \times n$ Hermitian positive-definite matrix, with a known generator, $\{ \mathbf{W}, \mathbf{W}\Sigma \}$, $\Sigma = \mathbf{I}_p \oplus -\mathbf{I}_q$ with respect to $\{\mathbf{Z}_n, \mathbf{Z}_n\}$. Consider the matrix,

$$\mathbf{A} \equiv \begin{bmatrix} \mathbf{B} & \mathbf{I}_n \\ \mathbf{I}_n & \mathbf{O} \end{bmatrix}. \tag{20}$$

Then by using the lemma in Sec 2, it is easy to see that $\{ \mathbf{X}, \mathbf{X}\Sigma \}$, where

$$\mathbf{X} \equiv \begin{bmatrix} \mathbf{w}_1 & \cdots & \mathbf{w}_p & \mathbf{e}_1 & \mathbf{w}_{p+1} & \cdots & \mathbf{w}_{p+q} & \mathbf{e}_1 \\ 0 & \cdots & 0 & \mathbf{e}_1/2 & 0 & \cdots & 0 & -\mathbf{e}_1/2 \end{bmatrix}, \quad \Sigma \equiv \mathbf{I}_{p+1} \oplus -\mathbf{I}_{q+1} \tag{21}$$

is a generator of **A** with respect to $\{\mathbf{Z}_n \oplus \mathbf{Z}_n, \mathbf{Z}_n \oplus \mathbf{Z}_n\}$. The length of the generator of $\mathbf{B}^{-1}$ obtained with the above **A** will be $p+q+2$. However, if the given generator $G_{p+q}(\mathbf{B}, \mathbf{Z}_n, \mathbf{Z}_n)$

satisfies a condition called *admissibility* [4], [16], then, as we shall see, we can obtain a generator of $\mathbf{B}^{-1}$ with a length less than $p+q+2$.

EXAMPLE 2 (Inversion with admissible generators).

A generator for a Hermitian matrix $\mathbf{B} \in C^{n \times n}$, $\{\mathbf{W}, \mathbf{W}\Sigma\}$, $\Sigma = \mathbf{I}_p \oplus -\mathbf{I}_q$ with respect to $\{\mathbf{Z}_n, \mathbf{Z}_n\}$ is called *admissible* if $\mathbf{e}_1 \in$ range $(\mathbf{W})$, i.e., if there is a linear combination of the columns of the generator that will give the unit vector.

Let $G_{p+q}(\mathbf{B}, \mathbf{Z}_n, \mathbf{Z}_n)$ be admissible, and

$$[\mu_1, \mu_2, \cdots, \mu_{p+q}]\mathbf{W}^* = \mathbf{e}_1^T.$$

Then it can be checked that the matrix,

$$\mathbf{A} \equiv \begin{bmatrix} \mathbf{B} & \mathbf{I}_n \\ \mathbf{I}_n & \eta \mathbf{I}_n \end{bmatrix}, \qquad \eta \equiv \sum_{i=1}^{p} |\mu_i|^2 - \sum_{i=p+1}^{p+q} |\mu_i|^2 \tag{22}$$

has a generator $\{\mathbf{X}, \mathbf{X}\Sigma\}$, with respect to $\{\mathbf{Z}_n \oplus \mathbf{Z}_n, \mathbf{Z}_n \oplus \mathbf{Z}_n\}$, where

$$\mathbf{X} \equiv \begin{bmatrix} \mathbf{w}_1 & \cdots & \mathbf{w}_p & \mathbf{w}_{p+1} & \cdots & \mathbf{w}_{p+q} \\ \mu_1 \mathbf{e}_1 & \cdots & \mu_p \mathbf{e}_1 & -\mu_{p+1}\mathbf{e}_1 & \cdots & -\mu_{p+q}\mathbf{e}_1 \end{bmatrix}, \qquad \Sigma \equiv \mathbf{I}_p \oplus -\mathbf{I}_q. \tag{23}$$

Since the Schur complement of $\mathbf{B}$ in (22) is $\eta \mathbf{I}_n - \mathbf{B}^{-1}$, we see that the generator of $\mathbf{B}^{-1}$ obtained with the $\mathbf{A}$ in (22) will have length $p+q+1$ if $\eta \neq 0$, or $p+q$ if $\eta = 0$, consistent with the results first obtained in [16].

For an example of a minimal admissible generator (besides generators of Toeplitz matrices), let us consider an $m \times n$ Toeplitz matrix $\mathbf{T} = (c_{i-j})$ with a full column rank. The matrix $\mathbf{T}^*\mathbf{T}$ has a minimal generator [4], $\{\mathbf{W}, \mathbf{W}\Sigma\}$, $\Sigma = \mathbf{I}_2 \oplus -\mathbf{I}_2$, with respect to $\{\mathbf{Z}_n, \mathbf{Z}_n\}$, where

$$\mathbf{w}_1 = \mathbf{T}^*\mathbf{t}_1/\|\mathbf{t}_1\|_2, \quad \mathbf{w}_2 = \mathbf{t}_2, \quad \mathbf{w}_3 = \mathbf{Z}_n \mathbf{Z}_n^* \mathbf{w}_1, \quad \mathbf{w}_4 = \mathbf{Z}_n \mathbf{l}_1, \tag{24a}$$

$$\mathbf{t}_1 = [\, c_0, c_1, \cdots, c_{m-1} \,]^*, \ \mathbf{t}_2 = [\, 0, c_{-1}, \cdots, c_{1-n} \,]^*, \ \mathbf{l}_1 = [\, c_{m-1}, \cdots, c_{m-n} \,]^*, \tag{24b}$$

and $\|\cdot\|_2$ denotes the Euclidean norm. This generator of $\mathbf{T}^*\mathbf{T}$ is admissible since

$$[1/\|\mathbf{t}_1\|_2, 0, -1/\|\mathbf{t}_1\|_2, 0]\mathbf{W}^* = \mathbf{e}_1^T. \tag{25}$$

Therefore, the matrix $\mathbf{A}$ in (22) would have the form

$$\mathbf{A} \equiv \begin{bmatrix} \mathbf{T}^*\mathbf{T} & \mathbf{I}_n \\ \mathbf{I}_n & \mathbf{O} \end{bmatrix}, \tag{26}$$

and the procedure will give a generator of $(\mathbf{T}^*\mathbf{T})^{-1}$ of length 4. The displacement representation of $(\mathbf{T}^*\mathbf{T})^{-1}$ is useful in solving Toeplitz least squares problems ($m \geq n$).

EXAMPLE 3 (Generator of $T_1^*T_2^{-1}T_1$).

Let $T_1 \in C^{n\times m}$ and $T_2 = (c_{i-j}) \in C^{n\times n}$ be Toeplitz, and Hermitian positive-definite Toeplitz, respectively. If we define

$$A \equiv \begin{bmatrix} T_2 & T_1 \\ T_1^* & O \end{bmatrix} \tag{27}$$

then A has a generator $\{ X, X\Sigma \}$, $\Sigma \equiv I_2 \oplus -I_2$, with respect to $\{Z_n \oplus Z_m, Z_n \oplus Z_m\}$, where

$$X \equiv \begin{bmatrix} v_1 & u_2 & v_2 & u_2 \\ u_1 & e_1/2 & u_1 & -e_1/2 \end{bmatrix},$$

v_1 = the first column of T_2 devided by $c_0^{1/2}$,

u_1 = the first column of T_1^*,

v_2 = same as v_1 with the first entry equals to zero,

u_2 = the first column of T_1 with the first entry equals to zero.

With the above A, we can obtain a generator of $T_1^*T_2^{-1}T_1$ with length 4.

The displacement representation of $T_1^*T_2^{-1}T_1$ is useful in solving weighted Toeplitz least squares problems ($n \geq m$), as arise in certain parametric time series identification problems.

REMARK 1. One can obtain a generator of $T_1^*T_1$ by setting T_2 in (27) with I_n. This procedure will need $O(mn)$ computations, which is of the same order as evaluating the closed form expression in (24a).

REMARK 2. It is interesting to note that $\alpha(T_1^*T_2^{-1}T_1, Z_m, Z_m) \leq 4$, whereas $\alpha(T_1^*T_2T_1, Z_m, Z_m) \leq 6$. The reason is that the first matrix can be identified as the Schur complement in a 2×2 block matrix, while to do so for $T_1^*T_2T_1$ requires going to a 3×3 block matrix whose displacement rank can be 6.

REMARK 3. Once one has a generator of $T_1^*T_2^{-1}T_1$, one can obtain a generator of $(T_1^*T_2^{-1}T_1)^{-1}$ using the matrix A in (20) and the generator in (21). This will give a generator of length 6. However, it turns out that minimal generators of $T_1^*T_2^{-1}T_1$ are admissible (with $\eta = 0$), and the displacement rank of $(T_1^*T_2^{-1}T_1)^{-1}$ is less than or equal to 4 (see Sec 4).

EXAMPLE 4 (Generator of the projection operator).

Let T be an $m \times n$ Toeplitz matrix with full column rank. If we define

$$A = \begin{bmatrix} T^*T & T^* \\ T & I_m \end{bmatrix}, \tag{28}$$

then $\{ X, X\Sigma \}$, $\Sigma \equiv I_2 \oplus -I_2$, where

$$X \equiv \begin{bmatrix} w_1 & w_2 & w_3 & w_4 \\ t_1/\|t_1\|_2 & e_1 & t_1/\|t_1\|_2 & 0 \end{bmatrix}, \quad w_i \text{ and } t_1 \text{ are as in (24).} \tag{29}$$

is a generator of A with respect to $\{Z_n \oplus Z_m, Z_n \oplus Z_m\}$. By applying the procedure in Sec 2 to the above matrix A, we can obtain the generator (of length 4) of the projection operator $I_m - T(T^*T)^{-1}T^*$ on the ($(m-n)$-dimensional) kernel of T^*. Also, in this case, the matrix M in (13) turns out to be the unitary basis of the range of T, because by (14a, b)

$$T^*T = LL^*, \quad \text{and} \quad T = ML^*, \quad \text{which implies} \quad M^*M = I_n, \quad M \in C^{m \times n}.$$

In fact, we have the QR factorization of T (see also [4]).

EXAMPLE 5 (Generator of the pseudo-inverse).

Let T be an $m \times n$ Toeplitz matrix with a full column rank. If we define

$$A \equiv \begin{bmatrix} T^*T & T^* \\ I_n & O_{n \times m} \end{bmatrix},$$

then by using the results in (25) and (29), we can see that A has a generator, $\{ X, Y \}$, with respect to $\{Z_n \oplus Z_n, Z_n \oplus Z_m\}$ where

$$X \equiv \begin{bmatrix} w_1 & w_2 & w_3 & w_4 \\ e_1/\|t_1\|_2 & 0 & e_1/\|t_1\|_2 & 0 \end{bmatrix}, \quad Y \equiv \begin{bmatrix} w_1 & w_2 & -w_3 & -w_4 \\ t_1/\|t_1\|_2 & e_1 & -t_1/\|t_1\|_2 & 0 \end{bmatrix},$$

and w_i and t_1 are as in (24). With the above generator, we can obtain a generator of the pseudo-inverse of T of length 4.

4. CONCLUDING REMARKS.

We have presented a constructive approach to the famous Gohberg-Semencul formula for the inverse of a Toeplitz matrix, and obtained various generalizations of it. We note that formulas of Gohberg and Semencul type are closely related to the problem of finding displacement representations (generators) of various matrices.

For further development, we may mention that the procedure for 2×2 block matrices given in Sec 2 can be easily generalized to $N \times N$ block matrices. For instance, by considering 3×3 block matrices, one can obtain a generator of $[A_{2,2} - A_{1,2}^* A_{1,1}^{-1} A_{1,2}]^{-1}$. As an example, we can obtain a generator of $(T_1^* T_2^{-1} T_1)^{-1}$ by working with the matrix

$$\mathbf{A} \equiv \begin{bmatrix} \mathbf{A}_{1,1} & \mathbf{A}_{1,2} \\ \mathbf{A}_{1,2}^* & \mathbf{O} \end{bmatrix}, \quad \mathbf{A}_{1,1} = \begin{bmatrix} \mathbf{T}_2 & \mathbf{T}_1 \\ \mathbf{T}_1^* & \mathbf{O} \end{bmatrix}, \quad \mathbf{A}_{1,2} = \begin{bmatrix} \mathbf{O} \\ \mathbf{I} \end{bmatrix}.$$

The length of the obtained generator will be 4. As another example, a generator of $\mathbf{T}_1^*\mathbf{T}_2\mathbf{T}_1$ can be obtained by choosing

$$\mathbf{A}_{1,1} = \begin{bmatrix} \mathbf{T}_2 & \mathbf{I} \\ \mathbf{I} & \mathbf{O} \end{bmatrix}, \quad \mathbf{A}_{1,2} = \begin{bmatrix} \mathbf{O} \\ \mathbf{T}_1 \end{bmatrix}.$$

We also remark that divide-and-conquer versions of the procedure in Sec 2 can be readily obtained [3]. By using this approach to compute the displacement representation of $(\mathbf{T}^*\mathbf{T})^{-1}$, one can, for instance, obtain least-squares solutions for Toeplitz systems in $O(m \log^2 m)$ operations.

Finally, we should note that several authors have explored the problem of fast inversion of various structured matrices by employing somewhat different, but related, definitions of displacement. We may mention the work of Heinig and Rost [12], Gohberg *et al* [8], [9], A. Ben-Artzi and T. Shalom [1], L. Lerer and M. Tismenetsky [15]. Some of the formulas therein are also generalizations of the Gohberg-Semencul formula. More work needs to be done to clarify the relationships between these different results and approaches.

REFERENCES

1. A. Ben-Artzi and T. Shalom, *On inversion of Toeplitz and close to Toeplitz matrices,* Linear Algebra and its Appl., 75 (1986), pp 173-192.
2. R. Brent, F. Gustavson and D. Yun, *Fast solution of Toeplitz systems of equations and computation of Pade approximants,* Journal of Algorithms, 1, (1980), pp. 259-295.
3. J. Chun and T. Kailath, *Divide-and-conquer solutions for least-squares problems for matrices with displacement structure,* Proc. Sixth Army conf. on Applied Math. and Comput., Boulder, CO, June, 1988.
4. J. Chun, T. Kailath and H. Lev-Ari, *Fast parallel algorithms for QR and triangular factorization,* SIAM J. Sci. Stat. Comput., vol. 8, No. 6, Nov., (1987), pp. 899-913.
5. B. Friedlander, M. Morf, T. Kailath and L. Ljung, *New inversion formula for matrices classified in terms of their distance from Toeplitz matrices,* Linear Algebra and its Appl., 27 (1979), pp. 31-60.
6. Ya. L. Geronimus, *Polynomials orthogonal on a circle and interval,* Pergamon press, New York, 1960.
7. I. Gohberg and I. Fel'dman, *Convolution equations and projection methods for their solutions,* Translations of Mathematical Monographs, vol. 41, Amer. Math. Soc., 1974.
8. I. Gohberg, T. Kailath and I. Koltracht, *Efficient solution of linear systems of equations with recursive structure,* Linear Algebra and its Appl., 80 (1986), pp 81-113.

9. I. Gohberg, T. Kailath, I. Koltracht and P. Lancaster, *Linear complexity parallel algorithms for linear systems of equations with recursive structure,* Linear Algebra and its Appl., 88 (1987), pp 271-315.

10. I. Gohberg and A. Semencul, *On the inversion of finite Toeplitz matrices and their continuous analogs,* Mat. Issled., 2 (1972), pp. 201-233.

11. U. Grenander and G. Szego *Toeplitz forms and their applications* 2nd ed., Chelsea publishing company, New York, 1984.

12. G. Heinig and K. Rost, Algebraic methods for Toeplitz-like matrices and operators, Akademie-Verlag, Berlin, 1984.

13. T. Kailath, S. Kung and M. Morf, *Displacement ranks of matrices and linear equations,* J. Math. Anal. Appl., 68 (1979) pp. 395-407. See also Bull. Amer. Math. Soc., 1 (1979), pp. 769-773.

14. T. Kailath, A. Vieira and M. Morf, *Inverses of Toeplitz operators, innovations, and orthogonal polynomial,* SIAM Review, vol. 20, No 1, Jan. (1978), pp. 106-119.

15 L. Lerer and M. Tismenetsky, *Generalized Bezoutian and matrix equations,* Linear Algebra and its Appl., 99 (1988), pp 123-160.

16. H. Lev-Ari, and T. Kailath, *Lattice filter parameterization and modeling of nonstationary process,* IEEE Trans. Inform. Theory, IT-30 (1984), pp. 2-16.

17. M. Morf, *Doubling algorithms for Toeplitz and related equations,* in Proceedings of the IEEE International Conf. on Acoustics, Speech and Signal Processing, Denver, (1980), pp. 954-959.

18. I. Schur, *Über Potenzreihen, die im Innern des Einheitskreises beschrankt sind,* J. für die Reine und Angewandte Mathematik, 147 (1917), pp. 205-232.

19. W. Trench, *An algorithm for inversion of finite Toeplitz matrices,* J. of SIAM, vol. 12.3 (1964), pp. 515-522.

Thomas Kailath and Joohwan Chun
Information Systems Laboratory,
Department of Electrical Engineering,
Stanford University,
Stanford, CA 94305.

Operator Theory:
Advances and Applications, Vol. 40

VARIATIONAL PROPERTIES AND RAYLEIGH QUOTIENT ALGORITHMS FOR SYMMETRIC MATRIX PENCILS

Peter Lancaster and Qiang Ye

Dedicated with respect and affection to Israel Gohberg on the occasion of his sixtieth birthday.

We consider matrix pencils $\lambda A - B$ in which λ is a complex parameter, A, B are both hermitian and A is nonsingular. Variational characterizations of the real eigenvalues (if any) are formulated. Rayleigh quotient algorithms for finding real eigenvalues are proposed and their local and global convergence properties are established and illustrated.

INTRODUCTION

In this paper we are concerned with the eigenvalue problem for hermitian, or real symmetric pencils of square matrices $\lambda A - B$, i.e. either A and B are hermitian, or both are real symmetric. We will assume throughout the paper that A is nonsingular. When $A = I$, the identity matrix or, more generally, when A is positive definite there are classical variational principles which characterize the eigenvalues (i.e. those λ for which $\det(\lambda A - B) = 0$), as well as other well-known properties of the Rayleigh quotient $(x^*Bx)/(x^*Ax)$ (see Lancaster and Tismentsky, [8], for example). These lead to Rayleigh quotient algorithms for computing eigenvalues. They are generally competitive when only a few extreme eigenvalues are required, mainly because of high local convergence rates in a neighbourhood of an eigenvalue, as well as favourable global convergence properties. The state of the art for these algorithms in 1980, and the history of their development up to that time are well-described by Parlett [10] [11].

The further advances made in this paper depend on the use of a canonical form for $\lambda A - B$ under congruence. Or, what is the same, the simultaneous reduction of A and B by congruence. If J is a Jordan canonical form for $A^{-1}B$, there is a corresponding canonical matrix P (described in detail in Theorem 1.1), and a nonsingular matrix X such that

$$X^*AX = P, \quad X^*BX = PJ$$

(Note that P and PJ are necessarily hermitian and that P and A have the same signature.) Then $A^{-1}B = XJX^{-1}$ and

$$X^* (\lambda A-B) X = X^*A (\lambda I-A^{-1}B) X = PX^{-1}(I\lambda-A^{-1}B) X$$

When A is positive definite P = I, and has no new role to play. Otherwise $P \neq I$ and plays a significant part in the analysis. In particular, the definition of P includes the assignment of +1 or −1 to each real Jordan block of J. An eigenvalue with only +1's (or only −1's) attached to its Jordan blocks is said to be of positive type or of negative type, respectively.

The notion of definite pencils has played an important part in the literature (see [2] [4] [10] [14]), and they can be defined as pencils $\lambda A - B$ with the property that, for some real α and β, $\alpha A + \beta B$ is positive definite. They have some simplifying properties (we also take advantage of them), and we give a new characterization (Theorem (1.3)) as those diagonable pencils with only real eigenvalues and for which the eigenvalues are separated, that is to say, all eigenvalues of positive type exceed all those of negative type, or vice versa. More generally, we consider diagonable pencils with all eigenvalues real and partially separated. That is, if the n eigenvalues of $\lambda A - B$ (counted with multiplicities) are $\lambda_1 \leq ... \leq \lambda_n$, there are integers $1 \leq r < s \leq n$, for which $\lambda_r < \lambda_{r+1}$, $\lambda_{s-1} < \lambda_s$, and $\lambda_1,...,\lambda_r$ are of one type, while $\lambda_s, ..., \lambda_n$ are of the other.

In Section 1 we present preliminary results on canonical forms and definite pencils and Section 2 contains variational characterizations of the extreme real eigenvalues in the case of partially separated real spectrum. In Section 3 we indicate extensions of these results to pencils with some non–real eigenvalues, provided that the set of real eigenvalues is partially separated.

The remainder of the paper is devoted to the analysis of numerical algorithms. In Section 4 an appropriate Rayleigh quotient algorithm is formulated for finding real eigenvalues. In Section 5 the very rapid (cubic) local convergence to real eigenvalues of classical cases is shown to extend to our indefinite problems and to the computation of eigenvectors. Then with the further hypothesis that the pencil is definite, global convergence results are established in Section 6. The results of these two sections are generalizations of those developed by Kahan and Parlett, [6], [11], [12].

A modified algorithm based on minimization of a Rayleigh quotient with respect to a real parameter is proposed in Section 7. This is found experimentally to have good global convergence properties and leads to the formulation of a two–stage algorithm initiated with that of Section 7 and followed by the more familiar algorithm with cubic local convergence.

Numerical experiments are presented in Section 8.

1. A Canonical Form for Hermitian Pencils and Definite Pencils

An hermitian matrix has the property that all its eigenvalues are real and it is diagonable. But this is not true for hermitian matrix pencils. Indeed, for the real case, we have that every real regular matrix pencil (or a real matrix) is equivalent to a real symmetric matrix pencil. It is well known that, for general regular matrix pencils, there is a Kronecker canonical form which extends appropriately the elementary divisor structure associated with the Jordan form for a single matrix. For hermitian (or real symmetric) matrix pencils the canonical form that exploits the symmetry has also been found. We quote the following theorem from [5], but mention that the notion of the sign characteristic of a real eigenvalue has a history going back to Weierstrass [18].

THEOREM 1.1: *If* A, B *are hermitian matrices with* A *invertible then there is a nonsingular matrix* X *such that*

$$X^*AX = P_{\epsilon,J}, \qquad X^*B\,X = P_{\epsilon,J}J$$

where $J = J_c \oplus J_r \oplus \bar{J}_c$ *is the Jordan matrix of* $A^{-1}B$, *with* $\sigma(J_r)$ *real and* $\lambda\epsilon\sigma(J_c)$ *implies* $\mathrm{Im}\lambda > 0$, *and* $P_{\epsilon,J}$ *is a canonical matrix defined by* J *and a sign characteristic* ϵ *in the following way: we have* $P_{\epsilon,J} = \begin{bmatrix} 0 & 0 & P_c \\ 0 & P_r & 0 \\ P_c & 0 & 0 \end{bmatrix}$ *and if* J_c, J_r *are expressed in terms of Jordan blocks by* $J_c = \mathrm{diag}[J_1,\dots,J_k]$, $J_r = \mathrm{diag}[J_{k+1},\dots,J_\ell]$, *then* P_c, P_r *have a corresponding block–diagonal structure:*

$$P_c = \mathrm{diag}[P_1,\dots,P_k], \qquad P_r = \mathrm{diag}[\epsilon_{k+1}P_{k+1},\dots,\epsilon_\ell P_\ell]$$

where P_i *is a sip matrix,* i.e. $P_i = \begin{bmatrix} 0 & \cdots & 1 \\ \vdots & & \vdots \\ 1 & \cdots & 0 \end{bmatrix}$ *and* $\epsilon_{k+1},\dots,\epsilon_\ell$ *are each equal to* $+1$ *or* -1. *The ordered set* $\epsilon = \left\{\epsilon_{k+1},\dots,\epsilon_\ell\right\}$, *which is called a sign characteristic of the pair* A,B, *is uniquely determined to within permutation of signs corresponding to equal blocks* J_i.

In a natural way, we may also associate a sign characteristic with each real eigenvalue of $\lambda A - B$. It is the set of $+1$'s and -1's associated with the Jordan blocks of the eigenvalue in question. In particular, an eigenvalue of mixed type may be viewed as a superposition of eigenvalues of positive and negative types. When $\lambda A-B$ is diagonable the number of entries in the sign characteristic of a real eigenvalue is just the multiplicity of the eigenvalue. A pencil $\lambda A - B$ with A invertible is said to be diagonable if $A^{-1}B$ is diagonable.

The following lemma will be a useful special case of Theorem 1.1.

LEMMA 1.1. *Let* $\lambda A - B$ *be an hermitian pencil with* A *invertible. If the pencil is diagonable and has all eigenvalues real, then there is a nonsingular matrix* X, *such that*

$$X^*AX = \overset{\quad k \quad n-k}{\begin{bmatrix} I & 0 \\ 0 & -I \end{bmatrix}}\begin{matrix} k \\ n-k \end{matrix}, \quad X^*BX = \overset{\quad k \quad n-k}{\begin{bmatrix} J_1 & 0 \\ 0 & -J_2 \end{bmatrix}}\begin{matrix} k \\ n-k \end{matrix}$$

where $J_1 = \mathrm{diag}[\lambda_1,\ldots,\lambda_k]$, $J_2 = \mathrm{diag}[\lambda_{k+1},\ldots,\lambda_n]$, $\lambda_1,\ldots,\lambda_k$ *are eigenvalues of positive type, and* $\lambda_{k+1},\ldots,\lambda_n$ *are eigenvalues of negative type.*

We say an hermitian matrix pencil $\lambda A - B$ (i.e. A, B are hermitian matrices) is definite if there exist $\alpha,\beta \in \mathbb{R}$ such that $\alpha A + \beta B$ is positive definite. One of the most important properties of this kind of pencil is its geometric characterization, i.e. that an hermitian pencil $\lambda A-B$ is definite if and only if $C(A,B) = \inf_{\|x\|=1} \{|x^*(A+iB)x|\} > 0.$

It is well-known that a definite pencil is diagonable and that all its eigenvalues are real. Conversely, is a diagonable pencil with all eigenvalues real necessarily definite? "Not necessarily" is the answer. Investigation of this question leads to the following spectral characterization of definite pencils.

THEOREM 1.2. *An hermitian pencil* $\lambda A - B$ *with* A *invertible is definite if and only if it is diagonable, has all eigenvalues real, and the eigenvalues of positive type and the eigenvalues of negative type are separated.*

PROOF: Necessity. If $\lambda A - B$ is definite, it is diagonable with real spectrum. So Lemma 1.1 holds and there is an invertible X, such that

$$X^*AX = \overset{\quad k \quad n-k}{\begin{bmatrix} I & 0 \\ 0 & -I \end{bmatrix}}\begin{matrix} k \\ n-k \end{matrix}, \quad X^*BX = \overset{\quad k \quad n-k}{\begin{bmatrix} J_1 & 0 \\ 0 & -J_2 \end{bmatrix}}\begin{matrix} k \\ n-k \end{matrix} \tag{1.1}$$

where $J_1 = \mathrm{diag}[\lambda_1,\ldots,\lambda_k]$, $J_2 = \mathrm{diag}[\lambda_{k+1},\ldots,\lambda_n]$, $\lambda_1,\ldots,\lambda_k$ are eigenvalues of positive type and $\lambda_{k+1},\ldots,\lambda_n$ are eigenvalues of negative type. Now, let $\alpha,\beta \in \mathbb{R}$ be such that $\alpha A + \beta B > 0$. Then (1.1) implies

$$\begin{bmatrix} \alpha I + \beta J_1 & 0 \\ 0 & -\alpha I - \beta J_2 \end{bmatrix} > 0$$

i.e. $\alpha + \beta\lambda_i > 0$ for $i = 1,\dots,k$ and $-\alpha - \beta\lambda_j > 0$ for $j = k+1,\dots,n$.

Case 1. $\beta = 0$. Then either $A > 0$ or $A < 0$. This implies that all eigenvalues are of positive (or negative) type.

Case 2. $\beta > 0$. Then $\lambda_i > -\frac{\alpha}{\beta} > \lambda_j$ for $i = 1,\dots,k$, $j = k+1,\dots,n$. So, $\{\lambda_i\}_{i=1}^{k}$ and $\{\lambda_j\}_{j=k+1}^{n}$ are separated.

Case 3. $\beta < 0$. Then $\lambda_j > -\frac{\alpha}{\beta} > \lambda_i$ for $i = 1,\dots,k$, $j = k+1,\dots,n$. So, $\{\lambda_i\}_{i=1}^{k}$ and $\{\lambda_j\}_{j=k+1}^{n}$ are separated.

Conversely, if $\lambda A - B$ is diagonable, and has all eigenvalues real, then Lemma 1.1 and equation (1.1) hold.

For $k = 0$ or n, we have $A > 0$ or $A < 0$. They are trivial cases. So we suppose $0 < k < n$. By hypothesis, $\{\lambda_i\}_{i=1}^{k}$ and $\{\lambda_j\}_{j=k+1}^{n}$ are separated. We discuss two cases.

Case 1. $\{\lambda_i\}_{i=1}^{k} > \{\lambda_j\}_{j=k+1}^{n}$. Let α be such that $\{\lambda_1,\dots,\lambda_k\} > \alpha > \{\lambda_{k+1},\dots,\lambda_n\}$. Then

$$X^*(B-\alpha A)\,X = \begin{bmatrix} J_1-\alpha I & 0 \\ 0 & -J_2+\alpha I \end{bmatrix} > 0.$$

where we notice that $\lambda_i - \alpha > 0$ for $i = 1,\dots,k$ and $-\lambda_j + \alpha > 0$ for $j = k+1,\dots,n$. So, $B - \alpha A > 0$, i.e. $\lambda A - B$ is a definite pencil.

Case 2. $\{\lambda_i\}_{i=1}^{k} < \{\lambda_j\}_{j=k+1}^{n}$. Let α be such that $\{\lambda_1,\dots,\lambda_k\} < \alpha < \{\lambda_{k+1},\dots,\lambda_n\}$. Then

$$X^*(-B+\alpha A)X = \begin{bmatrix} -J_1+\alpha I & 0 \\ 0 & J_2-\alpha I \end{bmatrix} > 0$$

where we notice that $-\lambda_i + \alpha > 0$ for $i = 1,\dots, k$ and $\lambda_j - \alpha > 0$ for $j = k+1,\dots,n$. So, $-B + \alpha A > 0$, i.e. $\lambda A - B$ is a definite pencil. □

From the proof of the theorem, we see that coefficients α,β can be found from the extreme eigenvalues λ_k and λ_{k+1}.

2.   Minimax Principle

The minimax principle is one of the most important characterizations of eigenvalues of an hermitian matrix. It was found while considering those conservative mechanical systems which can be reduced to an eigenvalue problem for a symmetric pencil $\lambda A - B$ with A positive definite. A lot of effort has been expended to generalize these results to non–conservative systems (e.g. [3], [13], [17]), and to general operators. For definite matrix pencils, Stewart [14] has a generalization in terms of certain angles. Textorius [16] discussed self–adjoint operators in an indefinite scalar product space, and his work extends that of Phillips [21], whose minimax characterization of eigenvalues is different from that given below.

In this section, we are going to give a direct generalization of the classical minimax principles to diagonable hermitian pencils. We notice that this result applies to some non–conservative systems. Indeed, we show that there is still a minimax characterization, provided that the eigenvalues of a diagonable pencil are partially separated.

THEOREM 2.1. *Let* $\lambda A - B$ *be a diagonable hermitian matrix pencil with* A *invertible and all eigenvalues real. Suppose that* $\lambda_1 \leq ... \leq \lambda_r < \lambda_{r+1} \leq ... \leq \lambda_k$ *are eigenvalues of negative type,* $\lambda_{k+1} \leq ... \leq \lambda_{s-1} < \lambda_s \leq ... \leq \lambda_n$ *are eigenvalues of positive type, and* $\lambda_r < \{\lambda_{r+1},...,\lambda_k, \lambda_{k+1},...,\lambda_{s-1}\} < \lambda_s$. *Then*

$$\lambda_{k+j} = \sup_{\dim S_j = n-j+1} \; \inf_{\substack{x \, \epsilon \, S_j \\ x^*Ax > 0}} \; \frac{x^*Bx}{x^*Ax}, \quad \textit{for } k+j \geq s, \tag{2.1}$$

$$\lambda_{k-j+1} = \inf_{\dim S_j = n-j+1} \; \sup_{\substack{x \, \epsilon \, S_j \\ x^*Ax < 0}} \; \frac{x^*Bx}{x^*Ax}, \quad \textit{for } k-j+1 \leq r. \tag{2.2}$$

PROOF: It follows from Lemma 1.1 that there is an invertible X, such that

$$X^*AX = \begin{array}{c} kn-k \\ \begin{bmatrix} -I & 0 \\ 0 & I \end{bmatrix} \begin{array}{c} k \\ n-k \end{array} \end{array}, \quad X^*BX = \begin{array}{c} kn-k \\ \begin{bmatrix} -J_1 & 0 \\ 0 & J_2 \end{bmatrix} \begin{array}{c} k \\ n-k \end{array} \end{array}$$

where $J_1 = \text{diag}[\lambda_1,...,\lambda_k]$, $J_2 = \text{diag}[\lambda_{k+1},...,\lambda_n]$. So, we can just consider the pencil

$$\lambda \begin{bmatrix} -I & 0 \\ 0 & I \end{bmatrix} - \begin{bmatrix} -J_1 & 0 \\ 0 & J_2 \end{bmatrix}, \text{ i.e. } A = \begin{bmatrix} -I & 0 \\ 0 & I \end{bmatrix}, \quad B = \begin{bmatrix} -J_1 & 0 \\ 0 & J_2 \end{bmatrix}. \text{ Now we establish (2.1) in two}$$

steps.

1. Let e_i denote the i–th unit coordinate vector in C^n. For any subspace S_j of C^n, with $\dim S_j = n-j+1$, we have

$$S_j \cap \mathrm{span}\{e_{k+1},\ldots,e_{k+j}\} \neq \{0\}$$

Let $\xi \in S_j \cap \mathrm{span}\{e_{k+1},\ldots,e_{k+j}\}$ with $\xi \neq 0$ and write $\xi = x_{k+1}e_{k+1} + \ldots + x_{k+j}e_{kj}$. Then $\xi^* A\xi = |x_{k+1}|^2 + \ldots + |x_{k+j}|^2 > 0$ and

$$\frac{\xi^*B\xi}{\xi^*A\xi} = \frac{\lambda_{k+1}|x_{k+1}|^2 + \ldots + \lambda_{k+j}|x_{k+j}|^2}{|x_{k+1}|^2 + \ldots + |x_{k+j}|^2} \leq \lambda_{k+j}$$

So, $\inf\limits_{\substack{x\in S_j \\ x^*Ax>0}} \frac{x^*Bx}{x^*Ax} \leq \lambda_{k+j}$. This implies that

$$\sup_{\dim S_j=n-j+1} \inf_{\substack{x\in S_j \\ x^*Ax>0}} \frac{x^*Bx}{x^*Ax} \leq \lambda_{k+j} \tag{2.3}$$

2. Let $T_j = \mathrm{span}\{e_1,\ldots,e_k, e_{k+j},\ldots,e_n\}$ so that $\dim T_j = n-j+1$. So for $x = x_1e_1 + \ldots + x_ke_k + x_{k+j}e_{k+j} + \ldots + x_ne_n \in T_j$, we have

$$x^*Ax = -|x_1|^2 - \ldots - |x_k|^2 + |x_{k+j}|^2 + \ldots + |x_n|^2.$$

and

$$x^*Bx = -\lambda_1|x_1|^2 - \ldots - \lambda_k|x_k|^2 + \lambda_{k+j}|x_{k+j}|^2 + \ldots + \lambda_n|x_n|^2.$$

Now, with $k+j \geq s$, we have $\lambda_1 \leq \ldots \leq \lambda_k < \lambda_s \leq \lambda_{k+j}$, i.e.

$-\lambda_1 \geq \ldots \geq -\lambda_k > -\lambda_{k+j}$. Hence

$$x^*Bx \geq -\lambda_{k+j}|x_1|^2 - \ldots - \lambda_{k+j}|x_k|^2 + \lambda_{k+j}|x_{k+j}|^2 + \ldots + \lambda_{k+j}|x_n|^2 = \lambda_{k+j}x^*Ax.$$

Therefore, for $x^*Ax > 0$,

$$\frac{x^*Bx}{x^*Ax} \geq \lambda_{k+j}$$

Thus,

$$\inf_{\substack{x\in T_j \\ x^*Ax>0}} \frac{x^*Bx}{x^*Ax} \geq \lambda_{k+j}$$

This implies

$$\sup_{\dim S_j=n-j+1} \inf_{\substack{x\in S_j \\ x^*Ax>0}} \frac{x^*Bx}{x^*Ax} \geq \lambda_{k+1} \tag{2.4}$$

So, (2.3) and (2.4) imply (2.1).

We can prove (2.2) by the same argument as above or by applying (2.1) to the pencil $\lambda A + B$. We omit the details. □

THEOREM 2.2. *Let* $\lambda A - B$ *be a diagonable hermitian matrix pencil with* A *invertible and all eigenvalues real. Suppose that* $\lambda_1 \leq \dots \leq \lambda_r < \lambda_{r+1} \leq \dots \leq \lambda_k$ *are eigenvalues of positive type,* $\lambda_{k+1} \leq \dots \leq \lambda_{s-1} < \lambda_s \leq \dots \leq \lambda_n$ *are eigenvalues of negative type, and* $\lambda_r < \{\lambda_{r+1},\dots,\lambda_k,\lambda_{k+1},\dots,\lambda_{s-1}\} < \lambda_s$. *Then*

$$\lambda_{k+j} = \sup_{\dim S_j = n-j+1} \inf_{\substack{x \in S_j \\ x^*Ax<0}} \frac{x^*Bx}{x^*Ax}, \quad \textit{for } k+j \geq s,$$

$$\lambda_{k-j+1} = \inf_{\dim S_j = n-j+1} \sup_{\substack{x \in S_j \\ x^*Ax>0}} \frac{x^*Bx}{x^*Ax}, \quad \textit{for } k+j \leq r.$$

PROOF: Simply apply the previous theorem to the pencil $\lambda(-A)-(-B)$ which has the same eigenvalues as $\lambda A - B$ with sign characteristics reversed. □

As special cases, the following two corollaries give a characterization for a definite matrix pencil.

COROLLARY 2.3. *Let* $\lambda A - B$ *be a diagonable hermitian matrix pencil with* A *invertible and all eigenvalues real. Suppose* $\lambda_1 \leq \dots \leq \lambda_k < \lambda_{k+1} \leq \dots \leq \lambda_n$ *are eigenvalues with* $\lambda_1,\dots,\lambda_k$ *negative type, and* $\lambda_{k+1},\dots,\lambda_n$ *positive type, then*

$$\lambda_i = \inf_{\dim S_i = n-k+i} \sup_{\substack{x \in S_i \\ x^*Ax<0}} \frac{x^*Bx}{x^*Ax}, \quad i = 1,\dots,k.$$

$$\lambda_j = \sup_{\dim S_j = n+k+1-i} \inf_{\substack{x \in S_j \\ x^*Ax>0}} \frac{x^*Bx}{x^*Ax}, \quad j = k+1,\dots,n.$$

In particular,

$$\lambda_k = \max_{x^*Ax<0} \frac{x^*Bx}{x^*Ax}, \quad \lambda_{k+1} = \min_{x^*Ax>0} \frac{x^*Bx}{x^*Ax}.$$

COROLLARY 2.4. *Let* $\lambda A - B$ *be a diagonable hermitian pencil with* A *invertible and all eigenvalues real. Suppose* $\lambda_1 \leq \dots \leq \lambda_k < \lambda_{k+1} \leq \dots \leq \lambda_n$ *are eigenvalues with* $\lambda_1,\dots,\lambda_k$ *positive type, and* $\lambda_{k+1},\dots,\lambda_n$ *negative type, then*

$$\lambda_i = \inf_{\dim S_i = n-k+i} \; \sup_{\substack{x \in S_i \\ x^*Ax>0}} \frac{x^*Bx}{x^*Ax}, \quad i = 1,\dots,k,$$

$$\lambda_j = \sup_{\dim S_j = n+k+1-j} \; \inf_{\substack{x \in S_j \\ x^*Ax<0}} \frac{x^*Bx}{x^*Ax}, \quad j = k+1,\dots,n.$$

In particular,

$$\lambda_k = \max_{x^*Ax>0} \frac{x^*Bx}{x^*Ax}, \quad \lambda_{k+1} = \min_{x^*Ax<0} \frac{x^*Bx}{x^*Ax}.$$

We make several remarks here.

REMARK 1: For an hermitian matrix H, we consider $\lambda I - H$. In this case all eigenvalues are of positive type. So, in a trivial way, we can regard the pencil $\lambda I - H$ as having negative type eigenvalues less than positive type eigenvalues, or vice versa. Then the Corollary 2.3 or Corollary 2.4 will apply and give the max–min or min–max characterization.

REMARK 2: The eigenvalues of an hermitian matrix have both max–min and min–max characterization. In contrast to this, the above results show that when eigenvalues of both types occur, our max–min and min–max characterizations apply only to eigenvalues of positive and negative types, respectively.

REMARK 3: Stewart [14] has found a different generalization of the classical minimax principle to definite pencils based on the analysis of certain angles in the complex plane determined by the properties of the eigenvalues. But the results here are applied directly to the eigenvalues themselves and depend on a Rayleigh quotient of classical form.

REMARK 4: If $\lambda A - B$ is a real symmetric pencil with all eigenvalues real, then it is easy to see that the X in Lemma 1.1 can be chosen to be real. So, all arguments in this section can be carried over within the real space $\mathbb{R}^n$. Then we obtain corresponding results of the same form with all subspace $S_i \subset \mathbb{R}^n$.

3. Minimax Principle in the Presence of Complex Eigenvalues

As we have seen in §1, a general hermitian pencil can have non–real eigenvalues. Because minimax theorems are established using the natural order of the real numbers, it seems impossible to characterize the non–real eigenvalues in this way. But for real eigenvalues, variational characterizations can be obtained using a projection method. We quote just one such result here. By a *simple* eigenvalue we mean one with index one (i.e. with only linear elementary divisors, or with a full complement of eigenvectors).

THEOREM 3.1. *Let* $\lambda A - B$ *be an hermitian matrix pencil with* A *invertible, let* $\lambda_1,\ldots,\lambda_m$ *be simple real eigenvalues,* $\lambda_{m+1},\ldots,\lambda_n$ *be non–real eigenvalues and let* $\mathcal{S}$ *be the spectral subspace associated with* $\lambda_1,\ldots,\lambda_m$. *Suppose* $\lambda_1 < \ldots < \lambda_r < \ldots < \lambda_k$ *are eigenvalues of negative type* $\lambda_{k+1} < \ldots < \lambda_s < \ldots < \lambda_m$ *are eigenvalues of positive type, and* $\lambda_r < \{\lambda_{r+1},\ldots,\lambda_{s-1}\} < \lambda_s$. *Then*

$$\lambda_{k+j} = \sup_{\substack{\dim \mathcal{S}_j = n-j+1 \\ \mathcal{S}_j \subset \mathcal{S}}} \ \inf_{\substack{x \in \mathcal{S}_j \\ x^*Ax>0}} \frac{x^*Bx}{x^*Ax}, \quad \textit{for} \ \ s \le k+j \le m,$$

$$\lambda_{k-j+1} = \inf_{\substack{\dim \mathcal{S}_j = n-j+1 \\ \mathcal{S}_j \subset \mathcal{S}}} \ \sup_{\substack{x \in \mathcal{S}_j \\ x^*Ax<0}} \frac{x^*Bx}{x^*Ax}, \quad \textit{for} \ \ k-j+1 \le r.$$

4. Rayleigh Quotient Iteration

The Rayleigh quotient iteration is a method for finding eigenvalues by using inverse iteration together with the Rayleigh quotient shift. Its local cubic convergence and global convergence properties make it a competitive method when only a few eigenvalues are needed. The discussion of local convergence for a hermitian matrix was started in Temple [15] and Crandall [1] and was analyzed rigorously and in detail in Ostrowski [9]. In a series of papers, Ostrowski also generalized it to non–hermitian matrices, and in Lancaster [7], its generalization to nonlinear eigenvalue problems was discussed. Then came the proof of global convergence for hermitian matrices in Kahan [6], Parlett and Kahan [12], and its generalization to normal matrices in Parlett [11]. Also, the corresponding results for symmetric matrix pencils $\lambda A - B$ with A positive definite can be found in Parlett [10]. But there has been no discussion for the case in which A is not positive definite; the problem that we now consider.

We first make a simple observation. For an hermitian matrix pencil $\lambda A - B$ with A invertible, and any vector $x \in \mathbb{C}^n$, we say $\rho(x) = \frac{x^*Bx}{x^*Ax}$ is the Rayleigh quotient of x if $x^*Ax \neq 0$. From this definition, we see the first difference: that $\rho(x)$ is not defined for A–isotropic vectors x. It is easy to see that if λ is a simple *real* eigenvalue, and x is an associated eigenvector, then $x^*Ax \neq 0$ (e.g. by Theorem 1.1), $\lambda = \rho(x)$, and x is a stationary point of $\rho(x)$.

With these observations, we write the Rayleigh quotient iteration process for $\lambda A - B$ with minor variations from the one matrix case. We use $\|\cdot\|$ to denote any vector norm on $\mathbb{C}^n$.

ALGORITHM 4.1: *Pick a starting vector* x_0 *with* $\|x_0\| = 1$ *and* $x_0^* A x_0 > 0$ (or $x_0^* A x_0 < 0$). *Then for* $k = 0,1,2,\ldots$

(i) *if* $x_k^* A x_k = 0$, *stop; otherwise*

(ii) *form* $\rho_k = \rho(x_k) = \dfrac{x_k^* B x_k}{x_k^* A x_k}$

(iii) *if* $\rho_k A - B$ *is singular, then solve* $(\rho_k A - B)\, v_{k+1} = 0$ *to get an approximation* (ρ_k, v_{k+1}) *and stop; otherwise*

(iv) *solve* $(\rho_k A - B)\, y_{k+1} = A x_k$

(v) *normalize* y_{k+1} *to get* $x_{k+1} = y_{k+1} / \|A y_{k+1}\|$.

Looking at the algorithm, we see that several difficulties can arise from the fact that A is indefinite. If there is some k such that $x_k^* A x_k = 0$, the iteration will break down and no information is obtained. Also, even if $x_k^* A x_k \neq 0$ but oscillates between positive and negative as k increases, there is no way to ensure convergence. Fortunately, it will be shown that these cases will not affect the local convergence to a simple real eigenvalue and will not happen even for global strategies for a definite pencil.

We remark that the norm chosen in the algorithm does not affect the Rayleigh quotient ρ_k and the direction of the iterative vector x_k , i.e. different normalizations will give the same ρ_k and the same direction of x_k .

Ostrowski [9] has discussed a generalized Rayleigh quotient method for general nonsymmetric matrices (in a so–called two–sided iteration). It is not hard to see that Algorithm 4.1 is equivalent to applying the generalized Rayleigh quotient method to $A^{-1}B$ with a special choice of initial vector pair, i.e. by taking $\xi_0 = x_0$ and $\zeta_0 = A x_0$ in two–sided iteration. Then Ostrowski's local convergence results can be applied to Algorithm 4.1. Under some conditions, (with A diagonable, for example) Ostrowski proved that the sequence of Rayleigh quotients $\{\rho_k\}$ converges cubically if it converges to an eigenvalue. But there has been no discussion about the convergence of Rayleigh iterative vectors. In the next section, we prove the local cubic convergence of Rayleigh iterative vectors under weak assumptions.

Finally, if the pencil is real, then eigenpairs to which we hope the algorithm will converge must be real. So we can take the starting vector x_0 to be real; hence all iteration will be performed in real spaces.

5. Locally Cubic Convergence

As pointed out, it is primarily the stationary property of the Rayleigh quotient that ensures cubic convergence for the Rayleigh quotient iteration. As the stationary property is valid for a simple real eigenvalue and eigenvector, it seems that we can carry over the local convergence results to a general hermitian pencil. A crucial point is how to choose a measure of the convergence and a related norm.

Let $\lambda A - B$ be an hermitian pencil with A invertible, and

$$X^{-1}(A^{-1}B)X = J \quad \text{or} \quad BX = AXJ \tag{5.1}$$

where $X = [e_0, e_1, \ldots, e_{n-1}]$ is an invertible matrix and $J = \begin{bmatrix} \lambda_0 & 0 \\ 0 & J_1 \end{bmatrix}$ is a Jordan matrix, with λ_0 a simple real eigenvalue. Then $e_0^* A e_0 \neq 0$. So we can normalize e_0 so that $|e_0^* A e_0| = 1$.

Without loss of generality, we suppose that there is only one Jordan block in J_1 which has order greater than one. i.e.

$$J_1 = \begin{bmatrix} J_2 & 0 \\ 0 & J_3 \end{bmatrix}$$

where J_2 is an $\ell \times \ell$ Jordan block with eigenvalue λ_1 and $J_3 = \text{diag}[\lambda_{\ell+1}, \ldots, \lambda_{n-1}]$. Then by (5.1)

$$\left.\begin{aligned} Be_1 &= \lambda_1 Ae_1 \\ Be_2 &= \lambda_1 Ae_2 + Ae_1 \\ &\cdots \\ Be_\ell &= \lambda_1 Ae_\ell + Ae_{\ell-1} \end{aligned}\right\} \tag{5.2}$$

and

$$Be_i = \lambda_i Ae_i \quad \text{for} \quad i \neq 1, \ldots, \ell.$$

Now, we prove a lemma.

LEMMA 5.1: *For any* $\alpha \notin \sigma(A^{-1}B)$ *and* $i = 1, \ldots, \ell$

$$(\alpha A - B)^{-1} Ae_i = \sum_{t=1}^{i} \frac{1}{(\alpha - \lambda_1)^t} e_{i-t+1} .$$

PROOF. The proof is by verification. We use Equations (5.2) to obtain

$$(\alpha A - B) \sum_{t=1}^{i} \frac{1}{(\alpha - \lambda_1)^t} e_{i-t+1}$$

$$= \sum_{t=1}^{i-1} \frac{1}{(\alpha-\lambda_1)^t}\left[(\alpha-\lambda_1)Ae_{i-t+1} - Ae_{i-t}\right] + \frac{1}{(\alpha-\lambda_1)^t}(\alpha-\lambda_1)Ae_1$$

$$= \sum_{t=1}^{i-1} \frac{1}{(\alpha-\lambda_1)^{t-1}} Ae_{i-t+1} - \sum_{t=1}^{i-1} \frac{1}{(\alpha-\lambda_1)^t} Ae_{i-t} + \frac{1}{(\alpha-\lambda_1)^{i-1}} Ae_1$$

$$= Ae_i + \sum_{t=1}^{i-2} \frac{1}{(\alpha-\lambda_1)^t} Ae_{i-t} - \sum_{t=1}^{i-2} \frac{1}{(\alpha-\lambda_1)^t} Ae_{i-t}$$

$$= Ae_i. \qquad \square$$

We turn to convergence analysis. We first introduce a norm. For any vector $x \in \mathbb{C}^n$, there is a decomposition

$$x = \sum_{i=0}^{n-1} \alpha_i e_i$$

and a norm associated with the basis defined by

$$\|x\|_* = \left[\sum_{i=0}^{n-1} |\alpha_i|^2\right]^{\frac{1}{2}}. \tag{5.3}$$

It is easy to see that $\|\cdot\|_*$ is a norm in $\mathbb{C}^n$. We can extend this norm to matrix space $\mathbb{C}^{n\times n}$ to get a consistent norm. Also, for any $x \in \mathbb{C}^n$, we have the decomposition

$$x = a\cdot e_0 + b\cdot u \tag{5.4}$$

where $a,b \in \mathbb{C}$, and $u \in \text{span}\{e_1,\dots,e_{n-1}\}$ with $\|u\|_* = 1$. This decomposition is unique if, in the representation $u = \sum_{j=1}^{n-1} \beta_j e_j$, the first non–zero β_j is a positive number.

Using this decomposition, for each Rayleigh iteration vector x_k of Algorithm 4.1, we can write, as in (5.4),

$$x_k = a_k e_0 + b_k \cdot u_k . \tag{5.5}$$

Then $c_k = \left|\frac{b_k}{a_k}\right|$ is a measure of how x_k approaches e_0 in direction. Notice that c_k only depends on the direction of x_k .

The following theorem and its corollary establish local cubic convergence for the sequence of approximate eigenvectors. They provide insights into this phenomenon and are not intended to provide computable estimates.

THEOREM 5.1. *Let* $\lambda A - B$ *be an hermitian matrix pencil with a simple real eigenvalue* λ_0 *and associated eigenvector* e_0. *Let* $\{x_k\}_{k=0}^{\infty}$ *be defined as in Algorithm*

4.1 *and* c_k *be defined as above. Then if* c_0 *is sufficiently small and* e_0 *is* A*–positive (or* A*–negative) then for all* k, x_k *is* A*–positive (or* A*–negative, respectively). Furthermore,* $c_{k+1} \le c_k^3 M$ *for some constant* M *where* $k = 0,1,2,\dots$.

PROOF. Without loss of generality, we can suppose $e_0^* A e_0 = 1$. We start from x_k. Let $x_k = a_k e_0 + b_k u_k$ with $u_k = \sum_{i=1}^{n-1} \alpha_i e_i$ and $\|u_k\|_*^2 = \sum_{i=1}^{n-1} |\alpha_i|^2 = 1$. Then, using Lemma 5.1,

$$y_{k+1} = (\rho_k A-B)^{-1} A x_k = a_k(\rho_k A-B)^{-1} A e_0 + b_k(\rho_k A-B)^{-1} A u_k = \frac{a_k}{\rho_k-\lambda_0} e_0 + b_k \cdot v_{k+1}$$

$$= a'_{k+1} e_0 + b'_{k+1} u_{k+1}$$

where $v_{k+1} = (\rho_k A-B)^{-1} A u_k$, $u_{k+1} = \frac{v_{k+1}}{\|v_{k+1}\|_* \gamma}$, $a'_{k+1} = \frac{a_k}{\rho_k-\lambda_0}$ and $b'_{k+1} = b_k \cdot \|v_{k+1}\|_* \gamma$, and γ is a complex number with $|\gamma| = 1$ for which the first non–zero e_j–component of u_{k+1} is a positive real number. Thus, with the norm $\|\cdot\|$ chosen in the algorithm,

$$x_{k+1} = \frac{y_{k+1}}{\|y_{k+1}\|} = \frac{a'_{k+1}}{\|y_{k+1}\|} e_0 + \frac{b'_{k+1}}{\|y_{k+1}\|} u_{k+1} = a_{k+1} e_0 + b_{k+1} u_{k+1} .$$

Hence

$$c_{k+1} = \left|\frac{b_{k+1}}{a_{k+1}}\right| = \left|\frac{b'_{k+1}}{a'_{k+1}}\right| = \left|\frac{b_k}{a_k}\right| \|v_{k+1}\|_* \cdot |\rho_k - \lambda_0| . \tag{5.6}$$

Now, using Lemma 5.1,

$$v_{k+1} = (\rho_k A-B)^{-1} A u_k = \sum_{i=1}^{\ell} \alpha_i(\rho_k A-B)^{-1} A e_i + \sum_{i=\ell+1}^{n-1} \alpha_i(\rho_k A-B)^{-1} A e_i$$

$$= \sum_{i=1}^{\ell} \alpha_i \sum_{t=1}^{i} \frac{1}{(\rho_k-\lambda_1)^t} e_{i-t+1} + \sum_{i=\ell+1}^{n-1} \frac{\alpha_i}{\rho_k-\lambda_i} e_i$$

$$= \sum_{t=1}^{\ell} \left[\sum_{i=t}^{\ell} \frac{\alpha_i}{(\rho_k-\lambda_1)^t} e_{i-t+1}\right] + \sum_{i=\ell+1}^{n-1} \frac{\alpha_i}{\rho_k-\lambda_i} e_i$$

$$= \sum_{t=2}^{\ell} \left[\sum_{i=t}^{\ell} \frac{\alpha_i}{(\rho_k-\lambda_1)^t} e_{i-t+1}\right] + \sum_{i=1}^{n-1} \frac{\alpha_i}{\rho_k-\lambda_i} e_i .$$

Therefore

$$\|v_{k+1}\|_* \le \sum_{t=2}^{\ell} \Big\| \sum_{i=t}^{\ell} \frac{\alpha_i}{(\rho_k-\lambda_1)^t} e_{i-t+1}\Big\|_* + \Big\| \sum_{i=1}^{n-1} \frac{\alpha_i}{\rho_k-\lambda_i} e_i\Big\|_*$$

$$= \sum_{t=2}^{\ell} \left[\sum_{i=t}^{\ell} \frac{|\alpha_i|^2}{|\rho_k-\lambda_1|^{2t}}\right]^{\frac12} + \left[\sum_{i=1}^{n-1} \frac{|\alpha_i|^2}{|\rho_k-\lambda_i|^2}\right]^{\frac12}.$$

So, if $|\rho_k-\lambda_0| \le \alpha = \frac12 \min_{i\neq 0} |\lambda_i-\lambda_0|$, then $|\rho_k-\lambda_i| \ge \alpha$ for $i \neq 0$. Hence

$$\|v_{k+1}\|_* \le \sum_{t=2}^{\ell} \frac{1}{\alpha^t}\left[\sum_{i=t}^{\ell} |\alpha_i|^2\right]^{\frac12} + \frac{1}{\alpha}\left[\sum_{i=1}^{n-1} |\alpha_i|^2\right]^{\frac12}$$

$$\le \sum_{t=2}^{\ell} \frac{1}{\alpha^t} + \frac{1}{\alpha} = \sum_{t=1}^{\ell} \frac{1}{\alpha^t} \tag{5.7}$$

Also

$$\rho_k - \lambda_0 = \frac{x_k^*(B-\lambda_0A)x_k}{x_k^* A x_k} = \frac{|b_k|^2\, u_k^*(B-\lambda_0A)u_k}{|a_k|^2 e_0^*Ae_0 + |b_k|^2\, u_k^*Au_k} = c_k^2 \frac{u_k^*(B-\lambda_0A)u_k}{1 + c_k^2\, u_k^*Au_k}$$

where we use the orthogonality property (see Theorem 2.5 of [5]): $e_0^* Au_k = \sum_{i=1}^{n-1} \alpha_i e_0^* Ae_i = 0$ together with $(B-\lambda_0A)e_0 = 0$. Then, if $1 - c_k^2\|A\|_* > 0$, we have

$$|\rho_k-\lambda_0| \le c_k^2 \frac{|u_k^*(B-\lambda_0A)u_k|}{1- c_k^2|u_k^*Au_k|} \le c_k^2 \frac{\|B-\lambda_0A\|_*}{1- c_k^2\|A\|_*}.$$

Thus, if $c_k < \delta$ for some sufficiently small positive number $\delta < \frac{1}{\sqrt{2\|A\|_*}}$, then $1 - c_k^2\|A\|_* > \frac12$, and hence

$$|\rho_k-\lambda_0| \le 2\|B-\lambda_0A\|_*\, c_k^2 = K\, c_k^2 < K\, \delta^2 \tag{5.8}$$

Notice $K = 2\|B-\lambda_0A\|_*$ is independent of δ. Now, we choose δ so small that $|\rho_k-\lambda_0| \le \alpha$ and (as in (5.7)) $\|v_{k+1}\|_* \le \sum_{t=1}^{\ell} \frac{1}{\alpha^t}$. So, we obtain from (5.6) and (5.8)

$$c_{k+1} = c_k^3\, K\left[\sum_{t=1}^{\ell} \frac{1}{\alpha^t}\right] =: Mc_k^3,$$

as required. Furthermore, for δ sufficiently small, we obtain $c_{k+1} \le c_k < \delta$, and also

$$x_{k+1}^* Ax_{k+1} = |a_{k+1}|^2 + |b_{k+1}|^2 u_{k+1}^* Au_{k+1} \ge a_{k+1}|^2 (1 - c_{k+1}^* \|A\|_*)$$

$$\ge |a_{k+1}|^2 (1 - \delta^2 \|A\|_*) > \frac12 |a_{k+1}|^2 > 0.$$

This completes the proof. □

Notice we only assume that c_0 is small enough, rather than the stronger hypotheses that $\{c_k\}$ converges to 0 or $\{x_k\}$ converges to an eigenvector.

The convergence in the above theorem is measured by c_k, or some kind of angle between vectors. But our next corollary shows that this can also be measured by residual norms.

COROLLARY 5.2: *With the hypotheses of Theorem* 5.1, *let the norm in the Algorithm* 4.1 *be given by* (5.3) *and let* $\epsilon_k = \frac{a_k}{|a_k|}$. *Then*

$$\|x_{k+1} - \epsilon_{k+1} e_0\|_* \le L \|x_k - \epsilon_k e_0\|_*^3, \quad k = 0,1,2,\ldots$$

for some constant L.

PROOF. Using equations (5.3) and (5.4) it is easy to see that $\|x_k\|_*^2 = |a_k|^2 + |b_k|^2 = 1$. Then

$$1 + c_k^2 = \frac{1}{|a_k|^2} = \left[\frac{\epsilon_k}{a_k}\right]^2,$$

and hence

$$\left[1 - \frac{\epsilon_k}{a_k}\right]\left[1 + \frac{\epsilon_k}{a_k}\right] = -c_k^2 .$$

Thus

$$\left|1 - \frac{\epsilon_k}{a_k}\right| \le \left|\left[1 - \frac{\epsilon_k}{a_k}\right]\left[1 + \frac{\epsilon_k}{a_k}\right]\right| = c_k^2 .$$

So,

$$\frac{\|x_{k+1}-\epsilon_{k+1}e_0\|_*^2}{\|x_k-\epsilon_k e_0\|_*^6} = \frac{|a_{k+1}-\epsilon_{k+1}|^2 + |b_{k+1}|^2}{[\,|a_k-\epsilon_k|^2 + |b_k|^2\,]^3} = \frac{\left[\left|1- \frac{\epsilon_{k+1}}{a_{k+1}}\right|^2 + c_{k+1}^2\right]|a_{k+1}|^2}{\left[\left[1 - \frac{\epsilon_k}{a_k}\right]^2 + c_k^2\right]^3 |a_k|^6}$$

$$= \frac{c_{k+1}^2}{c_k^6} \cdot \frac{1+\left[1- \frac{\epsilon_{k+1}}{a_{k+1}}\right]^2 / c_{k+1}^2}{\left[1+\left[1 - \frac{\epsilon_k}{a_k}\right]^2 / c_k^2\right]^3} \cdot \frac{|a_{k+1}|^2}{|a_k|^6} \le \frac{c_{k+1}^2}{c_k^6} \cdot \frac{1+c_{k+1}^2}{\left[1-c_k^2\right]^3} \cdot \frac{|a_{k+1}|^2}{|a_k|^6}$$

By Theorem 5.1, $c_k \longrightarrow 0$, then $0 < \delta \le |a_k|^2 \le 1$ for some δ, thus $\dfrac{1+c_{k+1}^2}{\left[1-c_k^2\right]^3} \dfrac{|a_{k+1}|^2}{|a_k|^6}$ is bounded. Therefore, $\dfrac{\|x_{k+1} - \epsilon_{k+1}\, e_0\|_*^2}{\|x_k - \epsilon_k\, e_0\|_*^6} \le L^2$ for some L. This proves the corollary. □

6. Global Convergence for Definite Pencils

From the point of view of numerical analysis of *definite* problems it should be remarked that an alternative strategy is available. Namely, to first compute real numbers α and β such that $\alpha A + \beta B > 0$, then make a shift of the parameter to create a pencil with positive definite leading term and apply more familiar algorithms to this problem. There are two major reasons for *not* doing this. First, the computation of α and β is itself a substantial task, so that computational efficiency (at the present state of knowledge) does not give clear guidance on the preferred line of attack. Second, our resolution of the direct approach to definite pencils may give some clues on the development of algorithms for indefinite pencils. Furthermore, our results show that the only significant advantage to be gained from making such a shift will be the improved stability resulting from a definite leading coefficient. There may also be some advantage in the freedom to decide whether positive or negative type eigenvalues are to be computed (after the shifting strategy is implemented this distinction is lost).

Note also that if Algorithm 4.1 is applied to the shifted pencil $\lambda M-B$, and to the original pencil $\lambda A-B$ two different recursions are obtained:

$$x_{k+1} = c_{k+1}(\mu_k M-B)^{-1} Mx_k ,$$

and

$$\tilde{x}_{k+1} = \tilde{c}_{k+1}(\mu_k M-B)^{-1} A\tilde{x}_k ,$$

respectively (see equation (6.7) below), where c_{k+1}, $\tilde{c}_{k+1}$ are scalars. So different sequences would be obtained from the same starting vector. Since $M > 0$, analysis for the first sequence is an easy extension of standard results (see references [11] and [12]). The presence of A in the second recursion demands the introduction of an indefinite scalar product and some new ideas in order to extend these standard results.

As we have mentioned in §4, if we start Algorithm 4.1 from an arbitrary vector x_0, it could happen that $x_k^* Ax_k$ oscillates between positive and negative numbers. So, when considering a global strategy, we first hope to retain the sign of $x_k^* Ax_k$ as k increases. It is shown in the following theorem that this is true for definite pencils.

(Notice that, in the following statement, if x represents x_k of Algorithm 4.1, then y is a scalar multiple of x_{k+1} .)

THEOREM 6.1. *Let* $\lambda A - B$ *be a definite pencil with* A *invertible, and* x *a vector for which* $x^*Ax \neq 0$ *and* $\rho(x) \notin \sigma(A^{-1}B)$. *Let* $y = (\rho(x)A-B)^{-1}Ax$ *and* $a = x^*Ax$, $b = y^*Ax$, $c = y^*Ay$. *Then* $3b^2 \leq 4ac$ *and* $ac > 0$.

PROOF. Without loss of generality, we can suppose $a = x^*Ax > 0$. Let t be a real parameter and

$$z = z(t) = y + tx = (\rho A-B)^{-1}Ax + tx$$

where $\rho = \rho(x)$. Then

$$(\rho A-B)z = Ax + t(\rho A-B)x. \tag{6.1}$$

Multiplying by x^*, and using the definition of $\rho(x)$, we have

$$x^*(\rho A-B)z = x^*Ax + tx^*(\rho A-B)x = x^*Ax. \tag{6.2}$$

Multiply (6.1) by z^*, and use (6.2) to obtain

$$\rho z^*Az - z^*Bz = z^*Ax + tz^*(\rho A-B)x = z^*Ax + tx^*Ax = y^*Ax + 2tx^*Ax.$$

Then for $z^*Az \neq 0$, we have

$$\frac{z^*Bz}{z^*Az} = \rho - \frac{y^*Ax + 2t\ x^*Ax}{z^*Az} = \rho - \frac{b + 2at}{z^*Az}. \tag{6.3}$$

Since $z = y + tx$, we also have

$$z^*Az = t^2x^*Ax + 2ty^*Ax + y^*Ay = at^2 + 2bt + c$$

where we notice that $b = y^*Ax = x^*Ay = x^*A(\rho A-B)^{-1}Ax$ is real.

Now, if $b^2 - ac < 0$, then $3b^2 < 4ac$ and $ac > 0$. If $b^2 - ac \geq 0$, then $at^2 + 2bt + c = (t-t_1)(t-t_2)$ with $at_1 = -b+\sqrt{b^2-ac}$ and $at_2 = -b - \sqrt{b^2-ac}$. Thus, $at^2 + 2bt + c \longrightarrow 0+$, as $t \longrightarrow t_1+$, and $b + 2at \longrightarrow 2(-b+\sqrt{b^2-ac}) + b = -b + 2\sqrt{b^2-ac}$ as $t \longrightarrow t_1+$. Also, $at^2 + 2bt + c \longrightarrow 0+$, as $t \longrightarrow t_2-$ and $b + 2at \longrightarrow -b - 2\sqrt{b^2-ac}$ as $t \longrightarrow t_2-$.

We show that $2\sqrt{b^2-ac} \leq |b|$ (which implies $3b^2 \leq 4ac$). Otherwise, suppose $2\sqrt{b^2-ac} > |b|$, i.e. $2\sqrt{b^2-ac} > b > -2\sqrt{b^2-ac}$, or $-b + 2\sqrt{b^2-ac} > 0$ and $b + 2\sqrt{b^2-ac} > 0$ and we see that when either $t \longrightarrow t_1+$ or $t \longrightarrow t_2-$, $b + 2at$ approaches a positive, or negative, limit respectively.

Then, from (6.3), we find that

$$\frac{z(t)^*Bz(t)}{z(t)^*Az(t)} = \rho - \frac{b + 2at}{at^2 + 2bt + c} \longrightarrow -\infty, \quad \text{as } t \longrightarrow t_1+$$

and

$$\frac{z(t)^*Bz(t)}{z(t)^*Az(t)} = \rho - \frac{b + 2at}{at^2 + 2bt + c} \longrightarrow +\infty, \quad \text{as } t \longrightarrow t_2-$$

with $z(t)^*A\,z(t) > 0$ in both cases. This contradicts either the Corollary 2.3 or Corollary 2.4. So, $2\sqrt{b^2-ac} \le |b|$. Hence $3b^2 \le 4ac$. From this $ac \ge 0$. Moreover, if $ac = 0$, then $b = c = 0$, hence $z^*(t)Az(t) = at^2 > 0$, for $t \neq 0$, and from (6.3),

$$\frac{z(t)^*Bz(t)}{z(t)^*Az(t)} = \rho - \frac{2at}{at^2} = \rho - \frac{2}{t} \longrightarrow -\infty, \quad \text{as } t \longrightarrow 0+$$

and

$$\frac{z(t)^*Bz(t)}{z(t)^*Az(t)} = \rho - \frac{2}{t} \longrightarrow +\infty, \quad \text{as } t \longrightarrow 0-.$$

This contradicts either the Corollary 2.3 or the Corollary 2.4 again. So, $ac > 0$, and the theorem is proved. □

The above theorem shows that if we start the iteration from a vector x_0 in the A–positive cone, i.e. $x_0^* Ax_0 > 0$ (or A–negative cone) the successive iterative vectors x_k will remain in the same cone.

In the case of Rayleigh quotient algorithms for normal matrices, it is the monotonicity of the norm of residual vectors that makes the global convergence possible. For our discussion, what is the appropriate norm? Also, what are the appropriate residual vectors? For a definite pencil, we immediately have a positive definite matrix in hand which defines a norm. In the following, we therefore discuss a definite pencil $\lambda A - B$ with $\alpha A + \beta B > 0$ for some real α and β.

Let $M = \alpha A + \beta B$ and denote the M^{-1}–norm by $\|\cdot\|$, i.e. $\|x\| = \|x\|_{M^{-1}} = \sqrt{x^*M^{-1}x}$. Also, we designate the norm which normalizes the vectors in Algorithm 4.1 to be this norm. First we prove a couple of lemmas.

LEMMA 6.1. *If* A, B *are hermitian matrices with* $M = \alpha A + \beta B > 0$ *for some* $\alpha,\beta \in \mathbb{R}$, *then* $AM^{-1}(uA+vB) = (uA+vB)M^{-1}A$ *and* $AM^{-1}(uA+vM) = (uA+vM)M^{-1}A$ *for any* $u,v \in \mathbb{R}$.

PROOF. Since $M = \alpha A + \beta B > 0$, A, B, M can be simultaneously reduced to diagonal matrices by congruence, i.e., there is an invertible matrix X, such that

$$X^*AX = P_A, \quad X^*BX = P_B, \quad X^*MX = P_M$$

where P_A, P_B, P_M are diagonal matrices. The result is clear after this reduction to diagonal forms. □

LEMMA 6.2. *Let* $\lambda A - B$ *be a definite pencil with* A *invertible and* $M = \alpha A + \beta B > 0$. *Then the Rayleigh quotients* ρ_k *defined by Algorithm* 4.1 *satisfy* $\alpha + \beta\rho_k \neq 0$.

PROOF. By Theorem 5.1, $x_k^* A x_k \neq 0$. Then $x_k^* M x_k > 0$, i.e. $\alpha x_k^* A x_k + \beta x_k^* B x_k > 0$, and hence $\alpha + \beta\rho_k \neq 0$. □

Now we introduce residual vectors r_k defined by

$$r_k = \frac{1}{\alpha + \beta\rho_k} (\rho_k A - B) x_k \tag{6.4}$$

and can establish the following monotonicity property.

THEOREM 6.2. *Let* $\lambda A - B$ *be a definite pencil with* A *invertible and* $M = \alpha A + \beta B > 0$. *Let* $\{x_k\}$ *be defined by Algorithm* 4.1 *and* M^{-1}*–norm* $\|\cdot\|$, *and* $\{r_k\}$ *be defined by* (6.4). *Then we have the monotonicity property* $\|r_{k+1}\| \leq \|r_k\|$.

PROOF. Let $\mu_k = \dfrac{1}{\alpha + \beta\rho_k} = \dfrac{x_k^* A x_k}{x_k^*(\alpha A + \beta B) x_k} = \dfrac{x_k^* A x_k}{x_k^* M x_k}$. With this μ_k, we have

$$\|(A - \mu_k M) x_{k+1}\|^2 = \|(A - \mu_{k+1} M) x_{k+1}\|^2 + (\mu_{k+1} - \mu_k)^2 \|M x_{k+1}\|^2 \tag{6.5}$$

where we notice that μ_k is a Rayleigh quotient. So

$$\|(A - \mu_{k+1} M) x_{k+1}\| \leq \|(A - \mu_k M) x_{k+1}\|. \tag{6.6}$$

Let $\tau_k = \dfrac{1}{\|A y_{k+1}\|}$ with $\{y_k\}$ defined in Algorithm 4.1. Then

$$x_{k+1} = (\rho_k A - B)^{-1} A x_k \cdot \tau_k , \tag{6.7}$$

and hence

$$\begin{aligned}(A - \mu_k M) x_{k+1} &= \mu_k[(\alpha + \beta\rho_k) A - M] x_{k+1} \\ &= \mu_k \cdot \beta(\rho_k A - B) x_{k+1} \\ &= (\mu_k \cdot \beta \cdot \tau_k) A x_k .\end{aligned}$$

i.e. $(A - \mu_k M) x_{k+1}$ has the same direction as $A x_k$. Since $\|A x_k\| = 1$,

$$\begin{aligned}\|(A - \mu_k M) x_{k+1}\| &= |(A x_k , (A - \mu_k M) x_{k+1})_{M^{-1}}| \\ &= |x_k^* A M^{-1} (A - \mu_k M) x_{k+1}| \\ &= |x_k^* (A - \mu_k M) M^{-1} A x_{k+1}| \quad \text{(by Lemma 6.1)} \\ &\leq \|(A - \mu_k M) x_k\| \cdot \|A x_{k+1}\| \quad \text{(by Schwartz inequality)} \\ &= \|(A - \mu_k M) x_k\|. \end{aligned} \tag{6.8}$$

This together with (6.6) implies

$$\|(A-\mu_{k+1}M)x_{k+1}\| \le \|(A-\mu_k M)x_k\|.$$

But $(A-\mu_k M)x_k = \mu_k \cdot \beta(\rho_k A-B)x_k = \beta\, r_k$, so, for $\beta \neq 0$, we get $\|r_{k+1}\| \le \|r_k\|$. For $\beta = 0$, i.e. $A > 0$ or $A < 0$, this has been proved (e.g. Parlett [10]). □

We need another lemma before proving the main result on global convergence, which is a generalization of the Kahan–Parlett global convergence theorem.

LEMMA 6.3. *With the hypothesis of Lemma* 6.2, *the sequence of Rayleigh quotients* $\{\rho_k\} = \left\{\dfrac{x_k^* Bx_k}{x_k^* Ax_k}\right\}$ *is bounded.*

PROOF. If $\beta = 0$, i.e. $A > 0$ or $A < 0$, this is a trivial case. So, we consider the case $\beta \neq 0$. Suppose there is a subsequence $\rho_{k_j} \longrightarrow \infty$. Since $\|Ax_k\| = 1$, $\{x_k\}$ lies in a compact subset of $\mathbb{C}^n$ and so there is a subsequence $\{x_{k_j}\}$ which is convergent. So, we can just suppose $x_{k_j} \longrightarrow z$ and $\rho_{k_j} \longrightarrow \infty$ for some subsequence and some z. Then

$$\mu_{k_j} = \frac{1}{\alpha + \beta\rho_{k_j}} \longrightarrow 0 \text{ and } r_{k_j} = \frac{1}{\alpha + \beta\,\mu_{k_j}}(\rho_{k_j}A-B)x_{k_j} = \frac{1}{\beta}(A-\mu_{k_j}M)x_{k_j} \longrightarrow \frac{1}{\beta}Az.$$

Since $\|Ax_k\| = 1$, we have $\|Az\| = 1$. Also, by Theorem 6.1, $x_k^* Ax_k \neq 0$ for all k, then

$$\mu_k = \frac{x_k^* Ax_k}{x_k^* Mx_k} \neq 0. \text{ Hence}$$

$$\|r_{k_j}\|^2 = \|\frac{1}{\beta}(A - \mu_{k_j}M)x_{k_j}\|^2 = \frac{1}{\beta^2}[\|Ax_{k_j}\|^2 - \mu_{k_j}^2\|Mx_{k_j}\|^2] < \frac{1}{\beta}\|AX_{k_j}\|^2 = \frac{1}{\beta^2}.$$

But, by Theorem 6.2, $\|r_k\|$ is monotonically decreasing, so

$$\|r_{k_j}\|^2 \ge \lim_{j\to\infty}\|r_{k_j}\|^2 = \|\frac{1}{\beta}Az\|^2 = \frac{1}{\beta^2}.$$

This is a contradiction and proves the lemma. □

THEOREM 6.3 (Global Convergence Theorem). *Let* $\lambda A - B$ *be an* n×n *definite pencil with* n *distinct eigenvalues,* A *invertible, and* $M = \alpha A + \beta B > 0$. *Let* $\{\rho_k, x_k\}$ *be the Rayleigh sequence defined by Algorithm* 4.1 *and the* M^{-1}*–norm. Then*

1. $\{\rho_k\}$ *converges, and either*
2. $(\rho_k, x_k) \longrightarrow (\lambda,z)$, *asymptotically cubically, where* $Bz = \lambda Az$, *or*
3. $x_{2k} \longrightarrow x_+$, $x_{2k+1} \longrightarrow x_-$, *linearly, where* x_+ *and* x_- *are the bisectors of*

a pair of eigenvectors whose eigenvalues have mean $\rho = \lim_k \rho_k$. *This situation is unstable under perturbations of* x_k.

PROOF. Since $\|r_k\|$ is decreasing, it converges. Let $\|r_k\| \to \gamma \geq 0$. We assume that $x_0^* Ax_0 > 0$ without loss of generality, and discuss two cases.

<u>CASE 1</u>. $\gamma = 0$. By Lemma 6.3, $\{\rho_k\}$ is bounded. Then $\{(\rho_k, x_k)\}$ has at least one accumulation point $(\bar{\rho}, z)$. Let $(\rho_{k_j}, x_{k_j}) \to (\bar{\rho}, z)$. Then $\|Az\| = \lim \|Ax_{k_j}\| = 1$, implies $z \neq 0$ and

$$\|(\bar{\rho}A-B)z\| = \lim \|(\rho_{k_j}A-B)x_{k_j}\| = |\alpha+\beta\bar{\rho}| \cdot \gamma = 0.$$

So $Bz = \bar{\rho}Az$, i.e. $(\bar{\rho}, z)$ is an eigenpair, and $\bar{\rho}$ is a simple eigenvalue by the hypothesis. Moroever, as $(\rho_{k_j}, x_{k_j}) \to (\bar{\rho}, z)$, we can find some j such that $|\rho_{k_j} - \bar{\rho}|$, $\|x_{k_j} - z\|$ are so small that the local convergence theorem will imply that all subsequent $|\rho_k - \bar{\rho}|$, $\|x_k - \bar{z}\|$ converge to 0 cubically. Thus, $\gamma = 0$ leads to the statements 1 and 2 of the theorem.

<u>CASE 2</u>. $\gamma > 0$. In this case, $\|r_{k+1}\|/\|r_k\| \to 1$.

<u>Step 1</u>. From (6.5) and (6.8), we have

$$\|r_{k+1}\|^2 = |r_k^* M^{-1}A x_{k+1}|^2 - \frac{1}{\beta^2}(\mu_{k+1}-\mu_k)^2\|Mx_{k+1}\|^2 \leq |r_k^* M^{-1}Ax_{k+1}|^2 \leq \|r_k\|^2.$$

So, $\|r_k\| \to \gamma$ implies

$$|r_k^* M^{-1}(Ax_{k+1})| \longrightarrow \gamma \tag{6.9}$$

and

$$(\mu_{k+1} - \mu_k)^2 \|Mx_{k+1}\| \longrightarrow 0$$

But $1 = \|Ax_{k+1}\| \leq \|AM^{-1}\| \|Mx_{k+1}\|$, i.e. $\|Mx_{k+1}\| \geq \|AM^{-1}\|^{-1} > 0$, hence

$$|\mu_{k+1} - \mu_k| \longrightarrow 0. \tag{6.10}$$

Also, by (6.8) and (6.7),

$$\begin{aligned} r_k^* M^{-1}(Ax_{k+1}) &= \frac{1}{\beta}(Ax_k, (A-\mu_k M)x_{k+1})_{M^{-1}} = \frac{1}{\beta}(Ax_k, \beta\cdot\mu_k(\rho_k A-B)x_{k+1})_{M^{-1}} \\ &= (Ax_k, \mu_k\cdot\tau_k Ax_k)_{M^{-1}} = \mu_k \tau_k \end{aligned} \tag{6.11}$$

Notice that by assuming $x_0^* Ax_0 > 0$ and using Theorem 6.1, we obtain

$\mu_k = \dfrac{x_k^* \, Ax_k}{x_k^* \, Mx_k} > 0$. Also, $\tau_k = \dfrac{1}{\|Ay_{k+1}\|} > 0$, and so we get

$$r_k^* \, M^{-1}(Ax_{k+1}) > 0.$$

Hence, by (6.9),

$$r_k^* \, M^{-1}(Ax_{k+1}) = |r_k^* \, M^{-1}(Ax_{k+1})| \longrightarrow \gamma.$$

Thus

$$\|r_k - Ax_{k+1} \, \|r_k\| \, \|^2 = \|r_k\|^2 - 2r_k^* \, M^{-1}(Ax_{k+1}) \, \|r_k\| + \|r_k\|^2 \longrightarrow 0 \tag{6.12}$$

and, by (6.11),

$$\mu_k \tau_k = r_k^* \, M^{-1}(Ax_{k+1}) \longrightarrow \gamma. \tag{6.13}$$

Observe also that $\{\rho_k\}$ is bounded (Lemma 6.3) and then (6.10) implies

$$|\rho_{k+1} - \rho_k| = |\tfrac{1}{\beta}(\alpha+\beta\rho_k)\,(\alpha+\beta\rho_{k+1})\,(\mu_{k+1}-\mu_k)| \longrightarrow 0 \tag{6.14}$$

Now, we have

$$\begin{aligned} &\|[(\rho_k - A^{-1}B)^2 - \mu_k^{-1}\,\tau_k\,\|r_k\|]x_k\| \\ &= \|(\rho_k - A^{-1}B)\,[(\rho_k - A^{-1}B)x_k - (\rho_k - A^{-1}B)^{-1}\,x_k \cdot \mu_k^{-1}\,\tau_k\,\|r_k\|]\,\|, \\ &= \|A^{-1}(\rho_k A - B)\,[\mu_k^{-1}\,A^{-1}\,r_k - \mu_k^{-1}\,\|r_k\| \cdot x_{k+1}]\|, \\ &= \|\mu_k^{-1}\,A^{-1}(\rho_k A - B)A^{-1}\,[r_k - \|r_k\|\,Ax_{k+1}]\|, \\ &\le \mu_k^{-1}\,\|A^{-1}(\rho_k A - B)A^{-1}\|\,\|r_k - \|r_k\|Ax_{k+1}\| \longrightarrow 0 \end{aligned} \tag{6.15}$$

where we use (6.12) and the boundness of ρ_k, μ_k^{-1}.

If $\bar{\rho}$ is an accumulation point of $\{\rho_k\}$, i.e. $\rho_{k_j} \longrightarrow \bar{\rho}$, then $\mu_{k_j}^{-1} = \alpha + \beta\,\rho_{k_j} \longrightarrow \bar{\mu} = \alpha + \beta\bar{\rho}$ and by (6.13)

$$\tau_{k_j} = \mu_{k_j}^{-1}\,\mu_{k_j}\tau_{k_j} \longrightarrow \tau = (\alpha+\beta\,\bar{\rho})\gamma = \bar{\mu}\,\gamma\,.$$

Hence

$$(\rho_{k_j} - A^{-1}B)^2 - \mu_{k_j}^{-1}\,\tau_{k_j}\,\|r_{k_j}\| \longrightarrow (\bar{\rho} - A^{-1}B)^2 - \tau^2.$$

So, (6.15) implies

$$\det[(\bar{\rho} - A^{-1}B)^2 - \tau^2] = 0.$$

Therefore, $\bar{\rho} = \lambda_i \pm \tau$ for some eigenvalue λ_i of $A^{-1}B$, i.e. $\bar{\rho} \in \{\lambda_i \pm \tau : \lambda_i \in \sigma(A^{-1}B)\}$, a finite set. So, $\{\rho_k\}$ has only finitely many possible accumulation points and (6.14) implies that $\bar{\rho}$ will be the only one, i.e. $\rho_k \longrightarrow \bar{\rho}$, and the first part of the theorem is proved. Furthermore, $\mu_k^{-1} \longrightarrow \bar{\mu}$, $\tau_k \longrightarrow \tau$.

Step 2. We now show that, when $\gamma > 0$, the subsequences $\{x_{2k}\}$ and $\{x_{2k+1}\}$ are convergent. First consider $\{x_{2k}\}$. Let x_+ be an accumulation point of $\{x_{2k}\}$, i.e. $x_{2k_j} \longrightarrow x_+$ for some subsequence k_j. Then, from (6.15) and the fact that $\bar{\mu}\gamma = \tau$ we have

$$(\bar{\rho} - A^{-1}B)^2 x_+ = \tau^2 x_+ \tag{6.16}$$

Also, by (6.7),

$$x_{2k_j-1} = A^{-1}(\rho_{2k_j-1} A-B)x_{2k_j}/\tau_{2k_j-1} \longrightarrow A^{-1}(\bar{\rho} A - B)x_+/\tau.$$

Let $x_- = A^{-1}(\bar{\rho} A-B)x_+/\tau$, then

$$(\bar{\rho} A-B)x_+ = \tau A x_- \tag{6.17}$$

This together with (6.16) implies

$$A^{-1}(\bar{\rho} A-B)x_- = (\bar{\rho} - A^{-1}B)^2 x_+/\tau = \tau x_+$$

i.e.

$$(\bar{\rho}A-B)x_- = \tau A x_+ \tag{6.18}$$

So, $(\bar{\rho} A-B)(x_+ \pm x_-) = \pm\tau A(x_+ \pm x_-)$, by (6.17) and (6.18). Now we show that $x_+ - x_- \neq 0$. Otherwise, if $x_+ = x_-$, then (6.17) gives $(\bar{\rho} A-B)x_+ = \tau A x_+$, i.e. x_+ is an eigenvector. Then the local convergence implies that $x_k \longrightarrow x_+$. And this reduces to the Case 1 with $\tau = 0$, a contradiction. So $x_+ - x_- \neq 0$. Similarly, $x_+ + x_- \neq 0$. This means that $(\bar{\rho} - \tau, x_+ + x_-)$ and $(\bar{\rho} + \tau, x_+ - x_-)$ are two eigenpairs and $\bar{\rho}$ is the mean of two eigenvalues.

Let P_1, P_2 be the projections onto the spectral subspace associated with $\bar{\rho} - \tau$ and $\bar{\rho} + \tau$, respectively, and $y_1 = P_1 x_0$, $y_2 = P_2 x_0$. It is easy to see that $P_1 x_k$ will have the same direction as $P_1 x_0$, and $P_2 x_k$ will have the same direction as $P_2 x_0$. Hence $P_1(x_+ + x_-)$ and $P_2(x_+ - x_-)$ have the same direction as $P_1 x_0$, $P_2 x_0$ respectively. Notice that $x_+ \pm x_-$ are eigenvectors, i.e., $P_1(x_+ + x_-) = x_+ + x_-$ and $P_2(x_+ - x_-) = x_+ - x_-$, we suppose

$$x_+ + x_- = 2sy_1 \quad , \quad x_+ - x_- = 2ty_2$$

for some complex s and t. Then

$$x_+ = sy_1 + ty_2 \quad , \quad x_- = sy_1 - ty_2 . \tag{6.19}$$

Notice that $\bar\rho = \lim \rho_k = \lim \rho_{2k_j}$, then from (6.17)

$$x_+^* Ax_- = \frac{1}{t} \lim x_{2k_j}^* (\bar\rho A - B) x_{2k_j} = \frac{1}{t} \lim (\bar\rho - \rho_{k_j}) \cdot x_{2k_j}^* A x_{2k_j} = 0.$$

Substitute from (6.19) and notice that $y_1^* A y_2 = 0$ to obtain

$$s^2 y_1^* A y_1 - t^2 y_2^* A y_2 = 0 \tag{6.20}$$

By the normalization, $x_+^* A M^{-1} Ax_+ = 1$ and $y_1^* A M^{-1} A y_2 = \dfrac{y_1^* A y_2}{\alpha + \beta(\bar\rho - \tau)} = 0$, we have

$$s^2 y_1^* A M^{-1} A y_1 + t^2 y_2^* A M^{-1} A y_2 = 1,$$

or

$$s^2 \frac{y_1^* A y_1}{\alpha + \beta(\bar\rho - \tau)} + t^2 \frac{y_2^* A y_2}{\alpha + \beta(\bar\rho + \tau)} = 1. \tag{6.21}$$

Equations (6.20) and (6.21) have a unique solution (s^2, t^2). Then there is a finite number of solutions for (s,t), i.e. (s,t) belongs to a finite set. Hence $x_+ + x_-$ and $x_+ - x_-$ belong to a finite set. This means that there are only finitely many accumulation points of $\{x_{2k})$ and $\{x_{2k-1}\}$.

Now,

$$\begin{aligned}
x_{i+1}^* A M^{-1} A x_{i-1} &= x_{i+1}^* A M^{-1} (\rho_{i-1} A - B) x_i / \tau_{i-1} \\
&= x_{i+1}^* A M^{-1} [(\rho_{i-1} - \rho_i) A + (\rho_i A - B)] x_i / \tau_{i-1} \\
&= [x_{i+1}^* A M^{-1} A x_i (\rho_{i-1} - \rho_i) + x_{i+1}^* A M^{-1} (\rho_i A - B) x_i] / \tau_{i-1} \\
&= x_{i+1}^* A M^{-1} A x_i (\rho_{i-1} - \rho_i) / \tau_{i-1} + x_{i+1}^* (\rho_i A - B) M^{-1} A x_i / \tau_{i-1} \\
&\qquad \text{(by Lemma 6.1)} \\
&= x_{i+1}^* A M^{-1} A x_i (\rho_{i-1} - \rho_i) / \tau_{i-1} + \frac{\tau_i x_i^* A M^{-1} A x_i}{\tau_{i-1}} \\
&= x_{i+1}^* A M^{-1} A x_i (\rho_{i-1} - \rho_i) / \tau_{i-1} + \tau_i / \tau_{i-1} \longrightarrow 1.
\end{aligned}$$

Then $\|Ax_{i+1} - Ax_{i-1}\|^2 = \|Ax_{i+1}\|^2 - 2x_{i+1}^* A M^{-1} A x_{i-1} + \|Ax_{i-1}\|^2 \longrightarrow 0$. Therefore

$$\|x_{i+1} - x_{i-1}\| \longrightarrow 0.$$

This implies $\{x_{2k}\}$ has only one accumulation point and $\{x_{2k+1}\}$ has only one accumulation point. Thus $\{x_{2k}\}$ converges to x_+ and $\{x_{2k+1}\}$ converges to x_-.

In the limit $\{x_{2k}\}$ and $\{x_{2k+1}\}$ behave like sequences obtained from an iteration process applied to $(\bar{\rho}-A^{-1}B)^2$ (see p. 79 of [10]). That implies that the convergence is linear. It only remains to establish the instability property of Statement 3.

Step 3. In considering the stability, we suppose $\beta \neq 0$ because the case $\beta = 0$ has been discussed in Parlett [10]. Let $w = (\bar{\rho}A-B)^{-1}Ax_-$ and $v = x_+ + \epsilon\, w$. Then,
$\mu(\epsilon) = \mu(v) = \frac{v^*Av}{v^*Mv} = \mu(x_+) + \mu_1\epsilon + 0(\epsilon^2)$ where $\mu_1 = \frac{2\,\tau(w^*A, x_-)}{\|Mx_+\|^2(\alpha+\beta\bar{\rho})}$. Hence

$$(A - \mu(v)M)v = (A-\mu(x_+)M)x_+ + [-\mu_1 Mx_+ + (A-\mu(x_+)M)w]\epsilon + 0(\epsilon^2)$$
$$= \frac{\beta}{\alpha + \beta\bar{\rho}}(\bar{\rho}A-B)x_+ + [-\mu_1 Mx_+ + \frac{\beta}{\alpha+\beta\bar{\rho}}(\bar{\rho}A-B)w]\,\epsilon + 0(\epsilon^2).$$

Therefore

$$\|(A-\mu(v)M)v\|^2 = \frac{\beta^2}{(\alpha + \beta\bar{\rho})^2}\|(\bar{\rho}A-B)x_+\|^2 + 2\epsilon\left[\frac{\beta}{\alpha + \beta\bar{\rho}}\right]^2 x_+^*(\bar{\rho}A-B)M^{-1}(\bar{\rho}A-B)w + 0(\epsilon^2)$$
$$= \beta^2\gamma^2 + 2\,\epsilon\,\tau\left[\frac{\beta}{\alpha + \beta\bar{\rho}}\right]^2 + 0(\epsilon^2)$$

where we use $x_+^*(\bar{\rho}A-B)M^{-1}(\bar{\rho}A-B)w = \tau\, x_-^*A\, M^{-1}Ax_- = \tau$. So,

$$\|r(v)\|^2 = \left\|\frac{1}{\alpha + \beta\cdot\rho(v)}(\rho(v)A-B)\right\|^2 = \frac{1}{\beta^2}\|(A - \mu(v)M)v\|^2$$
$$= \gamma^2 + 2\epsilon\frac{\tau}{(\alpha + \beta\bar{\rho})^2} + 0(\epsilon^2).$$

Thus, with perturbation of x_k which is close enough to x_+, the norms of residual vectors will go down below r. This prevents the Case 2 happening, i.e. it is unstable. □

7. A Modified Rayleigh Quotient Method for Definite Pencils

In this section, we propose a modification of the Rayleigh quotient iteration method for definite pencils. Preliminary investigations show that the algorithm has some favourable global convergence properties. Development of competitive, general purpose algorithms would, of course, require further investigation and development. These procedures also hold some promise for computation of the extreme eigenvalues of a given type (either positive or negative), and not just the extreme eigenvalues of the whole spectrum.

For simplicity, we consider a definite pencil $\lambda A - B$ with $\alpha A + B > 0$ and A invertible. (This is always true for pencils associated with over–damped quadratic polynomials. See Example 1 below.) Then if $\lambda_1 \geq \ldots \geq \lambda_k$ are eigenvalues of positive type, $\lambda_{k+1} \geq \ldots \geq \lambda_n$ are eigenvalues of negative type, we have $\lambda_k > -\alpha > \lambda_{k+1}$. Also, we can determine α from λ_k and λ_{k+1}. In Corollary 2.3, λ_k is characterized by minimization of the Rayleigh quotient. So we hope to have a minimization process at each iteration step in order to make the Rayleigh quotient approach λ_k. In another aspect, the Rayleigh quotient has no upper bound in the A–positive cone. Then with a careless choice of starting vector having a very big Rayleigh quotient, the convergence may be significantly slow. From this point of view, we also hope to have steep descent of the Rayleigh quotient at each step.

Given $x \in \mathbb{C}^n$ with $x^*Ax > 0$, and $\rho(x) \notin \sigma(A^{-1}B)$, we have the Rayleigh quotient iteration vector $y = (\rho(x)A-B)^{-1}Ax$. Let

$$z = z(t) = x + ty.$$

We try to find some t so that $z(t)$ is A–positive and has minimal Rayleigh quotient, i.e., a minimization problem

$$\min_{z(t)^*Az(t)>0} \frac{z(t)^*Bz(t)}{z(t)^*Az(t)} \tag{7.1}$$

in which x and y are fixed. As in Equation (6.3), we see that

$$\rho(t) = \frac{z(t)^*Bz(t)}{z(t)^*Az(t)} = \rho(x) - \frac{2at + b}{at^2 + 2bt + c}$$

where $a = x^*Ax$, $b = y^*Ax$, $c = y^*Ay$. Let

$$f(t) = \frac{2at + b}{at^2 + 2bt + c}.$$

Then the Problem (7.1) is transformed to

$$\max_{at^2+2bt+c>0} \frac{2at + b}{at^2 + 2bt + c} \tag{7.2}$$

Taking the derivitive, we get

$$f'(t) = -2\,\frac{a^2t^2 + abt + (b^2-ac)}{(at^2 + 2bt + c)^2}.$$

By Theorem 6.1, we have for the discriminant, Δ, of the numerator,

$$\Delta = (ab)^2 - 4a^2(b^2-ac) = a^2(4ac-3b^2) \geq 0,$$

so

$$t_{\pm} = \frac{-ab \pm \sqrt{\Delta}}{2a^2} = \frac{-b \pm \sqrt{4ac-3b^2}}{2a}$$

are the two stationary points of $f(t)$. Now we discuss three cases.

Case 1. $b^2 - ac = 0$. In this case, $b \neq 0$. Otherwise, $ac = 0$, this contradicts Theorem 6.1. Since $at^2 + 2bt + c = 0$ has only one zero $t_0 = -\frac{b}{a}$, then if $b < 0$, $\lim_{t\to t_0} f(t) = +\infty$ with $at^2 + 2bt + c > 0$ for $t \neq t_0$. This contradicts Corollary 2.3. So $b > 0$. Hence

$$\lim_{t\to t_0} f(t) = -\infty, \quad \lim_{t\to+\infty} f(t) = 0 \text{ and } f(t) < 0 \text{ for } t \in (-\infty, t_0).$$

This shows that $\max_{t\neq t_0} f(t) > 0$ and will be attained at some point in $(t_0, +\infty)$, which must be a stationary point. But $t_+ = \frac{-b + |b|}{2a} = 0 > t_- = -\frac{b}{a} = t_0$, so t_+ is the only stationary point in $(t_0, +\infty)$. Therefore, f(t) has a maximum at t_+, i.e. $\max_{at^2+2bt+c>0} f(t) = \max_{t\neq t_0} f(t) = f(t_+)$.

Case 2. $b^2 - ac > 0$. In this case, $at^2 + 2bt + c = 0$ has two zeros $t_{1,2} = \frac{-b \pm \sqrt{b^2-ac}}{a}$, and $at^2 + 2bt + c > 0$ if and only if $t \in (t_1,\infty)$ or $t \in (-\infty,t_2)$. By Corollary 2.3, we have $\lim_{t\to t_{1+}} f(t) = -\infty$, $\lim_{t\to t_{1-}} f(t) = +\infty$ and $\lim_{t\to t_{2+}} f(t) = +\infty$. Moreover, $\lim_{t\to\infty} f(t) = 0+$ and $f(t) < 0$ for $t \in (-\infty,t_2)$. This implies that f(t) has a maximum in (t_1,∞) and a minimum in (t_2,t_1) which are stationary points. But t_+ and t_- are the only stationary points and $t_+ > t_-$. So, f(t) has a maximum at t_+, i.e.

$$\max_{at^2+2bt+c>0} f(t) = \max_{t\in(-\infty,t_2)\cup(t_1,\infty)} f(t) = f(t_+).$$

Case 3. $b^2 - ac < 0$. Then $at^2 + 2bt + c > 0$ and f(t) is continuous in $(-\infty,\infty)$. Now $\lim_{t\to\infty} f(t) = 0$, $f(t) > 0$ for $t > -\frac{b}{2a}$ and $f(t) < 0$ for $t < -\frac{b}{2a}$. So f(t) has a maximum in $(-\frac{b}{2a}, +\infty)$ and a minimum in $(-\infty, -\frac{b}{2a})$, which are stationary points. But t_+ and t_- are the only stationary points and $t_+ > t_-$. Therefore, f(t) has a maximum at t_+, i.e. $\max_{at^2+2bt+c>0} f(t) = \max_{t\in(-\infty,\infty)} f(t) = f(t_+)$.

So, we have proved:

THEOREM 7.1. *Let* $\lambda A - B$ *be a definite pencil with* A *invertible and with positive type eigenvalues greater than negative type eigenvalues. Let* x *be a vector for which* $x^*Ax \neq 0$, $\rho(x) \notin \sigma(A^{-1}B)$,

$$y = (\rho(x)A-B)^{-1}Ax, \quad z = x + ty \quad \textit{and} \quad a = x^*Ax, \; b = y^*Ax, \; c = y^*Ay$$

where t *is a real parameter. Then*

$$\min_{z(t)^*Az(t)>0} \frac{z(t)^*Bz(t)}{z(t)^*Az(t)}$$

is attained at $t_+ = \frac{-b + \sqrt{4ac-3b^2}}{2a}$.

With this conclusion, we propose the following algorithm.

ALGORITHM 7.2. *Pick a starting iterative vector* x_0 *with* $\|x_0\| = 1$ *and* $x_0^* Ax_0 > 0$. *Then for* $k = 0,1,2,\dots$,

(i) *form* $\rho_k = \dfrac{x_k^* Bx_k}{x_k^* Ax_k}$

(ii) *if* $\rho_k A - B$ *is singular, then solve* $(\rho_k A-B)v_{k+1} = 0$ *to get the approximation* (ρ_k, v_{k+1}) *and stop; otherwise,*

(iii) *Solve* $(\rho_k A-B)y_{k+1} = Ax_k$

(iv) *Compute* $a = x_k^* Ax_k$, $b = y_{k+1}^* Ax_k$, $c = y_{k+1}^* Ay_{k+1}$,

$t = \dfrac{-b + \sqrt{4ac-3b^2}}{2a}$

(v) $z_{k+1} = x_{k+1} + ty_{k+1}$

(vi) *Normalize* z_{k+1} *to get* $x_{k+1} = z_{k+1}/ \|z_{k+1}\|$.

Similarly, if we start from x_0 with $x_0^* Ax_0 < 0$, we do the maximization process instead of the minimization.

From our construction, we see that the Rayleigh quotients $\{\rho_k\}$ are monotonically decreasing. This implies that $\{\rho_k\}$ converges. We do not have further analysis of convergence, but our numerical examples suggest that, in general, ρ_k will converge to the smallest positive type eigenvalue. The only exception arises when x_0 is chosen too close to an eigenvector with ρ_0 greater than the corresponding eigenvalue, in which case, (ρ_k,x_k) converges very fast to the corresponding eigenpair.

Because ρ_k is strictly decreasing, then even if a ρ_k is very close to an eigenvalue, but less than it, the subsequent ρ_k will not converge to this eigenvalue but keep going down. This suggests the use of a combination of two algorithms. We can start by using the Algorithm 7.2 for the first few steps, and then switch to Algorithm 4.1. This switch process can be controlled by the examination of the norm of residual vectors.

8. Numerical Examples

EXAMPLE 1. A family of examples can be obtained from reference [19]. We consider the quadratic matrix polynomials

$$L(\lambda,\epsilon) = \lambda^2 I + \epsilon\lambda\hat{B} + C \tag{8.1}$$

in which ϵ is a real parameter and

$$\hat{B} = \begin{bmatrix} 2 & 1 \\ 1 & 2 \end{bmatrix}, \quad C = \begin{bmatrix} 1 & 1 \\ 1 & 2 \end{bmatrix}.$$

The corresponding linear pencil is $\lambda A - B$ where

$$A = \begin{bmatrix} 2\epsilon & \epsilon & 1 & 0 \\ \epsilon & 2\epsilon & 0 & 1 \\ 1 & 0 & 0 & 0 \\ 0 & 1 & 0 & 0 \end{bmatrix}, \quad B = \begin{bmatrix} -1 & -1 & 0 & 0 \\ -1 & -2 & 0 & 0 \\ 0 & 0 & 1 & 0 \\ 0 & 0 & 0 & 1 \end{bmatrix}$$

The system represented by (8.1) is "over–damped" if and only if $\epsilon > \frac{5}{3}$. When $\epsilon = 2$ the spectrum of $\lambda A - B$ is

$$\{-5.5519331, -0.59927996, -0.18011744, -1.6686694\}$$

as determined by the IMSL routines. When Algorithm 4.1 above is applied with the starting vector $e_1 = [1,0,0,0]^T$, an eigenvalue estimate of -0.18011744 is obtained in 4 steps.

When $\epsilon = 1.2$ there is a conjugate pair of complex eigenvalues and two real eigenvalues. As determined by IMSL routines, they are

$$\{-0.3714440, -2.6918306, -0.8683375 \pm i\,0.4959737\}.$$

With initial vector e_1, we get rapid convergence. The Rayleigh quotient -0.3714944 is obtained at the 2nd step. But with initial vector e_2, there is oscillation in the first few steps. Then the Rayleigh quotient -0.37149440 is obtained at the 11th step.

EXAMPLE 2. The following matrices A and B are used in [20].

$$A = \begin{bmatrix} 4.3443 & -0.4696 & 0.1184 & 0.8482 & 2.3404 & -4.3342 \\ -0.4696 & -4.3485 & 6.4779 & 1.3731 & 0.1937 & -1.1516 \\ 0.1184 & 6.4779 & 2.7739 & 0.7720 & 0.8153 & 5.2281 \\ 0.8482 & 1.3731 & 0.7720 & 2.9806 & 0.6143 & -1.0325 \\ 2.3404 & 0.1937 & 0.8153 & 0.6143 & 1.9884 & -2.8104 \\ -4.3342 & -1.1516 & 5.2281 & -1.0325 & -2.8104 & 7.7535 \end{bmatrix},$$

$$B = \begin{bmatrix} 5.7850 & 8.1185 & 5.0490 & 1.7888 & 5.3932 & -0.7300 \\ 8.1185 & 23.2587 & -9.1936 & 1.8887 & 6.0846 & 19088 \\ 5.0490 & -9.1936 & 18.2674 & 5.1331 & -0.4157 & 0.4575 \\ 1.7888 & 1.8887 & 5.1331 & -1.2820 & 2.3567 & 1.4358 \\ 5.3932 & 6.0846 & -0.4157 & 2.3567 & 4.6237 & -3.8397 \\ -0.7300 & 1.9088 & 0.4575 & 1.4358 & -3.8397 & 5.9581 \end{bmatrix}$$

The spectrum of $\lambda A - B$ is

$$\{1.9996290, 3.9995092, -0.00041488241, -2.9999571, 2.0001686, -0.50014193\}$$

as determined by IMSL routines. Using Algorithm 4.1 with initial vector e_1, we get the Rayleigh quotient 1.9996289 at the 3rd step.

REFERENCES

1. Crandall, S.H.: Iterative procedures related to relaxation methods for eigenvalue problems, Proc. Roy. Soc. London, Ser. A. 207 (1951), 416–423.

2. Crawford, C.R.: A stable generalized eigenvalue problem, SIAM J. Num. Anal. 6 (1976), 854–860.

3. Duffin, R.J.: A minimax theory for overdamped networks, Arch. Rational Mech. Anal. 4 (1955), 221–233.

4. Elsner, L. and Lancaster, P.: The spectral variation of pencils of matrices, J. Comp. Math., 3 (1985), 262–274.

5. Gohberg, I., Lancaster, P. and Rodman, L.: Matrices and Indefinite Scalar Products, Birkhäuser, Basel, 1983.

6. Kahan, W.: Inclusion theorems for clusters of eigenvalues of hermitian matrices, Technical Report, Dept. of Comp. Sci., University of Toronto, 1967.

7. Lancaster, P.: A generalized Rayleigh quotient iteration for lambda–matrices, Arch. Rational Mech. Anal. 8 (1961), 309–322.

8. Lancaster, P. and Tismentsky, M.: The Theory of Matrices, Academic Press, Orlando, 1985.

9. Ostrowski, A.: On the convergence of the Rayleigh quotient iteration for the computation of characteristic roots and vectors. I–VI, Arch. Rational Mech. Anal., 1–4 (1958/1959), 233–241, 423–428, 325–340, 341–347, 472–481, 153–165.

10. Parlett, B.N.: The Symmetric Eigenvalue Problem, Prentice–Hall, Englewood Cliffs, N.J., 1980.

11. Parlett, B.N.: The Rayleigh quotient iteration and some generalizations for non–normal matrices, Math. Comp. 28 (1974), 679–693.

12. Parlett, B.N. and Kahan, W.: On the convergence of a practical QR algorithm, Information Processing 68, Vol. I Mathematics, Software, 114–118, North–Holland, Amsterdam, 1969.

13. Rogers, E.H.: A minimax theory for overdamped systems, Arch. Rational Mech. Anal. 16 (1964), 89–96.

14. Stewart, G.W.: Perturbation bounds for the definite generalized eigenvalue problem, Lin. Alg. & Appl. 23 (1979), 69–85.

15. Temple, G.: The accuracy of Rayleigh's method of calculating the natural frequencies of vibrating systems, Proc. Roy. Soc. London, Ser. A. 211 (1952), 204–224.

16. Textorius, B.: Minimaxprinzipe zur Bestimmung der Eigenwerte J–nichtnegativer Operatoren, Math. Scand. 35 (1974), 105–114.

17. Turner, R.: Some variational principles for a nonlinear eigenvalue problem, J. Math. Anal. Appl. 17 (1967), 151–165.

18. Weierstrass, K.: Zur Theorie der bilinearen und quadratischen Formen, Monatsber. Akad. Wiss. Berl. (1868), 310.

19. Gohberg, I., Lancaster, P. and Rodman, L.: Quadratic matrix polynomials with a parameter, Advances Appl. Math. 7 (1986), 253–281.

20. Ericsson, T. and Ruhe, A.: Lanczos algorithm and field of value rotations for symmetric matrix pencils, Linear Algebra Appl. 88/89 (1987), 733–746.

21. Phillips, R.S.: A minimax characterization for the eigenvalues of a positive symmetric operator in a space with an indefinite metric, J. Faculty Sci. Univ. Tokyo Sect. IA Math. 17 (1970), 51–59.

Department of Mathematics and Statistics
University of Calgary
Calgary, Alberta T2N 1N4
CANADA

Operator Theory:
Advances and Applications, Vol. 40

THE MATRIX QUADRATIC EQUATION AND FACTORIZATION OF MATRIX POLYNOMIALS

L. LERER

Dedicated to Professor I. C. Gohberg on his sixtieth birthday, with admiration and affection.

In this paper explicit connections are established between the problem of determining solutions of matrix quadratic equations and the factorization problem for matrix polynomials. It is shown that an adequate connecting link between the two problems is provided by the Bezout matrix of a quadruple of matrix polynomials.

0. INTRODUCTION

Consider the equation

$$AY - YB = YWY - C, \qquad \text{(E)}$$

for the p×q complex matrix Y, where A, B, W and C are also complex matrices of sizes p×p, q×q, q×p and p×q, respectively. Recall (see e.g. [C]) that if a solution Y_0 of (E) is known, then any solution of (E) is given by $Y = Y_0 + X$, where X is a solution of the equation

$$UX - WV = XWX, \qquad (E_1)$$

with coefficients

$$U = A - Y_0W, \ W = B + WY_0. \qquad (0.1)$$

The equation (E_1) is the main subject of study of this paper.

Note that equation (E) with $p = q$, $A = -B^*$, $D^* = D$ and $W \geq 0$, known as the algebraic Riccati equation, has been thoroughly investigated by many authors (see, e.g. [C], [Ku], [W], [Wi], [LR], [R1,2], [S1,2], [RR], [GLR2,3],

This research was supported by the Fund for Promotion of Research at the Technion.

[A] and references therein). The algebraic Riccati equation has diverse applications in many fields including various problems in optimal control, the theory of hamiltonian systems of differential equations, network theory and system theory (see, e.g. [B], [W], [Re], [KS], [AM], [Wo], [GR]). General quadratic equations of type (E) appear in the problem of factorization of rational matrix functions with value I at infinity into a product of two functions of the same type (see [BGK], sections 5.1-5.3).

Our motivation for the study of the quadratic equation (E_1) comes from a certain interpolation problem which is briefly stated now (for definitions of the relevant notions see, e.g. [GKLR3]). Given a controllable pair (V,Ψ) $(V \in \mathbb{C}^{q\times q}, \Psi \in \mathbb{C}^{q\times s})$ and an observable pair (Φ,U) $(\Phi \in \mathbb{C}^{s\times p}, U \in \mathbb{C}^{p\times p})$, describe all rational s×s matrix functions $\Omega(\lambda)$, with $\Omega(\infty) = I$, such that the zero pair of Ω is a restriction of (Φ,U) and the pole pair of Ω is a compression of (V,Ψ). It turns out that the formula

$$\Omega_X(\lambda) = I - \Phi X(\lambda I - V)^{-1}\Psi,$$

where X is a solution of the equation (E_1), with $W = \Psi\Phi$, establishes a bijective mapping $X \to \Omega_X$ between the set of solutions of (E_1), and the set of all rational functions with the desired properties. The McMillan degree of the matrix function $\Omega_X(\lambda)$ equals to rank X, and its inverse is found by

$$\Omega_X(\lambda)^{-1} = I + \Phi(\lambda I-U)^{-1}X\Psi.$$

The proof of the above result will appear in a separate publication. The line of inquiry of the present paper is slightly different. Here we relate the description of the set of solutions of (E_1) with a certain factorization problem for matrix polynomials. The existence of such relations could be guessed from a simple comparison of the known results for both problems (see, e.g. [GLR1,2,3], [BGK], [LR]). Our contribution lies in determining an adequate connecting link between the two problems. It turns out that a key ingredient of this link is the notion of a Bezoutian of a quadruple of matrix polynomials which we define below. First recall that if $\ell_j (j=1,\dots,n)$ are s×s complex matrices, the matrix valued function $L(\lambda) = \lambda^n I + \sum_{j=0}^{n-1} \lambda^j \ell_j$ is referred to as a ***monic* s×s *matrix polynomial of degree* n** (here I stands for the s×s identity matrix). By $\sigma(L)$ we denote the ***spectrum*** of $L(\lambda)$, i.e. $\sigma(L) = \{\lambda \in \mathbb{C} \mid \det L(\lambda)=0\}$. If $L(\lambda)$ is a linear pencil, $L(\lambda)=\lambda I-A$, we also write $\sigma(A):=\sigma(L)$.

Now let $M_1(\lambda)$, $M(\lambda)$ and $L_1(\lambda)$, $L(\lambda)$ be s×s monic matrix polynomials, with $\deg M = \deg M_1 = m$ and $\deg L = \deg L_1 = n$, such that

$$L_1(\lambda)M_1(\lambda) = L(\lambda)M(\lambda). \tag{0.2}$$

The corresponding *Bezoutian* $\mathbb{B} := \mathbb{B}(L_1,L;M_1,M)$ is defined as the block matrix $\mathbb{B} = [b_{ij}]_{i,j=1}^{n,m}$ whose entries b_{ij} are s×s matrices determined by the expansion

$$(\lambda-\mu)^{-1}[L_1(\lambda)M_1(\mu) - L(\lambda)M(\mu)] = \sum_{i,j=1}^{n,m} \lambda^{i-1}\mu^{j-1}b_{ij}.$$

This notion of Bezoutian has been introduced in [AJ] and subsequently studied in [BKAK], [LT1,2,3], [CK], [LRT] (in a slightly more general framework). In particular, it is proved in [LT1] that the dimension of Ker $\mathbb{B}(M_1,M;L_1,L)$ equals to the degree of the determinant of the greatest common (right) divisor of the polynomials $L_1(\lambda)$ and $L(\lambda)$.

Returning to the equation (E_1) we assume throughout that the pairs of matrices (W,U) and (V,W) are observable and controllable, respectively. Let $W = \Psi\Phi$ ($\Psi \in \mathbb{C}^{q\times s}$, $\Phi \in \mathbb{C}^{s\times p}$) be a rank decomposition of W and denote by n and m the minimal integers such that the matrices

$$\text{row}(V^{j-1}\Psi)_{j=1}^{m} := [\Psi,\ V\Psi,\dots,V^{m-1}\Psi],$$

$$\text{col}(\Phi U^{j-1})_{j=1}^{n} := \begin{bmatrix} \Phi \\ \Phi U \\ \vdots \\ \Phi U^{n-1} \end{bmatrix}$$

are of full rank. Now choose two distinct complex numbers c, $d \notin \sigma(U) \cup \sigma(V)$ and taking advantage of the theory of matrix polynomials as developed in [GLR1] produce monic s×s matrix polynomials $L_U(\lambda)$ and $L_V(\lambda)$, with $\deg L_U = n$ and $\deg L_V = m$, such that (Φ,U) is a restriction of the right standard pair of L_U, (V,Ψ) is a compression of the left standard pair of L_V, and $\sigma(L_U) = \sigma(U) \cup \{c\}$, $\sigma(L_V) = \sigma(V) \cup \{d\}$ (see section 1 of this paper for definitions and details). Introduce also the notations

$$T_U := [\text{col}(\Phi^{(n)}\hat{C}_{L_U}^{j-1})_{j=1}^{n}]^{-1}\ \text{col}(\Phi U^{j-1})_{j=1}^{n},$$

$$T_V := \text{row}(V^{j-1}\Psi)_{j=1}^{m}[\text{row}(C_{L_V}^{j-1}\Psi^{(m)})_{j=1}^{m}]^{-1},$$

where $\hat{C}_{L_U}$, C_{L_V} are companion matrices defined by (1.3), $\Phi^{(n)} := \text{row}(\delta_{nj}I)_{j=1}^{n}$,

$\Psi^{(m)} := \mathrm{col}(\delta_{mj}I)_{j=1}^{m}$. Note that T_U is left invertible and T_V is right invertible. We denote by $T_U^{(-1)}$ and $T_V^{(-1)}$ the one-sided inverses of these matrices. The following theorem is the key result of this paper.

THEOREM 0.1. *Any factorization of the matrix polynomial* $L_U(\lambda)L_V(\lambda)$ *into a product of two monic polynomials,*

$$L_U(\lambda)L_V(\lambda) = Q(\lambda)R(\lambda), \tag{0.3}$$

such that

$$\deg Q = n,\ \deg R = m,\ c \notin \sigma(R),\ d \notin \sigma(Q), \tag{0.4}$$

generates a solution X *of the equation* (E_1) *given by*

$$X = T_U^{(-1)}\mathbb{B}(L_U,Q;L_V,R)T_V^{(-1)}. \tag{0.5}$$

Conversely, if X *is a solution of* (E_1) *and* $S = [s_{ij}]_{i,j=1}^{n,m} := T_U X T_V$, *then the monic polynomials*

$$R(\lambda) := L_V(\lambda) - \sum_{k=1}^{m}\lambda^{k-1}s_{nk},\quad Q(\lambda) := L_U(\lambda) + \sum_{k=1}^{n}\lambda^{k-1}s_{km} \tag{0.6}$$

satisfy (0.3) *and* (0.4).

The above correspondence between the solutions of the equation (E_1) *and the factorizations* (0.3) *satisfying* (0.4) *is bijective.*

If the solution X *is given by* (0.5), *then* $\mathrm{rank}X = ms - \mathrm{degdet}\, D_r(\lambda)$, *where* $D_r(\lambda)$ *is a greatest common (right) divisor of* $L_V(\lambda)$ *and* $R(\lambda)$.

The relations between the equations (E) and (E_1) imply that if Y_0 is a solution of (E), then all solutions of (E) are obtained by the formula

$$Y = Y_0 + T_U^{(-1)}\mathbb{B}(L_U,Q;L_V,R)T_V^{(-1)},$$

where U, V are as in (0.1) and $Q(\lambda)$, $R(\lambda)$ satisfy (0.3) - (0.4).

Concerning the first assertion of Theorem 0.1 note that using the theory of matrix polynomials (see [GLR1]) one can explicitly construct the factors $Q(\lambda)$, $R(\lambda)$ in (0.3) in terms of certain subspaces in $\mathbb{C}^{(n+m)s}$ that are invariant for the companion matrix $C_{L_UL_V}$ of the polynomial $L_U(\lambda)L_V(\lambda)$ (see Propositions 2.6 and 5.6). In the special case that U and V are nonderogatory matrices one obtains all solutions of (E_1) directly in terms of zeroes of the characteristic polynomials of U and V (see Corollary 2.9).

The converse part of Theorem 0.1 solves, in fact, the following factorization problem: for a given monic matrix polynomial $G(\lambda)$ construct all factorizations $G(\lambda) = Q(\lambda)R(\lambda)$ with monic factors $Q(\lambda)$, $\deg Q = n$, and $R(\lambda)$, $\deg R = m$, given one factorization $G(\lambda) = L(\lambda)M(\lambda)$ of this type. To be more specific consider the following special case of the equation (E_1):

$$\hat{C}_L S - SC_M = S\Psi^{(m)}\Phi^{(n)}S. \qquad (\tilde{E}_1)$$

It follows from Theorem 0.1 that any solution $S = [s_{ij}]_{i,j=1}^{n,m}$ of the equation $(\tilde{E}_1)$ generates a factorization $G(\lambda) = Q(\lambda)R(\lambda)$ with

$$Q(\lambda) = L(\lambda) + \sum_{k=1}^{n} \lambda^{k-1} s_{km}, \quad R(\lambda) = M(\lambda) - \sum_{k=1}^{m} \lambda^{k-1} s_{nk} ; \qquad (0.7)$$

any factorization of $G(\lambda)$ with desired properties is obtained in this way, and the degree of the determinant of the greatest common (right) divisor of $M(\lambda)$ and $R(\lambda)$ is equal to ms - rankS. Note that the problem under discussion (with $n = m$) appears to be crucial in solving the problem of determining an $ns\times ns$ block Toeplitz (or block Hankel) matrix from the first block row and block column of its inverse (see [GL]). In this case one needs factorizations of $G(\lambda)$ such that $R(\lambda)$ and $M(\lambda)$ are right coprime, i.e. $\operatorname{Ker}R(\lambda) \cap \operatorname{Ker}M(\lambda) = (0)$, $\lambda \in \mathbb{C}$. It is clear that such factorizations are generated by invertible solutions S of $(\tilde{E}_1)$ (if any) (see Proposition 2.7 and Corollary 2.5).

Another interesting application of formulas (0.7) is connected with Wiener-Hopf factorizations of rational matrix polynomials $H(\lambda)=\sum_{j=-n}^{n} \lambda^j \ell_j$ with respect to a Cauchy contour in the complex plane (see section 2 for definitions of relevant notions). Several important problems in the theory of convolution type operators and in system theory lead to the following question: given a right canonical Wiener-Hopf factorization $H(\lambda)=H_+(\lambda)H_-(\lambda)$, $\lambda\epsilon\Gamma$, find necessary and sufficient conditions for the existence of a left canonical Wiener-Hopf factorization $H(\lambda)=F_-(\lambda)F_+(\lambda)$, $\lambda\epsilon\Gamma$, and provide explicit formulas for F_+ and F_-. Using formulas (0.7) we solve this problem for the case that the factors $H_\pm$ are given in the coefficient form, and the solution $F_\pm$ is found also in the coefficient form.

Note that in the special case of equation $(\tilde{E}_1)$ Theorem 0.1 implies, in particular, that if $L(\lambda)M(\lambda) = Q(\lambda)R(\lambda)$, with $\deg Q = n$, $\deg R = m$, the

Bezoutian $\mathbb{B}(L,Q;M,R)$ satisfies the equation $(\tilde{E}_1)$. This assertion was proved earlier by a different method in a nice paper by K. Clancey and B.A. Kon [CK]. Also, as I was informed by B.A. Kon after completing the manuscript of this paper, the fact that any solution of $(\tilde{E}_1)$ is a Bezoutian for some quadruple of monic matrix polynomials was proved by him without determining the factors $Q(\lambda)$ and $R(\lambda)$ in the explicit form (0.7) (see the abstract [K]).

Now consider the equation

$$V^*X - XV = XWX. \qquad (E_1^*)$$

The connection between this equation and the usual algebraic Riccati equation with $C = 0$ is obvious. Throughout we impose the standard conditions: $W \geq 0$ and the pair (V,W) is controllable. In the case of equation (E_1^*) one is especially interested in skew-hermitian solutions X. It turns out that such solutions are related to symmetric factorizations

$$L_V^*(\lambda)L_V(\lambda) = R^*(\lambda)R(\lambda). \qquad (0.8)$$

(Here we use the notation $L^*(\lambda) := [L(\bar{\lambda})]^*$). More specifically, let $W = \Psi\Psi^*$ be a rank decomposition of W, choose a real number $d \notin \sigma(V)$ and define $L_V(\lambda)$ as in the paragraph preceding Theorem 0.1. Then any symmetric factorization (0.8) generates a skew-hermitian solution of (E_1^*) given by

$$X_R = [T_V^{(-1)}]^*\mathbb{B}(L_V^*,R^*;L_V,R)T_V^{(-1)}. \qquad (0.9)$$

Conversely, if X is a skew-hermitian solution of (E_1^*) and $S=[s_{ij}]_{i,j=1}^m = T_V^*XT_V$, then the polynomial $L_V^*(\lambda)L_V(\lambda)$ admits the symmetric factorization (0.8) with

$$R(\lambda) = L_V(\lambda) - \sum_{k=1}^m \lambda^{k-1}s_{mk}. \qquad (0.10)$$

This correspondence between symmetric factorizations (0.8) and skew-hermitian solutions of (E_1^*) is bijective.

Furthermore, using the results of [LT1] we can explicitly express the number of eigenvalues of $R(\lambda)$ in the open upper (lower) half plane and on the real axis in terms of the inertia of the matrix iX, and vice versa. (Recall that the inertia of a matrix A is defined as the triple $\mathrm{in}(A) = (\pi(A), \nu(A), \delta(A))$, where $\pi(A)$, $\nu(A)$ and $\delta(A)$ denote the number of eigenvalues of A (counted with their algebraic multiplicities) with positive, negative and zero real parts, respectively.)

Also, it follows that given a monic polynomial $L(\lambda)$ of degree m, all symmetric factorization $L^*(\lambda)L(\lambda) = R^*(\lambda)R(\lambda)$ of the polynomial $L^*(\lambda)L(\lambda)$ are obtained from the skew-hermitian solutions $S = [s_{jk}]_{j,k=1}^m$ of the equation $C_L^*S - SC_L = S\Phi^{(m)}\Phi^{(m)*}S$ by (0.10) with $L_V = L$.

As is known (see e.g. [CG], [GLR2]) the nonnegative matrix polynomial $L_V^*(\lambda)L_V(\lambda)$ admits, in particular, the spectral factorizations: $L_V^*(\lambda)L_V(\lambda) = R_+^*(\lambda)R_+(\lambda)$, with $\mathrm{Im}\sigma(R_+) \leq 0$, and $L_V^*(\lambda)L_V(\lambda) = R_-^*(\lambda)R_-(\lambda)$, with $\mathrm{Im}\sigma(R_-) \geq 0$. It turns out that the solutions of (E_1^*) which correspond to R_+ and R_- according to formula (0.9) have important extremal properties. More specifically, $iX_{R_-} \leq iX \leq iX_{R_+}$ for any skew-hermitian solution X of (E_1^*),
$\mathrm{in}(iX_{R_+}) = (\nu(iV), 0, \delta(iV) + \pi(iV))$; $\mathrm{in}(iX_{R_-}) = (0, \pi(iV), \delta(iV)+\nu(iV))$
and
$\mathrm{in}(iV+iWX_{R_+}) = (0, \nu(iV)+\pi(iV), \delta(iV))$; $\mathrm{in}(iV+iWX_{R_-})= (\nu(iV)+\pi(iV), 0, \delta(iV))$.

Next, consider the equation

$$B^*Y - YB = YWY - C, \qquad (E^*)$$

with hermitian C, which we call the *algebraic skew-Riccati equation*. Assuming that a skew-hermitian solution Y_0 of (E^*) is known, we obtain all skew-hermitian solutions of (E^*) by the formula $Y_R = Y_0 + X_R$, where X_R is defined by (0.9), with $V := B+WY_0$, and $R(\lambda)$ satisfies (0.8). In particular, Y_{R_+} and Y_{R_-} are extremal solutions of (E^*) and we can describe their inertial properties. Note that existence and properties of externmal solutions of equations (E^*) and (E_1^*) have been established earlier by other methods (see, e.g., [C], [LR], [R 1,2], [S 1,2], [GLR 2], [RR]). The explicit connections between the skew-hermitian solutions and symmetric factorizations (in particular, spectral factorizations) given by formulas (0.9) - (0.10) seem to be new.

Note that when applying the main results of the present paper concerning the equation (E_1) (or (E_1^*)) to the corresponding equation with $C \neq 0$ we assume that (E) (or (E^*)) is solvable and a solution Y_0 of (E) (or a skew-hermitian solution Y_0 of (E^*)) is known. Criteria for solvability and explicit formulas for solutions of the equations (E) and (E^*) (which don't require the knowledge of a solution Y_0) will be presented in our future publication in terms of the generalized Bezoutian for a family of matrix polynomials introduced in [LT 2,3].

The rest of the paper is organized as follows. Section 1 contains necessary preliminaries. In section 2 we state Theorem 0.1 in the more simple case that $\mathrm{col}(\Phi U^{j-1})_{j=1}^{n}$ and $\mathrm{row}(V^{j-1}\Psi)_{j=1}^{m}$ are invertible matrices. This result is proved in section 3. Section 2 contains also several corollaries including the results concerning canonical factorization of rational matrix polynomials. In section 4 we define a dilation of the general equation (E_1) to an equation of type ($\tilde{E}_1$) so that a certain subset of the set of all solutions of ($\tilde{E}_1$) is in a one-to-one correspondence with the set of all solutions of (E_1). This subset of solutions of the equation ($\tilde{E}_1$) associated with (E) is completely described in section 5 which allows proving Theorem 0.1 (in a somewhat more general form). The applications to skew-Riccati equations are presented in section 6.

It is a great pleasure to dedicate this paper to Israel Gohberg, a great mathematician, a wonderful teacher, and a very good friend. His work and personality have had a very important impact on the present author.

It was a good fortune and great privilege for me to be introduced by I. Gohberg to many topics of his research activity and to work with him on some of them. Our collaboration on matrix polynomials, Wiener-Hopf factorization and interpolation problems is of particular relevance for the present paper.

1. PRELIMINARIES

Throughout this paper all matrices are assumed to have complex entries. When convenient we identify an $n\times m$ matrix A with its canonical representation as a linear transformation from $\mathbb{C}^m$ into $\mathbb{C}^n$. The superscript "$*$" (as in A^*) stands for the adjoint matrix or operator, while the superscript "τ" (as in A^τ) denotes the transposed matrix. The one-column block matrix whose i^{th} entry is the matrix A_i $(i=1,\dots,k)$, is denoted by $\mathrm{col}(A_i)_{i=1}^{k}$.

Similarly, $\mathrm{row}(A_i)_{i=1}^{k}$ denotes the one-row block matrix $[A_1, A_2, \ldots, A_k]$.

A pair of complex matrices (Φ, Q) is referred to as a *right admissible pair* of order p if Φ is of size s×p and Q is of size p×p. The number s will be fixed throughout the paper, while p may depend on the admissible pair. A pair (R, Ψ) with $R \in \mathbb{C}^{p\times p}$, $\Psi \in \mathbb{C}^{p\times s}$ is called a *left admissible pair* of order p. Note that as a rule we consider right admissible pairs, if not specified otherwise. When necessary one can reformulate the notions below for left admissible pairs using the obvious remark that (R, Ψ) is a left admissible pair if and only if (Ψ^T, R^T) is right admissible.

For a pair (Φ, A) we define the number

$$\mathrm{ind}(\Phi, A) := \min\{m \,|\, \mathrm{Kercol}(\Phi Q^{i-1})_{i=1}^{m} = \mathrm{Kercol}(\Phi Q^{i-1})_{i=1}^{m+1}\},$$

which is called the *index of stabilization* of the pair (Φ, Q). The *index of stabilization of a left admissible pair* (R, Ψ) is defined by $\mathrm{ind}(R, \Psi) := \mathrm{ind}(\Psi^T, R^T)$.

Two pairs (Φ_1, Q_1) and (Φ_2, Q_2) of order p are called *similar* if there is a p×p invertible matrix S such that $\Phi_1 = \Phi_2 S$ and $Q_1 = S^{-1} Q_2 S$. Clearly, similar pairs have the same index of stabilization. Given admissible pairs (Φ_1, Q_1) and (Φ_2, Q_2) of orders p_1 and p_2 $(p_1 \geq p_2)$, respectively, we say that the pair (Φ_1, Q_1) is an *extension* of (Φ_2, Q_2) or, which is equivalent, (Φ_2, Q_2) is a *restriction* of (Φ_1, Q_1), if there exists a $p_1 \times p_2$ matrix S of full rank such that $\Phi_1 S = \Phi_2$ and $Q_1 S = S Q_2$. In other words, the pair $(\Phi_1, Q_1)$is an extension of (Φ_2, Q_2) if it is similar to a pair of the form

$$\left([\Phi_2, \tilde{\Phi}_2], \begin{bmatrix} Q_2 & \hat{Q}_2 \\ 0 & \tilde{Q}_2 \end{bmatrix}\right),$$

where $\tilde{\Phi}_2, \tilde{Q}_2, \hat{Q}_2$ are some matrices of appropriate sizes. A pair (Φ, Q) is called a *common restriction* of the admissible pairs (Φ_1, Q_1) and (Φ_2, Q_2) if each of these pairs is an extension of (Φ, Q). A common restriction of the pairs (Φ_1, Q_1) and (Φ_2, Q_2), which is an extension of any other common restriction of these pairs, is referred to as a *greatest common restriction* of the pairs (Φ_1, Q_1) and (Φ_2, Q_2). A left admissible pair (R_2, Ψ_2) is called a *compression* of the left pair (R_1, Ψ_1) if the pair $({\Psi_2}^T, R_2^T)$ is a restriction of (Ψ_1^T, R_1^T). The notions of *common compression* and *greatest common compression* are defined in an obvious way.

Let $L(\lambda)=\sum_{j=0}^{n}\lambda^j \ell_j$ be an s×s ***matrix polynomial***, i.e., the coefficients ℓ_j are s×s matrices. If (Φ,Q) and (R,Ψ) are right and left admissible pairs, respectively, we denote

$$L(\Phi,Q):=\sum_{j=0}^{n}\ell_j\Phi Q^j,\quad L(R,\Psi):=\sum_{j=0}^{n}R^j\Psi\ell_j.$$

If $\Gamma(\lambda)=L_1(\lambda)L_2(\lambda)$, the following easily verified formulas hold true:

$$\Gamma(\Phi,Q)=L_1(\Phi,Q),Q);\ \Gamma(R,\Psi)=L_2(R,L_1(R,\Psi)). \tag{1.1}$$

We now recall some basic facts from the spectral theory of matrix polynomials (see the monograph [GLR1] for a detailed exposition). The point $\lambda_0\in\mathbb{C}$ is an ***eigenvalue*** of the polynomial $L(\lambda)$ if $\det L(\lambda_0)=0$. The set of all eigenvalues of $L(\lambda)$ is called the ***spectrum*** of $L(\lambda)$, and is denoted by $\sigma(L)$. The polynomial $L(\lambda)$ is said to be ***regular*** if $\sigma(L)\neq\mathbb{C}$. In this case the spectrum $\sigma(L)$ is either a finite set or else it is empty. Clearly, monic polynomials are regular. If $\lambda_0\in\sigma(L)$, then any non-zero column vector in $\operatorname{Ker}L(\lambda_0)$ is called a ***right eigenvector*** of $L(\lambda)$ corresponding to λ_0. A right admissible pair (Φ,Q) is called a ***right finite Jordan pair of a regular polynomial*** $L(\lambda)$ if its order is equal to $d:=\operatorname{degdet}L(\lambda)$, $L(\Phi,Q)=0$ and $\operatorname{rankcol}(\Phi Q^{j-1})_{j=1}^{n}=d$. Note that up to multiplication on the left by a matrix polynomial with a constant non-zero determinant, the polynomial $L(\lambda))$ is uniquely determined by its right finite Jordan pair. For the explanation of the spectral meaning and properties of Jordan pairs see [GLR1], [GKLR1].

Now assume that $L(\lambda)$ is a monic s×s matrix polynomial of degree n, i.e. $L(\lambda)=\lambda^nI+\sum_{j=0}^{n-1}\lambda^j\ell_j$, where I is the identity on $\mathbb{C}^s$, and let (Φ,Q) be a right finite Jordan pair of $L(\lambda)$. In this case Φ is an s×ns matrix, Q is an ns×ns matrix and $L(\lambda)$ is uniquely determined by its finite Jordan pair. In fact, $\operatorname{col}(\Phi Q^{j-1})_{j=1}^{n}$ is invertible and

$$L(\lambda)=\lambda^nI-\Phi Q^n(Y_1+\lambda Y_2+\dots+\lambda^{n-1}Y_n), \tag{1.2}$$

where $\operatorname{row}(Y_j)_{j=1}^{n}=[\operatorname{col}(\Phi Q^{j-1})_{j=1}^{n}]^{-1}$. A right finite Jordan pair of a monic polynomial $L(\lambda)$ is also called a ***right standard pair of*** $L(\lambda)$. Important examples of right standard pairs of the monic polynomial $L(\lambda)$ are provided by the *companion standard pairs* $(\Phi^{(1)},C_L)$ and $(\Phi^{(n)},\hat{C}_L)$, where $\Phi^{(k)}=\mathrm{row}(\delta_{kj}I)_{j=1}^{n}$ $(k = 1,2,\dots,n)$ and

$$C_L:=\begin{bmatrix} 0 & I & & \\ & & \ddots & \\ & & & I \\ -\ell_0 & -\ell_1 & \cdots & -\ell_{n-1} \end{bmatrix}, \qquad \hat{C}_{L}:=\begin{bmatrix} 0 & & & -\ell_0 \\ I & & & -\ell_1 \\ & \ddots & & \vdots \\ & & I & -\ell_{n-1} \end{bmatrix} \tag{1.3}$$

are the *first* and the *second companion matrices* of $L(\lambda)$, respectively. The following relation will be useful:

$$C_L = S_L^{-1}\hat{C}_L S_L, \tag{1.4}$$

where

$$S_L:=\begin{bmatrix} \ell_1 & \ell_2 & \cdots & \ell_{n-1} & I \\ \ell_2 & & \cdot^{\cdot^{\cdot}} & \cdot^{\cdot^{\cdot}} & \\ \vdots & \cdot^{\cdot^{\cdot}} & \cdot^{\cdot^{\cdot}} & & \\ \ell_{n-1} & \cdot^{\cdot^{\cdot}} & & & \\ I & & & & \end{bmatrix} \tag{1.5}$$

Now consider the following problem: given a right admissible pair (Φ,Q) of order p ($\leq ns$) such that $\mathrm{col}(\Phi Q^{j-1})_{j=1}^{n}$ is left invertible, construct a monic s×s matrix polynomial whose right standard pair is an extension of (Φ,Q). Solutions of this problem are given by formula (1.2), where the inverse of the matrix $\mathrm{col}(\Phi Q^{j-1})_{j=1}^{n}$ is replaced by any of its left inverses (see [GLR1]). A more delicate problem appears when one additionally requires that $\sigma(L) = \sigma(Q) \cup \{a\}$, where $a \notin \sigma(Q)$ is a prescribed point in $\mathbb{C}$. One easily sees that it is enough to solve this problem for the case that a = 0 and Q is invertible. In this case the solution is given again by formula (1.2), where $V = \mathrm{row}(Y_j)_{j=1}^{n}$ is a special left inverse of the matrix $\Omega = \mathrm{col}(\Phi Q^{j-1})_{j=1}^{n}$. Recall the definition of a special left inverse. Let Ω be a q×p matrix, and assume that $\mathrm{Ker}\Omega = (0)$, i.e., Ω has full rank, let $\eta_1,\dots,\eta_t$ be ordinal numbers (counting from the top) of rows in Ω which depend linearly on rows of Ω lying below them. These rows will be referred to as dependent rows. Let Ω_0 be the p×p matrix obtained from Ω by deleting all dependent rows. Then the *special left inverse* V of Ω is the p×q matrix with the following structure: the columns in V with ordinal numbers $\eta_1,\dots,\eta_t$ are all zero and after deleting these columns the remaining matrix is equal to Ω_0^{-1}.

Note that the above notions and results on right Jordan pairs have obvious "left" analogues. We mention that the left admissible pairs $(\hat{C}_L,\Psi^{(1)})$ and $(C_L,\Psi^{(n)})$, where $\Psi^{(k)} := \mathrm{col}(\delta_{kj}I)_{j=1}^n$ $(k = 1,\dots,n)$, provide examples of left standard pairs of the monic polynomial $L(\lambda) = \lambda^n I + \sum_{j=0}^{n-1} \lambda^j \ell_j$. The monic polynomial $L(\lambda)$ is uniquely determined by its left standard pair (R,Ψ). In fact,

$$L(\lambda) = \lambda^n I - (Z_1 + \lambda Z_2 + \dots + \lambda^{n-1} Z_n) R^n \Psi, \tag{1.6}$$

where $\mathrm{col}(Z_j)_{j=1}^n = [\mathrm{row}(R^{i-1}\Psi)_{i=1}^n]^{-1}$.

If (Φ,Q) is a right standard pair of $L(\lambda))$ and Y_n is defined as in (1.2), the triple of matrices (Φ,Q,Y_n) is called a ***standard triple*** of the monic polynomial $L(\lambda)$. It is clear that any triple (Γ,T,Λ) that is ***similar*** to (Φ,Q,Y_n), i.e. $\Gamma = \Phi S$, $T = S^{-1}QS$ and $\Lambda = S^{-1}Y_n$ for some invertible matrix S, is also a standard triple of $L(\lambda)$. If (R,Ψ) is a left standard pair of $L(\lambda)$ and Z_n is defined as in (1.6) then (Z_n, R, Ψ) is a standard triple of $L(\lambda)$. Important examples of standard triples of $L(\lambda)$ are provided by the triples $(\Phi^{(1)},C_L,\Psi^{(n)})$ and $(\Phi^{(n)},\hat{C}_L,\Psi^{(1)})$. Standard triples can be characterized as follows. A triple of matrices (Γ,T,Λ) where $\Gamma \in \mathbb{C}^{s\times ns}$, $T \in \mathbb{C}^{ns\times ns}$ and $\Lambda \in \mathbb{C}^{ns\times s}$ is a standard triple of a monic s×s matrix polynomial $L(\lambda)$ of degree n if and only if $L^{-1}(\lambda) = \Gamma(\lambda I-T)^{-1}\Lambda$.

Concerning the divisibility theory of matrix polynomials we need the following (see [GLR1], [GKLR1,2] for details and proofs). Given regular matrix polynomials $L(\lambda)$ and $D(\lambda)$, we say that $D(\lambda)$ is a ***right divisor*** of $L(\lambda)$ if there is a matrix polynomial $Q(\lambda)$ such that $L(\lambda) = Q(\lambda)D(\lambda)$. A matrix polynomial $D(\lambda)$ is called a ***common right divisor*** of matrix polynomials $L_1(\lambda)$ and $L_2(\lambda)$ if $D(\lambda)$ is a right divisor of each $L_i(\lambda)$ $(i = 1,2)$. A right common divisor $D_0(\lambda)$ of the polynomials $L_1(\lambda)$, $L_2(\lambda)$ is called a ***right greatest common divisor*** (abbreviated g.c.d.) of these polynomials if any right common divisor of $L_1(\lambda)$, $L_2(\lambda)$ is a right divisor of $D_0(\lambda)$ as well. If $D_0(\lambda) \equiv I$ is a greatest common right divisor of $L_1(\lambda)$ and $L_2(\lambda)$, we say that the polynomials $L_1(\lambda)$ and $L_2(\lambda)$ are ***right coprime***. The following result is basic: a regular matrix polynomial $D(\lambda)$ is a right divisor of a regular matrix polynomial $L(\lambda)$ if and only if the right finite Jordan pair of $D(\lambda)$ is a restriction of the right finite Jordan pair of $L(\lambda)$. Then it follows that a regular polynomial $D(\lambda)$ is a (greatest) common right divisor of regular polynomials $L_1(\lambda)$ and $L_2(\lambda)$ if and only if the right finite Jordan pair of $D(\lambda)$ is a (greatest) common restriction of the right finite Jordan pairs of $L_1(\lambda)$ and $L_2(\lambda)$. In particular, the polynomials $L_1(\lambda)$ and $L_2(\lambda)$ are right coprime if and only if $\mathrm{Ker} L_1(\lambda) \cap \mathrm{Ker}\ L_2(\lambda) = (0)$ for any $\lambda \in \mathbb{C}$. Of course, the above notions and results have obvious analogs concerning left divisors.

Now consider the following problem. Given a monic s×s matrix polynomial $L(\lambda)$ of degree ν, find all its factorizations $L(\lambda) = Q(\lambda)R(\lambda)$, where $Q(\lambda)$ and $R(\lambda)$ are monic polynomials. The solution of this problem can be given (see [GLR1]) in terms of supporting projectors. We say that P is a *supporting projector of degree* m for the standard triple (Γ,T,Λ) of $L(\lambda)$ if a) the subspace $\mathcal{M} := \mathrm{Im} P \in \mathbb{C}^{\nu s}$ is T-invariant; b) $\dim \mathcal{M} = ms$; c) the linear transformation $\mathrm{col}(\Gamma T^{j-1})_{j=1}^{m}|_{\mathcal{M}}: \mathcal{M} \to \mathbb{C}^{ms}$ is invertible. The hypothesis c) is equivalent to c′) the linear transformation $(I-P)[\mathrm{row}(T^{i-1}\Lambda)_{i=1}^{\nu-m}]: \mathbb{C}^{s(\nu-m)} \to \mathrm{Ker} P$ is invertible. Now any supporting projector P of degree m of the standard triple (Γ,T,Λ) of $L(\lambda)$ generates a factorization $L(\lambda) = Q(\lambda)R(\lambda)$, with $\deg R = m$, $\deg Q = n := \nu - m$, of which the factors are defined as follows:

$$\begin{aligned} R(\lambda) &:= \lambda^m I - \Gamma|_{\mathcal{M}}(T|_{\mathcal{M}})^m (Y_1 + \lambda Y_2 + \cdots + \lambda^{m-1} Y_m), \\ Q(\lambda) &:= \lambda^n I - (Z_1 + \lambda Z_2 + \cdots + \lambda^{n-1} Z_n)\tilde{P} T^n \tilde{P}\Lambda, \end{aligned} \tag{1.7}$$

where $\tilde{P} = I-P$ and

$$\begin{aligned} \mathrm{row}(Y_j)_{j=1}^{m} &= [\mathrm{col}(\Gamma|_{\mathcal{M}}(T|_{\mathcal{M}})^{i-1})_{i=1}^{m}]^{-1}, \\ \mathrm{col}(Z_j)_{j=1}^{n} &= [\mathrm{row}(\tilde{P}\Lambda \cdot \tilde{P} T^{i-1} \tilde{P})_{i=1}^{n}]^{-1} : \mathrm{Im}\tilde{P} \to \mathbb{C}^{ns}. \end{aligned} \tag{1.8}$$

Any factorization $L(\lambda) = Q(\lambda)R(\lambda)$ with $\deg R = m$ is obtained in this way by an appropriate choice of P.

Now consider the Bezoutian defined in the Introduction. Let $L_i(\lambda)$, $M_i(\lambda)$ (i=1,2) be monic s×s matrix polynomials, with $\deg L_1 = \deg L_2 = \nu$, $\deg M_1 = \deg M_2 = \mu$, such that $L_1(\lambda)M_1(\lambda) = L_2(\lambda)M_2(\lambda)$, and let $\mathbf{B} = \mathbf{B}(L_1,L_2;M_1,M_2)$ be the corresponding Bezoutian. Then the following basic results hold true (see [LT1,2,3]).

PROPOSITION 1.1. *If* (Φ,Q) *is a right admissible pair and* (R,Ψ) *is a left admissible pair, then*

$$\mathbf{B}\,\mathrm{col}(\Phi Q^{j-1})_{j=1}^{\mu} = S_{L_1}\mathrm{col}(M_1(\Phi,Q)Q^{j-1})_{j=1}^{\nu} - S_{L_2}\mathrm{col}(M_2(\Phi,Q)Q^{j-1})_{j=1}^{\nu},$$

$$-\mathrm{row}(R^{j-1}\Psi)_{j=1}^{\nu}\,\mathbf{B} = \mathrm{row}(R^{j-1}L_1(R,\Psi))_{j=1}^{\mu}S_{M_1} - \mathrm{row}(R^{j-1}L_2(R,\Psi))_{j=1}^{\mu}S_{M_2},$$

where S_{L_i} *and* S_{M_i} *are defined by* (1.5).

PROPOSITION 1.2. *Let* $D_r(\lambda)$ *denote a right g.c.d. of* $M_1(\lambda)$ *and* $M_2(\lambda)$, *and let* (Φ,Q) *be a finite Jordan pair of* $D_r(\lambda)$. *Then*

$$\mathrm{Ker}\mathbf{B} = \mathrm{Im}\,\mathrm{col}(\Phi Q^{j-1})_{j=1}^{\mu},$$

and in particular, $\dim \mathrm{Ker}\mathbf{B} = \deg \det D_r(\lambda)$.

2. MONIC DIVISORS OF MATRIX POLYNOMIALS AND THE MATRIX QUADRATIC EQUATION

Consider the quadratic equation

$$UX - XV = XWX, \qquad (E_1)$$

of which the coefficients $U \in \mathbb{C}^{ns\times ns}$, $V \in \mathbb{C}^{ms\times ms}$ and $W \in \mathbb{C}^{ms\times ns}$ are complex block matrices with $s\times s$ block entries. By $\mathcal{R}(E_1)$ we denote the set of all solutions of (E_1). Since $0\in\mathcal{R}(E_1)$, it is clear that $\mathcal{R}(E_1)$ is not empty.

It will be always assumed in this section that the block rank of W is equal to one, i.e. W can be factored as follows

$$W = \Psi\Phi, \quad \Psi \in \mathbb{C}^{ms\times s},\ \Phi \in \mathbb{C}^{s\times ns}, \qquad (2.1)$$

and

$$\det \mathrm{col}(\Phi U^{j-1})_{j=1}^{n} \neq 0,\ \det \mathrm{row}(V^{j-1}\Psi)_{j=1}^{m} \neq 0. \qquad (2.2)$$

Under the above conditions there exist $s\times s$ monic matrix polynomials $L_U(\lambda)$ and $L_V(\lambda)$ such that (Φ,U) is a right standard pair of L_U, while (V,Ψ) is a left standard pair of L_V. The degrees of the monic polynomials L_U and L_V are n and m, respectively. The pair $(\Phi^{(n)},\hat{C}_{L_U})$ also is a right standard pair of the polynomial $L_U(\lambda)$, and consequently, it is similar to the pair (Φ,U); namely,

$$U = T_U^{-1}\hat{C}_{L_U}T_U,\ \Phi = \Phi^{(n)}T_U, \qquad (2.3)$$

with

$$T_U := [\mathrm{col}(\Phi^{(n)}\hat{C}_{L_U}^{i-1})_{i=1}^{n}]^{-1}\mathrm{col}(\Phi U^{j-1})_{j=1}^{n}. \qquad (2.4)$$

Similarly, $(C_{L_V},\Psi^{(m)})$ and (V,Ψ) are left standard pairs of $L_V(\lambda)$, and hence

$$V = T_V C_{L_V} T_V^{-1}, \quad \Psi = T_V \Psi^{(m)}, \tag{2.5}$$

where

$$T_V := \mathrm{row}(V^{i-1}\Psi)_{i=1}^m [\mathrm{row}(C_{L_V}^{i-1}\Psi^{(m)})_{i=1}^m]^{-1}. \tag{2.6}$$

The expressions (2.4) and (2.6) can be written in a more transparent form involving the coefficients of the polynomials L_U and L_V. Indeed, using (1.4), we see that for $i = 0,1,\dots,n-1$

$$\Phi^{(n)}\hat{C}_{L_U}^i = \Phi^{(n)} S_{L_U} C_{L_U}^i S_{L_U}^{-1} = \Phi^{(1)} C_{L_U}^i S_{L_U}^{-1} = \Phi^{(i+1)} S_{L_U}^{-1},$$

and hence $[\mathrm{col}(\Phi^{(n)}\hat{C}_{L_U}^{i-1})_{i=1}^n]^{-1} = S_{L_U}$. In a similar way one checks that $[\mathrm{row}(C_{L_V}^{i-1}\Psi^{(m)})_{i=1}^m]^{-1} = S_{L_V}$. So, (2.4) and (2.6) can be written as

$$T_U = S_{L_U}\, \mathrm{col}(\Phi U^{j-1})_{j=1}^n, \quad T_V = \mathrm{row}(V^{i-1}\Psi)_{i=1}^m\, S_{L_V}. \tag{2.7}$$

Now introduce the following notation: for a monic polynomial $G(\lambda)$ (of degree $\geq m$) we denote by $\mathcal{D}(G;m)$ the set of all monic right divisors of degree m of $G(\lambda)$. The theorem below states that there is a one-to-one correspondence between the set $\mathcal{R}(E_1)$ of all solutions of (E_1) and the set $\mathcal{D}(G;m)$ of all right monic divisors of degree m of the polynomial $G(\lambda) := L_U(\lambda)L_V(\lambda)$. More precisely, we have the following result.

THEOREM 2.1. *Let* $R(\lambda)$ *be a right monic divisor of degree* m *of the matrix polynomial* $L_U(\lambda)L_V(\lambda)$, *and let* $Q(\lambda) := L_U(\lambda)L_V(\lambda)R^{-1}(\lambda)$. *Set*

$$\gamma(R) := T_U^{-1}\mathbb{B}(L_U,Q;L_V,R)T_V^{-1}. \tag{2.8}$$

Then (2.8) *defines a bijective mapping* γ *of* $\mathcal{D}(L_UL_V;m)$ *onto* $\mathcal{R}(E_1)$. *The inverse mapping* $\gamma^{-1}:\mathcal{R}(E_1) \to \mathcal{D}(L_UL_V;m)$ *is given as follows: if* $X \in \mathcal{R}(E_1)$ *and* $S = [s_{ij}]_{i,j=1}^{n,m} := T_U X T_V$, *then*

$$\gamma^{-1}(X) := R(\lambda) = L_V(\lambda) - S_n(\lambda), \tag{2.9}$$

where

$$S_n(\lambda) := \sum_{k=1}^{m} \lambda^{k-1} s_{nk}. \tag{2.10}$$

In this case the corresponding quotient $Q(\lambda) := L_U(\lambda)L_V(\lambda)R^{-1}(\lambda)$ *is given by*

$$Q(\lambda) = L_U(\lambda) + \tilde{S}_m(\lambda), \tag{2.11}$$

with

$$\tilde{S}_m(\lambda) := \sum_{k=1}^{n} \lambda^{k-1} s_{km}. \tag{2.12}$$

The proof of this theorem is postponed to the next section. Here we point out only that under the assumptions of this section the equation (E_1)can be transformed to the following equation with companion coefficients:

$$\hat{C}_{L_U} S - SC_{L_V} = S\Psi^{(m)}\Phi^{(n)}S. \tag{E_2}$$

This is easily deduced from (2.3) and (2.5) by setting $S := T_U X T_V$. Clearly, for equations of the form (E_2) the assertions of Theorem 2.1 become especially transparent. In particular, if $R(\lambda)$ is a right monic divisor of degree m of $L_U(\lambda)L_V(\lambda)$, then

$$S = \gamma(R) := \mathbb{B}(L_U, Q; L_V, R) \tag{2.8$'$}$$

is a solution of (E_2), where $Q := L_U L_V R^{-1}$. Conversely, if $S = [s_{ij}]_{i,j=1}^{n,m}$ is a solution of (E_2), then the matrix polynomial $L_U(\lambda)L_V(\lambda)$ admits the factorization

$$L_U(\lambda)L_V(\lambda) = Q(\lambda)R(\lambda), \tag{2.13}$$

where $R(\lambda)$ and $Q(\lambda)$ are defined by (2.9) - (2.12). Note that formulas (2.8′) and (2.9) - (2.12) show that a solution S of the equation (E_2) is uniquely determined by its last block row (or block column).

Now we present corollaries and applications of Theorem 2.1. First note that Proposition 1.2 leads to the following simple corollary.

COROLLARY 2.2. *If* $X = \gamma(R)$, $R \in \mathcal{D}(L_U L_V; m)$, *then*

$$\text{rank} X = ms - \text{degdet} D_r(\lambda) = ns - \text{degdet} D_\ell(\lambda), \tag{2.14}$$

where $D_r(\lambda)$ *denotes a right g.c.d. of* L_V *and* R *and* $D_\ell(\lambda)$ *stands for a left g.c.d of* L_U *and* $Q := L_U L_V R^{-1}$.

REMARK 2.3. It follows from formulas (2.9) and (2.11) that the polynomials $D_r(\lambda)$ and $D_\ell(\lambda)$ in (2.14) can be taken to be a right g.c.d. of $L_V(\lambda)$ and $S_n(\lambda)$ and a left g.c.d. of $L_U(\lambda)$ and $\tilde{S}_m(\lambda)$, respectively. This observation is especially useful in the case of equations of type (E_2), since in this case the polynomials $S_n(\lambda) = \sum_{k=1}^{m} \lambda^{k-1} s_{nk}$ and $\tilde{S}_m(\lambda) = \sum_{k=1}^{n} \lambda^{k-1} s_{km}$ are directly determined by the last block row and last block column of the solution $S = [s_{jk}]_{j,k=1}^{n,m}$ of (E_2).

REMARK 2.4. Theorem 2.1 and Corollary 2.2 yield that given an integer $r > 0$, there exists a solution $X \in \mathcal{R}(E_1)$ such that rank$S = r$ iff the matrix polynomial $L_U(\lambda)L_V(\lambda)$ has a right monic divisor $R(\lambda)$ of degree m such that the determinant of a right g.c.d. of L_V and R has degree $ms - r$. In particular, the equation (E_1), with $m = n$, has an invertible solution iff the polynomial $L_U(\lambda)L_V(\lambda)$ admits a factorization (2.13) such that L_V and R are right coprime or, which is equivalent, L_U and Q are left coprime.

Next, consider the linear matrix equation of Liapunov type

$$YU - VY = W, \qquad (E_3)$$

where the coefficients U,V,W satisfy (2.1) and (2.2). Observe that (E_3) has an invertible solution iff (E_1) has an invertible solution. To see this just set $X = Y^{-1}$. Thus combining Theorem 2.1 with Remark 2.4 we have

COROLLARY 2.5. *Under the assumptions* (2.1) *and* (2.2) *the equation* (E_3) *has an invertible solution if and only if* $n = m$ *and there are monic polynomials* $Q(\lambda)$ *and* $R(\lambda)$ *of degree* m *such that* L_V *and* R *are right coprime and* $L_U(\lambda)L_V(\lambda) = Q(\lambda)R(\lambda)$. *In this case* L_U *and* Q *are left coprime and the invertible solution* Y *of* (E_3) *is given by* $Y = T_V[\mathbb{B}(L_U,Q;L_V,R)]^{-1}T_U$.

Note that the first assertion of this corollary can be deduced from the results of [GKLR3].

Theorem 2.1 shows that the problem of determining solutions of the equation (E_1) is equivalent to the problem of determining right monic divisors of degree m of the polynomial $G(\lambda) := L_U(\lambda)L_V(\lambda)$. Let us specify both directions of this equivalence in a more constructive way.

PROPOSITION 2.6. *Let* (Γ,T,Λ) *be a standard triple of the polynomial* $G(\lambda) := L_U(\lambda)L_V(\lambda)$. *Then any supporting projector* P *of degree* m *of the triple* (Γ,T,Λ) *generates a solution* X_P *of* (E_1) *given by* $X_P := T_U^{-1}\mathbb{B}(L_U,Q;L_V,R)T_V^{-1}$, *where* $Q(\lambda)$ *and* $R(\lambda)$ *are defined by* (1.7) - (1.8). *All solutions of* (E_1) *are obtained in this way and if* $\mathrm{Im}P_1 \neq \mathrm{Im}P_2$, *then* $X_{P_1} \neq X_{P_2}$.

The *proof* follows immediately from Theorem 2.1 and Corollary 3.18 in [GLR1], where the explicit formulas (1.7) - (1.8) are established for monic divisors and corresponding quotients of a given monic polynomial. Of course, one can take the companion standard triple $(\Phi^{(1)}, C_G, \Psi^{(n+m)})$ as the triple (Γ, T, Λ) in the above proposition.

The converse direction of the equivalence mentioned in the paragraph preceding Propositon 2.6 can be interpreted as a solution of the problem of constructing all monic right divisors with a fixed degree m of a monic matrix polynomial $G(\lambda)$ $(\deg G > m)$, given one such divisor M (and the quotient GM^{-1}).

PROPOSITION 2.7. *Let* $G(\lambda)$ *be a monic matrix polynomial of degree* k, *let* $M(\lambda)$ *be a monic right divisor of degree* m $(<k)$ *of* $G(\lambda)$ *and set* $L(\lambda) = G(\lambda)M(\lambda)^{-1}$. *Then any monic right divisor* $R(\lambda)$ *of degree* m *of* $G(\lambda)$ *is given by the formula*

$$R(\lambda) := R_S(\lambda) = M(\lambda) - \sum_{i=1}^{m} \lambda^{i-1} s_{k-m,i}, \tag{2.15}$$

where $S = [s_{ji}]_{j,i=1}^{k-m,m}$ *is a solution of the equation*

$$\hat{C}_L S - SC_M = S\Psi^{(m)}\Phi^{(k-m)}S, \tag{E_2'}$$

and the corresponding quotient $Q(\lambda) = G(\lambda)R^{-1}(\lambda)$ *is given by*

$$Q(\lambda) := Q_S(\lambda) = L(\lambda) + \sum_{i=1}^{k-m} \lambda^{i-1} s_{im}. \tag{2.16}$$

If $D_r(\lambda)$ *(respectively,* $D_\ell(\lambda)$*) denotes the right (respectively, left) g.c.d. of* $M(\lambda)$ *and* $R_S(\lambda)$ *(respectively, of* $L(\lambda)$ *and* $Q_S(\lambda)$*), then*

$$\deg\det D_r(\lambda) = \dim\operatorname{Ker} S, \quad \deg\det D_\ell(\lambda) = (k-m)s - \operatorname{rank} S. \tag{2.17}$$

If $S_1 \neq S_2$, *then* $R_{S_1} \neq R_{S_2}$ *and* $Q_{S_1} \neq Q_{S_2}$.

The *proof* follows immediately from Theorem 2.1 and Corollary 2.2.

The problem solved in Proposition 2.7 is especially relevant in the theory of Wiener-Hopf factorizations of rational matrix polynomials. Let us introduce the necessary definitions (see, e.g. [CG]). Let Γ denote a Cauchy contour in the complex plane consisting of several non-intersecting simple smooth closed contours which form the positively oriented boundary of a finitely connected bounded domain Δ_+. We assume for convenience that $0 \in \Delta_+$. Denote $\Delta_- := [\mathbb{C} \cup \{\infty\}] \setminus [\Delta_+ \cup \Gamma]$. Let $H(\lambda)$ be a continuous $s \times s$ matrix function defined on Γ such that $\det H(\lambda) \neq 0$ for all $\lambda \in \Gamma$. A factorization

$$H(\lambda) = H_+(\lambda)H_-(\lambda), \quad \lambda \in \Gamma, \tag{2.18}$$

where $H_{\pm}(\lambda)$ are continuous $s\times s$ matrix functions on Γ, is called *right canonical* if $H_{-}(\lambda)$ and $H_{+}(\lambda)$ admit analytic continuation in Δ_{-} and Δ_{+}, respectively, with $\det H_{-}(\lambda) \neq 0$ for $\lambda \in \Delta_{-} \cup \Gamma$ and $\det H_{+}(\lambda) \neq 0$ for $\lambda \in \Delta_{+} \cup \Gamma$. It is easily seen that a right canonical factorization, if exists,is unique up to multiplication of $H_{-}(\lambda)$ by a constant matrix E on the left and simultaneous multiplication of $H_{+}(\lambda)$ by E^{-1} on the right. We shall fix *the* right canonical factorization by setting $\lim_{\lambda\to\infty} H_{-}(\lambda) = I$. Interchanging in (2.18) the places of H_{-} and H_{+}, we obtain the analogous definition of the *left canonical factorization* $H = H_{-}H_{+}$ of H.

The following question is important in the theory of singular integral operators and Toeplitz operators and in system theory. Given a right canonical factorization (2.18) of $H(\lambda)$, find necessary and sufficient conditions for the existence of a left canonical factorization

$$H(\lambda) = F_{-}(\lambda)F_{+}(\lambda) \qquad (\lambda \in \Gamma), \tag{2.19}$$

and provide explicit formulas for F_{+} and F_{-}. This problem has been solved in [BR] in the case that $H(\lambda)$ is a rational matrix function, with $H(\infty)=I$, and the factors $H_{\pm}$ and $F_{\pm}$ are in realization form. For the case that $H(\lambda)$ is a *rational* $s\times s$ *matrix polynomial*, i.e. $H(\lambda)= \sum_{j=-m}^{m} \lambda^j h_j$, and $H_{\pm}^{-1}$ and $F_{\pm}^{-1}$ are in realized form, a solution of the problem can be found in [GKL]. We solve here the problem under consideration in the case of a rational matrix polynomial $H(\lambda)$ with $h_m = I$, when the factors $H_{\pm}$ are given in coefficient form and the solution $F_{\pm}$ is found in coefficient form as well.

First mention the following easily verified facts. If $H(\lambda) = \sum_{j=-m}^{m} \lambda^j h_j$ ($h_m=I$) is a rational matrix polynomial, then $H_{+}(\lambda)$, $\tilde{H}_{-}(\lambda) := \lambda^m H_{-}(\lambda)$ and $F_{+}(\lambda)$, $\tilde{F}_{-}(\lambda) := \lambda^m F_{-}(\lambda)$ defined by (2.18)-(2.19) are monic polynomials of degree m. Conversely, if the monic matrix polynomial $\tilde{H}(\lambda) = \lambda^m H(\lambda)$ is factored as follows

$$\tilde{H}(\lambda) = H_{+}(\lambda)\tilde{H}_{-}(\lambda) , \tag{2.18'}$$

where H_{+} and $\tilde{H}_{-}$ are monic matrix polynomials of degree m, and

$$\sigma(H_{+}) \subset \Delta_{-}, \ \sigma(\tilde{H}_{-}) \subset \Delta_{+}, \tag{2.20}$$

then setting $H_-(\lambda) = \lambda^{-m}\tilde{H}_-(\lambda)$, we obtain the right canonical factorization (2.18). Similarly, if $\tilde{H}(\lambda)$ admits the factorization

$$\tilde{H}(\lambda) = \tilde{F}_-(\lambda)F_+(\lambda), \tag{2.19'}$$

where $\tilde{F}_-$ and F_+ are monic polynomials of degree m such that

$$\sigma(\tilde{F}_-) \subset \Delta_+,\ \sigma(F_+) \subset \Delta_-, \tag{2.21}$$

then setting $F_-(\lambda) = \lambda^{-m}\tilde{F}_-(\lambda)$, we obtain the left canonical factorization (2.19). Thus, the problem of determining the left canonical factorization (2.19) of $H(\lambda)$ from the given right canonical factorization (2.18) is equivalent to the problem of determining the representation (2.19′) of the monic polynomial $\tilde{H}(\lambda) := \lambda^m H(\lambda)$ as a product of two monic polynomials $\tilde{F}_-(\lambda)$ and $F_+(\lambda)$ of degree m satisfying (2.21), provided the representation (2.18′) with the properties (2.20) is given. We claim that the latter problem is equivalent to the problem of determining the representation (2.19′) with monic polynomials $\tilde{F}_-(\lambda)$ and $F_+(\lambda)$ such that $F_+(\lambda)$ and $\tilde{H}_-(\lambda)$ are right coprime, while $\tilde{F}_-(\lambda)$ and $H_+(\lambda)$ are left coprime. Indeed, it is clear that if we have (2.18′) with (2.20) and (2.19′) with (2.21), then $\operatorname{Ker}\tilde{H}_-(\lambda) \cap \operatorname{Ker}F_+(\lambda)=(0)$ and $\operatorname{Ker}H_+^{T}(\lambda) \cap \operatorname{Ker} \tilde{F}_-^{T}(\lambda)=(0)$ for all $\lambda \in \mathbb{C}$. Conversely, let us show that if $F_+(\lambda)$ and $\tilde{H}_-(\lambda)$ are right coprime, then $\sigma(F_+) \subset \Delta_-$. Assume $F_+(\lambda_0)\varphi_0 = 0$ ($\varphi_0 \neq 0$) for some $\lambda_0 \in \Delta_+$. Then

$$\tilde{H}(\lambda_0)\varphi_0 = H_+(\lambda_0)\tilde{H}_-(\lambda_0)\varphi_0 = \tilde{F}_-(\lambda_0)F_+(\lambda_0)\varphi_0 = 0.$$

In view of (2.20) $H_+(\lambda_0)$ is invertible, and hence $\tilde{H}_-(\lambda_0)\varphi_0 = 0$, which contradicts the right coprimeness of $\tilde{H}_-$ and F_+. In a similar way one sees that left coprimeness of $\tilde{F}_-$ and H_+ implies that $\sigma(\tilde{F}_-) \subset \Delta_+$. Now we can apply Proposition 2.7 to derive the following result.

THEOREM 2.8. *Let* $H(\lambda) = \sum_{j=-m}^{m} \lambda^j h_j$ ($h_m = I$) *be a rational* s×s *matrix polynomial that admits the right canonical factorization* (2.18) *with* $H_-(\infty) = I$. *Then* $H(\lambda)$ *admits a left canonical factorization* (2.19) *if and only if the (unique) solution of the equation*

$$Y\hat{C}_{H_+} - C_{\tilde{H}_-}Y = \Psi^{(m)}\Phi^{(m)} \tag{2.22}$$

is invertible, where $\widetilde{H}_-(\lambda) := \lambda^m H_-(\lambda)$. *If* Y *is the invertible solution of* (2.22) *and* $S = [s_{jk}]_{j,k=1}^m = Y^{-1}$, *then the factors in* (2.19) *are given by*

$$F_+(\lambda) = \lambda^m H_-(\lambda) - \sum_{i=1}^m \lambda^{i-1} s_{mi}, \quad F_-(\lambda) = \lambda^{-m}(H_+(\lambda) + \sum_{i=1}^m \lambda^{i-1} s_{im}). \tag{2.23}$$

REMARK 2.9. Since $\sigma(\widetilde{H}_-) \cap \sigma(H_+) = \emptyset$, the solution of (2.22) is given by the well known formula (see, e.g., [DK])

$$Y = -\frac{1}{2\pi i} \int_\Gamma (\lambda - C_{\widetilde{H}_-})^{-1} \Psi^{(m)} \Phi^{(m)} (\lambda - \hat{C}_{H_+})^{-1} d\lambda.$$

Also, to write the formulas (2.23) one has to solve only two block equations: $\mathrm{row}(s_{mj})_{j=1}^m Y = \Phi^{(m)}$ and $Y\mathrm{col}(s_{jm})_{j=1}^m = \Psi^{(m)}$.

The theory developed in this section is especially transparent if the matrix W in the right hand side of (E_1) is of rank s=1. Indeed, in this case the polynomials $L_U(\lambda)$ and $L_V(\lambda)$ are usual (scalar) polynomials with complex coefficients. Furthermore, if s=1, then condition (2.2) means that the matrices U and V are nonderogatory and the vectors $\Psi \in \mathbb{C}^m$, $\Phi^T \in \mathbb{C}^n$ are cyclic for the matrices V and U^T, respectively. Consequently, $L_U(\lambda)$ and $L_V(\lambda)$ coincide with the characteristic polynomials of U and V, respectively: $L_U(\lambda) = \det(\lambda I - U)$, $L_V(\lambda) = \det(\lambda I - V)$. Now from the results of this section we deduce the following result.

COROLLARY 2.10. *Consider the equation* (E_1), *where the matrices* $U \in \mathbb{C}^{n\times n}$ *and* $V \in \mathbb{C}^{m\times m}$ *are nonderogatory and assume that* $W = \Psi\Phi$, *where* $\Psi \in \mathbb{C}^m$ *and* $\Phi^T \in \mathbb{C}^n$ *are cyclic vectors of* V *and* U^T, *respectively. Let* $\lambda_1, \lambda_2, \ldots, \lambda_m$ *be the eigenvalues of* V *and let* $\lambda_{m+1}, \lambda_{m+2}, \ldots, \lambda_{m+n}$ *denote the eigenvalues of* U *(counted with their algebraic multiplicities). Then any collection of* m *points* $\Lambda = \{\lambda_{i_1}, \lambda_{i_2}, \ldots, \lambda_{i_m}\}$ *generates a solution* X_Λ *of* (E_1) *given by*

$$X = X_\Lambda := T_U^{-1} \mathbf{B}(L_U, Q; L_V, R) T_V^{-1},$$

where T_U *and* T_V *are defined by* (2.7) *and*

$$R_\Lambda(\lambda) = \prod_{k=1}^m (\lambda - \lambda_{i_k}), \quad Q_\Lambda(\lambda) = \prod_{j \notin \{i_1, \ldots, i_m\}} (\lambda - \lambda_j).$$

Any solution of (E_1) *is obtained in this way and if two collections* Λ_1, Λ_2 *are such that* $R_{\Lambda_1} \neq R_{\Lambda_2}$, *then* $X_{\Lambda_1} \neq X_{\Lambda_2}$. *Furthermore, if* $X = X_\Lambda$, *then* $\mathrm{rank} X = m - \#\{k (k=1,\ldots,m) \mid i_k \leq m\}$. *In particular, if* $m = n$, *the equation* (E_1) *has an invertible solution if and only if the matrices* U *and* V *don't have any common eigenvalue. Such a solution is unique and it is given by the formula* $X = T_U^{-1}\mathbb{B}(L_U,L_V;L_V,L_U)T_V^{-1}$.

Note that the last assertion of the above Corollary means that the Liapunov type equation (E_3), whose coefficients satisfy the assumptions of Corollary 2.10, has an invertible solution Y iff $\sigma(U) \cap \sigma(V) = \emptyset$ (cf. [H], [LLT], [GKLR3]), and $Y = T_V[\mathbb{B}(L_U,L_V;L_V,L_U)]^{-1}T_U$.

3. PROOF OF THE THEOREM 2.1

In this section we prove Theorem 2.1. In view of the observation made after the statement of Theorem 2.1 it is enough to prove the assertions of the Theorem in the case of the equation with companion coefficients

$$\hat{C}_{L_U}S - SC_{L_V} = S\Psi^{(m)}\Phi^{(n)}S. \tag{E_2}$$

Introduce the s×ns block row $\Lambda(\lambda) := \text{row}(\lambda^{j-1}I)_{j=1}^{n}$ and the ms×s block column $\mathcal{M}(\mu) := \text{col}(\mu^{j-1}I)_{j=1}^{m}$. If A is an ns×ms block matrix, we denote $A(\lambda,\mu) := \Lambda(\lambda)A\mathcal{M}(\mu)$. Also, write the polynomials L_U and L_V as follows

$$L_U(\lambda) = \lambda^n I + \sum_{j=0}^{n-1}\lambda^j \ell_U^{(j)}, \quad L_V(\lambda) = \lambda^m I + \sum_{j=0}^{m-1}\lambda^j \ell_V^{(j)}.$$

Now assume that $S = [s_{jk}]_{j,k=1}^{n,m}$ is a solution of (E_2), and multiply (E_2) by $\Lambda(\lambda)$ from the left and by $\mathcal{M}(\mu)$ from the right:

$$\Lambda(\lambda)\hat{C}_{L_U}S\mathcal{M}(\mu) - \Lambda(\lambda)SC_{L_V}\mathcal{M}(\mu) = \Lambda(\lambda)S\Psi^{(m)}\Phi^{(n)}S\mathcal{M}(\mu). \tag{3.1}$$

A simple calculation shows that

$$\Lambda(\lambda)\hat{C}_{L_U} = [\lambda I, \lambda^2 I, \ldots, \lambda^{n-1}I, -\sum_{j=0}^{n-1}\lambda^j\ell_U^{(j)}] = \lambda\Lambda(\lambda) - L_U(\lambda)\Phi^{(n)}, \tag{3.2}$$

and

$$C_{L_V}\mathcal{M}(\mu) = \mu\mathcal{M}(\mu) - \Psi^{(m)}L_V(\mu) . \tag{3.3}$$

Substituting (3.2), (3.3) into (3.1) we obtain

$$(\lambda-\mu)S(\lambda,\mu) - L_U(\lambda)\Phi^{(n)}S\mathcal{M}(\mu) + \Lambda(\lambda)S\Psi^{(m)}L_V(\mu) = \Lambda(\lambda)S\Psi^{(m)}\Phi^{(n)}S\mathcal{M}(\mu). \tag{3.4}$$

Next, one easily sees that

$$S_n(\mu) = \Phi^{(n)}S\mathcal{M}(\mu), \ \tilde{S}_m(\lambda) = \Lambda(\lambda)S\Psi^{(m)}, \tag{3.5}$$

where

$$\tilde{S}_m(\lambda) := \sum_{k=1}^{n} \lambda^{k-1} s_{km}, \quad S_n(\mu) := \sum_{k=1}^{m} \mu^{k-1} s_{nk}. \tag{3.6}$$

Using (3.5) we can rewrite (3.4) as follows

$$(\lambda-\mu)S(\lambda,\mu) - L_U(\lambda)S_n(\mu) + \tilde{S}_m(\lambda)L_V(\mu) = \tilde{S}_m(\lambda)S_n(\mu). \tag{3.7}$$

Setting here $\lambda = \mu$ we have, in particular,

$$\tilde{S}_m(\lambda)L_V(\lambda) - L_U(\lambda)S_n(\lambda) = \tilde{S}_m(\lambda)S_n(\lambda), \tag{3.8}$$

or equivalently,

$$L_U(\lambda)L_V(\lambda) = (L_U(\lambda) + \tilde{S}_m(\lambda))(L_V(\lambda) - S_n(\lambda)).$$

Therefore $R(\lambda) := L_V(\lambda) - S_n(\lambda)$ (which is monic and of degree m) is indeed a right divisor of $L_U(\lambda)L_V(\lambda)$ and

$$L_U(\lambda)L_V(\lambda) = Q(\lambda)R(\lambda) , \tag{3.9}$$

with $Q(\lambda) := L_U(\lambda) + \tilde{S}_m(\lambda)$. Now compute

$$Q(\lambda)R(\mu) - L_U(\lambda)L_V(\mu) = \tilde{S}_m(\lambda)L_V(\mu) - L_U(\lambda)S_n(\mu) - \tilde{S}_m(\lambda)S_n(\mu),$$

and rewrite (3.7) in the form

$$S(\lambda,\mu) = (\lambda-\mu)^{-1}[L_U(\lambda)L_V(\mu) - Q(\lambda)R(\mu)].$$

This means that $S = \mathbb{B}(L_U,Q;L_V,R)$.

Conversely, assume that a monic polynomial $R(\lambda)$ of degree m is a right divisor of $L_U(\lambda)L_V(\lambda)$, i.e. (3.9) holds true for some monic polynomial $Q(\lambda)$ of degree n. Consider the Bezoutian $\mathbb{B} = [b_{ij}]_{i,j=1}^{n,m} = \mathbb{B}(L_U,Q;L_V,R)$ defined by (3.9) i.e.

$$(\lambda-\mu)^{-1}[L_U(\lambda)L_V(\mu)-Q(\lambda)R(\mu)] = \sum_{i,j=1}^{n,m} \lambda^{i-1}\mu^{j-1}b_{ij} =: B(\lambda,\mu) . \tag{3.10}$$

We prove now that $\mathbb{B}$ is a solution of (E_2). Denote

$$B_j(\lambda) = \sum_{k=1}^{m} \lambda^{k-1} b_{jk} \quad (j=1,\dots,n), \quad \tilde{B}_j(\lambda) = \sum_{k=1}^{n} \lambda^{k-1} b_{kj} \quad (j=1,\dots,m),$$

and introduce the matrix $\Gamma := \hat{C}_{L_U}\mathbb{B} - \mathbb{B}C_{L_V}$. Using (3.2), (3.3) compute

$$\Lambda(\lambda)\Gamma\mathcal{M}(\mu) = (\lambda-\mu)B(\lambda,\mu) - L_U(\lambda)\Phi^{(n)}\mathbb{B}\mathcal{M}(\mu) + \Lambda(\lambda)\mathbb{B}\Psi^{(m)}L_V(\mu)$$

$$= (\lambda-\mu)B(\lambda,\mu) - L_U(\lambda)B_n(\mu) + \tilde{B}_m(\lambda)L_V(\mu).$$

Substituting $B(\lambda,\mu)$ from (3.10) we obtain

$$\Lambda(\lambda)\Gamma\mathcal{M}(\mu) = L_U(\lambda)L_V(\mu) - Q(\lambda)R(\mu) - L_U(\lambda)B_n(\mu) + \tilde{B}_m(\lambda)L_V(\mu). \tag{3.11}$$

Now rewrite (3.10) in the form

$$(\lambda-\mu)\sum_{k=1}^{m}\mu^{k-1}\tilde{B}_k(\lambda) = \sum_{k=0}^{m}\mu^k L_U(\lambda)\ell_V^{(k)} - \sum_{k=0}^{m}\mu^k Q(\lambda)r_k,$$

where $R(\lambda)=\sum_{j=0}^{m}\lambda^j r_j$ $(r_m=I)$. Comparison of the coefficients of μ^m on both sides of this equality yields

$$Q(\lambda) = \tilde{B}_m(\lambda) + L_U(\lambda). \tag{3.12}$$

By a similar argument one has

$$R(\mu) = L_V(\mu) - B_n(\mu) . \tag{3.13}$$

Substituting (3.12) and (3.13) in the right hand side of (3.11) we compute

$$\begin{aligned}\Lambda(\lambda)\Gamma\mathcal{M}(\mu) &= L_U(\lambda)L_V(\mu) - [L_U(\lambda) + \tilde{B}_m(\lambda)][L_V(\mu) - B_n(\mu)] \\ &- L_U(\lambda)B_n(\mu) + \tilde{B}_m(\lambda)L_V(\mu) = \tilde{B}_m(\lambda)B_n(\mu).\end{aligned} \tag{3.14}$$

Note that $\tilde{B}_m(\lambda) = \Lambda(\lambda)\mathbb{B}\Psi^{(m)}$ and $B_n(\mu) = \Phi^{(n)}\mathbb{B}\mathcal{M}(\mu)$. Thus, (3.14) can be rewritten as

$$\Lambda(\lambda)\Gamma\mathcal{M}(\mu) = \Lambda(\lambda)\mathbb{B}\Psi^{(m)}\Phi^{(n)}\mathbb{B}\mathcal{M}(\mu),$$

which implies

$$\hat{C}_{L_U}\mathbb{B} - \mathbb{B}C_{L_V} =: \Gamma = \mathbb{B}\Psi^{(m)}\Phi^{(n)}\mathbb{B},$$

i.e. $\mathbb{B}$ is a solution of equation (E_2).

To complete the proof of Theorem 2.1 it remains to show that the mapping γ: $\mathcal{D}(L_U L_V;m) \to \mathcal{R}(E_2)$ is injective. To this end, clearly, we have to show that if

$$L_U(\lambda)L_V(\lambda) = Q_1(\lambda)R_1(\lambda) = Q_2(\lambda)R_2(\lambda),$$

and

$$\mathbb{B}(L_U,Q_1;L_V,R_1) = \mathbb{B}(L_U,Q_2;L_V,R_2), \tag{3.15}$$

for some monic polynomials R_1,R_2 of degree m, then $R_1(\lambda)$ and $R_2(\lambda)$ coincide. But from the definition of the Bezoutian and from (3.15) we conclude that

$$Q_1(\lambda)R_1(\mu) = Q_2(\lambda)R_2(\mu)$$

for any $\lambda,\mu \in \mathbb{C}$. Writing this equality as

$$Q_2^{-1}(\lambda)Q_1(\lambda) = R_2(\mu)R_1^{-1}(\mu) \qquad (\lambda,\mu \in \mathbb{C}),$$

we infer that $R_2(\mu)R_1^{-1}(\mu)$ is a constant matrix. Since the polynomials $R_1(\mu)$ and $R_2(\mu)$ are monic of the same degree, we conclude, by letting $\mu \to \infty$, that $R_2(\mu)R_1^{-1}(\mu) = I$ for any $\mu \in \mathbb{C}$, $\mu \notin \sigma(R_1)$. □

4. DILATION OF THE QUADRATIC EQUATION

Consider the equation

$$UX - XV = XWX, \qquad (E_1)$$

with coefficients $U \in \mathbb{C}^{p\times p}$, $V \in \mathbb{C}^{q\times q}$, $W \in \mathbb{C}^{q\times p}$. In what follows our standing assumptions are that the pair (W,U) is observable and the pair (V,W) is controllable, i.e. $\mathrm{col}(WU^{j-1})_{j=1}^{p}$ and $\mathrm{row}(V^{j-1}W)_{j=1}^{q}$ are full rank matrices.

Write a rank decomposition of W:

$$W = \Psi\Phi \quad (\Psi \in \mathbb{C}^{q\times s},\ \Phi \in \mathbb{C}^{s\times p},\ s = \mathrm{rank}W)\ , \qquad (4.1)$$

and note that the controllability of (V,W) is equivalent to the controllability of (V,Ψ), while the observability of (W,U) is equivalent to the observability of (Φ,U). Denote $n = \mathrm{ind}(\Phi,U)$, $m = \mathrm{ind}(V,\Psi)$; then $\mathrm{col}(\Phi U^{j-1})_{j=1}^{n}$ is left invertible and $\mathrm{row}(V^{j-1}\Psi)_{j=1}^{m}$ is right invertible. Let $L_U(\lambda)$ (respectively, $L_V(\lambda)$) be a monic $s\times s$ matrix polynomial of degree n (respectively, m) such that (Φ,U) (respectively, (V,Ψ)) is a restriction (respectively, compression) of its right (respectively, left) standard pair.

Now we associate to (E_1) the following equation

$$\hat{C}_{L_U} Y - YC_{L_V} = Y\Psi^{(m)}\Phi^{(n)}Y. \qquad (E_2)$$

As in Section 2 (see (2.4), (2.7)) we define the matrices

$$\begin{aligned} T_U &= [\mathrm{col}(\Phi^{(n)}\hat{C}_{L_U}^{j-1})_{j=1}^{n}]^{-1}\mathrm{col}(\Phi U^{i-1})_{i=1}^{n} = S_{L_U}\mathrm{col}(\Phi U^{i-1})_{i=1}^{n}, \\ T_V &= \mathrm{row}(V^{i-1}\Psi)_{i=1}^{m}[\mathrm{row}(C_{L_V}^{j-1}\Psi^{(m)})_{j=1}^{m}]^{-1} = \mathrm{row}(V^{i-1}\Psi)_{i=1}^{m}S_{L_V}. \end{aligned} \qquad (4.2)$$

Under the assumptions of this section these matrices are not invertible but they have one-sided inverses $T_U^{(-1)}$ and $T_V^{(-1)}$. Next, we have

$$T_U U = \hat{C}_{L_U}T_U, \quad \Phi = \Phi^{(n)}T_U, \quad VT_V = T_V C_{L_V}, \quad \Psi = T_V\Psi^{(m)}. \qquad (4.3)$$

An important rôle in the sequel is played by *admissible solutions* of the equation (E_2) which are defined as solutions $Y \in \mathcal{R}(E_2)$ that satisfy

$$\mathrm{Im}Y \subset \mathrm{Im}T_U,\ \mathrm{Ker}\,Y \supset \mathrm{Ker}T_V. \qquad (4.4)$$

A detailed analysis and characterization of admissible solutions will be given in the next section. Here we prove that there is a one-to-one correspondence between the set $\mathcal{R}_a(E_2)$ of all admissible solutions of (E_2) and the set $\mathcal{R}(E_1)$ of all solutions of (E_1). More precisely, we have the following result.

THEOREM 4.1. *Let* $X \in \mathbb{C}^{p\times q}$ *be a solution of the equation* (E_1) *and set*

$$Y = \alpha(X) := T_U X T_V. \tag{4.5}$$

Then (4.5) *defines a bijective mapping of the set* $\mathcal{R}(E_1)$ *onto the set* $\mathcal{R}_a(E_2)$ *of all admissible solutions of the equation* (E_2). *The inverse mapping* α^{-1}: $\mathcal{R}_a(E_2) \to \mathcal{R}(E_1)$ *is given by*

$$\alpha^{-1}(Y) = T_U^{(-1)} Y T_V^{(-1)}. \tag{4.6}$$

In particular, (4.6) *doesn't depend on the choice of one-sided inverses* $T_U^{(-1)}$ *and* $T_V^{(-1)}$. *Furthermore, if* $X \in \mathcal{R}(E_1)$ *and* $X = \alpha^{-1}(Y)$, $Y \in \mathcal{R}_a(E_2)$, *then*

$$\operatorname{rank} X = \operatorname{rank} Y. \tag{4.7}$$

PROOF. Let $X \in \mathcal{R}(E_1)$ and multiply both sides of (E_1) by T_U from the left and by T_V from the right:

$$T_U U X T_V - T_U X V T_V = T_U X \Psi \Phi X T_V.$$

Using (4.3) one can rewrite this equation in the form

$$\hat{C}_{L_U} T_U X T_V - T_U X T_V C_{L_V} = T_U X T_V \Psi^{(m)} \Phi^{(n)} T_U X T_V,$$

which shows that $\alpha(X) = Y = T_U X T_V$ is a solution of (E_2). It is clear that the inclusions (4.4) hold true for Y, i.e. Y is an admissible solution of (E_2). Let us show that α is injective. Since α is a linear mapping, it is enough to show that if $Y = \alpha(X) = 0$, then $X = 0$. Assume $Y = 0$, then $\operatorname{Im} T_V \subset \operatorname{Ker} T_U X$. Since T_U is left invertible $\operatorname{Ker} T_U X = \operatorname{Ker} X$, and we have $\operatorname{Im} T_V \subset \operatorname{Ker} X$. But T_V is right invertible and hence $\operatorname{Im} T_V = \mathbb{C}^q$. This implies $\operatorname{Ker} X = \mathbb{C}^q$, i.e. $X = 0$.

Conversely, let $Y \in \mathcal{R}_a(E_2)$. Denote $P := I - T_V^{(-1)} T_V$. The operator P is a projector acting on $\mathbb{C}^{ms}$ with $\operatorname{Im} P = \operatorname{Ker} T_V$, and the second condition in (4.4) can be written as $YP = 0$, or equivalently,

$$Y T_V^{(-1)} T_V = Y. \tag{4.8}$$

Similarly, the first condition in (4.4) means that

$$T_U T_U^{(-1)} Y = Y. \tag{4.9}$$

Multiplying both sides of (E_2) by $T_U^{(-1)}$ from the left and by $T_V^{(-1)}$ from the right and using (4.8), (4.9), (4.3) one easily sees that $X = T_U^{(-1)} Y T_V^{(-1)}$ is a solution of the equation

$$UX - XV = X\Psi\Phi X.$$

Clearly, $\alpha(X) = T_U X T_V = Y$, which justifies the formula (4.6) for α^{-1}. It remains to check formula (4.7). Let $X = T_U^{(-1)} Y T_V^{(-1)}$, $Y \in \mathcal{R}_a(E_2)$. Then $Y = T_U X T_V$ and since T_V is right invertible, $\mathrm{Im}Y = \mathrm{Im}T_U X T_V = \mathrm{Im}T_U X$. But T_U is left invertible, i.e. injective, and hence $\dim\mathrm{Im}Y = \dim\mathrm{Im}T_U X = \dim\mathrm{Im}X$. □

COROLLARY 4.2. *Consider the equation* (E_1) *with* $p = q$. *A solution* $X \in \mathcal{R}(E_1)$ *is invertible if and only if at least one of the equalities:*

$$\mathrm{Im}Y = \mathrm{Im}T_U, \tag{4.10}$$

and

$$\mathrm{Ker}Y = \mathrm{Ker}T_V, \tag{4.11}$$

holds true for the solution $Y = T_U X T_V$ *of* (E_2). *If one of the conditions* (4.10), (4.11) *is satisfied, then the remaining one holds true as well.*

PROOF. Assume, for instance, that (4.10) holds true. Recall that $T_U: \mathbb{C}^p \to \mathbb{C}^{ns}$ is left invertible, and hence $\dim\mathrm{Im}T_U = p$. Then from (4.10) and (4.7) we have

$$\mathrm{rank}X = \mathrm{rank}Y = \dim\mathrm{Im}T_U = p,$$

i.e. X is invertible. A similar argument shows that (4.11) implies the invertibility of X.

Conversely, let X be invertible. Then from (4.7) $\mathrm{rank}Y = p$. We know already that $\dim\mathrm{Im}T_U = p$, and since for the admissible solution Y the inclusions (4.4) hold true, we infer that $\mathrm{Im}Y = \mathrm{Im}T_U$. To prove the validity of (4.11), note that since $T_V: \mathbb{C}^{ms} \to \mathbb{C}^q$ is right invertible, $\mathrm{rank}T_V = q$, i.e. $\dim \mathrm{Ker}T_V = ms-q$. From (4.7) we see that $\dim \mathrm{Ker}Y = ms - \mathrm{rank}\, X = ms - q$. Since Y is an admissible solution (i.e. (4.4) are satisfied) we conclude that $\mathrm{Ker}Y = \mathrm{Ker}T_V$. □

5. MAIN RESULTS

In this section we establish our main results concerning solvability of the equation

$$UX - XV = XWX, \tag{E_1}$$

where $U \in \mathbb{C}^{p\times p}$, $V \in \mathbb{C}^{q\times q}$ and $W \in \mathbb{C}^{q\times p}$. As in section 4 we write the rank decomposition of W

$$W = \Psi\Phi \quad (\Psi \in \mathbb{C}^{q\times s},\ \Phi \in \mathbb{C}^{s\times p},\ s = \text{rank } W), \tag{5.1}$$

and we assume that

$$\text{Kercol}(\Phi U^{j-1})_{j=1}^{n} = (0),\ \text{Imrow}(V^{j-1}\Psi)_{j=1}^{m} = \mathbb{C}^{q}, \tag{5.2}$$

where $n = \text{ind}(\Phi,U)$, $m = \text{ind}(V,\Psi)$.

Let $L_V(\lambda)$ be a monic matrix polynomial of degree m such that (V,Ψ) is a compression of its left standard pair. In other words, a left standard pair $(\hat{V}, \hat{\Psi})$ of $L_V(\lambda)$ is given by

$$\hat{V} = \begin{bmatrix} V & 0 \\ V_2 & V_1 \end{bmatrix},\quad \hat{\Psi} = \begin{bmatrix} \Psi \\ \Psi_1 \end{bmatrix}, \tag{5.3}$$

where $V_1 \in \mathbb{C}^{(ms-q)\times(ms-q)}$, $V_2 \in \mathbb{C}^{(ms-q)\times q}$, $\Psi_1 \in \mathbb{C}^{(ms-q)\times s}$ are some complex matrices such that the matrix $\text{row}(\hat{V}^{j-1}\hat{\Psi})_{j=1}^{m}$ is non-singular. Set $\hat{F} = \Psi^{(m)}[\text{row}(\hat{V}^{j-1}\hat{\Psi})_{j=1}^{m}]^{-1}$; then $(\hat{F},\hat{V},\hat{\Psi})$ is a standard triple of $L_V(\lambda)$. In accordance with (5.3) we split $\hat{F}$ as follows:

$$\hat{F} = [F,F_1],\ F \in \mathbb{C}^{s\times q},\ F_1 \in \mathbb{C}^{s\times(ms-q)}. \tag{5.4}$$

Analogously, let $L_U(\lambda)$ be a monic s×s matrix polynomial of degree n whose right standard pair is an extension of (Φ,U), i.e. a right standard pair $(\hat{\Phi}, \hat{U})$ of L_U is given by

$$\hat{\Phi} = [\Phi,\Phi_1],\ \hat{U} = \begin{bmatrix} U & U_2 \\ 0 & U_1 \end{bmatrix}, \tag{5.5}$$

where $\Phi_1 \in \mathbb{C}^{s\times(ns-p)}$, $U_1 \in \mathbb{C}^{(ns-p)\times(ns-p)}$ and $U_2 \in \mathbb{C}^{p\times(ns-p)}$ are complex matrices such that the matrix $\text{col}(\hat{\Phi}\hat{U}^{j-1})_{j=1}^{n}$ is non-singular. A standard triple of $L_U(\lambda)$ is given by $(\hat{\Phi}, \hat{U}, \hat{G})$, where $\hat{G} = [\text{col}(\hat{\Phi}\hat{U}^{j-1})_{j=1}^{n}]^{-1}\Psi^{(n)}$. We split $\hat{G}$ according to (5.5):

$$\hat{G} = \begin{bmatrix} G \\ G_1 \end{bmatrix}, \quad G \in \mathbb{C}^{p\times s}, \quad G_1 \in \mathbb{C}^{(ns-p)\times s}. \tag{5.6}$$

In the preceding section we have established a one-to-one correspondence between the set $\mathcal{R}(E_1)$ of all solutions of equation (E_1) and the set of admissible solutions

$$\mathcal{R}_a(E_2) = \{Y \in \mathcal{R}(E_2) \,|\, \mathrm{Im}Y \subset \mathrm{Im}T_U,\ \mathrm{Ker}Y \supset \mathrm{Ker}T_V\}$$

of the equation

$$\hat{C}_{L_U} Y - YC_{L_V} = Y\Psi^{(m)}\Phi^{(n)}Y. \tag{E_2}$$

In section 2 we introduced a bijective mapping γ: $\mathcal{D}(L_U L_V;m) \to \mathcal{R}(E_2)$ which maps the set $\mathcal{D}(L_U L_V;m)$ of all monic right divisors of degree m of $L_U(\lambda)L_V(\lambda)$ onto the set $\mathcal{R}(E_2)$ of all solutions of the equation (E_2). Our aim now is to characterize the set $\gamma^{-1}(\mathcal{R}_a(E_2))$ which we denote by $\mathcal{D}_a(L_U L_V;m)$.

PROPOSITION 5.1. *Let* $L_U(\lambda)$ *and* $L_V(\lambda)$ *be as above. Then the set* $\mathcal{D}_a(L_U L_V;m):=\gamma^{-1}(\mathcal{R}_a(E_2))$ *consists of all polynomials* $R\in\mathcal{D}(L_U L_V;m)$ *such that*

i) (F_1,V_1) *is a restriction of the right standard pair of* $R(\lambda)$;

ii) (U_1,G_1) *is a compression of the left standard pair of the polynomial* $Q(\lambda) = L_U(\lambda)L_V(\lambda)R^{-1}(\lambda)$.

PROOF. Since $(\Phi^{(1)},C_{L_V},\Psi^{(m)})$ is a standard triple of $L_V(\lambda)$, it is similar to the triple $(\hat{F},\hat{V},\hat{\Psi})$. So, there is an invertible operator Γ on $\mathbb{C}^{ms}$ such that

$$[F,F_1] = \Phi^{(1)}\Gamma^{-1}, \quad \Gamma C_{L_V}\Gamma^{-1} = \begin{bmatrix} V & 0 \\ V_2 & V_1 \end{bmatrix}, \quad \Gamma\Psi^{(m)} = \begin{bmatrix} \Psi \\ \Psi_1 \end{bmatrix}.$$

From these equalities we obtain two expressions for Γ:

$$\Gamma = \left[\mathrm{col}\Big([F,F_1] \begin{bmatrix} V & 0 \\ V_2 & V_1 \end{bmatrix}^{j-1}\Big)_{j=1}^{m}\right]^{-1} \tag{5.7}$$

and

$$\Gamma = \mathrm{row}\Big(\begin{bmatrix} V & 0 \\ V_2 & V_1 \end{bmatrix}^{j-1}\begin{bmatrix} \Psi \\ \Psi_1 \end{bmatrix}\Big)_{j=1}^{m}\left[\mathrm{row}(C_{L_V}^{\,j-1}\Psi^{(m)})_{j=1}^{m}\right]^{-1}. \tag{5.8}$$

From (5.7) we see that

$$\Gamma^{-1} = [\Gamma_2, \mathrm{col}(F_1 V_1^{j-1})_{j=1}^{m}], \tag{5.9}$$

where Γ_2 is a certain matrix of size ms×q. The expression (5.8) can be written as

$$\Gamma = \begin{bmatrix} T_V \\ \Gamma_1 \end{bmatrix}, \tag{5.10}$$

where Γ_1 is a certain matrix of size (ms-q)×ms. Equations (5.9), (5.10) yield, in particular, that $T_V \mathrm{col}(F_1 V_1^{j-1})_{j=1}^m = 0$, that is

$$\mathrm{Ker}\ T_V \supset \mathrm{Im}\ \mathrm{col}(F_1 V_1^{j-1})_{j=1}^m . \tag{5.11}$$

Recall that $T_V: \mathbb{C}^{ms} \to \mathbb{C}^q$ is right invertible, i.e. $\dim \mathrm{Ker} T_V = ms - q$. Also, note that the columns of the matrix $\mathrm{col}(F_1 V_1^{j-1})_{j=1}^m$ are linearly independent, as they are columns of the invertible matrix Γ^{-1}. So, $\dim \mathrm{Im}\,\mathrm{col}(F_1 V_1^{j-1})_{j=1}^m = ms - q$. But then (5.11) implies

$$\mathrm{Ker}\ T_V = \mathrm{Im}\ \mathrm{col}(F_1 V_1^{j-1})_{j=1}^m. \tag{5.12}$$

Now consider the standard triple $(\Phi^{(n)}, \hat{C}_{L_U}, \Psi^{(1)})$ of $L_U(\lambda)$, which is clearly similar to the triple $(\hat{\Phi}, \hat{U}, \hat{G})$. Let Λ be an invertible matrix such that

$$[\Phi, \Phi_1] = \Phi^{(n)}\Lambda, \ \Lambda^{-1}\hat{C}_{L_U}\Lambda = \begin{bmatrix} U & U_2 \\ 0 & U_1 \end{bmatrix}, \ \Lambda^{-1}\Psi^{(1)} = \begin{bmatrix} G \\ G_1 \end{bmatrix}.$$

From these equalities we have

$$\Lambda = [\mathrm{col}(\Phi^{(n)}\hat{C}_{L_U}^{j-1})_{j=1}^n]^{-1}\mathrm{col}([\Phi, \Phi_1]\begin{bmatrix} U & U_2 \\ 0 & U_1 \end{bmatrix}^{j-1})_{j=1}^n = [T_U, \Lambda_1], \tag{5.13}$$

where Λ_1 is a certain matrix of size ns×(ns-p), and

$$\Lambda^{-1} = \mathrm{row}(\begin{bmatrix} U & U_2 \\ 0 & U_1 \end{bmatrix}^{j-1}\begin{bmatrix} G \\ G_1 \end{bmatrix})_{j=1}^n = \begin{bmatrix} \Lambda_2 \\ \mathrm{row}(U_1^{j-1}G_1)_{j=1}^n \end{bmatrix}, \tag{5.14}$$

where Λ_2 is a certain p×ns matrix. From (5.13) and (5.14) we see that $\mathrm{row}(U_1^{j-1}G_1)_{j=1}^n T_U = 0$, which means that

$$\mathrm{Ker}\ \mathrm{row}(U_1^{j-1}G_1)_{j=1}^n \supset \mathrm{Im}\ T_U. \tag{5.15}$$

The operator $T_U: \mathbb{C}^p \to \mathbb{C}^{ns}$ is left invertible and the operator $\mathrm{row}(U_1^{j-1}G_1)_{j=1}^n: \mathbb{C}^{ns} \to \mathbb{C}^{ns-p}$ is right invertible. This means that $\dim \mathrm{Im} T_U = p$ and $\dim \mathrm{Ker}\ \mathrm{row}(U_1^{j-1}G_1)_{j=1}^n = p$, and hence (5.15) becomes

$$\mathrm{Im}\ T_U = \mathrm{Ker}\ \mathrm{row}(U_1^{j-1}G_1)_{j=1}^n. \tag{5.16}$$

Now let $Y \in \mathcal{R}_a(E_2)$ be an admissible solution of (E_2), i.e., in view of (5.12) and (5.16), the inclusions

$$\operatorname{Im} Y \subset \operatorname{Ker} \operatorname{row}(U_1^{j-1}G_1)_{j=1}^{n}, \quad \operatorname{Ker} Y \supset \operatorname{Im} \operatorname{col}(F_1V_1^{j-1})_{j=1}^{m} \tag{5.17}$$

hold true. Let $R = \gamma^{-1}(Y)$, i.e. $R(\lambda)$ is a monic polynomial of degree m such that the factorization $L_U(\lambda)L_V(\lambda) = Q(\lambda)R(\lambda)$ holds true for some monic polynomial $Q(\lambda)$ of degree n, and Y coincides with the Bezoutian associated with this factorization: $Y = \mathbb{B}(L_U,Q;L_V,R)$. Now apply Proposition 1.1 to this Bezoutian with $(\Phi,Q)=(F_1,V_1)$ and take into account that (F_1,V_1) is a restriction of the right standard pair of $L_V(\lambda)$, i.e. $L_V(F_1,V_1) = 0$, which follows clearly from (5.3) and (5.4). We have

$$Y\operatorname{col}(F_1V_1^{j-1})_{j=1}^{m} = -S_Q\operatorname{col}(R(F_1,V_1)V_1^{j-1})_{j=1}^{n}, \tag{5.18}$$

where S_Q is defined as in (1.5). The second inclusion in (5.17) means that $Y\operatorname{col}(F_1V_1^{j-1})_{j=1}^{m} = 0$, and hence (5.18) yields $R(F_1,V_1) = 0$, i.e. (F_1,V_1) is a restriction of the standard pair of the polynomial $R(\lambda)$.

Analogously, it follows from (5.5), (5.6) that (U_1,G_1) is a compression of the left standard pair of L_U, and hence $L_U(U_1,G_1) = 0$. Applying again Proposition 1.1 with $(R,\Psi) = (U_1,G_1)$ we obtain

$$-\operatorname{row}(U_1^{j-1}F_1)_{j=1}^{n}Y = \operatorname{row}(U_1^{j-1}Q(U_1,F_1))_{j=1}^{m}S_R, \tag{5.19}$$

where S_R is defined as in (1.5). As the first inclusion in (5.17) means that $\operatorname{row}(U_1^{j-1}F_1)_{j=1}^{n}Y = 0$, we infer from (5.19) that $Q(U_1,F_1) = 0$, i.e. (U_1,F_1) is a compression of the left standard pair of $Q(\lambda)$. □

Before stating the main result of this paper we recall that if $L_V(\lambda)$ is a monic matrix polynomial with a standard triple $(\hat{F},\hat{V},\hat{\Psi})$ given by (5.3), (5.4), and if $L_U(\lambda)$ is a monic matrix polynomial with a standard triple $(\hat{\Phi},\hat{U},\hat{G})$ given by (5.5), (5.6), then by $\mathcal{D}_a(L_UL_V;m)$ we denote the set of all monic divisors $R(\lambda)$ of degree m of L_UL_V which meet hypothesis i), ii) of Proposition 5.1.

THEOREM 5.2. *Let the coefficients of the equation* (E_1) *satisfy the standing assumptions* (5.1) *and* (5.2). *Let* $L_V(\lambda)$ *be a monic* s×s *matrix polynomial of degree* m *whose standard triple* $(\hat{F},\hat{V},\hat{\Psi})$ *is given by* (5.3), (5.4) *and let* $L_U(\lambda)$ *be a monic* s×s *matrix polynomial of degree* n *whose standard triple* $(\hat{\Phi},\hat{U},\hat{G})$ *is given by* (5.5), (5.6). *For any polynomial* $R(\lambda) \in \mathcal{D}_a(L_UL_V;m)$ *define*

$$X := \rho(R) := T_U^{(-1)} \mathbf{B}(L_U, Q; L_V, R) T_V^{(-1)}, \tag{5.20}$$

where T_U *and* T_V *are defined by* (4.2) *and* $Q = L_U L_V R^{-1}$. *Then* $X \in \mathcal{R}(E_1)$ *and the mapping* ρ: $\mathcal{D}_a(L_U L_V; m) \to \mathcal{R}(E_1)$ *defined by* (5.20) *is bijective. The inverse mapping* $\rho^{-1}: \mathcal{R}(E_1) \to \mathcal{D}_a(L_U L_V; m)$ *is defined as follows: if* $X \in \mathcal{R}(E_1)$ *and* $Y = [y_{jk}]_{j,k=1}^{n,m} = T_U X T_V$, *then*

$$R(\lambda) := \rho^{-1}(X) = L_V(\lambda) - \sum_{k=1}^{m} \lambda^{k-1} y_{nk}, \tag{5.21}$$

and

$$Q(\lambda) := L_U(\lambda) L_V(\lambda) R^{-1}(\lambda) = L_U(\lambda) + \sum_{k=1}^{n} \lambda^{k-1} y_{km}. \tag{5.22}$$

Furthermore, if $X = \rho(R)$, *then*

$$\operatorname{rank} X = ms - \operatorname{degdet} D_r(\lambda) = ns - \operatorname{degdet} D_\ell(\lambda), \tag{5.23}$$

where $D_r(\lambda)$ *is a right g.c.d. of* $L_V(\lambda)$ *and* $R(\lambda)$, *and* $D_\ell(\lambda)$ *is a left g.c.d. of* $L_U(\lambda)$ *and* $Q(\lambda)$.

PROOF. The proof follows immediately from Theorems 2.1, 4.1 and Proposition 5.1. In fact the mapping ρ defined by (5.20) can be written as $\rho = \alpha^{-1}\hat{\gamma}$, where the operator $\alpha: \mathcal{R}(E_1) \to \mathcal{R}_a(E_2)$ is defined in Theorem 4.1 and $\hat{\gamma}: \mathcal{D}_a(L_U L_V; m) \to \mathcal{R}_a(E_2)$ denotes the restriction of the mapping $\gamma: \mathcal{D}(L_U L_V; m) \to \mathcal{R}(E_2)$, defined in Theorem 2.1, to the set $\mathcal{D}_a(L_U L_V; m)$. Formula (5.23) follows from (4.7) and Proposition 1.2 on Bezoutians. □

We remark that the formulas in Theorem 5.2 depend heavily on the choice of the extensions $(\hat{\Phi}, \hat{U})$ and $(\hat{V}, \hat{\Psi})$, defined by (5.5) and (5.7), to right and left standard pairs of some monic matrix polynomials $L_U(\lambda)$ and $L_V(\lambda)$, respectively. Various extensions of this type can be found in [GLR1] (see also [GLeR]). In particular, it is possible to construct $(\hat{\Phi}, \hat{U})$ and $(\hat{V}, \hat{\Psi})$ so that $\sigma(U_1) = \{c\}$, $\sigma(V_1) = \{d\}$ (and even $U_2 = 0$, $V_2 = 0$), where $c \notin \sigma(U)$ and $d \notin \sigma(V)$ are arbitrary complex numbers. With such extensions the characterization of the set $\mathcal{D}_a(L_U L_V; m)$ becomes more transparent as the following proposition shows.

PROPOSITION 5.3 *Let* $c \neq d$ *be complex numbers such that* $c, d \notin \sigma(U) \cup \sigma(V)$ *and choose the extensions* (5.5) *and* (5.7) *so that* $\sigma(U_1) = \{c\}$, $\sigma(V_1) = \{d\}$. *Then*

$$\mathcal{D}_a(L_UL_V;m) = \{R \in \mathcal{D}(L_UL_V;m) \,|\, c \notin \sigma(R),\ d \notin \sigma(L_UL_VR^{-1})\}. \tag{5.24}$$

PROOF. Since (F_1,V_1) is a restriction of the standard pair of L_V, $L_V(F_1,V_1)=0$, and hence $(L_UL_V)(F_1,V_1)= L_U(L_V(F_1,V_1),V_1) = 0$. Let $R\in\mathcal{D}(L_UL_V;m)$ and $d \notin \sigma(Q)$, where $Q:= L_UL_VR^{-1}$. Then $0 = (QR)(F_1,V_1)=Q(R(F_1,V_1),V_1)$. If $R(F_1,V_1) \neq 0$, then the (non-trivial) pair $(R(F_1,V_1),V_1)$ is a restriction of the standard pair of $Q(\lambda)$, and in particular, $\sigma(V_1\} = \{d\} \subset \sigma(Q)$, which contradicts the assumption $d \notin \sigma(Q)$. So, $R(F_1,V_1) = 0$, i.e. condition i) in Proposition 5.1 holds true. In a similar way one shows that if $R \in \mathcal{D}(L_UL_V;m)$ and $c \notin \sigma(R)$, then condition ii) in Proposition 5.1 is satisfied. Thus, $\mathcal{D}_a(L_UL_V;m)$ contains the set in the right hand side of (5.24).

To prove the converse inclusion first note that from the assumptions of the Proposition one infers that $\lambda = c$ (respectively, $\lambda = d$) is a zero of the scalar polynomial $\det L_U(\lambda)L_V(\lambda) = \det(\lambda-\hat{U})\det(\lambda-\hat{V})$ of multiplicity ns-p (respectively, ms-q). Now let $R \in \mathcal{D}_a(L_UL_V;m)$ and assume that $c \in \sigma(R)$. Let ν be the multiplicity of c as a zero of $\det R(\lambda)$. Since $Q(U_1,G_1)=0$, the multiplicity of c as a zero of $\det Q(\lambda)$ is at least ns-p. But then the multiplicity of c as a zero of $\det L_U(\lambda)L_V(\lambda) = \det Q(\lambda)R(\lambda)$ is at least ns-p+ν, a contradiction. In a similar way one sees that $d \notin \sigma(Q)$. □

The above Proposition and Theorem 5.2 imply Theorem 0.1.

We pass now to the problem of existence of invertible solutions of the equation (E_1) with p = q, preserving the notations and assumptions of Theorem 5.2. Formula (5.23) yields that (E_1) has an invertible solution if and only if there is a factorization

$$L_U(\lambda)L_V(\lambda) = Q(\lambda)R(\lambda) \tag{5.25}$$

with $R \in \mathcal{D}_a(L_UL_V;m)$ such that

$$\operatorname{degdet} D_r(\lambda) = ms - q, \tag{5.26}$$

or equivalently,

$$\operatorname{degdet} D_\ell(\lambda) = ns - p. \tag{5.27}$$

It is clear that (F_1,V_1) is a restriction of the right standard pair of $L_V(\lambda)$, and (U_1,G_1) is a restriction of the left standard pair of $L_U(\lambda)$. Since the sizes of V_1 and U_1 are ms-q and ns-p, respectively, (5.26) and (5.27) mean that the finite Jordan pair of $D_r(\lambda)$ is (F_1,V_1), and the finite Jordan pair of $D_\ell(\lambda)$ is (U_1,G_1), respectively. If L_U and L_V are as in Proposition 5.3 the above considerations lead to the following result.

COROLLARY 5.4 *Consider the equation* (E_1) *with* $p = q$ *and assume that* (5.1) *and* (5.2) *are satisfied. Furthermore, preserve the assumptions of Proposition* 5.3. *Then* (E_1) *has an invertible solution if and only if there is a factorization* (5.25) *such that*

a) $c \notin \sigma(R)$, $d \notin \sigma(Q)$;

b) $\mathrm{Ker}L_V(\lambda) \cap \mathrm{Ker}R(\lambda) = (0)$, $\lambda \in \mathbb{C}\backslash\{d\}$,

or equivalently,

$$\mathrm{Ker}\ L_U^T \cap \mathrm{Ker}\ Q^T(\lambda) = (0),\ \lambda \in \mathbb{C}\backslash\{c\}.$$

Since the linear equation

$$YU - VY = W,\ (U,V,W \in \mathbb{C}^{p\times p}) \tag{E_3}$$

has an invertible solution Y if and only if the equation (E_1) has an invertible solution X $(= Y^{-1})$, Theorem 5.2 and Corollary 5.4 imply the following

COROLLARY 5.5 *Consider the equation* (E_3) *with* W *satisfying* (5.1), (5.2) *and* $p = q$. *Choose the polynomials* $L_U(\lambda)$ *as in Proposition* 5.3. *Then any factorization* (5.25) *of* $L_U(\lambda)L_V(\lambda)$ *that meets conditions* a) *and* b) *of Corollary* 5.4 *generates an invertible solution of* (E_3) *which is given by*

$$Y := Y_R = T_V[\mathbb{B}(L_U,Q;L_V,R)]^{-1}T_U, \tag{5.28}$$

where T_U *and* T_V *are defined by* (4.2). *Furthermore, any invertible solution of* (E_3) *is obtained in this way, and if* $R_1 \neq R_2$, *then* $Y_{R_1} \neq Y_{R_2}$.

In conclusion of this section we remark that using Theorem 5.2 one can extend the construction of solutions of (E_1) given in Proposition 2.6 to the general case under consideration. We state the result for the case when L_U and L_V are as in Proposition 5.3.

PROPOSITON 5.6 *Preserving the assumptions and notations of Theorem* 5.2 *and Proposition* 5.3, *let* (Γ,T,Λ) *be a standard triple of the polynomial* $G(\lambda) = L_U(\lambda)L_V(\lambda)$. *Then any supporting projector* P *of degree* m, *such that* $c \notin \sigma(T|_{\mathrm{Im}P})$, $d \notin \sigma((I-P)T|_{\mathrm{Im}(I-P)})$, *generates a solution* X_P *of* (E_1) *given by* $X_P := T_U^{(-1)}\mathbb{B}(L_U,Q;L_V,R)T_V^{(-1)}$, *where* $Q(\lambda)$ *and* $R(\lambda)$ *are defined by* (1.7) - (1.8). *All solutions of* (E_1) *are obtained in this way and if* $\mathrm{Im}P_1 \neq \mathrm{Im}P_2$, *then* $X_{P_1} \neq X_{P_2}$.

Note that choosing the extensions (5.3) and (5.5) so that $U_2=0$, $V_2=0$ one can modify the above proposition to a form which involves the invariant subspaces of the matrix $\begin{bmatrix} V & W \\ O & U \end{bmatrix}$. This will be done elsewhere in a more general framework using the generalized Bezoutians for a family of matrix polynomials as defined in [LT 2,3].

6. THE ALGEBRAIC SKEW-RICCATI EQUATION

In this section we study the equation

$$V^*X - XV = XWX , \qquad (E_4)$$

where V and W are p×p complex matrices and W is hermitian. In the case of equation (E_4) one is interested mainly in skew-hermitian solutions X, the set of which we denote by $\mathcal{R}_{sh}(E_4)$. To describe the set $\mathcal{R}_{sh}(E_4)$ the results obtained in the preceding sections have to be properly modified and refined. Note that setting $A=-iV$, $Y=iX$ one rewrites (E_4) as an algebraic Riccati equation

$$A^*Y + YA = YWY, \qquad (6.1)$$

and $X\in\mathcal{R}_{sh}(E_4)$ iff $Y = iX$ is a hermitian solution of (6.1). This justifies the name *algebraic skew-Riccati equation* for (E_4) and motivates our interest in the skew-hermitian solutions of (E_4). Of course, the results of this section concerning the set $\mathcal{R}_{sh}(E_4)$ can be rephrased in terms of hermitian solutions of the equation (6.1) in an obvious way. In the framework of the present paper it is more convenient to deal with the equation (E_4).

The description of the set $\mathcal{R}_{sh}(E_4)$ will be based on the notion of a *symmetric factorization* (relative to $\mathbb{R}$) of a monic s×s matrix polynomial $G(\lambda)$ which is defined as the representation

$$G(\lambda) = L^*(\lambda)L(\lambda), \qquad (6.2)$$

where $L(\lambda)$ is a monic polynomial of degree m and $L^*(\lambda) := [L(\bar{\lambda})]^*$. Clearly, a necessary condition for existence of the symmetric factorization (6.2) is that the polynomial $G(\lambda)$ is *nonnegative*, i.e. $\langle G(\lambda)x,x\rangle \geq 0$ for any $\lambda\in\mathbb{R}$, $x\in\mathbb{C}^s$. It turns out (see, e.g. [GLR2]) that conversely, any nonnegative monic matrix polynomial of degree 2m admits a symmetric factorization (6.2). Given such a polynomial G, we denote by $\mathcal{D}_{sym}(G)$ the set of all polynomials L that satisfy (6.2).

THEOREM 6.1. *Consider the equation* (E_4) *with* $W \geq 0$, *let* $W = \Phi\Phi^*$ $(\Phi \in \mathbb{C}^{p\times s})$ *be a rank decomposition of* W *and let* $\mathrm{Imrow}(V^{i-1}\Phi)_{i=1}^m = \mathbb{C}^p$ $(m = \mathrm{ind}(V,\Phi))$. *Choose a real number* $d \notin \sigma(V)$ *and let* $L_V(\lambda)$ *be a monic* $s\times s$ *matrix polynomial of degree* m *such that* (V,Φ) *is a compression of the left standard pair of* L_V *and* $\sigma(L_V) = \sigma(V) \cup \{d\}$. *Next, for any polynomial* $R \in \mathcal{D}_{sym}(L_V^*L_V)$ *define*

$$X := \hat{\rho}(R) = [T_V^{(-1)}]^*\mathbb{B}(L_V^*,R^*;L_V,R)T_V^{(-1)}, \tag{6.3}$$

where T_V *is defined by* (4.2). *Then* $X \in \mathcal{R}_{sh}(E_4)$ *and the mapping* $\hat{\rho}:\mathcal{D}_{sym}(L_V^*L_V) \to \mathcal{R}_{sh}(E_4)$ *is bijective. The inverse mapping* $\hat{\rho}^{-1}: \mathcal{R}_{sh}(E_4) \to \mathcal{D}_{sym}(L_V^*L_V)$ *is given as follows: if* $X \in \mathcal{R}_{sh}(E_4)$ *and* $Y=[y_{jk}]_{j,k=1}^m:=T_V^*XT_V$, *then*

$$R(\lambda) := \hat{\rho}^{-1}(X) = L_V(\lambda) - \sum_{k=1}^{m} \lambda^{k-1}y_{mk}. \tag{6.4}$$

PROOF. We shall deduce the assertions of the theorem from Theorem 5.2, where $L_U = L_V^*$. To do this we have to show that

$$\mathcal{D}_{sym}(L_V^*L_V) \subset \mathcal{D}_a(L_V^*L_V;m), \tag{6.5}$$

and that the mapping ρ, defined in Theorem 5.2, satisfies

$$\rho(\mathcal{D}_{sym}(L_V^*L_V)) = \mathcal{R}_{sh}(E_4). \tag{6.6}$$

Then $\hat{\rho}$ is defined as the restriction of ρ to the set $\mathcal{D}_{sym}(L_V^*L_V)$. (Note that in case $L_U = L_V^*$ one can take $T_U^{(-1)} = [T_V^{(-1)}]^*$.)

The inclusion (6.5) follows from the following fact which can be found in [LT1] (see Propositon 2.3 and Corollary 2.6). If $R \in \mathcal{D}_{sym}(L_V^*L_V)$, i.e. $L_V^*(\lambda)L_V(\lambda) = R^*(\lambda)R(\lambda)$, and if (Γ_0,T_0) (respectively, $(\tilde{\Gamma}_0,\tilde{T}_0)$) denotes the restriction of the right standard pair of $L_V(\lambda)$ (respectively, of $R(\lambda)$) that corresponds to all real eigenvalues, then (Γ_0,T_0) and $(\tilde{\Gamma}_0,\tilde{T}_0)$ are similar. Since $d \in \mathbb{R}$, it follows immediately that conditions i), ii) of Proposition 5.1 hold true for any $R \in \mathcal{D}_{sym}(L_V^*L_V)$.

To prove (6.6) note that $\mathbb{B}(L_V^*,R^*;L_V,R)$ is a skew-hermitian matrix (see [LT1,3]), and hence $X = \rho(R) \in \mathcal{R}_{sh}(E_4)$ for any $R \in \mathcal{D}_{sym}(L_V^*L_V)$. Conversely, if $X \in \mathcal{R}_{sh}(E_4)$, then $Y = T_V^*XT_V$ is skew-hermitian, and hence $y_{km} = -y_{mk}^*$

(k=1,...,m). So, $Q(\lambda)$ from (5.22) is equal to $L_V^*(\lambda)-\sum_{k=1}^{m}\lambda^{k-1}y_{mk}^* = R^*(\lambda)$, i.e. $\rho^{-1}(X)\in\mathcal{D}_{sym}(L_V^*L_V)$. □

For a more detailed study of the set $\mathcal{R}_{sh}(E_4)$ we need to describe the relation between the location of the eigenvalues of $R(\lambda)$ relative to the real axis and the location of the eigenvalues of $S=\rho(R)$ relative to the imaginary axis. Recall (see, e.g. [LaT]) that the *inertia of a matrix* A *relative to the imaginary axis* is defined as the triple $in(A) = (\pi(A),\nu(A),\delta(A))$, where $\pi(A),\nu(A)$ and $\delta(A)$ denote the number of eigenvalues of A (counted with their algebraic multiplicities) with positive, negative and zero real parts, respectively. The *inertia of* A *with respect to the imaginary axis* $\tilde{i}n(A)$ is defined by $\tilde{i}n(A):=(\nu(iA),\pi(iA),\delta(iA))$. For a regular matrix polynomial $M(\lambda)$ with a finite Jordan pair (Γ,T) we use the notations $\tilde{\pi}(M):=\tilde{\pi}(T)$, $\tilde{\nu}(M):=\tilde{\nu}(T)$. If $M(\lambda)$ is a monic polynomial we denote $\tilde{i}n(M):=\tilde{i}n(T)$. The celebrated Hermite's theorem, regarding root localization of scalar polynomials, has been extended to the case of regular matrix polynomials in [LT1]. For monic matrix polynomials this result, which is basic in what follows, states that if $M(\lambda)$ and $L(\lambda)$ are monic matrix polynomials such that $L^*(\lambda)L(\lambda) = M^*(\lambda)M(\lambda)$, and $\mathbb{B}:=\mathbb{B}(L^*,M^*;L,M)$, then

$$\tilde{i}n(M) = (\nu(i\mathbb{B})+\tilde{\pi}(L_0),\pi(i\mathbb{B})+\tilde{\nu}(L_0),\delta(i\mathbb{B})-\tilde{\pi}(L_0)-\tilde{\nu}(L_0)), \qquad (6.7)$$

where L_0 denotes a right g.c.d. of $L(\lambda)$ and $M(\lambda)$.

Now consider the special case of equation (E_4):

$$C_L^*S - SC_L = SW_0S, \qquad W_0:=\Psi^{(m)}\Psi^{(m)^*}, \qquad (E_5)$$

where $L(\lambda)$ is a monic s×s matrix polynomial of degree m. Clearly, Theorem 6.1 implies that the set $\mathcal{R}_{sh}(E_5)$ consists of matrices $S=\hat{\rho}(R) = \mathbb{B}(L^*,R^*;L,R)$, $R\in\mathcal{D}_{sym}(L^*L)$. Combining the converse part of Theorem 6.1 with the results of [LT1] cited above we obtain a complete description of all symmetric factorizations of the polynomial $L^*(\lambda)L(\lambda)$ along with the inertia of the factors in terms of the solutions of the equation (E_5).

COROLLARY 6.2. *Any skew-hermitian solution* $S=[s_{ij}]_{i,j=1}^m$ *of* (E_5) *generates a symmetric factorization of* $L^*(\lambda)L(\lambda)$:

$$L^*(\lambda)L(\lambda) = R_S^*(\lambda)R_S(\lambda),$$

where $R_S(\lambda) = L(\lambda) - S_m(\lambda)$, *with* $S_m(\lambda) := \sum_{k=1}^{m} \lambda^{k-1} s_{mk}$. *In this case*

$$\tilde{\text{in}}(R_S) = (\nu(iS) + \tilde{\pi}(D_0), \pi(iS) + \tilde{\nu}(D_0), \delta(iS) - \tilde{\pi}(D_0) - \tilde{\nu}(D_0)), \quad (6.8)$$

where $D_0(\lambda)$ *is a right g.c.d. of* $L(\lambda)$ *and* $S_m(\lambda)$.

All symmetric factorizations of $L^*(\lambda)L(\lambda)$ *are obtained in this way.*

Remark that using Corollary 6.2 one can solve the problem of determining a left canonical factorization (relative to the real axis) of a nonnegative rational polynomial, given its right canonical factorization (cf. Theorem 2.8). We omit the precise statement of this result.

We now pass to the description of the inertial characteristics of solutions of the equation (E_4). We need the following result.

LEMMA 6.3. *Let* $A \in \mathbb{C}^{\alpha\times\alpha}$ *and* $B \in \mathbb{C}^{\beta\times\beta}$ $(\alpha \geq \beta)$ *be hermitian matrices such that* $\text{rank}A = \text{rank}B$, *and let* $MAM^* = B$ *for some* $M \in \mathbb{C}^{\beta\times\alpha}$. *Then* $\text{in}(B) = (\pi(A), \nu(A), \delta(A) - \alpha + \beta)$.

The above result is known in the case $\alpha = \beta$ (see [LT1], p. 433, and [LaT], Theorem 3 of section 5.5). We shall use this in the proof.

PROOF. Set $\tilde{M} := \begin{bmatrix} M \\ 0_{\alpha-\beta,\alpha} \end{bmatrix}$, where $0_{p,q}$ denotes a zero matrix of size $p\times q$. Denote $\tilde{B} := \tilde{M}A\tilde{M}^*$ and write $\tilde{B} = \begin{bmatrix} B & 0_{\beta,\alpha-\beta} \\ 0_{\alpha-\beta,\beta} & 0_{\alpha-\beta,\alpha-\beta} \end{bmatrix}$. Then $\text{rank}A = \text{rank}\tilde{B}$ and applying the result for square matrices mentioned above we see that $\text{in}(A) = \text{in}(\tilde{B})$. It is clear that $\text{in}(\tilde{B}) = (\pi(B), \nu(B), \delta(B)+\alpha-\beta)$ and the desired result follows. □

In what follows we always preserve the assumptions of Theorem 6.1.

PROPOSITION 6.4. *Let* $R \in \mathcal{D}_{sym}(L_V^*L_V)$ *and* $X_R := \hat{\rho}(R)$. *Then*

$$\text{in}(iX_R) = (\tilde{\pi}(V) - \tilde{\pi}(D), \tilde{\nu}(V) - \tilde{\nu}(D), \tilde{\delta}(V) + \tilde{\pi}(D) + \tilde{\nu}(D)), \quad (6.9)$$

where $D(\lambda)$ *is a right g.c.d. of* $L_V(\lambda)$ *and* $R(\lambda)$.

PROOF. Consider the equation

$$C_{L_V}^* S - SC_{L_V} = S\Psi^{(m)}\Psi^{(m)*}S, \quad (E_6)$$

and let $\alpha:\mathcal{R}(E_4) \to \mathcal{R}_a(E_6)$ be the mapping defined in Theorem 4.1: $S = \alpha(X) = T_V^*XT_V$. The proof of Theorem 6.1 yields that any skew-hermitian solution of (E_6) is admissible, and hence the restriction $\hat{\alpha}$ of α to $\mathcal{R}_{sh}(E_4)$ maps $\mathcal{R}_{sh}(E_4)$ onto $\mathcal{R}_{sh}(E_6)$. Denote

$$S_R := \alpha(X_R) = \mathbb{B}(L_V^*, R^*; L_V, R). \tag{6.10}$$

Then using (6.7) we obtain

$$\text{in}(iS_R) = (\tilde{\pi}(L_V) - \tilde{\pi}(D), \tilde{\nu}(L_V) - \tilde{\nu}(D), \tilde{\delta}(L_V) + \tilde{\pi}(D) + \tilde{\nu}(D)).$$

In view of Theorem 4.1 $\text{rank}S_R = \text{rank}X_R$, and hence we can apply Lemma 6.3. It follows that

$$\text{in}(iX_R) = (\tilde{\pi}(L_V) - \tilde{\pi}(D), \tilde{\nu}(L_V) - \tilde{\nu}(D), \tilde{\delta}(L_V) + \tilde{\pi}(D) + \tilde{\nu}(D) - ms + p).$$

But $\tilde{\pi}(L_V) = \tilde{\pi}(V), \tilde{\nu}(L_V) = \tilde{\nu}(V)$ and $\tilde{\delta}(L_V) = \tilde{\delta}(V) + ms - p$, which obviously implies (6.9). □

Among all symmetric factorizations of a non-negative monic matrix polynomial $G(\lambda)$ of degree 2m the following two factorizations are of special importance: $G(\lambda) = R_+^*(\lambda)R_+(\lambda)$, with $\text{Im}\sigma(R_+) \leq 0$, which is called *right spectral* and $G(\lambda) = R_-^*(\lambda)R_-(\lambda)$, with $\text{Im}\sigma(R_-) \geq 0$, which is referred to as *left spectral*. The polynomials $R_+(\lambda)$ and $R_-(\lambda)$ are called *right* and *left spectral divisors* of G, respectively. A nonnegative polynomial G admits both right and left spectral factorizations which can be constructed explicitly (see [GLR2]). It turns out that the solutions of (E_4) that correspond to the spectral divisors of $L_V^*(\lambda)L_V(\lambda)$ are the extremal solutions investigated in [C], [LR], [R1,2], [S1,2]. More precisely, preserving the notations and assumptions of Theorem 6.1, we have the following result.

THEOREM 6.5. *Let* $X_+ = \hat{\rho}(R_+)$ *and* $X_- = \hat{\rho}(R_-)$ *be defined by* (6.3), *where* $R_\pm$ *are the spectral divisors of* $L_V^*L_V$. *Then for any* $X \in \mathcal{R}_{sh}(E_4)$ *we have*

$$iX_- \leq iX \leq iX_+. \tag{6.11}$$

Moreover,

$$\text{in}(iX_+) = (\tilde{\pi}(V), 0, \tilde{\delta}(V) + \tilde{\nu}(V)), \ \text{in}(iX_-) = (0, \tilde{\nu}(V), \tilde{\delta}(V) + \tilde{\pi}(V)), \tag{6.12}$$

and

$$\tilde{\text{in}}(V+WX_+) = (0, \tilde{\nu}(V)+\tilde{\pi}(V), \tilde{\delta}(V)), \ \tilde{\text{in}}(V+WX_-) = (\tilde{\nu}(V)+\tilde{\pi}(V), 0, \tilde{\delta}(V)). \tag{6.13}$$

PROOF. We first prove formulas (6.12). Denote by (Γ,T) the restriction of the standard pair of L_V with $\operatorname{Im}\sigma(T) < 0$. Since $L_V(\Gamma,T)=0$, we have $(L_V^*L_V)(\Gamma,T) = L_V^*(L_V(\Gamma,T),T) = 0$. Therefore, $0 = (R_+^*R_+)(\Gamma,T) = R_+^*(R_+(\Gamma,T),T)$, and since $\operatorname{Im}\sigma(R_+^*) \geq 0$, it follows that $R_+(\Gamma,T) = 0$. Thus, (Γ,T) is a restriction of the finite Jordan pair of the right g.c.d. $D(\lambda)$ of $L_V(\lambda)$ and $R_+(\lambda)$, and hence $\tilde{\nu}(D) = \tilde{\nu}(L_V) = \tilde{\nu}(V)$. Also, $\tilde{\pi}(D) = 0$ since R_+ has no eigenvalues in the open upper half plane. Now the formula for $\operatorname{in}(iX_+)$ in (6.12) follows from (6.9). In a similar way one proves the formula for $\operatorname{in}(iX_-)$ in (6.12).

To prove (6.11) denote by S_{R_+} the solution of (E_6) defined by (6.10) with $R = R_+$. Take an arbitrary $S \in \mathcal{R}_{sh}(E_6)$ and denote $Y = S - S_{R_+}$. One easily checks that Y satisfies the equation

$$(C_{L_V}^* - S_{R_+}W_0)Y - Y(C_{L_V} + W_0S_{R_+}) = YW_0Y \quad (W_0 = \Phi^{(m)}\Phi^{(m)*}). \qquad (E_7)$$

If $S_{R_+} = [s_{jk}^+]_{j,k=1}^m$, then by Theorem 6.1 $R_+(\lambda) = L_V(\lambda) - \sum_{k=1}^m \lambda^{k-1}s_{mk}^+$, and a simple calculation shows that $C_{L_V} + W_0S_{R_+} = C_{R_+}$. So, (E_7) can be written as

$$C_{R_+}^*Y - YC_{R_+} = YW_0Y, \qquad (E_7')$$

and Theorem 6.1 yields $Y = \mathbb{B}(R_+^*,M^*;R_+,M) = -\mathbb{B}(M^*,R_+^*;M,R_+)$, where $M(\lambda)$ is some monic polynomial of degree m such that $R_+^*(\lambda)R_+(\lambda) = M^*(\lambda)M(\lambda)$. Using the argument of the preceding paragraph we see that $\operatorname{in}(-iY) = (\tilde{\pi}(M),0,\tilde{\delta}(M)+\tilde{\nu}(M))$, and in particular $iY \leq 0$, i.e. $iS \leq iS_{R_+}$. Similarly one proves that $iS \geq iS_{R_-}$. Now (6.11) follows from the fact that any $X \in \mathcal{R}_{sh}(E_4)$ can be written as $X = [T_V^{(-1)}]^*ST_V^{(-1)}$, where $S \in \mathcal{R}_{sh}(E_6)$, and $X_\pm = [T_V^{(-1)}]^*S_{R_\pm}T_V^{(-1)}$.

Passing to the proof of (6.13) first note that from (4.3) and (6.3) one easily deduces that $(V+WX_+)T_V = T_V(C_{L_V}+W_0S_{R_+})$, and since $C_{L_V}+W_0S_{R_+} = C_{R_+}$, we have

$$(V+WX_+)T_V = T_VC_{R_+} . \qquad (6.14)$$

We claim that

$$\tilde{\nu}(V+WX_{+}) \geq \tilde{\nu}(C_{R_{+}}) \ . \tag{6.15}$$

Indeed, let λ_0, $\mathrm{Im}\lambda_0<0$, be an eigenvalue of $C_{R_{+}}$ of algebraic multiplicity α and let $\mathcal{M} \subset \mathbb{C}^{ms}$ be the root-subspace of $C_{R_{+}}$ corresponding to λ_0. From (6.14) we have $(V+WX_{+}-\lambda_0 I)^k T_V = T_V(C_{R_{+}}-\lambda_0 I)^k$ $(k=0,1,\ldots)$, and hence $x \in \mathcal{M}$ yields $(V+WX_{+}-\lambda_0 I)^{\alpha} T_V x = 0$. Let us show that if $0 \neq x_0 \in \mathcal{M}$, then $T_V x_0 \neq 0$. Indeed, we know from (5.12) that $\mathrm{Ker}T_V = \mathrm{Im}\,\mathrm{col}(F_1 V_1^{\,j-1})_{j=1}^{m}$, and hence assuming $T_V x_0 = 0$ we have some $y_0 \in \mathbb{C}^{ms-p}$ such that $x_0 = \mathrm{col}(F_1 V_1^{\,j-1} y_0)_{j=1}^{m}$. Since (F_1, V_1) is a restriction of the standard pair of $R_{+}(\lambda)$, we have

$$(C_{R_{+}}-\lambda_0 I)^k \mathrm{col}(F_1 V_1^{j-1})_{j=1}^{m} = \mathrm{col}(F_1 V_1^{j-1})_{j=1}^{m}\ (V_1-\lambda_0 I)^k \quad (k=0,1,\ldots).$$

It follows that $0 = (C_{R_{+}}-\lambda_0 I)^{\alpha} x_0 = \mathrm{col}(F_1 V_1^{j-1})_{j=1}^{m}(V_1-\lambda_0 I)^{\alpha} y_0$. As $\mathrm{col}(F_1 V_1^{j-1})_{j=1}^{m}$ is left invertible, we conclude that $(V_1-\lambda_0 I)^{\alpha} y_0 = 0$. But V_1 has real eigenvalues only, and hence $y_0 = 0$, which implies $x_0 = 0$, a contradiction. Now we can conclude that $\dim T_V\mathcal{M} = \alpha$ and the root-subspace of $V+WX_{+}$, corresponding to λ_0, contains $T_V\mathcal{M}$. This proves (6.15).

The same argument shows that if $\lambda_0 \in \sigma(V)$, $\lambda_0 \notin \sigma(V_1)$ is a real eigenvalue of $C_{R_{+}}$ of algebraic multiplicity β and $\mathcal{M}$ is the root-subspace of $C_{R_{+}}$ corresponding to this eigenvalue, then $\dim T_V\mathcal{M} = \beta$ and the root-subspace of $V+WX_{+}$ corresponding to λ_0 contains $T_V\mathcal{M}$. Since the multiplicity of such λ_0 as an eigenvalue of $C_{R_{+}}$ coincides with its multiplicity as an eigenvalue of V, we infer that

$$\delta(V+WX_{+}) \geq \delta(V). \tag{6.16}$$

Furthermore, it is clear that $\tilde{\nu}(R_{+}) = \tilde{\pi}(L_V)+\tilde{\nu}(L_V) = \tilde{\pi}(V) + \tilde{\nu}(V)$, and (6.15) can be written as

$$\tilde{\nu}(V+WX_{+}) \geq \tilde{\pi}(V) + \tilde{\nu}(V). \tag{6.17}$$

Since $\tilde{\pi}(V) + \tilde{\nu}(V) + \delta(V) = \tilde{\pi}(V + WX_{+}) + \tilde{\nu}(V + WX_{+}) + \delta(V+WX_{+}) = p$, the inequalities (6.16), (6.17) turn out to be equalities and $\tilde{\pi}(V+WX_{+}) = 0$. This proves the first formula in (6.13). The second one is proved analogously. □

The above Theorem and its proof imply immediately the following result.

COROLLARY 6.6. *Preserving the assumptions and notations of Theorem 6.1, the equation* (E_4) *has a unique skew-hermitian solution* $X = 0$ *if and only if the matrix* V *has real eigenvalues only.*

Now consider the equation

$$Q^*Y - YQ = QWQ - C \quad (Q,W,C \in \mathbb{C}^{p\times p},\ W^* = W, C^* = C). \tag{E_8}$$

It is well known and easily verified (see [C], [GLR3]) that if Y_0 is a skew-hermitian solution of (E_8), then any skew-hermitian solution of (E_8) is given by $Y=Y_0+X$, where X is a skew-hermitian solution of the equation

$$(Q^*-Y_0W)X - X(Q+WY_0) = XWX. \tag{$\hat{E}_4$}$$

THEOREM 6.7. *Consider the equation* (E_8) *with* $W \geq 0$, *let* $W = \Psi\Psi^*$ $(\Psi \in \mathbb{C}^{p\times s})$ *be a rank decomposition of* W *and let*

$$\operatorname{Imrow}(Q^{i-1}\Psi)_{i=1}^{m} = \mathbb{C}^p \quad (m = \operatorname{ind}(Q,\Psi)). \tag{6.18}$$

Let Y_0 *be a skew-hermitian solution of* (E_8) *and choose a real number* $d \notin \sigma(Q+WY_0)$. *Let* $L_{Q+WY_0}(\lambda)$ *be a monic* $s\times s$ *matrix polynomial of degree* m *such that* $(Q+WY_0,\Psi)$ *is a compression of its left standard pair and* $\sigma(L_{Q+WY_0}) = \sigma(Q+WY_0) \cup \{d\}$. *Then any symmetric factorization* $G(\lambda) = R^*(\lambda)R(\lambda)$ *of the polynomial* $G(\lambda) := L^*_{Q+WY_0}(\lambda)L_{Q+WY_0}(\lambda)$ *determines a skew-hermitian solution of* (E_8) *given by*

$$Y_R = Y_0 + [T^{(-1)}_{Q+WY_0}]^*\mathbb{B}(L^*_{Q+WY_0},R^*;L_{Q+WY_0},R)T^{(-1)}_{Q+WY_0}, \tag{6.19}$$

where T_{Q+WY_0} *is defined by* (4.2) *with* $V = Q+WY_0$. *All skew-hermitian solutions of* (E_8) *are obtained in this way.*

Furthermore, if $R_+(\lambda)$ *and* $R_-(\lambda)$ *are right and left spectral divisors of* $G(\lambda)$, *respectively, then* $iY_{R_-} \leq iY \leq iY_{R_+}$ *for any skew-hermitian solution of* (E_8), *and*

$$\begin{aligned} \widetilde{\operatorname{In}}(Q + WY_+) &= (0,\ \tilde{\nu}(Q+WY_0) + \tilde{\pi}(Q+WY_0),\ \tilde{\delta}(Q+WY_0)), \\ \widetilde{\operatorname{In}}(Q+WY_-) &= (\tilde{\nu}(Q+WY_0) + \tilde{\pi}(Q+WY_0),\ 0,\ \tilde{\delta}(Q+WY_0)). \end{aligned} \tag{6.20}$$

Moreover, for any $Y \in \mathcal{R}_{sh}(E_8)$

$$\mathrm{in}(iY_{R_+} - iY) = (\tilde{\pi}(Q+WY),\ 0,\ \gamma(Q+WY) + \tilde{\nu}(Q+WY)),$$

$$\mathrm{in}(iY - iY_{R_-}) = (\tilde{\nu}(Q+WY),\ 0,\ \gamma(Q + WY) + \tilde{\nu}(Q+WY)). \tag{6.21}$$

PROOF. It is well known (see e.g., [GLR3], Lemma 6.3.1) that (6.18) implies that $\mathrm{Imrow}(V^{i-1}\Psi)_{i=1}^{m} = \mathbb{C}^p$ for $V := Q+WY_0 = Q+\Psi\Psi^*Y_0$, where Y_0 is any matrix of suitable size. Thus we can apply Theorems 6.1, 6.6 to the equation $(\hat{E}_4)$. Now all the results stated in Theorem 6.10 follow from the relation between the equations (E_8) and $(\hat{E}_4)$ as described in the paragraph preceding Theorem 6.7. □

The following remark is in order. As established in [LR] the necessary and sufficient condition for existence of a skew-hermitian solution Y_0 of (E_8) is that the real eigenvalues of the matrix $T := \begin{bmatrix} Q & W \\ C & Q^* \end{bmatrix}$ (if any) have even partial multiplicities. If $Y_0 \in \mathcal{R}_{sh}(E_8)$, then

$$\begin{bmatrix} Q+WY_0 & W \\ 0 & Q^*-Y_0W \end{bmatrix} = \begin{bmatrix} I & 0 \\ -Y_0 & I \end{bmatrix} T \begin{bmatrix} I & 0 \\ Y_0 & I \end{bmatrix},$$

and consequently, formulas (6.20) can be rewritten as follows

$$\tilde{\mathrm{in}}(Q+WY_+) = (0,\ p - \tfrac{1}{2}\gamma(T),\ \tfrac{1}{2}\gamma(T))\ ,\ \tilde{\mathrm{in}}(Q+WY_-) = (p - \tfrac{1}{2}\gamma(T),\ 0,\ \tfrac{1}{2}\gamma(T)).$$

In conclusion note that the existence and properties of extremal solutions of (E_8) (in the framework of usual Riccati equations) have been established earlier by other methods (see, e.g. [C],, [LR], [R1,2], [S1,2]). Formulas (6.19) (with $R = R_\pm$) give explicit expressions for the extremal skew-hermitian solutions of (E_8) in terms of spectral factorizations of a certain non-negative matrix polynomial, provided a skew-hermitian solution Y_0 of (E_8) is known.

REFERENCES

[A] Ando, T.: Matrix quadratic equation, Hokkaido University, Sapporo, Japan, 1988.

[AJ] Anderson, B.D.O. and Jury, E.I.: Generalized Bezoutian and Sylvester matrices in multivariable linear control. IEEE Trans. Autom. Control, AC-21(1976), 551-556.

[AM] Anderson, B.D.O., Moore, J.B.: Optimal filtering, Prentice-Hall, Englewood Cliffs, N.J., 1979.

[BR] Ball, J.A., Ran, A.C.M.: Left versus right canonical factorization. Operator Theory: Advances and Applications, vol. 21, 1986, Birkhauser, Basel, 9-38.

[BGK] Bart, H., Gohberg, I., Kaashoek, M.A.: Minimal factorizations of matrix and operator functions. Birkhäuser, Basel, 1979.

[BKAK] Bitmead, R.R., Kung, S.Y., Anderson, B.D.O. and Kailath, T.: Greatest common divisors via generalized Sylvester and Bezout matrices. IEEE Trans. Autom. Control, AC-23(1978), 1043-1047.

[B] Brockett, R.: Finite dimensional linear systems. Wiley, New York, 1970.

[CG] Clancey, K. and Gohberg, I.: Factorization of matrix functions and singular integral operators. Operator Theory: Advances and Applications. Vol. 3, Birkhäuser, Basel, 1981.

[CK] Clancey, K. and Kon, B.A.: The Bezoutian and the algebraic Riccati equation. Linear and Multilinear Algebra, 15, (1984), 265-278.

[C] Coppel, C.A.: Matrix quadratic equations. Bull. Austral. Math. Soc. 10 (1974), 377-401.

[DK] Daleckii, Ju. L., Krein, M.G.: Stability of solutions of differential equations in Banach space. Amer. Math. Soc. Transl. Math. Monographs, Vol. 43, Providence, Rhode Island, 1974.

[GKL] Gohberg, I., Kaashoek, M.A., Lancaster, P.: General theory of regular matrix polynomials and band Toeplitz operators. Integral Equations and Operator Theory 6 (1988), 776-882.

[GKLR1] Gohberg, I., Kaashoek, M.A., Lerer, L. and Rodman, L.: Common multiples and common divisors of matrix polynomials, I.: Spectral method. Indiana Univ. Math. J. 30 (1981), 321-356.

[GKLR2] Gohberg, I., Kaashoek, M.A., Lerer, L. and Rodman, L.: Common multiples and common divisors of matrix polynomials, II: Vandermonde and resultant, Linear and Multilinear Algebra 12 (1982), 159-203.

[GKLR3] Gohberg, I., Kaashoek, M.A., Lerer, L. Rodman, L.: Minimal divisors of rational matrix functions with prescribed zero and pole structure. Operator Theory: Advances and Applications, 12, Birkhäuser, Basel, 1984, 241-275.

[GLR1] Gohberg, I., Lancaster, P. and Rodman, L.: Matrix Polynomials, Academic Press, New York, 1982.

[GLR2] Gohberg, I., Lancaster, P. and Rodman, L.: Matrices and indefinite scalar products. Operator Theory: Advances and Applications, Vol. 8, Birkäuser Verlag, Basel, 1983.

[GLR3] Gohberg, I., Lancaster, P. and Rodman, L.: Invariant subspaces of matrices with applications, John Wiley, New York, 1986.

[GL] Gohberg, I. and Lerer, L.: Matrix generalizations of M.G. Krein theorems on orthogonal polynomials, Operator Theory: Advances and Applications, Vol. 34, Birkhäuser, Basel, 1988, 137-202.

[GLeR] Gohberg, I., Lerer, L. and Rodman, L.: On factorization, indices and completely decomposable matrix polynomials. Technical Report 80-47, Tel-Aviv University, 1980.

[GR] Gohberg, I. and Rubinstein, S.: Proper contractions and their unitary minimal completions, Operator Theory: Advances and Applications, vol. 33, Birkhäuser, Basel, 1988, 233-247.

[H] Hearon, J.Z.: Nonsingular solutions of TA - BT = C, Linear Algebra and Appl. 16 (1977), 57-65.

[K] Kon, B.A.: The Bezoutian and the algebraic Riccati equation. Abstracts of the Haifa Conference on Matrix Theory, Haifa, December 1984.

[Ku] Kučera, V.: A review of the matrix Riccati equation, Kybernetika 9 (1973), 42-61.

[KS] Kwakernaak, H., Sivan, R.: Linear Optimal Control Systems. Wiley, New York, 1972.

[LLT] Lancaster, P., Lerer, L. and Tismenetsky, M.: Factored form of solutions of the equation AX-XB = C in matrices. Linear Algebra Appl., 62(1984), 19-49.

[LR] Lancaster, P., Rodman, L.: Existence and uniqueness theorems for algebraic Riccati equations. Int. J. Control 32 (1980), 285-309.

[LaT] Lancaster, P. and Tismenetsky, M.: The Theory of matrices. Academic Press, Orlando, 1985.

[LT1] Lerer, L. and Tismenetsky, M.: The eigenvalue separation problem for matrix polynomials. Integral Equations and Operator Theory 5, (1982), 386-445.

[LT2] Lerer, L. and Tismenetsky, M.: Bezoutian for several matrix polynomials and matrix equations. Technical Report 88.145, IBM-Israel Scientific Center, Haifa, November 1984.

[LT3] Lerer, L. and Tismenetsky, M.: Generalized Bezoutian and matrix equations. Linear Algebra Appl. 99(1988), 123-160.

[LRT] Lerer, L., Rodman, L. and Tismenetsky, M.: Bezoutian and the Schur-Cohn problem for operator polynomials, J. Math. Anal. Appl. 103 (1984), 83-102.

[RR] Ran, A.C.M. and Rodman, L.: The algebraic Riccati equation, Operator Theory: Advances and Applications, vol. 12, Birkhäuser, Basel, 1984, 351-381.

[Re] Reid, W.T.: Riccati differential equations. Academic Press, New York, 1972.

[R1] Rodman, L.: On extremal solutions of the algebraic Riccati equations. A.M.S. Lectures on Applied Math. 18 (1980), 311-327.

[R2] Rodman, L.: Maximal invariant neutral subspaces and an application to the algebraic Riccati equation. Manuscripts Math. 43 (1983), 1-12.

[S1] Shayman, M.A.: Geometry of the algebraic Riccati equation I. Siam J. Contr. Opt. 21 (1983), 375-394.

[S2] Shayman, M.A.: Geometry of the algebraic Riccati equation II. Siam J. Contr. Opt. 21 (1983), 395-409.

[W] Willems, J.C.: Least squares stationary optimal control and the algebraic Riccati equation, IEEE Trans. on Autom. Contr. 16 (1971), 621-634.

[Wi] Wimmer, H.K., The algebraic Riccati equation without complete controllability. Siam J. Alg. Discr. Meth. 3 (1982), 1-12.

[Wo] Wonham, W.M.: On a matrix Riccati equation of stochastic control. Siam J. Contr. 6 (1968), 681-697. Erratum, ibid. 7 (1969), 365.

L. Lerer
Department of Mathematics
Technion - Israel Institute of Technology
Haifa 32 000
Israel

Operator Theory:
Advances and Applications, Vol. 40

Inversion of Partially Specified Positive Definite Matrices by Inverse Scattering*

H. Nelis, P. Dewilde and E. Deprettere

Dedicated to I. Gohberg on the occasion of his 60th birthday.

Inverse scattering techniques such as the Wiener-Hopf factorization and the Schur algorithm can be used to determine an approximate inverse of a partially specified positive definite matrix. In this paper we explore the connection between inverse scattering and matrix extension theory from a mathematical and algorithmic point of view. We present fast algorithms for computing either the exact inverse of the maximum entropy extension of a partially specified positive definite matrix or a close approximation to it, depending on the structure of the set on which the matrix is specified. We aim at presenting a unification of various results which have appeared in the literature and present some new results as well.

1 Introduction

Suppose that $A = [a_{ij}]$, $i, j = 1, \ldots, n$, is a positive definite matrix. Furthermore, suppose that A is specified only on a subset $\mathcal{S}$ of the set of index pairs $\{(i,j) \mid i,j = 1, \ldots, n\}$. We assume that the diagonal entries in A are specified. A matrix that coincides with A on $\mathcal{S}$ is called an extension of A. In [1] Dym and Gohberg studied the case where $\mathcal{S}$ is a block band. They showed that there is a unique positive definite extension of A whose determinant is maximal, and that this matrix is the unique positive definite extension whose inverse is zero on the complement of $\mathcal{S}$. Because of the correspondence between this result and the maximum entropy inequality in spectral estimation theory (see e.g. [2]), we call this matrix the maximum entropy extension of A. In [3] Grone et al. generalized the above results to sets $\mathcal{S}$ that contain the diagonal pairs (i,i) but are arbitrary otherwise. They showed that a unique maximum

*This work was supported in part by the Dutch National Applied Science Foundation under grant FOM DEL 77.1260.

entropy extension of a positive definite matrix that is specified on such a set exists, and that its inverse vanishes on the complement of the set.

In the present paper we start out with a short review of the results mentioned above for as much as they are relevant to our purposes. In Section 3 we present a generalization of the Wiener-Hopf factorization theory to the case of general finite dimensional matrices that are specified on a block band $\mathcal{S}$. This theory provides the link between classical inverse scattering theory and matrix extension theory. It succeeds in constructing a global finite dimensional solution to a generalized inverse scattering problem which turns out to be equivalent to the maximum entropy matrix extension problem. We follow and adapt the methodology originally developed in [4] and [5]. In the following sections the interest shifts to the case where $\mathcal{S}$ is not a block band. A case of major physical interest is when $\mathcal{S}$ is a so-called multiple band. Bands of this type arise in applications with multi dimensional geometries, such as multi dimensional spectral estimation and finite element modelling of multi dimensional systems (see e.g. [6] and [7]). In contrast to the block band case, no closed solution to the maximum entropy extension problem for matrices that are specified on a multiple band exists. However, if the maximum entropy extension is a close approximant to the completely specified matrix (which in most applications is the case), then an approximate solution can be obtained. The approximate solution is the maximum entropy extension of a partially specified matrix that is close to the original and specified on the same set $\mathcal{S}$.

The method used in [1] to construct the maximum entropy extension of a positive definite matrix that is specified on a block band is based on the inversion of contiguous principal submatrices of that matrix. In [8] Delsarte et al. followed a similar approach to compute the triangular factors of the inverse of a completely specified positive definite matrix, thereby in fact generalizing an algorithm known in estimation theory as the Levinson algorithm [9]. The problem of computing the triangular factors of the inverse of a completely specified positive definite matrix can be viewed as a time variant estimation problem, since any positive definite matrix can be interpreted as a covariance matrix of a (part of a) time varying stochastic process. Computing the triangular factors of the inverse of the maximum entropy extension of a partially specified positive definite matrix then corresponds to solving a partial correlation (PARCOR) problem. In [10] Dewilde et al. showed how partial correlations for one dimensional time invariant stochastic processes can be determined by using an algorithm known in interpolation theory as the Schur algorithm [11]. It soon became apparent that the Schur algorithm can be used advantageously to determine partial correlations even for one dimensional time varying stochastic processes [12, 13]. This property of the Schur algorithm was exploited by Morf and Delosme to devise an algorithm for computing the triangular factors of the inverse of a completely specified positive definite matrix [14]. In [15] Dewilde and Deprettere showed how this algorithm can be used to compute the triangular factors of the inverse of the maximum entropy extension of a positive definite matrix that is specified on a staircase band. The algorithm requires $O(nb^2)$ operations and $O(nb)$ storage, where n is the size of the matrix and b is the average width of the staircase band. It is very well suited for implementation on an array processor of the wavefront or systolic type. In the same paper Dewilde and Deprettere showed that, except for a diagonal bias factor, the triangular factors of the inverse of the maximum entropy extension give an optimal approximation in the Frobenius norm (also known as the Hilbert-Schmidt norm) to the triangular factors of the inverse of the completely specified matrix. In the present paper we further explore these approximations and their import on the maximum entropy extension problem for matrices that are specified on a multiple band.

Several iterative algorithms for computing the maximum entropy extension of block-Toeplitz matrices that are specified on a multiple band have been proposed [6, 16, 17]. However, these algorithms either have trouble converging or are computationally very intensive. In [18] Dewilde and Deprettere proposed a fast algorithm for computing an approximate inverse of a positive definite matrix that is specified only on a triple band $\mathcal{S}$. They assumed that certain conditions on the completely specified matrix are satisfied. The resulting inverse is the inverse of a matrix that closely matches the partially specified matrix. It does not have zeros in all entries on the complement of $\mathcal{S}$ but can be represented and computed efficiently. In this paper we go one step further: we present a fast algorithm for computing an approximation to the inverse of the maximum entropy extension of a positive definite matrix that is specified on a multiple band $\mathcal{S}$. Our inverse has zeros on the complement of $\mathcal{S}$, is an extension of a partially specified matrix that is close to the original, and can be computed efficiently, i.e. with a complexity essentially equal to $n \times |\mathcal{S}|$, where n is the size of the matrix and $|\mathcal{S}|$ is the number of elements in $\mathcal{S}$.

2 Preliminaries

2.1 Notation and Basic Concepts

We denote matrices by italic uppercase letters. Matrices have complex entries, unless we state otherwise. The complex conjugate transpose of a matrix A is denoted by A^*. The direct sum of the matrices A and B is denoted by $A \oplus B$. The symbols I and 0 denote the identity matrix and the zero matrix. The size of I and 0 is defined by their context. If not, we use a subscript to indicate the size.

The symbols $\underline{\underline{P}}$ and $\underline{\underline{Q}}$ denote the projection operators that project a matrix on its upper triangular and lower triangular part respectively. For example, for a matrix $A = [a_{ij}]$,

$$(\underline{\underline{P}}A)_{ij} = \begin{cases} a_{ij} & \text{if} \quad i \leq j \\ 0 & \text{otherwise} \end{cases}$$

and

$$(\underline{\underline{Q}}A)_{ij} = \begin{cases} a_{ij} & \text{if} \quad i \geq j \\ 0 & \text{otherwise} \end{cases} .$$

The symbol $\underline{\underline{P}}_0$ denotes the projection operator that projects a matrix on its diagonal. The trace of A is denoted by tr$A$.

If A is positive definite, then the symbols L_A and M_A refer to the (unique) upper triangular matrices with positive diagonal entries that are such that $A = L_A L_A^* = M_A^* M_A$. The symbols U_A, V_A and D_A are defined as $U_A = \underline{\underline{P}}A$, $D_A = \underline{\underline{P}}_0 A$ and $V_A = (I - \underline{\underline{Q}})A$. In the sequel we assume that the diagonal entries in A are equal to one. This does not impair generality, because an arbitrary matrix can always be converted to $D_A{}^{-\frac{1}{2}} A D_A{}^{-\frac{1}{2}}$. Further attached to A (with $D_A = I$) are the *impedance matrix* $G_A = (I + 2V_A)$ and the *scattering matrix* $S_A = (G_A + I)^{-1}(G_A - I)$. G_A and S_A are related via a Cayley transformation. The following two equivalent properties should be obvious:

- $A = \frac{1}{2}(G_A + G_A^*)$ is positive definite,
- S_A is *contractive*, that is, $I - S_A^* S_A$ is positive definite.

If A is positive definite and only partially specified, and if the maximum entropy extension of A exists, then the symbol A_{ME} is used to denote this extension.

A set $\mathcal{S}$ is called a *staircase band* if it contains the diagonal pairs (i, i) and if it is such that if $(i, j) \in \mathcal{S}$ with $i \leq j$ $(i \geq j)$, then $(i + r, j - s) \in \mathcal{S}$ $((i - r, j + s) \in \mathcal{S})$ for all $r, s \geq 0$ such that $i + r \leq j - s$ $(i - r \geq j + s)$. The symbol J denotes the matrix

$$J = \begin{bmatrix} I & 0 \\ 0 & -I \end{bmatrix} .$$

A matrix Θ is *J-unitary* if $\Theta^* J \Theta = J$. An *elementary* J-unitary matrix is a rank-two correction to the matrix $I \oplus I$ of the form

$$
\begin{array}{c}
\\ \\ \\ \\ i \\ \\ \\ \\ j \\ \\ \\ \\
\end{array}
\begin{array}{c}
\begin{array}{ccccccccccc}
 & & & i & & & & j & & & \\
\end{array} \\
\left[\begin{array}{ccccccccccc}
1 & & & \vdots & & & & \vdots & & & \\
 & \ddots & & \vdots & & & & \vdots & & \mathbf{0} & \\
 & & 1 & \vdots & & & & \vdots & & & \\
\cdots & \cdots & \cdots & \mathrm{ch} & \cdots & \cdots & \cdots & \mathrm{sh} & \cdots & \cdots & \cdots \\
 & & & \vdots & 1 & & & \vdots & & & \\
 & & & \vdots & & \ddots & & \vdots & & & \\
 & & & \vdots & & & 1 & \vdots & & & \\
\cdots & \cdots & \cdots & \mathrm{sh}^* & \cdots & \cdots & \cdots & \mathrm{ch} & \cdots & \cdots & \cdots \\
 & & & \vdots & & & & \vdots & 1 & & \\
 & \mathbf{0} & & \vdots & & & & \vdots & & \ddots & \\
 & & & \vdots & & & & \vdots & & & 1
\end{array}\right]
\end{array},
$$

where $1 \leq i \leq n$, $n+1 \leq j \leq 2n$, n is the size of the identity, $\mathrm{ch} = (1-|\rho|^2)^{-\frac{1}{2}}$, $\mathrm{sh} = \rho(1-|\rho|^2)^{-\frac{1}{2}}$ and $|\rho| < 1$. The above matrix is denoted by $\Theta(i,j,\rho)$. Clearly, $\Theta^*(i,j,\rho)J\Theta(i,j,\rho) = J$. The Frobenius norm of a matrix $A = [a_{ij}]$, $i = 1,\ldots,m$, $j = 1,\ldots,n$, is defined as

$$||A||_F = (\frac{1}{mn}\sum_{i=1}^{m}\sum_{j=1}^{n}|a_{ij}|^2)^{\frac{1}{2}}.$$

We denote block matrices by bold uppercase letters. If we partition a matrix A as a block matrix, then the symbol $\mathbf{A}$ will refer to this block matrix. Conversely, if we interpret a block matrix $\mathbf{A}$ as a matrix with scalar entries, then this matrix is denoted by A. If $\mathbf{A}$ is a positive definite block matrix, then the symbols $\mathbf{L}_{\mathbf{A}}$ and $\mathbf{M}_{\mathbf{A}}$ refer to the (unique) upper triangular block matrices with upper triangular diagonal blocks with positive diagonal entries that are such that $\mathbf{A} = \mathbf{L}_{\mathbf{A}}\mathbf{L}^*_{\mathbf{A}} = \mathbf{M}^*_{\mathbf{A}}\mathbf{M}_{\mathbf{A}}$. For a block matrix $\mathbf{A}$ the symbol $\mathbf{A}(i,j)$ denotes the principal block matrix that lies in the rows and columns of $\mathbf{A}$ indexed by $i,\ldots,j$. Furthermore, the symbol $\nabla(\mathbf{A},(i,j))$ denotes the block matrix that is such that $\nabla(\mathbf{A},(i,j))(i,j) = \mathbf{A}$ and is zero otherwise. That is, $\nabla(\mathbf{A},(i,j))$ is an embedding of $\mathbf{A}$ in a zero matrix. The size of $\nabla(\mathbf{A},(i,j))$ is defined by its context.

To ease the notation we suppress as much of the subscripts as possible. For example, we write L_{ME} instead of $L_{A_{ME}}$ whenever the identity of L_{ME} is clear from the context.

2.2 The Maximum Entropy Extension

In this section we review some results on maximum entropy extensions that have appeared in the literature. We start out with the well-known inequality of Hadamard.

Theorem 1 (Hadamard's Inequality) *Let* $A = [a_{ij}]$, $i,j = 1,\ldots,n$, *be a positive definite matrix. Then,*

$$\det A \leq \prod_{i=1}^{n} a_{ii}.$$

Moreover, equality holds if and only if A *is diagonal.*

We can restate this result as follows. Suppose that A is a positive definite matrix, and suppose that only the diagonal entries in A are specified. Furthermore, suppose that $\mathcal{E}$ is the set of positive definite extensions of A. Then, there is a unique matrix B in $\mathcal{E}$ such that

$$\det B = \max\{\det E \mid E \in \mathcal{E}\}.$$

Moreover, B is the unique positive definite extension of A whose inverse is diagonal. Thus rephrased, the following result of Dym and Gohberg [1] becomes a generalization of Hadamard's inequality.

Theorem 2 ([1]) *Let* $A = [a_{ij}]$, $i,j = 1,\ldots,n$, *be a positive definite matrix that is specified on a band* $\mathcal{S} = \{(i,j) \mid |i-j| \leq m\}$. *Furthermore, let* $\mathcal{E}$ *be the set of positive definite extensions of* A. *Then, there is a unique matrix* B *in* $\mathcal{E}$ *such that*

$$\det B = \max\{\det E \mid E \in \mathcal{E}\}.$$

Moreover, B *is the unique positive definite extension of* A *whose inverse satisfies*

$$(B^{-1})_{ij} = 0 \quad \text{for all} \quad (i,j) \notin \mathcal{S}.$$

The following result of Grone et al. [3] in turn is a generalization of the result of Dym and Gohberg.

Theorem 3 ([3]) *Let* $A = [a_{ij}]$, $i,j = 1,\ldots,n$, *be a positive definite matrix that is specified on a set* $\mathcal{S}$ *that contains the diagonal pairs* (i,i) *but is arbitrary otherwise. Furthermore, let* $\mathcal{E}$ *be the set of positive definite extensions of* A. *Then, there is a unique matrix* B *in* $\mathcal{E}$ *such that*

$$\det B = \max\{\det E \mid E \in \mathcal{E}\}.$$

Moreover, B is the unique positive definite extension of A whose inverse satisfies

$$(B^{-1})_{ij} = 0 \quad \textit{for all} \quad (i,j) \notin \mathcal{S}.$$

As mentioned in the introduction, we call B the maximum entropy extension of A. We denote it by A_{ME}.

3 Maximum Entropy Extensions and Wiener-Hopf Equations

Suppose that $A = [a_{ij}]$, $i, j = 1, \ldots, n$, is a positive definite matrix that is specified on a set $\mathcal{S}$ that contains the diagonal pairs (i,i) but is arbitrary otherwise. In this section it is necessary to embed finite dimensional matrices in infinite dimensional ones. These are in fact doubly infinite and can be viewed as operators on l^2, the Hilbert space of doubly infinite sequences with quadratic norm. In the present context all infinite dimensional matrices are embeddings of finite dimensional matrices in doubly infinite identity or zero matrices. Operations with matrices of this type are bounded and coincide with well-defined actions of operators on l^2. In the sequel infinite dimensional matrices carry a '‾'.

Positive definite matrices like A and A_{ME} are generically embedded in doubly infinite identity matrices. The embedding of A is denoted by $\bar{A}$ and is defined as follows:

$$(\bar{A})_{ij} = \begin{cases} a_{ij} & \text{if} \quad i,j = 1,\ldots,n \\ \delta_{ij} & \text{otherwise} \end{cases},$$

where $\delta_{ij} = 1$ if $i = j$ and $\delta_{ij} = 0$ otherwise. In a similar way, U, G, L, M and A_{ME}, U_{ME}, G_{ME}, L_{ME}, M_{ME} are embedded in doubly infinite identity matrices. V, S and V_{ME}, S_{ME} are embedded in doubly infinite zero matrices. The symbols $\bar{I}$ and $\bar{0}$ denote the doubly infinite identity matrix and the doubly infinite zero matrix. The symbol J denotes the matrix

$$J = \begin{bmatrix} \bar{I} & \bar{0} \\ \bar{0} & -\bar{I} \end{bmatrix}.$$

With the notation developed so far we have that $\bar{A} = \bar{L}\bar{L}^* = \bar{M}^*\bar{M}$, $\bar{V} = \bar{U} - \bar{I}$, $\bar{G} = (\bar{I} + 2\bar{V})$, $\bar{S} = (\bar{G} + \bar{I})^{-1}(\bar{G} - \bar{I})$ and $\bar{A} = \frac{1}{2}(\bar{G} + \bar{G}^*)$. The inverses of $\bar{A}$, $\bar{L}$, $\bar{M}$, $\bar{U}$, $\bar{G}$ are well-defined as operators on l^2, they reduce to the inverses of the respective finite dimensional matrices. Similar relations hold for the doubly infinite matrices related to $\bar{A}_{ME}$.

The motivation for introducing doubly infinite matrices is the fact that we can write them as power series of a unitary matrix $\bar{Z}$. For a matrix $\bar{F}$ we write

$$\bar{F} = \sum_{i=-\infty}^{\infty} \bar{F}_i \bar{Z}^i,$$

where

$$\bar{Z} = \begin{bmatrix} \ddots & \ddots & \ddots & & \\ \ddots & 0 & 1 & 0 & \\ \ddots & 0 & \boxed{0} & 1 & \ddots \\ & 0 & 0 & 0 & \ddots \\ & & \ddots & \ddots & \ddots \end{bmatrix}$$

and $\bar{F}_i$ is a diagonal matrix (we use a box to mark the 00-entry of a doubly infinite matrix). Note that $\bar{Z}$ is unitary on l^2.

We denote the space of bounded operators on l^2 by $\mathcal{L}$. The symbols $\mathcal{H}$ and $\mathcal{K}$ denote the subspaces of $\mathcal{L}$ whose operators have a power series representation with vanishing coefficients of strictly negative and strictly positive powers of $\bar{Z}$ respectively. We call an operator in $\mathcal{H}$ upper triangular and an operator in $\mathcal{K}$ lower triangular. We extend the definition of the projection operators $\underline{\underline{P}}$ and $\underline{\underline{Q}}$ to the case of operators on l^2. In this section $\underline{\underline{P}}$ and $\underline{\underline{Q}}$ denote the projection operators that project an operator in $\mathcal{L}$ on $\mathcal{H}$ and $\mathcal{K}$ respectively. In the case of general operators on l^2 the above definitions need to be extended, but that is not necessary in this paper. We proceed with the following lemmas.

Lemma 1 *Let $A = [a_{ij}]$, $i, j = 1, \ldots, n$, be a positive definite matrix that is specified on a set $\mathcal{S}$ that contains the diagonal pairs (i,i) but is arbitrary otherwise. Then, there exist unique matrices $\bar{B}$, $\bar{C}$, $\bar{D}$, $\bar{E}$ such that*

$$\begin{bmatrix} \bar{I} & \bar{S}_{ME} \\ \bar{S}_{ME}^* & \bar{I} \end{bmatrix} = \begin{bmatrix} \bar{B} & \bar{0} \\ \bar{C} & \bar{I} \end{bmatrix}^{-*} \begin{bmatrix} \bar{B} & \bar{0} \\ \bar{C} & \bar{I} \end{bmatrix}^{-1} \tag{3.1}$$

$$= \begin{bmatrix} \bar{I} & \bar{D} \\ \bar{0} & \bar{E} \end{bmatrix}^{-*} \begin{bmatrix} \bar{I} & \bar{D} \\ \bar{0} & \bar{E} \end{bmatrix}^{-1}, \tag{3.2}$$

where i) $\bar{B}$, $\bar{E}$ and $\bar{C}$, $\bar{D}$ are embeddings of finite dimensional matrices in doubly infinite identity and doubly infinite zero matrices respectively, ii) $\bar{B} \in \mathcal{K}$ and $\bar{E} \in \mathcal{H}$ and iii) $\bar{B}$ and $\bar{E}$ have positive diagonal entries.

Proof Because S_{ME} is contractive, there exist unique matrices B, C, D, E such that

$$\begin{bmatrix} I & S_{ME} \\ S_{ME}^* & I \end{bmatrix}^{-1} = \begin{bmatrix} B & 0 \\ C & I \end{bmatrix} \begin{bmatrix} B & 0 \\ C & I \end{bmatrix}^* \tag{3.3}$$

$$= \begin{bmatrix} I & D \\ 0 & E \end{bmatrix} \begin{bmatrix} I & D \\ 0 & E \end{bmatrix}^*, \tag{3.4}$$

where B is lower triangular, E is upper triangular, and B and E have positive diagonal entries. When we embed S_{ME}, C, D in doubly infinite zero matrices and B, E in doubly infinite identity matrices, then

$$\begin{bmatrix} \bar{I} & \bar{S}_{ME} \\ \bar{S}_{ME}^* & \bar{I} \end{bmatrix}, \quad \begin{bmatrix} \bar{B} & \bar{0} \\ \bar{C} & \bar{I} \end{bmatrix} \text{ and } \begin{bmatrix} \bar{I} & \bar{D} \\ \bar{0} & \bar{E} \end{bmatrix}$$

are (boundedly) invertible as operators on $(l^2)^2$. Their inverses reduce to the inverses of the respective finite dimensional matrices. Furthermore,

$$\begin{bmatrix} \bar{I} & \bar{S}_{ME} \\ \bar{S}_{ME}^* & \bar{I} \end{bmatrix}^{-1} = \begin{bmatrix} \bar{B} & \bar{0} \\ \bar{C} & \bar{I} \end{bmatrix} \begin{bmatrix} \bar{B} & \bar{0} \\ \bar{C} & \bar{I} \end{bmatrix}^* \tag{3.5}$$

$$= \begin{bmatrix} \bar{I} & \bar{D} \\ \bar{0} & \bar{E} \end{bmatrix} \begin{bmatrix} \bar{I} & \bar{D} \\ \bar{0} & \bar{E} \end{bmatrix}^*. \tag{3.6}$$

We now prove the uniqueness of the factorization in Equation 3.5, the uniqueness of the factorization in Equation 3.6 is proved in a similar way. The main issue in the proof is that

$$\begin{bmatrix} \bar{B} & \bar{0} \\ \bar{C} & \bar{I} \end{bmatrix}$$

as well as its inverse is lower triangular and has positive diagonal entries. Suppose that

$$\begin{bmatrix} \bar{I} & \bar{S}_{ME} \\ \bar{S}_{ME}^* & \bar{I} \end{bmatrix}^{-1} = \mathbf{F}\mathbf{F}^* = \mathbf{G}\mathbf{G}^*,$$

where both $\mathbf{F}$, $\mathbf{G}$ and their inverses are lower triangular with lower triangular diagonal blocks with positive diagonal entries. Because $\mathbf{G}^{-1}\mathbf{F}$ is lower triangular, $\mathbf{G}^*\mathbf{F}^{-*}$ is upper triangular and $\mathbf{G}^{-1}\mathbf{F} = \mathbf{G}^*\mathbf{F}^{-*}$, it follows that $\mathbf{G}^{-1}\mathbf{F}$ is diagonal. In fact, the diagonal entries in $\mathbf{G}^{-1}\mathbf{F}$ can only be equal to one, so that $\mathbf{G}^{-1}\mathbf{F} = \mathbf{I}$ and hence, $\mathbf{F} = \mathbf{G}$. Indeed, the entries on the diagonal are equal to their reciprokes because $\mathbf{G}^{-1}\mathbf{F} = (\mathbf{G}^{-1}\mathbf{F})^{-*}$, and are positive because they evaluate to the products of the diagonal entries in $\mathbf{G}^{-1}$ and $\mathbf{F}$, which have positive diagonal entries. This suffices to prove uniqueness for our case where infinite dimensional matrices are embeddings of finite dimensional matrices in doubly infinite identity or zero matrices. A more general case is treated in [19]. ■

Lemma 2 *Let A and $\bar{B}$, $\bar{C}$, $\bar{D}$, $\bar{E}$ be as defined in Lemma 1. Then, $B+C = L_{ME}^{-*}$ and $D+E = M_{ME}^{-1}$ and similarly, $\bar{B}+\bar{C} = \bar{L}_{ME}^{-*}$ and $\bar{D}+\bar{E} = \bar{M}_{ME}^{-1}$.*

Proof It follows from Equation 3.3 that

$$S_{ME} = -B^{-*}C^{*} \tag{3.7}$$

and

$$B^{*}B - C^{*}C = I. \tag{3.8}$$

From these equations we derive that

$$\begin{aligned}(B+C)^{-*}(B+C)^{-1} &= (I - S_{ME})^{-1}B^{-*}B^{-1}(I - S_{ME})^{-*} \\ &= (I - S_{ME})^{-1}(I - S_{ME}S_{ME}^{*})(I - S_{ME})^{-*} \\ &= \frac{1}{2}(G_{ME} + G_{ME}^{*}) \\ &= A_{ME}.\end{aligned} \tag{3.9}$$

It follows from Equation 3.7 that $C = -S_{ME}^{*}B$ and hence, because S_{ME} is strictly upper triangular and B is lower triangular, that C is strictly lower triangular. Because B is lower triangular, C is strictly lower triangular and B has positive diagonal entries, we obtain from Equation 3.9 that $B+C = L_{ME}^{-*}$. The other equalities in the lemma are proved in a similar way. ■

Lemma 3 *Let A and $\bar{B}$, $\bar{C}$, $\bar{D}$, $\bar{E}$ be as defined in Lemma 1, and let*

$$\Theta = \begin{bmatrix} \bar{B} & \bar{D} \\ \bar{C} & \bar{E} \end{bmatrix}. \tag{3.10}$$

Then, Θ is J-unitary.

Proof The proof of the lemma follows by direct calculation and usage of the various relationships between $\bar{B}$, $\bar{C}$, $\bar{D}$, $\bar{E}$. ■

In the following lemmas we make use of the fact that if A is specified on a staircase band $\mathcal{S}$, then the related scattering matrix S is specified on the strictly upper triangular part of $\mathcal{S}$, and vice-versa. This can be seen from the relations

$$S = (G + I)^{-1}(G - I)$$

and

$$G = (I + S)(I - S)^{-1},$$

from which it follows that entries in S on the strictly upper triangular part of $\mathcal{S}$ are exclusively dependent on entries in G on that same part of $\mathcal{S}$, and vice-versa. Because G and G_{ME} coincide on the strictly upper triangular part of $\mathcal{S}$, it also follows that S and S_{ME} coincide on that part of the band.

Lemma 4 *Let $A = [a_{ij}]$, $i, j = 1, \ldots, n$, be a positive definite matrix that is specified on a staircase band $\mathcal{S}$. Then, the maximum entropy extension of*

$$\begin{bmatrix} I & S \\ S^* & I \end{bmatrix}$$

(in which i) the entries in the diagonal blocks, ii) the entries on the lower triangular part of S and iii) the entries in S on the strictly upper triangular part of $\mathcal{S}$ are specified) is equal to

$$\begin{bmatrix} I & S_{ME} \\ S_{ME}^* & I \end{bmatrix}.$$

Proof It follows from Equation 3.3 that

$$\det \begin{bmatrix} I & S_{ME} \\ S_{ME}^* & I \end{bmatrix} = |\det B|^{-2}. \tag{3.11}$$

Because $B + C = L_{ME}^{-*}$ (see Lemma 2), B is lower triangular and C is strictly lower triangular (see the proof of Lemma 2), we have that

$$\det B = \det L_{ME}^{-*}. \tag{3.12}$$

Substituting Equation 3.12 in Equation 3.11 we obtain that

$$\det \begin{bmatrix} I & S_{ME} \\ S_{ME}^* & I \end{bmatrix} = \det A_{ME}.$$

The chain of equalities leading to this result is independent of the maximum entropy property. For every positive definite extension E of A we have likewise that

$$\det \begin{bmatrix} I & S_E \\ S_E^* & I \end{bmatrix} = \det E.$$

Denoting the set of positive definite extensions of A by $\mathcal{E}$ we now obtain that

$$\max\{ \det \begin{bmatrix} I & S_E \\ S_E^* & I \end{bmatrix} \mid E \in \mathcal{E} \} = \max\{ \det E \mid E \in \mathcal{E} \} = \det A_{ME}$$

$$= \det \begin{bmatrix} I & S_{ME} \\ S_{ME}^* & I \end{bmatrix}.$$

■

Lemma 5 *Let $A = [a_{ij}]$, $i, j = 1, \ldots, n$, be a positive definite matrix that is specified on a band $\mathcal{S} = \{(i,j) \mid |i-j| \leq m\}$, and let $\bar{B}$, $\bar{C}$, $\bar{D}$, $\bar{E}$ be as defined in Equations 3.1 and 3.2. Then,*

$$\begin{array}{lcl} \bar{B} \in \mathcal{K} & & \bar{Z}^m \bar{B} \in \mathcal{H} \\ \bar{C} \in \bar{Z}^{-1}\mathcal{K} & \textit{and} & \bar{Z}^m \bar{C} \in \mathcal{H} \\ \bar{D} \in \bar{Z}\mathcal{H} & & \bar{Z}^{-m} \bar{D} \in \mathcal{K} \\ \bar{E} \in \mathcal{H} & & \bar{Z}^{-m} \bar{E} \in \mathcal{K} \end{array} .$$

Proof The left half of the inclusions has been shown in the proof of Lemma 2. The right half is proved as follows. Because by Lemma 4 the maximum entropy extension of

$$\begin{bmatrix} I & S \\ S^* & I \end{bmatrix}$$

is equal to

$$\begin{bmatrix} I & S_{ME} \\ S_{ME}^* & I \end{bmatrix},$$

and because by Equations 3.3 and 3.4

$$\begin{bmatrix} I & S_{ME} \\ S_{ME}^* & I \end{bmatrix}^{-1} = \begin{bmatrix} BB^* & BC^* \\ CB^* & I + CC^* \end{bmatrix} = \begin{bmatrix} I + DD^* & DE^* \\ ED^* & EE^* \end{bmatrix},$$

we have by Theorem 3 that BC^* vanishes on the upper triangular part of the complement of $\mathcal{S}$. Because B^{-1} is lower triangular, we also have that C^* vanishes on the upper triangular part of the complement of $\mathcal{S}$ and hence, that C vanishes on the lower triangular part of the complement of $\mathcal{S}$. It follows that $\bar{C} \in \bar{Z}^{-m}\mathcal{H}$, so that $\bar{Z}^m \bar{C} \in \mathcal{H}$. It also follows that $(I + C^*C)$ is zero on the complement of $\mathcal{S}$ and, because $I + C^*C = B^*B$ (see Equation 3.8) and B is lower triangular, that B is zero on the lower triangular part of the complement of $\mathcal{S}$. Therefore, $\bar{Z}^m \bar{B} \in \mathcal{H}$. Symmetric properties are true for $\bar{D}$ and $\bar{E}$. ■

Theorem 4 *Let A and $\bar{B}$, $\bar{C}$, $\bar{D}$, $\bar{E}$ be as defined in Lemma 5. Furthermore, let $\bar{F}_u = \underline{\underline{P}}(\bar{Z}^m \bar{S}^*)$ and $\bar{G} = \bar{Z}^m \bar{E} \bar{Z}^{*m}$, $\bar{H} = \bar{D}\bar{Z}^{*m}$, $\bar{K} = \bar{Z}^m \bar{C}$,*

$\bar{N} = \bar{B}$. Then, $\bar{G}$, $\bar{H}$, $\bar{K}$, $\bar{N}$ are uniquely determined by the generalized Wiener-Hopf equations

$$\left\{ \begin{array}{l} \bar{G} + \underline{P}(\bar{F}_u \bar{H}) = \bar{G}_0^{-*} \\ \underline{Q}(\bar{F}_u^* \bar{G}) + \bar{H} = \bar{0} \end{array} \right. \tag{3.13}$$

and

$$\left\{ \begin{array}{l} \bar{K} + \underline{P}(\bar{F}_u \bar{N}) = \bar{0} \\ \underline{Q}(\bar{F}_u^* \bar{K}) + \bar{N} = \bar{N}_0^{-*} \end{array} \right. . \tag{3.14}$$

Proof Suppose that $\bar{F} = \bar{Z}^m \bar{S}_{ME}^*$ and $\bar{F}_l = (\bar{I} - \underline{P})(\bar{Z}^m \bar{S}_{ME}^*)$. Then, $\bar{F} = \bar{F}_l + \bar{F}_u$ because $\bar{F}_u = \underline{P}(\bar{Z}^m \bar{S}^*) = \underline{P}(\bar{Z}^m \bar{S}_{ME}^*)$. From Equations 3.1 and 3.2 we find, e.g. by direct verification, that

$$\begin{aligned} \begin{bmatrix} \bar{I} & \bar{F} \\ \bar{F}^* & \bar{I} \end{bmatrix} &= \begin{bmatrix} \bar{0} & \bar{Z}^m \\ \bar{I} & \bar{0} \end{bmatrix} \begin{bmatrix} \bar{I} & \bar{S}_{ME} \\ \bar{S}_{ME}^* & \bar{I} \end{bmatrix} \begin{bmatrix} \bar{0} & \bar{I} \\ \bar{Z}^{*m} & \bar{0} \end{bmatrix} \\ &= \begin{bmatrix} \bar{0} & \bar{Z}^m \\ \bar{I} & \bar{0} \end{bmatrix} \begin{bmatrix} \bar{I} & \bar{D} \\ \bar{0} & \bar{E} \end{bmatrix}^{-*} \begin{bmatrix} \bar{0} & \bar{I} \\ \bar{Z}^{*m} & \bar{0} \end{bmatrix} \\ &\quad \begin{bmatrix} \bar{0} & \bar{Z}^m \\ \bar{I} & \bar{0} \end{bmatrix} \begin{bmatrix} \bar{I} & \bar{D} \\ \bar{0} & \bar{E} \end{bmatrix}^{-1} \begin{bmatrix} \bar{0} & \bar{I} \\ \bar{Z}^{*m} & \bar{0} \end{bmatrix} \\ &= \begin{bmatrix} \bar{Z}^m \bar{E} \bar{Z}^{*m} & \bar{0} \\ \bar{D} \bar{Z}^{*m} & \bar{I} \end{bmatrix}^{-*} \begin{bmatrix} \bar{Z}^m \bar{E} \bar{Z}^{*m} & \bar{0} \\ \bar{D} \bar{Z}^{*m} & \bar{I} \end{bmatrix}^{-1} \end{aligned}$$

and

$$\begin{aligned} \begin{bmatrix} \bar{I} & \bar{F} \\ \bar{F}^* & \bar{I} \end{bmatrix} &= \begin{bmatrix} \bar{0} & \bar{Z}^m \\ \bar{I} & \bar{0} \end{bmatrix} \begin{bmatrix} \bar{I} & \bar{S}_{ME} \\ \bar{S}_{ME}^* & \bar{I} \end{bmatrix} \begin{bmatrix} \bar{0} & \bar{I} \\ \bar{Z}^{*m} & \bar{0} \end{bmatrix} \\ &= \begin{bmatrix} \bar{0} & \bar{Z}^m \\ \bar{I} & \bar{0} \end{bmatrix} \begin{bmatrix} \bar{B} & \bar{0} \\ \bar{C} & \bar{I} \end{bmatrix}^{-*} \begin{bmatrix} \bar{0} & \bar{I} \\ \bar{Z}^{*m} & \bar{0} \end{bmatrix} \\ &\quad \begin{bmatrix} \bar{0} & \bar{Z}^m \\ \bar{I} & \bar{0} \end{bmatrix} \begin{bmatrix} \bar{B} & \bar{0} \\ \bar{C} & \bar{I} \end{bmatrix}^{-1} \begin{bmatrix} \bar{0} & \bar{I} \\ \bar{Z}^{*m} & \bar{0} \end{bmatrix} \\ &= \begin{bmatrix} \bar{I} & \bar{Z}^m \bar{C} \\ \bar{0} & \bar{B} \end{bmatrix}^{-*} \begin{bmatrix} \bar{I} & \bar{Z}^m \bar{C} \\ \bar{0} & \bar{B} \end{bmatrix}^{-1} . \end{aligned}$$

Hence,

$$\begin{bmatrix} \bar{I} & \bar{F} \\ \bar{F}^* & \bar{I} \end{bmatrix} \begin{bmatrix} \bar{G} \\ \bar{H} \end{bmatrix} = \begin{bmatrix} \bar{G}^{-*} \\ \bar{0} \end{bmatrix} \tag{3.15}$$

and

$$\begin{bmatrix} \bar{I} & \bar{F} \\ \bar{F}^* & \bar{I} \end{bmatrix} \begin{bmatrix} \bar{K} \\ \bar{N} \end{bmatrix} = \begin{bmatrix} \bar{0} \\ \bar{N}^{-*} \end{bmatrix}. \tag{3.16}$$

Projecting the equations on the first rows of Equations 3.15 and 3.16 on $\mathcal{H}$ and those on the second rows on $\mathcal{K}$ we obtain

$$\begin{cases} \underline{\underline{P}}\bar{G} + \underline{\underline{P}}(\bar{F}\,\bar{H}) = \underline{\underline{P}}\bar{G}^{-*} \\ \underline{\underline{Q}}(\bar{F}^*\bar{G}) + \underline{\underline{Q}}\bar{H} = \bar{0} \end{cases} \tag{3.17}$$

and

$$\begin{cases} \underline{\underline{P}}\bar{K} + \underline{\underline{P}}(\bar{F}\bar{N}) = \bar{0} \\ \underline{\underline{Q}}(\bar{F}^*\bar{K}) + \underline{\underline{Q}}\bar{N} = \underline{\underline{Q}}\bar{N}^{-*} \end{cases}. \tag{3.18}$$

It follows from the definition of $\bar{G}$, $\bar{H}$, $\bar{K}$, $\bar{N}$ and Lemma 5 that $\bar{G} \in \mathcal{H}$, $\bar{H} \in \mathcal{K}$, $\bar{K} \in \mathcal{H}$, $\bar{N} \in \mathcal{K}$ and hence, that $\underline{\underline{P}}\bar{G} = \bar{G}$, $\underline{\underline{Q}}\bar{H} = \bar{H}$, $\underline{\underline{P}}\bar{K} = \bar{K}$, $\underline{\underline{Q}}\bar{N} = \bar{N}$. Furthermore,

$$\underline{\underline{P}}(\bar{F}\bar{H}) = \underline{\underline{P}}((\bar{F}_l + \bar{F}_u)\bar{H}) = \underline{\underline{P}}(\bar{F}_u\bar{H}),$$
$$\underline{\underline{Q}}(\bar{F}^*\bar{G}) = \underline{\underline{Q}}((\bar{F}_l^* + \bar{F}_u^*)\bar{G}) = \underline{\underline{Q}}(\bar{F}_u^*\bar{G})$$

and $\underline{\underline{P}}\bar{G}^{-*} = \bar{G}_0^{-*}$, and

$$\underline{\underline{P}}(\bar{F}\bar{N}) = \underline{\underline{P}}((\bar{F}_l + \bar{F}_u)\bar{N}) = \underline{\underline{P}}(\bar{F}_u\bar{N}),$$
$$\underline{\underline{Q}}(\bar{F}^*\bar{K}) = \underline{\underline{Q}}((\bar{F}_l^* + \bar{F}_u^*)\bar{K}) = \underline{\underline{Q}}(\bar{F}_u^*\bar{K})$$

and $\underline{\underline{Q}}\bar{N}^{-*} = \bar{N}_0^{-*}$. Substituting these equalities in Equations 3.17 and 3.18 we obtain Equations 3.13 and 3.14. Uniqueness follows by remarking that Equations 3.13 and 3.14 are actually equivalent to Equations 3.15 and 3.16, which in turn are equivalent to Equations 3.1 and 3.2 in Lemma 1. ∎

Corollary 1 *Let $\bar{B}$, $\bar{C}$, $\bar{D}$, $\bar{E}$ and Θ be as defined in Lemma 5 and Equation 3.10. Then, $\bar{B}$, $\bar{C}$, $\bar{D}$, $\bar{E}$ and Θ are uniquely determined by Equations 3.13 and 3.14.*

Proof The proof of the corollary follows directly from Theorem 4. ∎

The Wiener-Hopf technique of Theorem 4 is due to Dym and Gohberg [4] (see also [5]). We now give the relation between the Θ matrix occuring in the LIS (Lossless Inverse Scattering) theorem of [15] and the Θ matrix occuring in [20]. The former is given by

$$\begin{bmatrix} \bar{B} & \bar{D} \\ \bar{C} & \bar{E} \end{bmatrix},$$

the latter is given by

$$\begin{bmatrix} \bar{N} & \bar{H} \\ \bar{K} & \bar{G} \end{bmatrix} = \begin{bmatrix} \bar{I} & \bar{0} \\ \bar{0} & \bar{Z}^{m} \end{bmatrix} \begin{bmatrix} \bar{B} & \bar{D} \\ \bar{C} & \bar{E} \end{bmatrix} \begin{bmatrix} \bar{I} & \bar{0} \\ \bar{0} & \bar{Z}^{*m} \end{bmatrix},$$

where $\bar{B}$, $\bar{C}$, $\bar{D}$, $\bar{E}$ and $\bar{G}$, $\bar{H}$, $\bar{K}$, $\bar{N}$ are as defined in Theorem 4. We proceed by exploring the connection between the above and LIS theory.

Suppose that $\bar{\Gamma}$ and $\bar{\Delta}$ are operators on l^2. Then, $[\bar{\Gamma}\ \bar{\Delta}]$ is called *admissible* if

1. $\bar{\Gamma}$ and $\bar{\Delta}$ are upper triangular,
2. $\bar{\Gamma}$ is boundedly invertible,
3. $\bar{\Gamma}^{-1}\bar{\Delta}$ is upper triangular and contractive.

For instance, $[\bar{I}\ \bar{S}]$ is admissible. We next show that the Θ matrix defined in Equation 3.10 solves an *inverse scattering* problem on $[\bar{I}\ \bar{S}]$ if $\bar{S}$ is related to a (positive definite) matrix that is specified on a block band.

Theorem 5 *Let A, $\bar{B}$, $\bar{C}$, $\bar{D}$, $\bar{E}$ and Θ be as defined in Lemma 5 and Equation 3.10. Furthermore, let $[\bar{I}\ \bar{S}]\Theta = [\bar{\Gamma}\ \bar{\Delta}]$. Then,*

1. *$[\bar{\Gamma}\ \bar{\Delta}]$ is admissible,*
2. *$\bar{\Delta}$ and $\bar{\Gamma}^{-1}\bar{\Delta}$ belong to $\bar{Z}^{m+1}\mathcal{H}$,*
3. *$\bar{S}$ can be written as*

$$\bar{S} = (\bar{a} + \bar{S}_L\bar{Z}^{m+1}\bar{b})^{-1}(\bar{c} + \bar{S}_L\bar{Z}^{m+1}\bar{d}), \tag{3.19}$$

where

$$\begin{bmatrix} \bar{a} & \bar{c} \\ \bar{b} & \bar{d} \end{bmatrix} = \begin{bmatrix} \bar{B}^* & -\bar{C}^* \\ -\bar{D}^* & \bar{E}^* \end{bmatrix} = \Theta^{-1}$$

and $\bar{S}_L$ is upper triangular and contractive,

4. *all extensions of $\bar{S}$ (specified on the strictly upper triangular part of S) can be obtained from Equation 3.19, when $\bar{S}_L$ is allowed to range over all upper triangular contractive matrices.*

Proof The proof proceeds by direct calculation. By definition,

$$[\bar{\Gamma}\ \bar{\Delta}] = [\bar{I}\ \bar{S}]\Theta = [(\bar{B} + \bar{S}\bar{C})\ (\bar{D} + \bar{S}\bar{E})].$$

Although $\bar{B}$ and $\bar{C}$ are lower triangular, $\bar{\Gamma} = \bar{B} + \bar{S}\bar{C}$ turns out to be upper triangular. Indeed, because $\bar{S}$ and $\bar{S}_{ME}$ coincide on the strictly upper triangular part of $\mathcal{S}$, we have that

$$\bar{\Gamma} = \bar{B} + \bar{S}\bar{C} = \bar{B} + (\bar{S}_{ME} + \bar{R}\bar{Z}^{m+1})\bar{C}, \tag{3.20}$$

where $\bar{R}$ is upper triangular. Combining

$$\bar{S}_{ME} = -\bar{B}^{-*}\bar{C}^{*}$$

and

$$\bar{B}^{*}\bar{B} - \bar{C}^{*}\bar{C} = \bar{I}$$

(cf. Equations 3.7 and 3.8) we obtain

$$\bar{B} + \bar{S}_{ME}\bar{C} = \bar{B}^{-*}.$$

Substituting this equation in Equation 3.20 we find that

$$\bar{\Gamma} = \bar{B}^{-*} + \bar{R}\bar{Z}^{m+1}\bar{C}$$

and hence, because $\bar{R}$ and $\bar{B}^{-*}$ are upper triangular and $\bar{Z}^{m+1}\bar{C}$ is strictly upper triangular (see Lemma 5 and the proof of that lemma), that $\bar{\Gamma}$ is upper triangular. Furthermore, because $\bar{B}^{-*}$ is upper triangular and boundedly invertible, $\bar{R}\bar{Z}^{m+1}\bar{C}$ is strictly upper triangular, and these matrices are embeddings of finite dimensional matrices in a doubly infinite identity and zero matrix, it follows that $\bar{\Gamma}$ is boundedly invertible. Because

$$\bar{\Delta} = \bar{D} + \bar{S}\bar{E}$$

and

$$\bar{S}_{ME} = -\bar{D}\bar{E}^{-1}$$

(see Equation 3.6) we find that

$$\bar{\Delta} = \bar{D} + \bar{S}\bar{E} = (\bar{S} + \bar{D}\bar{E}^{-1})\bar{E} = (\bar{S} - \bar{S}_{ME})\bar{E}.$$

Because $\bar{S}$ and $\bar{S}_{ME}$ coincide on the strictly upper triangular part of $\mathcal{S}$ and $\bar{E}$ is upper triangular (see Lemma 5), it follows that $\bar{\Delta}$ belongs to $\bar{Z}^{m+1}\mathcal{H}$ and hence, because $\bar{\Gamma}^{-1}$ is upper triangular, that $\bar{\Gamma}^{-1}\bar{\Delta}$ belongs to $\bar{Z}^{m+1}\mathcal{H}$ as well. Now, suppose that $\bar{\Gamma}^{-1}\bar{\Delta} = \bar{S}_L\bar{Z}^{m+1}$, where $\bar{S}_L$ is upper triangular. Then,

$$[\bar{I}\ \bar{S}]\Theta = [\bar{\Gamma}\ \bar{\Delta}] = \bar{\Gamma}[\bar{I}\ (\bar{S}_L\bar{Z}^{m+1})].$$

Because Θ is J-unitary and $\bar{Z}$ is unitary, it follows that

$$\bar{I} - \bar{S}\bar{S}^* = \bar{\Gamma}[\bar{I} - (\bar{S}_L\bar{Z}^{m+1})(\bar{S}_L\bar{Z}^{m+1})^*]\bar{\Gamma}^* = \bar{\Gamma}[\bar{I} - \bar{S}_L\bar{S}_L^*]\bar{\Gamma}^*$$

and, because $\bar{S}$ is contractive and $\bar{\Gamma}$ is invertible, that $\bar{S}_L\bar{Z}^{m+1}$ and $\bar{S}_L$ are contractive. Equation 3.19 now follows easily. The last assertion in the theorem follows from the fact that the construction given above is dependent only on the entries in S on the strictly upper triangular part of $\mathcal{S}$. ■

We terminate this section by showing how Theorem 4 leads to a system of linear equations that is based on a Hankel matrix whose entries are equal to the diagonals of $\bar{F}_u$ (and hence, the diagonals of $\bar{S}$ because $\bar{F}_u = \underline{\underline{P}}(\bar{Z}^m\bar{S}^*)$). With $s = m - 1$,

$$\bar{F}_u = \sum_{i=0}^{s} \bar{F}_i\bar{Z}^i, \quad \bar{G} = \sum_{i=0}^{s} \bar{G}_i\bar{Z}^i, \quad \bar{H} = \sum_{i=-s}^{0} \bar{H}_i\bar{Z}^i,$$

$$\bar{K} = \sum_{i=0}^{s} \bar{K}_i\bar{Z}^i, \quad \bar{N} = \sum_{i=-s}^{0} \bar{N}_i\bar{Z}^i$$

and the corresponding vectors and matrices

$$\mathbf{F} = \begin{bmatrix} \bar{F}_0 & \bar{F}_1\bar{Z} & \cdots & \bar{F}_s\bar{Z}^s \\ \bar{F}_1\bar{Z} & & \cdot^{\cdot^{\cdot}} & \\ \vdots & \cdot^{\cdot^{\cdot}} & & \\ \bar{F}_s\bar{Z}^s & & & 0 \end{bmatrix}, \quad \mathbf{G} = \begin{bmatrix} \bar{G}_0 \\ \bar{G}_1\bar{Z} \\ \vdots \\ \bar{G}_s\bar{Z}^s \end{bmatrix}, \quad \mathbf{G}_0 = \begin{bmatrix} \bar{G}_0^{-*} \\ \bar{0} \\ \vdots \\ \bar{0} \end{bmatrix},$$

$$\mathbf{H} = \begin{bmatrix} \bar{H}_0 \\ \bar{H}_{-1}\bar{Z}^* \\ \vdots \\ \bar{H}_{-s}\bar{Z}^{*s} \end{bmatrix}, \quad \mathbf{K} = \begin{bmatrix} \bar{K}_0 \\ \bar{K}_1\bar{Z} \\ \vdots \\ \bar{K}_s\bar{Z}^s \end{bmatrix}, \quad \mathbf{N} = \begin{bmatrix} \bar{N}_0 \\ \bar{N}_{-1}\bar{Z}^* \\ \vdots \\ \bar{N}_{-s}\bar{Z}^{*s} \end{bmatrix}, \quad \mathbf{N}_0 = \begin{bmatrix} \bar{N}_0^{-*} \\ \bar{0} \\ \vdots \\ \bar{0} \end{bmatrix}$$

Equations 3.13 and 3.14 reduce to

$$\begin{bmatrix} \mathbf{I} & \mathbf{F} \\ \mathbf{F}^* & \mathbf{I} \end{bmatrix} \begin{bmatrix} \mathbf{G} \\ \mathbf{H} \end{bmatrix} = \begin{bmatrix} \mathbf{G}_0 \\ \mathbf{0} \end{bmatrix}$$

and

$$\begin{bmatrix} \mathbf{I} & \mathbf{F} \\ \mathbf{F}^* & \mathbf{I} \end{bmatrix} \begin{bmatrix} \mathbf{K} \\ \mathbf{N} \end{bmatrix} = \begin{bmatrix} \mathbf{0} \\ \mathbf{N}_0 \end{bmatrix}.$$

These equations are definite because of Theorem 4. In fact,

$$\begin{bmatrix} \mathbf{I} & \mathbf{F} \\ \mathbf{F}^* & \mathbf{I} \end{bmatrix}$$

is the embedding of a positive definite matrix.

4 The Schur Algorithm

In this section we review the Schur algorithm presented in [15]. If A is a positive definite matrix that is specified on a staircase band, then this algorithm can be used to compute the triangular factors L_{ME}^{-*} and M_{ME}^{-1} of the inverse of the maximum entropy extension of A. The algorithm is based on the following theorem.

Theorem 6 ([15]) *Let $A = [a_{ij}]$, $i, j = 1, \ldots, n$, be a positive definite matrix that is specified on a staircase band $\mathcal{S}$, and let $\Gamma = U$ and $\Delta = V$. Then,*

1. *there are elementary J-unitary matrices $\Theta_1, \ldots, \Theta_m$ such that*

$$[\Gamma\ \Delta]\Theta_1 \cdots \Theta_m = [\Gamma^{(m)}\ \Delta^{(m)}], \tag{4.21}$$

where $\Gamma^{(m)}$ is an upper triangular matrix and $\Delta^{(m)}$ is a strictly upper triangular matrix with zeros on the strictly upper triangular part of $\mathcal{S}$.

2. *the product $\Theta_1 \cdots \Theta_m$ is such that*

$$\Theta_1 \cdots \Theta_m = \begin{bmatrix} U_{ME}^* & -V_{ME} \\ -V_{ME}^* & U_{ME} \end{bmatrix} \begin{bmatrix} L_{ME}^{-*} & 0 \\ 0 & M_{ME}^{-1} \end{bmatrix} \tag{4.22}$$

and hence, is equal to the Θ matrix defined in Equation 3.10.

For a proof of Theorem 6 we refer to [15].

Corollary 2 **([15])** *Let A and $\Theta_1, \ldots, \Theta_m$ be as defined in Theorem 6. Then,*

$$[I\ I]\Theta_1 \cdots \Theta_m = [L_{ME}^{-*}\ M_{ME}^{-1}]. \tag{4.23}$$

Proof The proof of the corollary follows directly from Equation 4.22.

■

We proceed by describing the algorithm. The triangular factors L_{ME}^{-*} and M_{ME}^{-1} of the inverse of the maximum entropy extension of A are computed in two steps. First, the elementary J-unitary matrices $\Theta_1, \ldots, \Theta_m$ defined in Equation 4.21 are computed recursively. Next, Equation 4.23 is evaluated. The computation of $\Theta_1, \ldots, \Theta_m$ proceeds as follows. Starting from $[\Gamma\ \Delta]$, where Γ and Δ are as defined in Theorem 6, Θ_1 is computed such that Δ_{12} is eliminated when $[\Gamma\ \Delta]$ is postmultiplied by Θ_1:

$$\Theta_1 = \Theta(1, 2, \rho_{12}), \quad \text{with } \rho_{12} = -\frac{\Delta_{12}}{\Gamma_{11}}.$$

Next, $[\Gamma\ \Delta]\Theta_1 = [\Gamma^{(1)}\ \Delta^{(1)}]$ is computed, with $\Delta_{12}^{(1)} = 0$. Note that Θ_1 is such that $\Gamma^{(1)}$ is upper triangular and $\Delta^{(1)}$ is strictly upper triangular. In a similar way, Θ_2 is computed such that $\Delta_{23}^{(1)}$ is eliminated if $[\Gamma^{(1)}\ \Delta^{(1)}]$ is postmultiplied by Θ_2:

$$\Theta_2 = \Theta(2, 3, \rho_{23}), \quad \text{with } \rho_{23} = -\frac{\Delta_{23}^{(1)}}{\Gamma_{22}^{(1)}}.$$

When for some l the entries in the first upper diagonal of $\Delta^{(l)}$ have been eliminated, Θ_{l+1} is computed such that the first entry in the second upper diagonal of $\Delta^{(l)}$ is eliminated if $[\Gamma^{(l)}\ \Delta^{(l)}]$ is postmultiplied by Θ_{l+1}, etc.. The recursion ends when for some m all entries in $\Delta^{(m)}$ on the strictly upper triangular part of the staircase band have been eliminated. The computation of Equation 4.23 is straightforward. Instead of $[\Gamma\ \Delta]$, $[I\ I]$ is postmultiplied by $\Theta_1 \cdots \Theta_m$. It is easy to verify that the Schur algorithm requires $O(nb^2)$ operations and $O(nb)$ storage, where n is the size of A and b is the average width of the staircase band. A flow-graph representation of the algorithm is shown in Figure 1, where $A = [a_{ij}]$, $i, j = 1, \ldots, 5$, is a positive definite matrix that is specified on a band $\{(i,j) \mid |i-j| \leq 2\}$. A node denotes a virtual processor, a box denotes a delay. The operation of a node is as follows. From the first two input values, say x and y (with $|x| > |y|$), $\rho = -y/x$ is computed. Also,

$$[x\ y]\frac{1}{\sqrt{1-|\rho|^2}}\begin{bmatrix} 1 & \rho \\ \rho^* & 1 \end{bmatrix} = [\sqrt{x^2 - y^2}\ 0]$$

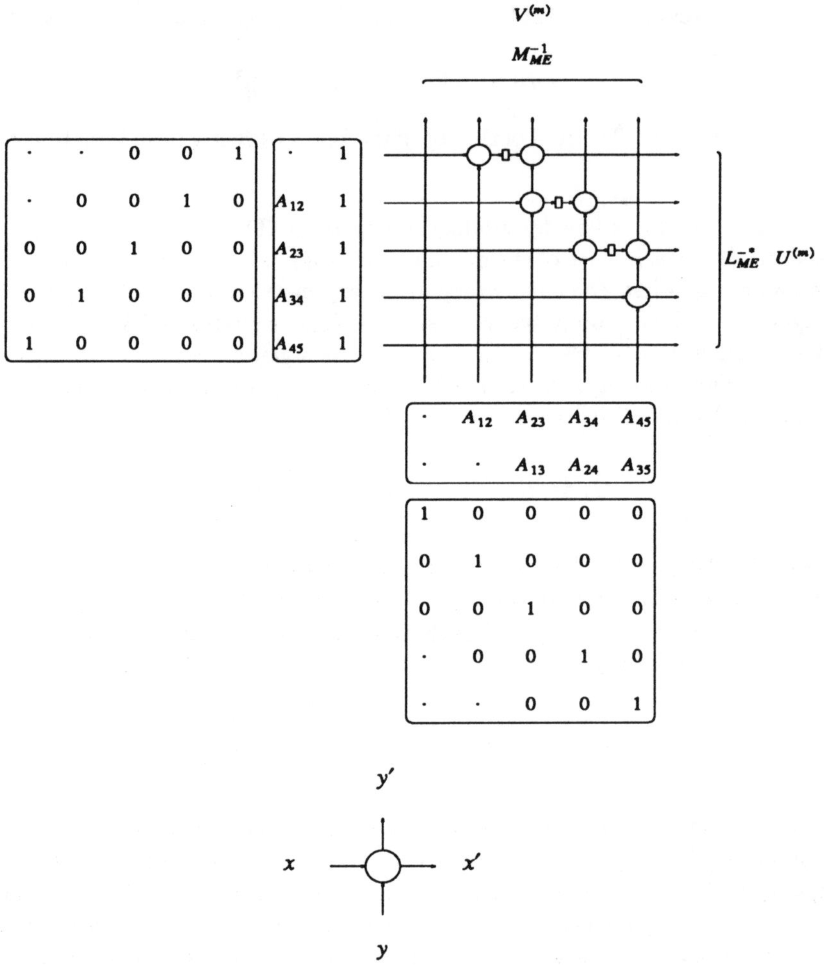

$$[x'\, y'] = [x\, y]\, \frac{1}{\sqrt{1-|\rho|^2}} \begin{bmatrix} 1 & \rho \\ \rho^* & 1 \end{bmatrix}$$

Figure 1: Flow-graph representation of the Schur algorithm. The symbol '·' denotes a 'don't care'.

is computed. This operation is called vectoring. For all subsequent input values x and y,

$$[x\ y]\frac{1}{\sqrt{1-|\rho|^2}}\begin{bmatrix} 1 & \rho \\ \rho^* & 1 \end{bmatrix} = [x'\ y']$$

is computed. This operation is called rotating. A node can be implemented by a pipelined CORDIC (Coordinate Rotation Digital Computer) device (see [21, 22, 23]). The CORDIC device described in [23] is capable of achieving a throughput of 10^7–10^8 floating point vectorizations or rotations per second. Its size is about 1 square centimeter.

We proceed by assessing the distance of the triangular factor L_{ME}^{-1} of the inverse of the maximum entropy extension of A to the triangular factor L^{-1} of the inverse of the completely specified matrix.

Theorem 7 *Let A be as defined in Theorem 6, let ρ_{ij} be as defined above, and let $k_i = \max\{ j \mid (i,j) \in \mathcal{S} \}$. Then,*

$$\|I - L_{ME}^{-1}L\|_F = \Big(2 - \frac{2}{n}\sum_{i=1}^{n}\prod_{j=k_i+1}^{n}(1-|\rho_{ij}|^2)^{\frac{1}{2}}\Big)^{\frac{1}{2}}. \tag{4.24}$$

To prove Theorem 7 we need the following lemma.

Lemma 6 *Let $A = [a_{ij}]$ be a positive definite matrix that is specified on a set $\mathcal{S}$ that contains the diagonal pairs (i,i) but is arbitrary otherwise. Then,*

$$\mathrm{tr}(L_{ME}^{-1} A L_{ME}^{-*}) = \mathrm{tr} I.$$

Proof Suppose that C is a matrix that is of the same size as A and has zeros off the set $\mathcal{S}$. Because $(A - A_{ME})$ has zeros on $\mathcal{S}$ and C has zeros off $\mathcal{S}$, we have that

$$\underline{\underline{P}}_0((A - A_{ME})C) = 0.$$

Substituting C by A_{ME}^{-1} we derive that

$$\underline{\underline{P}}_0(AA_{ME}^{-1}) = \underline{\underline{P}}_0 I.$$

Taking traces of the left and right-hand side of this equation we obtain that

$$\mathrm{tr}(AA_{ME}^{-1}) = \mathrm{tr} I.$$

Because similar matrices have equal traces, it follows that

$$\mathrm{tr}(L_{ME}^{-1} A L_{ME}^{-*}) = \mathrm{tr}(AA_{ME}^{-1}) = \mathrm{tr} I.$$

■

We proceed with the proof of Theorem 7.

Proof It follows from Equation 4.23 and the way in which $\Theta_1, \ldots, \Theta_m$ are constructed that

$$(L_{ME}^{-1})_{ii} = \prod_{j=i+1}^{k_i} (1 - |\rho_{ij}|^2)^{-\frac{1}{2}}.$$

When the staircase band equals the full set of indices $\{(i,j) \mid 1 \le i,j \le n\}$, then $A_{ME} = A$ and we obtain that

$$(L^{-1})_{ii} = \prod_{j=i+1}^{n} (1 - |\rho_{ij}|^2)^{-\frac{1}{2}},$$

because the Schur parametrization yields the same ρ_{ij} in both cases. It follows that

$$(L_{ME}^{-1} L)_{ii} = \prod_{j=k_i+1}^{n} (1 - |\rho_{ij}|^2)^{\frac{1}{2}}. \tag{4.25}$$

Furthermore, we have that

$$||I - L_{ME}^{-1} L||_F^2 = \frac{1}{n}(\mathrm{tr} I - 2\mathrm{tr}(L_{ME}^{-1} L) + \mathrm{tr}(L_{ME}^{-1} A L_{ME}^{-*})). \tag{4.26}$$

The proof of the theorem now follows by combining Lemma 6, Equation 4.25, and Equation 4.26. ∎

It was shown in [15] that of all upper triangular matrices with zeros off the staircase band the matrix $\underline{\underline{P}}_0(L_{ME}^{-1} L) L_{ME}^{-1}$ is the closest to L^{-1} in the $||I - \cdot L||_F$-norm. Furthermore, it was shown that

$$||I - \underline{\underline{P}}_0(L_{ME}^{-1} L) L_{ME}^{-1} L||_F = (1 - \frac{1}{n}\sum_{i=1}^{n} \prod_{j=k_i+1}^{n} (1 - |\rho_{ij}|^2))^{\frac{1}{2}}, \tag{4.27}$$

where ρ_{ij}, k_i and n are as defined in Theorem 7. Of course, the optimal matrix $\underline{\underline{P}}_0(L_{ME}^{-1} L) L_{ME}^{-1}$ is uncomputable, because L is unknown (L is a triangular factor of a partially specified matrix). However, it follows from Equation 4.24 and Equation 4.27 that the absolute difference between $||I - L_{ME}^{-1} L||_F$ and $||I - \underline{\underline{P}}_0(L_{ME}^{-1} L) L_{ME}^{-1} L||_F$ is small if the sum of products in Equation 4.24 is small. It follows from Equation 4.27 that the latter is the case if $\underline{\underline{P}}_0(L_{ME}^{-1} L) L_{ME}^{-1}$ is a good approximation of L^{-1}. Hence, L_{ME}^{-*} is a good approximation of L^{-1} whenever $\underline{\underline{P}}_0(L_{ME}^{-1} L) L_{ME}^{-1}$ is a good approximation of L^{-1}.

Now, suppose that A is a partially specified positive definite matrix, P is a permutation matrix and PAP^* is specified on a staircase band. Partially specified matrices of this type are encountered in the next section. The following theorem can be used to compute the inverse of the maximum entropy extension of A from the inverse of the maximum entropy extension of PAP^*.

Theorem 8 *Let $A = [a_{ij}]$ be a positive definite matrix that is specified on a set S that contains the diagonal pairs (i,i) but is arbitrary otherwise, and let P be a permutation matrix. Then, $A_{ME}^{-1} = P^*(PAP^*)_{ME}^{-1}P$.*

Proof The maximum entropy extension of a partially specified positive definite matrix is the unique positive definite extension of that matrix whose determinant is maximal. Because $\det(PAP^*) = \det P \det A \det P^*$ and the determinant of P is constant, we have that $(PAP^*)_{ME} = PA_{ME}P^*$. Hence, $A_{ME}^{-1} = P^*(PAP^*)_{ME}^{-1}P$. ∎

The triangular factors of the inverse of the maximum entropy extension of PAP^* can be computed by using the Schur algorithm, because PAP^* is a positive definite matrix that is specified on a staircase band. The computation of the inverse of the maximum entropy extension of PAP^* from its triangular factors requires only $O(nb^2)$ operations and $O(nb)$ storage, where n is the size of PAP^* and b is the average width of the staircase band of this matrix. This follows from the fact that the above mentioned factors are banded. The computation of PAP^* from A and the computation of the inverse of the maximum entropy extension of A from the inverse of the maximum entropy extension of PAP^* requires only the reindexing of the entries of A and the inverse of the maximum entropy extension of PAP^* respectively. This requires almost no computational effort. Thus, the computation of the inverse of the maximum entropy extension of A requires $O(nb^2)$ operations and $O(nb)$ storage, where n is the size of A and b is the average width of the staircase band of PAP^*.

Remember that we have assumed that the diagonal entries of A are equal to one. If this is not the case, then we normalize A to $A' = D^{-\frac{1}{2}}AD^{-\frac{1}{2}}$. Next, we compute the triangular factors $L_{A'_{ME}}^{-*}$ and $M_{A'_{ME}}^{-1}$ of the inverse of the maximum entropy extension of A' by using the Schur algorithm. By an argument similar to the argument used in the proof of Theorem 8, we can compute L_{ME}^{-*} and M_{ME}^{-1} as $L_{ME}^{-*} = D^{-\frac{1}{2}}L_{A'_{ME}}^{-*}$ and $M_{ME}^{-1} = D^{-\frac{1}{2}}M_{A'_{ME}}^{-1}$.

5 A Hierarchical Extension of the Schur Algorithm

If A is a positive definite matrix that is specified on a multiple band (see Figure 2), then the Schur algorithm presented in [15] can not be used to compute the triangular factors of the inverse of the maximum entropy extension of A. Indeed, it can only be used if a positive definite matrix is specified

$$\begin{bmatrix}
x & x & & & x & x & & & & & & \\
x & x & x & & x & x & x & & & & & \\
 & x & x & x & & x & x & x & & & & \\
 & & x & x & & & x & x & & & & \\
x & x & & & x & x & & & x & x & & \\
x & x & x & & x & x & x & & x & x & x & \\
 & x & x & x & & x & x & x & & x & x & x \\
 & & x & x & & & x & x & & & x & x \\
 & & & & x & x & & & x & x & & \\
 & & & & x & x & x & & x & x & x & \\
 & & & & & x & x & x & & x & x & x \\
 & & & & & & x & x & & & x & x
\end{bmatrix}$$

Figure 2: A positive definite matrix that is specified on a multiple band. Specified entries are marked with 'x', unspecified entries are blank.

on a staircase band, and a multiple band is clearly not a staircase band. Also, no permutation matrix P exists such that PAP^* is specified on a staircase band (see the last part of the previous section). In this section we present a hierarchical extension of the Schur algorithm which can be used to compute an approximate inverse of a positive definite matrix that is specified only on a multiple band. We assume that the maximum entropy extension of the partially specified matrix is a good approximation of the completely specified matrix. We also assume that the maximum entropy extensions of certain principal submatrices of the partially specified matrix are good approximations of the corresponding principal submatrices of the completely specified matrix. The resulting inverse is the inverse of a matrix that closely matches the partially specified matrix. It has zeros in the positions that correspond to unspecified entries in the partially specified matrix.

We start out with a description of the structure of the triangular factor $\mathbf{L}_{ME}^{-*}$ of the inverse of the maximum entropy extension of a positive definite block matrix $\mathbf{A} = [\mathbf{a}_{ij}]$ that is specified on a band $\{ (i,j) \mid |i-j| \leq m \}$.

Theorem 9 *Let* $\mathbf{A} = [\mathbf{a}_{ij}]$, $i,j = 1, .., n$, *be a positive definite block matrix with blocks* $\mathbf{a}_{ij}$ *of size* $n_i \times n_j$ *that is specified on a band* $\{ (i,j) \mid |i-j| \leq m \}$. *Then, the columns of* $\mathbf{L}_{ME}^{-*}$ *are such that for* $j = 1, \ldots, n-m-1$

$$\begin{aligned} (\mathbf{L}_{ME}^{-*})_{ij} &= (\mathbf{L}_{\mathbf{A}(j,j+m)}^{-*})_{(i-j+1)1} & i &= j, \ldots, j+m \\ (\mathbf{L}_{ME}^{-*})_{ij} &= 0 & i &= j+m+1, \ldots, n \end{aligned} \tag{5.28}$$

and for $j = n-m, \ldots, n$

$$(\mathbf{L}_{ME}^{-*})_{ij} = (\mathbf{L}_{\mathbf{A}(n-m,n)}^{-*})_{(i-(n-m)+1)(j-(n-m)+1)} \qquad i = j, \ldots, n.$$

Proof The proof follows that in [1]. We start out with introducing some notation. Let $\mathcal{S}$ denote the band of $\mathbf{A}$. For a block matrix $\mathbf{F}$ the symbol $\{\mathbf{F}\}_c$ denotes the block matrix that matches $\mathbf{F}$ on $\mathcal{S}$ and is zero otherwise. The symbol $\{\mathbf{F}\}_l$ denotes the lower triangular block matrix that matches the lower triangular part of $\mathbf{F}$ off the band and is zero otherwise. The size of $\{\mathbf{F}\}_c$ and $\{\mathbf{F}\}_l$ is the same as the size of $\mathbf{F}$. Now, suppose that $\mathbf{X} = [\mathbf{x}_{ij}]$ is an upper triangular block matrix with blocks $\mathbf{x}_{ij}$ of size $n_i \times n_j$, and that the columns of $\mathbf{X}^{-*}$ are such that for $j = 1, \ldots, n-m-1$

$$\begin{aligned} (\mathbf{X}^{-*})_{ij} &= (\mathbf{L}_{\mathbf{A}(j,j+m)}^{-*})_{(i-j+1)1} & i &= j, \ldots, j+m \\ (\mathbf{X}^{-*})_{ij} &= 0 & i &= j+m+1, \ldots, n \end{aligned} \tag{5.29}$$

and for $j = n-m, \ldots, n$

$$(\mathbf{X}^{-*})_{ij} = (\mathbf{L}_{\mathbf{A}(n-m,n)}^{-*})_{(i-(n-m)+1)(j-(n-m)+1)} \qquad i = j, \ldots, n$$

(cf. Equation 5.28). We shall prove that $\mathbf{X} = \mathbf{L}_{ME}$ and hence, $\mathbf{L}_{ME}^{-*}$ is as described in Equation 5.28. From Equation 5.29 it follows that $\mathbf{X}^{-*}$ has lower triangular diagonal blocks with positive diagonal entries, and that $\mathbf{X}^{-*}\mathbf{X}^{-1}$ has zeros off $\mathcal{S}$. It remains to prove that $\mathbf{X}\mathbf{X}^*$ is an extension of $\mathbf{A}$. We define

$$\mathbf{E} = \{\mathbf{E}\}_l + \{\mathbf{E}\}_c + \{\mathbf{E}\}_l^* \tag{5.30}$$

with

$$\{\mathbf{E}\}_c = \{\mathbf{A}\}_c \quad \text{and} \quad \{\mathbf{E}\}_l = -\{\{\mathbf{A}\}_c\mathbf{X}^{-*}\}_l\mathbf{X}^*. \tag{5.31}$$

We show that $\mathbf{E} = \mathbf{X}\mathbf{X}^*$, so that $\mathbf{X}\mathbf{X}^*$ is an extension of $\mathbf{A}$. From Equation 5.30 and Equation 5.31 and the fact that $\mathbf{X}^{-*}$ is lower triangular with zeros off $\mathcal{S}$ we have that

$$\begin{aligned} \{\mathbf{E}\mathbf{X}^{-*}\}_l &= \{\{\mathbf{E}\}_l\mathbf{X}^{-*}\}_l + \{\{\mathbf{E}\}_c\mathbf{X}^{-*}\}_l + \{\{\mathbf{E}\}_l^*\mathbf{X}^{-*}\}_l \\ &= \{\mathbf{E}\}_l\mathbf{X}^{-*} + \{\{\mathbf{A}\}_c\mathbf{X}^{-*}\}_l = 0 \end{aligned} \tag{5.32}$$

It follows from Equation 5.29 and Equation 5.32 that $\mathbf{EX}^{-*}$ is upper triangular. Furthermore, we have that

$$(\mathbf{X}^{-1}\mathbf{E})\mathbf{X}^{-*} = \mathbf{X}^{-1}(\mathbf{EX}^{-*}).$$

Because $\mathbf{X}^{-1}\mathbf{E}$ and $\mathbf{X}^{-*}$ are lower triangular, the left-hand side of this equation is lower triangular. For the same reason, the right-hand side is upper triangular. Therefore, $\mathbf{X}^{-1}\mathbf{EX}^{-*}$ is diagonal. It now follows from Equation 5.29 that $\mathbf{X}^{-1}\mathbf{EX}^{-*} = \mathbf{I}$, the identity matrix, and hence, that $\mathbf{E} = \mathbf{XX}^*$. This completes the proof of the theorem. ■

Now, let A be a positive definite matrix that is specified on a multiple band. If it were possible to partition A as $\mathbf{A} = [\mathbf{a}_{ij}]$, $i, j = 1, \ldots, n$, such that for some band $\{(i,j) \mid |i-j| \leq m\}$ the blocks on the band are completely specified and the blocks off its band are unspecified, then the triangular factor $\mathbf{L}_{ME}^{-*}$ of the inverse of the maximum entropy extension of $\mathbf{A}$ were found from the triangular factors of the inverses of the principal submatrices $\mathbf{A}(j, j+m)$, $j = 1, \ldots, n-m$ (see Theorem 9). Clearly, it is not possible to partition a matrix that is specified on a multiple band in this way. It is possible, however, to partition A as $\mathbf{A} = [\mathbf{a}_{ij}]$, $i, j = 1, \ldots, n$, such that for some band $\{(i,j) \mid |i-j| \leq m\}$ the partially specified principal submatrices $\mathbf{A}(j, j+m)$[1], $j = 1, \ldots, n-m$, can be permuted to positive definite matrices that are specified on a staircase band, and such that the blocks off the band are unspecified. For example, if A is as shown in Figure 2, then A can be partitioned as $\mathbf{A} = [\mathbf{a}_{ij}]$, $i, j = 1, 2, 3$, where the blocks $\mathbf{a}_{ij}$ are of size 4×4, so that the partially specified principal submatrices $\mathbf{A}(1,2)$ and $\mathbf{A}(2,3)$ can be permuted to positive definite matrices that are specified on a staircase band, and so that the blocks off the band $\{(i,j) \mid |i-j| \leq 1\}$ are unspecified. The partially specified principal submatrix $\mathbf{A}(1,2)$ and the permuted matrix $P\mathbf{A}(1,2)P^*$ (P denotes a permutation matrix) are shown in Figure 3.

We now assume that the maximum entropy extensions of the partially specified principal submatrices $\mathbf{A}(j, j+m)$, $j = 1, \ldots, n-m$, are good approximations of the corresponding principal submatrices of the completely specified matrix. For this reason, and because it is given that the maximum entropy extension of A is a good approximation of the completely specified matrix, we approximate the triangular factor L^{-*} of the inverse of the completely specified matrix by a lower triangular matrix that is built on the triangular factors of the inverses of the maximum entropy extensions of the partially specified principal submatrices $\mathbf{A}(j, j+m)$, $j = 1, \ldots, n-m$ (cf. Theorem 9). This lower triangular matrix is a triangular factor of the inverse of a matrix

[1] We mean that the block matrices $\mathbf{A}(j, j+m)$, interpreted as matrices with scalar entries, are partially specified.

$$\mathbf{A}(1,2) = \begin{bmatrix} x & x & & & x & x & & \\ x & x & x & & x & x & x & \\ & x & x & x & & x & x & x \\ & & x & x & & & x & x \\ x & x & & & x & x & & \\ x & x & x & & x & x & x & \\ & x & x & x & & x & x & x \\ & & x & x & & & x & x \end{bmatrix}$$

$$P\mathbf{A}(1,2)P^* = \begin{bmatrix} x & x & x & x & & & & \\ x & x & x & x & & & & \\ x & x & x & x & x & x & & \\ x & x & x & x & x & x & & \\ & & x & x & x & x & x & x \\ & & x & x & x & x & x & x \\ & & & & x & x & x & x \\ & & & & x & x & x & x \end{bmatrix}$$

Figure 3: The partially specified principle submatrix $\mathbf{A}(1,2)$ and the permuted matrix $P\mathbf{A}(1,2)P^*$.

which we call the hierarchical approximation of A. The adjective 'hierarchical' refers to the fact that, roughly speaking, we approximate the completely specified matrix by the maximum entropy extension of a block matrix that is specified on a block band and whose largest principal submatrices that are contained in the band are equal to the maximum entropy extensions of the corresponding partially specified principal submatrices of A. A precise definition is given below.

Let A be a positive definite matrix that is specified on a multiple band. Let A be partitioned as $\mathbf{A} = [\mathbf{a}_{ij}]$, $i,j = 1,\ldots,n$, where the blocks $\mathbf{a}_{ij}$ are of size $n_i \times n_j$, such that for some band $\{\,(i,j) \mid |i-j| \leq m\,\}$ the partially specified principal submatrices $\mathbf{A}(j, j+m)$, $j = 1,\ldots,n-m$, can be permuted to positive definite matrices that are specified on a staircase band, and such that the blocks off its band are unspecified. Then, the columns of $\mathbf{L}^{-*}_{\mathbf{A}_H}$ are defined for $j = 1,\ldots,n-m-1$ as

$$\begin{aligned} (\mathbf{L}^{-*}_{\mathbf{A}_H})_{ij} &= (\mathbf{L}^{-*}_{\mathbf{A}(j,j+m)_{ME}})_{(i-j+1)1} & i &= j,\ldots,j+m \\ (\mathbf{L}^{-*}_{\mathbf{A}_H})_{ij} &= 0 & i &= j+m+1,\ldots,n \end{aligned} \tag{5.33}$$

and for $j = n - m, \ldots, n$ as

$$(\mathbf{L}^{-*}_{\mathbf{A}_H})_{ij} = (\mathbf{L}^{-*}_{\mathbf{A}(n-m,n)_{ME}})_{(i-(n-m)+1)(j-(n-m)+1)} \qquad i = j, \ldots, n.$$

The *hierarchical* approximation of A is defined as $A_H = L_{A_H} L^*_{A_H}$.

We proceed by assessing the distance of the triangular factor L_H^{-1} of the inverse of the hierarchical approximation of A to the triangular factor L^{-1} of the inverse of the completely specified matrix.

Theorem 10 *Let A be as defined above, and let $\mathbf{I} = \oplus_{i=1}^{n} I_{n_i}$ and $n = \sum_{i=1}^{n} n_i$. Then,*

$$||\mathbf{I} - \mathbf{L}_H^{-1}\mathbf{L}||_F = (2 - \frac{2}{n}\mathrm{tr}(\mathbf{L}_H^{-1}\mathbf{L}) + \tag{5.34}$$

$$\frac{1}{n}\sum_{j=1}^{n-m-1} \mathrm{tr}(\oplus_{i=j+1}^{j+m} I_{n_i} - \mathbf{L}^{-1}_{\mathbf{A}(j,j+m)_{ME}(2,m+1)} \mathbf{A}(j+1, j+m)\mathbf{L}^{-*}_{\mathbf{A}(j,j+m)_{ME}(2,m+1)}))^{\frac{1}{2}}.$$

Proof Adding and subtracting a number of superfluous terms we obtain that

$$\mathrm{tr}(\mathbf{L}_H^{-1}\mathbf{A}\mathbf{L}_H^{-*}) = \sum_{j=1}^{n-m} \mathrm{tr}(\mathbf{L}^{-1}_{\mathbf{A}(j,j+m)_{ME}} \mathbf{A}(j, j+m)\mathbf{L}^{-*}_{\mathbf{A}(j,j+m)_{ME}}) \tag{5.35}$$

$$- \sum_{j=1}^{n-m-1} \mathrm{tr}(\mathbf{L}^{-1}_{\mathbf{A}(j,j+m)_{ME}(2,m+1)} \mathbf{A}(j+1, j+m)\mathbf{L}^{-*}_{\mathbf{A}(j,j+m)_{ME}(2,m+1)}).$$

By Lemma 6 we have that for $j = 1, \ldots, n - m$

$$\mathrm{tr}(\mathbf{L}^{-1}_{\mathbf{A}(j,j+m)_{ME}} \mathbf{A}(j, j+m)\mathbf{L}^{-*}_{\mathbf{A}(j,j+m)_{ME}}) = \mathrm{tr}(\oplus_{i=j}^{j+m} I_{n_i}). \tag{5.36}$$

Substituting Equation 5.36 in Equation 5.35 we derive that

$$\mathrm{tr}(\mathbf{L}_H^{-1}\mathbf{A}\mathbf{L}_H^{-*}) = \mathrm{tr}\mathbf{I} + \tag{5.37}$$

$$\sum_{j=1}^{n-m-1} \mathrm{tr}(\oplus_{i=j+1}^{j+m} I_{n_i} - \mathbf{L}^{-1}_{\mathbf{A}(j,j+m)_{ME}(2,m+1)} \mathbf{A}(j+1, j+m)\mathbf{L}^{-*}_{\mathbf{A}(j,j+m)_{ME}(2,m+1)}).$$

Furthermore, we have that

$$||\mathbf{I} - \mathbf{L}_H^{-1}\mathbf{L}||_F^2 = \frac{1}{n}(\mathrm{tr}\mathbf{I} - 2\mathrm{tr}(\mathbf{L}_H^{-1}\mathbf{L}) + \mathrm{tr}(\mathbf{L}_H^{-1}\mathbf{A}\mathbf{L}_H^{-*})). \tag{5.38}$$

The proof of the theorem follows by combining Equation 5.37 and Equation 5.38. ■

It was shown in [24] that under the conditions mentioned above $||I - L_H^{-1}L||_F$ is small. In the same paper it was shown that if $||I - L_H^{-1}L||_F$ is small, then both the entries of the hierarchical approximation of A and the completely specified matrix and the entries of the inverses of these matrices are close.

The hierarchical approximation of A has two problems. The first problem is that its inverse does not have zeros in all positions that correspond to unspecified entries in A. It has zeros in the positions that correspond to unspecified entries in A, except in those positions that correspond to unspecified entries in the blocks $\mathbf{a}_{ij}$ for which $|i-j| \leq m-1$, where $2 \leq i,j \leq n-1$. For example, if A is as shown in Figure 2, and if it is partitioned as before, then A_H^{-1} has zeros in the positions that correspond to unspecified entries in A, except in those positions that correspond to unspecified entries in the block $\mathbf{a}_{22}$. The second problem is that neither the triangular factors of the inverse of the hierarchical approximation of A nor this inverse itself can be computed efficiently. Although the inverses of the maximum entropy extensions of the partially specified principal submatrices $\mathbf{A}(j, j+m)$, $j = 1, \ldots, n-m$, can be computed efficiently (see the last part of Section 4), this is not the case for the triangular factors of these inverses. The cause of this is that the sparsity patterns of the inverses (multiple bands) are not preserved during triangular factorization. Unfortunately, the triangular factors are the ones that appear in Equation 5.33. To solve the first problem mentioned above we search for a 'small' matrix Z that is such that $(A_H^{-1} + Z)$, our new approximate inverse, has zeros in all positions that correspond to unspecified entries in A. Because $(A_H^{-1} + Z)$ must be positive definite, Z must be positive semi-definite. We adopt the following approach. We first search for a matrix X that is such that $(A_H^{-1} + X)$ has zeros in all positions that correspond to unspecified entries in A. Next, we search for a matrix Y that is as 'close' as possible to X, has zeros in the positions that correspond to unspecified entries in A and is such that $(X - Y)$ is positive semi-definite. Finally, we take $Z = X - Y$.

A matrix X is readily found. Indeed, $(A_H^{-1} + X)$ with

$$X = \sum_{j=1}^{n-m-1} \nabla((\mathbf{A}(j, j+m)_{ME}(2, m+1))^{-1}, (j+1, j+m)) \qquad (5.39)$$

has zeros in all positions that correspond to unspecified entries in A. This follows from the fact that

$$A_H^{-1} + X = \sum_{j=1}^{n-m} \nabla(\mathbf{A}(j, j+m)_{ME}^{-1}, (j, j+m)),$$

and this matrix clearly has zeros in all positions that correspond to unspecified entries in A. Note that X defined in Equation 5.39 is a convenient choice, because $(A_H^{-1} + X)$ can be computed efficiently. Indeed, we can compute $\mathbf{A}(j, j+m)_{ME}^{-1}$, $j = 1, \ldots, n-m$, as described in the last part of Section 4. The problem of finding Y can be formulated as a constrained nonlinear optimization problem [24], which can be solved by using standard techniques (see, for instance, [25]). These techniques, however, require considerable computational effort.

We now assume that the maximum entropy extensions of the partially specified principal submatrices $\mathbf{A}(j+1, j+m)$, $j = 1, \ldots, n-m-1$, are good approximations of the corresponding principal submatrices of the completely specified matrix. Because we already have assumed that the maximum entropy extensions of the partially specified principal submatrices $\mathbf{A}(j, j+m)$, $j = 1, \ldots, n-m$, are good approximations of the corresponding principal submatrices of the completely specified matrix, it follows that $\mathbf{A}(j+1, j+m)_{ME}$ is a good approximation of $\mathbf{A}(j, j+m)_{ME}(2, m+1)$, $j = 1, \ldots, n-m-1$. Hence,

$$Y = \sum_{j=1}^{n-m-1} \nabla(\mathbf{A}(j+1, j+m)_{ME}^{-1}, (j+1, j+m)) \tag{5.40}$$

is a good approximation for the matrix X defined in Equation 5.39. Clearly, Y has zeros in the positions that correspond to unspecified entries in A. The difference $Z = X - Y$, however, is not necessarily positive definite. We proceed with the following definition.

Let A be as defined above. Then, the ***banded-inverse*** approximation of A is defined as

$$A_{BI}^{-1} = \sum_{j=1}^{n-m} \nabla((\mathbf{A}(j, j+m)_{ME}^{-1}, (j, j+m)) -$$

$$\sum_{j=1}^{n-m-1} \nabla(\mathbf{A}(j+1, j+m)_{ME}^{-1}, (j+1, j+m)).$$

The inverse of the banded-inverse approximation of A has zeros in all positions that correspond to unspecified entries in A. It can be computed efficiently, because the matrices $\mathbf{A}(j, j+m)_{ME}^{-1}$, $j = 1, \ldots, n-m$, and $\mathbf{A}(j+1, j+m)_{ME}^{-1}$, $j = 1, \ldots, n-m-1$, can be computed as described in the last part of Section 4. The inverse of the hierarchical approximation of A can not be guaranteed to be positive definite. Indeed, it equals $A_H^{-1} + Z$ and Z is indefinite. Because Z is 'small', we conjecture that the inverse of the hierarchical approximation of A may fail to be positive definite only if the completely specified matrix is close to singular. This conjecture has been confirmed by numerical experiments [24].

Finally, note that if $\mathbf{A}$ is Toeplitz, then only $\mathbf{A}(1, m+1)_{ME}^{-1}$ and $\mathbf{A}(2, m+1)_{ME}^{-1}$ need to be computed to obtain A_{BI}^{-1}. This leads to an enormeous reduction in computation if, for example, the physical problem that underlies the partially specified matrix is stationary.

References

[1] H. Dym and I. Gohberg, Extensions of band matrices with band inverses, *Linear Algebra Appl.*, **36**:1–24, 1981.

[2] J.P. Burg, *Maximum-Entropy Spectral Analysis*, PhD thesis, Department of Geophysics, Stanford University, Stanford, California, 1975.

[3] R. Grone, C.R. Johnson, E. M. Sá, and H. Wolkowicz, Positive definite completions of partial Hermitian matrices, *Linear Algebra Appl.*, **58**:109–124, 1984.

[4] H. Dym and I. Gohberg, On an extension problem, generalized fourier analysis, and an entropy formula, *Integral Equations and Operator Theory*, **3/2**:144–215, 1980.

[5] H.J. Woerdeman, *Strictly contractive and positive completions for block matrices*, Technical Report WS 337, Vrije Universiteit Amsterdam, November 1987.

[6] S.W. Lang and J.H. McClellan, Multidimensional MEM spectral estimation, *IEEE Transactions on Acoustics, Speech, and Signal Processing*, **30**, 1982.

[7] Z.-Q Ning, P.M. Dewilde, and F.L. Neerhoff, Capacitance coefficients for VLSI multilevel metallization lines, *IEEE Transactions on Electron Devices*, **34**, 1987.

[8] Ph. Delsarte, Y. Genin, and Y. Kamp, A method of matrix inverse triangular decomposition, based on contiguous principal submatrices, *Linear Algebra Appl.*, **31**, 1980.

[9] N. Levinson, The Wiener rms (root mean square) error criterion in filter design and prediction, *Journal on Mathematical Physics*, **25**:261–278, 1947.

[10] P. Dewilde, A. Vieira, and T. Kailath, On a generalized Szegö-Levinson realization algorithm for optimal linear prediction based on a network synthesis approach, *IEEE Transactions on Circuits and Systems*, **25**, 1978.

[11] I. Schur, Über Potentzreihen die im Innnern des Einheitskreises beschrankt sind, *Journal für die Reine und Angewandte Mathematik*, **147**, 1917.

[12] E.F. Deprettere, Mixed-form time-variant lattice recursions, *Outils et Modèles Mathematiques pour l'Automatique, l'Analyse des Systèmes, et le Traitement du Signal*, 1981.

[13] H. Lev-Ari and T. Kailath, Schur and Levinson algorithms for nonstationary processes, In *Proceedings International Conference on Acoustics, Speech, and Signal Processing*, 1981.

[14] M. Morf and J.-M. Delosme, Matrix decompositions and inversions via elementary signature-orthogonal transformations, In *Proceedings International Symposium on Mini- and Micro computers in Control and Measurement*, 1981.

[15] P. Dewilde and E.F. Deprettere, *Approximate inversion of positive matrices with applications to modelling*, pages 211–238, Springer-Verlag, 1987.

[16] J. Lim and N. Malik, A new algorithm for two-dimensional maximum entropy power spectrum estimation, *IEEE Transactions on Acoustics, Speech, and Signal Processing*, **29**, 1981.

[17] N. Rozario and A. Papoulis, Spectral estimation from nonconsecutive data, *IEEE Transactions on Information Theory*, **33**, 1987.

[18] P. Dewilde and E.F. Deprettere, The generalized Schur algorithm: approximation and hierarchy, *Operator Theory: Advances and Applications*, **29**, 1988.

[19] M. Rosenblum and J. Rovnyak, *Hardy Classes and Operator Theory*, Oxford University Press, 1985.

[20] H. Dym and I. Gohberg, A new class of contractive interpolants and maximum entropy principles, *Operator Theory: Advances and Applications*, **29**, 1988.

[21] J. Volder, The Cordic trigonometric computing technique, *IRE Transactions on EC*, **8**, 1959.

[22] J. Walter, A unified algorithm for elementary functions, In *Proceedings Spring Joint Computer Conference*, 1971.

[23] J. de Lange, A. van der Hoeven, E.F. Deprettere, and J. Bu, An optimal floating-point pipeline CMOS CORDIC processor: algorithm, automated design, layout, and performance, In *Proceedings International Symposium on Circuits and Systems*, 1988.

[24] H. Nelis, E.F. Deprettere, and P. Dewilde, *Maximum-entropy and minimum-norm matrix extensions*, Technical Report NEL 88, Department of Electrical Engineering, Delft University of Technology, December 1988.

[25] G. Luenberger, *Introduction to Linear and Nonlinear Programming*, Addison-Wesley Publishing Company, Inc., 1973.

Operator Theory:
Advances and Applications, Vol. 40

FAST AND EFFICIENT PARALLEL INVERSION OF TOEPLITZ AND BLOCK TOEPLITZ MATRICES

Dedicated to Prof. I.C. Gohberg

Victor Pan

We call an $n \times n$ matrix A well-conditioned if $\log(\text{cond } A) = O(\log n)$. We compute the inverse of any $n \times n$ well-conditioned and diagonally dominant Hermitian Toeplitz matrix A (with errors $1/2^N$, $N = n^c$ for a constant c) by a numerically stable algorithm using $O(\log^2 n \log\log n)$ parallel arithmetic steps and $n \log^2 n / \log\log n$ processors. This dramatically improves the previous results. We also compute the inverse and all the coefficients of the characteristic polynomial of any $n \times n$ nonsingular Toeplitz matrix A filled with integers (and possibly ill-conditioned) by a distinct algorithm using $O(\log^2 n)$ parallel arithmetic steps, $O(n^2)$ processors, and the precision of $O(n \log(n\|A\|_1)$ binary digits. The results have several modifications, extensions, and further applications.

1. INTRODUCTION

Computing the inverse, the determinant, and the characteristic polynomial of Toeplitz and block Toeplitz matrices has numerous applications to the theory and practice of scientific and engineering computations, in particular, to the time series analysis, image processing, control theory, statistics, solution of integral and partial differential equations ([Bun]), Padé approximation ([G]), rational interpolation ([GY] and [BGY]), partial fraction decomposition, computations with polynomials ([vzG] and [vzG86a]) and with matrix polynomials ([BKAK] and [KK]). There are effective sequential algorithms that invert an $n \times n$ Toeplitz matrix $A = [a_{ij}]$, $a_{ij} = a_{i-j}$, $i,j = 0,1,..,n-1$, using $O(n \log^2 n)$ arithmetic operations ([BGY], [BA], [M] and [dH]). More precisely, the algorithms compute a *displacement generator* of the inverse matrix A^{-1} defined by its first and last columns; then any column of A^{-1} can be computed by means of the well-known formulae from [GSe] and [GF] using $O(n \log n)$ arithmetic operations (see Theorems 6.2 and 9.1 and Remark 6.3 below on these remarkable formulae and see Section 6 or [CKL-A] for the definition and some fundamental properties of displacement generators). (Hereafter, "computing

A^{-1}" will mean computing a displacement generator of A^{-1}.) The parallelization of these algorithms only leads to their acceleration by a factor of $\log^2 n$ or less, but even such a speed-up is considered practically important in the recent foremost survey, [Kai], p. 74.

The importance of the problem, its previous heavy investigation, and the inherently sequential character of the known fast algorithms for Toeplitz matrix inversion made it unlikely to expect a more substantial parallel acceleration. Nevertheless, in this paper, we present such a surprising parallel acceleration, which we obtain by simple, although unusual means and which promises to be practical and to become a springboard for devising effective algorithms for computations with other structured matrices.

Let us specify our results assuming that the input matrix A is Toeplitz, *well-conditioned* (that is, $\log(\|A\|_h \|A^{-1}\|_h) = O(\log n)$ for $h = 1,2,\infty$) and diagonally dominant, real symmetric or Hermitian. In this case, our algorithms numerically compute the inverse matrix A^{-1} (so that the 1-norm of the matrix of absolute errors is, at most, $2^{-N(n)}\|A^{-1}\|_1$ where $N(n) = n^c$, c is any fixed constant) yielding parallel arithmetic time $O(\log^2 n \log\log n)$ and thus accelerating the best sequential algorithms by roughly a factor of n, under a customary machine models of parallel arithmetic computations described below. So far, such an acceleration has been reached only by means of blowing up the number of the involved processors to more than n^2 and of allowing the precision of computations to exceed the input precision about n times ([BGH]). We do not need such a sacrifice: our algorithms are numerically stable and, moreover, self-correcting, and we only use $n \log^2 n / \log\log n$ processors in order to support the cited parallel time bound $O(\log^2 n \log\log n)$. Actually, we may speed up the computations $c \log\log n$ times for the price of increasing the processor bound by a factor of $(\log n)^{2c}$ for any positive constant c. Furthermore, we only need $O(\log^2 n)$ steps and n processors if the input Toeplitz matrix $A = [a_{i-j}]$ is *very strongly diagonally dominant,* that is, if

$$\|DA - I\|_\infty \leq q < 1 \text{ or } \|AD - I\|_1 \leq q < 1, \quad (1.1)$$

where I is the identity matrix, $D = I/a_0$, and q is a constant.

Here and hereafter, we assume the customary machine model of parallel arithmetic computations (see [BGH] and [vzG86]) where the computational cost is measured by the numbers of parallel steps and processors used, where each processor performs, at most, one arithmetic operation in each step, and where we may s times decrease the processor bound by slowing down the computations O(s) times.

We present the parallel time and processor bounds up to within constant factors.

Actually, we reduce all our Toeplitz computations to performing some multiplications of n×n triangular Toeplitz matrices by vectors, and each such an operation is further reduced to three applications of *fast Fourier transform (FFT)* at $N = O(n)$ points, so that the estimates of this paper hold under any model of parallel computation where $O(\log n)$ parallel arithmetic steps and n processors suffice in order to perform FFT at n points, which is a perfectly realistic assumption (see [Quinn]).

We extend our results to the inversion of well-conditioned real symmetric or Hermitian block Toeplitz matrices (see Remark 9.1 in Section 9) and then further to computations with any Toeplitz or Toeplitz-like matrix (see Appendix and [P88b]).

The algorithms rely on our new modification of Newton's iteration; they remain numerically stable and, moreover, self-correcting, even where the input matrix A is not positive definite, in which case the known fast algorithms for Toeplitz matrix inversion are unstable (see [Bun]).

In the next statement of our main theorem, we do not require the input matrix A be well-conditioned, but the computational cost of the inversion of A grows with the condition number of A, that is, our algorithm slows down if it is applied to the inversion of ill-conditioned Toeplitz matrices (but see an alternative in the Appendix).

THEOREM 1.1. *Let* $h=1,2,$ *or* ∞, *and let* $\tilde{\kappa}_h$ *denote an upper estimate available for* $\kappa_h = \kappa_h(A) = \|A\|_h \|A^{-1}\|_h$.

a) *Given a positive* ϵ *and an* n×n *real symmetric or Hermitian or (row- or column-) diagonally dominant Toeplitz matrix* A, *it suffices to use* $O((\log n)(\log(n\,\tilde{\kappa}_h)\log\log(n\,\tilde{\kappa}_h) + \log\log(1/\epsilon)))$ *parallel arithmetic steps and* $n\log^2(n\,\tilde{\kappa}_h)/\log\log(n\tilde{\kappa}_h)$ *processors in order to compute a matrix* $\tilde{A}^{-1}$ *such that*

$$\|\tilde{A}^{-1} - A^{-1}\|_h \leq \epsilon \|A^{-1}\|_h. \tag{1.2}$$

b) *Furthermore, for any positive* $c < 1$, $O((\log n)((1/c)\log(n\tilde{\kappa}_h) + \log\log(1/\epsilon)))$ *parallel arithmetic steps and* $n(\log(n\tilde{\kappa}_h))^{2+2c}/\log\log(n\tilde{\kappa}_h)$ *processors also suffice.*

REMARK 1.1. We do not have to specify h in Theorem 1.1 because $\log(n\kappa_h)$ is invariant in h within a constant factor.

Theorem 1.1 implies the cited bounds (that is, $O(\log^2 n \log\log n)$ steps and $n \log^2 n/\log\log n$ processors and, alternatively, $O((1/c)\log^2 n)$ and $n(\log n)^{2+2c}/\log\log n$) provided that $\log\log(1/\epsilon) = O(\log n)$ and A is a well-conditioned matrix. The estimates stated for a very strongly diagonally dominant matrix A do not follow from Theorem 1.1 but are yielded using the same algorithm that supports the theorem (see Remark 7.2 in Section 7).

Let us outline this algorithm, based on Newton's iteration

$$X_{g+1} = X_g\,(2I - W\,X_g), \tag{1.3}$$

$g=0,1,\ldots$, which rapidly converges to the inverse W^{-1} of a given matrix W provided that

$$\| W\,X_0 - I \|_h \le q < 1 \tag{1.4}$$

for h=1 or h=2 and for a constant q. (Alternatively, we could have relied on *any* other effective iterative algorithm for matrix inversion, compare [PS88].) If (1.4) holds, we will call the matrix X_0 an *approximate inverse* of W with respect to the h-norm of matrices and to a parameter q (hereafter, we will use the abbreviation *a.i.*(h,q) of W). The computational cost of the iteration step (1.3) is low if W is a Toeplitz matrix and if X_g is a structured Toeplitz-like matrix available with its displacement generator of small length d; in this case, the step (1.3) can be reduced to O(d) concurrent applications of *discrete Fourier transform (DFT)* performed by means of FFT's. Thus, to invert a given Toeplitz matrix A, it would be sufficient if we computed:

1°) an approximate inverse X_0 of A satisfying the inequalities (1.4) for W=A and having a displacement generator of small length and

2°) the matrices X_{g+1} with their displacement generators of bounded length for $g=0,1,\ldots$

Homotopic Variation of the Matrix Diagonal

Task 1^0) is trivially solved if $A = [a_{i-j}]$ is a very strongly diagonally dominant Toeplitz matrix (see (1.1)), for we just set $X_0 = I/a$ in this case. If the matrix A is real symmetric, Hermitian, or diagonally dominant (but not very strongly), then recursively compute an approximate inverse X_0 of A as follows: Start with a close approximation I/a to the inverse of the matrix $A_0 = A + aI$ (where we choose a sufficiently large value for the scalar a) and then recursively apply the iteration (1.3) with $W = A_j = A + ap^{\,j}I$ in order to numerically invert the matrices A_j (with high precision) for j=1,2,... and for a small positive p. The *key idea* is that an a.i.(h,1−p) of A_j is supplied for every j by the previous step of the inversion of the matrix A_{j-1}, for

$$\| A_j A_{j-1}^{-1} - I \|_h \leq 1-p.$$

Thus, we let $\tilde{A}_j^{-1}$ denote the computed numerical approximation to A_j^{-1} and successively compute the matrices

$A_0 = A + aI$, $\tilde{A}_0^{-1}$ by applying the iteration (1.3) with $X_0 = I/a$,

$A_1 = A + apI$, $\tilde{A}_1^{-1}$ by applying the iteration (1.3) with $X_0 = \tilde{A}_0^{-1}$,

$A_2 = A + ap^2I$, $\tilde{A}_2^{-1}$ by applying the iteration (1.3) with $X_0 = \tilde{A}_1^{-1}$,

....

Decreasing 1−p would improve the approximation to A_j^{-1} by A_{j-1}^{-1} and thus would speed up the convergence of the iteration (1.3), but decreasing p would accelerate the convergence of the matrices A_j to A and, consequently, of the matrices A_j^{-1} to A^{-1}. Actually, we will not need to update the matrix A_j for j=m if the computed matrix $\tilde{A}_m^{-1}$ is an a.i.(h,1−p) of A; at this point, we will numerically compute A^{-1} by applying the iteration (1.3) with $X_0 = \tilde{A}_m^{-1}$. We will estimate that $\tilde{A}_m^{-1}$ is an a.i.(h,1−p) of A for m being of an order of $\log(n\kappa_h)/\log(1/p)$ and that, for each j, the iteration (1.3) started with $\tilde{A}_{j-1}^{-1}$ converges to $\tilde{A}_j^{-1}$ in $O(\log\log \kappa_h + \log(1/p))$ steps. At this point, we may choose $1/p = O(1)$ and derive Theorem 1.1a, or we may choose 1/p of an order of $(\log n)^c$ for a constant $c > 0$ and derive Theorem 1.1b.

The presented method for computing an a.i.(h,1−p) of a matrix A is a new modification of the *variable diagonal techniques* of [P85] and [P87a]. We will call this modification the *homotopic variation of the matrix diagonal.* The method applies to the inversion of any nonsingular matrix A (not necessarily Toeplitz) and can be used for an alternative derivation of the complexity estimates of [Be] and [PR] for parallel inversion of well-conditioned general (nonToeplitz) matrices.

Newton's Iteration for the Inversion of Toeplitz Matrices

To exploit the displacement structure of the matrices W and X_g, we need to solve task 2^0) of computing displacement generators of appropriately bounded length d_g for the matrices X_g of (1.3). The available upper bound on the value $\log d_g$ grows proportionally to g as g grows large, which implies too large upper bounds on the overall computational cost of the above algorithm for the inversion of a Toeplitz matrix A. Thus, we modify the iteration (1.3) by adding steps that improve the structure of the computed approximation matrices X_g: we fix a monotone growing sequence of integers (g(0),g(1),...) where g(0) is sufficiently large and $g(s+1)-g(s) \leq 2$ for s=0,1,..., let the matrices X_{g+1} be defined by the iteration (1.3), unless g=g(s) for s=0,1,..., and let

$$X_{g+1} = \hat{X}_g(2I - W\,\hat{X}_g) \text{ for } g=g(s),\ s=0,1,... \tag{1.5}$$

Here, the matrix $\hat{X}_g$ is obtained with its displacement generator of length, at most, 2 by applying the already cited formula from [GSe]. This formula expresses the inverse W^{-1} of a Toeplitz matrix W through its first and its last columns, and, by means of the same formula, we express the matrix $\hat{X}_g$ through the first and the last columns of the matrix X_g, approximating to W^{-1} (see the equation (7.2) in Section 7).

We will show that the norm $\| \hat{X}_g - W^{-1} \|$ is proportional to the norm $\| X_g - W^{-1} \|$, which is small for a large enough g=g(0), since the iteration (1.3) very rapidly converges to W^{-1}. It follows that the modified iteration still exponentially rapidly converges to the solution. On the other hand, the transition from $X_{g(s)}$ to $\hat{X}_{g(s)}$ improves the structure of the approximation matrices, that is, the matrices $\hat{X}_{g(s)}$ for all s are computed with their displacement generators of length 2; this enables us to compute displacement generators of appropriately bounded length for the matrices X_g for all g, that is, to solve our task 2^0).

Our construction may serve as a specific example of the solution of a more general problem of imposing the desired structure on the auxiliary matrices computed in an iterative process and thus simplifying its every iterative step, without damaging the convergence property.

We will elaborate and substantiate the presented outline in the following order: In Section 2, we will recall some definitions and auxiliary results on matrix computations. In Section 3, we will recall the estimates for the convergence rate of Newton's iteration. In Sections 4 and 5, we will present our new iterative algorithm that computes an a.i. of a matrix A, and we will estimate the overall number of steps of Newton's iteration required by this algorithm for the numerical inversion of a general (nonToeplitz) matrix A. In Section 6, we will recall some auxiliary definitions and facts from the area of computations with structured matrices. In Section 7, we will complete the proof of Theorem 1.1 in the case of symmetric positive definite Toeplitz matrices A. In Section 8, we will discuss the extension of the algorithm to the inversion of any matrix having displacement generators of small length, and then, in Sections 8 and 9, we will specify such an extension and will substantiate the parallel cost bounds in the two cases: of diagonally dominant and of real symmetric Toeplitz matrices. All the results and proofs given in the real symmetric case can be routinely extended to the Hermitian case. In Section 9 (in Remark 9.1), we will comment on the block Toeplitz case.

The Ill Conditioned Case

The above approach performs poorly for ill-conditioned Toeplitz matrices A. In the Appendix, we describe a distinct algorithm that exactly computes all the coefficients of the characteristic polynomial and the inverse of any nonsingular $n \times n$ Toeplitz matrix filled with integers. This algorithm uses $O(\log^2 n)$ parallel arithmetic steps, n^2 processors, and the precision of computations of an order of the output precision. The output precision is generally high, however, since the output values are computed exactly, so, the algorithm seems to be more suitable for computer algebra than for numerical computations, and some of the several immediate applications of the algorithm to computer algebra are shown in the Appendix. On the other hand, in some applications, only few leading coefficients of the characteristic polynomial of A are sought, and then the algorithm of the Appendix can be performed with lower precision and turns into an effective numerical algorithm.

Acknowledgements. The author thanks Professors Dario Bini, George Cybenko, Thomas Kailath, Hanoch Lev-Ari, William Trench, Joachim von zur Gathen, and David Yun for the generous and very helpful supply of the copies of papers relevant to Toeplitz computations, the National Science Foundation for the support under the grant CCR 88 05782, and also Sally Goodall for her superb assistance with typing this paper.

2. SOME DEFINITIONS AND AUXILIARY RESULTS

We will use some customary definitions and will refer to some basic facts of the theory of matrix computations ([GL], [Par] and [W]). In particular, hereafter, we will write I to denote the $n \times n$ identity matrix; $\mathrm{diag}(a_1,\ldots,a_n)$ will denote the diagonal matrix with the diagonal entries $a_1,\ldots,a_n$; $\mathbf{v}^r$ will denote the vector obtained by reversing the order of the entries of a vector $\mathbf{v}$. A^T and $\mathbf{v}^T$ will denote the transposes of a matrix A and of a vector $\mathbf{v}$, respectively; $\|A\|_h$ will denote the h-norm of a matrix A; $\kappa_h(A) = \infty$ if A is a singular matrix, $\kappa_h(A) = \|A\|_h \, \|A^{-1}\|_h$ otherwise, for $h=1,2,\infty$. We will write $\kappa_h = \kappa_h(A)$.

PROPOSITION 2.1. *Let* $A = [a_{ij}]$ *be an* $n \times n$ *matrix. Then* $\| A \|_1 = \| A^T \|_\infty = \max_j \sum_i |a_{ij}|$, $\| A \|_h / \sqrt{n} \le \| A \|_2 \le \| A \|_h \sqrt{n}$, $\| A \|_h / n \le \max_{i,j} |a_{ij}| \le \| A \|_h$ *for* $h = 1,2,\infty$. *Furthermore,* $\|A\|_h \ge \|A\|_2$ *if* A *is a symmetric matrix.*

For a matrix $A = [a_{ij}]$, let $D(A) = \mathrm{diag}(1/a_{11},\ldots,1/a_{nn})$. A matrix $A = [a_{ij}]$ is *column-diagonally dominant* (c.-d.d.) if $\| AD(A) - I \|_1 < 1$, *row-diagonally dominant* (r.-d.d.) if $\| D(A)A - I \|_\infty < 1$, and *normalized* if $D(A) = I$.

Remark 2.1. The inversion of an r.-d.d. matrix B can be immediately reduced to the inversion of the c.-d.d. matrix $A = B^T$ (since $B^{-1} = (A^{-1})^T$) and, further, to the inversion of the n.c.-d.d. matrix $AD(A)$ (since $A^{-1} = D(A)(AD(A))^{-1}$).

In addition to the latter abbreviations and to the abbreviation a.i.(h,q) of A, introduced earlier, we will write *s.p.d.* for *symmetric positive definite,* that is, for real symmetric matrices having only positive eigenvalues and thus equal to the products $V^T V$ for some nonsingular matrices V.

PROPOSITION 2.2. *Let* A *be an* $n \times n$ *s.p.d. matrix having eigenvalues* $\lambda_1, \ldots, \lambda_n$, *such that* $0 < \lambda_n \le \ldots \le \lambda_1$. *Then*

$$\| A \|_2 = \lambda_1, \ \| A^{-1} \|_2 = 1/\lambda_n, \tag{2.1}$$

and, consequently,

$$\| A + aI \|_2 = \lambda_1 + a, \ \| (A + aI)^{-1} \|_2 = 1/(\lambda_n + a) \tag{2.2}$$

for any positive scalar a.

For simplicity, we will work with real symmetric matrices, but the extension to the complex Hermitian matrices is straightforward.

Hereafter, log and ln will denote logarithms to the base 2 and to the exponential base, respectively.

3. NEWTON'S ITERATION AND ITS EXPONENTIAL CONVERGENCE

We will use the following simple and well-known result:

PROPOSITION 3.1. *Let matrices* $X_1, X_2, \ldots$ *be defined by Newton's iteration (1.3), given matrices* W *and* X_0. *Let* $G = 2^g$ *for* $g = 1,2,\ldots$ *Then*

$$I - WX_g = (WX_{g-1} - I)^2, \ \| WX_g - I \| \le \| WX_{g-1} - I \|^2 \le \| WX_0 - I \|^G$$

for any fixed matrix norm and for $g=1,2,\ldots$ *Furthermore, if* $q = \| WX_0 - I\| < 1$, *then the matrix* W *is nonsingular, and*

$$\| W^{-1}\| \le \|X_0\| / (1-q),\ \| X_g - W^{-1}\| \le q^G \| W^{-1}\| \textit{ for } G=2^g,\ g=0,1,\ldots$$

4. NUMERICAL INVERSION OF A SYMMETRIC POSITIVE DEFINITE MATRIX

Hereafter, until Remark 5.2 of Section 5, A will denote an s.p.d. matrix, not necessarily Toeplitz matrix.

ALGORITHM 4.1. Input. An s.p.d. matrix $A = [a_{ij}]$ and a positive ϵ.

Output. A matrix $\tilde{A}^{-1}$ satisfying (1.2) for h=2.

The Initialization Stage. Fix a natural m and positive p, q, $\tilde{q}$ and δ such that $p = 1-q$, $\tilde{q} = 1-(p+p^2)/2$, and m and δ satisfy the bounds of Propositions 4.1, 5.3 and 5.4 below (also compare Remark 5.1 below); denote $A_{-1} = aI$; compute the scalar a and the matrix $\tilde{A}_{-1}^{-1}$ such that

$$a = n \max_{i,j} |a_{ij}| / q,\ \tilde{A}_{-1}^{-1} = A_{-1}^{-1} = I / a. \tag{4.1}$$

Stage j, j=0,1,...,m. Let

$$A_j = A + a_j I,\ a_j = ap^j,\ p=1-q,\ g = \lceil \log(\log \delta / \log \tilde{q}) \rceil,\ \tilde{q} = 1-(p+p^2)/2, \tag{4.2}$$

and apply g iteration steps (1.3) with $W = A_j$ and with $X_0 = \tilde{A}_{j-1}^{-1}$ in order to compute the matrix $\tilde{A}_j^{-1} = X_g$; we will deduce for $\delta = \tilde{q}^G$, $G = 2^g$ that

$$\| \tilde{A}_j^{-1} - A_j^{-1}\|_2 \le \delta \| A_j^{-1}\|_2. \tag{4.3}$$

Stage m+1. Apply the iteration (1.3) where $W = A$, $X_0 = \tilde{A}_m^{-1}$ in order to compute an approximation $\tilde{A}^{-1}$ to A^{-1} satisfying the bound (1.2) for h=2.

At Stage m of Algorithm 4.1, we compute a matrix $\tilde{A}_m^{-1}$ such that the inequality (4.3) holds for j=m and for $A_m = A+ap^mI$. Note that

$$A\, A_m^{-1} - I = (I - A_m A^{-1}) A\, A_m^{-1} = -ap^m A_m^{-1}. \tag{4.4}$$

Therefore, $\| A\, A_m^{-1} - I\| = ap^m \| A_m^{-1}\|$ for any matrix norm. Propositions 2.1 and 2.2 and the equations (4.1) and (4.2) imply that

$$q\, a \le n \| A\|_2,\ \| A_m^{-1}\|_2 \le \| A^{-1}\|_2.$$

We substitute these bounds into the equation (4.4), obtain that $\|A\,A_m^{-1}-I\|_2 \le p^m n\,\kappa_2/q$ and arrive at the following result:

PROPOSITION 4.1. *The matrix* A_m^{-1} *approximated at Stage* m *of Algorithm 4.1 is an a.i.*(2,q) *of* A *provided that the equations (4.1) and (4.2) hold and that*

$$m \ge \log(n\kappa_2/\,q^2)/\log(1/\,p). \tag{4.5}$$

5. THE COMPLEXITY OF THE INVERSION OF A SYMMETRIC POSITIVE DEFINITE MATRIX

PROPOSITION 5.1. *Let matrices* $A_0, A_1, \ldots$ *be defined by the equations (4.1) and (4.2). Let* $A_{-1} = aI$. *Then the matrix* A_{j-1}^{-1} *is an a.i.(2,q) of the matrix* A_j *for every* $j \ge 0$.

Since $A_0A_{-1}^{-1} - I = A/\,a$, Proposition 5.1 for j=0 immediately follows from Proposition 2.1. For $j \ge 1$, Proposition 5.1 is immediately implied by the following result to be applied to $B = A_j$, $C = A_{j-1}$, and $b = ap^{\,j-1}$:

PROPOSITION 5.2. *Let A be an s.p.d. matrix,* $B = A + bpI$, $C = A + bI$ *for two positive constants* b *and* p, p<1. *Let* q=1−p. *Then the matrix* C^{-1} *is an a.i.(2,q) of the matrix* B.

PROOF. $BC^{-1}-I = (C-bqI)C^{-1}-I = -bqC^{-1}$, so that $\|BC^{-1}-I\| = bq\|C^{-1}\|$ for any matrix norms. It remains to deduce from the equations (2.1) and (2.2) that

$$\|C^{-1}\|_2 = 1/\,(b + 1/\,\|A^{-1}\|_2) < 1/\,b. \tag{5.1}$$

Q.E.D.

If the value δ in the inequalities (4.3) is small enough, then, for each j, not only is the matrix A_{j-1}^{-1} is an a.i.(2,q) of A_j, but also the matrix $\tilde{A}_{j-1}^{-1}$ is an a.i.(2,$\tilde{q}$) of A_j where $\tilde{q} = \tilde{q}(\delta,q)$, $q < \tilde{q} < 1$. Indeed, start with the relations $\|A_jA_{j-1}^{-1}-I\| \le q < 1$ and $\|\tilde{A}_{j-1}^{-1}-A_{j-1}^{-1}\| \le \delta\,\|A_{j-1}^{-1}\|$ for the 2-norm of matrices and obtain that

$$\|A_j\tilde{A}_{j-1}^{-1}-I\| \le \|A_jA_{j-1}^{-1}-I\| + \|A_j(\tilde{A}_{j-1}^{-1}-A_{j-1}^{-1})\| \le q+\delta\,\|A_j\|\ \ \|A_{j-1}^{-1}\|\,. \tag{5.2}$$

The relations (5.1) for $C = A_{j-1}$ and for $b = a_{j-1} = ap^{\,j-1}$ imply that

$$\|A_{j-1}^{-1}\|_2 \le 1/\,(a_{j-1}+1/\,\|A^{-1}\|_2) < \min\,\{1/\,a_{j-1},\ \|A^{-1}\|_2\}. \tag{5.3}$$

On the other hand, the equations (4.2) imply that for any matrix norm $\| A_j \| \leq \| A \| + ap^j = \| A \| + pa_{j-1}$. Substitute the latter bound and the relations (5.3) into the inequality (5.2) and deduce that $\| A_j \tilde{A}_{j-1}^{-1} - I \|_2 \leq q + \delta\,(p + \kappa_2)$.

PROPOSITION 5.3. *The matrix* $\tilde{A}_{j-1}^{-1}$ *computed at Stage j of Algorithm 4.1 is an a.i.*$(2, \tilde{q})$ *of* A_j *for* $\tilde{q} = (1+u)q < 1$ *and for all* j *if* $\delta \leq uq/(p+\kappa_2) < 1$.

At this point, we set $u = p/2$, so that $\tilde{q} = 1 - p(p+1)/2 < 1$, combine Propositions 3.1 and 5.3 and deduce the bound (4.3) by induction on j.

Similarly, we prove the following result:

PROPOSITION 5.4. $\tilde{A}_m^{-1}$ *is an a.i.*$(2, \tilde{q})$ *of* A *for* $\tilde{q} = (1+u)q$ *if* $\tilde{q} < 1$, $\delta \leq uq/(p + \kappa_2) < 1$ *and* m *satisfies the inequality (4.5).*

PROOF. $\| A\, \tilde{A}_m^{-1} - I \| \leq \| A\, A_m^{-1} - I \| + \| A(\tilde{A}_m^{-1} - A_m^{-1}) \| \leq q + \delta \| A \| \; \| A_m^{-1} \|$ (due to Proposition 4.1 and to the inequality (4.3) for j=m); $\| A_m^{-1} \|_2 \leq \| A^{-1} \|_2$ (due to the bound (5.3)). Therefore, $\| A\, \tilde{A}_m^{-1} - I \|_2 \leq q + \delta\, \kappa_2 < q + \delta\,(p + \kappa_2)$. Q.E.D.

Combining Propositions 3.1, 4.1, 5.3 and 5.4 implies the following result:

COROLLARY 5.1. *Let* A *be an* n×n *s.p.d. matrix and* p, q, $\tilde{q}$ *and* ϵ *be positive scalars such that* $p = 1 - q$ *and* $\tilde{q} = 1 - (p + p^2)/2$. *Let a positive* δ *and an integer* m *satisfy the bounds of Propositions 4.1, 5.3 and 5.4 for* $u = p/2$ *and let*

$$s = (m+1) \lceil \log(\ln \delta / \ln \tilde{q}) \rceil; \; k(\epsilon) = \lceil \log(\ln \epsilon / \ln \tilde{q}) \rceil.$$

Then it takes, at most, s *steps (1.3) in Algorithm 4.1 to compute matrices* $\tilde{A}_j^{-1}$ *satisfying the bound (4.3) for* $j = 0,1,\ldots,m$; *furthermore, when the matrix* $\tilde{A}_m^{-1}$ *satisfying the bound (4.3) for* j=m *has been computed, it takes, at most,* $k(\epsilon)$ *further steps (1.3) in order to compute a matrix* $\tilde{A}^{-1}$ *satisfying the bound (1.2) for* h=2.

Here are the explicit expressions of Corollary 5.1 for s, $k(\epsilon)$, m and $1/\delta$ provided that $p < 1/2$:

$$s = (m+1) \left\lceil \log \frac{2 \ln(1/\delta)}{p+p^2} \right\rceil; \; k(\epsilon) = \left\lceil \log \frac{2 \ln(1/\epsilon)}{p+p^2} \right\rceil;$$

$$m \geq \frac{\ln(n\kappa_2/(1-p)^2)}{\ln(1/p)}, \; 1/\delta \geq 2(p+\kappa_2)/(p(1-p)).$$

Next, we will specify our upper bounds on $s + k(\epsilon)$ for some particular choices of p.

COROLLARY 5.2. *Let* p *be a small positive value,*

$$m = O(\ln(n\kappa_2)/\ln(1/p)),\ \ln\ln(1/\delta) = O(\log\log\kappa_2 + \log\log(1/p)). \tag{5.4}$$

Then the overall number of steps (1.3) in Algorithm 4.1 is bounded as follows:

$$s + k(\epsilon) = O(\log(n\kappa_2)(1 + \log\log\kappa_2/\log(1/p)) + \log(1/p) + \log\log(1/\epsilon)),$$

so that

$$s + k(\epsilon) = (\log(n\kappa_2) + \log\log(1/\epsilon))$$

if

$$\log\log\kappa_2 \leq (1/c)\log(1/p) \leq \log(n\kappa_2) \tag{5.5}$$

for a positive constant c*;*

$$s + k(\epsilon) = O(\log(n\kappa_2)\log\log\kappa_2 + \log\log(1/\epsilon))$$

if $1/p = O(1)$ *(say if* $p = 1/4$*).*

REMARK 5.1. Choosing m, p and δ that satisfy the relations (5.4) and (5.5) and the bounds of Propositions 4.1, 5.3 and 5.4, we assume the estimates for the values $\ln(n\kappa_2)$ and $\log\log\kappa_2$ available. (Note the helpful relations: $\kappa_2 \leq n\|X_g\|_1\|W\|_1 / (1-q(g))$ provided that $q(g) \geq \|I-W X_g\|_2$ and $g \geq 0$.) Alternatively, for a fixed value p (say, for $p = 1/4$), we may just test the inequalities $\sqrt{n}\ \|\tilde{A}_{j-1}^{-1}A_j - I\|_1 \leq \tilde{q}$ for the candidate values $\tilde{A}_{j-1}^{-1}$ and $\sqrt{n}\ \|\tilde{A}_m^{-1}A_j - I\|_1 \leq \tilde{q}$ for the candidate values $\tilde{A}_m^{-1}$.

REMARK 5.2. Algorithm 4.1 can be extended in order to invert any nonsingular matrix A (not necessarily s.p.d.) for we may invert the s.p.d. matrix A^TA and then compute $A^{-1} = (A^TA)^{-1}A^T$ (compare Remark 7.1 below).

6. DISPLACEMENT REPRESENTATION OF STRUCTURED MATRICES AND OF THEIR INVERSES

In the following sections we will deal with structured matrices A and B having (nonunique) *displacement representations*,

$$A = \sum_{i=1}^{d} L(\mathbf{x}^{(i)})\, U(\mathbf{y}^{(i)}), \tag{6.1}$$

$$B = \sum_{i=1}^{d^*} U(\mathbf{u}^{(i)})\, L(\mathbf{v}^{(i)}) \tag{6.2}$$

(see [KKM], [KVM], [FKML] and [CKL-A]). Here and hereafter, $L(\mathbf{w})$ and $U^T(\mathbf{z})$ denote the lower triangular Toeplitz matrices, defined by their first columns $\mathbf{w}$ and $\mathbf{z}$, respectively.

The following theorem motivates using the word "displacement" and clarifies the essence of the concepts of displacement representations:

THEOREM 6.1 ([KKM]). *The representations (6.1) and (6.2) hold for a pair of matrices* A *and* B, *respectively, if and only if*

$$A - Z\,A\,Z^T = \sum_{i=1}^{d} \mathbf{x}^{(i)}\mathbf{y}^{(i)T},\ B - Z^T B\,Z = \sum_{i=1}^{d} \mathbf{u}^{(i)r}(\mathbf{v}^{(i)r})^T$$

where $\mathbf{u}^{(i)r},\mathbf{v}^{(i)r}$ *denote the reverse vectors* $\mathbf{u}^{(i)},\mathbf{v}^{(i)}$, *respectively, and* Z *denotes the lower-shift (lower-displacement) matrix, zero everywhere, except for its first subdiagonal, filled with ones.*

In particular, a *Toeplitz matrix* $A = [a_{ij}]$ (where $a_{ij} = a_{i-j}$) has a nonunique representation $A = L + U = LI + IU = IL + UI$, so the equations (6.1) and (6.2) hold for $d = d^* = 2$. Furthermore, Theorem 6.1 enables us to compute the displacement representations (6.1), (6.2) of length, at most, $d \leq m+n$ for any $m\times n$ block matrix with Toeplitz blocks.

For any matrix A, the minimum integer $d = d(A)$ in its representation (6.1) is called the LU-*displacement rank* of A. For any displacement representation (6.1) of A, the pair of matrices (X,Y) formed by the d vector pairs $(\mathbf{x}^{(i)},\mathbf{y}^{(i)})$, i=1,2,...,d, is called an LU-*displacement generator* of length d for the matrix A and will be denoted $G_d(A)$. Similarly, the representation (6.2) defines the dual concepts of UL-displacement rank and generator. For brevity, we will mostly work with the LU-displacement representation (6.1), and will usually omit the dual properties of the UL-displacement representation (6.2); furthermore, we will usually omit the prefix LU.

Fact 6.1. *Given a vector* $\mathbf{v}$ *of length* n *and a displacement generator* $G_d(A)$ *of length* d *for an* $n\times n$ *matrix* A, *the vectors* $A\mathbf{v}$ *and* $\mathbf{v}^T A = (A^T\mathbf{v})^T$ *can be computed by means of* O(d) *concurrent applications of fast Fourier transform (FFT) at O(n) points and of two summations of d vectors of length* n.

THEOREM 6.2 ([CKL-A]). *Let a pair of* $n\times n$ *matrices* A *and* B *be given with their displacement generators of length* d_1 *and* d_2, *respectively. Then displacement generators of the matrices* A^TA *and* AB *of length, at most,* $d_1 + d_2 + 1$ *can be computed by means of* $O(d_1d_2)$ *concurrent applications of FFT at* O(n) *points and of*

$O(d_1 + d_2)$ *concurrent summations, each being the summation of* $O(d_1 + d_2)$ *vectors of length* n, *that is, the entire evaluation involves* $O(\log n)$ *parallel arithmetic steps and* $(d_1 + d_2)^2 n$ *processors.*

COROLLARY 6.1. *Let two* $n \times n$ *matrices* W *and* X_0 *be given with their displacement generators of length* $d \leq 2$ *and* $d_0 \leq 2$, *respectively; let* X_g *denote the matrix computed in* g *steps of Newton's iteration (1.3), and let* $G = 2^g$. *Then* $O(g \log n)$ *parallel arithmetic steps and* $G^2 n$ *processors suffice in order to compute a displacement generator of length, at most,* $d_g \leq 7G-5$ *for the matrix* X_g. *Furthermore, it suffices to slow down* $\lceil g/2^j \rceil$ *times the parallel implementation of the* $(g-j)$*-th steps (1.3) for* $j=1,2,\ldots, \lceil \log g \rceil$ *in order to decrease the processor bound by a factor of* g *preserving the asymptotic parallel step bound* $O(g \log n)$.

REMARK 6.1. For arbitrary d and d_0, the length of computed displacement generator of the matrix X_g is bounded as follows: $d_g \leq 2d_{g-1} + d + 3 \leq G\, d_0 + (G-1)(d+3)$, $G = 2^g$.

THEOREM 6.3. *Let* $W = [w_{ij}]$ *be the* $n \times n$ *leading principal submatrix of an* $(n+1) \times (n+1)$ *Toeplitz matrix* W^*, *both* W *and* W^* *be nonsingular; let* $\mathbf{x} = [x_0,\ldots,x_{n-1}]^T$ *and* $[x_0^*,\ldots,x_n^*]^T$ *be the first columns of the inverse matrices* W^{-1} *and* $(W^*)^{-1}$, *let* $\mathbf{y}^r = [y_{n-1},\ldots,y_0]^T$ *and* $[y_n^*,\ldots,y_0^*]^T$ *be the last columns of the same matrices. Let* $\mathbf{x}^* = [x_0^*,\ldots,x_{n-1}^*]^T$, $\mathbf{y} = [y_0,\ldots,y_{n-1}]^T$, $\mathbf{y}^* = [y_0^*,\ldots,y_{n-1}^*]^T$, $\mathbf{u} = [0,x_{n-1},\ldots,x_1]^T$, $\mathbf{v} = [0,y_{n-1},\ldots,y_1]^T$, $\mathbf{u}^* = [x_n^*,\ldots,x_1^*]^T$, $\mathbf{v}^* = [y_n^*,\ldots,y_1^*]^T$. *Then*

$$x_0 W^{-1} = L(\mathbf{x})U(\mathbf{y}) - L(\mathbf{v})U(\mathbf{u}), \tag{6.3}$$

$$x_0^* W^{-1} = L(\mathbf{x}^*)U(\mathbf{y}^*) - L(\mathbf{v}^*)U(\mathbf{u}^*), \tag{6.4}$$

$$x_0^* = y_0^* = \det W / \det W^*.$$

REMARK 6.2. We will use the expression (6.3) if $x_0 \neq 0$ and the expression (6.4) if $x_0 = 0$. In the latter case, $x_0^* = \det W/\det W^* \neq 0$. More specifically, the Toeplitz matrix W^* is completely defined by its submatrix W and by its two corner entries w_{n0}^* and w_{0n}^*; furthermore, $\det W^* \neq 0$ if $\det W \neq 0$, $x_0 = 0$, $w_{0n}^* = 1$, and $w_{n0}^* \neq 1$ (see [BGY]), so that Theorem 6.3 gives a displacement representation (6.1) of length 2 for the inverse of any nonsingular Toeplitz matrix W.

REMARK 6.3. Theorem 6.3 and its various extensions can be found in [GSe], [GF], p. 90, [T64], [T65], [BGY], pp. 277-279, [FKML], p. 34, [Heinig], [B-AS85], [B-AS86], [KC], [HR], [Tism] and [BA]. This theorem is a matrix analog of the Christoffel-Darboux formula for orthogonal polynomials.

In Section 8 we will refer to the following result:

THEOREM 6.4 ([KKM]). *Let a nonsingular* $n \times n$ *matrix* A *have an* LU- *(or a* UL-*) displacement rank* d. *Then the matrix* $B = A^{-1}$ *has a* UL- *(or an* LU-*) displacement rank d, respectively.*

7. MODIFIED NEWTON'S ITERATION FOR THE INVERSION OF SYMMETRIC POSITIVE DEFINITE MATRICES

In this section, we will combine the results of Sections 5 and 6 in order to arrive at Theorem 1.1. We will apply Algorithm 4.1 in order to invert an s.p.d. Toeplitz matrix A; at each stage j of Algorithm 4.1, we will replace the steps $g = g(s)$ of Newton's iteration (1.3) for $s = 0,1,\ldots$ by the iteration steps (1.5) where $g(0)$ is a large enough integer (see the inequality (7.3) below);

$$g(s+1) = g(s) + 2, \ s = 0,1,\ldots; \tag{7.1}$$

$$\hat{X}_g = (L(\mathbf{x}^{(g)})U(\mathbf{y}^{(g)}) - L(\mathbf{v}^{(g)})U(\mathbf{u}^{(g)})) \ / \ x_0^{(g)} \text{ for } g{=}g(0),g(1),\ldots; \tag{7.2}$$

$\mathbf{x}^{(g)}$ and $\mathbf{y}^{(g)}$ denote the first and the reverse last columns of the matrix X_g, respectively; and the vectors $\mathbf{u}^{(g)}$ and $\mathbf{v}^{(g)}$ and the scalar $x_0^{(g)}$ are defined by the vectors $\mathbf{x}^{(g)}$ and $\mathbf{y}^{(g)}$ in the same way as $\mathbf{u}$, $\mathbf{v}$, and x_0 are defined by the vectors $\mathbf{x}$ and $\mathbf{y}$ in Theorem 6.3. We will rely on the matrix equation (6.3). (Alternatively, we could have applied the similar iteration in order to invert a larger matrix W^* (defined in Theorem 6.3) and to recover W^{-1} using the matrix equation (6.4).) We will refer to this modification of Algorithm 4.1 as to **Algorithm 7.1**, and we will estimate its computational cost to prove Theorem 1.1.

Since the matrices $\hat{X}_g$ are available with their displacement generators of length 2, we compute the matrices X_g for all $g > g(0)$ with their displacement generators of length 23 or less (see the equations (7.1), Corollary 6.1 and also Remark 7.3 below), so that each step (1.3), (1.5) for $g > g(0)$ is reduced to O(1) DFT's and vector summations (see Theorem 6.2). Surely, such a reduction to DFT's and vector summations also applies to each step (7.2).

Generally, the transition to Algorithm 7.1 increases the number of steps (1.3), for approximation to W^{-1} by $\hat{X}_g$ is not as good as the approximation by X_g, but we will prove next that the double increase of the number of steps, suggested by the equation (7.1), will always suffice. We will deduce this by showing that the norm $\| \hat{X}_g - W^{-1} \|_1$ is proportional to $\| X_g - W^{-1} \|_1$ (see Proposition 7.1 below). If the norm $\| X_g - W^{-1} \|_1$ is small enough, the deterioration of the approximation at the step (7.2) is more than compensated in the two subsequent steps (1.3) (compare Proposition 3.1). Then it will remain to combine Corollaries 5.1, 5.2 and 6.1 in order to estimate the overall computational cost of approximating to A^{-1}.

Let us initially have a matrix X_0, an a.i.$(2,\tilde{q})$ of an s.p.d. matrix W where $\tilde{q} < 1$, and next prove that the norm $\| X_g - W^{-1} \|_1$ becomes sufficiently small in g(0) successive steps of the iteration (1.3), provided that

$$g(0) \geq \log_2(\log(101 \sqrt{n}\, \kappa_1^4(W))/ \log(1/\tilde{q})). \tag{7.3}$$

We will then apply Corollary 6.1 to deduce that the overall computational cost of the first g(0) iteration steps is sufficiently low.

We will start with the following result:

PROPOSITION 7.1. $\| \hat{X}_g - W^{-1} \|_1 \leq \nu_g(W) \| X_g - W^{-1} \|_1$ *for* $g = g(s)$ *and for all* s *provided that*

$$\nu_g(W) = (5\| W^{-1} \|_1 + 2\| X_g - W^{-1} \|_1) \;/\; |x_0| - \|X_g - W^{-1}\|_1).$$

PROOF. Let $\Delta(\mathbf{x}) = L(\mathbf{x}^{(g)}) - L(\mathbf{x})$, $\Delta(\mathbf{y}) = U(\mathbf{y}^{(g)}) - U(\mathbf{y})$, $\Delta(\mathbf{x},\mathbf{y}) = L(\mathbf{x}^{(g)})U(\mathbf{y}^{(g)}) - L(\mathbf{x})U(\mathbf{y})$, and similarly define $\Delta(\mathbf{u})$, $\Delta(\mathbf{v})$, and $\Delta(\mathbf{u},\mathbf{v})$. Then

$\| \Delta(\mathbf{x}) \|_1 \leq \| \mathbf{x}^{(g)} - \mathbf{x} \|_1 \leq \| X_g - W^{-1} \|_1$,

$\| \Delta(\mathbf{y}) \|_1 \leq \| \mathbf{y}^{(g)} - \mathbf{y} \|_1 \leq \| X_g - W^{-1} \|_1$,

$\| L(\mathbf{x}) \|_1 \leq \| W^{-1} \|_1$, $\| U(\mathbf{y}) \|_1 \leq \| W^{-1} \|_1$,

$\| U(\mathbf{y}^{(g)}) \|_1 \leq \| X_g \|_1 \leq \| W^{-1} \|_1 + \| X_g - W^{-1} \|_1$,

$\| \Delta(\mathbf{x},\mathbf{y}) \|_1 \leq \| \Delta(\mathbf{x}) \|_1 \| U(\mathbf{y}^{(g)}) \|_1 + \| L(\mathbf{x}) \|_1 \| \Delta(\mathbf{y}) \|_1 \leq$

$2\| X_g - W^{-1} \|_1 \| W^{-1} \|_1 + \| X_g - W^{-1} \|_1^2$.

Similarly, $\| \Delta(\mathbf{u},\mathbf{v}) \|_1 \leq 2\| X_g - W^{-1} \|_1 \| W^{-1} \|_1 + \| X_g - W^{-1} \|_1^2$. Now, recall the equations (6.3) and (7.2) and write $\hat{X}_g - W^{-1} = (\Delta(\mathbf{x},\mathbf{y}) - \Delta(\mathbf{u},\mathbf{v}))/ x_0 + (L(\mathbf{x}^{(g)})U(\mathbf{y}^{(g)}) - L(\mathbf{v}^{(g)})U(\mathbf{u}^{(g)}))(1/ x_0^{(g)} - 1/ x_0)$. The latter term on the right side equals $(x_0 - x_0^{(g)})\hat{X}_g / x_0$. Combine the resulting expression for $\hat{X}_g - W^{-1}$ with the above estimates for the norm of the matrices $\Delta(\mathbf{x},\mathbf{y})$ and $\Delta(\mathbf{u},\mathbf{v})$, recall that $|x_0 - x_0^{(g)}| \leq \| X_g - W^{-1} \|_1$, $\| \hat{X}_g \|_1 \leq \| \hat{X}_g - W^{-1} \|_1 + \| W^{-1} \|_1$, and deduce that $\|\hat{X}_g - W^{-1}\|_1 \leq (\|X_g - W^{-1}\|_1 / x_0)\;(5\|W^{-1}\|_1 + 2\|X_g - W^{-1}\|_1) + \|\hat{X}_g - W^{-1}\|_1 \; \|X_g - W^{-1}\|_1 / x_0$. Move the latter term to the left side of this inequality and deduce Proposition 7.1. Q.E.D.

Deduce from Proposition 7.1 that $\|W\hat{X}_g - I\|_1 \leq \|WX_g - I\|_1 \ \kappa_1(W)\nu_g(W)$, observe that $\nu_g(W) \leq \mu_g(W)$ where

$$\mu_g(W) = (5 + 2\| WX_g - I\|_1) \,/\, ((|x_0| \,/\, \|W^{-1}\|_1) - \|WX_g - I\|_1), \tag{7.4}$$

and obtain the following corollary:

COROLLARY 7.1. $\| W\hat{X}_g - I\|_1 \leq \| WX_g - I\|_1 \kappa_1(W)\mu_g(W)$, $\| WX_{g+l} - I\|_1 \leq (\| WX_g - I\|_1 \kappa_1(W)\mu_g(W))^L$ *for* $g = g(s)$, $L = 2^l$, $l = 1,2,\ldots,g(s+1)-g(s)$, $s = 0,1,\ldots$, *where the matrices* X_g, $\hat{X}_g$, X_{g+l} *appear in the modified Newton iteration (1.3), (1.5), (7.2) and where the scalar* $\mu_g(W)$ *is defined by the equation (7.4).*

Next, we will deduce the following result:

COROLLARY 7.2. *Let the inequality*

$$\| WX_g - I\|_1^{1/2} \kappa_1(W)\mu_g(W) \leq 1 \text{ for } g = g(s) \tag{7.5}$$

hold for $s = 0$; *let* $\| WX_0 - I\|_2 = \tilde{q} < 1$; *let* $g(s+1) = g(s) + 2$ *for* $s = 0,1,\ldots$ *Then the matrix* $X_{g(r)} = \tilde{W}^{-1}$ *computed in* $g(r) = g(0) + 2r$ *steps of the modified Newton iteration (1.3), (1.5), (7.2) satisfies the inequality* $\| \tilde{W}^{-1} - W^{-1}\|_1 \leq \gamma\| W^{-1}\|_1$ *provided that*

$$g(0) + r = g(r) - r \geq \log(\log \gamma / \log \tilde{q}). \tag{7.6}$$

PROOF. Suppose that the inequality (7.5) holds for s=0,1,... Then combining Proposition 3.1, Corollary 7.1 and the equations (7.1) would immediately imply that

$$\| WX_{g(s+1)} - I\|_1 \leq \| WX_{g(s)} - I\|_1^2 \text{ for } s = 0,1,\ldots, \tag{7.7}$$

and then Corollary 7.2 would follow. To complete its proof, it, therefore, remains to extend the bound (7.5) from the case s=0 to the cases s=1,2,... We will do this by induction on s.

Recall our assumption that $\| WX_0 - I\|_2 = \tilde{q} < 1$ and deduce that $\| WX_{g(0)} - I\|_2 < \tilde{q}^{\,G(0)}$, $G(0) = 2^{g(0)}$. We will choose g(0) such that $q^{G(0)} < 1/\sqrt{n}$. Then $\| WX_{g(0)} - I\|_1 < 1$, due to Proposition 2.1. The latter relation is inductively extended to the inequalities (7.5), (7.7), $\| WX_{g(s)} - I\|_1 < \| WX_{g(0)} - I\|_1 < 1$ and $\mu_{g(s)}(W) < \mu_{g(0)}(W)$ for $s = 1,2,\ldots$ Q.E.D.

Next, we will prove the following result:

PROPOSITION 7.2. *The inequality (7.5) holds for* $s = 0$ *as long as the inequality (7.3) holds.*

PROOF. We recall that W is a real symmetric matrix, apply the interlacing property of the eigenvalues of real symmetric matrices (see [GL], p. 269, or [Par], p. 186), and obtain that $1/|x_0| \leq \|W\|_2$. Therefore, $1/|x_0| \leq \|W\|_1$ (see Proposition 2.1), so $\|W^{-1}\|_1/|x_0| \leq \kappa_1(W)$. Combine the latter inequality with the equation (7.4) and with the following inequality, implied by the relations (7.3) and by Propositions 2.1 and 3.1: $2\|WX_{g(0)}-I\|_1\kappa_1(W) \leq 1$, and deduce that

$$\mu_g(W) \leq 2\,(5 + 2\,\|W\,X_g - I\|_1)\kappa_1(W).$$

Thus, the inequality (7.5) will follow for $s = 0$ if

$$4\|W\,X_{g(0)} - I\|_1\,\kappa_1^4(W)(5 + 2\,\|W\,X_{g(0)} - I\|_1)^2 \leq 1. \tag{7.8}$$

Let g(0) satisfy (7.3). Then, by virtue of Propositions 2.1 and 3.1,

$$\|W\,X_{g(0)} - I\|_1\ /\sqrt{n} \leq \|W\,X_{g(0)} - I\|_2 \leq 1/\,(101\sqrt{n}\ \kappa_1^4(W)).$$

This implies the bound (7.8) since $\kappa_1(W) \geq 1$. Q.E.D.

Now, we are ready to estimate the cost of approximating to A^{-1} by means of Algorithm 7.1. We will separately bound the cost C_0 of all the steps (1.3) for $g = 0,1,\ldots,g(0)$ in all the stages of Algorithm 7.1 and the cost C_1 of the remaining steps (1.3), as well as of all the steps (1.5) and (7.2).

Combining Corollaries 5.1, 5.2, 6.1 and Theorem 7.2, we estimate that the cost C_1 is $O((s+k(\epsilon))\log n)$ parallel arithmetic steps and n processors and the cost C_0 is $O(m\,g(0)\log n)$ parallel arithmetic steps and $n4^{g(0)}/g(0)$ processors. Here, we use the value $s+k(\epsilon)$ estimated in Corollaries 5.1 and 5.2.

Now, it remains to fix the values p, δ and m (see Propositions 4.1, 5.3 and 5.4 and the equations (5.4); also see more comments below on the choice of p), to let

$$g(0) = \lceil \log_2(\log(101\sqrt{n}\ \tilde{\kappa}_1^2)\ /\log(1/\tilde{q}))\ \rceil \tag{7.9}$$

(where $\tilde{\kappa}_1$ is an upper estimate for $\kappa_1(A)$ and $\tilde{q} = 1-p(p+1)/2$, and to deduce Theorem 1.1 for an s.p.d. Toeplitz matrix A by combining the above estimates for the parallel computational cost with the bounds of Section 5 and by observing that $\kappa_2 = \kappa_2(A) \geq \kappa_2(A_j)$ for all j and that $1/\log(1/\tilde{q})$ is a value of an order of 1/p as $p \to 0$. In particular, this way, the cost C_0 is estimated to be $O((\log\ln(n\tilde{\kappa}_2) + \log(1/p))\log n\ \ln(n\tilde{\kappa}_2)/\ln(1/p))$ parallel arithmetic steps and

$n\left(\frac{\ln(n\tilde{\kappa}_2)}{p}\right)^2 / \log\left(\frac{\ln(n\tilde{\kappa}_2)}{p}\right)$ processors. Similarly to Corollary 5.2, we first let $1/p = O(1)$ and deduce the part a) of Theorem 1.1 for an s.p.d. Toeplitz matrix A. Then we let $\log(1/p)$ be proportional to $\log\log(n\tilde{\kappa}_2)$ and yield the part b). The extension to the case of any real symmetric (or Hermitian) and/or diagonally dominant Toeplitz matrix A will be shown in Section 9.

REMARK 7.1. An a.i.(2,q) of a general $n \times n$ matrix A is readily available where $1-q$ is of an order of $n(\kappa_2(A))^2$, and then $O(\log(n\kappa_2(A)))$ iteration steps (1.3) suffice in order to compute an a.i.(2,1/2) of A^{-1} and then to invert the matrix A numerically. The overall computational cost bounds are on the same level as in Corollary 5.2 (see [Be] and [PR]). If, however, A is a symmetric Toeplitz matrix, then, in an order of $\log(n\kappa_2(A))$ steps (1.3), the displacement rank of the matrices X_g generally grows from the initial value 2 to the values of an order of n, blowing up the computational cost and making the approach inferior to ours in the case of Toeplitz matrix inversion.

REMARK 7.2. Suppose that $A = [a_{i-j}]$ is an $n \times n$ very strongly column-diagonally dominant Toeplitz matrix (see (1.1)), normalized so that $a_0 = 1$. Then $\kappa_1(A) = O(1)$, and $X_0 = I$ is an a.i.(1,q) of A for a constant $q < 1$, so that we may dispense with Algorithm 4.1 in this case and numerically compute the inverse matrix A^{-1} by applying modified Newton's iteration (1.3), (1.5), (7.2). Moreover, the inequalities (1.1) bound the diagonal entries of A^{-1} away from 0, and we may now satisfy the inequality (7.5) for $A = W$ and for $s = 0$ already where $g(0) = O(1)$. It follows that the matrices X_g are computed with their displacement generators of length $O(1)$ *for all* g, and, consequently, *the modified Newton iteration (1.3), (1.5), (7.2) for* $W = A$ *uses* $O(\log n \log\log(1/\epsilon))$ *parallel arithmetic steps and n processors in order to compute a matrix* $\tilde{A}^{-1}$ *that satisfies the inequality (1.2).* The transition from a matrix A to its transpose A^T enables us to extend this result to the inversion of a very strongly row-diagonally dominant Toeplitz matrix.

REMARK 7.3. If $\| WX_{g(0)} - I \|_1^{\alpha}\ \kappa_1(W)\mu_{g(0)}(W) \le 1$ for a constant $\alpha < 1/2$, then exponentially fast convergence (of order $2-2\alpha$) of the modified Newton iteration (1.3), (1.5), (7.2) can already be ensured if we replace (7.1) by setting $g(s+1) = g(s)+1$ for $s = 0,1,\ldots$ In this case, the matrices X_g for all $g > g(0)$ will be computed with their displacement generators of length, at most, 9, rather than, at most, 23, and this will respectively decrease the overhead constant in our asymptotic bound on the computational cost of the iteration.

8. EXTENSIONS TO THE INVERSION OF STRUCTURED MATRICES

In this section, we will consider the extension of our algorithm to the inversion of an arbitrary matrix A given with its displacement generator $G_d(A)$ of small length d. We may apply Algorithm 1.4 to invert the s.p.d. matrix A^TA, whose displacement generator $G_{2d+1}(A^TA)$ of length, at most, 2d+1 can be easily computed (see Theorem 6.2). To make the algorithm computationally simple (having low cost), we should exploit the displacement structure and apply the modified Newton iteration (1.3), (1.5).

We need, however, to extend the steps (7.2) to nonToeplitz matrices W in order to approximate to an LU- or a UL-displacement generator of smaller length for the matrices $B = (A^TA + a\ I)^{-1}$ and for positive scalars a. Such matrices have LU- and UL-displacement generators of length $d^* = 2d+2$, due to Theorems 6.2 and 6.4. The problem of approximating to such a generator can be solved either by using the new extensions of the Gohberg-Semencul formulas to the inverses of all matrices of small displacement ranks (see [KC]) or by following [P88b] and computing the singular value decomposition (SVD) of the auxiliary matrix of small rank associated with the generator (as an alternative to application of Theorem 6.3 in our construction), (this idea was suggested to the present author by T. Kailath). The resulting modification of our algorithm works for any matrix given with its displacement generator of small length, yielding asymptotic cost estimates that match the bounds of Theorem 1.1 over the class of Toeplitz matrices (up to within constant factors) but are still inferior to the estimates of this paper over the class of very strongly diagonally dominant Toeplitz matrices.

Furthermore, our results can be extended to computations with Vandermonde, Vandermonde-like, Hilbert and Hilbert-like matrices due to [P88c].

9. INVERSION OF TOEPLITZ AND BLOCK TOEPLITZ MATRICES

In this section, we will extend our algorithm to the inversion of symmetric (block) Toeplitz matrices and of diagonally dominant Toeplitz matrices using neither the formulae from [KC] nor the evaluation of the SVD of the auxiliary matrices. In this extension, problems may arise where the value $|x_0|$ in the formula (6.3) turns into 0 or approaches to 0. For some input matrices, we may circumvent the problem by referring to the formula (6.4) and to Remark 6.2, but we will avoid all these difficulties by applying the following result, due to [Heinig] (see also [Tism], [HR]):

THEOREM 9.1. *Let* $A = [a_{ij}]$ *be an* $n\times n$ *nonsingular Toeplitz matrix,* $a_{ij} = a_{i-j}$ *for* $i,j = 0,1,\ldots,n-1$. *Let* $\mathbf{a} = [b,a_{1-n},a_{2-n},\ldots,a_{-1}]^T$ *for any fixed scalar* b*;* $\mathbf{z} = A^{-1}\mathbf{a}$, $\mathbf{z} = [z_0,\ldots,z_{n-1}]^T$, $\mathbf{w} = [-1,z_{n-1},\ldots,z_1]^T$, $\mathbf{x}$ *and* $\mathbf{u}$ *be the two vectors defined in Theorem 6.3. Then*

$$A^{-1} = L(\mathbf{z})U(\mathbf{u}) - L(\mathbf{x})U(\mathbf{w}).$$

Next, we will indicate how to extend Algorithm 4.1 to the inversion of a normalized column-diagonally dominant (n.c.-d.d.) matrix A, which is not necessarily an s.p.d. matrix. It is sufficient to replace the 2-norm of matrices by their 1-norm throughout Algorithm 4.1 and also to replace the equations (4.1) by the following equations:

$$a = (1-q)/q, \quad \tilde{A}_{-1}^{-1} = I/(1+a). \tag{9.1}$$

We will call the resulting modification of Algorithm 4.1 by **Algorithm 9.1.** For $X_0 = \tilde{A}_{-1}^{-1}$, the equations (9.1) immediately imply that $\| A_0X_0 - I\|_1 = \| A - I\|_1 / (1+a) \le 1/(1+a) = q$.

Let us elaborate the respective changes in the proofs of other results of Sections 4 and 5, which we will extend provided that Algorithm 9.1 replaces Algorithm 4.1, the 1-norm of matrices replaces their 2-norm (so that each a.i.(2,q) is replaced by an a.i.(1,q)), and A is an n.c.-d.d. (but generally not s.p.d.) matrix.

We will first extend Proposition 4.1. We observe that, due to the equation (4.4), the matrix A_m^{-1} is an a.i. (1,q) of A if $m \ge \log(a\| A_m^{-1}\|_1/q)/\log(1/p) = \log((1-q)\| A_m^{-1}\|_1/q^2)/\log(1/p)$. On the other hand (see [A], p. 425), if $A_m = A+ap^mI$, then for any fixed matrix norm, $\| A_m^{-1}\| \le \| A^{-1}\| + ap^m\| A^{-1}\|^2/(1-ap^m\| A^{-1}\|)$. Therefore, $\| A_m^{-1}\|_1 \le \| A^{-1}\|_1/(1-c_m)$ provided that $c_m = ap^m\| A^{-1}\|_1 < 1$. We arrive at the following extension of Proposition 4.1:

PROPOSITION 9.1. *Let* A *be an n.c.-d.d. matrix,* q *be such that* $0 < q < 1$, $p=1-q$, $a=p/q$, m *be a natural number, such that* $m \ge \log(p\| A^{-1}\|_1/((1-c_m)q^2))/\log(1/p)$, *and* $c_m = ap^m\| A^{-1}\|_1 < 1$. *Then the matrix* A_m^{-1} *approximated at Stage* m *of Algorithm 9.1 is an a.i.*(1,q) *of* A.

To prove the rather straightforward extensions of Propositions 5.1 and 5.2, we only need to deduce that $b\| C^{-1}\|_1 \le 1$ provided that $C = A + bI$ and that A denotes an n.c.-d.d. matrix. In this case, $C/(b+1) = I-(I-A)/(b+1)$ and $\| I-A\|_1 = q_0 < 1$. It follows that $C^{-1} = \sum_{j=1}^{\infty} (I-A)^j/(b+1)^{j+1}$,

$$\| C^{-1}\|_1 \le (1/(b+1))/(1-q_0/(b+1)) = 1/(b+1-q_0) < 1/b. \tag{9.2}$$

Q.E.D.

To prove the extensions of Propositions 5.3 and 5.4, we apply the relations (9.2) to the matrix $C = A_{j-1}$ and to the scalar $b = a_{j-1} = ap^{\,j-1}$ and derive that

$$\| A_{j-1}^{-1}\|_1 \le 1/(a_{j-1}+1-\| I-A\|_1) < 1/(ap^{\,j-1}). \tag{9.3}$$

Substitute the latter relations and the equations (4.2) for A_j into the inequalities (5.2) and deduce that

$$\| A_j\tilde{A}_{j-1}^{-1}-I\|_1 \le q+\delta p+\delta\| A\|_1 \, \| A_{j-1}^{-1}\|_1. \tag{9.4}$$

On the other hand, $A^{-1} = (I-(I-A))^{-1} = \sum_{j=0}^{\infty}(I-A)^{\,j}$, so that $\| A^{-1}\|_1 \le 1/(1-\| I-A\|_1)$. Combining the latter inequality with the first inequality (9.3), we deduce that

$$\| A_{j-1}^{-1}\|_1 \le 1/(a_{j-1} + 1/\| A^{-1}\|_1) < \min\{1/a_{j-1}, \| A^{-1}\|_1\}. \tag{9.5}$$

Combining the relations (9.4) and (9.5) gives the desired extensions of Proposition 5.3. The inequalities (9.5) imply that $\| A_m^{-1}\|_1 < \| A^{-1}\|_1$. Using the latter bound, we may immediately extend Proposition 5.4 and Corollary 5.1.

The results of Section 7 are also extended, since we may apply Theorem 9.1 instead of Theorem 6.3. We arrive at Theorem 1.1 for an n.c.-d.d. matrix A and thus for all the diagonally dominant matrices A (compare Remark 2.1).

Then again, if we want to invert an arbitrary Toeplitz matrix A without computing the SVD of the auxiliary matrix, we may try to apply Theorem 9.1 and to modify Algorithm 4.1 by changing the definition of the values a_j as follows: $a_j = a\,p_j\exp(i\alpha_j)$ for certain real p_j and α_j, such that $0 \le \alpha_j < 2\pi$, $p^{\,j} \le p_j < 2p^{\,j}$. Then, surely, $\| A_0X_0 - I\|_1 \le q$, but Proposition 5.1 is not generally extended. The equations (4.2) imply that $\| A_jA_{j-1}^{-1} - I\| \le |a_{j-1}|\, q\, \| A_{j-1}^{-1}\|$ for any matrix norm, but the right side of the latter inequality may exceed 1 if $\| A_{j-1}^{-1}\|$ is large. To bound the right side, we need to choose a matrix norm and the values a_j such that, say,

$$\| A_j^{-1}\| \le \min\{\| A^{-1}\|, 1/|a_j|\} \text{ for all } j. \tag{9.6}$$

We may ensure the bounds (9.6) for a matrix A if we know the distribution of its eigenvalues on the complex plane (or even if we just know a trajectory $\{a_0,a_1,\ldots\}$ converging to 0 with a desired speed and passing far enough from all the eigenvalues of A). In particular, we may ensure (9.6) and, therefore, Theorem 1.1

in the case where the matrix A is *real symmetric or Hermitian* and thus has only real eigenvalues. In this case, we arrive at Theorem 1.1 by applying Theorem 9.1 and Algorithm 4.1, where we make the single change (and only in the equation (4.1)) by setting $a = n\sqrt{-1}\max_{i,j} |a_{ij}| / q$.

REMARK 9.1. The inversion formulae extending Theorem 6.3 are available for n×n Toeplitz matrices whose entries are m×m blocks (see [GH74] or [FKML]). Theorem 6.2 can also be extended to the block Toeplitz case, based on the transition, by means of the row and column interchange, from a given block Toeplitz matrix to an m×m matrix whose entries are n×n Toeplitz blocks, so, its displacement rank is, at most, 2m, due to Theorem 6.1. Therefore, Theorem 1.1 can be extended to this class of matrices, provided that they are well-conditioned and real symmetric or Hermitian. The previous proofs remain essentially the same, except that all the scalar entries, in particular, the entries x_0 of W^{-1} and $x_0^{(j)}$ of X_j, are replaced by m×m matrices, the values $|x_0|$ and $|x_0^{(j)}|$ are replaced by the norms of these matrices, and obtaining the required bounds on the norms relies on the interlacing property of the eigenvalues of real symmetric or Hermitian matrices and on Proposition 2.2. The resulting bounds on the computational cost depend on m, of course.

APPENDIX. THE ILL-CONDITIONED CASE

A.1. An Outline of the Algorithm

If a Toeplitz matrix A is ill-conditioned, then computing its inverse would require a high precision. Furthermore, we will assume the exact evaluation of A^{-1} in rational arithmetic provided that the entries of A are integers (if they are finite binary numbers, we may make them integers by scaling).

More precisely, the evaluation consists of two stages. In the first stage, we numerically invert the auxiliary Toeplitz matrices $I - q_jA$ by means of modified Newton's iteration. Here, the values $|q_j|$ are small, so the auxiliary matrices are very strongly diagonally dominant, and low precision computations suffice. In the second stage, we will use the computed approximations to the matrices $(I - q_jA)^{-1}$ in order to approximate to the matrices $A^2, A^3, \ldots$ Since the latter matrices are filled with integers, we recover the exact values of their entries by means of round-off. Then we use the exact rational arithmetic to compute first the integral coefficients of the characteristic polynomial of A, then adj A and, finally, A^{-1} as a pair of adj A and det A.

The algorithm is suggested for computer algebra applications rather than for numerical computations, due to the high precision computations required in the second stage. If, however, only few small powers of A or few first coefficients of the characteristic polynomial of A are sought, the algorithm is numerically stable and can be recommended for numerical computations. In the next two subsections, we will present this algorithm, and then will indicate some of its extensions and applications.

A.2. Computing Matrix Powers

DEFINITION A.1. The *canonical set of entries* of a square matrix is the set of all its entries in its first and last columns and on its diagonal.

Let us apply our ability to effectively invert very strongly diagonally dominant Toeplitz matrices in order to compute the canonical sets of entries of the powers A^k of a given $n \times n$ Toeplitz matrix A for $k=2,3,\dots,n$ where $\|A\|_1 \geq 1$. Let $m=2n$, $\omega = \exp(2\pi\sqrt{-1}/(m+1))$ be a primitive $(m+1)$-th root of 1, and q be such that

$$0 < q\,\|A\|_1 \leq q\,\|A\|_1^2 < 1/10,\ q_j = q\omega^j, \text{ for } j=0,1,\dots,m. \tag{A.1}$$

Then the matrices $W=I-q_jA$ are very strongly diagonally dominant for all j, so we may recall Remark 7.2 and apply the modified Newton iteration (1.3), (1.5), (7.2) in order to compute the canonical set of entries of the matrix

$$(I-q_jA)^{-1} = \sum_{k=0}^{\infty} (q_jA)^k = \sum_{k=0}^{\infty} (qA)^k\omega^{jk} \tag{A.2}$$

for each j with absolute error bound

$$E^* = 1/2^N,\ N = n^c \tag{A.3}$$

(where c is an arbitrary constant), for the cost of performing O(log n) DFT's at O(n) points.

Let $S_j = \sum_{k=0}^{m} (qA)^k\omega^{jk}$. We have already approximated to the matrices S_j by the matrices $(I - q_jA)^{-1}$ with high precision. Indeed,

$$\tilde{E} = \|(I-q_jA)^{-1} - S_j\|_1 \leq (10/9)(q\|A\|_1)^{m+1} \leq (q\,\|A\|_1)^m/9. \tag{A.4}$$

(see the relations (A.1), (A.2)). The computed approximations to the entries of $(I-q_jA)^{-1}$ approximate to the entries of S_j with absolute errors, at most, $E^*+\tilde{E}$ (see the equations (A.3), (A.4)). The cost of computing all these approximations for all j is $O(\log^2 n)$ parallel arithmetic steps and mn processors.

Next, apply inverse DFT's at m+1 points in order to compute the canonical set of entries of the matrices $(qA)^k$ for all $k \leq m$ (a single DFT at m+1 points is needed for each entry of the canonical set and for all $k \leq m$), and then divide the results by q^k to obtain the desired entries of A^k. The divisions by q^k increase the absolute errors q^k times; the increase would be the greatest for k near m. We will only need, however, the entries of A^k for $k \leq n = m/2$, whose approximations are obtained with absolute errors, at most,

$$(E^* + \tilde{E})/q^k < 1/(2^N q^n) + (q\|A\|_1^2)^n,$$

assuming the infinite precision computations. We perform DFT's by means of FFT's, recall that both Newton's iteration and FFT are stable, and, moreover, Newton's iteration is self-correcting (see [GS], [PR]), and extend the latter bound to the computations with finite precision as follows:

THEOREM A.1. *The canonical set of entries of the powers* A^k *of an* $n \times n$ *Toeplitz matrix for* $k=2,3,\ldots,n$ *can be computed with absolute errors less than*

$$E = O(1/(2^N q^n)+1/10^n),\ N = n^c,$$

using $O(\log^2 n)$ *parallel arithmetic steps,* n^2 *processors and the computation precision of* $O(n \log(\|A\|_1+(1/q)))$ *binary digits, where a positive* q *satisfies the bounds (A.1) and where* c *is an arbitrary constant. If all the entries of A are integers and if the error bound* E *is less than* 1/2, *then the exact values of the entries of the canonical sets of* A^k *can be recovered for all* $k \leq n$ *by rounding-off the computed approximations to the nearest integers.*

REMARK A.1. $O(n \log(\|A\|_1+(1/q)))$-bit precision is $O(n \log \|A\|_1)$-bit precision if $|\log q|=O(\log \|A\|_1))$. The algorithm can be restricted to computing the traces of A, $A^2,\ldots,A^l$ for a smaller l if we set $m = 2l$. Then $O(\log^2 n)$ parallel arithmetic steps, ln processors, and $O(l \log\|A\|_1 + (1/q))$-bit precision computation will suffice.

A.3. Csanky–LeVerrier Algorithm and the Overall Cost Bounds

Let us recall the well known adaptation by [Cs] of LeVerrier algorithm for computing the coefficients of the characteristic polynomial of a general matrix A. Hereafter, let

$$\mathbf{s} = [s_1,s_2,\ldots,s_n]^T,\ s_k = \mathrm{trace}(A^k),\ k=1,\ldots,n, \tag{A.5}$$

$$\mathbf{c} = (D+L)^{-1}\mathbf{s}, \tag{A.6}$$

so that $\mathbf{c} = [c_{n-1},\ldots,c_0]^T$ is the solution to the linear system $(D+L)\mathbf{c}=\mathbf{s}$ where $D = \mathrm{diag}(1,2,..,n)$, $L = L(\mathbf{p})$, $\mathbf{p} = [0,s_1,\ldots,s_{n-1}]^T$; as is well known ([Cs], [FF]), this solution gives the coefficient vector of the characteristic polynomial of A,

$$\det(\lambda I-A) = \lambda^n - \sum_{i=0}^{n-1} c_i\lambda^i = \prod_{j=1}^{n} (\lambda-\lambda_j),\ c_0=(-1)^n\det A. \qquad (A.7)$$

The Cayley-Hamilton theorem implies that

$$A^{-1} = (A^{n-1} - \sum_{j=1}^{n-1} c_j A^{j-1})/c_0.$$

ALGORITHM A.1 (Csanky-LeVerrier) ([Cs]). **Input:** A^k, $k=1,2,\ldots,n$. Successively compute the vectors $\mathbf{s} = [s_1,s_2,\ldots,s_n]^T$ and $\mathbf{c} = [c_{n-1},c_{n-2},\ldots,c_0]^T$ of the equations (A.5) and (A.6), $\det A = (-1)^n c_0$, and the matrix

$$\mathrm{adj}\ A = (-1)^n\ (A^{n-1} - \sum_{j=1}^{n-1} c_j A^{j-1}).$$

Finally, define A^{-1} as the pair (adj A, det A) or (if $c_0 \neq 0$) compute

$$A^{-1} = \mathrm{adj}\ A/\det A. \qquad (A.8)$$

When we apply Algorithm A.1 to a Toeplitz matrix A, we take the canonical sets of entries of the matrices A^k as the input, and we only need to compute the vector $\mathbf{c}$ and the first and the last columns of the matrices adj A and A^{-1} or, if $x_0 = 0$ in the equation (6.3) for W=A, we embed A=W into the $(n+1)\times(n+1)$ matrix W^* of Theorem 6.3 (choosing the entries w^*_{n0} and w^*_{0n} of W^* such that W^* is nonsingular), replace the matrix $A = W$ by W^*, and repeat the computation. We compute the vector $\mathbf{c}$ that satisfies the equation (A.6) (given the vector $\mathbf{s}$), by means of an algorithm of Newton type using $O(\log^2 n)$ parallel arithmetic steps and $n/\log n$ processors (see [P88b], [Sc]).

If we exclude the stage (A.8) of Algorithm A.1, then no divisions are involved in the entire algorithm, except for the division by $2,3,\ldots,2n$, needed in the transition from $\mathbf{s}$ to $\mathbf{c}$. Since the input matrix A is an integral matrix, all the outputs of Algorithm A.1 (except for the entries of A^{-1}) are integers. We perform all the computations modulo p^h where p is a prime, $p>2n$, and $0.5p^h$ exceeds the maximum absolute value of all the outputs of the algorithm. Then we immediately recover all the integral outputs from their values modulo p^h. To bound the output values, we recall that

$$|\det A| \leq \|A\|_2^n \leq (\sqrt{n}\,\|A\|_1)^n.$$

Finally, let us combine the resulting estimates for the cost of performing Algorithm A.1 (in the case of a Toeplitz matrix A) and of the computation of the input of this algorithm.

THEOREM A.2. *The coefficient vector* **c** *of the characteristic polynomial of a given* $n \times n$ *Toeplitz matrix* A *filled with integers,* adj A *and* det A, *as well as* $A^{-1} = \text{adj}\,A/\det A$ *if* $\det A \neq 0$, *can be evaluated using* $O(\log^2 n)$ *parallel arithmetic steps,* n^2 *processors, and the computation precision of* $O(n \log (n\,\|A\|_1))$ *binary digits.*

A.4. Extensions

COROLLARY A.1. $O(n \log^2 n)$ *parallel arithmetic steps and* n *processors suffice in order to approximate with the error* 2^{-N} *to all the eigenvalues of an* $n \times n$ *Toeplitz matrix* A *filled with integers in the range from* -2^N *to* 2^N *where* $N = n^c$, c *is a constant;* $O(\log^4 n)$ *parallel arithmetic steps and* n^2 *processors suffice in order to similarly approximate to all the eigenvalues of A if, in addition,* A *is symmetric;* $O(\log^3 n)$ *steps and* n^2 *processors suffice if a similar approximation to a single complex eigenvalue of A is sought.*

Corollary A.1 immediately follows from the bounds of Theorem A.2 on the cost of computing the coefficients of the characteristic polynomial of A and from the results of [P87b] and [P88a] on computing polynomial zeros.

COROLLARY A.2. *The resultant of two univariate polynomials of degree, at most,* n *and with coefficients whose absolute values are, at most,* N *can be computed using* $O(\log^2 n)$ *parallel arithmetic steps,* n^2 *processors, and the computation precision of* $O(n \log(n N))$ *binary digits.*

Corollary A.2 immediately follows form the extension of Theorem A.2 to Toeplitz matrices with Toeplitz blocks, for the resultant equals det A where

$$A = [A_1, A_2] \tag{A.9}$$

is a 1×2 block matrix with Toeplitz blocks A_1 and A_2. Since we may turn A into a block Toeplitz matrix with 2×2 blocks by a row (column) interchange, we may extend Theorem 6.3 respectively.

COROLLARY A.3. *The greatest common divisor of two given polynomials of degree, at most,* n *with integral coefficients whose absolute values are less than a fixed value* t *can be evaluated using* $O(\log^3 n)$ *parallel arithmetic steps and* n^2 *processors in* $O(n \log(nt))$*-bit precision computations.*

PROOF. Computing the *greatest common divisor (gcd)* of two polynomials p(x) and q(x) of degree, at most, n can be reduced to O(log n) steps of binary search; in each such a step, a linear system of equations is solved whose coefficient matrix is a Sylvester matrix or its submatrix, of the form (A.9) in both cases. The binary search relies on the fact that all the candidate linear systems of larger size also have solutions, and all the smaller size candidate linear systems are inconsistent (see [vzG], p. 809). Q.E.D.

The evaluation of the gcd of m polynomials of degree, at most, n can be immediately reduced to $\lceil \log_2 m \rceil$ parallel steps of the evaluation of the gcd's of pairs of such polynomials (where we need to handle, at most, m/2 pairs in each parallel step) using $O(\log^3 n \log m)$ parallel arithmetic steps and $n^2 m / \log m$ processors.

The evaluation of polynomial gcds has further applications to rational interpolation, Padé approximation and several polynomial computations (see [BGY] and [vzG]).

References

[A] K.E. Atkinson, *An Introduction to Numerical Analysis,* Wiley, 1978.

[B-AS85] A. Ben-Artzi and T. Shalom, "On Inversion of Block Toeplitz Matrices," *Integral Equations and Operator Theory*, vol. 8, pp. 751-779, 1985.

[B-AS86] A. Ben-Artzi and T. Shalom, "On Inversion of Toeplitz and Close to Toeplitz Matrices," *Linear Algebra and Its Applications*, vol. 75, pp. 173-192, 1986.

[Be] A. Ben-Israel, "A Note on Iterative Method for Generalized Inversion of Matrices," *Math. Computation*, vol. 20, pp. 439-440, 1966.

[BA] R.R. Bitmead and B.D.O. Anderson, "Asymptotically Fast Solution of Toeplitz and Related Systems of Linear Equations," *Linear Algebra and Its Applics.*, vol. 34, pp. 103-116, 1980.

[BKAK] R.R. Bitmead, S.-Y. Kung, B.D.O. Anderson, and T. Kailath, "Greatest Common Divisors via Generalized Sylvester and Bezout Matrices," *IEEE Trans. on Automatic Control*, vol. AC-23,6, pp. 1043-1047, 1978.

[BGH] A. Borodin, J. von zur Gathen, and J. Hopcroft, "Fast Parallel Matrix and GCD Computation," *Information and Control*, vol. 52,3, pp. 241-256, 1982.

[BGY] R.P. Brent, F.G. Gustavson, and D.Y.Y. Yun, "Fast Solution of Toeplitz Systems of Equations and Computation of Padé Approximations," *J. of Algorithms*, vol. 1, pp. 259-295, 1980.

[Bun] J.R. Bunch, "Stability of Methods for Solving Toeplitz Systems of Equations," *SIAM J. on Scientific and Statistical Computing*, vol. 6,2, pp. 349-364, 1985.

[CKL-A] J. Chun, T. Kailath, and H. Lev-Ari, "Fast Parallel Algorithm for QR-factorization of Structured Matrices," *SIAM J. on Scientific and Statistical Computing*, vol. 8,6, pp. 899-913, 1987.

[Cs] L. Csanky, "Fast Parallel Matrix Inversion Algorithm," *SIAM J. Computing*, vol. 5,4, pp. 618-623, 1976.

[dH] F.R. deHoog, "On the Solution of Toeplitz Systems," *Linear Algebra and Its Applics.*, vol. 88/89, pp. 123-138, 1987.

[FF] D.K. Faddeev and V.N. Faddeeva, *Computational Methods of Linear Algebra*, W.H. Freeman, San Francisco, 1963.

[FKML] B. Friedlander, T. Kailath, M. Morf, and L. Ljung, "Extended Levinson and Chandrasekar Equations for General Discrete-Time Linear Estimation Problems," *IEEE Trans. Automatic Control*, vol. AC-23,4, pp. 653-659, 1978.

[GS] W. Gentleman and G. Sande, "Fast Fourier Transform for Fun and Profit," *Proc. Fall Joint Comput. Conf.*, vol. 29, pp. 563-578, 1966.

[GF] I.C. Gohberg and I.A. Feldman, "Convolution Equations and Projection Methods for Their Solutions," *Translations of Math. Monographs*, vol. 41, Amer. Math. Soc., Providence, RI, 1974.

[GH74] I.C. Gohberg and G. Heinig, "Inversion of Finite Toeplitz Matrices with Entries Being Elements from a Noncommutative Algebra," *Rev. Roumaine Math. Pures Appl.*, vol. XIX,5, pp. 623-665, 1974.

[GSe] I.C. Gohberg and A.A. Semencul, "On the Inversion of Finite Toeplitz Matrices and Their Continuous Analogs," *Mat. Issled.*, vol. 2, pp. 201-233 (in Russian), 1972.

[GL] G.H. Golub and C.F. van Loan, *Matrix Computations*, Johns Hopkins Univ. Press, Baltimore, Maryland, 1983.

[G] W.B. Gragg, "The Padé Table and Its Relation to Certain Algorithms of Numerical Analysis," *SIAM Review*, vol. 14,1, pp. 1-62, 1972.

[GY] F.G. Gustavson and D.Y.Y. Yun, "Fast Algorithms for Rational Hermite Approximation and Solution of Toeplitz Systems," *IEEE Trans. Circuits and Systems*, vol. CAS-26,9, pp. 750-755, 1979.

[Heinig] G. Heinig, "Beitrage zur spektraltheorie von Operatorbuschen und zur algebraischen Theorei von Toeplitzmatrizen, Diss. B," *TH Karl-Marx-Stadt*, 1979.

[HR] G. Heining and K. Rost, "Algebraic Methods for Toeplitz-like Matrices and Operators," *Operator Theory*, vol. 13, Birkhauser, 1984.

[Kai] T. Kailath, "Signal Processing Applications of Some Moment Problems," *Proc. AMS Symp. in Applied Math.*, vol. 37, pp. 71-100, 1987.

[KC] T. Kailath and J. Chun, "Generalized Gohberg-Semencul Formulas for Matrix Inversion," *manuscript*, 1988.

[KKM] T. Kailath, S.-Y. Kung, and M. Morf, "Displacement Ranks of Matrices and Linear Equations," *J. Math. Anal. Appl.*, vol. 68,2, pp. 395-407, 1979.

[KVM] T. Kailath, A. Viera, and M. Morf, "Inverses of Toeplitz Operators, Innovations, and Orthogonal Polynomials," *SIAM Review*, vol. 20,1, pp. 106-119, 1978.

[KK] S. Kung and T. Kailath, "Fast Projection Methods for Minimal Design Problems in Linear System Theory," *Automatica*, vol. 16, pp. 399-403, 1980.

[M] B.R. Musicus, "Levinson and Fast Choleski Algorithms for Toeplitz and Almost Toeplitz Matrices," Internal Report, *Lab. of Electronics, M.I.T.*, 1981.

[P85] V. Pan, "Fast and Efficient Parallel Algorithms for the Exact Inversion of Integer Matrices," *Proc. Fifth Conference FST & TCS, Lecture Notes in Computer Science,* 206, pp. 504-521, Springer Verlag, 1985.

[P87a] V. Pan, "Complexity of Parallel Matrix Computations," *Theoretical Computer Science*, vol. 54, pp. 65-85, 1987.

[P87b] V. Pan, "Sequential and Parallel Complexity of Approximate Evaluation of Polynomial Zeros," *Computers and Mathematics (with Applications)*, vol. 14,8, pp. 591-622, 1987.

[P88a] V. Pan, "Fast and Efficient Parallel Evaluation of the Zeros of a Polynomial Having Only Real Zeros," *Technical Report 88-13, Computer Science Dept., SUNY Albany*, 1988.

[P88c] V. Pan, "A New Acceleration of the Hilbert-Vandermonde Matrix Computations by Their Reduction to Hankel-Toeplitz Computations," Tech. Rep. TR 88-34, Computer Science Dept., SUNY Albany, Albany, NY, 1988.

[P88b] V. Pan, "New Effective Methods for Computations with Structured Matrices," *Technical Report 88-28, Computer Science Dept., SUNY Albany*, 1988.

[PR] V. Pan and J. Reif, "Efficient Parallel Solution of Linear Systems," *Proc. 17-th Ann. ACM Symp. on Theory of Computing*, pp. 143-152, 1985.

[PS88] V. Pan and R. Schreiber, "An Improved Newton Iteration for the Generalized Inverse of a Matrix, with Applications," Technical Report 88-35, Computer Science Dept., SUNYA, 1988.

[Par] B.N. Parlett, *The Symmetric Eigenvalue Problem,* Prentice-Hall, 1980.

[Quinn] M.J. Quinn, *Designing Efficient Algorithms for Parallel Computers,* McGraw-Hill, New York, 1987.

[Sc] A. Schönhage, "The Fundamental Theorem of Algebra in Terms of Computational Complexity," manuscript, *Dept. of Math., University of Tübingen*, Tübingen, West Germany, 1982.

[Tism] M. Tismenetsky, "Besoutians, Toeplitz and Hankel Matrices in the Spectral Theory of Matrix Polynomials," *Ph.D. Thesis*, Technion, Haifa, 1981.

[T64] W.F. Trench, "An Algorithm for Inversion of Finite Toeplitz Matrices," *J. of SIAM*, vol. 12,3, pp. 515-522, 1964.

[T65] W.F. Trench, "An Algorithm for Inversion of Finite Hankel Matrices," *J. of SIAM*, vol. 13,4, pp. 1102-1107, 1965.

[vzG] J. von zur Gathen, "Parallel Algorithms for Algebraic Problems," *SIAM J. on Comp.*, vol. 13,4, pp. 802-824, 1984.

[vzG86] J. von zur Gathen, "Parallel Arithmetic Computations: A Survey," *Proc. Math. Foundation of Comp. Science, Lecture Notes in Computer Science*, vol. 233, pp. 93-112, Springer, 1986.

[vzG86a] J. von zur Gathen, "Representations and Parallel Computations for Rational Functions," *SIAM J. on Computing*, vol. 15,2, pp. 432-452, 1986.

[W] J.H. Wilkinson, *The Algebraic Eigenvalue Problem*, Clarendon Press, Oxford, 1965.

Dept. of Math., Lehman College
CUNY, Bronx, NY 10468
and
Computer Science Dept., SUNY Albany
Albany, New York 12222

Operator Theory:
Advances and Applications, Vol. 40

STABILITY OF INVARIANT LAGRANGIAN SUBSPACES II

*A. C. M. Ran and L. Rodman *)*

Dedicated to Professor Israel Gohberg on the occasion of his sixtieth birthday.

In this paper we consider various stability properties of real invariant lagrangian subspaces for real matrices which are either symmetric or skew-symmetric in a real quadratic form which may be symmetric or skew-symmetric itself. In particular, apart from ordinary stability we shall consider strong stability, which seems to be more desirable from a numerical point of view. For the classes of matrices we consider here stable subspaces are not always strongly stable, in contrast with the previous work. We shall completely characterize strongly stable invariant lagrangian subspaces, and in many cases also the stable ones. Invariant lagrangian subspaces with other stability properties, such as Lipschitz stability, are characterized as well.

0. Introduction

This paper is the second part of an investigation into various stability properties of invariant lagrangian subspaces. Such a subspace is invariant for a real matrix which is either symmetric or skew-symmetric in a real quadratic form (which itself may be symmetric or skew-symmetric), and it is maximal isotropic with respect to this form. Stability of such subspaces under perturbations of the matrix and the quadratic form is studied. In previous papers [RR1,2] we studied the cases when the matrix and the quadratic form are either both symmetric or both skew-symmetric.

Let us first recall some of the basic definitions from [RR2]. For $\xi=\pm 1, \eta=\pm 1$ let $L_n(\xi,\eta)$ denote the class of all pairs of real matrices (A,H) with H invertible and $H^T=\xi H, HA=\eta A^T H$. In case $\xi=-1$ we assume n is even in order to avoid the trivial case when $L_n(\xi,\eta)$ is empty.

For $(A,H) \in L_n(\xi,\eta)$, let $J(A,H)$ be the class of all A - invariant lagrangian subspaces $M \subset \mathbb{R}^n$. Here A-invariance means as usual $AM \subset M$. We call a subspace $M \subset \mathbb{R}^n$ *lagrangian* (with respect to H), or *H-lagrangian* if $(HM)^{\perp}=M$. A subspace $M \in J(A,H)$ is called *conditionally stable* if for every $\epsilon>0$ there is $\delta>0$ such that for any pair $(B,G) \in L_n(\xi,\eta)$ with $J(B,G) \neq \emptyset$ and

$$||G-H|| + ||B-A|| < \delta$$

* Partially supported by an NSF grant.

there is $M' \in J(B,G)$ with

$$\theta(M,M') < \epsilon.$$

Here θ denotes the gap metric on the set of subspaces of $\mathbb{R}^n$, which is defined as follows: for two subspaces M, M', $\theta(M,M')$ is defined by $\|P_M - P_{M'}\|$, where P_M and $P_{M'}$ denote the orthogonal projections on M and M', respectively. If in the above definition the condition $J(B,G) \neq \emptyset$ is omitted we say that M is *unconditionally stable.*

A subspace $M \in J(A,H)$ is called *Lipschitz conditionally stable* if there exist $\epsilon > 0$ and $K > 0$ such that for every pair $(B,G) \in L_n(\xi,\eta)$ with $J(B,G) \neq \emptyset$ and

$$\|A - B\| + \|H - G\| < \epsilon$$

there is $M' \in J(B,G)$ satisfying

$$\theta(M,M') \leqq K(\|A - B\| + \|H - G\|).$$

Again, if we leave out the condition $J(B,G) \neq \emptyset$, we shall say that M is *unconditionally Lipschitz stable.*

To introduce the concept of strong stability, let $(A,H) \in L_n(\xi,\eta)$, and choose sufficiently small positively oriented disjoint contours $\Gamma_j, j = 1,\ldots,k$ such that inside Γ_j is either precisely one real eigenvalue of A or precisely one pair of complex conjugate eigenvalues of A, and each eigenvalue of A is lying inside some Γ_j. Put $\Gamma = \bigcup_{j=1}^{k} \Gamma_j$. Then a subspace $M \in J(A,H)$ is called *conditionally strongly stable* if for any sequence $(A_m,H_m) \in L_n(\xi,\eta)$ with $J(A_m,H_m) \neq \emptyset, A_m \to A, H_m \to H$ and *any* sequence $M_m \in J(A_m,H_m)$ with

$$\dim P_{mj} M_m = \dim P_j M,$$

where P_{mj} (resp. P_j) is the spectral projection of A_m (resp. A) with respect to the eigenvalues inside Γ_j, we have

$$\theta(M_m,M) \to 0 \qquad \text{as} \qquad m \to \infty. \tag{0.1}$$

(Note that $\sigma(A_m) \cap \Gamma = \emptyset$ for m large enough, and so the projections P_{mj} are well defined for large m at least). Omitting the condition $J(A_m,H_m) \neq \emptyset$ we obtain the definition of *unconditionally strongly stable* subspace. Further, if we replace (0.1) by

$$\theta(M,M') \leqq K(\|A - A_m\| + \|H - H_m\|).$$

where $K > 0$ depends only on A, H and M, we shall call M *conditionally strongly Lipschitz stable* or *unconditionally strongly Lipschitz stable* according to whether or not we require

$J(A_m, H_m) \neq \emptyset$ in advance.

For further definitions and general theory the reader is referred to the first two sections of [RR2].

In the present paper we shall consider these notions of stability of invariant lagrangian subspaces in the cases when the matrix is symmetric in a skew-symmetric inner product or skew-symmetric in a symmetric inner product. Here for the first time we find subspaces which are stable but not strongly stable. In both cases we shall completely characterize the strongly stable invariant lagrangian subspaces, and in the latter case also the stable ones. In the former case we describe the stable subspaces for invertible matrices only.

To be more precise, let A be a symmetric matrix with respect to the skew-symmetric inner product given by H, i.e. $H=-H^T, HA=A^TH$. Then it will be shown that strongly stable invariant lagrangian subspaces do not exist, and that stable invariant lagrangian subspaces exist if and only if the geometric multiplicity of A at each of its eigenvalues is two. A full description is given of the stable subspaces in this case.

In case A is skew-symmetric with respect to the inner product given by H, i.e. $H=H^T$ and $HA=-A^TH$, it will be shown that conditionally strongly stable invariant lagrangian subspaces exist if and only if A is invertible and a certain condition on the partial multiplicities of A at pure imaginary eigenvalues and the signs corresponding to (A,H) is satisfied. Under these conditions it is shown that conditionally stable and conditionally strongly stable invariant lagrangian subspaces coincide. Finally an example is given to show that in case A is not invertible there may exist stable invariant lagrangian subspaces, which of course are not strongly stable.

There are in this paper also other phenomena differing considerably from the cases considered so far in the literature. In particular, in case A is skew symmetric with respect to the inner product given by a symmetric matrix H it will be shown that there are Lipschitz-stable invariant lagrangian subspaces which are not isolated in $J(A,H)$. Also, in case A is symmetric with respect to a skew-symmetric inner product it turns out that a stable subspace is always $\frac{1}{2}$-stable, meaning that for any pair (A',H') close to (A,H) there is $M' \in J(A',H')$ with

$$\theta(M,M') \leq K(\|A-A'\| + \|H-H'\|)^{\frac{1}{2}}$$

where $K>0$ depends on A, H and M only.

The following notations and conventions will be used in this paper. The block diagonal matrix with blocks $Z_1,\ldots,Z_q$ on the main diagonal is denoted $Z_1 \oplus \cdots \oplus Z_q$ or

$\oplus_{i=1}^{q} Z_i$. The transposed matrix is denoted by the superscript "T". The Jordan blocks (lower triangular) are designated as follows:

$$J_n(a)=\begin{pmatrix} a & & & \\ 1 & \cdot & 0 & \\ & \cdot & \cdot & \\ & 0 & \cdot & a \\ & & 1 & a \end{pmatrix}; \qquad J_n\begin{pmatrix} a & b \\ -b & a \end{pmatrix}=\begin{pmatrix} Z & & & \\ I_2 & \cdot & & \\ & \cdot & \cdot & \\ & & \cdot & \cdot \\ & & I_2 & Z \end{pmatrix},$$

where Z stands for the matrix $\begin{pmatrix} a & b \\ -b & a \end{pmatrix}$. Here a,b are real numbers and $b \neq 0$; the size of $J_n(a)$ is $n \times n$ and the size of $J_n\begin{pmatrix} a & b \\ -b & a \end{pmatrix}$ is $2n \times 2n$. The eigenvalues, partial multiplicities and algebraic multiplicities of real matrices are understood in the same way as for complex matrices, thus, $J_n\begin{pmatrix} a & b \\ -b & a \end{pmatrix}$ has two eigenvalues $a+ib$ and $a-ib$, each of geometric multiplicity one and algebraic multiplicity n. The standard inner product in $\mathbb{R}^n$ or $\mathbb{C}^n$ is denoted $<.,.>$. The superscript $\perp$ denotes the orthogonal complement (relative to the standard inner product). The range of a matrix X (i.e. its column space) is denoted Im X. The real root subspace of an $n \times n$ real matrix X corresponding to its real eigenvalue λ (resp. a pair of non-real eigenvalues $\lambda \pm i\mu$) is denoted $R(X,\lambda)$ (resp. $R(X,\lambda \pm i\mu)$). I, or I_n, stands for the $n \times n$ identity matrix. We denote by Inv (A) the lattice of all A-invariant subspces. For a subspace N we will denote by $A|_N$ the restriction of A to N. Finally, e_j stands for the standard j-th coordinate vector (i.e. the j-th coordinate is 1, all other coordinates are zeros) in $\mathbb{C}^p$ (the dimension p will be understood from the context).

1.The case $\xi=1,\eta=-1$

1.1.Canonical form and sign characteristic

Let $(A,H)\in L_n(1,-1)$,i.e. $H=H^T$ is real and invertible, and A is real and $HA=-A^TH$. We shall describe the canonical form of the pair (A,H) below. Denote

$$F_j=\begin{pmatrix} & & & 1 \\ & 0 & -1 & \\ & & \cdot & \\ & \cdot & & \\ & \cdot & 0 & \\ (-1)^{j-1} & & & \end{pmatrix},$$

so F_j is a $j \times j$ matrix which is symmetric if j is odd and skew -symmetric if j is even; and

$$G_j = \begin{bmatrix} & & & F_2^{j-1} \\ & 0 & -F_2^{j-1} & \\ & & \cdot & \\ & \cdot & & \\ & \cdot & 0 & \\ (-1)^{j-1}F_2^{j-1} & & & \end{bmatrix},$$

so G_j is a $2j \times 2j$ matrix which is symmetric for all j . The following result can be found in [DPWZ] (among other places).

THEOREM 1.1 *Given* $(A,H) \in L_n(1,-1)$ *there is an invertible matrix* S *such that*

$$S^{-1}AS = \bigoplus_{i=1}^{m} A_i, \quad S^T HS = \bigoplus_{i=1}^{m} H_i,$$

where the pairs of matrices (A_i, H_i) *are of one of the following types:*

$$\begin{cases} A_i = \bigoplus_{j=1}^{p} J_{2n_j+1}(0) \oplus \bigoplus_{j=1}^{q} \left[J_{n_{p+j}}(0) \oplus -J_{n_{p+j}}(0)^T \right], \\ H_i = \bigoplus_{j=1}^{p} \varkappa_j F_{2n_j+1} \oplus \bigoplus_{j=1}^{q} \begin{bmatrix} 0 & I_{n_{p+j}} \\ I_{n_{p+j}} & 0 \end{bmatrix} \end{cases} \tag{1.1}$$

where $n_{p+1}, \ldots, n_{p+q}$ *are even integers and* $\varkappa_1, \ldots, \varkappa_p$ *are signs* ± 1,

$$\begin{cases} A_i = \bigoplus_{j=1}^{p} J_{n_j}(a) \oplus -J_{n_j}(a)^T, \\ H_i = \bigoplus_{j=1}^{p} \begin{bmatrix} 0 & I_{n_j} \\ I_{n_j} & 0 \end{bmatrix} \end{cases} \tag{1.2}$$

where $a > 0$,

$$\begin{cases} A_i = \bigoplus_{j=1}^{p} J_{n_j} \begin{bmatrix} 0 & b \\ -b & 0 \end{bmatrix}, \\ H_i = \bigoplus_{j=1}^{p} \varkappa_j G_{n_j} \end{cases} \tag{1.3}$$

where $b>0$ *and* $\varkappa_1, \ldots, \varkappa_p$ *are signs* ± 1,

$$\begin{cases} A_i = \bigoplus_{j=1}^{p} \left(J_{n_j}\left(\begin{pmatrix} a & b \\ -b & a \end{pmatrix} \right) \oplus - \left(J_{n_j}\left(\begin{pmatrix} a & b \\ -b & a \end{pmatrix} \right) \right)^T \right), \\ H_i = \bigoplus_{j=1}^{p} \begin{pmatrix} 0 & I_{2n_j} \\ I_{2n_j} & 0 \end{pmatrix} \end{cases} \tag{1.4}$$

where $a,b>0$.

(Of course, the numbers a,b *as well as the signs* $\varkappa_j$ *and the numbers* p,q *may be different in different pairs of matrices* (A_i,H_i).*)*

Moreover this form is uniquely determined by the matrices A *and* H *, up to simultaneous permutations of pairs of blocks in* A_i,H_i.

Observe that if $(A,H)\in L_n(1,-1)$ then $(iA,H)\in L_n^c$, where L_n^c is the set of all pairs of complex matrices (A,H) with $HA=A^*H$ (here * denotes complex conjugate). In other words, the matrix iA is selfadjoint in the indefinite inner product induced in $\mathbb{C}^n$ by H. So there is a sign characteristic associated with (iA,H). For the definition and properties of the sign characteristic see, e.g. [GLR 1, RR 3]. This sign characteristic can be computed in terms of the signs $\varkappa_j$ which appear in (1.1) and (1.3) as follows.

THEOREM 1.2 *(i) Let (A,H) be of type (1.1). Then the sign in the sign characteristic of (iA,H) attached to the block* $J_{2n_j+1}(0)$ *is* $(-1)^{n_j}\varkappa_j$ *for* $j=1,\ldots,p$*, while the signs attached to the two blocks* $J_{n_{p+j}}(0)\oplus -J_{n_{p+j}}(0)^T$ *are 1 and -1, for* $j=1,\ldots,q$.

(ii) Let (A,H) be of type (1.3). Then the sign in the sign characteristic attached to the partial multiplicity n_j *corresponding to the eigenvalue b of iA is* $\varkappa_j$*, and the sign attached to* n_j *as a partial multiplicity of iA at -b is* $(-1)^{n_j-1}\varkappa_j$.

Proof. (i)The Jordan chain of $iJ_{2n+1}(0)$ for $n=n_j$ is $i^{2n}e_{2n+1},\ldots,ie_2,e_1$, so the sign attached to $J_{2n+1}(0)$ is $\langle \varkappa F_{2n+1}e_1, i^{2n}e_{2n+1}\rangle=(-1)^n\varkappa$, where $\varkappa=\varkappa_j$.

Next, with $n=\frac{1}{2}n_{p+j}$ two Jordan chains for $i\left(J_n(0)\oplus -J_n(0)^T\right)$ are given by

$$x_j=\frac{1}{\sqrt{2}}(i^{2n-j}e_{2n-j+1}+i(-i)^{2n-j}e_{2n+j}), \qquad (j=1,\ldots,2n),$$

$$y_j=\frac{1}{\sqrt{2}}(i^{2n-j}e_{2n-j+1}-i(-i)^{2n-j}e_{2n+j}), \qquad (j=1,\ldots,2n)$$

A calculation shows that

$$\left\langle \begin{bmatrix} 0 & I_{2n} \\ I_{2n} & 0 \end{bmatrix} x_1, x_{2n} \right\rangle = (-1)^{n+1}, \quad \left\langle \begin{bmatrix} 0 & I_{2n} \\ I_{2n} & 0 \end{bmatrix} y_1, y_{2n} \right\rangle = -(-1)^{n+1}$$

and

$$\left\langle \begin{bmatrix} 0 & I_{2n} \\ I_{2n} & 0 \end{bmatrix} x_1, y_{2n} \right\rangle = 0.$$

This proves (i).

(ii) First observe that the matrix $iJ_n \begin{pmatrix} 0 & b \\ -b & 0 \end{pmatrix}$, (with $b>0$) has Jordan chains

$$x_j = \frac{1}{\sqrt{2}} i^{n-j} (e_{2n-2j+1} - ie_{2n-2j+2}) \qquad j=1,\dots,n,$$
$$y_j = \frac{1}{\sqrt{2}} i^{n-j} (e_{2n-2j+1} + ie_{2n-2j+2}) \qquad j=1,\dots,n$$

corresponding to its eigenvalues $+b$ and $-b$, respectively. A computation shows that for n odd

$$\langle \varkappa G_n x_1, x_n \rangle = \varkappa = \langle \varkappa G_n y_1, y_n \rangle$$

while for n even

$$\langle \varkappa G_n x_1, x_n \rangle = \varkappa = -\langle \varkappa G_n y_1, y_n \rangle.$$

This implies (ii). □

1.2. Existence and uniqueness of invariant lagrangian subspaces

The next theorem deals with existence, uniqueness and description of invariant lagrangian subspaces.

THEOREM 1.3 *(i) Let $(A,H) \in L_n(1,-1)$. Then $J(A,H) \neq \emptyset$ if and only if for each pure imaginary eigenvalue of A the number of odd partial multiplicities is even and moreover the following holds:*

(a) if $2n_j+1$, $j=1,\dots,p$ are the odd partial multiplicities of A corresponding to zero, and $\varkappa_j$, $j=1,\dots,p$ are the corresponding signs in (1.1) then

$$\sum_{j=1}^{p} (-1)^{n_j} \varkappa_j = 0, \tag{1.5}$$

(b) if $n_1,\dots,n_p$ are the odd partial multiplicities of A corresponding to eigenvalues $\pm ib$, $b>0$, and $\varkappa_1,\dots,\varkappa_p$ are the corresponding signs in (1.3) then

$$\sum_{j=1}^{p} \varkappa_j = 0. \tag{1.6}$$

(ii) Let N be a real A-invariant subspace such that the eigenvalues of $A|_N$ are in the open right half plane, and let M_+ be the largest such subspace. Then there is a unique subspace $M \in J(A,H)$ such that $M \cap M_+ = N$ if and only if A is invertible and for each pure imaginary eigenvalue of A (if any) all partial multiplicities are even and all corresponding signs are equal.

Proof. By using the localization principle (Theorem 2.2 in [RR2]) we may assume that $(A,H)$is in one of the forms (1.1) -(1.4). First assume A has no pure imaginary eigenvalues, i.e. (A,H) is of the form (1.2) or (1.4). Observe that by simultaneous permutations of blocks (A,H) can be written in the form (A_1,H_1) where

$$A_1 = \begin{bmatrix} \tilde{A} & 0 \\ 0 & -\tilde{A}^T \end{bmatrix} \qquad H_1 = \begin{bmatrix} 0 & I_n \\ I_n & 0 \end{bmatrix}$$

with $\sigma(\tilde{A}) \cap \sigma(-\tilde{A}^T) = \varnothing$. Then any A_1 -invariant subspace M is of the form $M = N_1 \oplus N_2$, where $N_j \subset \mathbb{R}^n$, $j=1,2$. Such an M is lagrangian if and only if $N_2 = N_1^{\perp}$. Thus $M \in J(A_1,H_1)$ if and only if $M = N \oplus N^{\perp}$ for some $\tilde{A}$ -invariant subspace N. Obviously N and M determine each other uniquely. This gives the correspondence required in part (ii) for these cases. Note that this correspondence is a homeomorphism between $J(A,H)$ and the set of $\tilde{A}$-invariant subspaces, which we shall denote by Inv $(\tilde{A})$.

Next, suppose A has pure imaginary eigenvalues and assume $J(A,H) \neq \varnothing$. Considering A and H as complex matrices it is easily seen that also the set of all A-invariant lagrangian subspaces in $\mathbb{C}^n$ is non-empty. Using [RR3], Theorem 5.1 (see also [RR2], Proposition 1.3) combined with the description of the sign characteristic of (iA,H) given in Theorem 1.2 shows that the number of odd partial multiplicities at each pure imaginary eigenvalue is even, and the conditions (1.5),(1.6) hold.

For the converse in part (i) and the remainder of part (ii) first suppose $\sigma(A) = \{0\}$ and (A,H) is in the form (1.1), and moreover(1.5) holds. We have to show $J(A,H)$ contains at least two elements. If $p=0$ this is obvious,e.g.

$$\bigoplus_{j=1}^{q} \left(\mathbb{R}^{n_{p+j}} \oplus (0) \right) \in J(A,H), \quad \bigoplus_{j=1}^{q} \left((0) \oplus \mathbb{R}^{n_{p+j}} \right) \in J(A,H).$$

For the case $p \neq 0$ it is sufficient to consider the case $p=2, q=0$ and $(-1)^{n_1}\varkappa_1 = -(-1)^{n_2}\varkappa_2 = 1$. One easily checks that for $\epsilon = 1$and $\epsilon = -1$

$$\text{span } \{e_{n_1+1} + \epsilon e_{2n_1+1+n_2+1}, e_{n_1+2}, \ldots,$$

$$e_{2n_1+1}, e_{2n_1+1+n_2+2}, \ldots, e_{2n_1+1+2n_2+1}\} \in J(A,H).$$

This proves the theorem for the case $\sigma(A)=\{0\}$.

Finally assume (A,H) is of the form (1.3) and (1.6) holds. We show that $J(A,H) \neq \emptyset$ to prove (i), and that $J(A,H)$ consists of a single element if and only if the conditions in part (ii) hold. To prove that $J(A,H) \neq \emptyset$ we can assume without loss of generality either $p=1$ and n_1 is even or $p=2$, n_1 and n_2 are odd and $\varkappa_1=-\varkappa_2$. In the former case $(0)\oplus \mathbb{R}^{n_1} \in J(A,H)$. In the latter case we may also assume $n_1 \geqq n_2$ (otherwise interchange the blocks), and then for $\epsilon=\pm 1$

$$\text{span}\ \{e_{n_1+2}, \ldots, e_{2n_1}, e_{2n_1+n_2+2}, \ldots, e_{2n_1+2n_2},$$

$$e_{n_1}+\epsilon e_{2n_1+n_2+1}, -e_{n_1+1}+\epsilon e_{2n_1+n_2}\} \in J(A,H). \tag{1.7}$$

(in checking this use the equality $(-1)^{\frac{n-1}{2}} F_{\frac{n}{2}-1}=I$ for odd n). Formula (1.7) also shows that in case A has odd partial multiplicities $J(A,H)$ contains more than one element. So to prove that the conditions in (ii) must hold in case $J(A,H)$ consists of one element it remains to consider the case

$$A=J_{n_1}\begin{pmatrix} 0 & b \\ -b & 0 \end{pmatrix} \oplus J_{n_2}\begin{pmatrix} 0 & b \\ -b & 0 \end{pmatrix}, \quad H=G_{n_1}\oplus -G_{n_2};$$

where n_1 and n_2 are even, and to show that in this case $J(A,H)$ contains at least two elements. We assume $n_1 \geqq n_2$ without loss of generality. Then

$$\text{span}\ \{e_{n_1+1}, \ldots, e_{2n_1}, e_{2n_1+n_2+1}, \ldots, e_{2n_1+2n_2}\} \in J(A,H)$$

and

$$\text{span}\ \{e_{n_1+3}, \ldots, e_{2n_1}, e_{2n_1+n_2+3}, \ldots, e_{2n_1+2n_2},$$

$$e_{n_1-1}+e_{2n_1+n_2}, -e_{n_1}+e_{2n_1+n_2-1}, e_{n_1+1}+e_{2n_1+n_2+2}, -e_{n_1+2}+e_{2n_1+n_2+1}\} \in J(A,H),$$

as one readily checks.

For the converse in part (ii) suppose the hypothesis on partial multiplicities and signs of A described in (ii) hold true, and that $M_1 \neq M_2$, $M_j \in J(A,H)$ $(j=1,2)$ and $\sigma(A)=\{\pm ib\}$. Then, considering iA and H as complex matrices, there exist two different A-invariant lagrangian subspaces in $\mathbb{C}^n$. However, this contradicts [RR2], Theorem 2.2. □

We will need a more precise statement concerning the correspondence between N and M described in Theorem 1.3 (ii). Namely, assume that A is invertible and that for each pure imaginary eigenvalue of A all partial multiplicities are even and all signs are equal. Then the correspondence between M and N is Lipschitz in the following sense: there is a constant $C>0$ (which depends on A only) such that

$$\frac{1}{C}\theta(N,N')\leqq\theta(M,M')\leqq C\theta(N,N'),$$

where N,N' are real A-invariant subspaces such that the eigenvalues of $A|_N$ and $A|_{N'}$ lie in the open right halfplane, and $M,M'\in J(A,H)$ are such that $M\cap M_+=N$, $M'\cap M_+=N'$. The verification of this fact is again based on the reduction to the case when (A,H) is given by on of the formulas (1.2)-(1.4) and on using the form (A_1,H_1), as in the proof of Theorem 1.

1.3 Stability

The emphasis will be on strong stability in this section. We shall completely characterize strongly stable subspaces, and show that in this case the concepts of strong stability and stability do not coincide. The following theorem states some of our main results.

THEOREM 1.4. *Let* $(A,H)\in L_n(1,-1)$.

(i) There exists a conditionally strongly stable invariant lagrangian subspace if and only if A is invertible and for each pure imaginary eigenvalue ib of A the partial multiplicities of A at ib are even and the signs in the sign characteristic of (iA,H) corresponding to ib are all the same.

(ii) There exists an unconditionally strongly stable invariant lagrangian subspace if and only if $\sigma(A)\cap i\mathbb{R}=\emptyset$.

(iii) Suppose A is invertible. Then each (un)conditionally stable subspace in $J(A,H)$ *is (un)conditionally strongly stable in* $J(A,H)$.

(iv) Assume an (un)conditionally strongly stable lagrangian subspace exists. Then a subspace $M\in J(A,H)$ *is (un)conditionally strongly stable if and only if all the all the conditions (a)-(e) below are satisfied.*

(a) $M\cap R(A,\lambda)$ *is either* (0) *or* $R(A,\lambda)$ *whenever* $0\neq\lambda$ *is a real eigenvalue of A with* dim Ker $(A-\lambda)>1$ *, in this case* $M\cap R(A,-\lambda)$ *is* $R(A,-\lambda)$ *or* (0), *respectively,*

(b) $M\cap R(A,\lambda)$ *is an arbitrary even dimensional A-invariant subspace of* $R(A,\lambda)$ *whenever* $\lambda\neq 0$ *has geometric multiplicity one and the algebraic multiplicity of* λ *is even. In this case*

$$M\cap R(A,-\lambda)=[H(M\cap R(A,\lambda))]^{\perp}\cap R(A,-\lambda), \tag{1.8}$$

(c) $M\cap R(A,\lambda)$ *is an arbitrary A-invariant subspace of* $R(A,\lambda)$ *whenever* λ

has geometric multiplicity one and the algebraic multiplicity of λ *is odd. Again, in this case* $M\cap R(A,-\lambda)$ *is given by (1.8),*

(d) $M\cap R(A,a\pm ib)$ *is either* (0) *or* $R(A,a\pm ib)$ *whenever* $a\pm ib$, $a\neq 0$, $b\neq 0$ *are eigenvalues of* A *with geometric multiplicity at least two, in this case* $M\cap R(A,-a\pm ib)$ *is* $R(A,-a\pm ib)$ *or* (0) *,respectively,*

(e) $M\cap R(A,a\pm ib)$ *is an arbitrary* A*-invariant subspace of* $R(A,a\pm ib)$ *whenever* $a\pm ib$, $a\neq 0$, $b\neq 0$ *are eigenvalues of* A *with geometric multiplicity one. In this case*

$$M\cap R(A,-a\pm ib)=[H(M\cap R(A,a\pm ib))]^{\perp}\cap R(A,-a\pm ib). \tag{1.9}$$

Proof. By Theorem 2.2 in [RR2] we have to consider only the cases $\sigma(A)=\{a\pm ib,-a\pm ib\}$, $a>0$, $b>0$, $\sigma(A)=\{\lambda,-\lambda\}$, $\lambda>0$, $\sigma(A)=\{\pm ib\}$, $b>0$ and $\sigma(A)=\{0\}$.

In the first two cases the equivalence of conditional and unconditional stability follows from the fact that $J(A',H')\neq\varnothing$ for all $(A',H')\in L_n(1,-1)$ sufficiently close to (A,H). The rest of the theorem follows from Theorems 1.7 and 1.8 in [RR2] and from the homeomorphism between $J(A,H)$ and Inv $(\tilde{A})$ described in Theorem 1.3 and its proof. This establishes also (iv). The fact that in these cases there is no difference between (un)conditional stability and (un)conditional strong stability is a consequence of Lemma 1.11 in [RR2].

Next, let $\sigma(A)=\{0\}$. Let us show that there is no conditionally strongly stable subspace in $J(A,H)$. First suppose there is an even partial multiplicity corresponding to zero. Then write

$$A=J_n(0)\oplus -J_n(0)^T\oplus A_1\ ,\ H=\begin{bmatrix}0 & I_n\\ I_n & 0\end{bmatrix}\oplus H_1,$$

where n is even. Now consider the perturbation

$$A(\alpha)=J_n(\alpha)\oplus -J_n(\alpha)^T\oplus A_1\ ,\quad \alpha\in\mathbb{R}$$

Let M_1 be any A_1-invariant H_1-lagrangian subspace. Then $\operatorname{Im}\begin{bmatrix}I_n\\ 0\end{bmatrix}\oplus M_1\in J(A(\alpha),H)$ and $\operatorname{Im}\begin{bmatrix}0\\ I_n\\ 0\end{bmatrix}\oplus M_1\in J(A(\alpha),H)$ for all α. Letting $\alpha\to 0$ one sees that there is no strongly stable subspace in this case. Next suppose there are only odd partial multiplicities. According to Theorem 1.3 the number of these odd partial multiplicities is even in case $J(A,H)\neq\varnothing$. Assuming there exists a conditionally strongly stable subspace in $J(A,H)$, we can write

$$A = J_{2n_1+1}(0) \oplus -J_{2n_2+1}(0)^T \oplus A_1$$
$$H = \varkappa_1 F_{2n_1+1} \oplus \varkappa_1 (-1)^{n_1-n_2-1} F_{2n_2+1} \oplus H_1.$$

For the sake of simplicity assume A and H consist of only the first two blocks. Without loss of generality assume $n_1 \geqq n_2$. Consider the perturbation $A(\alpha)=A+Z$, $\alpha \in \mathbb{R}$, where Z has zero entries except for the $(2n_1+n_2+2 \, , n_1+1)$ entry and the $(n_1+1 \, , 2n_1+n_2+1)$ entry which are α. Then $\sigma(A(\alpha))=\{0,\alpha,-\alpha\}$ and $(A(\alpha),H) \in L_n(1,-1)$. One checks that

$$\operatorname{Ker}(A(\alpha)-\alpha I) = \operatorname{span}\,[0_{n_1},\alpha^{n_1},\alpha^{n_1-1},\ldots,\alpha,1,0_{n_1},\alpha^{n_1},\ldots,\alpha^{n_1-n_2}]^T,$$

where we denote by 0_p the $1 \times p$ zero row and

$$\operatorname{Ker}(A(\alpha)+\alpha I) = \operatorname{span}\,[0_{n_1},(-\alpha)^{n_1},\ldots,1,0_{n_1},-(-\alpha)^{n_1},\ldots,-(-\alpha)^{n_1-n_2}]^T,$$

Then

$$\operatorname{Ker}(A(\alpha)\mp\alpha I) \oplus \operatorname{span}\,\{e_{2n_1+1},\ldots,e_{n_1+2},e_{2n_1+2n_2+2},\ldots,e_{2n_1+n_2+3}\}$$
$$= \operatorname{span}\,\{e_{2n_1+1},\ldots,e_{n_1+2},e_{2n_1+2n_2+2},\ldots,e_{2n_1+n_2+3},e_{n_1+1}\pm e_{2n_1+n_2+2}\},$$

are both in $J(A(\alpha),H)$ for all $\alpha \in \mathbb{R}$. Letting $\alpha \to 0$ we see again that there cannot be a strongly conditionally stable subspace in $J(A,H)$.

It remains to consider the case $\sigma(A)=\{\pm ib\}$, $b>0$. First we shall show that in this case there is no unconditionally stable A- invariant lagrangian subspace, thereby establishing also (ii). In view of Theorem 1.3 it is sufficient to prove that for (A,H) given by either

$$A = J_n \begin{pmatrix} 0 & b \\ -b & 0 \end{pmatrix} , \quad H = G_n \quad (n>1, \quad b>0) \tag{1.10}$$

or

$$A = \begin{bmatrix} 0 & b & 0 & 0 \\ -b & 0 & 0 & 0 \\ 0 & 0 & 0 & b \\ 0 & 0 & -b & 0 \end{bmatrix}, \quad H = \begin{bmatrix} 1 & 0 & 0 & 0 \\ 0 & 1 & 0 & 0 \\ 0 & 0 & -1 & 0 \\ 0 & 0 & 0 & -1 \end{bmatrix} \quad (b>0) \tag{1.11}$$

and for arbitrary small $\epsilon>0$ there exists $A(\epsilon)$ such that $HA(\epsilon) = -A(\epsilon)^T H$, $\|A - A(\epsilon)\| \leqq \epsilon$ and there is a pure imaginary eigenvalue of $A(\epsilon)$ with algebraic multiplicity one. In case (1.11) take

$$A(\epsilon) = A + \begin{bmatrix} 0 & -\epsilon & 0 & 0 \\ \epsilon & 0 & 0 & 0 \\ 0 & 0 & 0 & 0 \\ 0 & 0 & 0 & 0 \end{bmatrix}$$

In case (1.10) with n odd take $A(\epsilon)=A+\epsilon B$, where B has 1 on the place $(n,n+1)$, -1 on the place $(n+1,n)$ and zeros elsewhere. In both cases $A(\epsilon)$ has an eigenvalue $i(b+\epsilon)$ with algebraic multiplicity one. If A,H are given by (1.10)and n is even, the perturbation is slightly more complicated. Put $A(\epsilon)=A+\epsilon C$, where C has -1 on the places $(n-1,n+1)$and $(n,n+2)$ and zeros elsewhere. A computation shows that $i(b^2+\epsilon\pm\sqrt{4\epsilon b^2})$are eigenvalues of $A(\epsilon)$ with algebraic multiplicity one.

Next we show that (in case $\sigma(A)=\{\pm ib\}$, $b\neq 0$) the existence of a conditionally stable subspace implies that the partial multiplicities of A are all even and the signs in the sign characteristic of $(iA,H)$are all equal. Since $J(A,H)\neq\varnothing$ by assumption Theorem 1.3 implies that we can write (by rearranging blocks if necessary)

$$A=J_{n_1}\begin{pmatrix}0 & b\\ -b & 0\end{pmatrix}\oplus\dots\oplus J_{n_{2q+r}}\begin{pmatrix}0 & b\\ -b & 0\end{pmatrix},$$

$$H=\varkappa_1 G_{n_1}\oplus\cdots\oplus\varkappa_{2q+r}G_{n_{2q+r}},$$

where $n_1,\dots,n_{2q}$ are odd, and $n_{2q+1},\dots,n_{2q+r}$are even, and $\varkappa_{2j-1}=-\varkappa_{2j}=1$ for $j=1,\dots,q$. (We implicitly assume that both odd n_j values and even n_j values are present; if all n_j are odd, or all are even the changes in the subsequent argument are obvious.) For a positive ϵ, let $A(\epsilon)$ be the matrix obtained from A by replacing b by $b+j\epsilon$ in the blocks $J_{n_{2j-1}}\begin{pmatrix}0 & b\\ -b & 0\end{pmatrix}$ and $J_{n_{2j}}\begin{pmatrix}0 & b\\ -b & 0\end{pmatrix}$ $(j=1,\dots,q)$, and in the blocks $J_{n_j}\begin{pmatrix}0 & b\\ -b & 0\end{pmatrix}$ $(j=2q+1,\dots,2q+r)$. Clearly $A(\epsilon)\rightarrow A$ as $\epsilon\rightarrow 0$, $(A(\epsilon),H)\in L_n(1,-1)$,and by Theorem 1.3 also $J(A(\epsilon),H)\neq\varnothing$. Since M is conditionally stable there is $M(\epsilon)\in J(A(\epsilon),H)$ such that $\lim_{\epsilon\rightarrow 0}\theta(M(\epsilon),M)=0$. Since each $M(\epsilon)$, $\epsilon\neq 0$ must be the sum of its intersections with the root subspaces of $A(\epsilon)$, it follows that

$$M(\epsilon)=M_1(\epsilon)\oplus\dots\oplus M_{q+r}(\epsilon), \tag{1.12}$$

where $M_j(\epsilon)\subset\mathbb{R}^{2n_{2j-1}+2n_{2j}}$ for $j=1,\dots,q$ and $M_{q+j}(\epsilon)\subset\mathbb{R}^{2n_{2q+j}}$ for $j=1,\dots,r$. Passing to the limit in (1.12) we obtain that M has an analogous decomposition

$$M=M_1\oplus\dots\oplus M_{q+r}.$$

Here for $j=1,\dots,q$ the subspace $M_j\subset\mathbb{R}^{2n_{2j-1}+2n_{2j}}$ is $J_{n_{2j-1}}\begin{pmatrix}0 & b\\ -b & 0\end{pmatrix}\oplus J_{n_{2j}}\begin{pmatrix}0 & b\\ -b & 0\end{pmatrix}$ -invariant and lagrangian with respect to $G_{n_{2j-1}}\oplus G_{n_{2j}}$. Moreover, it is easily seen that M_j is conditionally stable as an element of

$$J(J_{n_{2j-1}}\begin{pmatrix}0 & b\\ -b & 0\end{pmatrix}\oplus J_{n_{2j}}\begin{pmatrix}0 & b\\ -b & 0\end{pmatrix},G_{n_{2j-1}}\oplus G_{n_{2j}}).$$

(See [RR2], Proposition 2.5 .) Analogous statement holds also for the subspaces M_j when $j=q+1,\ldots,q+r$. By the uniqueness statement of Theorem 1.3 we have that

$$M_{q+j} = \text{span}\,\{e_{n_{2q+j}+1},\ldots,e_{2n_{2q+j}}\} \quad j=1,\ldots,r.$$

Also, the direct sums of type $\oplus M_{j_k}$ are conditionally stable with respect to the appropriate pairs (A,H). So to prove our claim it remains to verify two statements:

1) if $A=J_{n_1}\begin{pmatrix} 0 & b \\ -b & 0 \end{pmatrix} \oplus J_{n_2}\begin{pmatrix} 0 & b \\ -b & 0 \end{pmatrix}$ $H=\varkappa_1 G_{n_1} \oplus \varkappa_2 G_{n_2}$ and n_1 and n_2 are odd, $\varkappa_1 \neq \varkappa_2$, then there is no conditionally stable subspace in $J(A,H)$.

2) if $A=J_{n_1}\begin{pmatrix} 0 & b \\ -b & 0 \end{pmatrix} \oplus J_{n_2}\begin{pmatrix} 0 & b \\ -b & 0 \end{pmatrix}$ $H=\varkappa_1 G_{n_1} \oplus \varkappa_2 G_{n_2}$ and n_1 and n_2 are even, $\varkappa_1 \neq \varkappa_2$, then there does not exist a conditionally stable subspace.

We shall consider the second case first. We may assume $n_1 \geqq n_2$. Let Z be the $2n_2 \times 2n_2$ matrix with zeros everywhere except at the $(1,2n_2-1)$ and the $(2,2n_2)$ entries, where it is ϵ. Put, for $\mu=\pm 1$:

$$A(\mu,\epsilon)=A+\begin{pmatrix} 0 & 0 & 0 & 0 \\ 0 & Z & 0 & -\mu Z \\ 0 & 0 & 0 & 0 \\ 0 & \mu Z & 0 & -Z \end{pmatrix},$$

where 0 on the main block diagonal stands for the $n_1-n_2 \times n_1-n_2$ zero matrix. Since H can be block decomposed as

$$H=\begin{pmatrix} 0 & 0 & H_1 & 0 \\ 0 & \varkappa_1 G_{n_2} & 0 & 0 \\ H_1^T & 0 & 0 & 0 \\ 0 & 0 & 0 & \varkappa_2 G_{n_2} \end{pmatrix}$$

and $\varkappa_1 \neq \varkappa_2$ one checks that $(A(\mu,\epsilon),H) \in L_n(1,-1)$. One now checks that $\sigma(A(\mu,\epsilon)=\{\pm bi\}$ and Ker $(A(\mu,\epsilon)\pm bi)$ is one-dimensional. (For instance by seeing that there is essentially only one Jordan chain at those eigenvalues.) So $J(A(\mu,\epsilon),H)$ consists of one element only. It is convenient to denote the j-th unit coordinate vector in the first (resp. second) block of $2n_1$ (resp. $2n_2$) coordinates by e_{1j} (resp. e_{2j}). Then the unique element in $J(A(\mu,\epsilon),H)$ can be written as follows:

$$M(\mu) = \text{span}\,\{e_{1,2n_1},\ldots,e_{1,n_1+n_2+1}, e_{1,n_1+n_2}+\mu e_{2,2n_2}, \ldots, e_{1,n_1-n_2+1}+\mu e_{2,1}\}$$

(compare the proof of [RR2], Theorem 3.4). Letting $\epsilon \to 0$ one sees that a conditionally stable subspace in $J(A,H)$ should at once equal $M(1)$ and $M(-1)$. Since $M(1) \neq M(-1)$ this is clearly impossible. So in this case there does not exist a conditionally stable subspace, as required.

Next, we prove the first case. Now let Z be the $2n_2 \times 2n_2$ matrix with zeros everywhere, except for ϵ in the $(1,2n_2)$ entry and $-\epsilon$ in the $(2,2n_2-1)$ entry. We shall assume $n_1 \geqq n_2$. Consider for $\mu = \pm 1$:

$$A(\mu,\epsilon) = A + \begin{bmatrix} 0 & 0 & 0 & 0 \\ 0 & -\mu Z & 0 & Z \\ 0 & 0 & 0 & 0 \\ 0 & -Z & 0 & \mu Z \end{bmatrix},$$

where again the zeros on the main block diagonal stand for the $(n_1-n_2)\times(n_1-n_2)$ zero matrix. Similar arguments as above show that since $\varkappa_1 \neq \varkappa_2$, $(A(\mu,\epsilon),H) \in L_n(1,-1)$; and again one checks that $\sigma(A(\mu,\epsilon) = \{\pm bi\}$ and Ker $(A(\mu,\epsilon) \pm bi)$ is one-dimensional. Again the only element in $J(A(\mu,\epsilon),H)$ is the subspace

$$M(\mu) = \text{ span } \{e_{1,2n_1},\ldots,e_{1,n_1+n_2+1},e_{1,n_1+n_2}+\mu e_{2,2n_2}, \ldots, e_{1,n_1-n_2+1}+\mu e_{2,1}\}$$

Since $M(1) \neq M(-1)$ we see that also in the first case there is no conditionally stable subspace in $J(A,H)$.

Finally we show the converse in (*i*) for the case $\sigma(A) = \{\pm ib\}$. If all conditions are satisfied, by Theorem 1.3 there exists a unique element in $J(A,H)$. Then [RR2], Theorem 2.4 shows that this unique element is conditionally strongly stable.

The Theorem is proved completely. □

Our next step is to show that the condition of invertibility of A in part (*iii*) of the previous theorem cannot be omitted. In other words, we show that the concepts of stability and strong stability do not coincide.

Example.1.1.

Let $A = \begin{bmatrix} 0 & 0 \\ 0 & 0 \end{bmatrix}$, $H = \begin{bmatrix} 1 & 0 \\ 0 & -1 \end{bmatrix}$. The only perturbations A' of A such that $(A',H) \in L_n(1,-1)$ are of the form $A(\alpha) = \begin{bmatrix} 0 & \alpha \\ \alpha & 0 \end{bmatrix}$. Now $J(A,H)$ consists of two elements, namely span $\begin{bmatrix} 1 \\ 1 \end{bmatrix}$ and span $\begin{bmatrix} 1 \\ -1 \end{bmatrix}$, and they also constitute $J(A(\alpha),H)$. So in this case both these subspaces are unconditionally stable, but clearly they are not unconditionally strongly stable. □

Theorem 1.4 and the above example leave open the problem of describing stable lagrangian subspaces in the case when $\sigma(A) = \{0\}$. Some examples in this direction are given in Section 1.4.

We next study Lipschitz stability.

THEOREM 1.5.*Let* $(A,H)\in L_n(1,-1)$. *Then there exists a conditionally strongly Lipschitz stable subspace in* $J(A,H)$ *if and only if* $\sigma(A)\cap i\mathbb{R}=\emptyset$. *In that case the following are equivalent for a subspace* $M\in J(A,H)$:

(i) M is Lipschitz unconditionally stable,

(ii) M is Lipschitz unconditionally strongly stable,

(iii) M is Lipschitz conditionally stable,

(iv) M is Lipschitz conditionally strongly stable,

(v) M is the sum of root subspaces of A.

Proof. Suppose $\sigma(A)\cap i\mathbb{R}=\emptyset$.Then the spectral subspace of A corresponding to the open right half plane is conditionally strongly stable. Also, since in this case $J(A',H')\neq\emptyset$ for any $(A',H')\in L_n(1,-1)$ with $\|A-A'\|+\|H-H'\|$ small enough, classes of conditional and unconditional stability coincide. So $(i)$and (iii) are equivalent, and also (ii) and (iv). It remains to show the equivalence of (iii),(iv) and (v) in this case. Clearly (v) implies (iv) implies (iii). Suppose (iii) holds. We may suppose (A,H) is of the form

$$A=\begin{pmatrix}\tilde{A} & 0\\ 0 & -\tilde{A}^T\end{pmatrix},\quad H=\begin{pmatrix}0 & I\\ I & 0\end{pmatrix}$$

with $\mathrm{Re}\,\sigma(\tilde{A})>0$, and

$$M=\{\begin{pmatrix}x\\ y\end{pmatrix}\mid x\in N,\ y\in N^{\perp}\}$$

for some $\tilde{A}$-invariant subspace N. Since $J(A,H)$ and $\mathrm{Inv}\,(\tilde{A})$ are homeomorphic (see e.g. the proof of Theorem 1.3) N is Lipschitz stable as an $\tilde{A}$-invariant subspace. Then [GLR2], Theorem 15.9.7 implies N and hence also M, is a spectral subspace, i.e. M is the sum of root subspaces.

Finally we prove the converse in the first statement of the theorem . Suppose there exists a conditionally strongly Lipschitz stable subspace M in $J(A,H)$. Then M is certainly strongly conditionally stable so by Theorem 1.4 $0\notin\sigma(A)$. Suppose $ib\in\sigma(A)$, $b>0$. Then we may assume by Theorem 1.4

$$A=\bigoplus_{j=1}^{p}J_{n_j}\begin{pmatrix}0 & b\\ -b & 0\end{pmatrix}\quad H=\bigoplus_{j=1}^{p}G_{n_j}$$

with n_j even. Consider the perturbation

$$A(\alpha)=A+Z$$

where Z is the matrix with zeros everywhere except at the $(1,2n_1-1)$ and the $(2,2n_1)$ entry, where it is α. Clearly $(A(\alpha),H)\in L_n(1,-1)$. Let $\alpha>0$ in case $n_1=4m+2$ for some m and $\alpha<0$ in case $n_1=4m$. In that case $J(A(\alpha),H)\neq\emptyset$. Now apply the argument in the proof of Theorem 15.9.7 in [GLR2], to see that there does not exist a conditionally Lipschitz stable subspace. □

1.4 Stability for the case of nilpotent A

In this section we consider some examples of stable invariant lagrangian subspaces for the pair $(A,H)\in L_n(1,-1)$ in the case when A is nilpotent. The general problem of characterizing all these subspaces remains open (for nilpotent A).

Example 1.2. Let $A=\begin{bmatrix}0&0\\0&0\end{bmatrix}$ $H=\begin{bmatrix}1&0\\0&-1\end{bmatrix}$ There are two invariant lagrangian subspaces for (A,H), namely span $\begin{bmatrix}1\\1\end{bmatrix}$ and span $\begin{bmatrix}1\\-1\end{bmatrix}$, and both are conditionally stable. They are also unconditionally stable, because there is no small perturbation A' of A such that $(A',H)\in L_n(1,-1)$ and A' has pure imaginary non-zero eigenvalues (cf. formula (1.3)).

Example 1.3. Let

$$A=\begin{bmatrix}0&0&0&0\\1&0&0&0\\0&0&0&-1\\0&0&0&0\end{bmatrix}\quad H=\begin{bmatrix}0&0&1&0\\0&0&0&1\\1&0&0&0\\0&1&0&0\end{bmatrix}$$

One can show (by considering the general perturbation A' of A such that $(A',H)\in L_n(1,-1)$) that the subspace $\operatorname{Ker} A=\operatorname{span}\{e_2,e_3\}$ is conditionally stable invariant lagrangian subspace. We leave out the tedious proof of this statement.

We conjecture that all conditionally stable subspaces for the case of nilpotent A are described as follows.

Conjecture 1.1. *Let (A,H) be given by (1.1) and assume that $J(A,H)\neq\emptyset$. There exists a conditionally stable invariant lagrangian subspace for (A,H) if and only if* $\dim\operatorname{Ker}A=2$, *i.e. either $p=2$, $q=0$ or $p=0$, $q=1$ in (1.1). In the former case the only two conditionally stable subspaces are given by*

$$\operatorname{span}\{e_{n_1+1}\pm e_{2n_1+1+n_2+1},e_{n_1+2},\ldots,e_{2n_1+1},e_{2n_1+1+n_2+2},\ldots,e_{2n_1+1+2n_2+1}\}.$$

In the latter case the only conditionally stable subspace is $\operatorname{Ker}A^{\frac{n_1}{2}}$.

1.5 Stability and isolatedness

In this section we indicate the connection between stable and isolated invariant lagrangian subspaces. Let $(A,H)\in L_n(1,-1)$. An invariant lagrangian subspace M is called *isolated* if M is isolated as an element of $J(A,H)$, i.e. there is $\epsilon>0$ such that M is the only element in $J(A,H)$ whose distance (in the gap metric) form M is less than ϵ. Using the result of Theorem 1.4 and the description of the connected components of the set of all invariant subspaces for real matrices (which is given, e.g., in [GLR2]) we obtain the following.

THEOREM 1.6 *Let $(A,H)\in L_n(1,-1)$, and assume that there are (un)conditionally strongly stable invariant lagrangian subspaces for (A,H). If $M\in J(A,H)$ is (un)conditionally strongly stable, then M is isolated as an element in $J(A,H)$. Conversely, every isolated element in $J(A,H)$ is (un)conditionally strongly stable provided A has no real eigenvalues with geometric multiplicity one and even algebraic multiplicity.*

2 The case $\xi=-1,\eta=1$

2.1 The canonical form

The canonical form in this case can be described as follows. Let $(A,H)\in L_n(-1,1)$; then there exists an invertible real matrix S, such that $(S^{-1}AS, S^THS)$ is a block diagonal sum of blocks (A_i, H_i) of the following types:

$$A_i=\bigoplus_{j=1}^{p}(J_{n_j}(a)\oplus J_{n_j}(a)^T)$$
$$H_i=\bigoplus_{j=1}^{p}\begin{pmatrix}0 & I_{n_j}\\ -I_{n_j} & 0\end{pmatrix} \tag{2.1}$$

where a is real,

$$A_i=\bigoplus_{j=1}^{p}\left(J_{n_j}\begin{pmatrix}a & b\\ -b & a\end{pmatrix}\oplus J_{n_j}\begin{pmatrix}a & b\\ -b & a\end{pmatrix}^T\right)\quad (b>0)$$
$$H_i=\bigoplus_{j=1}^{p}\begin{pmatrix}0 & I_{2n_j}\\ -I_{2n_j} & 0\end{pmatrix} \tag{2.2}$$

Clearly $J(A,H)\neq\emptyset$, and never consists of one element. Indeed, in case of (2.1) take

$$M=\mathbb{R}^{n_1}\oplus(0)\oplus\mathbb{R}^{n_2}\oplus(0)\oplus\cdots\oplus\mathbb{R}^{n_p}\oplus(0)$$

$$M'=(0)\oplus\mathbb{R}^{n_1}\oplus(0)\oplus\mathbb{R}^{n_2}\oplus\cdots\oplus(0)\oplus\mathbb{R}^{n_p}$$

In case of (2.2) just replace $\mathbb{R}^j$ by $\mathbb{R}^{2j}$ above, to establish that $J(A,H)$ consists of more than one element.

2.2 Stability of invariant lagrangian subspaces

Note that since $J(A,H)\neq\emptyset$ for every pair $(A,H)\in L_n(-1,1)$ the notions of conditional and unconditional stability coincide.

First we shall show that strong stability does not occur in this case. By Theorem 2.2 of [RR2] we may assume that (A,H) is either of the form (2.1) or of the form (2.2). In both cases consider the perturbation $A+\alpha I$, $\alpha\in\mathbb{R}$, then $(A+\alpha I,H)\in L_n(-1,1)$. Clearly the subspaces M and M' mentioned in the previous section are in $J(A,H)$ for all $\alpha\in\mathbb{R}$. Letting $\alpha\to 0$ one sees that there are two (constant) converging sequences, namely M and M', which do not converge to the same subspace as they should in case a strongly stable subspace existed. Hence strong stability does not occur in this case.

The next theorem describes the stable elements in $J(A,H)$. We assume that (A,H) is in canonical form with respect to the standard basis $\{e_{jk}\}_{j=1}^{p}{}_{k=1}^{2n_j}\cup\{e_{jk}\}_{j=p+1}^{q}{}_{k=1}^{4n_j}$

$$A=\mathop{\oplus}_{j=1}^{p}\left[J_{n_j}(a_j)\ \oplus J_{n_j}(a_j)^T\right]\ \oplus$$

$$\mathop{\oplus}_{j=p+1}^{q}\left[J_{n_j}\begin{pmatrix} a_j & b_j\\ -b_j & a_j\end{pmatrix}\oplus J_{n_j}\begin{pmatrix} a_j & b_j\\ -b_j & a_j\end{pmatrix}^T\right], \tag{2.3}$$

$$H=\mathop{\oplus}_{j=1}^{p}\begin{bmatrix} 0 & I_{n_j}\\ -I_{n_j} & 0\end{bmatrix}\oplus\mathop{\oplus}_{j=p+1}^{q}\begin{bmatrix} 0 & I_{n_j}\\ -I_{n_j} & 0\end{bmatrix},$$

with $b_j>0$.

THEOREM 2.1 *There exists a stable element in J(A,H) if and only if the geometric multiplicity at each eigenvalue of A is two. In that case $M\in J(A,H)$ is stable if and only if the following conditions hold:*

(i)for $1\leq j\leq p$ and n_j even

$$M\cap R(A,a_j)=\operatorname{Ker}(A-a_jI)^{\frac{n_j}{2}},$$

(ii)for $1\leq j\leq p$ and n_j odd

$$M\cap R(A,a_j)=\operatorname{Ker}(A-a_jI)^{\frac{n_j-1}{2}}\oplus\operatorname{span}\{\alpha e_{j,\frac{n_j+1}{2}}+\beta e_{j,n_j+\frac{n_j-1}{2}}\}$$

for some real α,β,

(iii)for $p+1\leq j\leq q$ and n_j even

$$M \cap R(A, a_j \pm ib_j) = \text{span } \{e_{j,n_j+1}, \ldots, e_{j,n_{3n_j}}\},$$

(iv)for $p+1 \leq j \leq q$ and n_j odd

$$M \cap R(A, a_j \pm ib_j) = \text{span } \{e_{j,n_j+1}, \ldots, e_{j,n_{3n_j}-2},$$

$$\alpha e_{j,n_j} + \beta e_{j,3n_j-1}, \alpha e_{j,n_j-1} + \beta e_{j,3n_j}\},$$

for some real α,β

Generically the geometric multiplicity of A at its eigenvalues (real or non-real) will be two, and all partial multiplicities will be one. So generically there is a continuum of invariant lagrangian subspaces (this holds for all $(A,H) \in L_n(-1,1)$) and they are all stable. It is instructive to compare this situation with the complex case. Here generically there will be no real eigenvalues and all multiplicities (both geometric and algebraic) will be one. Then there is only a finite number of complex invariant lagrangian subspaces, and again they are all stable, as well as strongly stable.

The proof of the theorem will be given in several steps, which will be presented as independent lemmas. First we shall show that if there exists a stable element in $J(A,H)$ then the geometric multiplicity of A at each of its eigenvalues is two. Next we show that a stable $M \in J(A,H)$ must have the form described in the theorem. Finally, for the the converse, we show that each subspace as described in the theorem is in fact stable. In each case we may restrict our attention to the case when (A,H) is either of the form (2.1) or of the form (2.2), by Theorem 2.2 in [RR2].

LEMMA 2.2 *Let $(A,H) \in L_n(-1,1)$ be given by (2.1) or (2.2). Suppose there exists a stable element in J(A,H). Then we have $p=1$, i.e. the geometric multiplicity of A is two.*

Proof. Assume $p>1$. First, let $\epsilon_1, \ldots, \epsilon_p$ be different real numbers. Consider the perturbation

$$A(\epsilon) = A + \epsilon_1 I_{2n_1} \oplus \cdots \oplus \epsilon_p I_{2n_p},$$

in case (2.1), or

$$A(\epsilon) = A + \epsilon_1 I_{4n_1} \oplus \cdots \oplus \epsilon_p I_{4n_p},$$

in case (2.2). Then $(A(\epsilon),H) \in L_n(-1,1)$ and every element $M' \in J(A(\epsilon),H)$ looks like

$$M' = M_1' \oplus \ldots . \oplus M_p'$$

where $M_j' \subset \mathbb{R}^{2n_j}$ in case (2.1), and $M_j' \subset \mathbb{R}^{4n_j}$ in case (2.2). Letting $\epsilon \to 0$ for all i we see that if M is stable in $J(A,H)$ then M is of the form

$$M=M_1 \oplus \ldots . \oplus M_p \tag{2.4}$$

where $M_j \subset \mathbb{R}^{2n_j}$ in case (2.1), and $M_j \subset \mathbb{R}^{4n_j}$ in case (2.2).

Now from the next lemma it follows that for each subspace $M \in J(A,H)$ of the form (2.3) there is an invertible S such that $S^{-1}AS=A$, $S^T HS=H$ and SM is not of the form (2.3). In view of Theorem 2.3 in [RR2] we see that this implies the statement of the lemma. □

LEMMA 2.3 *Suppose* $M_1, M_2 \in J(A,H)$, *and* $A|_{M_1}$ *and* $A|_{M_2}$ *are similar. Then there exists an invertible real matrix S such that* $S^{-1}AS=A$, $S^T HS=H$ *and* $SM_1=M_2$.

Proof. Let $\{x_1,\ldots,x_{\frac{n}{2}}\}$ be an orthonormal basis for M_1, then $\{Hx_i\}_{i=1}^{\frac{n}{2}}$ is an orthonormal basis for $M_1{}^{\perp}$. With respect to the basis $\{x_1,\ldots,x_{\frac{n}{2}},Hx_1,\ldots,Hx_{\frac{n}{2}}\}$ A and H are given by

$$A=\begin{pmatrix} A_1 & X \\ 0 & A_1{}^T \end{pmatrix}, \quad H=\begin{pmatrix} 0 & I \\ -I & 0 \end{pmatrix}$$

Likewise, for an orthonormal basis $\{z_1,\ldots,z_{\frac{n}{2}},Hz_1,\ldots,Hz_{\frac{n}{2}}\}$ of $M_2 \oplus M_2{}^{\perp}$ we have

$$A=\begin{pmatrix} A_2 & Z \\ 0 & A_2{}^T \end{pmatrix}, \quad H=\begin{pmatrix} 0 & I \\ -I & 0 \end{pmatrix}$$

Because $A|_{M_1}$ and $A|_{M_2}$ are similar there is an invertible $V:M_1 \to M_2$ such that $V^{-1}A_2V=A_1$. Consider V^T as a mapping from $M_2{}^{\perp}$ to itself, with respect to the basis $\{Hx_i\}_{i=1}^{\frac{n}{2}}$. Then

$$\begin{pmatrix} V^{-1} & 0 \\ 0 & V^T \end{pmatrix} \begin{pmatrix} A_2 & Z \\ 0 & A_2{}^T \end{pmatrix} \begin{pmatrix} V^{-1} & 0 \\ 0 & V^T \end{pmatrix} = \begin{pmatrix} A_1 & V^{-1}ZV^{-T} \\ 0 & A_1{}^T \end{pmatrix},$$

$$\begin{pmatrix} V^T & 0 \\ 0 & V^{-1} \end{pmatrix} \begin{pmatrix} 0 & I \\ -I & 0 \end{pmatrix} \begin{pmatrix} V & 0 \\ 0 & V^{-T} \end{pmatrix} = \begin{pmatrix} 0 & I \\ -I & 0 \end{pmatrix}$$

Put $V^{-1}ZV^{-T}=Y$ and $Vz_i=y_i$, $V^{-T}Hz_i=Hy_i$. Let $U:M_1 \oplus M_1^{\perp} \to M_2 \oplus M_2^{\perp}$ be given by $Ux_i=z_i$, $UHx_i=Hz_i$. Then U is unitary. Put

$$S=\begin{pmatrix} V & 0 \\ 0 & V^{-T} \end{pmatrix} U.$$

Then, with respect to $\{x_1, \ldots, x_{\frac{n}{2}}, Hx_1, \ldots, Hx_{\frac{n}{2}}\}$ we have:

$$S^T HS = U^T \begin{pmatrix} 0 & I \\ -I & 0 \end{pmatrix} U = \begin{pmatrix} 0 & I \\ -I & 0 \end{pmatrix}$$

Indeed

$$\langle S^T HSx_i, x_j \rangle = \langle \begin{pmatrix} V^T & 0 \\ 0 & V^{-1} \end{pmatrix} H \begin{pmatrix} V & 0 \\ 0 & V^{-T} \end{pmatrix} z_i, z_j \rangle = 0,$$

and similar formulas hold for the other basis elements. Further, with respect to the same basis we have

$$S^{-1}AS = U^{-1} \begin{pmatrix} V^{-1} & 0 \\ 0 & V^T \end{pmatrix} \begin{pmatrix} A_2 & Z \\ 0 & A_2{}^T \end{pmatrix} \begin{pmatrix} V^{-1} & 0 \\ 0 & V^T \end{pmatrix} U$$

$$= \begin{pmatrix} A_1 & U^{-1}V^{-1}ZV^{-T}U \\ 0 & A_1{}^T \end{pmatrix}.$$

Then $X = U^{-1}YU$. So $S^{-1}AS = A$, $S^T HS = H$ and

$$\operatorname{span}\{Sx_i\}_{i=1}^{\frac{n}{2}} = SM_1 = \operatorname{span}\{Vz_i\}_{i=1}^{\frac{n}{2}} = M_2. \square$$

Our next step is to show that in case $M \in J(A,H)$ is stable it must have the form described in the theorem. We shall start with the case (2.1), when A has only a real eigenvalue, which we may assume to be zero without loss of generality.

LEMMA 2.4 *Suppose* $A = J_n(0) \oplus J_n(0)^T$, $H = \begin{pmatrix} 0 & I_n \\ -I_n & 0 \end{pmatrix}$ *Suppose* $M \in J(A,H)$ *is stable. In case n is even we have* $M = \operatorname{Ker} A^{\frac{n}{2}}$, *in case n is odd*

$$M = \operatorname{Ker} A^{\frac{n-1}{2}} \oplus \operatorname{span}\{\alpha e_{\frac{n+1}{2}} + \beta e_{n+\frac{n+1}{2}}\}$$

for some real α, β.

Proof. First suppose $n=1$. Then $A = \begin{pmatrix} 0 & 0 \\ 0 & 0 \end{pmatrix}$, $H = \begin{pmatrix} 0 & 1 \\ -1 & 0 \end{pmatrix}$. Any perturbation $(A',H)\in L_n(-1,1)$ is of the form $A'=aI$ with $|a|$ small. Then $J(A',H)=J(A,H)$, and hence every element in $J(A,H)$ is stable.

Now let $n>1$. We shall show that if $M\in J(A,H)$ is stable then span $\{e_n,e_{n+1}\}\subset M$. Let $M\in J(A,H)$ be such that at least one of the eigenvectors e_n and e_{n+1} is not contained in M. Then $A|_M$ is similar to $J_n(0)$, and by combining Lemma 2.3 with Theorem 2.3 in [RR2] we conclude that either all of such M's are stable or none of them is. Let $X=X^T$ be an $n\times n$ matrix with and $XJ_n(0)=J_n(0)^TX$. Then $M=\operatorname{Im}\begin{pmatrix}I\\X\end{pmatrix}$ is in $J(A,H)$ and $A|_M$ is similar to $J_n(0)$. We claim that such an M cannot be stable. Indeed, consider for $\epsilon\neq 0$

$$A(\epsilon)=\begin{pmatrix}J(\epsilon) & 0\\ 0 & J(\epsilon)^T\end{pmatrix},$$

where $J(\epsilon)$ is given by

$$J(\epsilon)=\begin{pmatrix}(n-1)\epsilon & & & & \\ 1 & (n-2)\epsilon & & & \\ & 1 & \cdot & & \\ & & \cdot\ \cdot & & \\ & & & \cdot\ \cdot & \\ & & & \cdot & \epsilon \\ & & & 1 & 0\end{pmatrix}.$$

Then $(A(\epsilon),H)\in L_n(-1,1)$. Further, every $M(\epsilon)\in J(A(\epsilon),H)$ is of the form

$$M(\epsilon)=\operatorname{span}\{x_0(\epsilon),\ldots,x_{n-1}(\epsilon)\}$$

where $x_j(\epsilon)\in\operatorname{Ker}(A(\epsilon)-j\epsilon)$, $j=0,\ldots,n-1$. Put

$$p_j(\epsilon)=(0,\ldots,0,j!\epsilon^j,\ldots,j(j-1)\epsilon^2,j\epsilon,1,0,\ldots,0)^T,$$

where the zeros are in the first $n-j-1$ and the last n entries. Also, let

$$q_j(\epsilon)=(0,\ldots,0,j!\epsilon^j,\ldots,j(j-1)\epsilon^2,j\epsilon,1,0,\ldots,0)^T,$$

where the zeros are in the first n and the last j places. Then $\operatorname{Ker}(A(\epsilon)-j\epsilon)=\operatorname{span}\{p_j(\epsilon),q_j(\epsilon)\}$.

Suppose $M(\epsilon)\to M$ in gap for some choice $x_j(\epsilon)=\alpha_j p_j(\epsilon)+\beta_j(\epsilon)q_j(\epsilon)$. Taking $x_j(\epsilon)$ uniformly bounded in norm we have $\alpha_j(\epsilon)$, $\beta_j(\epsilon)$ bouded, and passing to a subsequence of ϵ's if necessary, we may assume $\alpha_j(\epsilon)\to\alpha_j$, $\beta_j(\epsilon)\to\beta_j$. Suppose one of the α_j's is zero. Then for this j we have $x_j(\epsilon)\to\beta_j e_{n+1}$, so this would imply $e_{n+1}\in M=\operatorname{Im}\begin{pmatrix}I\\X\end{pmatrix}$.

Clearly this is impossible, so all α_j's are non-zero. Then we can assume $\alpha_j(\epsilon)\neq 0$ for all j, and all ϵ. Dividing by $\alpha_j(\epsilon)$ we can assume $x_j(\epsilon)=p_j(\epsilon)+\beta_j(\epsilon)q_j(\epsilon)$. Then

$$M(\epsilon)=\text{Im}\begin{bmatrix}X_1(\epsilon)\\X_2(\epsilon)\end{bmatrix}=\text{Im}\begin{bmatrix}I\\X_2(\epsilon)X_1(\epsilon)^{-1}\end{bmatrix},$$

where the $n\times n$ matrices $X_1(\epsilon)$ and $X_2(\epsilon)$ are given by

$$\begin{bmatrix}X_1(\epsilon)\\0_{n\times n}\end{bmatrix}=(p_{n-1}(\epsilon),p_{n-2}(\epsilon),\ .\ .\ .\ ,p_0(\epsilon)),$$

$$\begin{bmatrix}0_{n\times n}\\X_2(\epsilon)\end{bmatrix}=(\beta_{n-1}(\epsilon)q_{n-1}(\epsilon),\beta_{n-2}(\epsilon)q_{n-2}(\epsilon),\ldots,\beta_0(\epsilon)q_0(\epsilon))$$

Put $X(\epsilon)=X_2(\epsilon)X_1(\epsilon)^{-1}$. We will compute the first column of $X(\epsilon)$. For this we need the first column of $X_1(\epsilon)^{-1}$. Using the lower triangular form of $X_1(\epsilon)$ one computes that the first column of $X_1(\epsilon)^{-1}$ is given by $\epsilon^{-n+1}(\delta_1,\ .\ .\ .\ ,\delta_n)^T$, where

$$\delta_j=\frac{(-1)^{j-1}}{(j-1)!(n-j)!}.$$

Then one computes that the first column of $X(\epsilon)$ is given by

$$\left(\epsilon^{-n+i}\frac{(-1)^{n-i}}{(n-i)!}\sum_{j=0}^{n-i}\binom{n-i}{j}\beta_j(\epsilon)(-1)^j\right)_{i=1}^{n}.$$

Consider the first column of $\begin{bmatrix}I\\X(\epsilon)\end{bmatrix}$. Multiplying by $\epsilon^{n-1},\epsilon^{n-2},\ldots,\epsilon$ successively, and then letting $\epsilon\to 0$ one sees that for $i=1,\ldots,n-1$ we have

$$\sum_{j=0}^{n-i}\binom{n-i}{j}\beta_j(-1)^j=0\ ,$$

where $\beta_j=\lim_{\epsilon\to 0}\beta_j(\epsilon)$. Taking $i=n-1$ on sees that from this we have $\beta_0=\beta_1$. In fact it is easily shown by induction that all β_j's are equal. Clearly, since $M=\text{Im}\begin{bmatrix}I\\X\end{bmatrix}=\lim_{\epsilon\to 0}M(\epsilon)=\lim_{\epsilon\to 0}\text{Im}\begin{bmatrix}I\\X(\epsilon)\end{bmatrix}$ we have $X=\lim_{\epsilon\to 0}X(\epsilon)$. Now if all β_j's are zero we would get $X=0$. In case $\beta_0\neq 0$ (and hence $\beta_j\neq 0$ for all j) we see from $X(\epsilon)=X_2(\epsilon)X_1(\epsilon)^{-1}$ and the triangular forms of $X_2(\epsilon)$ and $X_1(\epsilon)^{-1}$ that X has the form

$$X=\begin{bmatrix}0 & . & . & . & 0 & \beta_0\\ . & & & & . & * \\ . & & & . & * & \\ . & & . & * & & \\ 0 & * & & & & * \\ \beta_0 & & & & & \end{bmatrix},$$

We conclude that if $M=\operatorname{Im}\begin{bmatrix} I \\ X \end{bmatrix}\in J(A,H)$ is stable, then necessarily X has zero in the top left corner. Consequently, $\operatorname{Im}\begin{bmatrix} I \\ X_0 \end{bmatrix}\in J(A,H)$ where X_0 is the matrix with one in the top left corner and zeros everywhere else, is not stable. Hence (by Lemma 2.3 and Theorem 2.3 in [RR2]) every subspace in $J(A,H)$ of the form $\operatorname{Im}\begin{bmatrix} I \\ X \end{bmatrix}$ is not stable. It is clear now that any stable element M in $J(A,H)$ contains the vectors e_n and e_{n+1}. Since M is lagrangian it follows also that $M\subset \operatorname{span}\{e_2,\ldots,e_{2n-1}\}$.

We proceed to prove Lemma 2.4 by induction. For $n=1$ and $n=2$ we are done by the arguments above. So suppose $n>2$, and assume the statement of the lemma holds for $m<n$. For any vector $x\in\mathbb{R}^{2n}$ let $\hat{x}\in\mathbb{R}^{2n-4}$ be obtained from x by deleting coordinates 1,n,n+1 and 2n, i.e.

$$\hat{x}=(x_2,\ldots,x_{n-1},x_{n+2},\ldots,x_{2n-1})^T.$$

Clearly the map $x\to\hat{x}$ is a linear map of norm 1. Also, let $\hat{A},\hat{H}$ be obtained from A,H by crossing out rows and columns $1,n,n+1$ and $2n$. Clearly

$$\hat{H}=-\hat{H}^T\ ,\ \hat{H}\hat{A}=\hat{A}^T\hat{H},$$

i.e. $(\hat{A},\hat{H})\in L_{2n-4}(-1,1)$. Put

$$\hat{M}=\{\hat{x}\ |\ x\in M\}$$

We shall show that $\hat{M}\in J(\hat{A},\hat{H})$ and $\hat{M}$ is stable. Let us verify that $\hat{M}\in J(\hat{A},\hat{H})$. Indeed, take $\hat{x},\hat{y}$ in $\hat{M}$, $x,y\in M$. Then

$$\langle \hat{H}\hat{x},\hat{y}\rangle=\langle Hx,y\rangle=0,$$

since the first and last coordinate of x and y are zero (recall that we have already shown that $M\subset\operatorname{span}\{e_2,\ldots,e_{2n-1}\}$). So $\hat{M}$ is lagrangian. Likewise

$$\hat{A}\,\hat{x}=\hat{A}\,(x_2,\ .\ .\ .\ ,x_{n-1},x_{n+2},\ .\ .\ .\ ,x_{2n-1})^T=$$

$$=(0,x_2,\ldots,x_{n-2},x_{n+3},\ .\ .\ .\ ,x_{2n-1},0)=\hat{Ax}\in\hat{M}.$$

Now it remains to show that $\hat{M}$ is a stable element in $J(\hat{A},\hat{H})$. Let $\tilde{A}_k$ be a sequence of matrices with $\tilde{A}_k\to\hat{A}$ and $(\tilde{A}_k,\hat{H})\in L_{2n-4}(-1,1)$. Define A_k such that $\hat{A}_k=\tilde{A}_k$, and in the rows and columns 1,n,n+1 and 2n the entries of A_k coincide with those of A, except for the entries (1,1), (n,n),(n+1,n+1) and (2n,2n), where we have $\epsilon_k,\delta_k,\epsilon_k$ and δ_k, respectively. Here ϵ_k and δ_k are real numbers not in the spectrum of $\tilde{A}_k$, and such that $\epsilon_k\to 0,\delta_k\to 0$. Then $A_k\to A$ and $(A_k,H)\in L_{2n}(-1,1)$. Let $M_k\in J(A_k,H)$ be such that

$M_k \to M$ (since M is stable such M_k exists). Because of the canonical form and the choice of ϵ_k and δ_k each M_k contains a one dimensional subspace from Ker $(A_k - \epsilon_k)$ and a one dimensional subspace from Ker $(A_k - \delta_k)$. Let $x_k \in$ Ker $(A_k - \epsilon_k) \cap M_k$, $\|x_k\| = 1$ and $y_k \in$ Ker $(A_k - \delta_k) \cap M_k$, $\|y_k\| = 1$. There exists an A_k-invariant subspace $N_k \subset M_k$ such that $M_k = N_k \oplus$ span $\{x_k, y_k\}$, because of our choice of ϵ_k and δ_k. Since $M_k \to M$ we have $N_k \to N \subset M$ for some $n-2$ dimensional subspace N. Consider $M'_k = N_k \oplus$ span $\{e_n, e_{n+1}\}$. Since $e_n \in$ Ker $(A_k - \delta_k)$ and $e_{n+1} \in$ Ker $(A_k - \epsilon_k)$ and $\sigma(A_k \mid_{N_k}) \cap \{\epsilon_k, \delta_k\} = \varnothing$ we have that span $\{e_n, e_{n+1}\}$ and N_k are H-orthogonal, and that $N_k \cap$ span $\{e_n, e_{n+1}\} = \varnothing$. So dim $M'_k = n$, and hence $M'_k \in J(A_k, H)$. Also $M'_k \to M$ since N_k converges to a subspace contained in M. Clearly, since span $\{e_n, e_{n+1}\} \subset M'_k$ and M'_k is lagrangian we have $M'_k \subset$ span $\{e_2, \ldots, e_{2n-1}\}$. But then $\hat{M}'_k$ is $\hat{A}_k = \tilde{A}_k$-invariant and $\hat{H}$-lagrangian, i.e. $\hat{M}'_k \in J(\hat{A}_k, \hat{H})$ and $\hat{M}'_k \to \hat{M}$. So $\hat{M}$ is a stable element in $J(\hat{A}, \hat{H})$. Now apply induction: Lemma 2.4 holds true for $(\hat{A}, \hat{H})$. So $\hat{M} =$ Ker $\hat{A}^{\frac{n-2}{2}}$ if n is even and $\hat{M} =$ Ker $\hat{A}^{\frac{n-2}{2}} \oplus$ span $\{\alpha e_{\frac{n-3}{2}} + \beta e_{n-2+\frac{n-1}{2}}\}$ for some α, β in case n is odd. It remains to note that on can retrieve M from $\hat{M}$, knowing that span $\{e_n, e_{n+1}\} \subset M$. With this the lemma is proved. □

We proceed by showing that in case (A, H) is given by (2.2), where we may assume $a = 0$ without restriction, a stable subspace $M \in J(A, H)$ necessarily has the form described in the theorem.

LEMMA 2.5 *Suppose*

$$A = J_n \begin{pmatrix} 0 & b \\ -b & 0 \end{pmatrix} \oplus J_n \begin{pmatrix} 0 & b \\ -b & 0 \end{pmatrix}^T, \quad H = \begin{pmatrix} 0 & I_{2n} \\ -I_{2n} & 0 \end{pmatrix},$$

and suppose $M \in J(A, H)$ is stable. In case n is even $M =$ span $\{e_{n+1}, \ldots, e_{3n}\}$, in case n is odd $M =$ span $\{e_{n+1}, \ldots, e_{3n-2}, \alpha e_n + \beta e_{3n-1}, \alpha e_{n-1} + \beta e_{3n}\}$.

Proof. The proof is essentially the same as the proof of Lemma 2.4. One first checks that M must contain the vectors $e_{2n-1}, e_{2n}, e_{2n+1}, e_{2n+2}$. (Note: if M contains e_{2n} it contains e_{2n-1} and conversely, and likewise $e_{2n+1} \in M$ if and only if $e_{2n+2} \in M$.) This is accomplished in the same way as in the previous lemma. One then applies an induction argument to finish the proof, as above. □

Next, we show the converse, i.e. we show that if $M \in J(A, H)$ is given as in the theorem, then M is stable. We start by considering the case (2.1).

LEMMA 2.6 *Assume* $A = J_n(0) \oplus J_n(0)^T$, $H = \begin{pmatrix} 0 & I_n \\ -I_n & 0 \end{pmatrix}$. *If n is even then*

Ker $A^{\frac{n}{2}}$ *is stable. If* n *is odd all subspaces of the form* Ker $A^{\frac{n-1}{2}} \oplus$ span $\{\alpha e_{\frac{n+1}{2}} + \beta e_{n+\frac{n-1}{2}}\}$, *with* α,β *real and not both zero are stable.*

Proof. First consider the case when n is even. Suppose Ker $A^{\frac{n}{2}}$ is not stable. Then there exists a sequence of matrices $A_m \to A$ and an $\epsilon > 0$ such that $(A_m, H) \in L_n(-1,1)$ and such that for all $M' \in J(A_m, H)$ we have

$$\theta(M', \text{Ker } A^{\frac{n}{2}}) \geqq \epsilon.$$

Choose

$$\gamma_m = (\max_{\frac{n}{2} \leqq j \leqq n-1} ||A_m^j - A^j||)^{½}.$$

Note that $\gamma_m \to 0$ as $m \to \infty$. Put

$$x_m = -\gamma_m e_1 + e_{\frac{n}{2}+1} + \alpha e_{\frac{n}{2}+n} + \gamma e_{2n},$$

where $\alpha > 0$ independent of m is such that $x_m, A_m x_m, \ldots, A_m^{n-1} x_m$ are linearly independent. Since $x_m, Ax_m, \ldots, A^{n-1} x_m$ are independent for all $\alpha > 0$, such an α exists.

Consider the subspace

$$M_m = \text{span } \{x_m, A_m x_m, \ldots, A_m^{n-1} x_m\} =$$

$$= \text{span } \{x_m, A_m x_m, \ldots, A_m^{\frac{n}{2}-1} x_m, \frac{1}{\gamma_m} A_m^{\frac{n}{2}} x_m, \ldots, \frac{1}{\gamma_m} A_m^{n-1} x_m\}$$

This subspace is A_m-invariant since the minimal polynomial of A_m has degree n at most, as can be seen from the canonical form.

It is easily shown that for every pair $(\tilde{A}, \tilde{H}) \in L_n(-1,1)$ all matrices $\tilde{H}\tilde{A}^j$ $(j \geqq 0)$ are skew symmetric. From this it follows that M_m is lagrangian. So $M_m \in J(A_m, H)$.

Now for $0 \leqq j \leqq \frac{n}{2} - 1$ we have

$$A_m^j x_m \to e_{\frac{n}{2}+j+1} + \alpha e_{\frac{3n}{2}-j} \quad (m \to \infty). \tag{2.5}$$

Note that because of our choice of γ_m for any entry a_{ik} in $A_m^j - A^j$ we have $\frac{a_{ik}}{\gamma_m} \to 0$ as $m \to \infty$ in case $\frac{n}{2} \leqq j \leqq n-1$. Hence for these j's

$$\gamma_m A_m^j x_m \to -e_{j+1} + e_{2n-j} \quad (m\to\infty). \tag{2.6}$$

The limit vectors in (2.4) and (2.5) are all in $\operatorname{Ker} A^{\frac{n}{2}}$. Since $\alpha>0$ it is easy to see that in fact they span $\operatorname{Ker} A^{\frac{n}{2}}$. So we obtain $M_m \to \operatorname{Ker} A^{\frac{n}{2}}$ which is a contradiction. Hence $\operatorname{Ker} A^{\frac{n}{2}}$ is stable.

Now let us turn to the case when n is odd. By Lemma 2.3 all subspaces

$$\operatorname{Ker} A^{\frac{n-1}{2}} \oplus \operatorname{span}\{\alpha e_{\frac{n+1}{2}} + \beta e_{n+\frac{n-1}{2}}\} \tag{2.7}$$

(where α, β are real numbers not both zero) are in the same orbit under transformations $M \to SM$ where S are real invertible matrices such that $S^{-1}AS=A$, $S^T HS=H$. By Theorem 2.3 of [RR2] either all subspaces (2.7) are stable or all are unstable. We proceed by showing that for the choice $\alpha=1, \beta=-1$ this subspace is stable. Suppose it is not stable. As above choose a sequence $A_m \to A$ and an $\epsilon>0$ such that $(A_m,H)\in L_n(-1,1)$ and for all $M'\in J(A_m,H)$

$$\theta(\operatorname{Ker} A^{\frac{n-1}{2}} \oplus \operatorname{span}\{e_{\frac{n+1}{2}} - e_{n+\frac{n-1}{2}}\}, M') \geqq \epsilon$$

Choose $\gamma_m = (\max_{\frac{n-1}{2}\leqq j\leqq n-1} \|A_m^j - A^j\|)^{1/2}$ and put

$$x_m = -\gamma_m e_1 + e_{\frac{n+1}{2}+1} + \alpha e_{2n-\frac{n+1}{2}} + \gamma_m e_{2n}$$

where $\alpha>0$ is such that $x_m, A_m x_m, \ldots, A_m^{n-1} x_m$ are independent. As above one sees that such an α exists. Again consider

$$M_m = \operatorname{span}\{x_m, A_m x_m, \ldots, A_m^{n-1} x_m\} =$$

$$= \operatorname{span}\{x_m, A_m x_m, \ldots, A_m^{\frac{n-3}{2}} x_m, \frac{1}{\gamma_m} A_m^{\frac{n-1}{2}} x_m, \ldots, \frac{1}{\gamma_m} A_m^{n-1} x_m\}$$

One checks that $M_m \in J(A_m,H)$.

Now for $0 \leqq j \leqq \frac{n-3}{2}$ we have

$$A_m^j x_m \to e_{\frac{n+1}{2}+j+1} + \alpha e_{2n-\frac{n+1}{2}-j} \quad (m\to\infty). \tag{2.8}$$

while for $\frac{n-1}{2} \leqq j \leqq n-1$

$$\frac{1}{\gamma_m} A_m^j x_m \to e_j - e_{2n-j} \quad (m \to \infty). \tag{2.9}$$

So $M_m \to \operatorname{Ker} A^{\frac{n-1}{2}} \oplus \operatorname{span}\{e_{\frac{n+1}{2}} - e_{n+\frac{n-1}{2}}\}$ as one easily checks. This is a contradiction, so $\operatorname{Ker} A^{\frac{n-1}{2}} \oplus \operatorname{span}\{e_{\frac{n+1}{2}} - e_{n+\frac{n-1}{2}}\}$ is stable. This proves the lemma. □

Finally we consider the case (2.2).

LEMMA 2.7 *Assume*

$$A = J_n \begin{pmatrix} 0 & b \\ -b & 0 \end{pmatrix} \oplus J_n \begin{pmatrix} 0 & b \\ -b & 0 \end{pmatrix}^T, \quad H = \begin{pmatrix} 0 & I_{2n} \\ -I_{2n} & 0 \end{pmatrix},$$

If n is even then $\operatorname{span}\{e_{n+1},\ldots,e_{3n}\}$ *is stable. If n is odd then*

$$\operatorname{span}\{e_{n+1},\ldots,e_{3n-2}, \alpha e_n + \beta e_{3n-1}, \alpha e_{n-1} + \beta e_{3n}\}$$

is stable for all $\alpha, \beta \in \mathbb{R}$ (not both zero).

Proof. First, let n be even, and suppose $M := \operatorname{span}\{e_{n+1},\ldots,e_{3n}\}$ is not stable. Select a sequence $A_m \to A$ and an $\epsilon > 0$ such that $(A_m, H) \in L_n(-1,1))$ and for all $M' \in J(A_m, H)$ we have $\theta(M, M') \geqq \epsilon$.

Choose

$$\gamma_m = \left(\max_{n \leqq j \leqq 2n-1} \|A_m^j - A^j\| \right)^{1/2},$$

$$x_m = -\gamma_m e_1 + e_{n+1} + \alpha e_{3n} + \gamma e_{4n},$$

where α is such that $x_m, \ldots, A_m^{2n-1} x_m$ are independent. Take

$$M_m = \operatorname{span}\{x_m, \ldots, A_m^{2n-1} x_m\}.$$

Since the minimal polynomial of A_m has degree at most $2n$, M_m is A_m-invariant. Also M_m is lagrangian, so $M_m \in J(A_m, H)$. One checks that M_m converges to M in essentially the same way as in the previous lemma. This is a contradiction, so M is stable.

For the case when n is odd first observe that all subspaces given in the lemma are in the same orbit under the transformations $M \to SM$, where S are real invertible matrices such that $S^{-1}AS = A$, $S^T HS = H$. So by Theorem 2.3 in [RR2] it suffices to show that one of them is stable. Take $\alpha = 1, \beta = -1$. One shows that this subspace is stable in essentially the same way as above. □

The lemmas above combine to prove Theorem 2.1.

2.3 Lipschitz stability and isolatedness

We consider here Lipschitz stability of invariant lagrangian subspaces for a pair $(A,H)\in L_n(-1,1)$.

First, we consider the notion of stability slightly weaker than Lipschitz stability. Let $(A,H)\in L_n(-1,1)$ and $M\in J(A,H)$. We say that M is $\frac{1}{2}$*-stable* if there exist positive constants K and ϵ such that for every pair $(A',H')\in L_n(-1,1)$ with

$$||A-A'||+||H-H'||<\epsilon$$

there is a A'-invariant H'-invariant subspace M' satisfying

$$\theta(M,M')\leqq K\{||A'-A||+||H'-H||\}^{\frac{1}{2}}.$$

As in the proof of Theorem 2.1 of [RR2] one verifies that M is $\frac{1}{2}$-stable if and only if M is $\frac{1}{2}$-stable with fixed H, i.e. there exist $K,\epsilon>0$ such that for every pair $(A',H)\in L_n(-1,1)$ with $||A-A'||<\epsilon$ there is an A'-invariant H-lagrangian subspace M' satisfying $\theta(M,M')\leqq K\,||A-A'||^{\frac{1}{2}}$. Clearly, every $\frac{1}{2}$-stable subspace is stable, and every Lipschitz stable subspace is $\frac{1}{2}$-stable.

It turns out that in the framework of the class $L_n(-1,1)$ the stable subspaces are also $\frac{1}{2}$-stable.

THEOREM 2.8 *Let* $(A,H)\in L_n(-1,1)$. Then a subspace $M\in J(A,H)$ *is stable if and only if it is* $\frac{1}{2}$*-stable.*

Proof. Suppose $M\in J(A,H)$ is stable but not $\frac{1}{2}$-stable. We may assume (A,H) is in either of the forms considered in Lemma 2.6 and 2.7, and M is as described there. There exists a sequnce $A_m\to A$ such that $(A_m,H)\in L_n(-1,1)$ and for all $M'\in J(A_m,H)$ we have

$$\frac{\theta(M,M')}{||A-A_m||^{\frac{1}{2}}}\to\infty \qquad (m\to\infty).$$

Choose γ_m,x_m and the subspace M_m as in the proof of Lemma 2.6 or 2.7. Then it is easily seen that in fact

$$\frac{\theta(M,M_m)}{\|A-A_m\|^{\frac{1}{2}}}$$

remains bounded. Contradiction, so M is $\frac{1}{2}$-stable. □

The criterium for existence and description of all Lipschitz stable invariant lagrangian subspaces is given in the following theorem.

THEOREM 2.9. *Let* $(A,H)\in L_n(-1,1)$ *be given by formulas (2.3) where* $a_1,..,a_p$ *are distinct real numbers and* $a_{p+1}+ib_{p+1},...,a_q+ib_q$ *are distinct non-real numbers. Then there exists a Lipschitz stable element in* $J(A,H)$ *if and only if* $n_1=n_2=...=n_p=n_{p+1}=...=n_q=1$. *In such case every element in* $J(A,H)$ *is Lipschitz stable.*

Note that if not all numbers $a_1,..,a_p,a_{p+1}+ib_{p+1},...,a_q+ib_q$ are different, then by Lemma 2.2 there is no stable element in $J(A,H)$, let alone Lipschitz stable.

Proof. By the localization principle (Theorem 2.2 in [RR2]) without loss of generality we can restrict our attention to two cases:

$$A=J_n(0)\ \oplus J_n(0)^T;\qquad H=\begin{pmatrix}0 & I_n\\ -I_n & 0\end{pmatrix}; \tag{a}$$

$$A=J_n\begin{pmatrix}0 & 1\\ -1 & 0\end{pmatrix}\ \oplus J_n\begin{pmatrix}0 & 1\\ -1 & 0\end{pmatrix}^T;\qquad H=\begin{pmatrix}0 & I_{2n}\\ -I_{2n} & 0\end{pmatrix}. \tag{b}$$

Consider first case (a). If $n=1$, then trivially any one-dimensional subspace in $\mathbb{R}^2$ belongs to $J(A,H)$ and is Lipschitz stable. Assume that $n\geqq 2$ and n is even. In view of Theorem 2.1 we have to show that the stable subspace $M=$ span $\{e_{\frac{n}{2}+1},...,e_{\frac{3n}{2}}\}$ is not Lipschitz stable. For $\epsilon>0$ close to zero consider the matrix

$$A(\epsilon)=\begin{bmatrix}0&0&0&.&0&\epsilon\\ 1&0&0&&&.\\ &.&.&&&.\\ &&.&.&.&.\\ &&&.&.&0\\ 0&&&.&1&0\end{bmatrix}\oplus\begin{bmatrix}0&1&0&.&.&0\\ 0&0&.&&&0\\ .&&.&.&&.\\ .&&&.&&.\\ 0&&&&.&1\\ \epsilon&0&.&.&.&0\end{bmatrix}. \tag{2.10}$$

The eigenvalues of the matrix $A(\epsilon)$ are the n-th roots of ϵ, and any $A(\epsilon)$-invariant lagrangian subspace $M(\epsilon)$ must contain an eigenvector corresponding to the positive n-th root of

ϵ, call it η. This eigenvector has the form

$$x = (\eta^{n-1}y, \ldots, \eta y, y, z, \eta z, \ldots, \eta^{n-1}z)^T \tag{2.11}$$

for some real numbers y and z (not both zero). Denoting by P the orthogonal projection on M, we have

$$\theta(M(\epsilon), M)^2 \geq \frac{\|x - Px\|^2}{\|x\|^2} = \frac{\sum_{j=\frac{n}{2}}^{n-1} \eta^{2j}(|y|^2 + |z|^2)}{\sum_{j=0}^{n-1} \eta^{2j}(|y|^2 + |z|^2)} \geq \frac{1}{2}\eta^n$$

for ϵ close enough to zero. So

$$\theta(M(\epsilon), M) \geq \frac{1}{\sqrt{2}}\eta^{\frac{n}{2}} = \frac{1}{\sqrt{2}}\|A(\epsilon) - A\|^{\frac{1}{2}}$$

which shows that M is not Lipschitz stable.

Assume now $n \geq 2$ and n is odd. Let $M \in J(A, H)$ be of the form

$$\text{span}\,\{e_{\frac{n+1}{2}+1}, \ldots, e_n, e_{n+1}, \ldots, e_{n+\frac{n-1}{2}}, \alpha e_{\frac{n+1}{2}} + \beta e_{n+\frac{n+1}{2}}\}$$

for some real α, β not both zero. Letting $A(\epsilon)$ be as in (2.10), and letting η to be the positive n-th root of ϵ, every $A(\epsilon)$-invariant lagrangian subspace $M(\epsilon)$ must contain an eigenvector x (given by (2.11)) corresponding to η. Arguing as above we obtain

$$\theta(M(\epsilon), M)^2 \geq \frac{\|x - Px\|^2}{\|x\|^2} = \frac{\sum_{j=\frac{n+1}{2}}^{n-1} \eta^{2j}(|y|^2 + |z|^2)}{\sum_{j=0}^{n-1} \eta^{2j}(|y|^2 + |z|^2)} \geq \frac{1}{2}\eta^{n+1}$$

for ϵ close enough to zero. Then

$$\theta(M(\epsilon), M) \geq \frac{1}{\sqrt{2}}\eta^{\frac{n+1}{2}} = \frac{1}{\sqrt{2}}\|A(\epsilon) - A\|^{\frac{n+1}{2n}}$$

and again M is not Lipschitz stable. In view of Theorem 2.1 this settles the case (a).

We pass now to the case (b), and consider first the case $n = 1$. Using the canonical form (2.1),(2.2) it is easy to see that the canonical form of any perturbation A' (sufficiently close to A) such that $(A', H) \in L_n(-1,1)$ is $\begin{pmatrix} a & b \\ -b & a \end{pmatrix} \oplus \begin{pmatrix} a & -b \\ b & a \end{pmatrix}$ for some real a close to zero and some real b close to one. Moreover, any two-dimensional (real) A'-

invariant subspace M' is H-lagrangian. A general theorem (see[GR]) on perturbations that preserve Jordan structure now implies that any element in $J(A,H)$ is Lipschitz stable.

Next, assume $n>1$ and n is even. Denote by D the 2×2 matrix $\begin{bmatrix} 0 & 1 \\ -1 & 0 \end{bmatrix}$, and consider the following perturbation of A:

$$A(\epsilon)=\begin{bmatrix} D & 0 & & & 0 & \epsilon I_2 \\ I_2 & D & & & & 0 \\ 0 & I_2 & \cdot & & & \cdot \\ \cdot & & \cdot & \cdot & & \cdot \\ \cdot & & & \cdot & \cdot & \cdot \\ \cdot & & & & D & 0 \\ 0 & 0 & \cdot & \cdot & I_2 & D \end{bmatrix} \oplus \begin{bmatrix} D & 0 & & & 0 & \epsilon I_2 \\ I_2 & D & & & & 0 \\ 0 & I_2 & \cdot & & & \cdot \\ \cdot & & \cdot & \cdot & & \cdot \\ \cdot & & & \cdot & \cdot & \cdot \\ \cdot & & & & D & 0 \\ 0 & 0 & \cdot & \cdot & I_2 & D \end{bmatrix}^T$$

where ϵ is a small positive number. One checks that $A(\epsilon),H)\in L_n(-1,1)$. Further, letting

$$Z_j=\eta\begin{bmatrix} \cos\frac{2\pi j}{n} & \sin\frac{2\pi j}{n} \\ -\sin\frac{2\pi j}{n} & \cos\frac{2\pi j}{n} \end{bmatrix}, \quad j=0,..,n-1,$$

where $\eta=|\epsilon|^{\frac{1}{n}}$, one verifies that

$$A(\epsilon)\begin{bmatrix} W & 0 \\ 0 & \tilde{W} \end{bmatrix}= \tag{2.12}$$

$$\begin{bmatrix} W & 0 \\ 0 & \tilde{W} \end{bmatrix}((Z_0+D)\oplus\cdots\oplus(Z_{n-1}+D)\oplus(Z_0+D)^T\oplus\cdots\oplus(Z_{n-1}+D)^T),$$

where W is the matrix

$$\begin{bmatrix} Z_0^{n-1} & \cdots & Z_{n-1}^{n-1} \\ \cdot & & \cdot \\ \cdot & & \cdot \\ Z_0 & & Z_{n-1} \\ I_2 & \cdots & I_2 \end{bmatrix}$$

and $\tilde{W}$ is the matrix obtained from W by reversing the order of the rows. In particular, the eigenvalues of $A(\epsilon)$ are $\pm i+\eta\epsilon_1, \ldots, \pm i+\eta\epsilon_n$, where $\epsilon_1,..,\epsilon_n$ are the n-th roots of 1. We also conclude from (2.12) that any two dimensional (real) $A(\epsilon)$-invariant subspace M must be of the form

$$M = \text{Im}\left[(Z_0^{n-1}X)^T..(Z_0X)^TX^TY^T(Z_0Y)^T..(Z_0^{n-1}Y)^T\right]^T,$$

for some real 2×2 matrices X and Y. One easily verifies (cf. the proof in the case (a)) that for every such subspace M the inequality

$$\theta(M, \text{span}\,\{e_{n+1},..,e_{3n}\}) \geqq C\,||A(\epsilon)-A\,||^{\frac{1}{2}}$$

holds, with a constant C independent of ϵ. In view of Theorem 2.1 we conclude that there are no Lipschitz stable subspaces in case (b) when $n>1$ is even. If in case (b) $n>1$ is odd, the proof is analogous. We omit the details. □

Our final remark concerns the isolatedness of subspaces in $J(A,H)$. It turns out that stable elements in $J(A,H)$ (when they exist) are never isolated; this in contrast with the stability properties of general real matrices (without additional symmetries); see [BGK] or [GLR2]. For example let

$$A = J_n(0)\ \oplus J_n(0), \quad H = \begin{bmatrix} 0 & I_n \\ -I_n & 0 \end{bmatrix}$$

with even n. Then

$$M(\alpha) = \text{span}\,\{e_{n+1}+\alpha e_{\frac{n}{2}},..,e_{\frac{3n}{2}}+\alpha e_1, e_{\frac{n}{2}+1},..,e_n\}$$

(α is a real parameter) is a continuous family of A-invariant lagrangian subspaces, and the stable subspace is obtained when $\alpha=0$.

References

[BGK] H.Bart, I.Gohberg and M.A.Kaashoek: Minimal factorization of matrix and operator functions, Birkhäuser Verlag, Basel, 1979.

[DPWZ] D.Z.Djokovic, J.Potera, P.Winternitz and H.Zassenhaus: Normal forms of elements of classical real and complex Lie and Jordan algebras, Journal of Math. Physics 24 (1983), 1363-1374.

[GLR1] I.Gohberg, P.Lancaster and L.Rodman: Matrices and indefinite scalar products, Birkhäuser Verlag, Basel, 1983.

[GLR2] I.Gohberg, P.Lancaster and L.Rodman: Invariant subspaces of matrices with applications, J.Wiley, New York, 1986.

[GR] I.Gohberg and L.Rodman: On the distance between lattices of invariant subspaces, Linear Algebra Appl. 76 (1986), 85-120.

[RR1] A.C.M.Ran and L.Rodman: Stable real invariant semidefinite subspaces and stable factorizations of symmetric rational matrix functions, Linear and

Multilinear Algebra 22 (1987), 25-55.

[RR2] A.C.M.Ran and L.Rodman: Stability of invariant lagrangian subspaces I. Integral Equations and Operator Theory, to appear.

[RR3] A.C.M.Ran and L.Rodman: Stability of invariant maximal semidefinite subspaces I, Linear Algebra Appl. 62 (1984), 51-86.

André C.M.Ran
Faculteit Wiskunde en Informatica
Vrije Universiteit
De Boelelaan 1081
1081 HV Amsterdam
The Netherlands

Leiba Rodman
Department of Mathematics
College of William and Mary in Virginia
Williamsburg, Virginia 23185
USA

Operator Theory:
Advances and Applications, Vol. 40

On strong α-stability of invariant subspaces of matrices

A.C.M. Ran and L.Roozemond

Dedicated to professor I.Gohberg on the occasion of his sixtieth birthday

0.Introduction

Stability properties of invariant subspaces of matrices have been studied extensively the last decade. The first results on stability of invariant subspaces were obtained independently in 1979 by Campbell and Daughtry [CD] and Bart, Gohberg and Kaashoek [BGK]. Recently a complete theory on stability of invariant subspaces was laid down in a book by Gohberg, Lancaster and Rodman [GLR]. The development of this theory was chiefly done by mathematicians from the 'Gohberg school'. Our aim in this paper is to add a little bit to this beautiful theory.

In the first section we shall give our main theorem, which will be proved in the second section. In the third section we shall give an application to algebraic Riccati equations, while in the last section we give an application to factorization of monic matrix polynomials.

1.The main theorem

Before stating our main result, let us introduce some notions and notations. Let A be an $n \times n$ complex matrix. The set of invariant subspaces of A will be denoted by Inv (A). By $\theta(M,N)$ we shall denote the gap between two subspaces M and N, i.e.

$$\theta(M,N) = ||P_M - P_N||,$$

where P_M, P_N are the orthogonal projections on M and N, respectively. Here $||.||$ stands for the usual norm of matrices as operators on $\mathbb{C}^n$ equipped with the Euclidean norm; e.g.

$$||A|| = \max_{||x||=1} ||Ax||.$$

A subspace $M \in \mathrm{Inv}\,(A)$ will be called α-stable if there exist positive constants K and ϵ such that every $n \times n$ matrix B with $\|B-A\|<\epsilon$ has an invariant subspace N with $\theta(M,N) \leqq K\|B-A\|^{\frac{1}{\alpha}}$. This notion was first introduced in [GLR] (see page 513). Note that, except for the trivial case $M=(0)$ or $M=\mathbb{C}^n$ the best one can expect is $\alpha=1$ i.e. Lipschitz stability. Therefore, we shall assume henceforth that $\alpha \geqq 1$. Also note that M is certainly stable if M is α-stable (see [GLR] for the definition of stable invariant subspace). Clearly, if M is α-stable, M is also β-stable for $\beta>\alpha$.

Let A be an $n \times n$ matrix and Γ a positively oriented contour in the complex plane such that no eigenvalues of A lie on Γ. The spectral projection of A with respect to Γ is defined by

$$P(\Gamma,A)=\frac{1}{2\pi i}\int_\Gamma(\lambda-A)^{-1}d\lambda.$$

In case only one eigenvalue, say λ_0 lies inside Γ the image of $P(\Gamma,A)$ is denoted by $R_{\lambda_0}(A)$; it is the span of eigenvectors and generalized eigenvectors of A corresponding to λ_0.

Next, we introduce the notion of *strong α-stability*. Let A be an $n \times n$ matrix, and let $\lambda_1, \ldots, \lambda_r$ be its different eigenvalues. Choose for each $j=1,\ldots,r$ a contour Γ_j such that λ_j is inside Γ_j and λ_i is outside Γ_j for $i \neq j$. A subspace $M \in \mathrm{Inv}\,(A)$ is called *strongly α-stable* if there exists a positive constant K such that for any sequence $A_n \to A$ and *any* $M \in \mathrm{Inv}\,(A_n)$ with

$$\dim P_{nj}M_n = \dim P_jM \qquad (j=1,\ldots,r), \tag{1.1}$$

where P_j (resp. P_{nj}) is the spectral projection of A (resp. A_n) with respect to Γ_j we have

$$\theta(M_n,M) \leqq K\|A_n-A\|^{\frac{1}{\alpha}}. \tag{1.2}$$

Note that if condition (1.1) is violated in the long run, the subspaces M_n cannot converge to M. So, roughly speaking, strong α-stability of M means that any sequence of subspaces $M_n \in \mathrm{Inv}\,(A_n)$ which 'has a chance' of converging to M really does so, and with speed specified by (1.2). From numerical point of view it thus seems that strong α-stability is more desirable than just α-stability. Again, strong α-stability implies stability and also strong β-stability for $\beta>\alpha$. (The notion of *strong stability* was first introduced in [RR] for a certain class of subspaces.) The definition of strong α-stability can be rephrased as follows. A stable subspace

$M \in \text{Inv}(A)$ is strongly α-stable if there exist positive constants K and ϵ such that for $\|B-A\|<\epsilon$ and *any* $N \in \text{Inv}(B)$ sufficiently close to M we have (1.2).

We next state our theorem which characterizes strongly α-stable subspaces in $\text{Inv}(A)$. Here and in the sequel we shall use the notation $R_\lambda(A)$ for the spectral subspace of a matrix A corresponding to its eigenvalue λ.

Theorem 1.1 *Let $M \in \text{Inv}(A)$ and let $\lambda_1, \ldots, \lambda_r$ be the different eigenvalues of A. Write $M = \oplus_{j=1}^{r} N_j$ where $N_j \subset R_{\lambda_j}(A)$. Then M is strongly α-stable if and only if the following three conditions hold*

(i) $N_i=(0)$ *or* $N_i=R_{\lambda_i}(A)$ *whenever* $\dim \text{Ker}(\lambda_i - A)>1$,

(ii) $N_i=(0)$ *or* $N_i=R_{\lambda_i}(A)$ *whenever whenever* $\dim \text{Ker}(\lambda_i - A)=1$, *and* $\alpha < \dim R_{\lambda_i}(A)$,

(iii) N_i *is an arbitrary element of* $\text{Inv}(A)$ *contained in* $R_{\lambda_i}(A)$ *whenever* $\dim \text{Ker}(\lambda_i - A)=1$ *and* $\alpha \geqq \dim R_{\lambda_i}(A)$.

In particular, if (i), (ii) and (iii) hold M is α-stable.

Let us draw some conclusions from Theorem 1.1. First, if M is strongly α-stable with $\alpha<2$ it is Lipschitz stable (i.e. 1-stable). Indeed, in that case M will be a spectral subspace, and hence Lipschitz stable. Note that we use the notion of Lipschitz stability here for a single subspace, and not for a lattice of subspaces as in [GLR]. Second, denote by $m(A)$ the order of the largest Jordan block coreseponding to eigenvalues of A of geometric multiplicity one ($m(A)$ is the so called *height* of A, see [GLR]). Then every stable invariant subspace of A is strongly α-stable for any $\alpha \geqq m(A)$. In particular, every stable invariant subspace of the $n \times n$ matrix A is strongly n-stable. This follows immediately from Theorem 1.1 and the description of stable invariant subspaces (see [CD],[BGK] or [GLR]).

2. Proof of Theorem 1.1

Before we start the proof, we first present a lemma, which allows us to treat the problem locally.

Lemma 2.1 *Suppose A_1, A_2 are $n_1 \times n_1$ and $n_2 \times n_2$ matrices, respectively, and $\sigma(A_1) \cap \sigma(A_2) = \emptyset$. Introduce an $m \times m$ $(m=n_1+n_2)$ matrix $A=A_1 \oplus A_2$ and denote $R_i=R_{\sigma(A_i)}(A)$. Let M_i be A_i-invariant subspaces in R_i, for $i=1,2$. Then the subspace $M=M_1 \oplus M_2 \in \text{Inv}(A)$, is strongly α-stable if and only if M_i is strongly α-stable as an element of $\text{Inv}(A_i)$.*

Proof. Suppose M is strongly α-stable. Take a sequence $B_{n1} \to A_1$ arbitrarely and $M_{n1} \in \text{Inv}(B_{n1})$ with $\dim M_{n1} = \dim M_1$. Consider $B_n = B_{n1} \oplus A_2$.

Then $M_n = M_{n1} \oplus M_2 \in$ Inv (B_n) and for n large enough we have by the strong α-stability of M that

$$\theta(M_n, M) = \theta(M_{n1}, M_1) \leqq K \, \| B_n - A \|^{\frac{1}{\alpha}} = K \, \| B_{n1} - A_1 \|^{\frac{1}{\alpha}}$$

for some positive K. Hence M_1 is strongly α-stable. Likewise one shows that M_2 is strongly α-stable.

Conversely, assume M_1 and M_2 are strongly α-stable. Take a sequence of matrices $B_n \to A$. By the Lipschitz stability of R_i we can decompose $\mathbb{C}^m$ for n large enough as $\mathbb{C}^m = N_{n1} \oplus N_{n2}$, where

$$\theta(N_{ni}, R_i) \leqq K_1 \| B_n - A \| .$$

By Lemma 13.3.2 in [GLR] there exists $S_n : \mathbb{C}^m \to \mathbb{C}^m$ such that $S_n N_{ni} = R_i$ and

$$\max(\| S_n - I \| , \| S_n^{-1} - I \|) \leqq K_2(\theta(N_{n1}, R_1) + \theta(N_{n2}, R_2)) \leqq K_3 \| B_n - A \| \quad (2.1)$$

for some K_3 independent of n.

Put $\tilde{B}_n = S_n B_n S_n^{-1} = B_{n1} \oplus B_{n2}$ with respect to the decomposition $\mathbb{C}^m = R_1 \oplus R_2$. Then $\tilde{B}_n \to A$, $B_{ni} \to A_i$. Now take any $M_n \in$ Inv (B_n) with $M_n = M_{n1} \oplus M_{n2}, M_{ni} \subset N_{ni}$ and $\dim M_{ni} = \dim M_i$. We have to show

$$\theta(M_n, M) \leqq K \, \| B_n - A \|^{\frac{1}{\alpha}} \quad (2.2)$$

for some K independent of n. Put $\tilde{M}_n = S_n M_n \in$ Inv $\tilde{B}_n$ and $\tilde{M}_{ni} = S_n M_{ni} \in$ Inv (B_{ni}). Since M_1 and M_2 are strongly α-stable we have, using (2.1)

$$\theta(\tilde{M}_{ni}, M_i) \leqq L_i \, \| B_{ni} - A_i \|^{\frac{1}{\alpha}} \leqq K \, \| B_n - A \|^{\frac{1}{\alpha}} .$$

Then

$$\theta(M_n, M) \leqq \theta(M_{n1} \oplus M_{n2}, \tilde{M}_{n1} \oplus M_{n2}) +$$
$$+ \theta(\tilde{M}_{n1} \oplus M_{n2}, \tilde{M}_{n1} \oplus \tilde{M}_{n2}) + \theta(\tilde{M}_{n1} \oplus \tilde{M}_{n2}, M_{n1} \oplus M_{n2})$$
$$\leqq \theta(M_{n1}, \tilde{M}_{n1}) + \theta(M_{n2}, \tilde{M}_{n2}) + \theta(M_1, \tilde{M}_{n1}) + \theta(M_2, \tilde{M}_{n2}).$$

Now by (2.1)

$$\theta(M_{ni}, \tilde{M}_{ni}) \leqq \| P_{M_{ni}} - S_n P_{M_{ni}} S_n^{-1} \| \leqq$$

$$\leqq \| P_{M_{ni}} - S_n P_{M_{ni}} \| + \| S_n P_{M_{ni}} (I - S_n^{-1}) \| \leqq K_5 \| B_n - A \| \leqq K_6 \| B_n - A \|^{\frac{1}{\alpha}}$$

(recall that $\alpha \geqq 1$), for n large enough. Combining the inequalities above we obtain (2.2). Hence M is strongly α-stable. □

We proceed by proving Theorem 1.1

Proof of Theorem 1.1. Because of the lemma just proved, we may assume $\sigma(A)$ consists of one point, say λ.

In case dim Ker $(A-\lambda)>1$ and M is strongly α-stable we see from the stability of M that (i) holds (see [BGK],[CD],[GLR]). Conversely, if (i) holds $M=(0)$ or the whole space and hence trivially strongly α-stable.

So consider the case dim Ker $(A-\lambda)=1$. Without loss of generality we may assume $\lambda=0$ and $A=J_n$ is the $n\times n$ Jordan block with zero eigenvalue. Let M be the k-dimensional subspace in Inv (A), i.e.

$$M=\text{ span }\{e_1,\ldots,e_k\} \qquad (1\leqq k<n).$$

Take α arbitrarely. We have to show that in case $\alpha\geqq n$ M is strongly α-stable, and in case $\alpha<n$ M is not strongly α-stable.

Suppose $\alpha\geqq n$. In the proof of Lemma 16.5.2 in [GLR] the following is shown. There exist positive constants ϵ and K such that if $\|B-A\|<\epsilon$ then for every k-dimensional subspace $N\in$ Inv (B) one has

$$\theta(M,N)\leqq K\|B-A\|^{\frac{1}{n}}.$$

In particular, M is strongly n-stable, and hence also strongly α-stable.

Finally assume $\alpha<n$. Consider the matrices

$$B_\epsilon=\begin{pmatrix} 0 & 1 & 0 & . & . & . & 0\\ . & . & . & & & & .\\ . & & . & . & & & .\\ . & & & . & . & & .\\ . & & & & . & . & 0\\ 0 & & & & & . & 1\\ \epsilon & 0 & . & . & . & . & 0\end{pmatrix}.$$

Denote $\epsilon_j=|\epsilon|^{\frac{1}{n}}\exp\frac{2\pi i j}{n}$, the eigenvalues of B_ϵ. Further, let

$$y_j=(1,\epsilon_j,\epsilon_j^2,\ldots,\epsilon_j^{n-1})^T$$

be the corresponding eigenvectors. Put $M_\epsilon=$ span $\{y_1,\ldots,y_k\}$. Clearly

$$M_\epsilon=\text{Im}\begin{pmatrix}R_1\\ R_2\end{pmatrix}=\text{Im}\begin{pmatrix}I\\ R_2R_1^{-1}\end{pmatrix},$$

where

$$R_1=\begin{bmatrix} 1 & \cdots & 1 \\ \epsilon_1 & & \epsilon_k \\ \cdot & & \cdot \\ \cdot & & \cdot \\ \cdot & & \cdot \\ \epsilon_1^{k-1} & \cdots & \epsilon_k^{k-1} \end{bmatrix}, \quad R_2=\begin{bmatrix} \epsilon_1^k & \cdots & \epsilon_k^k \\ \cdot & & \cdot \\ \cdot & & \cdot \\ \cdot & & \cdot \\ \epsilon_1^{n-1} & \cdots & \epsilon_k^{n-1} \end{bmatrix}.$$

Compute the last column of $R_2R_1^{-1}$. This is most easily done by computing first the last column of the inverse of the Vandermonde matrix R_1, using $R_1^{-1} = (\det R_1)^{-1}\operatorname{adj}R_1$, and the formula $\det R_1 = \prod_{i<j}(\epsilon_j-\epsilon_i)$ Then an easy argument shows that the last column of $R_2R_1^{-1}$ equals

$$(p_1(\epsilon_1,..,\epsilon_k), \ldots ,p_{n-k}(\epsilon_1,..,\epsilon_k))^T,$$

where p_j is the homogeneous polynomial of degree j given by

$$p_j(y_1,\ldots,y_k)=\sum y_1^{\alpha_1}y_2^{\alpha_2}\cdots y_k^{\alpha_k}$$

where the sum is taken over all k-tuples of nonnegative integers $(\alpha_1,..,\alpha_k)$ such that their sum is j. Now put

$$u=(0,\ldots,0,1,p_1(\epsilon_1,..,\epsilon_k),\ldots,p_{n-k}(\epsilon_1,..,\epsilon_k))^T.$$

Then, since $M_\epsilon = \operatorname{Im}\begin{bmatrix} I \\ R_2R_1^{-1}\end{bmatrix}$, we have $u \in M_\epsilon$. Therefore

$$\|P_{M_\epsilon}-P_M\|^2 \geqq \frac{1}{\|u\|^2}\|(P_{M_\epsilon}-P_M)u\|^2=$$

$$=\frac{1}{\|u\|^2}\|u-e_k\|^2 \geqq \frac{1}{\|u\|^2}|p_1(\epsilon_1,\ldots,\epsilon_k)|^2=$$

$$\frac{1}{\|u\|^2}|\epsilon_1+\ldots+\epsilon_k|^2 \geqq \frac{1}{4}|\epsilon_1+\ldots+\epsilon_k|^2,$$

for $|\epsilon|$ small enough. Hence

$$\theta(M_\epsilon,M) \geqq c\,|\epsilon_1+\ldots+\epsilon_k|$$

for ϵ small enough and c independent of ϵ. So

$$\theta(M_\epsilon,M) \geqq c\,|\epsilon|^{\frac{1}{n}}\,\Big|\sum_{j=1}^{k}\exp\frac{2\pi ij}{n}\Big| = c_1|\epsilon|^{\frac{1}{n}}$$

with c_1 independent of ϵ. This means that M cannot be strongly α-stable for $\alpha<n$. □

3. Application to algebraic Riccati equations

In this section we give applications of Theorem 1.1 to stability of solutions of algebraic Riccati equations. We start by considering the algebraic Riccati equation

$$XA_{21}X+XA_{22}-A_{11}X-A_{12}=0 \tag{3.1}$$

where the A_{ij}'s are matrices. A solution X is called strongly α-stable if there exist positive constants K and ϵ such that for any matrices B_{ij} with $\max_{i,j=1,2}\|A_{ij}-B_{ij}\|<\epsilon$ and any solution Y of

$$YB_{21}Y+YB_{22}-B_{11}Y-B_{12}=0$$

sufficiently close to X we have

$$\|Y-X\|\leqq K(\max_{i,j=1,2}\|A_{ij}-B_{ij}\|)^{\frac{1}{\alpha}}.$$

Introduce the matrix $A=\begin{pmatrix}A_{11} & A_{12}\\ A_{21} & A_{22}\end{pmatrix}$. The following theorem describes strongly α-stable solutions of equation (3.1).

Theorem 3.1. *The following are equivalent:*

(i) X is a strongly α-stable solution of (3.1),

(ii) Im $\begin{pmatrix}X\\ I\end{pmatrix}$ *is strongly α-stable as an A-invariant subspace,*

(iii) each common eigenvalue of $A_{11}-XA_{21}$ and $A_{22}+A_{21}X$ is an eigenvalue of A of geometric multiplicity one and algebraic multiplicity $\leqq\alpha$.

Proof. From Lemma 7.2 in [BGK] we see that X is strongly α-stable if and only if Im $\begin{pmatrix}X\\ I\end{pmatrix}$ is strongly α-stable as an A-invariant subspace. Thus the equivalence of (i) and (ii) is straightforward. It remains to show that (ii) and (iii) are equivalent. To see this note that

$$\begin{pmatrix}I & -X\\ 0 & I\end{pmatrix}\begin{pmatrix}A_{11} & A_{12}\\ A_{21} & A_{22}\end{pmatrix}\begin{pmatrix}I & X\\ 0 & I\end{pmatrix}=\begin{pmatrix}A_{11}-XA_{21} & 0\\ A_{21} & A_{21}X+A_{22}\end{pmatrix}.$$

Denote the latter matrix by $\tilde{A}$. It follows that Im $\begin{pmatrix}X\\ I\end{pmatrix}$ is strongly α-stable as an

A-invariant subspace if and only if $\operatorname{Im}\begin{bmatrix}0\\ I\end{bmatrix}$ is strongly α-stable as an $\tilde{A}$-invariant subspace. Now from Theorem 1.1 it easily follows that this is equivalent to the statement (iii). □

4. Applications to factorization of matrix polynomials

In this section we consider the following problem: given a matrix polynomial $L(\lambda)=\sum_{j=0}^{l}\lambda^j A_j$, with $A_l=I$, describe all factorizations $L(\lambda)=L_1(\lambda)L_2(\lambda)$, with $L_2(\lambda)=\sum_{j=0}^{k}\lambda^j A_{2,j}$ and $A_{2,k}=I$, which are strongly α-stable. To be precise, the factorization above is called strongly α-stable if there exists a positive constant K such that for any monic polynomial $\tilde{L}(\lambda)=\sum_{j=0}^{l}\lambda^j B_j$ with coefficients close enough to those of L, and any factorization $\tilde{L}=\tilde{L}_1\tilde{L}_2$, with $\tilde{L}_2(\lambda)=\sum_{j=0}^{k}\lambda^j B_{2,j}$, $B_{2,k}=I$ with coefficients close to those of L_2 we have in fact

$$\sum_{j=0}^{k-1}\|A_{2,j}-B_{2,j}\|\leqq\Big(\sum_{j=0}^{l-1}\|A_j-B_j\|\Big)^{\frac{1}{\alpha}}.$$

The complex number λ is called an *eigenvalue* of the matrix polynomial L in case $\operatorname{Ker} L(\lambda)\neq(0)$. In that case $\dim\operatorname{Ker} L(\lambda)$ is called the *geometric multiplicity* of L at λ and the multiplicity of λ as a zero of $\det L(\lambda)$ is called the *algebraic multiplicity* of L at λ.

Using the methods of proof employed in Chapter 17, Sections 1,2,3 of [GLR], and Theorem 17.1.2 in particular, one obtains the following result, of which we omit the details of the proof.

Theorem 4.1. *The factorization $L(\lambda)=L_1(\lambda)L_2(\lambda)$ is strongly α-stable if and only if each common eigenvalue of L_1 and L_2 is an eigenvalue of L of geometric multiplicity one and algebraic multiplicity $\leqq\alpha$.*

References

[BGK] Bart,H.,Gohberg,I. and Kaashoek,M.A.: Minimal Factorization of Matrix and Operator Functions, Birkhäuser, Basel, 1979.

[CD] Campbell,S. and Daughtry,J.: The stable solutions of quadratic matrix equations, Proc. AMS 74 (1979), 19-23.

[GLR] Gohberg,I.,Lancaster,P. and Rodman,L.: Invariant Subspaces of Matrices with Applications, John Wiley & Sons, New York, 1986.

[RR] Ran, A.C.M. and Rodman,L.: Stability of Invariant Lagrangian Subspaces I, in: Topics in Operator Theory, Constantin Apostol memorial issue, (ed: I.Gohberg), OT 32, Birkhäuser, Basel, 1988.

A.C.M.Ran
Faculteit Wiskunde en Informatica
Vrije Universiteit
De Boelelaan 1081
1081 HV Amsterdam
The Netherlands

L.Roozemond
Koninklijke/Shell Exploratie en Produktie Laboratorium
P.O.Box 60
2280 AB Rijswijk ZH
The Netherlands

Operator Theory:
Advances and Applications, Vol. 40

On Classification of Invariant Subspaces of a Linear Operator

Boris Reichstein

Dedicated to Professor Israel Gohberg
on the occasion of his sixtieth birthday.

The problem of the classification of invariant subspaces of a linear operator is shown to be at least as complex as the problem of the classification of arbitrary pairs of square matrices up to simultaneous similarity.

Let

$$\{\mathbf{C}^n, \mathbf{A}, \mathbf{S}\} \tag{1}$$

be a three-tuple where $\mathbf{C}^n$ is a complex n-dimensional linear space, $\mathbf{A} : \mathbf{C}^n \to \mathbf{C}^n$ is a linear operator and $\mathbf{S} \subset \mathbf{C}^n$ is a subspace invariant for $\mathbf{A}$, i.e. $\mathbf{AS} \subset \mathbf{S}$. If

$$\{\tilde{\mathbf{C}}^n, \tilde{\mathbf{A}}, \tilde{\mathbf{S}}\} \tag{2}$$

is another three-tuple, we call the two tuples *equivalent* if there exists a linear non-singular map $\mathbf{M} : \mathbf{C}^n \to \tilde{\mathbf{C}}^n$ such that

$$\tilde{\mathbf{A}} = \mathbf{MAM}^{-1} \tag{3}$$

and

$$\tilde{\mathbf{S}} = \mathbf{MS}. \tag{4}$$

The following theorem shows how this definition can be restated in matrix form.

THEOREM 1 *Let (1) and (2) be two three-tuples,*

$$\{\mathbf{v}_1, \mathbf{v}_2, \ldots, \mathbf{v}_n\} \tag{5}$$

an arbitrary basis of $\mathbf{C}^n$, $\mathbf{B}$ *the matrix of* $\mathbf{A}$ *in this basis. Further, let the* m *vectors*

$$\sum_{j=1}^{j=n} c_{ij}\mathbf{v}_j \quad (i = 1, 2, \ldots, m) \tag{6}$$

span $\mathbf{S}$. *Then the tuples (1) and (2) are equivalent if and only if there exists a basis*

$$\{\tilde{\mathbf{v}}_1, \tilde{\mathbf{v}}_2, \ldots, \tilde{\mathbf{v}}_n\} \tag{7}$$

of $\mathbf{C}^n$ *such that the matrix of* $\tilde{\mathbf{A}}$ *in this basis is* $\mathbf{B}$ *and the* m *vectors*

$$\sum_{j=1}^{j=n} c_{ij}\tilde{\mathbf{v}}_j \quad (i = 1, 2, \ldots, m) \tag{8}$$

span $\tilde{\mathbf{S}}$.

PROOF: If (1) and (2) are equivalent and $\mathbf{M}$ is as in (3) and (4), we define the basis (7) by the identities $\tilde{\mathbf{v}}_i = \mathbf{M}\mathbf{v}_i$ $(i = 1, 2, \ldots, n)$. It is a trivial exercise to check that the basis (7) so defined has all the properties required by the theorem, namely, the matrix of $\tilde{\mathbf{A}}$ in this basis is $\mathbf{B}$ and vectors (8) span $\tilde{\mathbf{S}}$.

Conversely, if (5) and (7) are two bases of $\mathbf{C}^n$ and $\tilde{\mathbf{C}}^n$, respectively, such that the matrix of $\mathbf{A}$ in basis (5) is the same as the matrix of $\tilde{\mathbf{A}}$ in basis (7) and the vectors (6) span $\mathbf{S}$ and the vectors (8) span $\tilde{\mathbf{S}}$, then the map $\mathbf{M} : \mathbf{C}^n \to \tilde{\mathbf{C}}^n$ defined by the identities $\mathbf{M}\mathbf{v}_i = \tilde{\mathbf{v}}_i$ for all $i = 1, 2, \ldots, n$ satisfies (3) and (4). Hence, the three-tuples (1) and (2) are equivalent. Q.E.D.

The problem that we would like to solve is to describe all classes of non-equivalent three-tuples and to find a canonical representation for each class. The problem turns out to be closely related to the problem of classifying block-triangular matrices up to block-triangular equivalence. We now explain what it means. Let

$$\mathbf{T} = \begin{pmatrix} \mathbf{P} & \mathbf{Q} \\ \mathbf{0} & \mathbf{R} \end{pmatrix} \tag{9}$$

and

$$\tilde{\mathbf{T}} = \begin{pmatrix} \tilde{\mathbf{P}} & \tilde{\mathbf{Q}} \\ \mathbf{0} & \tilde{\mathbf{R}} \end{pmatrix} \tag{10}$$

be two $n \times n$-matrices where $\mathbf{P}$ and $\tilde{\mathbf{P}}$ are $m \times m$-matrices. We say that $\mathbf{T}$ and $\tilde{\mathbf{T}}$ are *block-triangular equivalent* if there exists an $n \times n$-matrix

$$\mathbf{E} = \begin{pmatrix} \mathbf{F} & \mathbf{G} \\ \mathbf{0} & \mathbf{H} \end{pmatrix} \tag{11}$$

with regular $m \times m$-matrix $\mathbf{F}$ and regular $(n-m) \times (n-m)$-matrix $\mathbf{H}$ such that

$$\tilde{\mathbf{T}} = \mathbf{ETE}^{-1}. \tag{12}$$

THEOREM 2 *Let* $\mathbf{T}$ *and* $\tilde{\mathbf{T}}$ *be two block-triangular matrices (9)-(10). Let* $\mathbf{C}^n$ *and* $\tilde{\mathbf{C}}^n$ *be two n-dimensional linear spaces, (5) ((7)) an arbitrary basis of* $\mathbf{C}^n$ $(\tilde{\mathbf{C}}^n)$, $\mathbf{A}$ $(\tilde{\mathbf{A}})$ *be a linear operator* $\mathbf{C}^n \to \mathbf{C}^n$ $(\tilde{\mathbf{C}}^n \to \tilde{\mathbf{C}}^n)$ *defined via its matrix (9) ((10)) in the basis (5) ((7)). If* $\mathbf{S} = span\{\mathbf{v}_1, \mathbf{v}_2, \ldots, \mathbf{v}_m\}$ *and* $\tilde{\mathbf{S}} = span\{\tilde{\mathbf{v}}_1, \tilde{\mathbf{v}}_2, \ldots, \tilde{\mathbf{v}}_m\}$ *then* $\tilde{\mathbf{T}}$ *is block-triangular equivalent to* $\mathbf{T}$ *if and only if the three-tuple* $(\tilde{\mathbf{C}}^n, \tilde{\mathbf{A}}, \tilde{\mathbf{S}})$ *is equivalent to the three-tuple* $(\mathbf{C}^n, \mathbf{A}, \mathbf{S})$.

PROOF: First let $\tilde{\mathbf{T}}$ be block-triangular equivalent to $\mathbf{T}$ and the matrix (11) realize the equivalence, i.e. (12) holds. Given the bases (5) of $\mathbf{C}^n$ and (7) of $\tilde{\mathbf{C}}^n$ we define a map $\mathbf{M} : \mathbf{C}^n \to \tilde{\mathbf{C}}^n$ via its matrix (11). It is obvious that for this map $\mathbf{M}$ the identity (3) holds. The identity (4) follows from the definition of the subspaces $\mathbf{S}$ and $\tilde{\mathbf{S}}$, the block structure of the matrix $\mathbf{E}$ and the regularity of $\mathbf{F}$.

Conversely, let the three-tuples $(\tilde{\mathbf{C}}^n, \tilde{\mathbf{A}}, \tilde{\mathbf{S}})$ and $(\mathbf{C}^n, \mathbf{A}, \mathbf{S})$ defined in the statement of the theorem be equivalent and $\mathbf{M}$ be a map that realizes the equivalency, i.e. the identities (3) and (4) hold. Since (4) holds, the matrix of $\mathbf{M}$ in bases (5), (7) has the block-triangular form,

$$\mathbf{M} = \begin{pmatrix} \mathbf{F} & \mathbf{G} \\ 0 & \mathbf{H} \end{pmatrix}, \quad det(\mathbf{F}) \neq 0, \quad det(\mathbf{H}) \neq 0.$$

Now the identity (3) written in the block form becomes

$$\begin{pmatrix} \tilde{\mathbf{P}} & \tilde{\mathbf{Q}} \\ 0 & \tilde{\mathbf{R}} \end{pmatrix} = \begin{pmatrix} \mathbf{F} & \mathbf{G} \\ 0 & \mathbf{H} \end{pmatrix} \begin{pmatrix} \mathbf{P} & \mathbf{Q} \\ 0 & \mathbf{R} \end{pmatrix} \begin{pmatrix} \mathbf{F} & \mathbf{G} \\ 0 & \mathbf{H} \end{pmatrix}^{-1}$$

which means that the matrices $\mathbf{T}$ and $\tilde{\mathbf{T}}$ are block-triangular equivalent. Q.E.D.

In the next statement we prove that the problem of the classification of three-tuples is at least as complex as the problem of the classification of arbitrary pairs of square matrices up to simultaneous similarity.

THEOREM 3 *Let*

$$\{\mathbf{P}(p_{ij}), \mathbf{Q}(q_{ij})\}, \quad \{\tilde{\mathbf{P}}(\tilde{p}_{ij}), \tilde{\mathbf{Q}}(\tilde{q}_{ij})\} \tag{13}$$

be two pairs of $n \times n$*-matrices. Let* $\mathbf{C}^{25n}$ *and* $\tilde{\mathbf{C}}^{25n}$ *be two* $25n$*-dimensional spaces,*

$$\{\mathbf{a}_{11}, \mathbf{a}_{21}, \ldots, \mathbf{a}_{n1}, \mathbf{b}_{11}, \mathbf{b}_{21}, \ldots, \mathbf{b}_{n1}, \mathbf{b}_{12}, \mathbf{b}_{22}, \ldots, \mathbf{b}_{n2}, \mathbf{c}_{11}, \mathbf{c}_{21}, \ldots, \mathbf{c}_{n1}, \ldots, \mathbf{c}_{15}, \mathbf{c}_{25}, \ldots, \mathbf{c}_{n5},$$

$$\mathbf{d}_{11},\mathbf{d}_{21},\ldots,\mathbf{d}_{n1},\ldots,\mathbf{d}_{17},\mathbf{d}_{27},\ldots,\mathbf{d}_{n7},\mathbf{e}_{11},\mathbf{e}_{21},\ldots,\mathbf{e}_{n1},\ldots,\mathbf{e}_{19},\mathbf{e}_{29},\ldots,\mathbf{e}_{n9}\} \tag{14}$$

be a basis of $\mathbf{C}^{25n}$ *and*

$$\{\tilde{\mathbf{a}}_{11},\tilde{\mathbf{a}}_{21},\ldots,\tilde{\mathbf{a}}_{n1},\tilde{\mathbf{b}}_{11},\tilde{\mathbf{b}}_{21},\ldots,\tilde{\mathbf{b}}_{n1},\tilde{\mathbf{b}}_{13},\tilde{\mathbf{b}}_{23},\ldots,\tilde{\mathbf{b}}_{n3},\tilde{\mathbf{c}}_{11},\tilde{\mathbf{c}}_{21},\ldots,\tilde{\mathbf{c}}_{n1},\ldots,\tilde{\mathbf{c}}_{15},\tilde{\mathbf{c}}_{25},\ldots,\tilde{\mathbf{c}}_{n5},$$

$$\tilde{\mathbf{d}}_{11},\ldots,\tilde{\mathbf{d}}_{n1},\ldots,\tilde{\mathbf{d}}_{17},\tilde{\mathbf{d}}_{27},\ldots,\tilde{\mathbf{d}}_{n7},\tilde{\mathbf{e}}_{11},\tilde{\mathbf{e}}_{21},\ldots,\tilde{\mathbf{e}}_{n1},\ldots,\tilde{\mathbf{e}}_{19},\tilde{\mathbf{e}}_{29},\ldots,\tilde{\mathbf{e}}_{n9}\} \tag{15}$$

be a basis of $\tilde{\mathbf{C}}^{25n}$. *Define an operator* $\mathbf{A}:\mathbf{C}^{25n}\to\mathbf{C}^{25n}$ *by the identities*

$$\mathbf{A}\mathbf{f}_{ij}=\mathbf{f}_{i,j-1},\quad \mathbf{f}_{i,0}=0 \tag{16}$$

where $\mathbf{f}$ *is any of the symbols* $\mathbf{a},\mathbf{b},\mathbf{c},\mathbf{d},\mathbf{e}$, $i=1,2,\ldots,n$ *and* j *runs over all possible values for the corresponding* $\mathbf{f}$ *(thus,* $\mathbf{A}$ *is a nilpotent operator whose Jordan form consists of* n 1×1*-blocks,* n 3×3*-blocks,* n 5×5*-blocks,* n 7×7*-blocks and* n 9×9 *blocks). Similarly, define an operator* $\tilde{\mathbf{A}}$ *acting in* $\mathbf{C}^{25n}$ *by the identities*

$$\tilde{\mathbf{A}}\tilde{\mathbf{f}}_{ij}=\tilde{\mathbf{f}}_{i,j-1},\quad \tilde{\mathbf{f}}_{i,0}=0. \tag{17}$$

Next, define $2n$ *vectors in* $\mathbf{C}^{25n}$*:*

$$\mathbf{v}_i=\mathbf{a}_{i1}+\mathbf{c}_{i3}+\mathbf{d}_{i4}+\sum_{j=1}^{j=n}p_{ij}\mathbf{e}_{j5},\quad \mathbf{w}_i=\mathbf{b}_{i2}+\mathbf{c}_{i3}+\sum_{j=1}^{j=n}q_{ij}\mathbf{d}_{j4}+\mathbf{e}_{i5}, \tag{18}$$

and, similarly, $2n$ *vectors in* $\tilde{\mathbf{C}}^{25n}$*:*

$$\tilde{\mathbf{v}}_i=\tilde{\mathbf{a}}_{i1}+\tilde{\mathbf{c}}_{i3}+\tilde{\mathbf{d}}_{i4}+\sum_{j=1}^{j=n}\tilde{p}_{ij}\tilde{\mathbf{e}}_{j5},\quad \tilde{\mathbf{w}}_i=\tilde{\mathbf{b}}_{i2}+\tilde{\mathbf{c}}_{i3}+\sum_{j=1}^{j=n}\tilde{q}_{ij}\tilde{\mathbf{d}}_{j4}+\tilde{\mathbf{e}}_{i5}. \tag{19}$$

If $\mathbf{S}$ *is the minimal subspace invariant for* $\mathbf{A}$ *and containing all the vectors* $\mathbf{v}_i$ *and* $\mathbf{w}_i$*, and* $\tilde{\mathbf{S}}$ *is the minimal subspace invariant for* $\tilde{\mathbf{A}}$ *and containing all the vectors* $\tilde{\mathbf{v}}_i$ *and* $\tilde{\mathbf{w}}_i$*, then the three-tuples*

$$(\mathbf{C}^{25n},\mathbf{A},\mathbf{S}),\quad (\tilde{\mathbf{C}}^{25n},\tilde{\mathbf{A}},\tilde{\mathbf{S}}) \tag{20}$$

are equivalent if and only if the pairs (13) of matrices are simultaneously similar.

PROOF: Assume first that the pairs (13) are simultaneously similar, i.e.

$$\tilde{\mathbf{P}}=\mathbf{R}^{-1}\mathbf{P}\mathbf{R},\quad \tilde{\mathbf{Q}}=\mathbf{R}^{-1}\mathbf{Q}\mathbf{R} \tag{21}$$

for some non-singular $n\times n$-matrix $\mathbf{R}(r_{ij})$. Define a map $\mathbf{M}:\mathbf{C}^{25n}\to\tilde{\mathbf{C}}^{25n}$ by the identities

$$\mathbf{M}\mathbf{f}_{ij}=\sum_{k=1}^{k=n}r_{ik}\tilde{\mathbf{f}}_{kj} \tag{22}$$

where, as above, $\mathbf{f}$ runs over all symbols $\mathbf{a}, \mathbf{b}, \mathbf{c}, \mathbf{d}, \mathbf{e}$. For any $\mathbf{f}$ we have:

$$\mathbf{MAf}_{ij} = \mathbf{Mf}_{i,j-1} = \sum_{k=1}^{k=n} r_{ik}\tilde{\mathbf{f}}_{k,j-1} = \sum_{k=1}^{k=n} r_{ik}\tilde{\mathbf{A}}\tilde{\mathbf{f}}_{kj} = \tilde{\mathbf{A}}(\sum_{k=1}^{k=n} r_{ik}\mathbf{f}_{kj}) = \tilde{\mathbf{A}}\mathbf{Mf}_{ij},$$

or $\tilde{\mathbf{A}} = \mathbf{MAM}^{-1}$. Next, the identities (18) and (22) yield:

$$\mathbf{Mv}_i = \mathbf{M}(\mathbf{a}_{i1} + \mathbf{c}_{i3} + \mathbf{d}_{i4} + \sum_{j=1}^{j=n} p_{ij}\mathbf{e}_{j5}) = \sum_{k=1}^{k=n} r_{ik}(\tilde{\mathbf{a}}_{k1} + \tilde{\mathbf{c}}_{k3} + \tilde{\mathbf{d}}_{k4}) + \sum_{j=1}^{j=n}\sum_{k=1}^{k=n} p_{ij}r_{jk}\tilde{\mathbf{e}}_{k5}. \quad (23)$$

From the first identity (21) it follows that

$$\sum_{k=1}^{k=n} p_{ik}r_{kj} = \sum_{k=1}^{k=n} r_{ik}\tilde{p}_{kj}$$

and, therefore, the expression (23) for $\mathbf{Mv}_i$ can be rewritten as

$$\mathbf{Mv}_i = \sum_{k=1}^{k=n} r_{ik}(\tilde{\mathbf{a}}_{i1} + \tilde{\mathbf{c}}_{i3} + \tilde{\mathbf{d}}_{i4} + \sum_{j=1}^{j=n} \tilde{p}_{kj}\tilde{\mathbf{e}}_{j5}) = \sum_{k=1}^{k=n} r_{ik}\tilde{\mathbf{v}}_k.$$

Similarly,

$$\mathbf{Mw}_i = \sum_{k=1}^{k=n} r_{ik}\tilde{\mathbf{w}}_k.$$

From the last two equalities and regularity of $\mathbf{R}$ it follows that $\mathbf{MS} = \tilde{\mathbf{S}}$.

Now assume that, conversely, the three-tuples (20) defined in the statement of the theorem are equivalent and a map $\mathbf{M} : \mathbf{C}^{25n} \to \tilde{\mathbf{C}}^{25n}$ realizes the equivalence, i.e.

$$\tilde{\mathbf{A}} = \mathbf{MAM}^{-1}, \quad \tilde{\mathbf{S}} = \mathbf{MS}. \quad (24)$$

We shall prove that the pairs (13) are simultaneously similar. According to (16), the matrix of $\mathbf{A}$ in basis (14) and the matrix of $\tilde{\mathbf{A}}$ in basis (15) can be written in a block form as

$$\mathbf{A} = \tilde{\mathbf{A}} = \begin{pmatrix} \mathbf{A}_1 & \mathbf{0} & \mathbf{0} & \mathbf{0} & \mathbf{0} \\ \mathbf{0} & \mathbf{A}_2 & \mathbf{0} & \mathbf{0} & \mathbf{0} \\ \mathbf{0} & \mathbf{0} & \mathbf{A}_3 & \mathbf{0} & \mathbf{0} \\ \mathbf{0} & \mathbf{0} & \mathbf{0} & \mathbf{A}_4 & \mathbf{0} \\ \mathbf{0} & \mathbf{0} & \mathbf{0} & \mathbf{0} & \mathbf{A}_5 \end{pmatrix} \quad (25)$$

where $\mathbf{A}_1 = \mathbf{0}_{n\times n}$, $\mathbf{A}_2$ is $3n \times 3n$- , $\mathbf{A}_3$ $5n \times 5n$- , $\mathbf{A}_4$ $7n \times 7n$- and $\mathbf{A}_5$ is $9n \times 9n$-matrix. If each of the matrices $\mathbf{A}_2$, $\mathbf{A}_3$, $\mathbf{A}_4$ and $\mathbf{A}_5$ is partitioned into $n \times n$-blocks, then each $(i, i+1)$-block is $\mathbf{I}_{n\times n}$ ($i = 1, 2$ for $\mathbf{A}_2$, $i = 1, 2, 3, 4$ for $\mathbf{A}_3$, $i = 1, 2, \ldots, 6$ for $\mathbf{A}_4$ and $i = 1, 2, \ldots, 8$ for $\mathbf{A}_5$), while each of the remaining blocks is $\mathbf{0}_{n\times n}$.

Next, let $\mathbf{M}$ be the matrix of $\mathbf{M}$ in the bases (14)-(15) and

$$\mathbf{M} = \begin{pmatrix} \mathbf{M}_{11} & \mathbf{M}_{12} & \dots & \mathbf{M}_{15} \\ \mathbf{M}_{21} & \mathbf{M}_{22} & \dots & \mathbf{M}_{25} \\ \dots & \dots & \dots & \dots \\ \mathbf{M}_{51} & \mathbf{M}_{52} & \dots & \mathbf{M}_{55} \end{pmatrix} \tag{26}$$

be its block decomposition corresponding to the decomposition (25) of $\mathbf{A}$. Equating the corresponding blocks in the both sides of the identity $\mathbf{MA} = \tilde{\mathbf{A}}\mathbf{M}$ (which is equivalent to (24)) we arrive at the equations

$$\mathbf{M}_{ij}\mathbf{A}_j = \mathbf{A}_i\mathbf{M}_{ij} \quad (i, j = 1, 2, 3, 4, 5). \tag{27}$$

Taking into account the structure of the matrices $\mathbf{A}_i$ described above and partitioning each of the matrices $\mathbf{M}_{ij}$ into $n \times n$-blocks we conclude, after writing each of the identities (27) in the block form, that each of the matrices $\mathbf{M}_{ij}$ is an upper triangular block Toeplitz matrix of corresponding size. It means that if $\mathbf{M}_{ij}$ is an $np \times nq$-matrix partitioned into pq $n \times n$-blocks $\mathbf{M}_{ij,kl}$ $(k = 1, 2, \dots, p;\ l = 1, 2, \dots, q)$, then $\mathbf{M}_{ij,kl} = \mathbf{M}_{ij,l-k}$ where each of $\mathbf{M}_{ij,m}$ is an $n \times n$-matrix and $\mathbf{M}_{ij,m} = \mathbf{0}_{n\times n}$ if $m < max(0, q - p)$.

Let $\mathbf{V}$ be the $25n \times 2n$-matrix whose columns are the coordinates of vectors (18) in the basis (14). It is easy to see that, due to (18),

$$\mathbf{V} = \begin{pmatrix} \mathbf{V}_1 \\ \mathbf{V}_2 \\ \mathbf{V}_3 \\ \mathbf{V}_4 \\ \mathbf{V}_5 \end{pmatrix} \tag{28}$$

where

$$\mathbf{V}_1 = \begin{pmatrix} \mathbf{I} & \mathbf{0} \end{pmatrix}, \quad \mathbf{V}_2 = \begin{pmatrix} \mathbf{0} & \mathbf{0} \\ \mathbf{0} & \mathbf{I} \\ \mathbf{0} & \mathbf{0} \end{pmatrix}, \quad \mathbf{V}_3 = \begin{pmatrix} \mathbf{0} & \mathbf{0} \\ \mathbf{0} & \mathbf{0} \\ \mathbf{I} & \mathbf{I} \\ \mathbf{0} & \mathbf{0} \\ \mathbf{0} & \mathbf{0} \end{pmatrix},$$

$$\mathbf{V}_4 = \begin{pmatrix} \mathbf{0} & \mathbf{0} \\ \mathbf{0} & \mathbf{0} \\ \mathbf{0} & \mathbf{0} \\ \mathbf{I} & \mathbf{Q}^t \\ \mathbf{0} & \mathbf{0} \\ \mathbf{0} & \mathbf{0} \\ \mathbf{0} & \mathbf{0} \end{pmatrix}, \quad \mathbf{V}_5 = \begin{pmatrix} \mathbf{0} & \mathbf{0} \\ \mathbf{0} & \mathbf{0} \\ \mathbf{0} & \mathbf{0} \\ \mathbf{0} & \mathbf{0} \\ \mathbf{P}^t & \mathbf{I} \\ \mathbf{0} & \mathbf{0} \\ \mathbf{0} & \mathbf{0} \\ \mathbf{0} & \mathbf{0} \\ \mathbf{0} & \mathbf{0} \end{pmatrix}. \tag{29}$$

Here the symbol $\mathbf{R}^t$ means the matrix transpose of $\mathbf{R}$. The columns of the matrix $\tilde{\mathbf{V}} = \mathbf{MV}$ are the coordinates of the vectors $\mathbf{Mv}_i$ and $\mathbf{Mw}_i$ in the basis (15). A straigthforward multiplication of the matrices $\mathbf{M}$ and $\mathbf{V}$ shows that

$$\tilde{\mathbf{V}} = \begin{pmatrix} \tilde{\mathbf{V}}_1 \\ \tilde{\mathbf{V}}_2 \\ \tilde{\mathbf{V}}_3 \\ \tilde{\mathbf{V}}_4 \\ \tilde{\mathbf{V}}_5 \end{pmatrix} \tag{30}$$

where

$$\tilde{\mathbf{V}}_1 = \begin{pmatrix} \mathbf{M}_{11,0} & \mathbf{M}_{23,2} \end{pmatrix}, \tilde{\mathbf{V}}_2 = \begin{pmatrix} \mathbf{M}_{23,2} & * \\ \mathbf{0} & \mathbf{M}_{22,0} \\ \mathbf{0} & \mathbf{0} \end{pmatrix}, \tilde{\mathbf{V}}_3 = \begin{pmatrix} * & * \\ * & * \\ \mathbf{M}_{33,0} & \mathbf{M}_{33,0} \\ \mathbf{0} & \mathbf{0} \\ \mathbf{0} & \mathbf{0} \end{pmatrix},$$

$$\tilde{\mathbf{V}}_4 = \begin{pmatrix} * & * \\ * & * \\ * & * \\ \mathbf{M}_{44,0} & \mathbf{M}_{44,0}\mathbf{Q}^t \\ \mathbf{0} & \mathbf{0} \\ \mathbf{0} & \mathbf{0} \\ \mathbf{0} & \mathbf{0} \end{pmatrix}, \quad \tilde{\mathbf{V}}_5 = \begin{pmatrix} * & * \\ * & * \\ * & * \\ * & * \\ \mathbf{M}_{55,0}\mathbf{P}^t & \mathbf{M}_{55,0} \\ \mathbf{0} & \mathbf{0} \\ \mathbf{0} & \mathbf{0} \\ \mathbf{0} & \mathbf{0} \\ \mathbf{0} & \mathbf{0} \end{pmatrix}. \tag{31}$$

We have denoted by $*$ the $n \times n$-matrices that will not play a role in the further consideration, although they can be found easily.

On the other hand, the columns of the matrix $\tilde{\mathbf{V}}$ are coordinates of linear combinations of vectors (19) and vectors from $\tilde{\mathbf{S}}' = \tilde{\mathbf{A}}\tilde{\mathbf{S}}$. Let

$$\mathbf{M}\mathbf{v}_i = \sum_{j=1}^{j=n}(x_{ji}\tilde{\mathbf{v}}_j + y_{ji}\tilde{\mathbf{w}}_j) + \tilde{\mathbf{v}}_i', \quad \mathbf{M}\mathbf{w}_i = \sum_{j=1}^{j=n}(z_{ji}\tilde{\mathbf{v}}_j + u_{ji}\tilde{\mathbf{w}}_j) + \tilde{\mathbf{w}}_i'$$

where $\tilde{\mathbf{v}}_i', \tilde{\mathbf{w}}_i' \in \tilde{\mathbf{S}}'$ $(i = 1, 2, \ldots, n)$. Let $\mathbf{X}, \mathbf{Y}, \mathbf{Z}, \mathbf{U}$ be the $n \times n$-matrices:

$$\mathbf{X} = (x_{ij}), \ \mathbf{Y} = (y_{ij}), \ \mathbf{Z} = (z_{ij}), \ \mathbf{U} = (u_{ij}).$$

As it is easy to see, the matrix $\tilde{\mathbf{V}}$ can be now written in the form (30) with

$$\tilde{\mathbf{V}}_1 = \begin{pmatrix} \mathbf{X} & \mathbf{Z} \end{pmatrix}, \ \tilde{\mathbf{V}}_2 = \begin{pmatrix} \mathbf{0} & * \\ \mathbf{Y} & \mathbf{U} \\ \mathbf{0} & \mathbf{0} \end{pmatrix}, \ \tilde{\mathbf{V}}_3 = \begin{pmatrix} * & * \\ * & * \\ \mathbf{X}+\mathbf{Y} & \mathbf{Z}+\mathbf{U} \\ \mathbf{0} & \mathbf{0} \\ \mathbf{0} & \mathbf{0} \end{pmatrix},$$

$$\tilde{\mathbf{V}}_4 = \begin{pmatrix} * & * \\ * & * \\ * & * \\ \mathbf{X}+\tilde{\mathbf{Q}}^t\mathbf{Y} & \mathbf{Z}+\tilde{\mathbf{Q}}^t\mathbf{U} \\ \mathbf{0} & \mathbf{0} \\ \mathbf{0} & \mathbf{0} \\ \mathbf{0} & \mathbf{0} \end{pmatrix}, \ \tilde{\mathbf{V}}_5 = \begin{pmatrix} * & * \\ * & * \\ * & * \\ * & * \\ \tilde{\mathbf{P}}^t\mathbf{X}+\mathbf{Y} & \tilde{\mathbf{P}}^t\mathbf{Z}+\mathbf{U} \\ \mathbf{0} & \mathbf{0} \\ \mathbf{0} & \mathbf{0} \\ \mathbf{0} & \mathbf{0} \\ \mathbf{0} & \mathbf{0} \end{pmatrix}. \tag{32}$$

Equating the expressions (31) and (32) for matrices $\mathbf{V}_i$ we obtain the following identities:

$$\mathbf{X} = \mathbf{M}_{11,0}, \ \mathbf{Z} = \mathbf{M}_{23,2}, \ \mathbf{M}_{23,2} = \mathbf{0}, \ \mathbf{Y} = \mathbf{0}, \ \mathbf{U} = \mathbf{M}_{22,0}, \ \mathbf{X}+\mathbf{Y} = \mathbf{M}_{33,0}, \ \mathbf{Z}+\mathbf{U} = \mathbf{M}_{33,0},$$

$$\mathbf{X}+\tilde{\mathbf{Q}}^t\mathbf{Y} = \mathbf{M}_{44,0}, \ \mathbf{Z}+\tilde{\mathbf{Q}}^t\mathbf{U} = \mathbf{M}_{44,0}\mathbf{Q}^t, \ \mathbf{Y}+\tilde{\mathbf{P}}^t\mathbf{X} = \mathbf{M}_{55,0}\mathbf{P}^t, \ \mathbf{U}+\tilde{\mathbf{P}}^t\mathbf{Z} = \mathbf{M}_{55,0}.$$

From the last identities it follows easily that

$$\mathbf{Y} = \mathbf{Z} = \mathbf{0}, \ \mathbf{X} = \mathbf{U} = \mathbf{M}_{11,0} = \mathbf{M}_{22,0} = \mathbf{M}_{33,0} = \mathbf{M}_{44,0} = \mathbf{M}_{55,0}, \ \mathbf{X}\mathbf{P}^t = \tilde{\mathbf{P}}^t\mathbf{X}, \ \mathbf{X}\mathbf{Q}^t = \tilde{\mathbf{Q}}^t\mathbf{X}.$$

Since the operator **M** is non-degenerate, **X** is a regular matrix. Hence, the last two equalities can be rewritten as

$$\tilde{P} = (X^t)^{-1} P X^t, \quad \tilde{Q} = (X^t)^{-1} Q X^t,$$

i.e., the pairs (13) are simultaneously similar. Q.E.D.

The result proved in the theorem 3 was announced in [1].

I express my deep gratitude to an anonymous referee who responded very promptly to my paper. His/her advice to rewrite the proof of the last theorem in a matrix form rather than in a vector form, as it was in my original manuscript, helped me to improve the presentation.

REFERENCES

1. B. Reichstein, On the problem of classification of invariant subspaces of a linear operator, Uspekhi Matemat. Nauk, XXXII, 1(193), 1977, p. 201-202.

Department of Mathematics,
The Catholic University of America,
Washington, D.C. 20064, USA

Operator Theory:
Advances and Applications, Vol. 40

ON THE INVERSE OF BLOCK TRIDIAGONAL MATRICES WITH APPLICATIONS TO THE INVERSES OF BAND MATRICES AND BLOCK BAND MATRICES

Pál Rózsa (1), Roberto Bevilacqua, Paola Favati and Francesco Romani

Dedicated to Professor I. Gohberg on his 60th birthday.

In the present paper the authors make an attempt to give a uniform description of the main properties of tridiagonal, band, block tridiagonal and block band matrices and their inverses. Some basic concepts are recalled and also some new results are presented.

INTRODUCTION

The number of papers dealing with basic properties of band matrices and block tridiagonal matrices, has been increasing continuously in recent years. It is remarkable that in spite of the significant demand for increasing the efficiency of algorithms there is a definite interest in studying the structural properties of the mentioned classes of matrices together with those of their inverses. In the present paper an attempt is made to establish a uniform treatment of the chosen topics and to get results which can be considered as generalizations of some special ones already known.

As a simple example let us recall the *symmetric tridiagonal* matrices, called also *Jacobian* matrices or *continuant* matrices in the literature. Probably the first significant step was the result of Gantmacher and Krein [12]: they proved that under certain conditions the inverse of a symmetric tridiagonal matrix is a so called *one-pair* matrix with positive elements. Barret [3] showed that the result was valid under weaker conditions as well. It is interesting to remark that this basic property was discovered by other authors again and again (e.g. see [8]); in the references, however, one can hardly find the original work [12]. The inverse of a symmetric tridiagonal matrix is often called a *Green* matrix as it was used by Asplund [2] in a generalized sense. His result concerning the structure of the Green matrix can be regarded as a basic step in generalizing the result of Gantmacher and Krein. Barret and Feinsilver [4] related the vanishing of a certain set of minors in a

---

(1) Visiting at the Dipartimento di Informatica of the University of Pisa under the support of GNAFA-CNR

matrix to the vanishing of a corresponding set of minors in the inverse; as a corollary the first theorem of Asplund can be obtained. They introduced the concept of "triangle property" of matrices. Making use of their methods and introducing the "quasi-triangle property" of matrices, Rizvi [19] succeeded in generalizing their result for block tridiagonal matrices. Haley [13] established the so called "projection recurrence" method to obtain the inverse of a band matrix. In his paper a comprehensive list of references can be found concerning the recent literature on the structure of the inverse of band matrices. Capovani [10], [11] expressed the inverse of a tridiagonal matrix in terms of some determinantal recurrence relations and showed the structure of the inverse of a tridiagonal nonsymmetric matrix (the same structure was rediscovered ten years later by Lewis [16]). Bevilacqua and Capovani [5], [6] extended the structural results to band and square blocks case, exploiting an additive structure of the inverse of a band matrix in the symmetric case. Other significant properties of the inverse of band matrices and block tridiagonal matrices have been found by the authors [7], [20], [21], [22], among others the additive structure of the inverse of band matrices was investigated further, the concept of semi-separable matrices was introduced, sufficient and necessary conditions have been found for matrices to be band matrices or semi-separable matrices.

The use of difference equations proved to be appropriate as an approach to look at structural properties of the inverse from another direction. Amato [1] reduced the higher order difference equations to a first order vector difference equation, his method was combined with that of Kounias [15] by Uppuluri and Carpenter [26] to get the inverse of a band matrix when solving a boundary value problem for the corresponding difference equation. Making use of the linearly independent solutions of certain difference equations and generalizing the idea of Torii [25], Oohashi [18] presented a method to obtain the inverse of band matrices. Similar considerations were applied by Yamamoto and Ikebe [27]. In another paper Ikebe [14] presented a method for the inverse of a block Hessenberg matrix (this result is a straightforward consequence of the results of [2], [12], nevertheless his single reference is [8]). His work was extended for a block generalized Hessenberg matrix by Cao and Stewart [9].

It should be mentioned that the inverse of a band matrix can be obtained after an LU factorization as it was suggested by Neuman [17] and D. and F. Szynal [24]. The idea of factorization was applied for block tridiagonal matrices by Rizvi [19] when he made use of the corresponding results of Schechter [23].

This short survey shows the numerous aspects and ways the structural problems - and also numerical problems - can be attacked from and therefore the endeavour of the authors of this paper might be understandable: "viribus unitis" they try to establish a uniform treatment for - at least - some of the problems sketched above.

In Section 1 some elementary relationships are presented concerning the Schur complements and the inverses of certain submatrices and also an important identity due to Jacobi will be recalled. This collection of known formulae will help the reader to follow the principal line of our considerations.

In Section 2 the concept of (p,q) partitioning of a matrix will be introduced; this concept enables us to handle the important class of the so called (p,q) block tridiagonal matrices. Their characteristic property is that the blocks along the codiagonal are square matrices. Then, the (q,p) block semi-separable matrices [21] will be introduced together with the "everted" block tridiagonal matrix S, which can be considered as the generalization of block skew matrices, in a certain sense. By means of these definitions the structure of the inverse of proper (p,q) block tridiagonal matrices can be characterized; the inverse problem will be proved also and explicit formulae will be given for the determinant of a proper (q,p) block semi-separable matrix. Theorem 2.3 can be considered as the main result, presenting necessary and sufficient conditions for a non-singular block matrix to be a proper (p,q) block tridiagonal matrix.

In Section 3 the special case of proper (p,q) block tridiagonal matrices will be considered when the super- and sub-diagonal blocks are non-singular lower and upper triangular matrices, respectively. This class of block tridiagonal matrices turns out to be equivalent to the class of strict {p,q} band matrices the order of which is equal to a multiple of p+q and thus from Section 2 the corresponding theorems for band matrices and their inverses can be obtained as corollaries.

In Section 4 the concept of block tridiagonal block matrices and block semi-separable block matrices will be introduced: they are double compound block matrices where the blocks themselves are consisting of blocks instead of scalar elements. As special cases of such double compound matrices the block band matrices and the semiseparable block matrices will be defined, finally necessary and sufficient conditions will be given for a nonsingular block matrix to be proper (p,q) block band matrix.

1. PRELIMINARIES

Let us consider a square matrix A partitioned into four blocks:

$$A = \begin{bmatrix} X_{11} & X_{12} \\ X_{21} & X_{22} \end{bmatrix} \tag{1.1}$$

The partitioning will be called *persymmetric partitioning* if the blocks X_{12} and X_{21} are square matrices say of order q and p, respectively. If X_{12} is non-singular the following factorization of A holds:

$$A = \begin{bmatrix} I & 0 \\ X_{22}X_{12}^{-1} & I \end{bmatrix} \begin{bmatrix} X_{12} & 0 \\ 0 & X_{21} - X_{22}X_{12}^{-1}X_{11} \end{bmatrix} \begin{bmatrix} X_{12}^{-1}X_{11} & I \\ I & 0 \end{bmatrix} \tag{1.2}$$

where $X_{21} - X_{22} X_{12}^{-1} X_{11}$ is the *Schur complement* for X_{12}. From (1.2) immediately follows that the determinant of A is

$$(1.3) \qquad \det A = (-1)^{pq} \det X_{12} \det (X_{21} - X_{22} X_{12}^{-1} X_{11})$$

and hence, in the case of non-singular X_{12}, A is non-singular iff the Schur complement for X_{12} is non-singular.

Assuming that A is non-singular, from (1.2) it is easy to obtain the following expression for the inverse of A:

$$(1.4) \quad A^{-1} = \begin{bmatrix} 0 & 0 \\ X_{12}^{-1} & 0 \end{bmatrix} + \begin{bmatrix} I \\ -X_{12}^{-1} X_{11} \end{bmatrix} (X_{21} - X_{22} X_{12}^{-1} X_{11})^{-1} [\, -X_{22} X_{12}^{-1} \quad I \,]$$

Analogously, if X_{21} is non-singular, the determinant of A can be obtained as

$$(1.5) \qquad \det A = (-1)^{pq} \det X_{21} \det (X_{12} - X_{11} X_{21}^{-1} X_{22})$$

where $X_{12} - X_{11} X_{21}^{-1} X_{22}$ is the Schur complement for X_{21} and the inverse can be obtained as

$$(1.6) \quad A^{-1} = \begin{bmatrix} 0 & X_{21}^{-1} \\ 0 & 0 \end{bmatrix} + \begin{bmatrix} -X_{21}^{-1} X_{22} \\ I \end{bmatrix} (X_{12} - X_{11} X_{21}^{-1} X_{22})^{-1} [\, I \quad -X_{11} X_{21}^{-1} \,]$$

From (1.4) and (1.6) simple expressions can be obtained for calculating the inverse of a submatrix if the inverse of the given matrix is known. Let the inverse of A be partitioned according to the partitioning of (1.1), where the order of P_{12} and P_{21} is equal to the order of X_{21} and X_{12} respectively:

$$(1.7) \qquad A^{-1} = \begin{bmatrix} P_{11} & P_{12} \\ P_{21} & P_{22} \end{bmatrix}$$

From (1.4) it is easy to see that the inverse of the non-singular submatrix X_{12} can be obtained as

$$(1.8) \qquad X_{12}^{-1} = P_{21} - P_{22} P_{12}^{-1} P_{11}.$$

Analogously from (1.6) we get

$$(1.9) \qquad X_{21}^{-1} = P_{12} - P_{11} P_{21}^{-1} P_{22}$$

These results can be formulated in the following lemma.

LEMMA 1.1. *The inverse of a submatrix of a given non-singular matrix, if it exists, is equal to the Schur complement for the corresponding block of the inverse of the given matrix.*

From the above expressions we get immediately the interesting and important equality among certain minors of a matrix and its inverse due to Jacobi. Let us write the analogous expression of (1.8) for the inverse of the corresponding block of A^{-1} in (1.7)

$$P_{12}^{-1} = X_{21} - X_{22} X_{12}^{-1} X_{11}$$

(i.e. P_{12} is the inverse of the Schur complement for X_{12}). Substituting into (1.3) we obtain

(1.10) $\det X_{12} = (-1)^{pq} \det A \ \det P_{12}$

In a similar way, according to (1.9) we may write

$$P_{21}^{-1} = X_{12} - X_{11} X_{21}^{-1} X_{22}$$

and from (1.5) we get

(1.11) $\det X_{21} = (-1)^{pq} \det A \ \det P_{21}$

2. BLOCK TRIDIAGONAL MATRICES

Let us consider a block tridiagonal matrix of the form

$$(2.1) \qquad A = \begin{bmatrix} A_1 & B_1 & 0 & & \cdots & & \\ C_1 & A_2 & B_2 & & \cdots & & \\ 0 & C_2 & A_3 & & \cdots & & \\ & \cdot & \cdot & \cdot & \cdot & \cdot & \\ & & & & \cdots & & B_{2k-1} \\ & & & \cdots & & C_{2k-1} & A_{2k} \end{bmatrix}$$

where A_{2i-1} are qxp matrices, A_{2i} are pxq matrices, consequently all blocks in the codiagonals are square matrices alternating of order p and q, respectively (an example of the shape of A is shown in Fig.1). Let us introduce the following definitions.

DEFINITION 2.1. If the order of a given matrix is a multiple of p+q and it is partitioned according to (2.1), then it will be called a *block matrix of (p,q) partitioning* .

DEFINITION 2.2. A block tridiagonal matrix will be called a *proper (p,q) block tridiagonal matrix* if it is a block matrix of (p,q) partitioning and if all blocks in the codiagonals are non-singular.

The main goal of the present paper is to examine under what conditions the inverse of a proper block tridiagonal matrix exists, how its structure can be characterized and what kind of

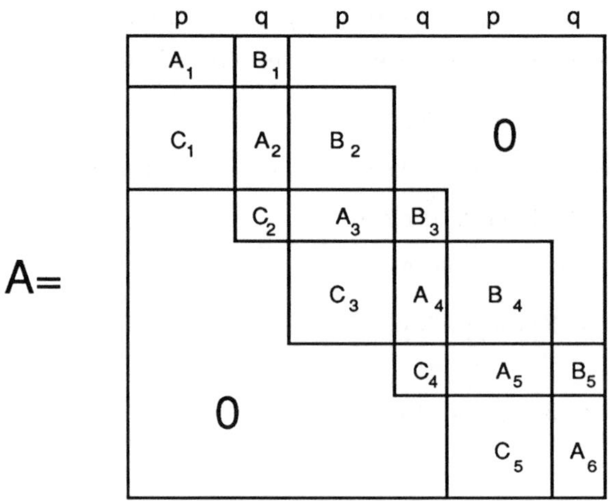

Fig.1 Example of the shape of A in the case k=3.

inverse theorems can be proved.

Assuming that the inverse of A exists, let us try to get the blocks of it. The basic idea of the method is the same as that presented in [7], the block tridiagonal matrix is bordered by the first "block unit vector" * (above) and by the 2k+1-st "block unit vector" (right), thus a lower block triangular matrix will be obtained (see Fig.2 for an example of the case k=3):

$$
(2.2) \qquad A_L = \begin{bmatrix} I_p & 0 & 0 & \cdots & & 0 \\ A_1 & B_1 & 0 & \cdots & & 0 \\ C_1 & A_2 & B_2 & \cdots & & 0 \\ 0 & C_2 & A_3 & \cdots & & \\ & \cdots & \cdots & \cdots & & \\ & & & \cdots & B_{2k-1} & 0 \\ & & \cdots & C_{2k-1} & A_{2k} & I_p \end{bmatrix}
$$

As the blocks B_i are non-singular, the inverse of A_L exists and since it is a lower block triangular matrix, its inverse can easily be calculated. Let the blocks of the inverse be denoted according to the following scheme (the shape is shown in Fig.3):

* The meaning of the "block unit vector" is obvious from the block matrix (2.2).

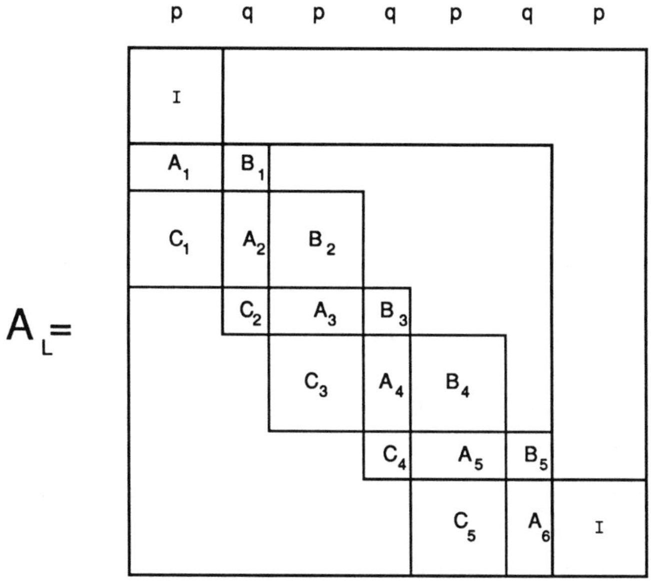

Fig. 2 . Example of the shape of A_L in the case k=3.

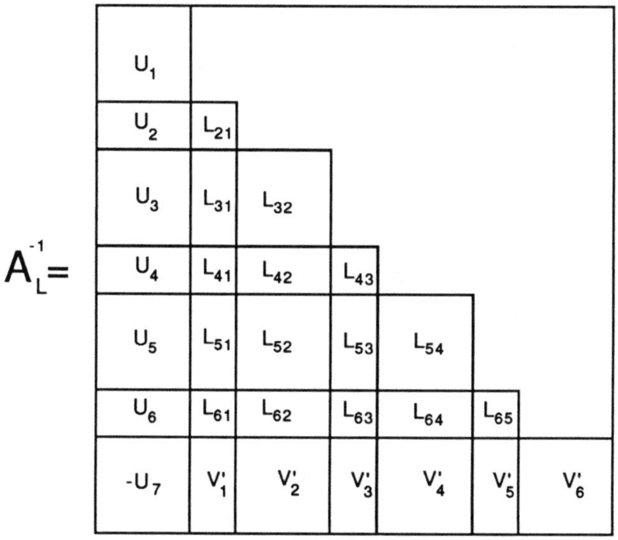

Fig 3. Example of the shape of A_L^{-1} for k=3, $V'_i = U_7 V_i$.

$$(2.3)\qquad A_L^{-1} = \begin{bmatrix} U_1 & 0 & 0 & \dots & & & 0 \\ U_2 & L_{21} & 0 & \dots & & & 0 \\ U_3 & L_{31} & L_{32} & 0 & \dots & & 0 \\ \dots & \dots & \dots & \dots & & & \\ U_{2k} & L_{2k,1} & \dots & & & L_{2k,2k-1} & 0 \\ -U_{2k+1} & U_{2k+1}V_1 & \dots & & & & U_{2k+1}V_{2k} \end{bmatrix}$$

where obviously $L_{ij}=0$ for $i\le j$. Making use of formula (1.11) we may write now

$$(2.4)\qquad \det A = (-1)^{pk(p+q)} \left(\prod_{i=1}^{2k-1} \det B_i \right) \det(-U_{2k+1})$$

and hence if the given proper (p,q) block tridiagonal matrix is non-singular, the block U_{2k+1} is non-singular as well. Furthermore, since the given block tridiagonal matrix is the lower left submatrix of (2.2), in order to get its inverse, the formula (1.9) can be applied and for the blocks of the matrix $R = A^{-1}$ the expressions

$$(2.5)\qquad R_{ij} = L_{ij} + U_i V_j, \qquad (L_{ij} = 0 \text{ for } i \le j)$$

are obtained.

On the other hand, if (2.1) is bordered by the first block unit vector from the left and by the 2k+1-st block unit vector from below, then a lower block triangular matrix (say A_M) will be obtained:

$$(2.6)\qquad A_M = \begin{bmatrix} I_q & A_1 & B_1 & 0 & \dots & & 0 \\ 0 & C_1 & A_2 & & \dots & & 0 \\ 0 & 0 & C_2 & & \dots & & \\ & \dots & \dots & \dots & \dots & & \\ & & & \dots & & A_{2k-1} & B_{2k-1} \\ 0 & & \dots & & 0 & C_{2k-1} & A_{2k} \\ 0 & & & \dots & 0 & 0 & I_q \end{bmatrix}$$

Because of the non-singularity of the blocks C_i, the inverse of this upper block triangular matrix can be calculated. Let us write the inverse according to the following scheme:

$$(2.7)\qquad A_M^{-1} = \begin{bmatrix} W_0Z_1 & W_0Z_2 & & \cdots & W_0Z_{2k} & -W_0 \\ 0 & M_{12} & M_{13} & \cdots & & W_1 \\ 0 & 0 & M_{23} & \cdots & & W_2 \\ & \cdots & \cdots & \cdots & & \\ & & & \cdots & M_{2k-1,2k} & W_{2k-1} \\ 0 & \cdots & & & 0 & W_{2k} \end{bmatrix}$$

where obviously $M_{ij}=0$ for $i\geq j$. Making use of formula (1.10) we get

$$(2.8)\qquad \det A = (-1)^{qk(p+q)} \left(\prod_{i=1}^{2k-1} \det C_i \right) \det(-W_0)$$

and hence the non-singularity of A implies the non-singularity of the block W_0. In this case the block tridiagonal matrix A is the upper right submatrix of (2.6), therefore formula (1.8) can be applied to obtain its inverse R. The blocks of the inverse can be written as:

$$(2.9)\qquad R_{ij} = M_{ij} + W_iZ_j, \quad (M_{ij} = 0 \text{ for } i \geq j)$$

Comparison of (2.5) and (2.9) implies

$$(2.10)\qquad R_{ij} = \begin{cases} U_iV_j & \text{for } i \leq j \\ W_iZ_j & \text{for } i \geq j \end{cases}$$

Further

$$(2.11)\qquad L_{ij} = W_iZ_j - U_iV_j, \quad \text{for } i \geq j$$

$$(2.12)\qquad M_{ij} = U_iV_j - W_iZ_j, \quad \text{for } i \leq j$$

and hence

$$(2.13)\qquad L_{ii} = M_{ii} = U_iV_i - W_iZ_i = 0, \; i=1,2,\ldots,2k.$$

Moreover the diagonal blocks of the matrices (2.2) and (2.6) are the nonsingular blocks B_i and C_i, of the block tridiagonal matrix A and for their inverses we get from (2.3) and (2.7):

$$(2.14)\qquad B_i^{-1} = L_{i+1,\,i}, \quad i=1,2,\ldots,2k-1,$$

$$(2.15)\qquad C_i^{-1} = M_{i,\,i+1}, \quad i=1,2,\ldots,2k-1.$$

Following the ideas of some previous results of the authors [21], [22], let us introduce the following definition.

DEFINITION 2.3. A block matrix R of (q,p) partitioning will be called a *(q,p) block semi-separable matrix* * if its blocks can be expressed as

$$(2.16) \qquad R_{ij} = \begin{cases} U_i V_j & \text{for } i \leq j \\ W_i Z_j & \text{for } i \geq j \end{cases}$$

Obviously (2.16) implies

$$(2.17) \qquad U_i V_i - W_i Z_i = 0, \text{ for } i=1,2,\dots,2k.$$

Moreover a (q,p) block semi-separable matrix will be called *proper* if

$$(2.18) \qquad \det(U_{i+1} V_i - W_{i+1} Z_i) \neq 0, \text{ for } i=1,2,\dots,2k-1,$$

$$(2.19) \qquad \det(U_i V_{i+1} - W_i Z_{i+1}) \neq 0, \text{ for } i=1,2,\dots,2k-1.$$

Thus our results can be formulated in the following theorem.

THEOREM 2.1. *The inverse of a non-singular proper (p,q) block tridiagonal matrix is a proper (q,p) block semi-separable matrix.*

In order to obtain the blocks of the inverse of a non-singular proper (p,q) block tridiagonal matrix, the well known recurrences defining the first column and the last row of the inverse of a lower block triangular matrix and the first row and the last column of the inverse of an upper block triangular matrix can be used. The list of the recurrences can be found in [7]. It should be noted that the total number of parameters of the given matrix is $k(p+q)^2+(k-1)(p^2+q^2)$, while the number of parameters of its inverse calculated as sketched above is $2k(p+q)^2-p^2-q^2$. That means we have 2kpq redundant parameters corresponding to the conditions (2.17).

Now we want to approach the properties of the inverse of a block tridiagonal matrix from another direction. For this purpose let us recall the following property of one-pair matrices [12]. Consider the one-pair real matrix $R = [r_{ij}]$ with elements

$$(2.20) \qquad r_{ij} = \begin{cases} u_i v_j & \text{for } i \leq j \\ v_i u_j & \text{for } i \geq j \end{cases}$$

The skew-symmetric matrix $S = [s_{ij}]$ can be formed with the help of the vectors $\mathbf{u} = [u_i]$ and $\mathbf{v} = [v_j]$:

$$(2.21) \qquad S = \mathbf{u}\,\mathbf{v}^T - \mathbf{v}\,\mathbf{u}^T = [\,\mathbf{u} \;\; \mathbf{v}\,] \begin{bmatrix} \mathbf{v}^T \\ -\mathbf{u}^T \end{bmatrix}$$

---

* The authors want to thank Professor I.Gohberg for suggesting the use of the expression of "semi-separable" matrices.

This matrix multiplication can be arranged as follows.

$$
(2.22)\qquad
\begin{array}{cc}
 & \begin{bmatrix} v_1 & v_2 & \cdots & & v_n \\ -u_1 & -u_2 & \cdots & & -u_n \end{bmatrix} \\
\begin{bmatrix} u_1 & v_1 \\ u_2 & v_2 \\ & \cdots \\ & \\ u_n & v_n \end{bmatrix} &
\begin{bmatrix} 0 & s_{12} & \cdots & & s_{1n} \\ s_{21} & 0 & s_{23} & \cdots & s_{2n} \\ & & \cdots & & \\ & & & & \\ s_{n1} & s_{n2} & \cdots & s_{n,n-1} & 0 \end{bmatrix}
\end{array}
$$

The elements along the main diagonal are trivially equal to zero and the elements along the codiagonals are necessarily different from zero if the one pair matrix is the inverse of a strict tridiagonal matrix (i.e. with non-zero elements along the codiagonals, see Definition 3.1) [12]. Now, in a similar way, let us introduce the block matrix S generated by the block vectors U, V, W and Z, whose blocks are U_i, V_i,W_i, Z_i, i=1,2,...,2k, partitioned according to Fig. 4.

$$
(2.23)\qquad S = U V - W Z = [U \; W] \begin{bmatrix} V \\ -Z \end{bmatrix}
$$

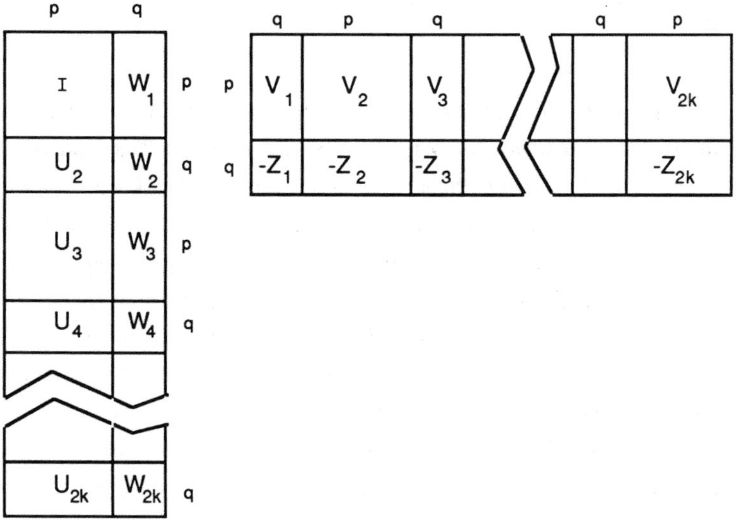

Fig.4. Partitioning of matrices U, V, W, Z.

If the blocks U_i, V_i, W_i, Z_i, i=1,2,...,2k, are defined in the same way as in (2.10) then S is equal to M - L and has the following properties:

(2.24) $S_{ii} = 0$, i=1,2,...,2k,

(2.25) $S_{i+1,i} = -L_{i+1,i} = -B_i^{-1}$, i=1,2,...,2k-1,

(2.26) $S_{i,i+1} = M_{i,i+1} = C_i^{-1}$, i=1,2,...,2k-1,

therefore the codiagonal blocks of S are necessarily non-singular matrices. On the other hand if (2.24) holds and the codiagonal blocks of S are non-singular matrices then U, V, W, Z define a proper (q,p) block semi-separable matrix R via (2.16). The shape of S in the case k=3 is shown in Fig. 5. Comparing the structure of S with that of the block matrix (2.1), we may say that S is an "everted" proper block tridiagonal matrix.

Now let us turn to the inverse problem: let R be a given proper (q,p) block semi-separable matrix and we want to characterize the structure of its inverse , its determinant and to get a method for calculating the blocks of the inverse. According to Definition 2.3 any proper (q,p) block semi-separable matrix can be written as the sum of a lower (q,p) block triangular matrix L (with null diagonal blocks and non-singular subdiagonal blocks) and a block outer product (block dyad) UV:

(2.27) $R = L + U V$.

In a similar way, it can be regarded as the sum of an upper (q,p) block triangular matrix M (with null diagonal blocks and non-singular superdiagonal blocks) and a block outer product (block dyad) WZ:

(2.28) $R = M + W Z$.

Note first that the invertibility of R, the special structure of M and L, and equalities (2.27)-(2.28) imply that the matrices U_1, V_{2k}, Z_1, W_{2k} are invertible. The expressions (2.27) and (2.28) can be regarded as the Schur complements for the bordered block matrices R_L (which has the same structure as A_L^{-1} in eq. (2.3) with $U_{2k+1}= I$) and R_M (which has the same structure as A_M^{-1} in eq. (2.7) with $W_0= I$), respectively. Since R_L is a lower, R_M is an upper block triangular matrix , their inverses (which necessarily exist) are block triangular matrices as well. From the corresponding partitioning of these inverses it is to be seen that, according to (1.9), the Schur complement (2.27) is the inverse of the lower left submatrix of R_L^{-1} and, according to (1.8), the Schur complement (2.28) is the inverse of the upper right submatrix of R_M^{-1}. Since the non-singular proper (q,p) block semi-separable matrix R has a unique inverse, these two matrices are identical and this is possible only if they are proper (p,q) block tridiagonal matrices. Thus the following theorem holds:

THEOREM 2.2. *The inverse of a non-singular proper (q,p) block semi-separable matrix is a proper (p,q) block tridiagonal matrix.*

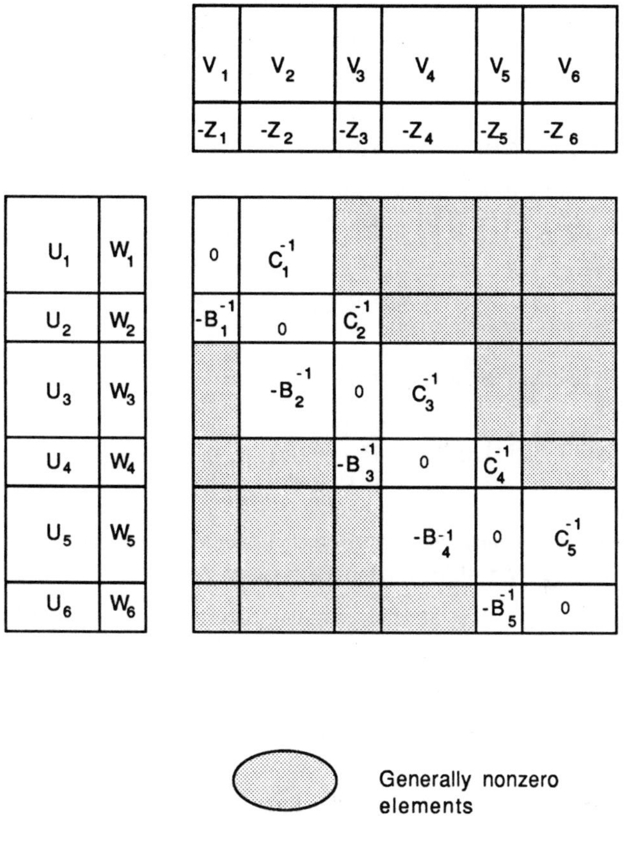

Fig.5. The shape of S for k=3.

As a consequence of Theorems 2.1 and 2.2 we can formulate our result in the following theorem.

THEOREM 2.3. *A non-singular (p,q) block matrix is a proper (p,q) block tridiagonal matrix if and only if its inverse is a proper (q,p) block semi-separable matrix .*

Now let us turn to the conditions for a proper (q,p) block semi-separable matrix to be non-singular. To this purpose let us recall the expression (1.5) and apply it for calculating the determinant of R_L:

(2.29) $$\det R_L = (-1)^{pk(p+q)} (-1)^p \det(L + U\,V)$$

The diagonal blocks $L_{i+1,i}$ of R_L are non-singular according to (2.11) and (2.18), thus the semi-separable matrix $R = L + U\,V$ is invertible if and only if

(2.30) $$\det U_1 \neq 0 \quad \text{and} \quad \det V_{2k} \neq 0,$$

and its determinant can be calculated according to the formula

(2.31) $$\det R = (-1)^{p[k(p+q)+1]} \det U_1 \left(\prod_{i=1}^{2k-1} \det(-S_{i+1,i}) \right) \det V_{2k}$$

A similar expression can be obtained when applying (1.3) for calculating the determinant of R_M:

(2.32) $$\det R_M = (-1)^{qk(p+q)} (-1)^q \det(M + W\,Z)$$

The diagonal blocks $M_{i,i+1}$ of R_M are non-singular according to (2.12) and (2.19) thus the semi-separable matrix $R = M + W\,Z$ is invertible if and only if

(2.33) $$\det Z_1 \neq 0 \quad \text{and} \quad \det W_{2k} \neq 0,$$

and its determinant can be calculated according to the formula

(2.34) $$\det R = (-1)^{q[k(p+q)+1]} \det Z_1 \left(\prod_{i=1}^{2k-1} \det S_{i,i+1} \right) \det W_{2k}$$

Conditions (2.30) and (2.33) are obviously equivalent.

Below we give two expressions for det R which will be convenient for further discussions. From (2.23) and (2.24) we can write the following identities

(2.35) $$\begin{bmatrix} U_i & W_i \\ U_{i+1} & W_{i+1} \end{bmatrix} \begin{bmatrix} V_{i-1} & V_i \\ -Z_{i-1} & -Z_i \end{bmatrix} = \begin{bmatrix} S_{i,i-1} & 0 \\ S_{i+1,i-1} & S_{i+1,i} \end{bmatrix}, \quad i=2,3,\dots,2k-1,$$

(2.36) $$\begin{bmatrix} U_{2k} & W_{2k} \\ I & 0 \end{bmatrix} \begin{bmatrix} V_{2k-1} & V_{2k} \\ -Z_{2k-1} & -Z_{2k} \end{bmatrix} = \begin{bmatrix} S_{2k,2k-1} & 0 \\ V_{2k-1} & V_{2k} \end{bmatrix}$$

Making use of the determinantal form of (2.35) and (2.36) and substituting into (2.31) we get

$$(2.37)\quad \det R = (-1)^{(k+1)pq} \det U_1 \prod_{i=1}^{k-1} \begin{vmatrix} U_{2i} & W_{2i} \\ U_{2i+1} & W_{2i+1} \end{vmatrix} \prod_{i=1}^{k} \begin{vmatrix} V_{2i-1} & V_{2i} \\ Z_{2i-1} & Z_{2i} \end{vmatrix} \det W_{2k}$$

Analogously we get the formula

$$(2.38)\quad \det R = (-1)^{kpq} \det Z_1 \prod_{i=1}^{k} \begin{vmatrix} U_{2i-1} & W_{2i-1} \\ U_{2i} & W_{2i} \end{vmatrix} \prod_{i=1}^{k-1} \begin{vmatrix} V_{2i} & V_{2i+1} \\ Z_{2i} & Z_{2i+1} \end{vmatrix} \det V_{2k}$$

Finally let us calculate the blocks of the inverse of a proper (q,p) block semi-separable matrix. Since the structure of the inverse is known, according to (2.25) and (2.26) the codiagonal blocks can be obtained immediately from

(2.39) $\quad B_i = -S_{i+1,i}^{-1} = (W_{i+1}Z_i - U_{i+1}V_i)^{-1}, \quad i=1,2,\ldots,2k-1$

(2.40) $\quad C_i = S_{i,i+1}^{-1} = (U_iV_{i+1} - W_iZ_{i+1})^{-1}, \quad i=1,2,\ldots,2k-1$

The diagonal blocks A_i can be obtained from the simple consideration that the subdiagonal blocks of R_L can easily be calculated from the identity $R_L^{-1} R_L = I$ and observing that the lower left submatrix of R_L^{-1} is equal to R^{-1}. It is not difficult to verify that

(2.41) $\quad U_2 = -B_1^{-1} A_1 U_1,$

(2.42) $\quad -S_{i+1,i-1} = -B_i^{-1} A_i B_{i-1}^{-1}, \quad i=2,3,\ldots,2k-1,$

and hence

(2.43) $\quad A_1 = -B_1 U_2 U_1^{-1},$

(2.44) $\quad A_i = B_i S_{i+1,i-1} B_{i-1}, \quad i=2,3,\ldots,2k-1.$

According to similar considerations for the superdiagonal blocks of R_M we get

(2.45) $\quad W_{2k-1} = -C_{2k-1}^{-1} A_{2k} W_{2k},$

and hence

(2.46) $\quad A_{2k} = -C_{2k-1} W_{2k-1} W_{2k}^{-1}.$

3. BAND MATRICES

In this section it will be shown that a certain class of band matrices can be regarded as special block tridiagonal matrices, consequently the results of Section 2 can be applied for them. First let us introduce some basic definitions. Let us consider real (or complex) square matrices $A = [a_{ij}]$ of order n.

DEFINITION 3.1. A matrix is called a *{p,q} band matrix* if $a_{ij} = 0$, for $j - i > p$ and $i - j > q$. If in addition

(3.1) $a_{ij} \neq 0$, for $j - i = p$ and $i - j = q$
then it will be called a *strict* {p,q} band matrix. If the order of a strict {p,q} band matrix is a multiple of (p+q), say

(3.2) $n = k\,(p+q)$

then, obviously it can be partitioned in the form of (2.1); in this case we will speak about a *(p,q) partitioning of a strict {p,q} band matrix* (see Fig.6).

It is evident that the (p,q) partitioning of a strict {p,q} band matrix of order n=k(p+q) is a proper (p,q) block tridiagonal matrix and thus the results of Section 2 can be applied. Moreover we see that the superdiagonal blocks of a (p,q) partitioning of a strict {p,q} band matrix are non-singular lower triangular matrices and its subdiagonal blocks are non-singular upper triangular matrices. Thus we get information about the mentioned class of band matrices when taking the special structure of the corresponding block tridiagonal matrices into consideration.

Making use of the definition of (q,p) block semi-separable matrices, Theorem 2.1 and the notation of Section 2, the square blocks B_i and consequently their inverses:

(3.3) $$B_i^{-1} = L_{i+1,\,i} = -\,S_{i+1,\,i}\,, \quad i=1,2,\ldots,2k-1.$$

are lower triangular matrices, further the blocks C_i and consequently their inverses:

(3.4) $$C_i^{-1} = M_{i,\,i+1} = S_{i,\,i+1}\,, \quad i=1,2,\ldots,2k-1.$$

are upper triangular matrices (see (2.25) and (2.26)). That means, the block matrix $S = [S_{ij}] =$ $=UV-WZ$ (see (2.23)) regarded as an ordinary k(p+q) x k(p+q) matrix, has null entries in a band strip containing p-1 subdiagonals and and q-1 superdiagonals as it is illustrated in Fig. 7. In other words we may say that S regarded as an ordinary matrix is an "everted" strict {p,q} band matrix.This property of S implies that

i) any submatrix consisting of the i,i+1,...,i+p+q-1 rows and the i+q,i+q+1,...,i+p+2q-1 columns of S is a nonsingular upper triangular matrix, i=1,2,...,(k-2)(p+q)+p+1.

ii) any submatrix consisting of the i,i+1,...,i+p+q-1 rows and the i-p,i-p+1,...,i+q-1 columns of S is a nonsingular lower triangular matrix, i=p+1,p+2,...,(k-1)(p+q)+1.

In order to get a general formula for the inverse of strict {p,q} band matrices, let us introduce the following notation for the elements of the block vectors U, V, W, Z:

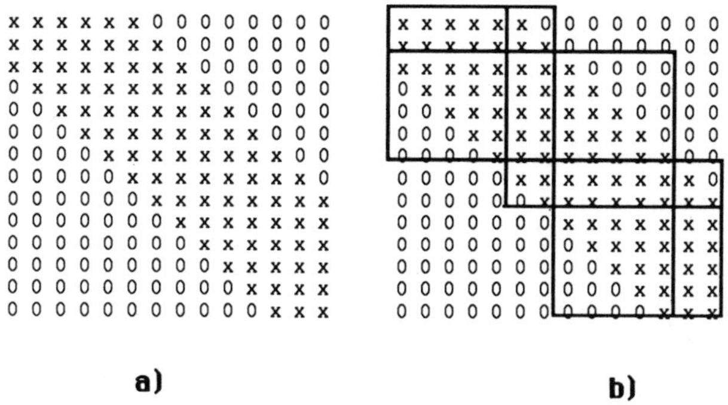

Fig. 6. a) a {5,2} band matrix, b) the same as a (5,2) block tridiagonal matrix

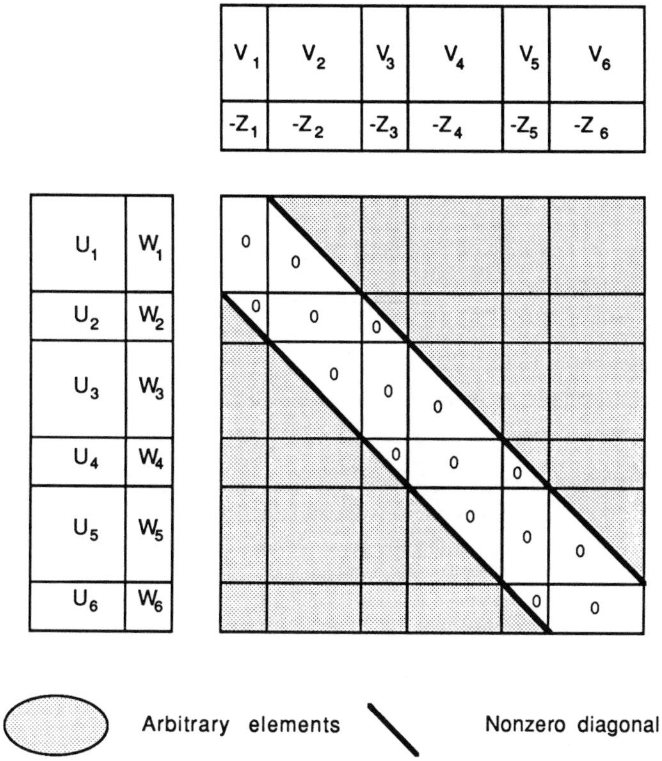

Fig.7. The shape of S for k=3, in the case of band matrices

$$U = [\, u_{\alpha\mu}], \quad W = [\, w_{\alpha\nu}], \quad V = [\, v_{\mu\beta}], \quad Z = [\, z_{\nu\beta}], \qquad \left\} \begin{array}{l} \alpha, \beta = 1,2,\ldots,n, \\ \mu = 1,2,\ldots,p, \\ \nu = 1,2,\ldots,q \end{array} \right. \tag{3.5}$$

By means of these notations the elements of the inverse $R = [r_{\alpha\beta}]$ of a strict {p,q} band matrix A can be written in the following way:

$$r_{\alpha\beta} = \begin{cases} \sum\limits_{\mu=1}^{p} u_{\alpha\mu} v_{\mu\beta} & \text{if } \alpha - \beta < p \\ \sum\limits_{\nu=1}^{q} w_{\alpha\nu} z_{\nu\beta} & \text{if } \beta - \alpha < q \end{cases} \tag{3.6}$$

According to (2.17)-(2.19) the conditions for the q-th super- and p-th subdiagonal elements and for the null elements of S can be written as

$$\sum_{\mu=1}^{p} u_{\alpha\mu} v_{\mu\beta} - \sum_{\nu=1}^{q} w_{\alpha\nu} z_{\nu\beta} \neq 0 \quad \text{for } \alpha - \beta = p, \ \beta - \alpha = q \tag{3.7}$$

$$\sum_{\mu=1}^{p} u_{\alpha\mu} v_{\mu\beta} - \sum_{\nu=1}^{q} w_{\alpha\nu} z_{\nu\beta} = 0 \quad \text{for } -q < \alpha - \beta < p \tag{3.8}$$

For the class of matrices with elements satisfying the conditions (3.6)-(3.8) let us introduce the following definition.

DEFINITION 3.2. A matrix $R = [r_{\alpha\beta}]$ is called a *{q,p} semi-separable matrix* if its elements satisfy the conditions (3.6)-(3.8).

Thus as a consequence of Theorem 2.1 the following theorem holds.

THEOREM 3.1. *The inverse of a non-singular (p,q) partitioning of a strict {p,q} band matrix is a {q,p} semi-separable matrix.*

It should be noted that the same result can be found in some previous papers of the authors obtained in a different way and without the restrictions (3.2) for the order of the matrices (e.g. see [20], [22]).

If the order of a {q,p} semi-separable matrix satisfies (3.2), i.e. if it is a multiple of p+q, the reverse theorem is a straightforward consequence of Theorem 2.2:

THEOREM 3.2. *If $n=k(p+q)$ then the inverse of a non-singular {q,p} semi-separable matrix is a strict {p,q} band matrix.*

For proving the theorem it is sufficient to consider the matrix S generated by the matrices U, V, W, Z determining the given {q,p} semi-separable matrix. Since S is a (q,p) partitioning of a block matrix with null blocks in the main diagonal, non singular upper triangular blocks in the superdiagonal and non-singular lower triangular blocks in the subdiagonal, the inverse of the given {q,p} semi-separable matrix of order k(p+q) is a proper (p,q) block tridiagonal matrix which can be considered as a strict {p,q} band matrix.

As a consequence of Theorems 3.1 and 3.2 we can formulate the following result.

THEOREM 3.3. *A non-singular matrix is a (p,q) partitioning of a strict {p,q} band matrix if and only if its inverse is a {q,p} semi-separable matrix.*

It should be noted that the theorem holds for matrices of arbitrary order, as shown in [22] thus the restriction "a (p,q) partitioning of" in Theorem 3.3 can be omitted.

4. BLOCK BAND MATRICES

In the previous section it was shown that the {p,q} band matrices can be regarded as special (p,q) block tridiagonal matrices if their order is a multiple of p+q. Now the question arises whether similar considerations could help us in establishing corresponding results with respect to block band matrices. In order to answer this question let us now consider proper (p,q) block tridiagonal matrices where the blocks are consisting of blocks instead of scalar elements. The only restriction with respect to the partitioning is that the square blocks along the codiagonals should symmetrically be partitioned; in other words: all blocks in the main diagonal of the codiagonal blocks should be square matrices (see Fig.8). Obviously all theorems of Section 2 are valid for these "double compound" block matrices when replacing the elements by the corresponding blocks. In order to distinguish this class of block matrices from that of the block tridiagonal matrices in Section 2 (see Definition 1.2), let us introduce the definition of block tridiagonal block matrices.

DEFINITION 4.1. A proper (p,q) block tridiagonal matrix with symmetrically partitioned non-singular pxp and qxq block matrices along the codiagonals will be called a *proper (p,q) block tridiagonal block matrix.*

As a special case for the block tridiagonal block matrices let us consider the class of block matrices where the blocks in the superdiagonals are non-singular lower block triangular matrices and the blocks in the subdiagonals are non-singular upper block triangular matrices (see Fig.9). The structure of this class of block matrices shows that it can be regarded as a block band matrix, more exactly the following definition can be introduced.

DEFINITION 4.2. A proper (p,q) block tridiagonal block matrix with non-singular lower block triangular matrices in the superdiagonals and non-singular upper block triangular matrices in the subdiagonals will be called *a (p,q) partitioning of a proper {p,q} block band matrix.*

This definition implies that the order of a (p,q) partitioning of a {p,q} block band matrix (with respect to the number of block rows and block columns, respectively) is equal to a multiple of p+q.

In a similar way the (q,p) block semi-separable block matrices and the proper (q,p) block semi-separable block matrices are defined in the following way.

DEFINITION 4.3. If the factors U_i, V_j, W_i, Z_j of a (q,p) block semi-separable matrix $R = [R_{ij}]$ with

$$(4.1) \qquad R_{ij} = \begin{cases} U_i V_j & \text{for } i \le j \\ W_i Z_j & \text{for } i \ge j \end{cases}$$

are partitioned in such a way that the block matrices

$$(4.2) \qquad U_i V_{i+1} - W_i Z_{i+1} \qquad \text{for } i=1,2,\dots,2k-1 ,$$

and

$$(4.3) \qquad U_{i+1} V_i - W_{i+1} Z_i \qquad \text{for } i=1,2,\dots,2k-1$$

turn out to be symmetrically partitioned block matrices and

$$(4.4) \qquad U_i V_i - W_i Z_i = 0 \qquad \text{for } i=1,2,\dots,2k$$

then R is called a *(q,p) block semi-separable block matrix.*
Moreover if the block matrices (4.2) and (4.3) are non-singular then R is called a *proper (q,p) block semi-separable block matrix.*

This definition implies that the matrix

$$(4.5) \qquad S = U V - W Z$$

generated by the block matrices U_i, V_j, W_i, Z_j is an "everted" proper (p,q) block tridiagonal block matrix, i.e. S is a block matrix of (q,p) partitioning with null blocks in the main diagonal and with symmetrically partitioned non-singular block matrices in the codiagonals (see Fig. 10).

In the special case if (4.2) are non-singular upper block triangular matrices and (4.3) are non-singular lower block triangular matrices, i.e. the matrix S generated according to (4.5) is the (q,p) partitioning of an "everted" proper {p,q} block band matrix then the concept of {p,q} semi-separable block matrix can be defined as follows.

DEFINITION 4.4. If the factors U_i, V_j, W_i, Z_j of a (q,p) block semi-separable matrix $R = [R_{ij}]$ with blocks (4.1) are partitioned such that the block matrices (4.2) are non-singular upper block triangular matrices and (4.3) are non-singular lower block triangular matrices and further (4.4) holds, then R is called a *{q,p} semi-separable block matrix.*

As corollaries of Theorems 2.3 and 3.3 now we can formulate the main results in the following theorems.

THEOREM 4.1. *A non-singular double compound block matrix is a proper (p,q) block tridiagonal block matrix if and only if its inverse is a proper (q,p) block semi-separable block matrix.*

THEOREM 4.2. *A non-singular block matrix is a (p,q) partitioning of a proper {p,q} block band matrix if and only if its inverse is a {q,p} semi-separable block matrix.*

Fig. 8. A (3,2) block tridiagonal block matrix.

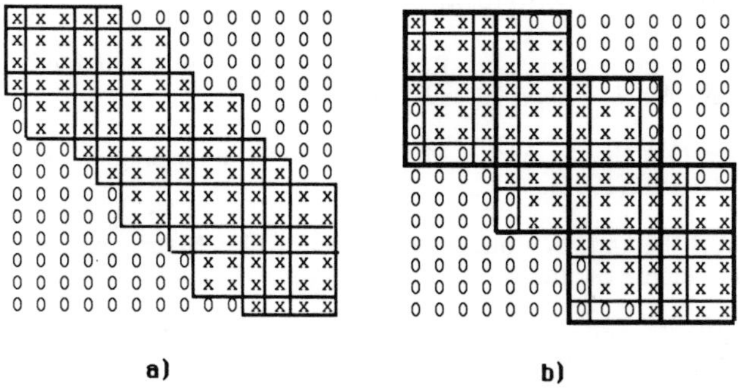

Fig. 9. a) a {3,2} block band matrix. b) the same as a (3,2) block tridiagonal block matrix

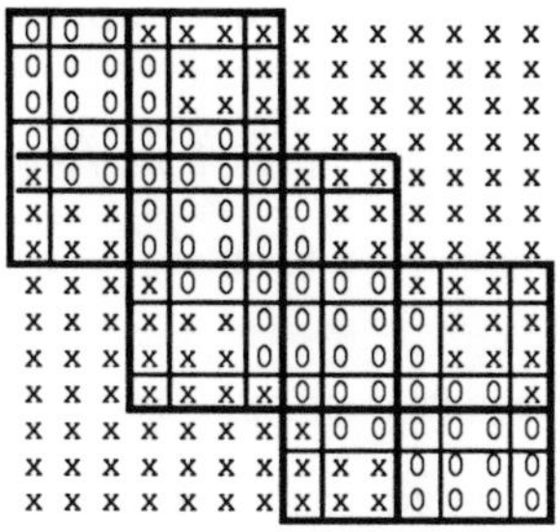

Fig. 10. An "everted" (3,2) block tridiagonal block matrix.

REFERENCES

1 V.Amato, A method for the solution of difference equations, *La scuola in Azione* 13:109-116 (1962-63).

2 E.Asplund, Inverses of matrices $\{a_{ij}\}$ which satisfy $a_{ij} = 0$ for $j > i+p$, *Math. Scand.* 7:57-60 (1959).

3 W.W.Barret, A theorem on inverses of tridiagonal matrices, *Linear Algebra Appl.* 27:211-217 (1979).

4 W.W.Barret, P.J.Feinsilver, Inverses of band matrices, *Linear Algebra Appl.* 41:111-130 (1981).

5 R.Bevilacqua, M.Capovani, *Proprietà delle matrici tridiagonali ad elementi ed a blocchi*, Editrice Tecnico Scientifica, Pisa, 1972.

6 R.Bevilacqua, M.Capovani, Proprietà delle matrici a banda ad elementi ed a blocchi, *Boll. Un. Mat. Ital.* B 13: 844-861 (1976).

7 R.Bevilacqua, B.Codenotti and F.Romani, Parallel solution of block tridiagonal linear systems, *Linear Algebra Appl.* 104:39-57 (1988).

8 B.Bukhberger, G.A.Emel'yanenko, Methods of inverting tridiagonal matrices, *Zh. Vychisl. Mat. i Fiz.* 13:10-20 (1973).

9 W.L.Cao, W.J.Stewart, A note on Hessenberg-like Matrices, *Linear Algebra Appl.* 76:233-240 (1986).

10 M.Capovani, Sulla determinazione della inversa delle matrici tridiagonali e tridiagonali a blocchi, *Calcolo* 7:295-303 (1970).

11 M.Capovani, Su alcune proprietà delle matrici tridiagonali e pentadiagonali, *Calcolo* 8:149-159 (1971).

12 F.R.Gantmacher, M.G.Krein, *Oszillationsmatrizen, Oszillationskerne und kleine Schwingungen Mechanischer Systeme*, Akademie Verlag, Berlin, 1960.

13 S.B.Haley, Solution of band matrix equations by projection-recurrence, *Linear Algebra Appl.* 32:33-48 (1980).

14 Y.Ikebe, On inverses of Hessenberg matrices, *Linear Algebra Appl.* 24:93-97 (1979).

15 E.G.Kounias, An inversion technique for certain patterned matrices, *J. Math. Anal. Appl.* 21:695-698 (1968).

16 J.W.Lewis, Inversion of tridiagonal matrices, *Numer. Math.* 38:333-345 (1982).

17 E.Neuman, The inversion of certain band matrices, *Rocz.Pol.Tow. Mat. Ser.3* 9:15-24 (1977).

18 T.Oohashi, Some representation for inverses of band matrices, *TRU Math.* 14-2:39-47 (1978).

19 S.A.H.Rizvi, Inverses of quasi-tridiagonal matrices, *Linear Algebra Appl.* 56:177-184 (1984).

20 F.Romani, On the additive structure of the inverses of banded matrices, *Linear Algebra Appl.* 80:131-140 (1986).

21 P.Rózsa, Band matrices and semi-separable matrices, *Colloq.Math. Soc. János Bolyai* 50:229-237 (1986).

22 P.Rózsa, On the inverse of band matrices, *Integral Equations Operator Theory* 10:82-95 (1987).

23 S.Schechter, Quasi-tridiagonal matrices and type-insensitive difference equations, *Quart. Appl. Math* . 18:285-295 (1960-61).

24 D.Szynal, J.Szynal, A propos de l'inversion des matrices généralisées de Jacobi, *Apl. Mat.* 17:28-32 (1972).

25 T.Torii, Inversion of tridiagonal matrices and the stability of tridiagonal systems of linear equations, *Tech. Rep. Osaka Univ.* 16:403-414 (1966).

26 V.R.R.Uppuluri, J.A.Carpenter, An inversion method for band matrices, *J. Math. Anal. Appl.* 31:554-558 (1970).

27 T.Yamamoto, Y.Ikebe, Inversion of band matrices, *Linear Algebra Appl.* 24:105-111 (1979).

Department of Mathematics, Technical University of Budapest,
Stoczek-u. 2-4 ,
1111 BUDAPEST, HUNGARY.

Dipartimento di Informatica, University of Pisa,
Corso Italia 40,
56100 PISA, ITALY.

Istituto di Elaborazione dell'Informazione - CNR,
Via S.Maria 46,
56100 PISA, ITALY.

Dipartimento di Informatica, University of Pisa,
Corso Italia 40,
56100 PISA, ITALY.

Operator Theory:
Advances and Applications, Vol. 40

DIVISIBILITY RELATIONS SATISFIED BY THE INVARIANT FACTORS OF A MATRIX PRODUCT

Robert C. Thompson

I wish to thank Israel Gohberg for the pleasure that I have found studying some of the beautiful books he has coauthored.

A combinatorial proof is given that a family of divisibility relations for the invariant factors of a matrix product possesses a recursive structure similar to that of the Horn-Lidksii inequalities for the eigenvalues of a sum of Hermitian matrices.

1. INTRODUCTION.

Let $\mathbf{R}$ be a commutative principal ideal domain, and A an $n \times n$ matrix over $\mathbf{R}$. For brevity, we call a matrix with entries in $\mathbf{R}$ an *integral* matrix. It is well known, see [3] or [16] for example, that integral unimodular matrices U and V exist such that UAV is a diagonal matrix,

$$UAV = \operatorname{diag}(\alpha_1,\ldots,\alpha_n),$$

with the diagonal entries forming a divisibility chain: $\alpha_n \mid \cdots \mid \alpha_1$. (The symbol $\mid$ denotes divisibility.) This is the Smith form theorem, and the diagonal elements in its diagonal form are called the *invariant factors* of A. In this paper an ongoing study by several authors of the characterization of the invariant factors of a product of integral matrices will be continued. The special case in which $\mathbf{R}$ is the polynomial ring in a single variable over a field is particularly important in applications, and is frequently mentioned in the Gohberg, Lancaster, Rodman books [3, 4].

We consider nonsingular integral matrices A, B, C, all $n \times n$, with $C = AB$. Let the invariant factors of A, B, C be

$$\alpha_n \mid \cdots \mid \alpha_1, \qquad \beta_n \mid \cdots \mid \beta_1, \qquad \gamma_n \mid \cdots \mid \gamma_1, \tag{1}$$

respectively. By assumption, these are nonzero. We are interested in the behaviour of invariant factors under matrix multiplication, and specifically how those of C depend on those of A and B. In the context of polynomial matrices, this question has been of interest since the 1979 publication of the Gohberg-Kaashoek paper [2]. Moreover, in the context of ring and group theory the question has a history reaching back to 1955, and earlier, as will be explained below. It is now known [23] that

$$\gamma_{k_1}\gamma_{k_2}\cdots\gamma_{k_r} \mid \alpha_{i_1}\alpha_{i_2}\cdots\alpha_{i_r}\beta_{j_1}\beta_{j_2}\cdots\beta_{j_r} \qquad (2)$$

when the subscripts are numbered so that

$$1 \le i_1 < \ldots < i_r \le n, \quad 1 \le j_1 < \ldots < j_r \le n, \quad 1 \le k_1 < \ldots < k_r \le n,$$

and under this numbering satisfy certain implicitly defined combinatorial constraints, described below, involving Young tableau. The purpose of this paper is to show that these implicitly defined combinatorial constraints have a recursive presentation, also to be defined below.

One of the inequalities (2), that in which $i_1 = k_1, \ldots, i_r = k_r$, and $j_1 = 1, \ldots, j_r = r$, appears in [4 and 20] and is called the *Sigal inequality*. A known [20, 23] generalization of it restoring the symmetry between the i and j indices will be explained below.

It is generally believed that the family of divisibility relations (2), with indices given by the recursive family mentioned above, and specifying equality (in place of divisibility) in (2) when $r = n$, yields a complete description of the allowable invariant factors of a product $C = AB$ of integral matrices when the invariant factors of the constituents A and B are assumed known. A strategy invented by the author about ten years ago is to use combinatorics alone to reduce this issue to another for which a complete solution was found by T. Klein [10] by algebraic methods. Thus we have a division of labour: the algebraic aspect is [10], and the combinatorial aspect is being analysed.

This approach is only one of the available techniques for studying the invariant factors of a matrix product. Another is the construction of an argument linking (by representation theory) this problem to the announced solution by B. V. Lidskii [12] of the characterization of the spectrum of a sum of two Hermitian matrices. Unlikely as it may seem, these two problems do relate to each other, in a nontrivially deep fashion. A brief sketch of this connection is in [22]. Yet another and more direct approach is in the report of Thijsse [20]; see also his earlier paper [19].

It is also worth noting that the Sigal inequality mentioned above originally appeared in the context of the spectrum of a sum of Hermitian matrices, and there carries the name of V. B. Lidskii [13]. A treatment of V. B. Lidskii's inequality by Lie group representation theory appears in [1], a paper that is without question central to this circle of ideas. A direct treatment of the invariant factor problem for a product within the setting of group representations thus seems naturally to be called for. In this context the book of I. G. Macdonald [14] on symmetric polynomials contains much valuable material bearing on all aspects of our question.

2. A COMBINATORIAL APPROACH. An initial observation is that the study of the invariant factors of a product of integral (and nonsingular) matrices is equivalent to a module theoretic problem.

To describe this, recall a standard fact that a finitely generated $\mathfrak{R}$ module $\mathcal{M}$ decomposes as a direct sum of cyclic submodules $\langle g_i \rangle$, with generators g_i,

$$\mathfrak{R} = \langle g_1 \rangle \oplus \langle g_2 \rangle \oplus \cdots \oplus \langle g_n \rangle.$$

Here the ideals $\mathfrak{I}_i$ of $\mathfrak{R}$ annihilating the individual cyclic direct summands, $\mathfrak{I}_i \langle g_i \rangle = 0$, are to form a divisibility chain: $\mathfrak{I}_1 \subseteq \mathfrak{I}_2 \subseteq \cdots \subseteq \mathfrak{I}_n$. The *invariant factors* of the module are by definition these annihilating ideals. Often we use generators s_i of the annihilating ideals $\mathfrak{I}_i$ in place of the ideals themselves. Then the invariant factors of $\mathcal{M}$ are elements s_i of $\mathfrak{R}$ forming a divisibility chain, $s_n \mid s_{n-1} \mid \cdots \mid s_1$, and unique only to within multiplication by units (from $\mathfrak{R}$).

Now let $\mathfrak{C}$ denote a finitely generated $\mathfrak{R}$ module, with $\mathcal{A}$ a submodule of $\mathfrak{C}$ and $\mathfrak{B} = \mathfrak{C}/\mathcal{A}$. Then it is known that product C = AB of integral matrices exists with A, B, and C having the prescribed invariant factors shown in (1) if, and only if, there exists an $\mathfrak{R}$ module $\mathfrak{C}$ containing a submodule $\mathcal{A}$ such that $\mathcal{A}$, $\mathfrak{B} = \mathfrak{C}/\mathcal{A}$, and $\mathfrak{C}$, respectively, have the invariant factors (1). A description of this relationship between matrices and modules appears in several places, see [23] for example. Thus the invariant factor problem for a product of integral (and nonsingular) matrices is equivalent to a module theoretic problem involving torsion modules over $\mathbf{R}$.

Now a finitely generated torsion $\mathbf{R}$ module decomposes as a direct sum of p-modules, for various prime elements p of $\mathbf{R}$. (The Sylow theorem for abelian groups.) The study of the relation $\mathfrak{B} = \mathfrak{C}/\mathcal{A}$ then may be considered at each direct summand. For matrices, this means that *elementary divisors* rather than invariant factors are looked at, where elementary divisors are (as usual) the prime power constituents of the invariant factors. Indeed, the divisibility relation (2) holds for invariant factors if, and only if, it is valid at the individual powers of each fixed prime p present, that is, precisely when it holds for elementary divisors.

Thus the invariant factor problem for a matrix product is equivalent to the study of the invariant factors belonging to a p module $\mathfrak{C}$ having a submodule $\mathcal{A}$ and a quotient $\mathfrak{B} = \mathfrak{C}/\mathcal{A}$.

This last problem was studied by T. Klein in close detail, in [10] in which the existence question is addressed, and [11] in which the count of the number of inequivalent solutions is examined. Her work was done under the direction of the group theorist J. A. Green, who in turn followed the lead provided by the group theorist Philip Hall. Hall appears to have given two talks [5, 6], on the module theoretic version of the problem, in 1955 and 1959, but published extremely sparingly on it. Interesting historical comments tracing Hall's interest in the abelian group version to 1938 may be found in [15]. Surprisingly, there is a 1900 conjecture of Steinitz anticipating some of Hall's statements; see [15]. Returning to Klein, she produced in [10] a necessary and sufficient condition for the existence of a triple of p-modules $\mathcal{A}, \mathfrak{B}, \mathfrak{C}$ with $\mathcal{A} \subseteq \mathfrak{C}$ and $\mathfrak{B} = \mathfrak{C}/\mathcal{A}$, such that $\mathcal{A}, \mathfrak{B}, \mathfrak{C}$ have prescribed invariant factors. To explain her result, we need new notation. Let

$$\alpha_i = p^{e_i}, \qquad \beta_i = p^{f_i}, \qquad \gamma_i = p^{g_i}, \qquad i = 1,2,\ldots,n, \tag{3}$$

with nonnegative weakly decreasing rational integer exponents:

$$e_1 \geq e_2 \geq \ldots \geq e_n, \qquad f_1 \geq f_2 \geq \ldots \geq f_n, \qquad g_1 \geq g_2 \geq \ldots \geq g_n. \tag{4}$$

(In the terminology of [26], the vector $e = (e_1,\ldots, e_n)$ is called the *Segre characteristic* of the module $\mathcal{A}$.) Then one of several equivalent versions of Klein's theorem is this:

There exist p-modules $\mathcal{A}, \mathfrak{B}, \mathfrak{C}$ *with* $\mathfrak{B} = \mathfrak{C}/\mathcal{A}$ *and with invariant factors specified by (3) and (4) if, and only if, a rectangular array of nonnegative integers*

$$\begin{array}{cccc} \sigma_{01} & \sigma_{02} & \ldots\ldots & \sigma_{0n} \\ \sigma_{11} & \sigma_{12} & \ldots\ldots & \sigma_{1n} \\ \cdot & \cdot & \ldots\ldots & \cdot \\ \sigma_{r1} & \sigma_{r2} & \ldots\ldots & \sigma_{rn} \end{array},$$

exists in which the entries satisfy the following conditions:

(i) *The top row is* $e_1, e_2,\ldots, e_n$;

(ii) *The bottom row is* $g_1, g_2,\ldots, g_n$;

(iii) *Each row is weakly decreasing (= nonincreasing) when read from left to right;*

(iv) *Each column is weakly increasing, with increases only in steps of* 0 *or* 1, *that is,* $\sigma_{i+1,j} = \sigma_{i,j}$ or $\sigma_{i+1,j} = \sigma_{i,j} + 1$, *for all* i *and* j;

(v) *The partial increase from one row to the next lying to the right of any fixed vertical line does not grow when passing downward through the array, that is,*

$$\Sigma_{j=k}^{n}\sigma_{i+1,j} - \Sigma_{j=k}^{n}\sigma_{i,j}$$

weakly decreases as i *increases, for all* i *and each fixed* k.

(vi) There are precisely $f_t - f_{t+1}$ *rows for which the total increase over the preceding row is* t, *that is,*

$$\Sigma_{j=1}^{n}\sigma_{i+1,j} - \Sigma_{j=1}^{n}\sigma_{i,j} = t$$

holds for precisely $f_t - f_{t+1}$ *values of* i, $0 \leq i < r$, *for each* $t = 1,2,\ldots, n$, *where* $f_{n+1} = 0$.

These conditions force $r = f_1$. Their significance is that they implicitly

describe the allowable triples of exponents $e = (e_1,\ldots,e_n)$, $f = (f_1,\ldots,f_n)$, $g = (g_1,\ldots, g_n)$ *on the elementary divisors belonging to a prime* p *in a product* C = AB *of integral matrices.*

We say "implicit" because to test the allowability of e, f, g requires determining whether Klein's array exists. Another defect is also evident: they are not divisibility conditions, not saying that a product of some invariant factors from C must divide (or be divisible by) another product built from invariant factors of A and B.

The structure of the combinatorial approach may now be described, in two phases, (i) and (ii), each having two parts.

(ia). To show that the Klein implicit conditions imply another (but still implicit) family of divisibility conditions on the invariant factors.

(ib). To show that this family of (implicit) divisibility conditions imply the Klein implicit conditions.

Thus (ia) and (ib) together are to present necessary and sufficient conditions in the form of divisibility conditions for the existence of a product C = AB of integral matrices with prescribed invariant factors.

As this is written it appears that (ia) has been achieved, with (ib) not yet investigated.

(iia). To endow the implicit divisibility conditions with a recursive structure.

(iib). To show that the recursively defined structure for the divisibility conditions implies the implicit divisibility conditions.

The announcement [12] by B. V. Lidskii seems to imply (via Lie representation theory and an appeal to [1]) that both (iia) and (iib) have been achieved. Since the proofs to acompany [12] are unpublished this conclusion remains somewhat uncertain, although it probably is correct.

The four parts, when completed, will show that the recursive divisibility conditions are necessary and sufficient for the existence of a triple of integral matrices A, B, C = AB with prescribed invariant factors.

Part (ia) of this program was successfully carried out in [23], using a rather intricate lattice path argument. (Essentially the same type of lattice path reasoning appears elsewhere in the combinatorial literature, for example, in [25].) The present paper will do (iia) using only basic properties of tableaux. A strategy for a purely combinatorial approach to (iib) that begins with the tableau insertion algorithm of Schensted (as amplified by G. P. Thomas, see [21]) is planned, but is not yet very far developed. If successful, the details will be reported in a later paper. An approach to (ib) based on the minimal path concept developed by I. Zaballa (unpublished) is probably possible. Thus there is a reasonable prospect that all parts of this combinatorial approach can be successfully done.

The very interesting papers [19, 20] of Thijsse should be mentioned, in which the problem of the invariant factors of a product is solved for matrices of dimension seven or smaller, over the ring of polynomials in a single variable. The arguments there will probably work for matrices over a general principal ideal domain. Whether the same ideas can establish necessity and/or sufficiency for the recursive divisibility conditions is unclear. There is also an earlier paper of Rodman-Schaps [17]. Clearly, though, parts of the very active study of polynomial matrices fit naturally into ring theory.

We also draw attention to the important second paper of Klein [11], the results of which (after a transfer from modules to matrices) yield information on the number of inequivalent ways a product C = AB may be found with A, B, C all having given invariant factors. The same module theoretic ideas in expanded form are described in detail in Macdonald's book [14] and his historical paper [15].

3. THE IMPLICIT DIVISIBILITY CONDITIONS. We next describe a family of conditions that three sets of positive integers

$$i_1 < \dots < i_r, \qquad j_1 < \dots < j_r, \qquad k_1 < \dots < k_r,$$

with $i_r, j_r, k_r \le n$ may satisfy:

There are to exist nonnegative integers ρ_{pq}, $1 \le p \le r$, $1 \le q \le p$, *such that*

$$\{i_p - p\} + \rho_{rp} + \dots + \rho_{pp} = \{k_p - p\}, \qquad 1 \le p \le r, \tag{5}$$

$$\rho_{pp} + \rho_{p,p-1} + \dots + \rho_{p1} = \{j_p - p\}, \qquad 1 \le p \le r, \tag{6}$$

$$\{i_p - p\} + \rho_{rp} + \dots + \rho_{tp} \le \{i_{p+1} - (p+1)\} + \rho_{r,p+1} + \dots + \rho_{t+1,p+1}, \quad 1 \le p < r,\ p \le t \le r, \tag{7}$$

$$\rho_{pp} + \rho_{p,p-1} + \cdots + \rho_{p,p-q} \geq \rho_{p-1,p-1} + \cdots + \rho_{p-1,p-q-1},$$
$$0 \leq q < p-1,\ 2 \leq p \leq r. \qquad (8)$$

We have elected not to introduce separate notation for the weakly increasing sequences $i_1-1 \leq \ldots \leq i_r-r$, $j_1-1 \leq \ldots \leq j_r-r$, $k_1-1 \leq \ldots \leq k_r-r$, (usually called *partitions*) even though to do so is customary and convenient. Now we have this important fact, part (i)a of our program:

If nonnegative integers ρ_{pq} *exist to satisfy these conditions, then the divisibility relation (2) is valid for the invariant factors of a product of integral matrices.*

This divisibility statement is equivalent to

$$\sum_{t=1}^{r} g_{k_t} \leq \sum_{t=1}^{r} e_{i_t} + \sum_{t=1}^{r} f_{j_t}.$$

The proof is in [23], where the result is deduced from the Klein theorem described in the previous section by a purely combinatorial lattice path argument. Although the algebraic conditions (5)-(8) are seemingly murky and unintuitive, they do have a reasonably intuitive combinatorial form which we now explain.

Form a tableau consisting of rows of zeros, with row lengths (reading from the top row, called the rth, to the bottom row, called the 1st) as follows:

$$\begin{array}{l} i_r - r, \\ i_{r-1} - (r-1), \\ \cdots\cdots\cdots \\ i_1 - 1. \end{array}$$

(See the display below, illustrating the $r = 6$ case. In the terminology of [26], the vector $i = (i_r-r,\ldots,i_1-1)$ is called a *Weyr characteristic.*) Augment these rows by adjoining symbols x_r at the right end of each row; the number of symbols x_r adjoined at the end of row t is ρ_{rt}, for $t = r, r-1,\ldots,1$. A total of j_r-r symbols x_r are thus adjoined. Then adjoin symbols x_{r-1} at the end of each row, except the top row; the number of symbols x_{r-1} adjoined at the end of row t is $\rho_{r-1,t}$, for $t = r-1, r-2,\ldots,1$, a total of $j_{r-1}-(r-1)$ symbols x_{r-1}. Continue in this way, adjoining further symbols $x_{r-2}, x_{r-3},\ldots, x_1$. The symbol x_m is to be adjoined only at the ends of rows $m, m-1,\ldots,1$, and the number of adjuctions of it at the end of row t is ρ_{mt}, for t = m, m-1,...,1, altogether j_m-m symbols x_m. After all these adjunctions, the row lengths (top row first) are to be

$$k_r\text{-}r,$$
$$k_{r-1} - (r-1),$$
$$\dots\dots\dots$$
$$k_1\text{-}1.$$

Furthermore, after the adjunctions of symbol x_t in a row p, with p < r, the length of row p through to its rightmost symbol x_t is not to exceed the length of the next higher row, p+1, through to its rightmost symbol x_{t+1}. This is to hold for all t = r,...,p, where x_{r+1} = 0. Thus the symbols x_r, x_{r-1},..., x_1 appearing in a single column of the completed tableau occur in it in strictly decreasing order when it is read from top to bottom, under the order defined by $x_r > x_{r-1} > ... > x_1$. Moreover, in each row of the completed tableau, the nonzero symbols weakly decrease when read from left to right (under the same order). The case r = 6 of these conditions is illustrated below. The numbers inside each box here specifies the length of the box, that is, the number of symbols filling it. The left most box shown (if nonempty) in each row is filled with 0 symbols; then the next box shown (if nonempty) with x_6 symbols; then the box next shown (if nonempty) with x_5 symbols, etc. The total lengths of the rows displayed here (top row first) are k_6-6, k_5-5,..., k_1-1. The partial length of each row through to its rightmost symbol x_t does not exceed the partial length of the next higher

row 6	$i_6\text{-}6$						ρ_{66}
row 5	$i_5\text{-}5$					ρ_{65}	ρ_{55}
row 4	$i_4\text{-}4$				ρ_{64}	ρ_{54}	ρ_{44}
row 3	$i_3\text{-}3$			ρ_{63}	ρ_{53}	ρ_{43}	ρ_{33}
row 2	$i_2\text{-}2$		ρ_{62}	ρ_{52}	ρ_{42}	ρ_{32}	ρ_{22}
row 1	$i_1\text{-}1$	ρ_{61}	ρ_{51}	ρ_{41}	ρ_{31}	ρ_{21}	ρ_{11}

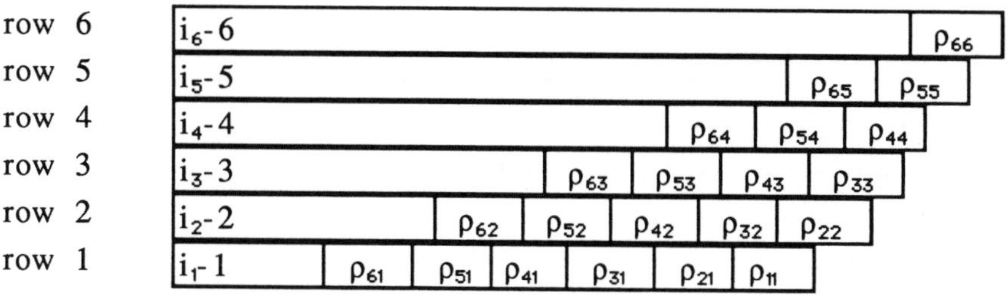

row through to its rightmost symbol x_{t+1}, for every t = 1,...,6. (x_7 is 0.) The total number of x_6 symbols, that is, the total $\rho_{66} + \cdots + \rho_{61}$ down the highest slant, is to be j_6-6, the total number of x_5 symbols, that is, the total $\rho_{55} + \cdots + \rho_{51}$ down the next slant, is to be j_5-5, etc.

This description encompasses all conditions (5)-(8) except (8). The final condition, (8), imposed on the adjoined symbols x_r, x_{r-1},..., x_1 is usually called *the lattice word condition*, and amounts to this: Let a word be formed by reading the adjoined symbols x_r,..., x_1 right to left across each row, first across the top row from its right end, then continuing across the next to top row from its right end,..., finally across the bottom row from its right end. Condition (8) then is: if this word is read from its initial letter to its last letter, at every stage in the reading process the number of symbols x_p so far seen weakly exceeds the number of symbols x_{p-1} already seen, and this is to be true of every symbol x_p for p = r, r-1,..., 2.

The lattice word condition is perhaps better understood as a massive set of majorization conditions, which for r = 6 are just

$$\rho_{66} \geq \rho_{55} \geq \rho_{44} \geq \rho_{33} \geq \rho_{22} \geq \rho_{11},$$

$$\rho_{66}+\rho_{65} \geq \rho_{55}+\rho_{54} \geq \rho_{44}+\rho_{43} \geq \rho_{33}+\rho_{32} \geq \rho_{22}+\rho_{21},$$

$$\rho_{66}+\rho_{65}+\rho_{64} \geq \rho_{55}+\rho_{54}+\rho_{53} \geq \rho_{44}+\rho_{43}+\rho_{42} \geq \rho_{33}+\rho_{32}+\rho_{31},$$

$$\rho_{66}+\rho_{65}+\rho_{64}+\rho_{63} \geq \rho_{55}+\rho_{54}+\rho_{53}+\rho_{52} \geq \rho_{44}+\rho_{43}+\rho_{42}+\rho_{41},$$

$$\rho_{66}+\rho_{65}+\rho_{64}+\rho_{63}+\rho_{62} \geq \rho_{55}+\rho_{54}+\rho_{53}+\rho_{52}+\rho_{51}.$$

An alternative statement is that these numbers give the box sizes in a left standardized tableau, see below for the r = 6 case.

ρ_{66}	ρ_{65}	ρ_{64}	ρ_{63}	ρ_{62}	ρ_{61}
ρ_{55}	ρ_{54}	ρ_{53}	ρ_{52}	ρ_{51}	
ρ_{44}	ρ_{43}	ρ_{42}	ρ_{41}		
ρ_{33}	ρ_{32}	ρ_{31}			
ρ_{22}	ρ_{21}				
ρ_{11}					

All these combinatorial conditions are difficult to check since one has to verify that an unwieldy set of linear inequalities and equalities has a nonnegative integer solution. A formulation omitting reference to the ρ_{pq} is needed and recursion may yield one.

There is, however, a case in which the combinatorial constraints on the ρ_{pq} may obviously be satisfied. Indeed, take

$$\rho_{rr} = j_r - r,\ \rho_{r-1,r-1} = j_{r-1} - (r-1), \ldots, \rho_{11} = j_1 - 1,\ \rho_{ij} = 0 \text{ for all } i \neq j.$$

Here the adjoined letter x_t occurs only in row t, for t = r,...,1. In this case $k_t = i_t + j_t - t$ for all t. Thus we have:

The invariant factors of a matrix product satisfy

$$\prod_{t=1}^{r} \gamma_{i_t+j_t-t} \mid \prod_{t=1}^{r} \alpha_{i_t} \prod_{t=1}^{r} \beta_{j_t} \tag{9}$$

whenever $i_1 < \ldots < i_r$ *and* $j_1 <. \ldots < j_r$ *are positive integers with* $i_r+j_r-r \leq n$.

This inequality (9) appears in both [20] and [23], but in fact has a history going back to the late 1960's, when it was discovered by the present author [24] in the context of the spectrum of a sum of Hermitian matrices. In this context an equivalent but rather more complicated statement appears in an announcement by J. Hersch and B. P. Zwahlen [7], with proof by B. P. Zwahlen alone in [27], and this pair of articles are perhaps properly regarded as the first occurrence of the inequality. The tableau corresponding to it (in the 6×6 case) is:

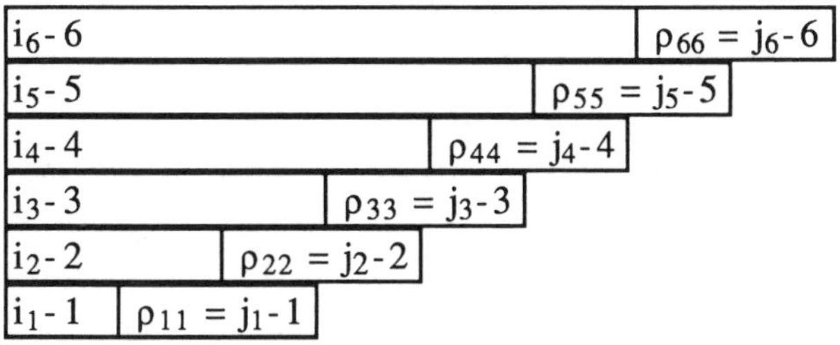

Of course, the early papers just mentioned did not recognize that this inequality is naturally described in terms of tableaux. The first recognition of the connection with tableaux is probably due to S. Johnson as part of his study of spectral inequalities and the Schubert calculus [9, unpublished].

The special case $j_t = t$ for all t gives the Sigal inequality.

The inequality (9) appears in so many different situations involving matrix spectra that it deserves a name. This is especially true since it is the cleanest and simplest of the inequalities defined by tableaux. It is not unreasonable to call it the *standard inequality*.

4. THE RECURSIVE DIVISIBILITY CONDITIONS. The objective of part (ii) of the combinatorial program is to convert the implicitly presented divisibility conditions to a recursive form. To explain this, the first remark is that in quite another context a recursive definition was given by A. Horn [8] for the index sets in a family of eigenvalue inequalities for the spectrum of a sum of Hermitian matrices. The purpose of the present paper may now be stated:

The index sets $i_1,\ldots, i_r, j_1,\ldots, j_r, k_1,\ldots, k_r$ *appearing in the divisibility conditions above satisfy the Horn recursion.*

To explain this in more detail, we need some notation.

Let $\mathrm{Tab}_r(n)$ denote the set of ordered triples (i, j, k) of ordered r-tuples,

$$\begin{aligned} i &= (i_1,\ldots, i_r), && 1 \le i_1 < \ldots < i_r \le n, \\ j &= (j_1,\ldots, j_r), && 1 \le j_1 < \ldots < j_r \le n, \qquad (10)\\ k &= (k_1,\ldots, k_r), && 1 \le k_1 < \ldots < k_r \le n, \end{aligned}$$

such that the constraints (5), (6), (7), (8) have a nonnegative solution for the integers ρ_{pq}. Our main result in this paper is then the following theorem.

THEOREM. *Suppose that* $(i, j, k) \in \mathrm{Tab}_r(n)$, *and that* $(u, v, w) \in \mathrm{Tab}_s(r)$, *where*

$$\begin{aligned} u &= (u_1,\ldots, u_s), && 1 \le u_1 < \ldots < u_s \le r, \\ v &= (v_1,\ldots, v_s), && 1 \le v_1 < \ldots < v_s \le r, \\ w &= (w_1,\ldots, w_s), && 1 \le w_1 < \ldots < w_s \le r. \end{aligned}$$

Then

$$\Sigma_{t=1}^{s} i_{u_t} + \Sigma_{t=1}^{s} j_{v_t} \le \Sigma_{t=1}^{s} k_{w_t} + \frac{s(s+1)}{2}, \qquad (11)$$

with equality when $s = r$.

Inequality (11) is the same as

$$\Sigma_{t=1}^{s}(i_{u_t} - u_t) \quad + \quad \Sigma_{t=1}^{s}(j_{v_t} - v_t) \;\leq\; \Sigma_{t=1}^{s}(k_{w_t} - w_t). \qquad (11')$$

The proof of this theorem, in the form (11′), is below.

5. THE HORN RECURSION. Let us say that triples (i, j, k) of r-tuples of strictly increasing integers in [1,n] belong to $\mathrm{Horn}_r(n)$ if (11) is valid for all triples (u, v, w) of strictly increasing sequences in $\mathrm{Horn}_s(r)$ for $s < r$, together with equality in (11) when $s = r$. (When $s = r$, $u = v = w = (1,2,...,r)$.)

The distinction between $\mathrm{Tab}_r(n)$ and $\mathrm{Horn}_r(n)$ is that the set of inequalities (11) (with equality for $s = r$) is (by the theorem above) a proved assertion for the sequences in $\mathrm{Tab}_r(n)$, whereas the sequences in $\mathrm{Horn}_r(n)$ are specified recursively by requiring that they satisfy the full family of inequalities (11) based on previously defined sequences in $\mathrm{Horn}_s(r)$ for all $s < r$, together with the equality (11) when $s = r$.

Naturally, one suspects that $\mathrm{Tab}_r(n) = \mathrm{Horn}_r(n)$ for all r and n, and the completion of this step is part (iib) of our combinatorial project.

Although it has been folklore knowledge for some years that the inequalities (2) for the $\mathrm{Horn}_r(n)$ indices, $1 \leq r \leq n$, with equality when $r = n$, precisely describe the invariant factors of a product of integral matrices (as well as the eigenvalues of a sum of Hermitian matrices when $|$ is replaced by $\leq$), published details are scanty, and the present paper is a contribution to the published literature on these problems. It is to be emphasized, though, that it is a *modest* contribution to this literature.

6. PROOF OF THE THEOREM. The fact that $(u,v,w) \in \mathrm{Tab}_s(r)$ means that nonnegative integers σ_{yz} exist, $1 \leq z \leq y \leq s$, such that

$$u_y - y + \sigma_{sy} + \sigma_{s-1,y} + \cdots + \sigma_{yy} = w_y - y, \qquad y = 1,...,s, \qquad (12a)$$

$$v_y - y = \sigma_{yy} + \sigma_{y,y-1} + \cdots + \sigma_{y1}, \qquad y = 1,...,s, \qquad (12b)$$

$$\begin{aligned} &u_y - y + \sigma_{sy} + \sigma_{s-1,y} + \cdots + \sigma_{ty} && s \geq t \geq y, \\ &\quad \leq u_{y+1} - (y+1) + \sigma_{s,y+1} + \cdots + \sigma_{t+1,y+1}, && 1 \leq y < s, \end{aligned} \qquad (12c)$$

$$\begin{aligned} &\sigma_{yy} + \sigma_{y,y-1} + \cdots + \sigma_{y,y-t} && 0 \leq t < y-1, \\ &\quad \geq \sigma_{y-1,y-1} + \cdots + \sigma_{y-1,y-t-1}, && 1 < y \leq s. \end{aligned} \qquad (12d)$$

The left side of (11′) equals

$$\Sigma_{t=1}^{s}(i_{u_t} - u_t) + \Sigma_{t=1}^{s}(\rho_{v_t,v_t} +\cdots+ \rho_{v_t 1})$$

$$\leq \Sigma_{t=1}^{s}(i_{u_t} - u_t) + \Sigma_{t=1}^{s}(\rho_{v_t+u_1-1,v_t+u_1-1} +\cdots+ \rho_{v_t+u_1-1,u_1}) \tag{13}$$

using the lattice word condition (8). (By (12b) for $y = s$ and (12c) for $t = s$ and $y = 1,2,\ldots,s$, the largest subscript $v_s + u_1 - 1 \leq u_s + \sigma_{ss} = w_s \leq r$, so is in the allowable range.)

Let T be fixed, $0 \leq T \leq s$, and define integers $U_1,\ldots, U_s$ and $V_1,\ldots, V_s$, all dependent on T, by

$$U_t = u_t + \sigma_{st} + \sigma_{s-1,t} +\cdots+ \sigma_{s-T+t,t}, \qquad t = 1,\ldots,T,$$

$$U_t = u_t, \qquad t = T+1,\ldots,s,$$

$$V_t = v_t - \sigma_{t1} - \sigma_{t,2} -\cdots- \sigma_{t,t+T-s}, \qquad t = s,\ldots,s-T+1,$$

$$V_t = v_t, \qquad t = s-T,\ldots,1.$$

Using (12b),

$$V_t - t = \sigma_{tt} + \sigma_{t,t-1} +\cdots+ \sigma_{t,T+1-s+t}, \qquad t = s,\ldots,s-T+1. \tag{14}$$

Owing to the row length conditions (12c) imposed on the partially completed tableau, we have $1 \leq U_1 < \cdots < U_s \leq u_s + \sigma_{ss} = w_s \leq r$. And, owing to the lattice word condition (12d), we have $1 \leq V_1 < \cdots < V_s \leq r$. Furthermore, for $T = 0$, we have $U_1 = u_1,\ldots, U_s = u_s$, $V_1 = v_1,\ldots, V_s = v_s$. We shall prove by induction on T that the expression (13) is $\leq$

$$\Sigma_{t=1}^{T}\{(i_{U_t} - U_t) + \rho_{rU_t} + \rho_{r-1,U_t} +\cdots+ \rho_{V_{s-T+t}+U_t-t,U_t}\}$$

$$+ \Sigma_{t=T+1}^{s}\{i_{U_t} - U_t\}$$

$$+ \Sigma_{t=1}^{s-T}\{\rho_{V_t+U_1-1,V_t+U_1-1} +\cdots+ \rho_{V_t+U_1-1,U_1}\}$$

$$+ \Sigma_{t=1}^{T}\{\rho_{V_{s-T+t}+U_t-t,V_{s-T+t}+U_t-t} +\cdots+ \rho_{V_{s-T+t}+U_t-t,U_t+1}\}. \tag{15}$$

For $T = 0$, (15) is the same as (13). This starts the induction. Let $0 \leq T < s$. Note that each of the subscripts in the various parts of (15) is within its allowable range. For example, the largest first subscript in the $\Sigma_{t=1}^{s-T}$ part is

$$\begin{aligned}
V_{s-T} + U_1 - 1 &= (s-T) + \sigma_{s-T,s-T} + \cdots + \sigma_{s-T,2} \\
&\qquad + (u_1-1) + \sigma_{s1} + \cdots + \sigma_{s-T+1,1} + \sigma_{s-T,1} \\
&\leq (s-T) + \sigma_{s-T,s-T} + \cdots + \sigma_{s-T,3} \\
&\qquad + (u_2-2) + \sigma_{s2} + \cdots + \sigma_{s-T+1,2} + \sigma_{s-T,2} \\
&\leq \cdots \\
&\leq (s-T) \\
&\qquad + (u_{s-T} - (s-T)) + \sigma_{s,s-T} + \cdots + \sigma_{s-T,s-T} \\
&= w_{s-T} \leq r.
\end{aligned}$$

And the largest subscript in the last $\Sigma_{t=1}^{T}$ is

$$\begin{aligned}
V_s + U_T - T &= s + \sigma_{ss} + \cdots + \sigma_{s,T+1} + U_T - T \\
&\leq s + \sigma_{ss} + \cdots + (\sigma_{s,T+1} + U_{T+1} - (T+1)) \\
&= s + \sigma_{ss} + \cdots + (\sigma_{s,T+1} + u_{T+1} - (T+1)) \\
&\leq s + \sigma_{ss} + \cdots + \sigma_{s,T+2} + (u_{T+2} - (T+2)) \\
&\leq \cdots \leq s + \sigma_{ss} + u_s - s = w_s \leq r.
\end{aligned}$$

And also $V_{s-T+t} + U_t - t \geq (s-T+t) + U_t - t = s-T + U_t \geq 1 + U_t$.

To continue the induction, we apply inequality (12d) to each set of braces in the last of the four summations (15), and so replace the last Σ_1^T with the weakly larger quantity

$$\begin{aligned}
&\Sigma_{t=1}^{T} \left\{ \rho_{V_{s-T+t}+U_{t+1}-(t+1),V_{s-T+t}+U_{t+1}-(t+1)} + \cdots + \rho_{V_{s-T+t}+U_{t+1}-(t+1),U_{t+1}} \right\} \\
= \; &\Sigma_{t=1}^{T} \left\{ \rho_{V_{s-(T+1)+(t+1)}+U_{t+1}-(t+1),V_{s-(T+1)+(t+1)}+U_{t+1}-(t+1)} + \cdots \right\} \qquad (16)
\end{aligned}$$

(The largest subscript here is $V_s + U_{T+1} - (T+1)$, and as seen above is at most $\sigma_{ss} + u_s = w_s \leq r$, so is in the allowable range.) Then we shift the term with $t = s - T$ in the next last summand of (15) to be united with (16), so that the last two summations of (15) have been converted to the larger quantity

$$\Sigma_{t=1}^{s-(T+1)}\left\{\rho v_{t+U_1-1, V_t+U_1-1} + \cdots + \rho v_{t+U_1-1, U_1}\right\}$$

$$+ \quad \Sigma_{t=1}^{T+1}\left\{\rho v_{s-(T+1)+t+U_t-t, V_{s-(T+1)+t}+U_t-t} + \cdots + \rho v_{s-(T+1)+t+U_t-t, U_t}\right\}. \qquad (17)$$

We now take the last term from each of the braces in the $\Sigma_{t=1}^{T+1}$ part of (17), and put it into the braces in the first $\Sigma_{t=1}^{T}$ part of (15), respectively, except that the term with t = T+1 is united with the

$$i_{U_{T+1}} - U_{T+1}$$

term from the $\Sigma_{t=T+1}^{s}$ part of (15). Thus (15) is $\leq$

$$\Sigma_{t=1}^{T}\left\{(i_{U_t} - U_t) + \rho_{rU_t} + \cdots + \rho v_{s-T+t+U_t-t, U_t} + \rho v_{s-(T+1)+t+U_t-t, U_t}\right\}$$

$$+ \quad \left\{(i_{U_{T+1}} - U_{T+1}) + \rho v_{s-(T+1)+(T+1)+U_{T+1}-(T+1), U_{T+1}}\right\}$$

$$+ \quad \Sigma_{t=T+2}^{s}\left\{i_{U_t} - U_t\right\}$$

$$+ \quad \Sigma_{t=1}^{s-(T+1)}\left\{\rho v_{t+U_1-1, V_t+U_1-1} + \cdots + \rho v_{t+U_1-1, U_1}\right\}$$

$$+ \quad \Sigma_{t=1}^{T+1}\left\{\rho v_{s-(T+1)+t+U_t-t, V_{s-(T+1)+t}+U_t-t} + \cdots + \rho v_{s-(T+1)+t+U_t-t, U_t+1}\right\}$$

$$\leq \quad \Sigma_{t=1}^{T+1}\left\{(i_{U_t} - U_t) + \rho_{rU_t} + \cdots + \rho v_{s-(T+1)+t+U_t-t, U_t}\right\}$$

$$+ \quad \Sigma_{t=T+2}^{s}\left\{i_{U_t} - U_t\right\}$$

$$+ \quad \Sigma_{t=1}^{s-(T+1)}\left\{\rho v_{t+U_1-1, V_t+U_1-1} + \cdots + \rho v_{t+U_1-1, U_1}\right\}$$

$$+ \quad \Sigma_{t=1}^{T+1}\left\{\rho v_{s-(T+1)+t+U_t-t, V_{s-(T+1)+t}+U_t-t} + \cdots + \rho v_{s-(T+1)+t+U_t-t, U_t+1}\right\}. \qquad (18)$$

We set

$$U'_t = U_t + \sigma_{s-T-1+t,t}, \qquad t = 1,\dots,T+1,$$

$$U'_t = U_t, \qquad t = T+2,\dots,s,$$

$$V'_t = V_t - \sigma_{t,t+T+1-s}, \qquad t = s,\dots,s-T,$$

$$V'_t = V_t, \qquad t = s-T-1,\dots,1.$$

Thus the U′ and the V′ are the U and V for parameter T+1.

To the typical expression in braces in the $\Sigma_{t=1}^{s-(T+1)}$ part of (18), we apply the lattice word condition as follows:

$$\rho_{V_t+U_t-1,V_t+U_t-1} + \cdots + \rho_{V_t+U_t-1,U_t}$$

$$\leq \rho_{V_t+U'_t-1,V_t+U'_t-1} + \cdots + \rho_{V_t+U'_t-1,U'_t}$$

$$= \rho_{V'_t+U'_t-1,V'_t+U'_t-1} + \cdots + \rho_{V'_t+U'_t-1,U'_t},$$

and obviously, for the typical $\Sigma_{t=T+2}^{s}$ terms we have

$$i_{U_t} - U_t = i_{U'_t} - U'_t$$

We operate with the typical terms in the two $\Sigma_{t=1}^{T+1}$ parts of (18) as follows, using first the row length inequality (7) in the first collection of terms, then shifting the last term in the second collection to be a new last term in the first:

$$\begin{aligned}
&\left\{(i_{U_t} - U_t) + \rho_{r,U_t} + \cdots + \rho_{V_{s-(T+1)+t}+U_t-t,U_t}\right\} \\
+ &\left\{\rho_{V_{s-(T+1)+t}+U_t-t,V_{s-(T+1)+t}+U_t-t} + \cdots + \rho_{V_{s-(T+1)+t}+U_t-t,U_t+1}\right\} \qquad (19)\\
\leq &\left\{(i_{U_t+1} - (U_t+1)) + \rho_{r,U_t+1} + \cdots + \rho_{V_{s-(T+1)+t}+(U_t+1)-t,U_t+1}\right. \\
&\qquad \left. + \rho_{V_{s-(T+1)+t}+U_t-t,U_t+1}\right\} \\
+ &\left\{\rho_{V_{s-(T+1)+t}+U_t-t,V_{s-(T+1)+t}+U_t-t} + \cdots + \rho_{V_{s-(T+1)+t}+U_t-t,U_t+2}\right\}
\end{aligned}$$

$$= \left\{ (i_{U_t+1} - (U_t+1)) + \rho_{r,U_t+1} + \cdots + \rho_{(V_{s-(T+1)+t}-1)+(U_t+1)-t,U_t+1} \right\}$$

$$+ \left\{ \rho_{(V_{s-(T+1)+t}-1)+(U_t+1)-t,(V_{s-(T+1)+t}-1)+(U_t+1)-t} + \cdots + \right.$$

$$\left. \rho_{(V_{s-(T+1)+t}-1)+(U_t+1)-t,(U_t+1)+1} \right\}. \qquad (20)$$

Note that (20) has the same structure as (19), except that U_t is replaced with $U_t + 1$ and $V_{s-(T+1)+t}$ is replaced with $V_{s-(T+1)+t} - 1$. We may interate this process and so eventually replace

$$U_t \quad \text{by} \quad U_t + \sigma_{s-T+t-1,t} = U_t'$$

$$V_{s-(T+1)+t} \quad \text{by} \quad V_{s-(T+1)+t} - \sigma_{s-(T+1)+t,t} = V_{s-(T+1)+t}',$$

$$1 \leq t \leq T+1.$$

That is, (19) is $\leq$ (19) with the symbols U and V (with attached subscripts) replaced by the symbols U′ and V′ (with corresponding attached subscripts.) Since the U′ and V′ are U and V for T+1 instead of T, this completes the proof that (15) for parameter T is $\leq$ (15) for parameter T+1.

Thus the left hand side of (11′) is $\leq$ (15) with T = s in (15). But (15) for T = s is just

$$\Sigma_{t=1}^{s} \left\{ (i_{U_t} - U_t) + \rho_{rU_t} + \rho_{r-1,U_t} + \cdots + \rho_{V_t+U_t-t,U_t} \right\}$$

$$+ \quad \Sigma_{t=1}^{s} \left\{ \rho_{V_t+U_t-t,V_t+U_t-t} + \cdots + \rho_{V_t+U_t-t,U_t+1} \right\}. \qquad (21)$$

Moreover, for T = s,

$$U_t = u_t + \sigma_{st} + \cdots + \sigma_{tt} = w_t,$$

$$V_t - t = 0, \qquad t=1,\ldots,s,$$

so that $U_t = w_t$ and $V_t = t$, for t =1,..,s.

Thus the second $\Sigma_{t=1}^{s}$ in (21) is

$$\Sigma_{t=1}^{s}\{\rho_{U_t,U_t} + \cdots + \rho_{U_t,U_t+1}\} \tag{22}$$

in which the second subscripts decrease from first term to last. We therefore have a sum of empty braces, and so (22) is zero. The first term in (21) is

$$\Sigma_{t=1}^{s}\{(i_{w_t} - w_t) + \rho_{rw_t} + \cdots + \rho_{w_t,w_t}\} = \Sigma_{t=1}^{s}\{k_{w_t} - w_t\},$$

since the expression in braces is precisely the row length of the tableau for row w_t. This completes the proof that the left side of (11′) is at most the right side. The equality statement in the theorem is immediate upon summing the tableau row lengths.∎

7. ACKNOWLEDGMENTS. The theorem above was proved by the author some years ago, but is only now offered for publication. Over the intervening time span the author has received financial support from the National Science Foundation, from the Airforce Office of Scientific Research, and from the Flight Dynamics Lab at Wright Patterson Airforce Base. The author wishes to acknowledge his indebtedness to these scientific organizations.

8. REFERENCES.

1. F. Berezin and I. Gel'fand, Some remarks on spherical functions on symmetric Riemannian manifolds, Tr. Mosk. Mat. Obshch., 5, 1956, 311-351.

2. I. Gohberg and M. A. Kaashoek, Unsolved problems in matrix and operator theory, II. Partial multiplicities for products. Integral equations Operator Theory, 2, 1979, 116-120.

3. I. Gohberg, P. Lancaster, and L. Rodman, Matrix polynomials, Academic Press, 1982.

4. I. Gohberg, P. Lancaster, and L. Rodman, Invariant subspaces of matrices with applications, Wiley-Interscience, 1986.

5. P. Hall, The algebra of partitions, Canadian Mathematical Congress Proceedings Banff 1959, 147-159. (This has been available at the library of the University of Alberta, Edmonton.)

6. P. Hall, Colloquium, St. Andrews, 1955. (Apparently unobtainable, see a footnote in [10].)

7. J. Hersch and B. P. Zwahlen, Évaluations par défaut pour une somme quelconque de valeurs γ_k d'un operateur C = A + B à l'aide de valeurs α_i de A et β_j de B, C. R. Acad. Sci. Paris, 254, 1962, 1559-1561.

8. A. Horn, Eigenvalues of a sum of Hermitian matrices, Pacific J. Math., 12, 1962, 225-241.

9. S. Johnson, The Schubert calculus and eigenvalue inequalities for sums of Hermitian matrices, University of California at Santa Barbara, 1979.

10. T. Klein, The multiplication of Schur functions and extensions of p-modules, J. London Math. Soc., 43, 280-284, 1968.

11. T. Klein, The Hall polynomial, J. Algebra, 12, 1969, 61-78.

12. B. V. Lidskii, Spectral polyhedron of a sum of two Hermitian matrices, Functional Anal. Appl., 10, 76-77 (Russian), 139-140 (English), 1982.

13. V. B. Lidskii, Characteristic numbers of the sum and product of symmetric matrices, Dokl. Akad. Nauk SSSR, 75, 1950, 769-772.

14. I. G. Macdonald, Symmetric functions and Hall polynomials, Oxford, 1979.

15. I. G. Macdonald, The algebra of partitions, Group theory: Essays for Philip Hall, London Mathematical Society (Academic Press), 1984, 315-333.

16. M. Newman, Integral matrices, Academic Press, 1972.

17. L. Rodman and M. Schaps, On the partial multiplicities of a product of matrix polynomials, Integral Equations Operator Theory, 2/4, 1979, 565-599.

18. E. I. Sigal, Partial multiplicities of a product of operator functions, Mat. Issled., 8(4), 1973, 65-79.

19. G. P. A. Thijsse, Rules for the partial multiplicities of the product of holomorphic matrix functions, Integral Equations Operator Theory, 3-4, 1980, 515-528.

20. G. P. A. Thijsse, Partial multiplicities of products of holomorphic matrix functions, Rapport nr. 294, Wiskundig Seminarium, Vrije Universiteit, Amsterdam, 1985.

21. G. P. Thomas, On Schensted's construction and the multiplication of Schur functions, Advances in Math., 30, 1978, 8-32; reprinted in J. P. S Kung, Young tableaux in combinatorics, invariant theory, and algebra, Academic Press, 1982, 81-105.

22. R. C. Thompson, Invariant factors of algebraic combinations of matrices, in Frequency domain and state space methods for linear systems, C. Byrnes and A. Lindquist, editors, Elsevier, 1986, 73-88.

23. R. C. Thompson, Smith invariants of a product of integral matrices, Contemporary Mathematics, American Mathematical Society, 47, 1985, 401-434.

24. R. C. Thompson and L. Freede, Eigenvalues of a sum of Hermitian matrices, Linear Algebra and its Applications, 4, 1971, 369-376.

25. G. Viennot, Une forme geometrique de la correspondance de Robinson-Schensted, in Combinatoire et Representation du Groupe Symétrique, Lecture Notes in Mathematics, 579, Strasbourg, 1976.

26. I. Zaballa, Inequalities for the Weyr characteristic of modules, Algebra lineal y aplicaciones, Universidad del Pais Vasco, 1984, 432-442.

27. B. P. Zwahlen, Über die Eigenwerte der Summe zweier selbstadjungierter Operatoren, Comment. Math. Helv., 40, 1966, 81-116.

Robert C. Thompson,
Mathematics, University of California,
Santa Barbara, CA 93106, USA.

Table of contents of Volume II